HOLT McDOUGAL

Mathematics
Grade 6

Jennie M. Bennett

Edward B. Burger

David J. Chard

Earlene J. Hall

Paul A. Kennedy

Freddie L. Renfro

Tom W. Roby

Janet K. Scheer

Bert K. Waits

HOLT McDOUGAL

 HOUGHTON MIFFLIN HARCOURT

COMMON CORE

EDITION

Cover Photo: Sam Dudgeon/Houghton Mifflin Harcourt

Jennie M. Bennett, Ed.D., is a recently retired mathematics teacher at Hartman Middle School in Houston, Texas. She is past president of the Benjamin Banneker Association, the former First Vice-President of NCSM, and a former board member of NCTM.

Edward B. Burger, Ph.D., is Professor of Mathematics and Chair at Williams College and is the author of numerous articles, books, and videos. He has won many prestigious writing and teaching awards offered by the Mathematical Association of America. In 2006, Dr. Burger was named Reader's Digest's "Best Math Teacher" in its "100 Best of America" issue. He has made numerous television and radio appearances and has given countless mathematical presentations around the world.

David J. Chard, Ph.D., is the Leon Simmons Dean of the School of Education and Human Development at Southern Methodist University. He is a Past President of the Division for Research at the Council for Exceptional Children, a member of the International Academy for Research on Learning Disabilities, and has been the Principal Investigator on numerous research projects for the U.S. Department of Education. He is the author of several research articles and books on instructional strategies for students struggling in school.

Earlene J. Hall, Ed.D., is the Middle School Mathematics Supervisor for the Detroit Public Schools district. She teaches graduate courses in Mathematics Leadership at University of Michigan Dearborn. Dr. Hall has traveled extensively throughout Africa and China and has made numerous presentations including topics such as Developing Standards Based Professional Development and Culture Centered Education. She was a member of the NCTM 2009 Yearbook Panel.

Paul A. Kennedy, Ph.D., is a professor in the Department of Mathematics at Colorado State University. Dr. Kennedy is a leader in mathematics education. His research focuses on developing algebraic thinking by using multiple representations and technology. He is the author of numerous publications.

Freddie L. Renfro, MA, has 35 years of experience in Texas education as a classroom teacher and director/coordinator of Mathematics PreK-12 for school districts in the Houston area. She has served as a reviewer and TXTEAM trainer for Texas Math Institutes and has presented at numerous math workshops.

Tom W. Roby, Ph.D., is Associate Professor of Mathematics and Director of the Quantitative Learning Center at the University of Connecticut. He founded and co-directed the Bay Area-based ACCLAIM professional development program. He also chaired the advisory board of the California Mathematics Project and reviewed content for the California Standards Tests.

Janet K. Scheer, Ph.D., Executive Director of Create A Vision™, is a motivational speaker and provides customized K-12 math staff development. She has taught and supervised internationally and nationally at all grade levels.

Bert K. Waits, Ph.D., is a Professor Emeritus of Mathematics at The Ohio State University and cofounder of T^3 (Teachers Teaching with Technology), a national professional development program. Dr. Waits is also a former board member of NCTM and an author of the original NCTM Standards.

PROGRAM REVIEWERS

FIELD TEST PARTICIPANTS

Wendy Black
Southmont Jr. High
Crawfordsville, IN

Barbara Broeckelman
Oakley Middle School
Oakley, KS

Cindy Bush
Riverside Middle School
Greer, SC

Cadian Collman
Cutler Ridge Middle School
Miami, FL

Dora Corcini
Eisenhower Middle School
Oregon, OH

Deborah Drinkwalter
Sedgefield Middle School
Goose Creek, SC

Susan Gomez
Glades Middle School
Miami, FL

LaChandra Hogan
Apollo Middle School
Hollywood, FL

Ty Inlow
Oakley Middle School
Oakley, KS

Leighton Jenkins
Glades Middle School
Miami, FL

Heather King
Clever Middle School
Clever, MO

Dianne Marrett
Pines Middle School
Pembroke Pines, FL

Angela J. McNeal
Audubon Middle School
Los Angeles, CA

Wendy Misner
Lakeland Middle School
LaGrange, IN

Vanessa Nance
Pines Middle School
Pembroke Pines, FL

Teresa Patterson
Damonte Ranch High School
Reno, NV

Traci Peters
Cario Middle School
Mount Pleasant, SC

Ashley Piatt
East Forsyth Middle School
Kernersville, NC

Jeannine Quigley
Wilbur Wright Middle School
Dayton, OH

Shioban Smith-Haye
Apollo Middle School
Hollywood, FL

Jill Snipes
Bunn Middle School
Bunn, NC

Cathy Spencer
Oakridge Junior High
Oakridge, OR

Connie Vaught
K.D. Waldo School
Aurora, IL

Shelley Weeks
Lewis Middle School
Valparaiso, FL

Jennie Woo
Gaithersburg Middle School
Gaithersburg, MD

Reggie Wright
West Hopkins School
Nebo, KY

Operations and Properties

Learn It Online
Online Resources **go.hrw.com**

Introduction to Algebra

Learn It Online
Online Resources **go.hrw.com**

(all) Pat and Chuck Blackley

Decimals

Number Theory and Fractions

Learn It Online
Online Resources **go.hrw.com**

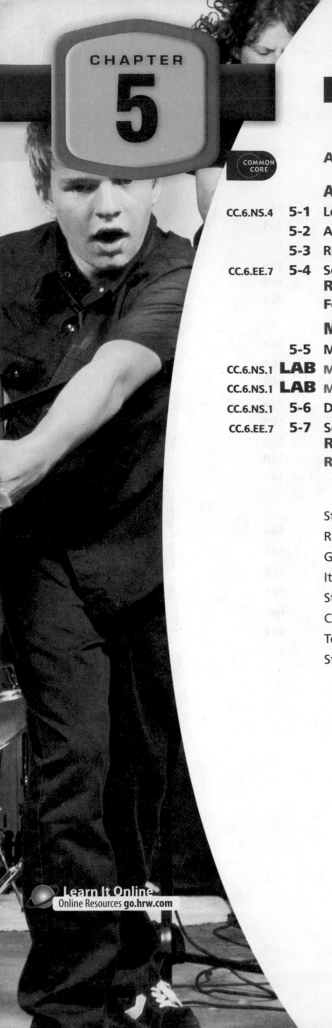

CHAPTER 5

Fraction Operations

COMMON CORE

Learn It Online
Online Resources **go.hrw.com**

(all) Michelle Pedone/zefa/Corbis

Data Collection and Analysis

COMMON CORE

Learn It Online
Online Resources **go.hrw.com**

(bkgd) Eastcott Momatiuk/Getty Images

Proportional Relationships

COMMON
CORE

Learn It Online
Online Resources go.hrw.com

Measurement and Geometry

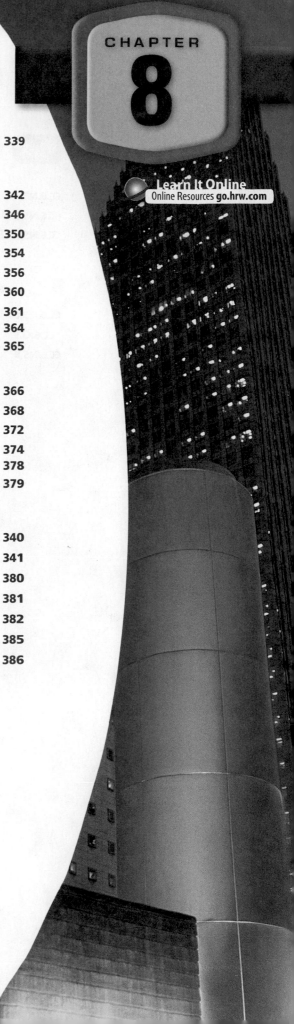

Learn It Online
Online Resources **go.hrw.com**

Richard Cummins/Corbis

Integers and the Coordinate Plane

COMMON CORE

Learn It Online
Online Resources **go.hrw.com**

Functions

Learn It Online
Online Resources **go.hrw.com**

Bruce Wheadon/Alamy

Standards for Mathematical Content
Correlation for Holt McDougal Mathematics Grade 6

Standard	Descriptor	Page Citations
CC.6.RP	**RATIOS AND PROPORTIONAL RELATIONSHIPS**	
Understand ratio concepts and use ratio reasoning to solve problems		
CC.6.RP.1	Understand the concept of a ratio and use ratio language to describe a ratio relationship between two quantities	**SE:** 286–289, 300, 305, 327, 330, 333, 336
CC.6.RP.2	Understand the concept of a unit rate a/b associated with a ratio $a:b$ with $b \neq 0$, and use rate language in the context of a ratio relationship[1] [1]Expectations for unit rates in this grade are limited to non-complex fractions	**SE:** 287–289, 306, 330, 333, 337
CC.6.RP.3	Use ratio and rate reasoning to solve real-world and mathematical problems, e.g., by reasoning about tables of equivalent ratios, tape diagrams, double number line diagrams, or equations	**SE:** 287–289, 291–293, 306, 330, 333
CC.6.RP.3a	Make tables of equivalent ratios relating quantities with whole number measurements, find missing values in the tables, and plot the pairs of values on the coordinate plane. Use tables to compare ratios	**SE:** 290–293, 298–299, 306, 330, 333, 443–444, 448
CC.6.RP.3b	Solve unit rate problems including those involving unit pricing and constant speed	**SE:** 287–289, 306, 330, 333, 337
CC.6.RP.3c	Find a percent of a quantity as a rate per 100 (e.g., 30% of a quantity means 30/100 times the quantity); solve problems involving finding the whole, given a part and the percent.	**SE:** 308–316, 326–327, 332–333, 337
CC.6.RP.3d	Use ratio reasoning to convert measurement units; manipulate and transform units appropriately when multiplying or dividing quantities	**SE:** 342–349
CC.6.NS	**THE NUMBER SYSTEM**	
Apply and extend previous understandings of multiplication and division to divide fractions by fractions		
CC.6.NS.1	Interpret and compute quotients of fractions, and solve word problems involving division of fractions by fractions, e.g., by using visual fraction models and equations to represent the problem	**SE:** 216–229, 234–235, 239
Compute fluently with multi-digit numbers and find common factors and multiples		
CC.6.NS.2	Fluently divide multi-digit numbers using the standard algorithm	**SE:** 10–13
CC.6.NS.3	Fluently add, subtract, multiply, and divide multi-digit decimals using the standard algorithm for each operation	**SE:** 104–109, 112, 123–125, 129–132, 135–137, 140–141, 166, 197, 201, 223, 283
CC.6.NS.4	Find the greatest common factor of two whole numbers less than or equal to 100 and the least common multiple of two whole numbers less than or equal to 12. Use the distributive property to express a sum of two whole numbers 1–100 with a common factor as a multiple of a sum of two whole numbers with no common factor	**SE:** 27–29, 35, 37, 40, 57, 151–154, 156–160, 166, 185, 187, 189, 194–197, 209–210, 227, 232, 235, 289

SE = Student Edition

Standard	Descriptor	Page Citations
Apply and extend previous understandings of numbers to the system of rational numbers		
CC.6.NS.5	Understand that positive and negative numbers are used together to describe quantities having opposite directions or values (e.g., temperature above/below zero, elevation above/below sea level, credits/debits, positive/negative electric charge); use positive and negative numbers to represent quantities in real-world contexts, explaining the meaning of 0 in each situation	**SE:** 392–395, 399, 403, 423
CC.6.NS.6	Understand a rational number as a point on the number line. Extend number line diagrams and coordinate axes familiar from previous grades to represent points on the line and in the plane with negative number coordinates	**SE:** 392–394, 399, 404–411
CC.6.NS.6a	Recognize opposite signs of numbers as indicating locations on opposite sides of 0 on the number line; recognize that the opposite of the opposite of a number is the number itself, e.g., $-(-3) = 3$, and that 0 is its own opposite	**SE:** 392–395, 399, 402, 420
CC.6.NS.6b	Understand signs of numbers in ordered pairs as indicating locations in quadrants of the coordinate plane; recognize that when two ordered pairs differ only by signs, the locations of the points are related by reflections across one or both axes	**SE:** 402, 404–407, 412–415
CC.6.NS.6c	Find and position integers and other rational numbers on a horizontal or vertical number line diagram; find and position pairs of integers and other rational numbers on a coordinate plane	**SE:** 241, 272, 279, 296–297, 392–394, 401, 405–411, 418, 421, 423, 427, 429
CC.6.NS.7	Understand ordering and absolute value of rational numbers	**SE:** 177, 393–394, 396–399, 401, 420, 423
CC.6.NS.7a	Interpret statements of inequality as statements about the relative position of two numbers on a number line diagram	**SE:** 396, 398
CC.6.NS.7b	Write, interpret, and explain statements of order for rational numbers in real-world contexts	**SE:** 397–399
CC.6.NS.7c	Understand the absolute value of a rational number as its distance from 0 on the number line; interpret absolute value as magnitude for a positive or negative quantity in a real-world situation	**SE:** 254–257, 392–393
CC.6.NS.7d	Distinguish comparisons of absolute value from statements about order	**SE:** 254–257, 393–394
CC.6.NS.8	Solve real-world and mathematical problems by graphing points in all four quadrants of the coordinate plane. Include use of coordinates and absolute value to find distances between points with the same first coordinate or the same second coordinate	**SE:** 402, 406–411, 414–415, 418, 421, 423, 427
CC.6.EE	**EXPRESSIONS AND EQUATIONS**	
Apply and extend previous understandings of arithmetic to algebraic expressions		
CC.6.EE.1	Write and evaluate numerical expressions involving whole-number exponents	**SE:** 14–16, 18, 25, 35, 37, 41, 65, 297
CC.6.EE.2	Write, read, and evaluate expressions in which letters stand for numbers	**SE:** 46–57, 60, 75, 89, 129, 445

Standard	Descriptor	Page Citations
CC.6.EE.2a	Write expressions that record operations with numbers and with letters standing for numbers	**SE:** 50–57, 60, 65, 89, 129
CC.6.EE.2b	Identify parts of an expression using mathematical terms (sum, term, product, factor, quotient, coefficient); view one or more parts of an expression as a single entity	**SE:** 46–53, 156–159
CC.6.EE.2c	Evaluate expressions at specific values of their variables. Include expressions that arise from formulas used in real-world problems. Perform arithmetic operations, including those involving whole number exponents, in the conventional order when there are no parentheses to specify a particular order (Order of Operations)	**SE:** 22–25, 350–353, 356–359, 361–363, 368–371, 374–377
CC.6.EE.3	Apply the properties of operations to generate equivalent expressions	**SE:** 26–27, 29, 40, 58–59, 88, 156–159
CC.6.EE.4	Identify when two expressions are equivalent (i.e., when the two expressions name the same number regardless of which value is substituted into them)	**SE:** 62–65, 80, 85, 87, 156–159
Reason about and solve one-variable equations and inequalities		
CC.6.EE.5	Understand solving an equation or inequality as a process of answering a question: which values from a specified set, if any, make the equation or inequality true? Use substitution to determine whether a given number in a specified set makes an equation or inequality true	**SE:** 62–65, 80, 89
CC.6.EE.6	Use variables to represent numbers and write expressions when solving a real-world or mathematical problem; understand that a variable can represent an unknown number, or, depending on the purpose at hand, any number in a specified set	**SE:** 67, 69, 72, 74, 78–80, 86–87, 89, 126–127, 208–210
CC.6.EE.7	Solve real-world and mathematical problems by writing and solving equations of the form $x + p = q$ and $px = q$ for cases in which p, q and x are all nonnegative rational numbers	**SE:** 67–69, 73–76, 80, 86–87, 91, 101, 105–107, 113–115, 125–128, 130, 136–137, 154, 206–208, 214, 224–228, 233–235, 289, 389, 416, 422–423, 429, 435, 439
CC.6.EE.8	Write an inequality of the form $x > c$ or $x < c$ to represent a constraint or condition in a real-world or mathematical problem. Recognize that inequalities of the form $x > c$ or $x < c$ have infinitely many solutions; represent solutions of such inequalities on number line diagrams	**SE:** 446–449
Represent and analyze quantitative relationships between dependent and independent variables		
CC.6.EE.9	Use variables to represent two quantities in a real-world problem that change in relationship to one another; write an equation to express one quantity, thought of as the dependent variable, in terms of the other quantity, thought of as the independent variable. Analyze the relationship between the dependent and independent variables using graphs and tables, and relate these to the equation	**SE:** 440, 450, 456–457, 461

SE = Student Edition

Standard	Descriptor	Page Citations
CC.6.G	**GEOMETRY**	
Solve real-world and mathematical problems involving area, surface area, and volume		
CC.6.G.1	Find the area of right triangles, other triangles, special quadrilaterals, and polygons by composing into rectangles or decomposing into triangles and other shapes; apply these techniques in the context of solving real-world and mathematical problems	**SE:** 350–353, 356–359, 361–364, 382–383, 385
CC.6.G.2	Find the volume of a right rectangular prism with fractional edge lengths by packing it with unit cubes of the appropriate unit fraction edge lengths, and show that the volume is the same as would be found by multiplying the edge lengths of the prism. Apply the formulas $V = l\,w\,h$ and $V = b\,h$ to find volumes of right rectangular prisms with fractional edge lengths in the context of solving real-world and mathematical problems	**SE:** 366–371, 378–379, 384–385
CC.6.G.3	Draw polygons in the coordinate plane given coordinates for the vertices; use coordinates to find the length of a side joining points with the same first coordinate or the same second coordinate. Apply these techniques in the context of solving real-world and mathematical problems	**SE:** 408–411
CC.6.G.4	Represent three-dimensional figures using nets made up of rectangles and triangles, and use the nets to find the surface area of these figures. Apply these techniques in the context of solving real-world and mathematical problems	**SE:** 372–377
CC.6.SP	**STATISTICS AND PROBABILITY**	
Develop understanding of statistical variability		
CC.6.SP.1	Recognize a statistical question as one that anticipates variability in the data related to the question and accounts for it in the answers	**SE:** 254–257
CC.6.SP.2	Understand that a set of data collected to answer a statistical question has a distribution which can be described by its center, spread, and overall shape	**SE:** 245–249, 254–258, 260–265, 268–273, 276–281
CC.6.SP.3	Recognize that a measure of center for a numerical data set summarizes all of its values with a single number, while a measure of variation describes how its values vary with a single number	**SE:** 246–249, 254–257, 268–271, 276, 279, 281
Summarize and describe distributions		
CC.6.SP.4	Display numerical data in plots on a number line, including dot plots, histograms, and box plots	**SE:** 254–257, 260–263, 268–271
CC.6.SP .5	Summarize numerical data sets in relation to their context, such as by	**SE:** 260–266, 268–271
CC.6.SP.5a	Reporting the number of observations	**SE:** 156, 260–266, 269–271
CC.6.SP.5b	Describing the nature of the attribute under investigation, including how it was measured and its units of measurement	**SE:** 268–271
CC.6.SP.5c	Giving quantitative measures of center (median and/or mean) and variability (interquartile range and/or mean absolute deviation), as well as describing any overall pattern and any striking deviations from the overall pattern with reference to the context in which the data were gathered	**SE:** 254–257, 268–271
CC.6.SP.5d	Relating the choice of measures of center and variability to the shape of the data distribution and the context in which the data were gathered	**SE:** 268–271

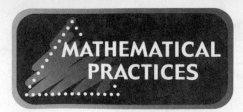

Mastering the Standards

for Mathematical Practice

The topics described in the Standards for Mathematical Content will vary from year to year. However, the *way* in which you learn, study, and think about mathematics will not. The Standards for Mathematical Practice describe skills that you will use in all of your math courses. These pages show some features of your book that will help you gain these skills and use them to master this year's topics.

1 Make sense of problems and persevere in solving them.

Mathematically proficient students start by explaining to themselves the meaning of a problem... They analyze givens, constraints, relationships, and goals. They make conjectures about the form... of the solution and plan a solution pathway...

In your book

Focus on Problem Solving describes a four-step plan for problem solving. The plan is introduced at the beginning of your book, and practice appears throughout.

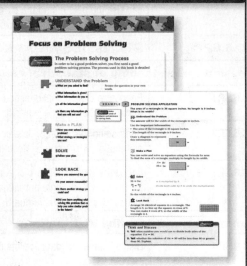

2 Reason abstractly and quantitatively.
3 Construct viable arguments and critique the reasoning of others.

Mathematically proficient students... justify their conclusions, [and]... distinguish correct... reasoning from that which is flawed.

In your book

Think and Discuss asks you to evaluate statements, explain relationships, apply mathematical principles, and justify your reasoning.

> **MATHEMATICAL PRACTICES**
>
> **Think and Discuss**
>
> 1. **Give an example** of a situation in which you would use mental math to solve a problem. When would you use paper and pencil?
> 2. **Tell** how you could use mental math in Example 1B if the problem were $867 + 59$.

> **MATHEMATICAL PRACTICES**
>
> **Think and Discuss**
>
> 1. **Explain** why $6 + 7 \times 10 = 76$ but $(6 + 7) \times 10 = 130$.
> 2. **Tell** how you can add parentheses to the numerical expression $2^2 + 5 \times 3$ so that 27 is the correct answer.

Getty Images/PhotoDisc

④ Model with mathematics.

Mathematically proficient students can apply... mathematics... to... problems... in everyday life, society, and the workplace...

In your book

Application exercises and **Real-World Connections** apply mathematics to other disciplines and in real-world scenarios.

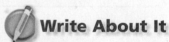

⑤ Use appropriate tools strategically.

Mathematically proficient students consider the available tools when solving a... problem... [and] are... able to use technological tools to explore and deepen their understanding...

In your book

Hands-on Labs and **Technology Labs** use concrete and technological tools to explore mathematical concepts.

⑥ Attend to precision.

Mathematically proficient students... communicate precisely... with others and in their own reasoning... [They] give carefully formulated explanations...

In your book

Reading and Writing Math and **Write About It** help you learn and use the language of math to communicate mathematics precisely.

⑦ Look for and make use of structure.
⑧ Look for and express regularity in repeated reasoning.

Mathematically proficient students... look both for general methods and for shortcuts...

In your book

Lesson examples group similar types of problems together, and the solutions are carefully stepped out. This allows you to make generalizations about—and notice variations in—the underlying structures.

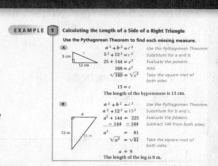

Countdown to Mastery

DAY 1

There are 1,932,704 cars in Oklahoma. Which of the states in the table have more cars than Oklahoma?

State	Number of Cars
Kentucky	1,914,028
Louisiana	1,960,105
South Carolina	1,933,281

- (A) Kentucky and Louisiana
- (B) Louisiana and South Carolina
- (C) Kentucky and South Carolina
- (D) Kentucky, Louisiana, and South Carolina

DAY 2

The table shows what Elena spends each day during a business trip. About how much does she spend altogether during the four-day trip?

Category	Daily Cost
Hotel	$108
Food	$29
Transportation	$11

- (F) $150
- (G) $300
- (H) $450
- (J) $600

DAY 3

Principal Meyers is arranging chairs in the gym for an assembly. She puts 11 chairs in a row and makes 17 rows. About how many chairs are in the gym?

- (A) 100
- (B) 150
- (C) 500
- (D) 200

DAY 4

Jerome uses metal strips to make rectangular frames that are 8 inches long and 4 inches wide. What is the total length of the metal needed to make 5 frames?

- (F) 17 inches
- (G) 60 inches
- (H) 120 inches
- (J) 160 inches

DAY 5

In a school auditorium, the first row has 15 seats. The second row has 18 seats, the third row has 21 seats, and the fourth row has 24 seats. Suppose the pattern continues. How many seats are in the sixth row?

- (A) 27
- (B) 30
- (C) 33
- (D) 36

DAY 1

The table shows how many people attended the school play at each performance. Round to the nearest hundred to find about how many people saw the play over the whole weekend.

(A) 1,000

(B) 1,200

(C) 1,400

(D) 1,600

Play Attendance	
Performance	Attendance
Friday night	289
Saturday night	412
Sunday matinee	162
Sunday night	347

DAY 2

The table shows the number of passengers that traveled through four airports in 2007. Which of the airports had the fewest passengers in 2007?

Airport Statistics, 2007	
Airport	Number of Passengers
Detroit Metropolitan	36,126,555
London Gatwick	35,218,399
Narita International	35,530,035
Singapore Changi	36,701,556

(F) Detroit Metropolitan

(G) London Gatwick

(H) Narita International

(J) Singapore Changi

DAY 3

A florist is making flower arrangements for a party. He has 24 roses, 56 tulips, and 40 irises. He uses all the flowers to make 8 arrangements, each with the same number of flowers. How many flowers are in each arrangement?

(A) 8

(B) 12

(C) 15

(D) 20

DAY 4

Jill drew a diagram of her room. What is the area of Jill's room?

(F) 18 square feet

(G) 36 square feet

(H) 40 square feet

(J) 80 square feet

8 ft

10 ft

DAY 5

Michael has 4 pairs of red socks and 5 pairs of white socks. How many socks does Michael have in total?

(A) 9 socks

(B) 11 socks

(C) 18 socks

(D) 20 socks

DAY 1

The table shows how many people competed in the annual bike race each year. Round to the nearest hundred to find about how many people in all have competed in the five years of races.

(A) 30,500
(B) 31,000
(C) 33,000
(D) 34,800

Annual Bike Race	
Year	Number of Racers
2001	8,432
2002	5,711
2003	6,204
2004	7,377
2005	7,114

DAY 2

The table shows the number of gallons a typical heart pumps in different amounts of time. What expression can you use to find the number of gallons a heart pumps in *h* hours?

Hours	Gallons
1	80
2	160
3	240
4	320

(F) $h + 80$
(G) $80 \div h$
(H) $\frac{h}{80}$
(J) $80h$

DAY 3

The distance around the rectangle is 398 feet. The width *w* of the rectangle is 41 feet. Which is the best estimate for the length ℓ of the rectangle?

(A) 10 feet
(B) 160 feet
(C) 320 feet
(D) 360 feet

w

ℓ

DAY 4

Claire is 6 years older than Brian. Let *b* represent Brian's age. Which is an expression for Claire's age?

(F) $b - 6$
(G) $6b$
(H) $6 - b$
(J) $b + 6$

DAY 5

There are *s* students in Mr. Chen's class. Each student brought in 10 pennies for a math project. Mr. Chen brought in 25 pennies for the project. What expression can you use to find the total number of pennies in the class?

(A) $10s + 25$
(B) $s + 10 + 25$
(C) $25s + 10$
(D) $25 \times 10s$

DAY 1

Chuck is 2 inches shorter than his sister, Jan. If j is Jan's height, what equation can you use to find Chuck's height c?

(A) $j + 2 = c$

(B) $c - j = 2$

(C) $c = j - 2$

(D) $c = 2j$

DAY 2

Cara wants to cover a wall with fabric. The wall is 19 feet by 49 feet. About how much fabric should Cara buy?

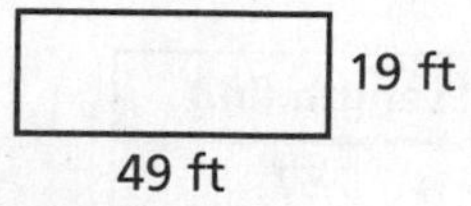

19 ft

49 ft

(F) 450 square feet

(G) 600 square feet

(H) 850 square feet

(J) 1,000 square feet

DAY 3

Alicia bought n notebooks that cost $3 each. She paid for the notebooks with a $20 bill. Assuming there is no sales tax, what expression shows the amount of change Alicia should receive?

(A) $3n - 20$

(B) $20 - 3 - n$

(C) $3n + 20$

(D) $20 - 3n$

DAY 4

Ann extends the pattern shown here by adding additional rows. Which row of the pattern has 13 circles?

Row 1   ○

Row 2   ○○○

Row 3   ○○○○○

Row 4 ○○○○○○○

(F) Row 6

(G) Row 7

(H) Row 12

(J) Row 14

DAY 5

What expression gives the missing value in the table?

Kirk's Age	9	10	11	12	n
Sandra's Age	14	15	16	17	?

(A) $n - 5$

(B) $n + 5$

(C) $5n$

(D) $n \div 5$

DAY 1

Keith's hamster had 2.1 ounces of food in its bowl. After the hamster ate, 1.3 ounces were left. Which equation could Keith use to find out the amount x the hamster ate?

A $x + 2.1 = 1.3$

B $x - 1.3 = 2.1$

C $x = 2.1 - 1.3$

D $x = 2.1 + 1.3$

DAY 2

A serving of 10 strawberries contains 0.8 grams of protein. What is the total amount of protein you consume by eating 10 strawberries on Monday, 30 strawberries on Tuesday, and 20 strawberries on Wednesday?

F 0.8 grams

G 2.4 grams

H 4.8 grams

J 8 grams

DAY 3

Kris has four pet turtles. Last week he measured each turtle. What is the order of the turtles from shortest to longest?

A Carly, Patty, Bennie, Charley

B Patty, Bennie, Charley, Carly

C Patty, Carly, Bennie, Charley

D Bennie, Patty, Carly, Charley

Turtle	Length (in.)
Bennie	5.67
Charley	5.75
Patty	5.07
Carly	5.5

DAY 4

What is the area of the shaded region?

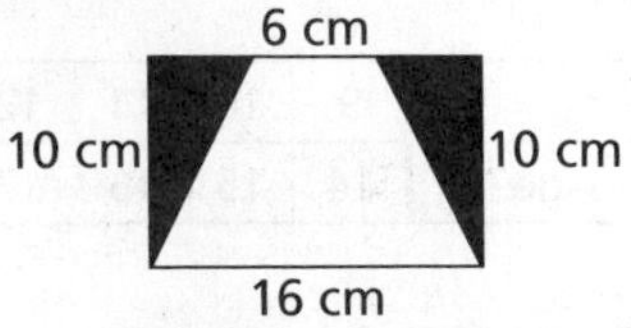

6 cm

10 cm 10 cm

16 cm

F 25 square centimeters

G 50 square centimeters

H 110 square centimeters

J 160 square centimeters

DAY 5

Toni is placing photos into a scrapbook. She has 74 photos, and can fit 6 photos on a page. How many pages will she need for the scrapbook?

A 11

B 12

C 13

D 14

DAY 1

The table shows the lengths of several hiking trails at Olympic National Park in Washington. The Chavez family hikes the three shortest trails. What is the total distance they hike?

Trails at Olympic National Park	
Trail	Length (mi)
Terrace Loop	1.5
Second Beach	0.8
Mt. Storm King	1.7
Third Beach	1.4
Spruce Nature	1.25

- (A) 3.45 miles
- (B) 3.55 miles
- (C) 3.7 miles
- (D) 4.6 miles

DAY 2

The manager of a furniture store bought 25 vases at a total cost of $450. She plans to sell each vase for $23. What is the fewest number of vases she must sell in order to make a profit?

- (F) 19
- (G) 20
- (H) 23
- (J) 25

DAY 3

If Sarah wants to buy a dozen roses and two dozen irises, how much will she spend?

Flower prices (dozen)	
Roses	$15.99
Irises	$6.75

- (A) $9.24
- (B) $22.74
- (C) $29.49
- (D) $31.98

DAY 4

A factory produces 3,200 shirts each day. The shirts are packed in boxes. Each box holds 8 shirts. How many boxes are needed each day to pack the shirts?

- (F) 40
- (G) 80
- (H) 400
- (J) 800

DAY 5

Jon grew 4.25 inches in two years. His brother Ben grew 3.575 inches. How many more inches did Jon grow than his brother?

- (A) 0.6 inch
- (B) 0.675 inch
- (C) 6.75 inches
- (D) 7.825 inches

DAY 1

Sam is growing a tomato plant in his garden. Last week, Sam picked one tomato that had a mass of 213.5 grams and another tomato that had a mass of 190.62 grams. What is the difference in mass of the two tomatoes?

(A) 22.43 grams

(B) 22.88 grams

(C) 23.05 grams

(D) 23.12 grams

DAY 2

Michael bought art supplies for his painting class. He spent $3.98 on a brush, $20.08 on paints, $10.49 on paint thinner, and $17.47 for some canvas. How much did Michael spend on art supplies?

(F) $48.62

(G) $50.09

(H) $52.02

(J) $52.74

DAY 3

Lena is making gift bags for a party. She has 24 gel pens, 48 sheets of stickers, and 32 note pads. She wants all the gift bags to be identical and she wants to use all the items. What is the greatest number of gift bags she can make?

(A) 6

(B) 8

(C) 12

(D) 24

DAY 4

The distance from Denver to Tulsa is 694 miles. Serena drives at an average speed of 51.1 miles per hour. About how many hours will the drive take?

(F) 8 hours

(G) 12 hours

(H) 14 hours

(J) 16 hours

DAY 5

The table shows the distances Margo walked during one week. How many miles did she walk in all?

Day	M	T	W	Th	F
Distance Walked (mi)	0.725	0.7	0.62	0.665	0.71

(A) 2.71

(C) 3.37

(B) 2.79

(D) 3.42

DAY 1

Use the table of Andrea's chores. How much time does it take Andrea to complete all three chores?

(A) 1.6 hours

(B) 1.7 hours

(C) 2.5 hours

(D) 2.6 hours

Andrea's Chores	
Chore	Time (hours)
Mow lawn	1.35
Do dishes	0.25
Clean room	0.9

DAY 2

To make biscuits, Lilly needs 16.45 ounces of butter. She needs 9.7 ounces of butter to make muffins. How much more butter does Lilly need for the biscuits than she needs for the muffins?

(F) 6.75 ounces

(G) 7.38 ounces

(H) 16.35 ounces

(J) 26.15 ounces

DAY 3

Eric's science class grew plants from bean seeds. The table shows how much each student's plant grew in two weeks. Put the plants in order from least change to greatest change.

Student	Miguel	Eric	Jane	Trisha	Cindy
Plant Heights (in.)	$\frac{1}{2}$	$\frac{5}{12}$	$\frac{3}{16}$	$\frac{1}{8}$	$\frac{4}{5}$

(A) $\frac{1}{2}, \frac{5}{12}, \frac{3}{16}, \frac{1}{8}, \frac{4}{5}$

(B) $\frac{1}{8}, \frac{3}{16}, \frac{5}{12}, \frac{1}{2}, \frac{4}{5}$

(C) $\frac{1}{2}, \frac{4}{5}, \frac{1}{8}, \frac{5}{12}, \frac{3}{16}$

(D) $\frac{1}{2}, \frac{1}{8}, \frac{3}{16}, \frac{4}{5}, \frac{5}{12}$

DAY 4

A magazine has p pages. A stack of 15 copies of the magazine has a total of 960 pages. What equation can you use to find the number of pages in the magazine?

(F) $15 \div p = 960$

(G) $p \div 15 = 960$

(H) $15p = 960$

(J) $960p = 15$

DAY 5

A geologist has four rock samples whose masses are 1.2 kilogram, 1.48 kilogram, 1.55 kilogram, and 1.6 kilogram. She needs a sample whose mass is as close as possible to $1\frac{1}{2}$ kilogram. Which sample should she use?

(A) 1.2 kilogram

(B) 1.48 kilogram

(C) 1.55 kilogram

(D) 1.6 kilogram

Countdown to Mastery

WEEK 9

DAY 1

The table shows the amount of water needed to cook $\frac{1}{6}$ cup of several different grains. Which grain requires the greatest amount of water?

Cooking Instructions	
Grain	**Amount of Water**
Buckwheat	$\frac{1}{3}$ cup
Millet	$\frac{5}{12}$ cup
Oats	$\frac{2}{3}$ cup
Wild Rice	$\frac{1}{2}$ cup

(A) Buckwheat (C) Oats

(B) Millet (D) Wild Rice

DAY 2

Which of the following is NOT equivalent to 4.4?

(F) $4\frac{2}{5}$

(G) $\frac{22}{5}$

(H) 4.40

(J) $4\frac{4}{5}$

DAY 3

Tom swims one lap every 5 minutes. Rob swims one lap every 4 minutes. If they start together, in how many minutes will they start a lap together again?

(A) 9

(B) 10

(C) 20

(D) 40

DAY 4

Mei has 67 baseball cards. She arranges the cards in rows. She makes as many rows as possible with 7 cards per row. How many cards does she have left over?

(F) None

(G) 3

(H) 4

(J) 6

DAY 5

It takes $1\frac{3}{4}$ cups of sauce to make one pizza. How many cups of sauce are needed to make $5\frac{1}{2}$ pizzas?

(A) $5\frac{3}{8}$ cups

(B) $7\frac{1}{4}$ cups

(C) $9\frac{5}{8}$ cups

(D) $12\frac{5}{6}$ cups

DAY 1

Jack ate $\frac{1}{2}$ of a pizza. Andy ate $\frac{1}{4}$ of a pizza. Which picture correctly models how much pizza the boys ate in all?

DAY 2

The table shows the results of a survey of 40 people who were asked to choose their favorite fruit. Which fraction shows the number of people who named strawberry?

Fruit	Number of People
Apple	18
Orange	10
Strawberry	12

- (F) $\frac{1}{4}$
- (G) $\frac{3}{10}$
- (H) $\frac{9}{20}$
- (J) $\frac{11}{20}$

DAY 3

Carla has $3\frac{1}{3}$ times as many stamps in her collection as Holly. Andy has $2\frac{1}{2}$ times as many stamps as Carla. If Andy has 300 stamps in his collection, how many stamps does Holly have?

- (A) 36
- (B) 90
- (C) 120
- (D) 2500

DAY 4

In most places, it is only possible to see 2,000 stars in the nighttime sky due to light pollution. This is $\frac{4}{15}$ as many stars as you can expect to see in the sky at Bryce Canyon National Park in Utah. How many stars can you expect to see at Bryce Canyon?

- (F) 533
- (G) 2000
- (H) 2667
- (J) 7500

DAY 5

The measure of the snake is actually 20% less than its true length. What is its true length?

18 in.

- (A) 14.4 in.
- (B) 18.9 in.
- (C) 20.8 in.
- (D) 22.5 in.

DAY 1

Allison took three quizzes. Her scores on the first two quizzes were 6 and 9. The mean of her three scores was 8. What was her score on the third quiz?

- (A) 6
- (B) 7
- (C) 8
- (D) 9

DAY 2

Peter has $\frac{4}{5}$ yard of fabric. Robert has $\frac{3}{7}$ yard of fabric. How much more fabric does Peter have?

- (F) $\frac{1}{35}$ yard
- (G) $\frac{7}{35}$ yard
- (H) $\frac{13}{35}$ yard
- (J) $\frac{1}{2}$ yard

DAY 3

Mitch made a long sandwich for a birthday party. A guest cut off $\frac{2}{3}$ of the sandwich. Then another guest cut off $\frac{1}{2}$ of the remainder. After these two cuts, the sandwich was 4 inches long. What was the original length of the sandwich?

- (A) 12 inches
- (C) 18 inches
- (B) 16 inches
- (D) 24 inches

DAY 4

Jeff drew this model of an airplane. What is the length of the wing written as a decimal?

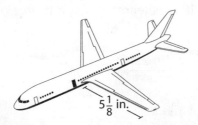

$5\frac{1}{8}$ in.

- (F) 5.1 in.
- (H) 5.625 in.
- (G) 5.125 in.
- (J) 5.8 in.

DAY 5

Tomas has $8\frac{5}{10}$ feet of fishing line and Mike has $2\frac{8}{16}$ feet of fishing line. How many feet of fishing line do they have together?

- (A) 6
- (B) 10
- (C) $10\frac{1}{2}$
- (D) 11

DAY 1

A hot-air balloon rises at 42.1 feet per minute. It descends at twice the rate that it rises. If it descends at a constant rate, how many feet will the hot-air balloon descend in 20 minutes?

- (A) 842 feet
- (B) 1684 feet
- (C) 2105 feet
- (D) 4210 feet

DAY 2

The table shows the number of electoral votes for several states. Given that the median number of electoral votes for these states is 4.5, how many electoral votes does Nebraska have?

State	Electoral Votes
Hawaii	4
Kansas	6
Nebraska	?
Vermont	3

- (F) 2
- (G) 4
- (H) 5
- (J) 7

DAY 3

Cara has $\frac{5}{8}$ yard of fabric. She used $\frac{1}{2}$ yard of the fabric to make a doll's dress. Which picture correctly models how much fabric Cara has left?

- (A)
- (C)
- (B)
- (D)

DAY 4

If 24 apples are needed to make 3 pies, how many apples are needed to make 2 pies?

- (F) 8
- (G) 12
- (H) 14
- (J) 16

DAY 5

Vignesh has quiz scores of 88, 79, 83, 93, 85, and 83. What is the range of these data?

- (A) 9
- (B) 14
- (C) 83
- (D) 93

DAY 1

The data set shows the number of wins by the Cleveland Indians baseball team from 1996 to 2006.

99 86 89 97 90 91 74 68 80 93 78

What is the median of the data?

- (A) 85.9
- (B) 86
- (C) 89
- (D) 90

DAY 2

The distance from Chandra's house to the park is $3\frac{1}{2}$ miles. She starts at home and walks $1\frac{1}{4}$ miles before stopping for lunch. Then she walks another $\frac{1}{2}$ mile and stops to talk to a friend. How much further must Chandra walk to reach the park?

- (F) $1\frac{1}{4}$ miles
- (G) $1\frac{1}{2}$ miles
- (H) $1\frac{3}{4}$ miles
- (J) $2\frac{1}{4}$ miles

DAY 3

The table shows the number of people who attended a concert. Round to the nearest hundred to find about how many people in all attended the concert.

- (A) 2,800
- (B) 3,200
- (C) 3,600
- (D) 4,200

Day	M	T	W	Th	F
Number of People	789	805	643	595	821

DAY 4

Sandy bought 2.75 liters of cranberry juice, 3.5 liters of pineapple juice, and 4.2 liters of orange juice for punch for a party. How many liters of punch will this make?

- (F) 3.52 liters
- (H) 9.45 liters
- (G) 7.7 liters
- (J) 10.45 liters

DAY 5

In a frog-jumping contest, Ben's frog jumped 20.75 centimeters in one hop. Billy's frog jumped 24.09 centimeters in one hop. How much farther did Billy's frog jump than Ben's frog?

- (A) 2.34 centimeters
- (B) 3.34 centimeters
- (C) 3.35 centimeters
- (D) 4.66 centimeters

DAY 1

Mia enlarges a rectangular photo that is 6.4 inches long and 4.2 inches wide. What is the area of the photo to the nearest tenth?

6.4 in.

4.2 in.

- (A) 21.6 square inches
- (B) 25.4 square inches
- (C) 26.1 square inches
- (D) 26.9 square inches

DAY 2

One week, Karl ate $\frac{1}{3}$ of a dozen oranges and his sister ate $\frac{1}{4}$ of a dozen oranges. Which picture correctly models how many oranges Karl and his sister ate?

- (F)
- (G)
- (H)
- (J)

DAY 3

A machine can make 10 widgets in 6 minutes. A worker sets the machine to make 15 widgets. A bell rings every 30 seconds while the widgets are being made. How many times does the bell ring while the 15 widgets are being made?

- (A) 9
- (B) 12
- (C) 15
- (D) 18

DAY 4

The ratio of girls to boys at a summer camp is $\frac{2}{3}$. There are 20 children at the camp. How many girls are there?

- (F) 2
- (G) 8
- (H) 12
- (J) 16

DAY 5

The dance club has 11 more members than the soccer club. There are 34 students in the soccer club. What equation can you solve to find the number of students in the dance club?

- (A) $d + 11 = 34$
- (B) $d + 34 = 11$
- (C) $d - 11 = 34$
- (D) $d = 34 - 11$

Countdown to Mastery

WEEK 15

DAY 1

The Hawks' mean score in two football games was 26. They scored 18 points in the first game. How many points did they score in the second game?

(A) 8
(B) 22
(C) 34
(D) 44

DAY 2

Chris bought $\frac{7}{8}$ pound of peanuts and ate $\frac{3}{4}$ pound. How many pounds of peanuts remain?

(F) $\frac{1}{8}$ pound
(H) $\frac{1}{2}$ pound
(G) $\frac{4}{8}$ pound
(J) $\frac{2}{3}$ pound

DAY 3

The table shows how much a seedling grew each day for five days. On which days did the seedling grow less than $\frac{3}{4}$ in.?

(A) Monday and Friday
(B) Tuesday and Wednesday
(C) Wednesday and Thursday
(D) Thursday and Friday

Day	M	T	W	Th	F
Growth (in.)	$\frac{4}{5}$	$\frac{5}{6}$	$\frac{7}{10}$	$\frac{5}{8}$	$\frac{4}{5}$

DAY 4

In the chess club, 50% of the students are girls. Of the girls, 50% are playing in a tournament. There are 7 girls from the club playing in the tournament. How many students are in the club altogether?

(F) 14
(G) 21
(H) 28
(J) 70

DAY 5

As she cooked, Sue used $3\frac{2}{8}$ cups of milk, $2\frac{4}{16}$ cups of water and $\frac{1}{2}$ cup of orange juice. How much liquid did she use?

(A) 5 cups
(B) $5\frac{3}{4}$ cups
(C) 6 cups
(D) $6\frac{1}{4}$ cups

DAY 1

The figure shows a pattern of tiles on the top of a table. Jared writes the ratio of black tiles to white tiles as n:6. What is the value of n?

(A) 1

(C) 3

(B) 2

(D) 12

DAY 2

On both Monday and Tuesday, Franco ran $4\frac{1}{2}$ miles and Nick ran $2\frac{2}{3}$ miles. How much farther did Franco run than Nick over the course of the two days?

(F) $2\frac{5}{6}$ miles

(G) $3\frac{2}{3}$ miles

(H) $4\frac{5}{6}$ miles

(J) $5\frac{1}{6}$ miles

DAY 3

Two towns are 143 miles apart. If Lorena drives at 35 miles per hour, how long will it take her to drive from one town to the other?

(A) about 2 hours

(B) about 4 hours

(C) about 5 hours

(D) about 10 hours

DAY 4

What is the mean number of candles sold per month?

(F) 25

(G) 30

(H) 40

(J) 45

Candles Sold Per Month

Jan. Feb. Mar. Apr.

🕯 = 5 candles

DAY 5

The point A is shown on the graph. What are the coordinates of point A?

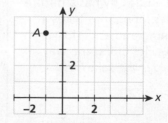

(A) $(4, -1)$

(C) $(1, 4)$

(B) $(-1, 4)$

(D) $(-1, -4)$

DAY 1

A rope is 17 feet long. Natasha cuts the rope into pieces that are each $1\frac{3}{8}$ feet long. What is the maximum number of such pieces that she can cut from the rope?

- (A) 9
- (B) 12
- (C) 13
- (D) 15

DAY 2

In the 2004 Olympics, the ratio of gold medals to silver medals won by the team from Hungary was 4:3. The ratio of silver medals to bronze medals won by the team was 2:1. The team won 3 bronze medals. How many gold medals did they win?

- (F) 4
- (G) 6
- (H) 8
- (J) 12

DAY 3

Kirsten is making a pictograph that shows the number of people who saw the school play each day for a week. In her pictograph, each stick figure represents 5 people who saw the play. If 30 people saw the school play on Monday, what should she draw on her pictograph for Monday?

- (A)
- (C)
- (B)
- (D)

DAY 4

Powell Gardens in Kansas City has a nature trail that is 3.25 miles long. Rosa takes a photo at the beginning and end of the trail and every 0.25 miles along the way. How many photos does she take?

- (F) 4
- (G) 12
- (H) 13
- (J) 14

DAY 5

Frank took six history exams. On each exam, the highest possible score was 100. His scores on the first five exams were 90, 82, 90, 93, and 85. The range of his scores was 19. What was Frank's score on the sixth exam?

- (A) 71
- (B) 74
- (C) 82
- (D) 99

DAY 1

Marianne earns money baby-sitting. When she baby-sits 3 hours, she earns $21; for 5 hours, she earns $35; and for 6 hours, she earns $42. Suppose h is the number of hours Marianne baby-sits and m is the amount she earns. Which equation describes the situation?

(A) $m = 3h$ (C) $m = 7h$

(B) $m = h + 18$ (D) $m = \frac{h}{7}$

DAY 2

A trapezoid has base lengths of 6 cm and 9 cm. Its height is 10 cm. Find the area of the trapezoid.

(F) 30 cm²   (H) 75 cm²

(G) 54 cm²   (J) 80 cm²

DAY 3

Sherri surveyed the ages of children who visited the doctor's office on Tuesday. What is the mode of this data set?

12, 9, 8, 15, 10, 13, 12

(A) 7   (C) 12

(B) 11.3   (D) 15

DAY 4

It takes Ari 40 minutes to walk 2 miles. How long will it take him to walk 4 miles?

(F) 60 minutes

(G) 70 minutes

(H) 80 minutes

(J) 90 minutes

DAY 5

What is the mean of the number of TVs repaired in June, July, and August?

(A) 14

(B) 21

(C) 28

(D) 63

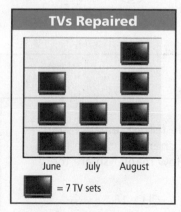

TVs Repaired

June   July   August

= 7 TV sets

DAY 1

In Derek's class, 18 of the 25 students belong to an after-school club. Which of the following describes the ratio of students **not** in an after-school club to students in an after-school club?

Ⓐ $\frac{7}{18}$ Ⓒ 25:18

Ⓑ 18 to 25   Ⓓ $\frac{7}{25}$

DAY 2

The radius of a circle is 18 inches. A snail crawls along the diameter of the circle at a rate of 3 inches per minute. How long does it take the snail to make the trip?

Ⓕ 3 minutes

Ⓖ 6 minutes

Ⓗ 9 minutes

Ⓙ 12 minutes

DAY 3

The picture shows the shirts Teresa owns. What is the ratio of red shirts to blue shirts?

Ⓐ 3 to 9   Ⓒ 6 to 3

Ⓑ 9 to 6   Ⓓ 6 to 9

DAY 4

The ratio of male fish to female fish in an aquarium is 2:5. There are 6 male fish in the aquarium. How many fish are there altogether?

Ⓕ 14   Ⓗ 18

Ⓖ 15   Ⓙ 21

DAY 5

If 30 buses can carry 1,500 people, how many people can 5 buses carry?

Ⓐ 200   Ⓒ 500

Ⓑ 250   Ⓓ 750

DAY 1

Which value satisfies the compound inequality?

$x < 3$ or $x > 10$

(A) 3

(B) 6

(C) 10

(D) 12

DAY 2

Which expression best represents the value of y?

x	2	4	6	8	10
y	1	2	3	4	5

(F) $x - 1$

(G) $2x$

(H) $\frac{x}{2}$

(J) $x + 1$

DAY 3

In Katie's class, 65% of the students have a pet. What fraction of the class does NOT have a pet?

(A) $\frac{7}{50}$

(B) $\frac{7}{20}$

(C) $\frac{1}{2}$

(D) $\frac{13}{20}$

DAY 4

The width of a rectangle is 75% of the length. The length of the rectangle is 12 feet. What is the perimeter of the rectangle?

(F) 9 feet

(G) 21 feet

(H) 42 feet

(J) 108 feet

DAY 5

If it takes Pat 4 hours to knit a child's cap, how many hours will it take to knit 3 caps?

4 hours   ? hours

(A) 6 hours

(B) 8 hours

(C) 10 hours

(D) 12 hours

DAY 1

Which of the following shows the values −3, 4, |−2|, and 0 in increasing order?

- (A) 0, |−2|, 3, 4
- (B) −3, 0, |−2|, 4
- (C) 4, −3, |−2|, 0
- (D) −3, |−2|, 0, 4

DAY 2

What is the area of triangle *BCD*?

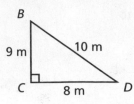

- (F) 22.5 m²
- (G) 27 m²
- (H) 36 m²
- (J) 72 m²

DAY 3

The table shows low temperatures for 4 cities in January. Which city has the lowest temperature?

January Low Temperatures	
City	Temperature (°F)
Smithfield	−6
Canton	9
Kingstown	−7
Fairville	8

- (A) Smithfield
- (B) Canton
- (C) Kingstown
- (D) Fairville

DAY 4

Which ordered pair is located in quadrant IV of the coordinate plane?

- (F) (−2, 5)
- (G) (2, 5)
- (H) (−2, −5)
- (J) (2, −5)

DAY 5

Mark wants to frame a painting. If the painting is 2.75 feet by 4.25 feet, what is the best estimate for the number of feet of wood Mark will need?

- (A) 7 feet
- (B) 12 feet
- (C) 14 feet
- (D) 16 feet

DAY 1

A rectangular prism has dimensions of 4 inches, 5 inches, and 6 inches. What is the surface area of the prism?

Ⓐ 74 in²

Ⓑ 120 in²

Ⓒ 136 in²

Ⓓ 148 in²

DAY 2

A box of crackers is a rectangular prism with a volume of 128 cubic inches. The length of the box is 8 inches and the width is 4 inches. What is the height of the box?

Ⓕ 2 inches

Ⓖ 4 inches

Ⓗ 8 inches

Ⓙ 16 inches

DAY 3

Jimmy ran 0.82 miles. What is this decimal written as a fraction in lowest terms?

Ⓐ $\frac{82}{100}$

Ⓑ $\frac{8}{10}$

Ⓒ $\frac{41}{50}$

Ⓓ $\frac{4}{5}$

DAY 4

Jose plots the points *A, B, C,* and *D* as shown and connects them to form a square. Then he moves the square one unit to the right. Which of these is NOT a point on the square after it is moved?

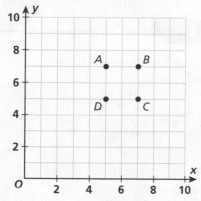

Ⓕ (6, 5)

Ⓖ (6, 7)

Ⓗ (7, 6)

Ⓙ (8, 5)

DAY 5

Which location has an ordered pair of the form (*a, a*), for some number *a*?

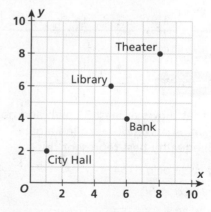

Ⓐ Bank

Ⓑ City Hall

Ⓒ Library

Ⓓ Theater

Countdown to Mastery

WEEK 23

DAY 1

Each card in a set of 12 cards is marked with the letter *A* or *B*. When you choose a card at random, the probability of choosing a card marked *A* is $\frac{2}{3}$. How many cards are marked *A*?

Ⓐ 4
Ⓑ 6
Ⓒ 8
Ⓓ 9

DAY 2

A triangle has two angles that each measure 21°. What is the measure of the third angle of the triangle?

Ⓕ 21°
Ⓖ 42°
Ⓗ 48°
Ⓙ 138°

DAY 3

What is the area of this figure?

Ⓐ 44 square yards
Ⓑ 90 square yards
Ⓒ 100 square yards
Ⓓ 120 square yards

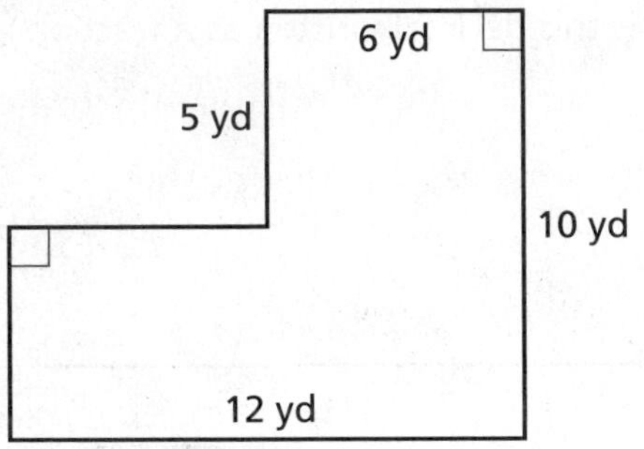

6 yd
5 yd
10 yd
12 yd

DAY 4

A wind that blows at least 39 mi/h and not more than 54 mi/h hour is called a gale. Which inequality best represent this?

Ⓐ $g < 39$ or $g > 54$
Ⓑ $39 < g < 54$
Ⓒ $g \geq 39$ or $g \leq 54$
Ⓓ $39 \leq g \leq 54$

DAY 5

Which equation describes the function in the table?

x	1	2	3	4
y	4	9	14	19

Ⓐ $y = x + 3$
Ⓑ $y = 4x$
Ⓒ $y = 3x + 1$
Ⓓ $y = 5x - 1$

DAY 1

A flower bed is 12 feet long and 4 feet wide. Judy covers 75% of the flower bed's area with mulch. How many square feet are covered with mulch?

(A) 12 square feet

(B) 24 square feet

(C) 27 square feet

(D) 36 square feet

DAY 2

Joe wants to tile the floor of the room shown in this diagram. How much tile does Joe need to buy?

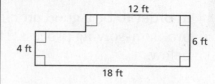

(F) 48 ft²   (H) 72 ft²

(G) 60 ft²   (J) 96 ft²

DAY 3

Triangle ABC is translated 4 units left. What are the coordinates of the image of point B?

(A) (−1, 4)

(B) (2, 4)

(C) (−2, 4)

(D) (2, 8)

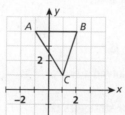

DAY 4

Ted wants to make a small fountain in his garden. The diagram shows the dimensions of the fountain. How much water will Ted need to fill the fountain?

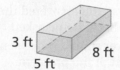

(F) 18 cubic feet

(H) 40 cubic feet

(G) 80 cubic feet

(J) 120 cubic feet

DAY 5

A television weather forecaster reported that temperatures the previous night had stayed between −6 °F and 2 °F. Which of the following might have been the temperature the previous night?

(A) −7 °F

(B) −3 °F

(C) 3 °F

(D) 9 °F

Focus on Problem Solving

The Problem Solving Process

In order to be a good problem solver, you first need a good problem-solving process. The process used in this book is detailed below.

UNDERSTAND the Problem

- **What are you asked to find?** — Restate the question in your own words.

- **What information is given?** — Identify the facts in the problem.

- **What information do you need?** — Determine which facts are needed to answer the question.

- **Is all the information given?** — Determine whether all the facts are given.

- **Is there any information given that you will not use?** — Determine which facts, if any, are unnecessary to solve the problem.

Make a PLAN

- **Have you ever solved a similar problem?** — Think about other problems like this that you successfully solved.

- **What strategy or strategies can you use?** — Determine a strategy that you can use and how you will use it.

SOLVE

- **Follow your plan.** — Show the steps in your solution. Write your answer as a complete sentence.

LOOK BACK

- **Have you answered the question?** — Be sure that you answered the question that is being asked.

- **Is your answer reasonable?** — Your answer should make sense in the context of the problem.

- **Is there another strategy you could use?** — Solving the problem using another strategy is a good way to check your work.

- **Did you learn anything while solving this problem that could help you solve similar problems in the future?** — Try to remember the problems you have solved and the strategies you used to solve them.

Using the Problem Solving Process

During summer vacation, Nicholas will visit first his cousin and then his grandmother. He will be gone for 5 weeks and 2 days, and he will spend 9 more days with his cousin than with his grandmother. How long will he stay with each family member?

UNDERSTAND the Problem

Identify the important information.

- Nicholas's visits will total 5 weeks and 2 days.
- He will spend 9 more days with his cousin than with his grandmother.

The answer will be how long he will stay with each family member.

Make a PLAN

You can draw a diagram to show how long Nicholas will stay. Use boxes for the length of each stay. The length of each box will represent the length of each stay.

SOLVE

Think: There are 7 days in a week, so 5 weeks and 2 days is 37 days in all. Your diagram might look like this:

| Cousin | ? days | 9 days | = 37 days |

| Grandmother | ? days |

| Cousin | 14 days | 9 days | $37 - 9 = 28$ |

| Grandmother | 14 days | $28 \div 2 = 14$ |

So Nicholas will stay with his cousin for 23 days and with his grandmother for 14 days.

LOOK BACK

Twenty-three days is 9 days longer than 14 days. The total of the two stays is $23 + 14$, or 37 days, which is the same as 5 weeks and 2 days. This solution fits the description of Nicholas's trip given in the problem.

Using Your Book for Success

This book has many features designed to help you learn and study math. Becoming familiar with these features will prepare you for greater success on your exams.

Learn

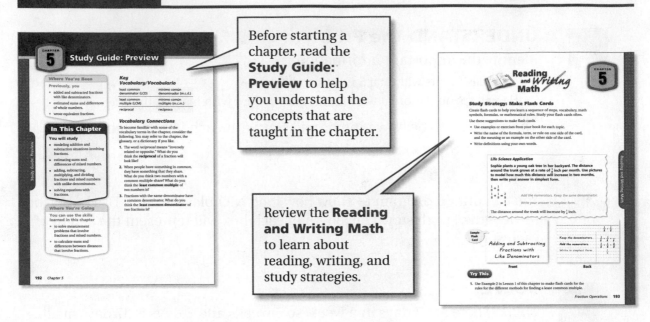

Before starting a chapter, read the **Study Guide: Preview** to help you understand the concepts that are taught in the chapter.

Review the **Reading and Writing Math** to learn about reading, writing, and study strategies.

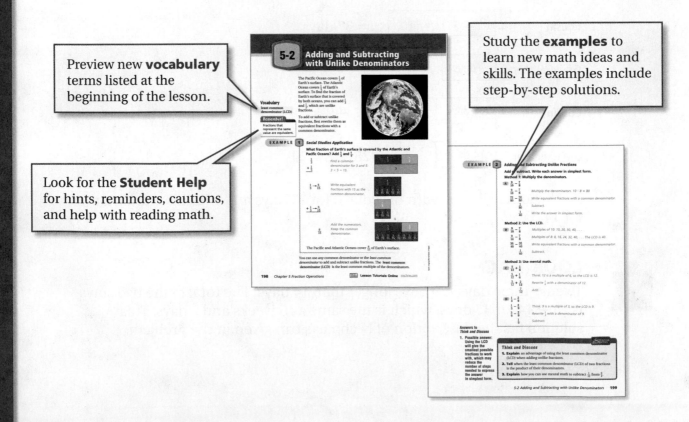

Preview new **vocabulary** terms listed at the beginning of the lesson.

Look for the **Student Help** for hints, reminders, cautions, and help with reading math.

Study the **examples** to learn new math ideas and skills. The examples include step-by-step solutions.

Practice

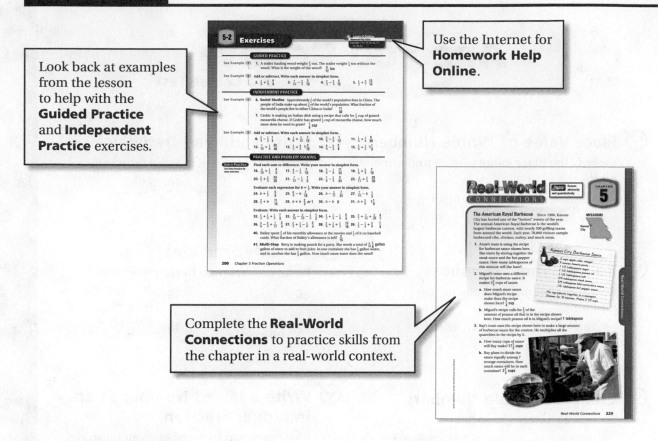

Look back at examples from the lesson to help with the **Guided Practice** and **Independent Practice** exercises.

Use the Internet for **Homework Help Online**.

Complete the **Real-World Connections** to practice skills from the chapter in a real-world context.

Review

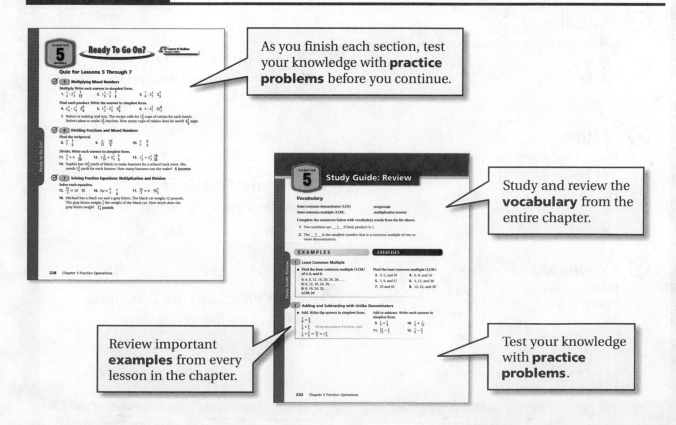

As you finish each section, test your knowledge with **practice problems** before you continue.

Study and review the **vocabulary** from the entire chapter.

Review important **examples** from every lesson in the chapter.

Test your knowledge with **practice problems**.

ARE YOU READY?

Pre-Course Test

✓ Place Value of Whole Numbers

Identify the place value of each underlined digit.

1. 6<u>4</u>,253　　　　　**2.** 8<u>1</u>3,479

✓ Round Whole Numbers

Round each number to the nearest hundred.

3. 8,297　　　　　**4.** 42,631

✓ Compare Whole Numbers

Compare. Write <, >, or =.

5. 512 ■ 521　　　　　**6.** 417 ■ 328

✓ Multiples

List the first four multiples of each number.

7. 9　　　　　**8.** 14

✓ Factors

Find all the whole-number factors of each number.

9. 20　　　　　**10.** 121

✓ Exponents

Find each value.

11. 3^4　　　　　**12.** 16^2

✓ Write and Read Decimals

Write each decimal in word form.

13. 6.29　　　　　**14.** 9.834

✓ Simplify Fractions

Write each fraction in simplest form.

15. $\frac{3}{15}$　　　　　**16.** $\frac{8}{12}$

17. $\frac{18}{30}$　　　　　**18.** $\frac{15}{21}$

✓ Write a Mixed Number as an Improper Fraction

Write each mixed number as an improper fraction.

19. $4\frac{2}{5}$　　　　　**20.** $8\frac{5}{6}$

✓ Write Equivalent Fractions

Write three equivalent fractions for each given fraction.

21. $\frac{1}{3}$　　　　　**22.** $\frac{2}{9}$

✓ Compare Fractions

Compare. Write >, <, or =.

23. $\frac{3}{7}$ ■ $\frac{7}{3}$　　　　　**24.** $\frac{2}{6}$ ■ $\frac{3}{9}$

✓ Write Fractions as Decimals

Write each fraction as a decimal.

25. $\frac{3}{4}$　　　　　**26.** $\frac{7}{8}$

✓ Write Ratios

Write the ratio.

27. red squares to all squares

28. blue squares to red squares

✓ Whole Number Operations

Add, subtract, multiply, or divide.

29.
$$\begin{array}{r} 34 \\ + 42 \end{array}$$

30.
$$\begin{array}{r} 28 \\ \times 16 \end{array}$$

31.
$$\begin{array}{r} 545 \\ - 217 \end{array}$$

32. $6\overline{)174}$

33.
$$\begin{array}{r} 317 \\ \times 25 \end{array}$$

34.
$$\begin{array}{r} 245 \\ + 576 \end{array}$$

35. $31\overline{)1426}$

36.
$$\begin{array}{r} 905 \\ - 438 \end{array}$$

✓ Decimal Operations

Multiply.

37. 3.27×41

38. 7.4×6.3

✓ Simplify Numerical Expressions

Simplify each expression.

39. $\frac{1}{2}(7 + 9)$

40. $2.6(4)^2$

✓ Evaluate Expressions

Evaluate each expression for the given value of the variable.

41. $2(5 - x)$ for $x = 2.7$

42. $4y^2$ for $y = 3.1$

✓ Solve One-Step Equations

Solve each equation.

43. $t + 4.8 = 7.0$

44. $\frac{h}{3} = 24$

✓ Solve Proportions

Solve for n.

45. $\frac{4}{6} = \frac{n}{15}$

46. $\frac{n}{5} = \frac{21}{15}$

✓ Graph Ordered Pairs

Graph each ordered pair.

47. $A(3, 7)$

48. $B(8, 1)$

✓ Identify Polygons

Tell how many sides and angles each polygon has.

49.

50.

Why Learn This?

Patterns are visible all around us. In nature, we see patterns in the lines formed by strata in rock formations over millions of years and exposed by erosion. You can use whole number estimation to estimate the number of lines seen.

Learn It Online
Chapter Project Online

Chapter

• Use the order of operations.

• Use properties to find equivalent expressions.

(all) age fotostock/SuperStock

Are You Ready?

✓ Vocabulary

Choose the best term from the list to complete each sentence.

1. The answer in a multiplication problem is called the _____?_____.

2. 5,000 + 400 + 70 + 5 is a number written in _____?_____ form.

3. A(n) _____?_____ tells about how many.

4. The number 70,562 is written in _____?_____ form.

5. Ten thousands is the _____?_____ of the 4 in 42,801.

place value

estimate

product

expanded

standard

period

Complete these exercises to review skills you will need for this chapter.

✓ Compare Whole Numbers

Compare. Write <, >, or =.

6. 245 ▮ 219

7. 5,320 ▮ 5,128

8. 64 ▮ 67

9. 784 ▮ 792

✓ Round Whole Numbers

Round each number to the nearest hundred.

10. 567

11. 827

12. 1,642

13. 12,852

14. 1,237

15. 135

16. 15,561

17. 452,801

Round each number to the nearest thousand.

18. 4,709

19. 3,399

20. 9,825

21. 26,419

22. 12,434

23. 4,561

24. 11,784

25. 468,201

✓ Whole Number Operations

Add, subtract, multiply, or divide.

26. 18×22

27. $135 \div 3$

28. $247 + 96$

29. $358 - 29$

✓ Simplify Numerical Expressions

Simplify each expression.

30. $3 \times 4 \times 2$

31. $20 + 100 - 40$

32. $5 \times 20 \div 4$

33. $6 \times 12 \times 5$

Where You've Been

Previously, you

- compared and ordered whole numbers to the hundred thousands.
- divided whole numbers.
- used the order of operations without exponents.

In This Chapter

You will study

- using the order of operations, including exponents.
- using properties to compute whole-number operations mentally.
- representing whole numbers by using exponents.

Where You're Going

You can use the skills learned in this chapter

- to express numbers in scientific and standard notation in science classes.
- to work with expressions involving other types of numbers.

Key Vocabulary/Vocabulario

Associative Property	propiedad asociativa
base	base (en numeración)
Commutative Property	propiedad conmutativa
Distributive Property	propiedad distributiva
dividend	dividendo
divisor	divisor
exponent	exponente
numerical expression	expresión numérica
order of operations	orden de las operaciones

Vocabulary Connections

To become familiar with some of the vocabulary terms in the chapter, consider the following. You may refer to the chapter, the glossary, or a dictionary if you like.

1. An *order* is the way things are arranged one after the other. How do you think an **order of operations** will help you solve math problems?

2. The word *numerical* means "of numbers." The word *expression* can refer to a mathematical symbol or combination of symbols. What do you think a **numerical expression** is?

3. To *divide* means to separate a number into a given number of equal parts. What do you think a **divisor** is?

Reading and Writing Math

Reading Strategy: Use Your Book for Success

Understanding how your textbook is organized will help you locate and use helpful information.

As you read through an example problem, pay attention to the **margin notes,** such as Reading Math notes, Writing Math notes, Helpful Hints, and Caution notes. These notes will help you understand concepts and avoid common mistakes.

Reading Math
A group of four ta
marks with a line
through it means

Writing Math
To write a repeati
decimal, you can
show three dots

Helpful Hint
Estimating before
you add or subtra
will help you chec

Caution!
When you write a
expression for data
a table, check that

The **Glossary** is found in the back of your textbook. Use it as a resource when you need the definition of an unfamiliar word or property.

The **Index** is located at the end of your textbook. Use it to locate the page where a particular concept is taught.

The **Skills Bank** is found in the back of your textbook. These pages review concepts from previous math courses, including geometry skills.

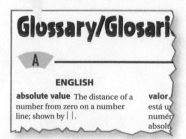

Glossary/Glosari

A

ENGLISH

absolute value The distance of a number from zero on a number line; shown by | |.

valor
está u
numér
absolu

Index

A

Aaron, Hank, 36
Abacus, 9
Absolute value, 762
Accuracy, 767

in sca
37
in sim
solvi
tiles, 63
variable
Algebra t
Algebraic
writing,
Alternate
Alternate
Alvin sub

Skills Bank

Place Value—Trillions

You can use a place-value chart to read and write numbers.

Try This

Use your textbook.

1. Use the glossary to find the definitions of *bisect* and *factor tree*.

2. Name two sections of the Skills Bank that can help you review how to round numbers.

3. Use the Problem Solving Handbook to list the four steps of the problem-solving plan and two different problem-solving strategies.

4. Use the index to find the pages where *exponent* and *properties* appear.

1-1 Estimating with Whole Numbers

Sometimes in math you do not need an exact answer. Instead, you can use an *estimate*. **Estimates** are close to the exact answer but are usually easier and faster to find.

When estimating, you can round the numbers in the problem to *compatible numbers*. **Compatible numbers** are close to the numbers in the problem, and they can help you do math mentally.

Vocabulary

estimate

compatible number

underestimate

overestimate

"WELL, MAYBE UMPTEEN ZILLION WAS TOO GENERAL A COST ESTIMATE."

EXAMPLE 1 Estimating a Sum or Difference by Rounding

Estimate each sum or difference by rounding to the place value indicated.

Remember!

When rounding, look at the digit to the right of the place to which you are rounding.

• If that digit is 5 or greater, round up.
• If that digit is less than 5, round down.

A 5,439 + 7,516; thousands

$$\begin{array}{ll} 5,000 & \text{Round 5,439 down.} \\ +\ 8,000 & \text{Round 7,516 up.} \\ \hline 13,000 \end{array}$$

The sum is about 13,000.

B 62,167 − 47,511; ten thousands

$$\begin{array}{ll} 60,000 & \text{Round 62,167 down.} \\ -\ 50,000 & \text{Round 47,511 up.} \\ \hline 10,000 \end{array}$$

The difference is about 10,000.

An estimate that is less than the exact answer is an **underestimate**.

An estimate that is greater than the exact answer is an **overestimate**.

Cartoon Stock

Video **Lesson Tutorials Online** my.hrw.com

EXAMPLE **2** **Estimating a Product by Rounding**

Ms. Escobar is planning a graduation celebration for the entire eighth grade. There are 9 eighth-grade homeroom classes of 27 students. Estimate how many cups Ms. Escobar needs to buy for the students if they all attend the celebration.

Find the number of students in the eighth grade.

$9 \times 27 \rightarrow 9 \times 30$ *Overestimate the number of students.*

$9 \times 30 = 270$ *The actual number of students is **less than** 270.*

If Ms. Escobar buys 270 cups, she will have enough for every student.

EXAMPLE **3** **Estimating a Quotient Using Compatible Numbers**

Mrs. Byrd will drive 120 miles to take Becca to the state fair. She can drive 65 mi/h. About how long will the trip take?

To find how long the trip will be, divide the miles Mrs. Byrd has to travel by how many miles per hour she can drive.

miles ÷ miles per hour

$120 \div 65 \rightarrow 120 \div 60$ *120 and 60 are compatible numbers. **Underestimate** the speed.*

$120 \div 60 = 2$ *Because she **underestimated** the speed, the actual time will be **less than** 2 hours.*

It will take Mrs. Byrd about two hours to reach the state fair.

Think and Discuss

MATHEMATICAL PRACTICES

1. **Suppose** you are buying items for a party and you have $50. Would it be better to overestimate or underestimate the cost of the items?

2. **Suppose** your car can travel between 20 and 25 miles on a gallon of gas. You want to go on a 100-mile trip. Would it be better to overestimate or underestimate the number of miles per gallon your car can travel?

3. **Describe** situations in which you might want to estimate.

Gabe Palmer/Alamy

GUIDED PRACTICE

See Example 1 — **Estimate each sum or difference by rounding to the place value indicated.**

    1. 4,689 + 2,469; thousands   **2.** 50,498 − 35,798; ten thousands

See Example 2 — **3.** The graph shows the number of bottles of water used in three bicycle races last year. If the same number of riders enter the races each year, estimate the number of bottles that will be needed for races held in May over the next five years.

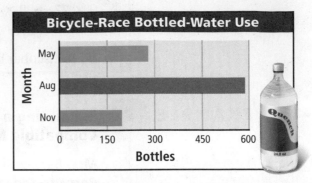

Bicycle-Race Bottled-Water Use

See Example 3 — **4.** If a local business provided half the bottled water needed for the August bicycle race, about how many bottles did the company provide?

    5. Carla drives 80 miles on her scooter. If the scooter gets about 42 miles per gallon of gas, about how much gas did she use?

INDEPENDENT PRACTICE

See Example 1 — **Estimate each sum or difference by rounding to the place value indicated.**

    6. 6,570 + 3,609; thousands   **7.** 49,821 − 11,567; ten thousands

    8. 3,912 + 1,269; thousands   **9.** 37,097 − 20,364; ten thousands

See Example 2 — **10.** The recreation center has provided softballs every year to the city league. Use the table to estimate the number of softballs the league will use in 5 years.

See Example 3 — **11.** The recreation center has a girls' golf team with 8 members. About how many golf balls will each girl on the team get?

Recreation Center Balls Supplied	
Sport	**Number of Balls**
Basketball	21
Golf	324
Softball	28
Table tennis	95

12. If the recreation center loses about 4 table tennis balls per year, and they are not replaced, about how many years will it take until the center has none left?

PRACTICE AND PROBLEM SOLVING

Extra Practice
See Extra Practice for more exercises.

Estimate each sum or difference by rounding to the greatest place value.

13. 152 + 269   **14.** 797 − 234   **15.** 242 − 179

16. 6,152 − 3,195   **17.** 9,179 + 2,206   **18.** 10,982 + 4,821

19. 82,465 − 38,421   **20.** 38,347 + 17,039   **21.** 51,201 + 16,492

22. 639,069 + 283,136   **23.** 777,060 − 410,364   **24.** 998,927 − 100,724

Use the bar graph for Exercises 25–31.

25. On one summer day there were 2,824 sailboats on Lake Erie. Estimate the number of square miles available to each boat.

26. If the areas of all the Great Lakes are rounded to the nearest thousand, which two of the lakes would be the closest in area?

27. About how much larger is Lake Huron than Lake Ontario?

28. The Great Lakes are called "great" because of the huge amount of fresh water they contain. Estimate the total area of all the Great Lakes combined.

29. **?** **What's the Question?** Lake Erie is about 50,000 square miles smaller. What is the question?

30. **Write About It** Explain how you would estimate the areas of Lake Huron and Lake Michigan to compare their sizes.

31. **Challenge** Estimate the average area of the Great Lakes.

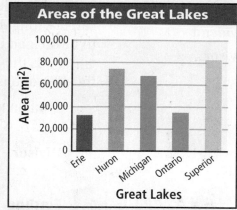

Areas of the Great Lakes

Area includes the water surface and drainage basin within the United States and Canada.

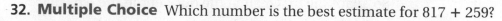

32. Multiple Choice Which number is the best estimate for $817 + 259$?

Ⓐ 10,000 Ⓑ 2,000 Ⓒ 1,100 Ⓓ 800

33. Short Response The National Football League requires home teams to have 36 new footballs for outdoor games and 24 new footballs for indoor games. Estimate how many new footballs the Washington Redskins must buy for 8 outdoor games. Explain how you determined your estimate.

1-2 Divide Multi-Digit Whole Numbers

COMMON CORE

CC.6.NS.2 Fluently divide multi-digit numbers using the standard algorithm

Vocabulary
dividend
divisor

Every year students take the school bus to and from school. There are about 480,000 school buses in the United States, and there are 25,920,000 total students who take the bus. You can use division to find out how many students are on each bus.

To divide multi-digit numbers, you can use long division. The number to be divided is the **dividend**. The **divisor** is the number by which the dividend is divided.

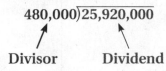

$$480,000\overline{)25,920,000}$$

Divisor   Dividend

EXAMPLE 1 **Finding Group Size Using Division**

A school wants to separate 364 students into equal-sized homeroom classes. There are 13 classrooms in the school that can be used for a homeroom. How many students will be in each homeroom?

Step 1: Decide where to place the first digit in the quotient.

$$\begin{array}{r} x \\ 13\overline{)364} \end{array}$$ no   *You cannot divide 3 by 13.*

$$\begin{array}{r} x\blacksquare \\ 13\overline{)364} \end{array}$$ yes   *You can divide 36 by 13.*

So, place the first digit of the quotient in the tens place.

Step 2: Divide the tens. $13\overline{)36}$

$$\begin{array}{r} 2 \\ 13\overline{)364} \\ -26 \\ \hline 10 \end{array}$$ *Multiply. 13 × 2*
   Subtract. 36 − 26
   Compare. 10 < 13

Step 3: Divide the ones. $13\overline{)104}$

$$\begin{array}{r} 28 \\ 13\overline{)364} \\ -26\downarrow \\ \hline 104 \\ -104 \\ \hline 0 \end{array}$$ *Multiply. 13 × 8*

   Subtract. 104 − 104

So, each homeroom will have 28 students.

In the previous example, division is used to separate a large group into a certain number of smaller groups to find out how many each smaller group will have. In the following example, division is used to separate a large group into groups of a certain size to find out how many groups there will be.

EXAMPLE 2

Finding Number of Groups Using Division

A high school's administrators rent school buses to transport 1,056 students. Each bus holds 52 students. How many buses will be needed?

Step 1: Use an estimate to place the first digit in the quotient.

Divide: $1{,}056 \div 52 = n$ $\qquad 52\overline{)1{,}056}$

Estimate: $1{,}000 \div 50 = 20$ $\qquad$ So, $n \approx 20$.

So, the first digit of the quotient will be in the tens place.

Step 2: Divide the tens. $52\overline{)105}$

$$\begin{array}{r} 2 \\ 52\overline{)1{,}056} \\ -104 \\ \hline 1 \end{array}$$

$\qquad$ *Multiply.* 52×2
$\qquad$ *Subtract.* $105 - 104$
$\qquad$ *Compare.* $1 < 52$

Step 3: Divide the ones. $52\overline{)16}$

Think: Since 52 > 16, write a zero in the ones place in the quotient.

$$\begin{array}{r} 20 \text{ r}16 \\ 52\overline{)1{,}056} \\ -104\downarrow \\ \hline 16 \\ -0 \\ \hline 16 \end{array}$$

$\qquad$ *Multiply.* 52×0

$\qquad$ *Subtract.* $16 - 0$
$\qquad$ *Compare.* $16 < 52$

Twenty buses will not be enough to transport all of the students. The high school will need to rent another bus to transport the remaining 16 students. The quotient must be rounded up to the next whole number.

Since 21 is close to the estimate of 20, the answer is reasonable. So, the high school will need 21 buses.

Think and Discuss

1. Tell how you decide where to write the first digit of your quotient.

2. Explain how you know when you need to write a zero in the quotient.

GUIDED PRACTICE

See Example **1**

1. **Money** Amanda wants to save $1,450 for a summer trip to Europe. She has 25 weeks to save the money. How much does she need to save each week in order to have enough for the trip?

2. An aquarium has 29 large fish tanks. A total of 1,423 fish need to be kept in the tanks. If the owner wants to split the fish into the tanks as evenly as possible, what is the greatest number of fish that will be in one tank?

See Example **2**

3. **Environment** One of the most fuel-efficient automobiles gets 51 highway miles to the gallon. The automobile is able to travel about 607 highway miles on a tank of gas. About how many gallons of gas does the car's fuel tank hold?

4. **School** A class of 34 students pick a total of 1,115 apples on an apple-picking field trip. Their teacher wants to split the total apples evenly so each student brings home the same number. How many whole apples will each student get?

INDEPENDENT PRACTICE

See Example **1**

5. A total of 1,232 people visit the top of a skyscraper one afternoon. There were a total of 77 elevator trips, and each elevator held an equal number of people. How many people were in each elevator?

6. The distance from Camp V on Mt. Everest to the peak of the mountain is 7,058 feet. Starting at Camp V, a climber ascends to the peak and returns back. If a climber wants to do this within a 13-hour period, how many feet must she travel each hour?

See Example **2**

7. **Gardening** A landscaper needs 1,225 pounds of topsoil to complete a project. If the soil comes in 40-pound bags, how many will the landscaper need to buy?

8. **Manufacturing** A peanut butter manufacturer packs its jars of peanut butter into cases that hold 40 jars each. If the company produces 3,528 jars of peanut butter in one day, how many cases can it pack?

PRACTICE AND PROBLEM SOLVING

Extra Practice
See Extra Practice for more exercises.

Find each quotient.

9. $1,392 \div 58$

10. $5,756 \div 36$

11. $7,045 \div 15$

12. $9,223 \div 50$

13. $18,207 \div 27$

14. $32,544 \div 36$

15. $24,826 \div 32$

16. $45,025 \div 25$

17. **Transportation** A train travels 2,982 miles at an average speed of 42 miles per hour. At that speed, how long will the train take to complete its trip?

18. Life Science A male adult dolphin at an aquarium eats 576 pounds of fish during a 30-day month. On average, how many pounds of fish does the dolphin eat each day?

19. Earth Science A scientist monitors Old Faithful, a geyser in Yellowstone National Park, for a period of 2,880 minutes. During this time the geyser erupts a total of 34 times. At this rate, how often does Old Faithful erupt?

20. Critical Thinking Describe how the problem $24,000 \div 50$ could be solved without just dividing 24,000 by 50. Then find the answer.

21. Multi-Step Claudia's parents bought an entertainment center for $1,176. They plan to pay for it with 14 equal monthly payments. How much will each payment be if a $4.50 service charge is added every month?

22. What's the Error? A student solved the division problem $1,182 \div 12$ as shown. His answer was 98.6. Explain the error and write the correct quotient.

$$\begin{array}{r} 98 \\ 12\overline{)\,1{,}182} \\ -108 \\ \hline 102 \\ -96 \\ \hline 6 \end{array}$$

23. Write About It A professor needs 2,025 sheets of paper to print classroom materials. The professor can buy packs of paper which have 200 sheets each. Explain how to find how many packs of paper the professor must buy.

24. Challenge The population of Jackson, TN, was 59,643 in 2000. In 2006 the population had increased by 3,068 people. The area of the city is approximately 112 square kilometers. What was the population density of Jackson, TN, in 2006, rounded to the nearest person per square kilometer?

Test Prep

25. Multiple Choice A small airplane has a total weight capacity of 3,000 pounds for its passengers and crew. If the average weight of each passenger and crew member is 189 pounds, what is the greatest number of passengers and crew that can fit on the airplane?

(A) 15 (B) 15.87 (C) 16 (D) 17

26. Short Response A long-distance bike rider travels 1,220 miles from Tulsa, OK, to Orlando, FL, in 24 days. How many miles per day did the rider average on the journey?

COMMON CORE

CC.6.EE.1 Write and evaluate numerical expressions involving whole-number exponents

Since 1906, the height of Mount Vesuvius in Italy has increased by about 7^3 feet. How many feet is this?

The number 7^3 is written with an exponent. An **exponent** tells how many times a number called the **base** is used as a factor.

Vocabulary

exponent

base

exponential form

The most recent eruption of Mount Vesuvius took place in 1944.

Exponent

Base → 7^3 = $7 \times 7 \times 7 = 343$

So the height of Mount Vesuvius has increased by about 343 ft.

Interactivities Online ▶ A number is in **exponential form** when it is written with a base and an exponent.

Exponential Form	Read	Multiply	Value
10^1	"10 to the 1st power"	10	10
10^2	"10 squared," or "10 to the 2nd power"	10×10	100
10^3	"10 cubed," or "10 to the 3rd power"	$10 \times 10 \times 10$	1,000
10^4	"10 to the 4th power"	$10 \times 10 \times 10 \times 10$	10,000

EXAMPLE **1** **Writing Numbers in Exponential Form**

Write each expression in exponential form.

A $4 \times 4 \times 4$

4^3 *4 is a factor 3 times.*

B $9 \times 9 \times 9 \times 9 \times 9$

9^5 *9 is a factor 5 times.*

EXAMPLE **2** **Finding the Value of Numbers in Exponential Form**

Find each value.

A 2^7

$2^7 = 2 \times 2 \times 2 \times 2 \times 2 \times 2 \times 2$

$= 128$

B 6^4

$6^4 = 6 \times 6 \times 6 \times 6$

$= 1,296$

Video **Lesson Tutorials Online** my.hrw.com

Corbis/Bettmann

EXAMPLE **3** **PROBLEM SOLVING APPLICATION**

If Dana's school closes, a phone tree is used to contact each student's family. The secretary calls 3 families. Then each family calls 3 other families, and so on. How many families will be notified during the 6th round of calls?

1. Understand the Problem

The **answer** will be the number of families called in the 6th round.

List the **important information:**
- The secretary calls 3 families.
- Each family calls 3 families.

2. Make a Plan

You can draw a diagram to see how many calls are in each round.

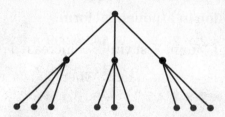

Secretary

1st round—3 calls

2nd round—9 calls

3. Solve

Notice that in each round, the number of calls is a power of 3.
1st round: 3 calls = 3 = 3^1
2nd round: 9 calls = 3 × 3 = 3^2

So during the 6th round there will be 3^6 calls.
$3^6 = 3 × 3 × 3 × 3 × 3 × 3 = 729$
During the 6th round of calls, 729 families will be notified.

4. Look Back

Drawing a diagram helps you visualize the pattern, but the numbers become too large for a diagram after the third round of calls. Solving this problem by using exponents can be easier and faster.

MATHEMATICAL PRACTICES

Think and Discuss

1. Read each number: 4^8, 12^3, 3^2.

2. Explain which has the greater value, 3^4 or 4^3.

GUIDED PRACTICE

See Example **1** Write each expression in exponential form.

1. $8 \times 8 \times 8$ **2.** 7×7 **3.** $6 \times 6 \times 6 \times 6 \times 6$

4. $4 \times 4 \times 4 \times 4$ **5.** $5 \times 5 \times 5 \times 5 \times 5$ **6.** 1×1

See Example **2** Find each value.

7. 4^2 **8.** 3^3 **9.** 5^4 **10.** 8^2 **11.** 7^3

See Example **3** **12.** At Russell's school, one person will contact 4 people and each of those people will contact 4 other people, and so on. How many people will be contacted in the fifth round?

INDEPENDENT PRACTICE

See Example **1** Write each expression in exponential form.

13. $2 \times 2 \times 2 \times 2 \times 2 \times 2$ **14.** $9 \times 9 \times 9 \times 9$ **15.** 8×8

16. $1 \times 1 \times 1$ **17.** $6 \times 6 \times 6 \times 6 \times 6$ **18.** $5 \times 5 \times 5$

19. $7 \times 7 \times 7 \times 7 \times 7 \times 7 \times 7$ **20.** $3 \times 3 \times 3 \times 3$ **21.** 4×4

See Example **2** Find each value.

22. 2^4 **23.** 3^5 **24.** 6^2 **25.** 9^2 **26.** 7^4

27. 8^3 **28.** 1^4 **29.** 16^2 **30.** 10^8 **31.** 12^2

See Example **3** **32.** To save money for a video game, you put one dollar in an envelope. Each day for 5 days you double the number of dollars in the envelope from the day before. How much will be saved on the fifth day?

PRACTICE AND PROBLEM SOLVING

Extra Practice

See Extra Practice for more exercises.

Write each expression as repeated multiplication.

33. 16^3 **34.** 22^2 **35.** 31^6 **36.** 46^5 **37.** 50^3

38. 4^1 **39.** 1^9 **40.** 17^6 **41.** 8^5 **42.** 12^4

Find each value.

43. 10^6 **44.** 73^1 **45.** 9^4 **46.** 80^2 **47.** 10^5

48. 19^2 **49.** 2^9 **50.** 57^1 **51.** 5^3 **52.** 11^3

Compare. Write $<$, $>$, or $=$.

53. 6^1 ▨ 5^1 **54.** 9^2 ▨ 20^1 **55.** 10^1 ▨ $1{,}000{,}000^1$

56. 7^3 ▨ 3^7 **57.** 5^5 ▨ 25^1 **58.** 100^2 ▨ 10^4

You are able to grow because your body produces new cells. New cells are made when old cells divide. Single-celled bodies, such as bacteria, divide by *binary fission*, which means "splitting into two parts." A cycle is the length of time a cell needs to divide once.

59. In science lab, Carol has a dish containing 4^5 cells. How many cells are represented by this number?

60. A certain colony of bacteria triples in length every 15 minutes. Its length is now 1 mm. How long will it be in 1 hour? (*Hint:* There are four cycles of 15 minutes in 1 hour.)

Use the bar graph for Exercises 61–64.

61. Determine how many times cell type A will divide in a 24-hour period. If you begin with one type A cell, how many cells will be produced in 24 hours?

62. Multi-Step If you begin with one type B cell and one type C cell, what is the difference between the number of type B cells and the number of type C cells produced in 24 hours?

63. 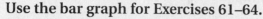 **Write About It** Explain how to find the number of type A cells produced in 48 hours.

64. ⭐ **Challenge** How many hours will it take one C cell to divide into at least 100 C cells?

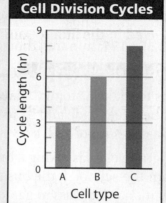

Cell Division Cycles

This plant cell shows the anaphase stage of mitosis. Mitosis is the process of nuclear division in complex cells called eukaryotes.

Test Prep

65. Multiple Choice Which of the following shows the expression $4 \times 4 \times 4$ in exponential form?

Ⓐ 64　　　　Ⓑ 444　　　　Ⓒ 3^4　　　　Ⓓ 4^3

66. Multiple Choice Which expression has the greatest value?

Ⓕ 2^5　　　　Ⓖ 3^4　　　　Ⓗ 4^3　　　　Ⓙ 5^2

CHAPTER 1 SECTION A

Quiz for Lessons 1 Through 3

 1 **Estimating with Whole Numbers**

Estimate each sum or difference by rounding to the place value indicated.

1. 61,582 + 13,281; ten thousands

2. 86,125 − 55,713; ten thousands

3. 7,903 + 2,654; thousands

4. 34,633 − 32,087; thousands

5. 1,896,345 + 3,567,194; hundred thousands

6. 56,129,482 − 37,103,758; ten millions

7. Marcus wants to make a stone walkway in his garden. The rectangular walkway will be 3 feet wide and 21 feet long. Each 2-foot by 3-foot stone covers an area of 6 square feet. How many stones will Marcus need?

8. Jenna's sixth-grade class is taking a bus to the zoo. The zoo is 156 miles from the school. If the bus travels an average of 55 mi/h, about how long will it take the class to get to the zoo?

9. Robin's class is contacting families from her school as part of a fundraiser. If there are 471 families at the school and 27 students in Robin's class, about how many families will each student contact?

 2 **Divide Multi-Digit Whole Numbers**

Find each quotient.

10. $1{,}280 \div 64$ 11. $2{,}682 \div 39$ 12. $2{,}631 \div 24$ 13. $13{,}284 \div 27$

14. There were 954 swimmers at the state meet last month. If 53 teams competed and each team had the same number of members, how many swimmers were on each team?

3 **Exponents**

Write each expression in exponential form.

15. $7 \times 7 \times 7$ 16. $5 \times 5 \times 5 \times 5$

17. $3 \times 3 \times 3 \times 3 \times 3 \times 3$ 18. $10 \times 10 \times 10 \times 10$

19. $1 \times 1 \times 1 \times 1 \times 1$ 20. $4 \times 4 \times 4 \times 4$

Find each value.

21. 3^3 22. 2^4 23. 6^2 24. 8^3

25. To start reading a novel for English class, Sara read 1 page. Each day for 4 days she reads double the number of pages she read the day before. How many pages will she read on the fourth day?

Focus on Problem Solving

MATHEMATICAL PRACTICES — Make sense of problems and persevere in solving them.

Solve

Solve

• **Choose the operation: addition or subtraction**

Read the whole problem before you try to solve it. Determine what action is taking place in the problem. Then decide whether you need to add or subtract in order to solve the problem.

If you need to combine or put numbers together, you need to add. If you need to take away or compare numbers, you need to subtract.

Action	Operation	Picture
Combining Putting together	Add	
Removing Taking away	Subtract	
Comparing Finding the difference	Subtract	

Read each problem. Determine the action in each problem. Choose an operation in order to solve the problem. Then solve.

Most hurricanes that occur over the Atlantic Ocean, the Caribbean Sea, or the Gulf of Mexico occur between June and November. Since 1886, a hurricane has occurred in every month except April.

Use the table for problems 1 and 2.

Number of Out-of-Season Hurricanes Since 1886	
Month	Number
Jan	1
Feb	1
Mar	1
May	14
Dec	10

❶ How many out-of-season hurricanes have occurred in all?

❷ How many more hurricanes have occurred in May than in December?

❸ There were 14 named storms during the 2000 hurricane season. Eight of these became hurricanes, and three others became major hurricanes. How many of the named storms were not hurricanes or major hurricanes?

Focus on Problem Solving **19**

Technology LAB

Explore the Order of Operations

Use with Order of Operations

Learn It Online
Lab Resources Online

Use appropriate tools strategically.
CC.6.EE.2 Write, read, and evaluate expressions in which letters stand for numbers *Also CC.6.EE.2c*

Look at the expression 3 + 2 · 8. To evaluate this expression, decide whether to add first or multiply first. Knowing the correct *order of operations* is important. Without this knowledge, you could get an incorrect result.

Activity 1

Use pencil and paper to evaluate 3 + 2 · 8 two different ways.

Add first, and then multiply by 8.	3 + 2 = 5 5 · 8 = 40
Multiply first, and then add 3.	2 · 8 = 16 16 + 3 = 19

Now evaluate 3 + 2 · 8 using a graphing or scientific calculator.

The result, 19, shows that this calculator multiplied first, even though addition came first in the expression.

If there are no parentheses, then multiplication and division are done before addition or subtraction. If the addition is to be done first, parentheses *must* be used.

When you evaluate (3 + 2) · 8 on a calculator, the result is 40. Because of the parentheses, the calculator adds before multiplying.

Graphing and scientific calculators follow a logical system called the algebraic order of operations. The order of operations tells you to multiply and divide before you add or subtract.

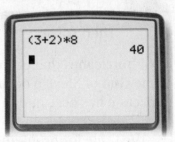

Think and Discuss

1. In 4 + 15 ÷ 5, which operation do you perform first? How do you know?

2. Tell the order in which you would perform the operations in the expression 8 ÷ 2 + 6 · 3 − 4.

Try This

Evaluate each expression with pencil and paper. Check your answer with a calculator.

1. 4 · 12 − 7   **2.** 15 ÷ 3 + 10   **3.** 4 + 2 · 6   **4.** 10 − 4 ÷ 2

Activity 2

What should you do if the same operation appears twice in an expression? Use a calculator to decide which subtraction is done first in the expression $7 - 3 - 2$.

If $7 - 3$ is done first, the value of the expression is $4 - 2 = 2$.

If $3 - 2$ is done first, the value of the expression is $7 - 1 = 6$.

On the calculator, the value of $7 - 3 - 2$ is 2. The subtraction on the left, $7 - 3$, is done first.

Addition and subtraction (or multiplication and division) are done from left to right.

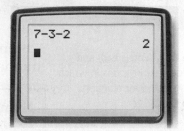

Think and Discuss

1. In $15 + 5 + 4$, does it matter which operation you perform first? Explain.

2. Does it matter which operation you perform first in $15 - 5 + 4$? Explain.

Try This

Evaluate each expression. Check your answer with a calculator.

1. $8 - 6 - 1$ **2.** $20 \div 5 \div 2$ **3.** $3 \cdot 6 \cdot 2$ **4.** $19 + 6 + 5$

Activity 3

Without parentheses, the expression $8 + 2 \cdot 10 - 3$ equals 25. Insert parentheses to make the value of the expression 22.

What happens if you add first?

$(8 + 2) \cdot 10 - 3$

$10 \cdot 10 - 3$

$100 - 3$

97

What happens if you subtract first?

$8 + 2 \cdot (10 - 3)$

$8 + 2 \cdot 7$

$8 + 14$

22

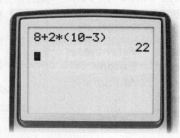

For the expression to equal 22, the subtraction must be done first.

Think and Discuss

1. To evaluate $13 + 5 \cdot 255$ on a calculator, you type $13 + 5$ and then press the $\boxed{\times}$ key. But before you can type in the 255, the display changes to 18!

   a. Does this calculator follow the correct order of operations? Why?

   b. How could you use this calculator to evaluate $13 + 5 \cdot 255$?

Try This

Insert parentheses to make the value of each expression 12.

1. $56 - 40 + 4$ **2.** $3 - 1 \cdot 10 - 4$ **3.** $18 \div 2 + 1 + 6$ **4.** $100 + 8 \div 2 \cdot 2 + 5$

1-4 Order of Operations

COMMON CORE

CC.6.EE.2 Write, read, and evaluate expressions in which letters stand for numbers
Also CC.6.EE.2c

A **numerical expression** is a mathematical phrase that includes only numbers and operation symbols.

Numerical Expressions	$4 + 8 \div 2 \times 6$	$371 - 203 + 2$	$5{,}006 \times 19$

Vocabulary

numerical expression

simplify

order of operations

When you **simplify** a numerical expression, you find its value.

Erika and Jamie each simplified $3 + 4 \times 6$. Their work is shown below. Whose answer is correct?

When an expression has more than one operation, you must know which operation to do first. To make sure that everyone gets the same answer, we use the **order of operations**.

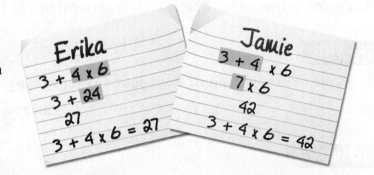

Erika
$3 + 4 \times 6$
$3 + 24$
27
$3 + 4 \times 6 = 27$

Jamie
$3 + 4 \times 6$
7×6
42
$3 + 4 \times 6 = 42$

Remember!

The first letters of these words can help you remember the order of operations.

Please	*Parentheses*
Excuse	*Exponents*
My	*Multiply/*
Dear	*Divide*
Aunt	*Add/*
Sally	*Subtract*

ORDER OF OPERATIONS

1. Perform operations in **parentheses**.
2. Find the values of numbers with **exponents**.
3. **Multiply** or **divide** from left to right as ordered in the problem.
4. **Add** or **subtract** from left to right as ordered in the problem.

$3 + 4 \times 6$	*There are no parentheses or exponents. Multiply first.*
$3 + 24$	*Add.*
27	*Erika has the correct answer.*

EXAMPLE 1 **Using the Order of Operations**

Simplify each expression.

A $9 + 12 \times 2$

$9 + 12 \times 2$	*There are no parentheses or exponents.*
$9 + \quad 24$	*Multiply.*
33	*Add.*

Video **Lesson Tutorials Online** <u>my.hrw.com</u>

Simplify each expression.

B $7 + (12 \times 3) \div 6$

$7 +$	(12×3)	$\div 6$	
$7 +$	36	$\div 6$	*Perform operations within parentheses.*
$7 +$		6	*Divide.*
13			*Add.*

EXAMPLE 2 Using the Order of Operations with Exponents

Simplify each expression.

A $3^3 + 8 - 16$

$3^3 + 8 - 16$	*There are no parentheses.*
$27 + 8 - 16$	*Find the values of numbers with exponents.*
$35 \;\; - 16$	*Add*
19	*Subtract.*

B $8 \div (1 + 3) \times 5^2 - 2$

$8 \div (1 + 3) \times 5^2 - 2$	
$8 \div \quad 4 \quad \times 5^2 - 2$	*Perform operations within parentheses.*
$8 \div \quad 4 \quad \times 25 - 2$	*Find the values of numbers with exponents.*
$2 \;\; \times 25 - 2$	*Divide.*
$50 \quad - 2$	*Multiply.*
48	*Subtract.*

EXAMPLE 3 *Consumer Application*

Regina bought 5 carved wooden beads for \$3 each and 8 glass beads for \$2 each. Simplify $5 \times 3 + 8 \times 2$ to find the amount Regina spent for beads.

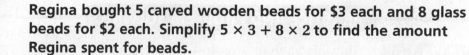

$5 \times 3 + 8 \times 2$

$15 \;\; + \;\; 16$

31

Regina spent \$31 for beads.

Think and Discuss

1. Explain why $6 + 7 \times 10 = 76$ but $(6 + 7) \times 10 = 130$.

2. Tell how you can add parentheses to the numerical expression $2^2 + 5 \times 3$ so that 27 is the correct answer.

Sam Dudgeon/HMH

Video Lesson Tutorials Online my.hrw.com

GUIDED PRACTICE

See Example **1** Simplify each expression.

1. $36 - 18 \div 6$ **2.** $7 + 24 \div 6 \times 2$ **3.** $62 - 4 \times (15 \div 5)$

See Example **2** **4.** $11 + 2^3 \times 5$ **5.** $5 \times (28 \div 7) - 4^2$ **6.** $5 + 3^2 \times 6 - (10 - 9)$

See Example **3** **7.** Coach Milner fed the team after the game by buying 24 Chicken Deals for $4 each and 7 Burger Deals for $6 each. Simplify $24 \times 4 + 7 \times 6$ to find the cost of the food.

INDEPENDENT PRACTICE

See Example **1** Simplify each expression.

8. $9 + 27 \div 3$ **9.** $2 \times 7 - 32 \div 8$ **10.** $45 \div (3 + 6) \times 3$

11. $(6 + 2) \times 4$ **12.** $9 \div 3 + 6 \times 2$ **13.** $5 + 3 \times 2 + 12 \div 4$

See Example **2** **14.** $4^2 + 48 \div (10 - 4)$ **15.** $100 \div 5^2 + 7 \times 3$ **16.** $6 \times 2^2 + 28 - 5$

17. $6^2 - 12 \div 3 + (15 - 7)$ **18.** $21 \div (3 + 4) \times 9 - 2^3$ **19.** $(3^2 + 6 \div 2) \times (36 \div 6 - 4)$

See Example **3** **20.** The nature park has a pride of 5 adult lions and 3 cubs. The adults eat 8 lb of meat each day and the cubs eat 4 lb. Simplify $5 \times 8 + 3 \times 4$ to find the amount of meat consumed each day by the lions.

21. Angie read 4 books that were each 150 pages long and 2 books that were each 325 pages long. Simplify $4 \times 150 + 2 \times 325$ to find the total number of pages Angie read.

PRACTICE AND PROBLEM SOLVING

Extra Practice
See Extra Practice for more exercises.

Simplify each expression.

22. $12 + 3 \times 4$ **23.** $25 - 21 \div 3$ **24.** $1 + 7 \times 2$

25. $60 \div (10 + 2) \times 4^2 - 23$ **26.** $10 \times (28 - 23) + 7^2 - 37$ **27.** $(5 - 3) \div 2$

28. $72 \div 9 - 2 \times 4$ **29.** $12 + (1 + 7^2) \div 5$ **30.** $25 - 5^2$

31. $(15 - 6)^2 - 34 \div 2$ **32.** $(2 \times 4)^2 - 3 \times (5 + 3)$ **33.** $16 + 2 \times 3$

Add parentheses so that each equation is correct.

34. $2^3 + 6 - 5 \times 4 = 12$ **35.** $7 + 2 \times 6 - 4 - 3 = 53$

36. $3^2 + 6 + 3 \times 3 = 36$ **37.** $5^2 - 10 + 5 + 4^2 = 36$

38. $2 \times 8 + 5 - 3 = 23$ **39.** $9^2 - 2 \times 15 + 16 - 8 = 11$

40. $5 + 7 \times 2 - 3 = 21$ **41.** $4^2 \times 3 - 2 \div 4 = 4$

42. Critical Thinking Jon says the answer to $1 + 3 \times (6 + 2) - 7$ is 25. Julie says the answer is 18. Who is correct? Explain.

Archaeologists study cultures of the past by uncovering items from ancient cities. An archaeologist has chosen a site in Colorado for her team's next dig. She divides the location into rectangular plots and labels each plot so that uncovered items can be identified by the plot in which they were found.

43. The archaeologist must order a cover for the plot where the team is digging. Simplify the expression $3 \times (2^2 + 6)$ to find the area of the plot in square meters.

Tourists assist archaeologists at Shields Pueblo in Colorado.

44. In the first week, the archaeology team digs down 2 meters and removes a certain amount of dirt. Simplify the expression $3 \times (2^2 + 6) \times 2$ to find the volume of the dirt removed from the plot in the first week.

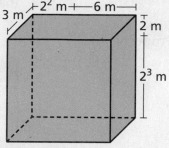

45. Over the next two weeks, the archaeology team digs down an additional 2^3 meters. Simplify the expression $3 \times (2^2 + 6) \times (2 + 2^3)$ to find the total volume of dirt removed from the plot after 3 weeks.

46. ✐ **Write About It** Explain why the archaeologist must follow the order of operations to determine the area of each plot.

47. ★ **Challenge** Write an expression for the volume of dirt that would be removed if the archaeologist's team were to dig down an additional 3^2 meters after the first three weeks.

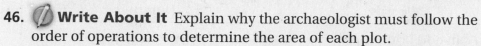

Test Prep

48. **Multiple Choice** Which operation should you perform first when you simplify $81 - (6 + 30 \div 2) \times 5$?

   Ⓐ Addition   Ⓑ Division   Ⓒ Multiplication   Ⓓ Subtraction

49. **Multiple Choice** Which expression does NOT have a value of 5?

   Ⓕ $2^2 + (3 - 2)$ Ⓖ $(2^2 + 3) - 2$ Ⓗ $2^2 + 3 - 2$ Ⓙ $2^2 - (3 + 2)$

50. **Gridded Response** What is the value of the expression $3^2 + (9 \div 3 - 2)$?

1-5 Properties and Mental Math

COMMON CORE

CC.6.EE.3 Apply the properties of operations to generate equivalent expressions *Also CC.6.NS.4*

Vocabulary

Commutative Property

Associative Property

Distributive Property

Mental math means "doing math in your head." Daniel Tammet is extremely good at mental math. When he was asked to calculate 37 × 37 × 37 × 37, he multiplied mentally and gave the correct answer of 1,874,161 in under a minute!

Many mental math strategies use number properties that you already know to make equivalent expressions that may be easier to simplify.

Caution!

The Commutative and Associative Properties do not apply to subtraction or division.

COMMUTATIVE PROPERTY (Ordering)

Words	Numbers
You can add or multiply numbers in any order.	$18 + 9 = 9 + 18$ $15 \times 2 = 2 \times 15$

ASSOCIATIVE PROPERTY (Grouping)

Words	Numbers
When you are only adding or only multiplying, you can group any of the numbers together.	$(17 + 2) + 9 = 17 + (2 + 9)$ $(12 \times 2) \times 4 = 12 \times (2 \times 4)$

EXAMPLE **1** **Using Properties to Add and Multiply Whole Numbers**

A Simplify $12 + 4 + 18 + 46$.

$12 + 4 + 18 + 46$	*Look for sums that are multiples of 10.*
$12 + 18 \ + \ 4 + 46$	*Use the Commutative Property.*
$(12 + 18) + (4 + 46)$	*Use the Associative Property to make*
$30 \quad + \quad 50$	*groups of compatible numbers.*
80	*Use mental math to add.*

Colin McPherson/Corbis

Video **Lesson Tutorials Online** my.hrw.com

B Simplify $5 \times 12 \times 2$.

$5 \times 12 \times 2$	*Look for products that are multiples of 10.*
$12 \times 5 \times 2$	*Use the Commutative Property.*
$12 \times (5 \times 2)$	*Use the Associative Property to group*
$12 \times \quad 10$	*compatible numbers.*
$\quad 120$	*Use mental math to multiply.*

To multiply a number by a sum, such as $6 \times (10 + 4)$, you can use the order of operations, or you can use the *Distributive Property*.

DISTRIBUTIVE PROPERTY

Words	Numbers
To multiply a number by a sum, multiply by each number in the sum and then add.	$6 \times (10 + 4) = (6 \times 10) + (6 \times 4)$ $= \quad 60 \quad + \quad 24$ $= \quad\quad 84$

When you multiply two numbers, you can "break apart" one of the numbers into a sum and then use the Distributive Property.

EXAMPLE **2** **Using the Distributive Property to Multiply**

Use the Distributive Property to find each product.

A 4×23

$4 \times 23 = 4 \times (20 + 3)$	*"Break apart" 23 into 20 + 3.*
$= (4 \times 20) + (4 \times 3)$	*Use the Distributive Property.*
$= \quad 80 \quad + \quad 12$	*Use mental math to multiply.*
$= \quad\quad 92$	*Use mental math to add.*

B 8×74

$8 \times 74 = 8 \times (70 + 4)$	*"Break apart" 74 into 70 + 4.*
$= (8 \times 70) + (8 \times 4)$	*Use the Distributive Property.*
$= \quad 560 \quad + \quad 32$	*Use mental math to multiply.*
$= \quad\quad 592$	*Use mental math to add.*

MATHEMATICAL PRACTICES

Think and Discuss

1. **Give examples** of the Commutative Property and the Associative Property.

2. **Name** some situations in which you might use mental math.

Learn It Online
Homework Help Online
Exercises 1–30, 31, 39, 41, 45, 51

GUIDED PRACTICE

See Example **1** **Simplify.**

1. $13 + 9 + 7 + 11$ **2.** $19 + 18 + 11 + 32$ **3.** $25 + 7 + 13 + 5$

4. $5 \times 14 \times 4$ **5.** $4 \times 16 \times 5$ **6.** $5 \times 17 \times 2$

See Example **2** **Use the Distributive Property to find each product.**

7. 5×24 **8.** 8×52 **9.** 4×39 **10.** 6×14

11. 3×33 **12.** 2×78 **13.** 9×12 **14.** 2×87

INDEPENDENT PRACTICE

See Example **1** **Simplify.**

15. $15 + 17 + 3 + 5$ **16.** $14 + 7 + 16 + 13$ **17.** $6 + 21 + 14 + 9$

18. $5 \times 25 \times 2$ **19.** $2 \times 32 \times 10$ **20.** $6 \times 12 \times 5$

See Example **2** **Use the Distributive Property to find each product.**

21. 3×36 **22.** 4×42 **23.** 6×71 **24.** 2×94 **25.** 6×23

26. 5×25 **27.** 6×62 **28.** 7×21 **29.** 8×41 **30.** 2×94

PRACTICE AND PROBLEM SOLVING

Extra Practice
See Extra Practice for more exercises.

Use mental math to find each sum or product.

31. $8 + 13 + 7 + 12$ **32.** $2 \times 25 \times 4$ **33.** $4 + 22 + 16 + 18$

34. $5 \times 8 \times 12$ **35.** $5 + 98 + 95$ **36.** $6 \times 5 \times 14$

37. $11 + 75 + 25$ **38.** $8 \times 11 \times 5$ **39.** $19 + 1 + 11 + 39$

40. Paul is writing a story for the school newspaper about the landscaping done by his class. The students planted 15 vines, 12 hedges, 8 trees, and 35 flowering plants. How many plants were used in the project?

41. Earth Science The temperature on Sunday was 58 °F. The temperature is predicted to rise 4 °F on Monday, then rise 2 °F more on Tuesday, and then rise another 6 °F by Saturday. What is the predicted temperature on Saturday?

42. Multi-Step Janice wants to order disks for her computer. She needs to find the total cost, including shipping and handling. If Janice orders 7 disks, what will her total cost be?

Description	Number	Unit Cost with Tax	Price
Computer Disk	7	$24.00	
		Shipping & Handling	$7.00
		Total	

Multiply using the Distributive Property.

43. 9 × 17   **44.** 4 × 27   **45.** 11 × 18   **46.** 7 × 51

Determine if each pair of expressions is equivalent. If so, state the property shown.

47. 8 × 35 and (8 × 30)(8 × 5)

48. 14 + 7 + 6 and 6 + 14 + 7

49. (9 × 7) × 6 and 9 × (7 × 6)

50. 24 ÷ 6 ÷ 2 and 6 ÷ 24 ÷ 2

51. Life Science Poison-dart frogs can breed underwater, and the females lay from 4 to 30 eggs. What would be the total number of eggs if four female poison-dart frogs each laid 27 eggs?

Use the table for Exercises 52 and 53.

52. Rickie wants to buy 3 garden hoses. How much will they cost?

53. The boys in Josh's family are saving money to buy 4 ceiling fans. How much will they need to save?

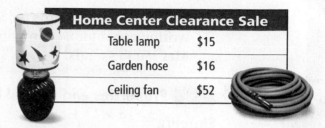

Home Center Clearance Sale	
Table lamp	$15
Garden hose	$16
Ceiling fan	$52

54. Critical Thinking Give a problem that you could simplify using the Commutative and Associative Properties. Then, show the steps to solve the problem and label the Commutative and Associative Properties.

55. What's The Error? A student wrote 5 + 24 + 25 + 6 = 5 + 25 + 24 + 6 by the Associative Property. What error did the student make?

56. Write About It Why can you simplify 5(50 + 3) using the Distributive Property? Why can't you simplify 5(50) + 3 using the Distributive Property?

57. Challenge Explain how you could find the product of 5^2 × 112 using the Distributive Property. Simplify the expression.

Test Prep

58. Multiple Choice Which expression does NOT have the same value as 7 × (4 + 23)?

Ⓐ 7 × 27   Ⓑ (7 × 4) + (7 × 23)   Ⓒ 7 × 4 + 23   Ⓓ 28 + (7 × 23)

59. Gridded Response Michelle flew 1,240 miles from Los Angeles to Dallas, and another 718 miles from Dallas to Atlanta. From Atlanta, she flew 760 miles to New York City. How many miles did Michelle fly in all?

Quiz for Lessons 4 Through 5

 4 Order of Operations

Simplify each expression.

1. $2 + 6 \times 3$

2. $3 \times 4 \div (10 - 4)$

3. $5^2 + 10 \div 2 - 1$

4. $4 + (12 - 8) \times 6$

5. $(2^3 + 2) \times 10$

6. $14 - 3 \times (9 - 6)$

7. Mrs. Webb buys 7 cards for $2 each, 3 metallic pens for $1 each, and 1 pad of writing paper for $4. Simplify $7 \times 2 + 3 \times 1 + 1 \times 4$ to find the total amount Mrs. Webb spends.

 5 Properties and Mental Math

Simplify.

8. $4 + 21 + 9 + 6$

9. $8 \times 12 \times 5$

10. $45 + 19 + 1 + 55$

11. $2 \times 17 \times 10$

12. $2 + 13 + 8 + 7$

13. $3 \times 2 \times 5$

Use the Distributive Property to find each product.

14. 5×62

15. 9×41

16. 4×23

17. 7×14

18. 5×34

19. 11×32

20. The Suarez family was on vacation and traveled by car between tourist attractions. One day, they traveled 8 miles, then 63 miles, then 7 miles, and finally 12 miles. How many miles in total did they travel that day?

Ready to Go On?

Real-World CONNECTIONS

UConn Women's Basketball The University of Connecticut, located in Storrs, is home to one of the nation's best women's basketball teams. In fact, the Huskies won the national championship in 2002, 2003, and 2004. The team's success has made them a favorite of sports fans throughout Connecticut and around the country.

CONNECTICUT

Storrs

1. The table shows the number of field goals and free throws that were made by some of the team's players during the 2007–2008 season. Estimate the total number of free throws that were made by these players. Explain how you made your estimate.

UConn Women's Basketball: 2007–2008 Season			
Player	Two-Point Field Goals	Three-Point Field Goals	Free Throws
Tina Charles	202	0	86
Renee Montgomery	91	63	96
Mel Thomas	22	35	17
Ketia Swanier	47	39	13
Meghan Gardler	17	5	21

2. To find the total number of points a player scored, multiply the number of two-point field goals by 2, multiply the number of three-point field goals by 3, and multiply the number of free throws by 1. Then add these values.

   a. To find the number of points scored by Ketia Swanier, a fan writes the expression $47 \times 2 + 39 \times 3 + 13 \times 1$. Explain how to evaluate this expression. Then find the number of points Ketia Swanier scored.

   b. Which of the five players scored the greatest number of points?

3. In a 2008 game against Georgetown, the UConn team scored $2^6 + 4^2$ points. The two teams scored a total of 2^7 points. What was the final score of the game?

(c) Royalty Free/Corbis; (bl) Icon Sports Media, Inc./Corbis

Real-World Connections

Game Time

Palindromes

A *palindrome* is a word, phrase, or number that reads the same forward and backward.

Examples:
race car   Madam, I'm Adam.   3710173

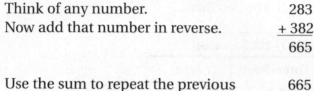

You can turn almost any number into a palindrome with this trick.

Think of any number.	283
Now add that number in reverse.	+ 382
	665

Use the sum to repeat the previous	665
step and keep repeating until the	+ 566
final sum is a palindrome.	1,231

1,231
+ 1,321
2,552

It took only three steps to create a palindrome by starting with the number 283. What happens if you start with the number 196? Do you think you will ever create a palindrome if you start with 196? One man who started with 196 did these steps until he had a number with 70,928 digits and he still had not created a palindrome!

Spin-a-Million

The object of this game is to create the number closest to 1,000,000.

Taking turns, spin the pointer and write the number on your place-value chart. The number cannot be moved once it has been placed.

After six turns, the player whose number is closest to one million wins the round and scores a point. The first player to get five points wins the game.

A complete copy of the rules and game pieces are available online.

Learn It Online
Game Time Extra

Jenny Thomas/HMH

Materials
- plastic DVD case
- card stock
- markers
- scissors
- glue stick
- library pocket
- index cards
- brass fastener
- large paper clip

It's in the Bag!

PROJECT **Picture This**

Make a game in an empty DVD case to review concepts from this chapter.

Directions

1 Cut a piece of card stock that can be folded in half to fit inside the DVD case. Lay the card stock flat and draw a path for a board game. Be sure to have a start and a finish. **Figure A**

2 Close the game board and decorate the front. Glue a library pocket onto the front to hold the index cards. **Figure B**

3 On the index cards, write problems that can be solved using math from the chapter. Place the cards in the pocket.

4 Cut a piece of card stock to fit the other side of the DVD box. Glue directions for your game at the top. At the bottom, make a spinner the size of a DVD. Attach a brass fastener to the middle of the spinner, and then attach a paper clip to the fastener. **Figure C**

Putting the Math into Action

Play your game with a partner. Use buttons or coins as playing pieces. Players should take turns spinning the spinner and then be required to solve a problem correctly in order to move their piece.

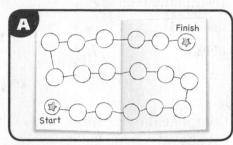

HMH

Study Guide: Review

Vocabulary

Associative Property

base

Commutative Property

compatible numbers

Distributive Property

dividend

divisor

estimate

exponent

exponential form

numerical expression

order of operations

overestimate

simplify

underestimate

Complete the sentences below with vocabulary words from the list above.

1. When you write $6 \times (5 + 2)$ as $6 \times 5 + 6 \times 2$, you are using the ___?___.

2. In the expression 8^5, 8 is the ___?___, and 5 is the ___?___.

3. The ___?___ is a set of rules used to evaluate an expression that contains more than one operation.

4. When you ___?___ a numerical expression, you find its value.

EXAMPLES

EXERCISES

1 Estimating with Whole Numbers

■ **Estimate the sum 837 + 710 by rounding to the hundreds place.**
$800 + 700 = 1,500$
The sum is about 1,500.

■ **Estimate the quotient of 148 and 31.**
$150 \div 30 = 5$
The quotient is about 5.

Estimate each sum or difference by rounding to the place value indicated.

5. $4,671 - 3,954$; thousands

6. $3,123 + 2,987$; thousands

7. $53,465 - 27,465$; ten thousands

8. Ralph has 38 photo album sheets with 22 baseball cards in each sheet. About how many baseball cards does he have?

2 Dividing Multi-Digit Whole Numbers

■ Find the quotient $675 \div 13$.

$$
\begin{array}{r}
51 \\
13\overline{)675} \\
-65\downarrow \\
\hline
25 \\
-13 \\
\hline
12
\end{array}
$$

Multiply. 13×5
Subtract. $67 - 65$
Compare. $2 < 13$
Multiply. 13×1
Subtract. $25 - 13$

$$675 \div 13 = 51\frac{12}{13}$$

Find each quotient.

9. $467 \div 12$ **10.** $8{,}452 \div 29$

11. $14{,}102 \div 32$ **12.** $57{,}645 \div 45$

13. The 1,296 graduates this year are to be seated in the auditorium in rows of 48 students each. How many rows of chairs are needed?

3 Exponents

■ Write 6×6 in exponential form.

6^2 *6 is a factor 2 times.*

Find each value.

■ 5^2 ■ 6^3

$5^2 = 5 \times 5$ $6^3 = 6 \times 6 \times 6$
$ = 25$ $ = 216$

Write each expression in exponential form.

14. $5 \times 5 \times 5$ **15.** $3 \times 3 \times 3 \times 3 \times 3$

16. $7 \times 7 \times 7 \times 7$ **17.** 8×8

18. $4 \times 4 \times 4 \times 4$ **19.** $1 \times 1 \times 1$

Find each value.

20. 4^4 **21.** 2^4 **22.** 6^3

23. 3^3 **24.** 1^5 **25.** 7^4

26. 5^3 **27.** 10^2 **28.** 9^2

4 Order of Operations

■ Simplify $8 \div (7 - 5) \times 2^2 - 2 + 9$.

$8 \div (7 - 5) \times 2^2 - 2 + 9$

$8 \div 2 \times 2^2 - 2 + 9$ *Subtract in parentheses.*

$8 \div 2 \times 4 - 2 + 9$ *Simplify the exponent.*

$4 \times 4 - 2 + 9$ *Divide.*

$16 - 2 + 9$ *Multiply.*

$14 + 9$ *Subtract.*

23 *Add.*

Simplify each expression.

29. $9 \times 8 - 13$

30. $21 \div 3 + 4$

31. $6 + 4 \times 5$

32. $19 - 12 \div 6$

33. $30 \div 2 - 5 \times 2$

34. $(7 + 3) \div 2 \times 3^2$

35. Jerome bought 4 shirts for $12 each and 5 pairs of pants for $18 each. The tax for his purchase was $11. Simplify $4 \times 12 + 5 \times 18 + 11$ to find the amount Jerome spent for clothes.

Study Guide: Review

5 Properties and Mental Math

Simplify.

■ 4 + 13 + 6 + 7
4 + 6 + 13 + 7
(4 + 6) + (13 + 7)
  10 + 20
      30

■ 5 × 9 × 6
5 × 6 × 9
(5 × 6) × 9
30 × 9
270

■ Use the Distributive Property to find 3 × 16.

3 × 16 = 3 × (10 + 6)
      = (3 × 10) + (3 × 6)
      = 30 + 18 = 48

Simplify.

36. 9 + 5 + 1 + 15   **37.** 8 × 13 × 5

38. 31 + 16 + 19 + 14   **39.** 6 × 12 × 15

40. 17 + 12 + 8 + 3   **41.** 16 × 5 × 4

Use the Distributive Property to find each product.

42. 7 × 24   **43.** 9 × 15

44. 6 × 34   **45.** 8 × 19

Study Guide: Review

Chapter Test

Estimate each sum or difference by rounding to the place value indicated.

1. 8,743 + 3,198; thousands

2. 62,524 − 17,831; ten thousands

Estimate.

3. Kaitlin's family is planning a trip from Washington, D.C., to New York City. New York City is 227 miles from Washington, D.C., and the family can drive an average of 55 mi/h. About how long will the trip take?

4. An auditorium can hold 572 people. If 109 people have come in through the north entrance, and 218 people have come in through the south entrance, about how many more people can fit in the auditorium?

Find each quotient.

5. $278 \div 12$

6. $1,607 \div 24$

7. $4,815 \div 15$

8. $12,956 \div 38$

9. The school cafeteria can seat 660 people. If there are 55 tables and each table seats the same number of students, how many seats are at each table?

Write each expression in exponential form.

10. $4 \times 4 \times 4 \times 4 \times 4$

11. $10 \times 10 \times 10$

12. $6 \times 6 \times 6 \times 6$

Find each value.

13. 2^3

14. 5^2

15. 4^4

16. 11^2

17. 9^3

Simplify each expression.

18. $12 + 8 \div 2$

19. $3^2 \times 5 + 10 - 7$

20. $12 + (28 - 15) + 4 \times 2$

Simplify.

21. $15 + 23 + 47 + 5$

22. $5 \times 48 \times 2$

23. $2 \times 5 \times 11$

24. $44 + 18 + 12 + 6$

Use the Distributive Property to find each product.

25. 3×32

26. 52×6

27. 24×5

28. 81×6

29. 6×21

Test Tackler

STANDARDIZED TEST STRATEGIES

Multiple Choice: Eliminate Answer Choices

You can solve some math problems without doing detailed calculations. You can use mental math, estimation, or logical reasoning to help you eliminate answer choices and save time.

EXAMPLE 1

Which number is the closest estimate for 678 + 189?

   Ⓐ 700   Ⓒ 1,000

   Ⓑ 900   Ⓓ 5,000

You can use logical reasoning to eliminate choice A because it is too small. The estimated sum has to be greater than 700 because 678 + 189 is greater than 700.

Choice D may also be eliminated because the value is too large. The estimated sum will be less than 5,000.

Round 678 up to 700 and 189 up to 200. Then find the sum of 700 and 200: 700 + 200 = 900. You can eliminate choice C because it is greater than 900.

Choice B is the closest estimate.

EXAMPLE 2

Which of the following numbers is the standard form of four million, six hundred eight thousand, fifteen?

   Ⓕ 468,015   Ⓗ 4,068,150

   Ⓖ 4,608,015   Ⓙ 4,600,815,000

Logical reasoning can be used to eliminate choices. Numbers that have a place value in the millions must have at least seven but no more than nine digits. Choices F and J can be eliminated because they do not have the correct number of digits.

Both choices G and H have the correct range of digits, so narrow it down further. The number must end in 15. Choice H ends in 50, so it cannot be correct. Eliminate it.

The correct answer choice is G.

Read each item and answer the questions that follow.

Item A
Which number is the greatest?

Ⓐ 599,485   Ⓒ 5,569,003

Ⓑ 5,571,987   Ⓓ 5,399,879

1. Are there any answer choices you can eliminate immediately? If so, which ones and why?

2. Describe how you can find the correct answer.

City Middle School Populations	
Central Middle School	652
Eastside Middle School	718
Northside Middle School	663
Southside Middle School	731
Westside Middle School	842

Item B
The school district receives $30 a day in state funding for every student enrolled in a public school. Find the approximate number of students that attend all of the city middle schools.

Ⓕ 2,000   Ⓗ 3,600

Ⓖ 3,300   Ⓙ 4,000

3. Can F be eliminated? Why or why not?

4. Can H be eliminated? Why or why not?

5. Explain how to use mental math to solve this problem.

Item C
Which expression does NOT have the same value as 8 × (52 + 12)?

Ⓐ 8 × 64

Ⓑ (8 × 52) + (8 × 12)

Ⓒ 8(60) + 8(4)

Ⓓ 8 × 52 + 12

6. Which answer choice can be eliminated immediately? Explain.

7. Explain how you can use the Distributive Property to solve this problem.

Item D
Stacey is beginning a new exercise program. She plans to cycle 2 kilometers on her first day. Each day after that, she will double the number of kilometers she cycled from the day before. Which expression shows how many kilometers she will cycle on the sixth day?

Ⓕ 2×6 Ⓗ 2^6

Ⓖ $2 + 2 + 2 + 2 + 2 + 2$ Ⓙ 6^2

8. Are there any answer choices you can eliminate immediately? If so, which choices and why?

9. Explain how you can use a table to help you solve this problem.

Item E
James is driving to his aunt's house. If he drives about 55 miles per hour for 5 hours, about how many miles will he have driven?

Ⓐ 12 miles   Ⓒ 60 miles

Ⓑ 300 miles   Ⓓ 600 miles

10. Which answer choice(s) can be immediately eliminated and why?

11. Explain how to solve this problem.

Test Tackler

Cumulative Assessment

Multiple Choice

1. Jonah has 31 boxes of baseball cards. If each box contains 183 cards, about how many baseball cards does Jonah have in his collection?

Ⓐ 3,000 cards   Ⓒ 9,000 cards

Ⓑ 6,000 cards   Ⓓ 12,000 cards

2. Which of the following does NOT have a value of 27?

Ⓕ 3^3 Ⓗ $3 \times 3 + 18$

Ⓖ $3^2 + 3 \times 7$ Ⓙ $9^2 \div 3$

3. Which of the following is the quotient $5,892 \div 18$?

Ⓐ 327   Ⓒ $327\frac{1}{3}$

Ⓑ $327\frac{1}{18}$ Ⓓ $327\frac{7}{18}$

4. Which of the following correctly shows the use of the Distributive Property to find the product of 64 and 8?

Ⓕ $64 \times 8 = (8 \times 60) + (8 \times 4)$

Ⓖ $64 \times 8 = 8 \times 64$

Ⓗ $64 \times 8 = 8 + (60 + 4)$

Ⓙ $64 \times 8 = (8 \times 4) \times 60$

5. What is five billion, two hundred fifty-two million, six hundred thousand, three hundred eleven in standard form?

Ⓐ 5,252,603,011   Ⓒ 5,252,600,311

Ⓑ 52,526,311   Ⓓ 5,252,060,311

6. The attendance at a local library is shown in the table below. How many people visited the library last week?

Last Week's Attendance	
Sunday	Closed
Monday	78
Tuesday	125
Wednesday	122
Thursday	96
Friday	104
Saturday	225

Ⓕ 450   Ⓗ 650

Ⓖ 550   Ⓙ 750

7. Which number is the greatest?

Ⓐ 5,432,873   Ⓒ 5,221,754

Ⓑ 5,201,032   Ⓓ 5,332,621

8. What is $6 \times 6 \times 6 \times 6$ written in exponential form?

Ⓕ 24^4

Ⓖ 1,296

Ⓗ 6^4

Ⓙ $1000 + 200 + 90 + 6$

9. The expression $6 \times 3 \times 4 = 3 \times 6 \times 4$ is an example of which property?

Ⓐ Associative   Ⓒ Distributive

Ⓑ Commutative   Ⓓ Exponential

10. Which list of numbers is in order from least to greatest?

   (F) 1,231; 1,543; 1,267; 1,321

   (G) 3,210; 3,357; 3,366; 3,401

   (H) 4,321; 4,312; 4,211; 4,081

   (J) 5,019; 5,187; 5,143; 5,314

11. The Theater Club made $572 from ticket sales at a performance of the Fall Play. How many tickets were sold if the Club charged $13 per ticket?

   (A) 44 tickets

   (B) 559 tickets

   (C) 585 tickets

   (D) 25,168 tickets

 HOT TIP! When you read a word problem, underline the information you need to help you answer the question.

Gridded Response

12. What is the value of
    $3 + 8 \times 6 - (12 \div 4)$?

13. What is the value of 2^4?

14. A library has 1,206 books in its collection. If the library shelves each hold 18 books, how many shelves are there in the library?

15. At 2:00 P.M., the water temperature in the pool was 88 °F. By 10:00 P.M. the water temperature in the pool was 75 °F. By how many degrees did the water temperature drop?

16. Estimate the sum of 3,820 and 4,373 by rounding to the nearest thousand.

17. What is the base of 6^3?

Short Response

S1. Megan deposited $2 into her savings account on the first Friday of the month. Each week she doubles her deposit from the week before.

   a. If this pattern continues, how much money will she deposit in week 4?

   b. What is the total amount in Megan's account after her fourth deposit? Explain how you found your answer.

S2. Create a numerical expression that can be simplified in four steps. Include one set of parentheses and an exponent. The same mathematical operation may be used no more than two times. Show how to simplify your expression.

Extended Response

E1. The student population at Southside Middle School is listed in the table below.

Student Population at Southside Middle School		
	Boys	**Girls**
6th Grade	98	102
7th Grade	89	105
8th Grade	123	117

   a. Use the information in the table to find the total number of students who attend Southside Middle School. Show your work.

   b. About how many more girls are enrolled in the school than boys? Show your work. Explain how you found your answer.

   c. The school board wants the school to have one teacher for every 20 students. If there are 8 sixth-grade teachers, does the school need to hire more sixth-grade teachers? If so, how many more? Explain your answer.

Chapter
- Write expressions and equations for given situations.
- Evaluate expressions.
- Solve one-step equations.

Why Learn This?

Rafting is a popular activity in many parts of the country. If you know how long you rafted and the distance you traveled, you can solve an equation to find the average speed of the river.

Learn It Online
Chapter Project Online

(all) Pat and Chuck Blackley

 **Are You Ready?**

 **Learn It Online**
Resources Online

✓ Vocabulary

Choose the best term from the list to complete each sentence.

1. Multiplication is the ___?___ of division.

2. The ___?___ of 12 and 3 is 36.

3. The ___?___ of 12 and 3 is 15.

4. Addition, subtraction, multiplication, and division are called ___?___.

5. The answer to a division problem is called the ___?___.

dividend

factor

inverse

operations

product

quotient

sum

Complete these exercises to review skills you will need for this chapter.

✓ Multiplication Facts

Multiply.

6. 7×4 7. 8×9 8. 9×6 9. 7×7

10. 6×5 11. 3×8 12. 5×5 13. 2×9

✓ Division Facts

Divide.

14. $64 \div 8$ 15. $63 \div 9$ 16. $56 \div 7$ 17. $54 \div 6$

18. $49 \div 7$ 19. $30 \div 5$ 20. $32 \div 4$ 21. $18 \div 3$

✓ Whole Number Operations

Add, subtract, multiply, or divide.

22. $\begin{array}{r} 28 \\ + 15 \end{array}$ 23. $\begin{array}{r} 71 \\ + 38 \end{array}$ 24. $\begin{array}{r} 1{,}218 \\ + 430 \end{array}$ 25. $\begin{array}{r} 2{,}218 \\ + 1{,}135 \end{array}$

26. $\begin{array}{r} 72 \\ - 35 \end{array}$ 27. $\begin{array}{r} 98 \\ - 45 \end{array}$ 28. $\begin{array}{r} 1{,}642 \\ - 249 \end{array}$ 29. $\begin{array}{r} 3{,}408 \\ - 1{,}649 \end{array}$

30. 6×13 31. 8×15 32. 16×22 33. 20×35

34. $9\overline{)72}$ 35. $7\overline{)84}$ 36. $16\overline{)112}$ 37. $23\overline{)1{,}472}$

Study Guide: Preview

Where You've Been

Previously, you

- wrote numerical expressions involving whole numbers.

- solved problems using addition, subtraction, multiplication, and division of whole numbers.

In This Chapter

You will study

- writing algebraic expressions involving whole numbers.

- using addition, subtraction, multiplication, and division to solve one-step equations involving whole numbers.

- determining whether a number is a solution to an equation.

Where You're Going

You can use the skills learned in this chapter

- to solve one-step equations involving decimals and fractions.

- to solve one-step inequalities.

Key Vocabulary/Vocabulario

algebraic expression	expresión algebraica
constant	constante
equation	ecuación
solution of an equation	solución de una ecuación
variable	variable

Vocabulary Connections

To become familiar with some of the vocabulary terms in the chapter, consider the following. You may refer to the chapter, the glossary, or a dictionary if you like.

1. *Algebra* is a type of math that uses letters to represent numbers. The word *algebraic* means "relating to algebra." What do you think an **algebraic expression** contains?

2. When something is *constant*, it does not change. If there is a **constant** in an expression, do you think the number changes? Explain.

3. When something is *variable*, it is able to vary, or change. What do you think a **variable** in an expression is able to do?

4. An *equation* shows that two expressions are equal. What mathematical symbol would you expect to see in an **equation**?

Reading and Writing Math

Writing Strategy: Use Your Own Words

Sometimes when you are reading about a new math concept for the first time from a textbook, the concept is difficult to understand.

As you go through each lesson, do the following:

- Look for the key ideas.
- Rewrite explanations given as paragraphs as steps or a list.
- Add an example when possible.

What Lupe Reads

When you multiply two numbers, you can "break apart" one of the numbers into a sum and then use the Distributive Property.

What Lupe Writes

Multiply Using Mental Math

Step 1: Break one of the numbers into a sum.
Step 2: Use the Distributive Property.
Step 3: Use mental math to multiply; then add.

Example: 5×27

Break one number into a sum: $5 \times (20 + 7)$

Use the Distributive Property: $(5 \times 20) + (5 \times 7)$

Use mental math to multiply; $100 + 35$
then add: 135

Try This

Rewrite the paragraph in your own words.

1. Sometimes in math you do not need an exact answer. Instead, you can use an estimate. Estimates are close to the exact answer but are usually easier and faster to find. When estimating, you can round the numbers in the problem to compatible numbers. Compatible numbers are close to the numbers in the problem, and they can help you do math mentally.

CC.6.EE.2 Write, read, and evaluate expressions in which letters stand for numbers **Also CC.6.EE.2b**

Vocabulary

variable

constant

algebraic expression

evaluate

Inflation is the rise in prices that occurs over time. For example, you would have paid about $7 in the year 2000 for something that cost only $1 in 1950.

With this information, you can convert prices in 1950 to their equivalent prices in 2000.

Input

Output

1950	2000
$1	$7
$2	$14
$3	$21
$p	$p × 7

A **variable** is a letter or symbol that represents a quantity that can change. In the table above, p is a variable that stands for any price in 1950. A **constant** is a quantity that does not change. For example, the price of something in 2000 is always 7 times the price in 1950.

An **algebraic expression** contains one or more variables and may contain operation symbols. So $p \times 7$ is an algebraic expression.

Algebraic Expressions	NOT Algebraic Expressions
$150 + y$	$85 \div 5$
$35 \times w + z$	$10 + 3 \times 5$

To **evaluate** an algebraic expression, substitute a number for the variable and then find the value by simplifying.

EXAMPLE 1 **Evaluating Algebraic Expressions**

 Interactivities Online ►

Evaluate each expression to find the missing values in the tables.

A

w	$w \div 11$
55	5
66	▪
77	▪

Substitute for w in $w \div 11$.

$w = 55$; $55 \div 11 = 5$

$w = 66$; $66 \div 11 = 6$

$w = 77$; $77 \div 11 = 7$

The missing values are 6 and 7.

Video **Lesson Tutorials Online** my.hrw.com

Evaluate each expression to find the missing values in the tables.

B

n	$4 \times n + 6^2$
1	40
2	
3	

Substitute for n in $4 \times n + 6^2$.
Use the order of operations.
$n = 1;\ 4 \times 1 + 36 = 40$
$n = 2;\ 4 \times 2 + 36 = \mathbf{44}$
$n = 3;\ 4 \times 3 + 36 = \mathbf{48}$

The missing values are 44 and 48.

Writing Math

When you are multiplying a number times a variable, the number is written first. Write "3x" and not "x3." Read 3x as "three x."

You can write multiplication and division expressions without using the symbols $\times$ and $\div$.

Instead of . . .	You can write . . .
$x \times 3$	$x \cdot 3 \quad x(3) \quad 3x$
$35 \div y$	$\dfrac{35}{y}$

EXAMPLE 2 **Evaluating Expressions with Two Variables**

A rectangle is 2 units wide. What is the area of the rectangle if it is 4, 5, 6, or 7 units long?

You can multiply length and width to find area, which is measured in square units. Let ℓ be length and w be width.

ℓ	w	$\ell \times w$
4	2	8
5	2	
6	2	
7	2	

Make a table to help you find the number of square units for each length.
$\ell = 4;\ 4 \times 2 = 8$ *square units*
$\ell = 5;\ 5 \times 2 = \mathbf{10}$ *square units*
$\ell = 6;\ 6 \times 2 = \mathbf{12}$ *square units*
$\ell = 7;\ 7 \times 2 = \mathbf{14}$ *square units*

The rectangle will cover 8, 10, 12, or 14 square units.

Check

Draw a rectangle 2 units wide. Then count the total number of square units when the rectangle is 4, 5, 6, and 7 units long.

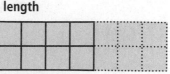

length

width

MATHEMATICAL PRACTICES

Think and Discuss

1. Name a quantity that is a variable and a quantity that is a constant.

2. Explain why $45 + x$ is an algebraic expression.

Exercises

Learn It Online
Homework Help Online
Exercises 1–6, 7, 9, 11, 15, 19, 21, 23

GUIDED PRACTICE

See Example 1   Evaluate each expression to find the missing values in the tables.

1.

n	$n + 7$
38	45
49	■
58	■

2.

x	$12x + 2^3$
8	104
9	■
10	■

See Example 2   **3.** A rectangle is 4 units wide. How many square units does the rectangle cover if it is 6, 7, 8, or 9 units long?

INDEPENDENT PRACTICE

See Example 1   Evaluate each expression to find the missing values in the tables.

4.

x	$4x$
50	200
100	■
150	■

5.

n	$2n - 3^2$
10	11
16	■
17	■

See Example 2   **6.** A builder is designing a rectangular patio that has a length of 12 units. Find the total number of square units the patio will cover if the width is 4, 5, 6, or 7 units.

PRACTICE AND PROBLEM SOLVING

Extra Practice

See Extra Practice for more exercises.

7. Estimation Bobby drives his truck at a rate of 50 to 60 miles per hour.
  a. Approximately how far can Bobby drive in 2, 3, 4, and 5 hours?
  b. Bobby plans to take an 8-hour trip, which will include a 1-hour stop for lunch. What is a reasonable distance for Bobby to drive?

8. Multi-Step Each table in the cafeteria seats 8 people. Find the total number of people that can be seated at 7, 8, 9, and 10 tables. If the average bill per person is $12, how much money can the cafeteria expect from 7, 8, 9, and 10 tables that have no empty seats?

9. Measurement When traveling in Europe, Jessika converts the temperature given in degrees Celsius to a Fahrenheit temperature by using the expression $9x \div 5 + 32$, where x is the Celsius temperature. Find the temperature in degrees Fahrenheit when it is 0 °C, 10 °C, and 25 °C.

10. Geometry To find the area of a triangle, you can use the expression $b \times h \div 2$, where b is the base of the triangle and h is its height. Find the area of a triangle with a base of 5 and a height of 6.

Evaluate each expression for the given value of the variable.

11. $3h + 2$ for $h = 10$ **12.** $2x^2$ for $x = 3$ **13.** $t - 7$ for $t = 20$

14. $4p - 3$ for $p = 20$ **15.** $\frac{c}{7}$ for $c = 56$ **16.** $10 + 2r$ for $r = 5$

17. $3x + 17$ for $x = 13$ **18.** $5p$ for $p = 12$ **19.** $s^2 - 15$ for $s = 5$

20. $14 - 2c$ for $c = 2$ **21.** $10x$ for $x = 11$ **22.** $4j + 12$ for $j = 9$

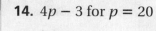

Money

Why does a Polish coin show Australia and a kangaroo? This coin honors Pawel Edmund Strzelecki, a Pole who explored and mapped much of Australia.

23. Money The zloty is the currency in Poland. In 2005, 1 U.S. dollar was worth 3 zlotys. How many zlotys were equivalent to 8 U.S. dollars?

24. Use the graph to complete the table.

Cups of Water	Number of Lemons
8	▧
12	▧
16	▧
w	▧

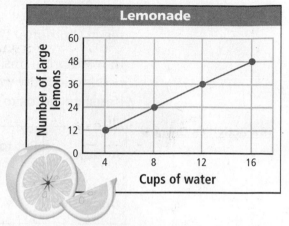

Lemonade

25. What's the Error? A student evaluated the expression $x \div 2$ for $x = 14$ and gave an answer of 28. What did the student do wrong?

26. Write About It How would you evaluate the expression $2x + 5$ for $x = 1, 2, 3,$ and 4?

27. Challenge Using the algebraic expression $3n - 5$, what is the smallest whole-number value for n that will give you a result greater than 100?

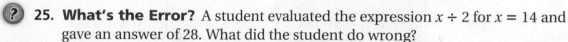

Test Prep

28. Multiple Choice Evaluate $8m - 5$ for $m = 9$.

    Ⓐ 67   **Ⓑ** 83   **Ⓒ** 84   **Ⓓ** 94

29. Gridded Response Evaluate the expression $4p + 18$ for $p = 5$.

Translating Between Words and Math

COMMON CORE

CC.6.EE.2 Write, read, and evaluate expressions in which letters stand for numbers *Also CC.6.EE.2a, CC.6.EE.2b*

The distance from Charlotte, North Carolina, to Charlotte, Tennessee, is 470 miles. Beth drove c miles from Charlotte, NC, toward Charlotte, TN. How many more miles must she drive to reach Charlotte, TN?

In word problems, you may need to identify the action to translate words to math.

Interactivities Online ▶

Action	Put together or combine	Find how much more or less	Put together groups of equal parts	Separate into equal groups
Operation	Add	Subtract	Multiply	Divide

To solve this problem, you need to find how many more miles Beth must drive. To find *how much more*, subtract.

$$470 - c$$

Beth must drive $470 - c$ more miles to reach Charlotte, TN.

E X A M P L E **Social Studies Applications**

> **A** The Nile River is the world's longest river. Let n stand for the length in miles of the Nile. The Amazon River is 4,000 miles long. Write an expression to show how much longer the Nile is than the Amazon.
>
> To *find how much longer,* subtract the **length of the Amazon** from the **length of the Nile**.
>
> $$n \qquad - \qquad 4{,}000$$
>
> The Nile is $n - 4{,}000$ miles longer than the Amazon.
>
> **B** Let s represent the number of senators that each of the 50 states has in the U.S. Senate. Write an expression for the total number of senators.
>
> To *put together 50 equal groups of s,* multiply 50 times s.
>
> $$50s$$
>
> There are $50s$ senators in the U.S. Senate.

Video **Lesson Tutorials Online** my.hrw.com

Richard Cummins/SuperStock

There are several different ways to write math expressions with words.

Operation	✚	➖	✖	➗
Numerical Expression	$37 + 28$	$90 - 12$	8×48 or $8 \cdot 48$ or $(8)(48)$ or $8(48)$ or $(8)48$	$327 \div 3$ or $\frac{327}{3}$
Words	• 28 **added** to 37 • 37 **plus** 28 • the **sum** of 37 and 28 • 28 **more than** 37	• 12 **subtracted** from 90 • 90 **minus** 12 • the **difference** of 90 and 12 • 12 **less than** 90 • **take away** 12 from 90	• 8 **times** 48 • 48 **multiplied** by 8 • the **product** of 8 and 48 • 8 **groups of** 48	• 327 **divided** by 3 • the **quotient** of 327 and 3
Algebraic Expression	$x + 28$	$k - 12$	$8 \cdot w$ or $(8)(w)$ or $8w$	$n \div 3$ or $\frac{n}{3}$
Words	• 28 **added** to x • x **plus** 28 • the **sum** of x and 28 • 28 **more than** x	• 12 **subtracted** from k • k **minus** 12 • the **difference** of k and 12 • 12 **less than** k • **take away** 12 from k	• 8 **times** w • w **multiplied** by 8 • the **product** of 8 and w • 8 **groups of** w	• n **divided** by 3 • the **quotient** of n and 3

EXAMPLE **2** **Translating Words into Math**

Write each phrase as a numerical or algebraic expression.

A 287 plus 932

$287 + 932$

B b divided by 14

$b \div 14$ or $\frac{b}{14}$

EXAMPLE **3** **Translating Math into Words**

Write two phrases for each expression.

A $a - 45$
- a minus 45
- take away 45 from a

B $(34)(7)$
- the product of 34 and 7
- 7 multiplied by 34

Think and Discuss

1. Tell how to write each of the following phrases as a numerical or algebraic expression: 75 less than 1,023; the product of 125 and z.

2. Give two examples of "$a \div 17$" expressed with words.

GUIDED PRACTICE

See Example **1**

1. **Social Studies** The Big Island of Hawaii is the largest Hawaiian island, with an area of 4,028 mi². The next biggest island is Maui. Let m represent the area of Maui. Write an expression for the difference between the two areas.

See Example **2**

Write each phrase as a numerical or algebraic expression.

2. 279 minus 125   3. the product of 15 and x 4. 17 plus 4

5. p divided by 5   6. the sum of 9 and q 7. 149 times 2

See Example **3**

Write two phrases for each expression.

8. $r + 87$ 9. 345×196 10. $476 \div 28$ 11. $d - 5$

INDEPENDENT PRACTICE

See Example **1**

12. **Social Studies** In 2005, California had 21 more seats in the U.S. Congress than Texas had. If t represents the number of seats Texas had, write an expression for the number of seats California had.

13. Let x represent the number of television show episodes that are taped in a season. Write an expression for the number of episodes taped in 5 seasons.

See Example **2**

Write each phrase as a numerical or algebraic expression.

14. 25 less than k 15. the quotient of 325 and 25

16. 34 times w 17. 675 added to 137

18. the sum of 135 and p 19. take away 14 from j

See Example **3**

Write two phrases for each expression.

20. $h + 65$ 21. $243 - 19$ 22. $125 \div n$ 23. $342(75)$

24. $\frac{d}{27}$ 25. $45 \cdot 23$ 26. $629 + c$ 27. $228 - b$

PRACTICE AND PROBLEM SOLVING

Extra Practice

See Extra Practice for more exercises.

Translate each phrase into a numerical or algebraic expression.

28. 13 less than z 29. 15 divided by d

30. 874 times 23   31. m multiplied by 67

32. the sum of 35, 74, and 21   33. 319 less than 678

34. **Critical Thinking** Paula and Manda were asked to write an expression to find the total number of shoes in a closet. Let s represent the number of pairs of shoes. Paula wrote s and Manda wrote $2s$. Who is correct? Explain.

 35. **Write About It** Write a situation that could be modeled by the expression $x + 5$.

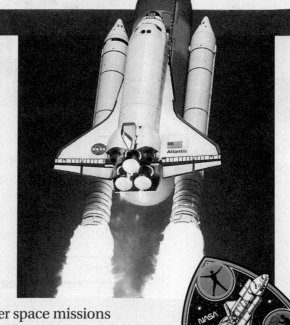

Science LINK

The graph shows the number of U.S. space exploration missions from 1961 to 2005.

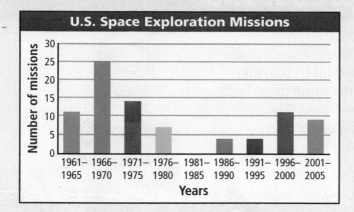

U.S. Space Exploration Missions

(Bar graph: y-axis "Number of missions" from 0 to 30; x-axis "Years" with categories 1961–1965, 1966–1970, 1971–1975, 1976–1980, 1981–1985, 1986–1990, 1991–1995, 1996–2000, 2001–2005)

36. Between 1966 and 1970, the Soviet Union had m fewer space missions than the United States. Write an algebraic expression for this situation.

37. Let d represent the number of dollars that the United States spent on space missions from 1986 to 1990. Write an expression for the cost per mission.

38. 🖊 **Write a Problem** Use the data in the graph to write a word problem that can be answered with a numerical or algebraic expression.

39. Critical Thinking Let p stand for the number of missions between 1996 and 2000 that had people aboard. What operation would you use to write an expression for the number of missions without people? Explain.

40. ⭐ **Challenge** Write an expression for the following: two more than the number of missions from 1971 to 1975, minus the number of missions from 1986 to 1990. Then evaluate the expression.

Test Prep

41. Multiple Choice Which expression represents the product of 79 and x?

Ⓐ $79 + x$ Ⓑ $x - 79$ Ⓒ $79x$ Ⓓ $\frac{x}{79}$

42. Extended Response Tim is driving from Ames, Iowa to Canton, Ohio. He is 280 miles from Ames when he stops for gas. Write an expression to represent the number of miles Tim has left to drive. Explain. Translate your expression into two different word phrases.

COMMON CORE

CC.6.EE.2: Write, read, and evaluate expressions in which letters stand for numbers *Also CC.6.EE.2a*

In 2004, International Chess Master Andrew Martin broke a world record by playing 321 games of chess at the same time. Each game required 32 chess pieces. The table shows the number of pieces needed for different numbers of games.

Games	Pieces
1	32
2	64
3	96
n	$32n$

The number of pieces is always 32 times the number of games. For n games, the expression $32n$ gives the number of pieces that are needed.

EXAMPLE 1 **Writing an Expression**

Write an expression for the missing value in each table.

A

Reilly's Age	Ashley's Age
9	11
10	12
11	13
12	14
n	

Ashley's age is Reilly's age plus 2.

$9 + 2 = 11$
$10 + 2 = 12$
$11 + 2 = 13$
$12 + 2 = 14$
$n + 2$

When Reilly's age is n, Ashley's age is $n + 2$.

B

Eggs	Dozens
12	1
24	2
36	3
48	4
e	

The number of dozens is the number of eggs divided by 12.

$12 \div 12 = 1$
$24 \div 12 = 2$
$36 \div 12 = 3$
$48 \div 12 = 4$
$e \div 12$

When there are e eggs, the number of dozens is $e \div 12$, or $\frac{e}{12}$.

Video **Lesson Tutorials Online** my.hrw.com

You can look for a pattern in a table to help you write an expression.

EXAMPLE 2 **Writing an Expression for a Sequence**

Write an expression for the sequence in the table.

Position	1	2	3	4	5	n
Value of Term	3	5	7	9	11	■

Look for a relationship between the positions and the values of the terms in the sequence. Use guess and check.

Guess $2n$.	Guess $2n + 1$.
Check by substituting 3.	Check by substituting 3.
$2 \times 3 \neq 7$ ✗	$2 \times 3 + 1 = 7$ ✔

The expression $2n + 1$ works for the entire sequence.

$2 \times 1 + 1 = 3, 2 \times 2 + 1 = 5, 2 \times 3 + 1 = 7,$
$2 \times 4 + 1 = 9, 2 \times 5 + 1 = 11$

The expression for the sequence is $2n + 1$.

Caution!

When you write an expression for data in a table, check that the expression works for *all* of the data in the table.

EXAMPLE 3 **Writing an Expression for the Area of a Figure**

A triangle has a base of 8 inches. The table shows the area of the triangle for different heights. Write an expression that can be used to find the area of the triangle when its height is *h* inches.

Base (in.)	Height (in.)	Area (in^2)	
8	1	4	$8 \times 1 = 8, \quad 8 \div 2 = 4$
8	2	8	$8 \times 2 = 16, 16 \div 2 = 8$
8	3	12	$8 \times 3 = 24, 24 \div 2 = 12$
8	4	16	$8 \times 4 = 32, 32 \div 2 = 16$
8	h	■	$8 \times h = 8h, 8h \div 2$

In each row of the table, the area is half the product of the base and the height. The expression is $\frac{8h}{2}$, or $4h$.

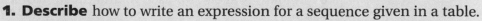

Think and Discuss

1. Describe how to write an expression for a sequence given in a table.

2. Explain why it is important to check your expression for all of the data in a table.

GUIDED PRACTICE

See Example **1**   Write an expression for the missing value in each table.

1.

Go-Carts	1	2	3	4	n
Wheels	4	8	12	16	■

See Example **2**   Write an expression for the sequence in the table.

2.

Position	1	2	3	4	5	n
Value of Term	9	10	11	12	13	■

See Example **3**   **3.** A rectangle has a length of 5 inches. The table shows the area of the rectangle for different widths. Write an expression that can be used to find the area of the rectangle when its width is w inches.

Length (in.)	Width (in.)	Area (in²)
5	2	10
5	4	20
5	6	30
5	8	40
5	w	■

INDEPENDENT PRACTICE

See Example **1**   Write an expression for the missing value in each table.

4.

Players	Soccer Teams
22	2
44	4
66	6
88	8
n	■

5.

Weeks	Days
4	28
8	56
12	84
16	112
n	■

See Example **2**   Write an expression for the sequence in the table.

6.

Position	1	2	3	4	5	n
Value of Term	7	12	17	22	27	■

See Example **3**   **7.** The table shows the area of a square with different side lengths. Write an expression that can be used to find the area of a square when its side length is s feet.

Length (ft)	2	4	6	8	s
Area (ft²)	4	16	36	64	■

Make a table for each sequence. Then write an expression for the sequence.

8. 2, 4, 6, 8, . . . **9.** 6, 7, 8, 9, . . . **10.** 10, 20, 30, 40, . . .

11. Earth Science The planet Mercury takes 88 days to make a complete orbit of the Sun. The table shows the number of orbits and the number of days it takes to make the orbits. Write an expression for the number of days it takes Mercury to make n orbits.

Orbits	Days
1	88
2	176
3	264
n	▨

12. Multi-Step The entry fee for a county fair is $10. Each ride at the fair costs $2. The table shows the total cost to go on various numbers of rides. Write an expression for the cost of r rides. Then use the expression to find the cost of 12 rides.

Number of Rides	1	3	5	8	10	r
Total Cost ($)	12	16	20	26	30	▨

13. Critical Thinking Write two different expressions that describe the relationship in the table.

14. Write About It Explain how you can make a table of values for the expression $4n + 3$.

Position (n)	Value of Term
3	10

15. Challenge Can there be more than one expression that describes a set of data in a table? Explain.

Test Prep

16. Multiple Choice Which expression describes the sequence in the table?

Position	1	2	3	4	5	n
Value of Term	6	11	16	21	26	▨

Ⓐ $n + 5$ Ⓑ $5n + 1$ Ⓒ $6n$ Ⓓ $6n - 1$

17. Multiple Choice Find the missing value in the sequence 1, 3, 5, ▨, 9, ...

Ⓕ 6 Ⓖ 7 Ⓗ 8 Ⓙ 9

Hands-on LAB
Explore Area and Perimeter of Rectangles

Use with Translating Between Tables and Expressions

Learn It Online
Lab Resources Online

Use appropriate tools strategically.
CC.6.EE.3 Apply the properties of operations to generate equivalent expressions *Also CC.6.EE.2*

REMEMBER
- Perimeter is the distance around a figure.
- Area is the amount of space a figure covers. It is measured in square units.

You can use graph paper to model the area of different rectangles.

Activity 1

Sarita is digging rectangular vegetable gardens. To prevent weeds from growing she will cover each garden with a mesh sheet the exact size of the garden before planting the vegetables. Complete the table to find the size of sheet needed for each garden.

Each sheet will be the same size as the garden it covers. Complete the table at right to show the area of each garden.

	Areas of Gardens		
Garden	Length (ℓ)	Width (w)	Area (A)
A	4	2	8
B	4	3	▪
C	▪	▪	▪
D	▪	▪	▪

Garden A
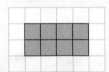

Garden B
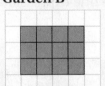

Garden C
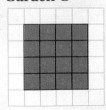

Garden D
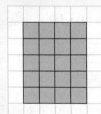

Think and Discuss

1. If you had a garden with a length of 4 and an area of 24, what would the width be? How did you get your answer?

2. The area of each garden is equal to its length times its width. Using the variables ℓ and w, what expression can you use to find the area of a rectangle? $A = $ _____.

Try This

Complete a table like the one in Activity 1 to find the area of each rectangle.

1. length = 10, width = 5 **2.** length = 10, width = 6 **3.** length = 10, width = 7

You can use graph paper to model the perimeters of different rectangles.

Activity 2

Jorge's family has many pictures that they want to frame, and they decide to make their own frames. The amount of wood needed for each frame is the perimeter of the frame. Complete the table to find the amount of wood needed for each frame.

Frame A

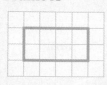

Frame B

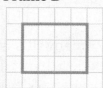

Frame C

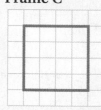

Frame D

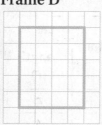

Perimeters of Picture Frames			
Frame	Length (ℓ)	Width (w)	Perimeter (P)
A	4	2	12
B	4	3	▪
C	▪	▪	▪
D	▪	▪	▪

Think and Discuss

1. How did you find the perimeter of each frame?

2. A rectangle has one pair of sides with the same measure, called the length, and another pair with the same measure, called the width. We can say two lengths and two widths equal the perimeter. Using the variables ℓ and w, what expression can you use to find the perimeter of a rectangle?
$P =$ _____.

3. Use the Distributive Property to write another expression for the perimeter of a rectangle:
$P =$ _____.

Try This

Complete a table like the one in Activity 2 to find the perimeter of each rectangle.

1. length = 8, width = 3 **2.** length = 20, width = 4 **3.** length = 7, width = 7

Ready To Go On?

Quiz for Lessons 1 Through 3

1 Variables and Expressions

Evaluate each expression to find the missing values in the tables.

1.

y	23 + y
17	40
27	
37	

2.

w	w × 3 + 10
4	22
5	
6	

3. Stephanie's CD holder holds 6 CDs per page. How many CDs does Stephanie have if she fills 2, 3, 4, or 5 pages?

2 Translating Between Words and Math

4. The small and large intestines are part of the digestive system. The small intestine is longer than the large intestine. Let n represent the length in feet of the small intestine. The large intestine is 5 feet long. Write an expression to show how much longer the small intestine is than the large intestine.

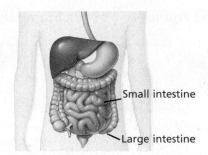
Small intestine

Large intestine

5. Let h represent the number of times your heart beats in 1 minute. Write an expression for the total number of times it beats in 1 hour. (*Hint:* 1 hour = 60 minutes)

Write each phrase as a numerical or algebraic expression.

6. 719 plus 210   **7.** t multiplied by 7   **8.** the sum of n and 51

Write two phrases for each expression.

9. $n + 19$ **10.** $12 \cdot 13$ **11.** $72 - x$ **12.** $\frac{t}{12}$ **13.** $15s$

3 Translating Between Tables and Expressions

Write an expression for the missing value in the table.

14.

Position	1	2	3	4	5	n
Value of Term	8	16	24	32	40	

Make a table for each sequence. Then write an expression for the sequence.

15. 3, 4, 5, 6, . . .   **16.** 4, 7, 10, 13, . . .

Focus on Problem Solving

MATHEMATICAL PRACTICES

Make sense of problems and persevere in solving them.

Understand the Problem

• **Identify too much or too little information**

Problems often give too much or too little information. You must decide whether you have enough information to work the problem.

Read the problem and identify the facts that are given. Can you use any of these facts to arrive at an answer? Are there facts in the problem that are not necessary to find the answer? These questions can help you determine whether you have too much or too little information.

If you cannot solve the problem with the information given, decide what information you need. Then read the problem again to be sure you haven't missed the information in the problem.

Copy each problem. Circle the important facts. Underline any facts that you do not need to answer the question. If there is not enough information, list the additional information you need.

1 The reticulated python is one of the longest snakes in the world. One was found in Indonesia in 1912 that was 33 feet long. At birth, a reticulated python is 2 feet long. Suppose an adult python is 29 feet long. Let *f* represent the number of feet the python grew since birth. What is the value of *f*?

2 The largest flying flag in the world is 7,410 square feet and weighs 180 pounds. There are a total of 13 horizontal stripes on it. Let *h* represent the height of each stripe. What is the value of *h*?

3 The elevation of Mt. McKinley is 20,320 ft. People who climb Mt. McKinley are flown to a base camp located at 7,200 ft. From there, they begin a climb that may last 20 days or longer. Let *d* represent the distance from the base camp to the summit of Mt. McKinley. What is the value of *d*?

4 Let *c* represent the cost of a particular computer in 1981. Six years later, in 1987, the price of the computer had increased to $3,600. What is the value of *c*?

PhotoDisc/Getty Images

2-4 Equations and Their Solutions

COMMON CORE

CC.6.EE.5 Understand solving an equation or inequality as a process of answering a question: which values from a specified set, if any, make the equation or inequality true? Use substitution to determine whether a given number in a specified set makes an equation or inequality true
Also CC.6.EE.4

Vocabulary

equation

solution

<u>Interactivities Online</u> ▶

Reading Math

The symbol ≠ means "is not equal to."

An **equation** is a mathematical statement that two expressions are equal. You can think of a correct equation as a balanced scale.

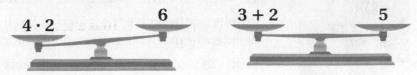

Equations may contain variables. If a value for a variable makes an equation true, that value is a **solution** of the equation.

You can test a value to see whether it is a solution of an equation by substituting the value for the variable.

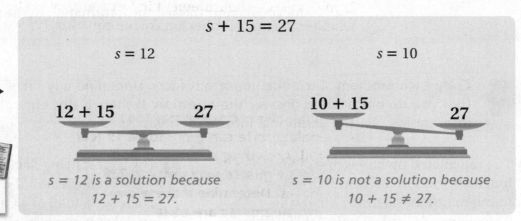

$s + 15 = 27$

$s = 12$ $s = 10$

$12 + 15$ 27 $10 + 15$ 27

s = 12 is a solution because   *s = 10 is not a solution because*
12 + 15 = 27.   *10 + 15 ≠ 27.*

EXAMPLE 1   **Determining Solutions of Equations**

Determine whether the given value of the variable is a solution.

   A $a + 23 = 82$ for $a = 61$

      $a + 23 = 82$

      $61 + 23 \overset{?}{=} 82$ *Substitute 61 for a.*

        $84 \overset{?}{=} 82$ *Add.*

84 82

Since 84 ≠ 82, 61 is not a solution of $a + 23 = 82$.

Determine whether the given value of the variable is a solution.

B $60 \div c = 6$ for $c = 10$

$60 \div c = 6$

$60 \div 10 \overset{?}{=} 6$ *Substitute 10 for c.*

$6 \overset{?}{=} 6$ *Divide.*

6   6

Because $6 = 6$, 10 is a solution of $60 \div c = 6$.

You can use equations to check whether measurements given in different units are equal.

For example, there are 12 inches in one foot. If you have a measurement in feet, multiply by 12 to find the measurement in inches: $12 \cdot \text{feet} = \text{inches}$, or $12f = i$.

If you have one measurement in feet and another in inches, check whether the two numbers make the equation $12f = i$ true.

EXAMPLE 2   **Life Science Application**

One science book states that a male giraffe can grow to be 19 feet tall. According to another book, a male giraffe may grow to 228 inches. Determine if these two measurements are equal.

$12f = i$

$12 \cdot 19 \overset{?}{=} 228$ *Substitute.*

$228 \overset{?}{=} 228$ *Multiply.*

Because $228 = 228$, 19 feet is equal to 228 inches.

Reading Math

An equation has an equal sign, but an expression does not. An equation can be solved, but an expression can only be evaluated or simplified.

Think and Discuss

1. Tell which of the following is the solution of $y \div 2 = 9$: $y = 14$, $y = 16$, or $y = 18$. How do you know?

2. Give an example of an equation with a solution of 15.

Eric Nathan/Alamy

Exercises

Learn It Online
Homework Help Online
Exercises 1–21, 25, 27, 29, 35, 37, 39, 41

GUIDED PRACTICE

See Example 1 **Determine whether the given value of the variable is a solution.**

1. $c + 23 = 48$ for $c = 35$

2. $z + 31 = 73$ for $z = 42$

3. $96 = 130 - d$ for $d = 34$

4. $85 = 194 - a$ for $a = 105$

5. $75 \div y = 5$ for $y = 15$

6. $78 \div n = 13$ for $n = 5$

See Example 2 **7. Social Studies** An almanac states that the Minnehaha Waterfall in Minnesota is 53 feet tall. A tour guide said the Minnehaha Waterfall is 636 inches tall. Determine if these two measurements are equal.

INDEPENDENT PRACTICE

See Example 1 **Determine whether the given value of the variable is a solution.**

8. $w + 19 = 49$ for $w = 30$

9. $d + 27 = 81$ for $d = 44$

10. $g + 34 = 91$ for $g = 67$

11. $k + 16 = 55$ for $k = 39$

12. $101 = 150 - h$ for $h = 49$

13. $89 = 111 - m$ for $m = 32$

14. $116 = 144 - q$ for $q = 38$

15. $92 = 120 - t$ for $t = 28$

16. $80 \div b = 20$ for $b = 4$

17. $91 \div x = 7$ for $x = 12$

18. $55 \div j = 5$ for $j = 10$

19. $49 \div r = 7$ for $r = 7$

See Example 2 **20. Money** Kent earns $6 per hour at his after-school job. One week, he worked 12 hours and received a paycheck for $66. Determine if Kent was paid the correct amount of money. (*Hint:* $6 · hours = total pay)

21. Measurement The Eiffel Tower in Paris, France, is 300 meters tall. A fact page states that it is 30,000 centimeters tall. Determine if these two measurements are equal. (*Hint:* 1 m = 100 cm)

PRACTICE AND PROBLEM SOLVING

Extra Practice
See Extra Practice for more exercises.

Determine whether the given value of the variable is a solution.

22. $93 = 48 + u$ for $u = 35$

23. $112 = 14 \times f$ for $f = 8$

24. $13 = m \div 8$ for $m = 104$

25. $79 = z - 23$ for $z = 112$

26. $64 = l - 34$ for $l = 98$

27. $105 = p \times 7$ for $p = 14$

28. $94 \div s = 26$ for $s = 3$

29. $v + 79 = 167$ for $v = 88$

30. $m + 36 = 54$ for $m = 18$

31. $x - 35 = 96$ for $x = 112$

32. $12y = 84$ for $y = 7$

33. $7x = 56$ for $x = 8$

34. Estimation A large pizza has 8 slices. Determine whether 6 large pizzas will be enough for 24 people, if each person eats 2 to 3 slices of pizza.

35. Multi-Step Rebecca has 17 one-dollar bills. Courtney has 350 nickels. Do the two girls have the same amount of money? (*Hint*: First find how many nickels are in a dollar.)

Replace each ▇ with a number that makes the equation correct.

36. $4 + 1 = ▇ + 2$

37. $2 + ▇ = 6 + 2$

38. $▇ - 5 = 9 - 2$

39. $5(4) = 10(▇)$

40. $3 + 6 = ▇ - 4$

41. $12 \div 4 = 9 \div ▇$

42. Critical Thinking Linda is building a rectangular playhouse. The width is x feet. The length is $x + 3$ feet. The distance around the base of the playhouse is 36 feet. Is 8 the value of x? Explain.

43. Choose a Strategy What should replace the question mark to keep the scale balanced?

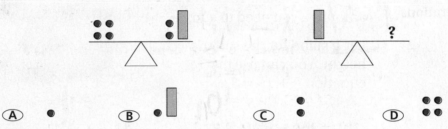

44. Write About It Explain how to determine if a value is a solution to an equation.

45. Challenge Is $n = 4$ a solution for $n^2 + 79 = 88$? Explain.

Test Prep

46. Multiple Choice For which equation is $b = 8$ a solution?

Ⓐ $13 - b = 8$　　Ⓑ $8 + b = 21$　　Ⓒ $b - 13 = 21$　　Ⓓ $b + 13 = 21$

47. Multiple Choice When Paul gets 53 more postcards, he will have 82 cards in his collection. Solve the equation $n + 53 = 82$ to find how many postcards Paul has in his collection now.

Ⓕ 135　　　　Ⓖ 125　　　　Ⓗ 29　　　　Ⓙ 27

CC.6.EE.7 Solve real-world and mathematical problems by writing and solving equations of the form $x + p = q$ and $px = q$ for cases in which p, q and x are all nonnegative rational numbers *Also CC.6.EE.6*

COMMON CORE

Vocabulary
inverse operations

Some surfers recommend that the length of a beginner's surfboard be 14 inches greater than the surfer's height. If a surfboard is 82 inches, how tall should the surfer be to ride it?

The height of the surfer *combined* with 14 inches equals 82 inches. To combine amounts, you need to add.

Let h stand for the surfer's height. You can use the equation $h + 14 = 82$.

The equation $h + 14 = 82$ can be represented as a balanced scale.

To find the value of h, you need h by itself on one side of a balanced scale.

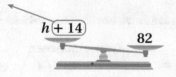

To get h by itself, first take away 14 from the left side of the scale. Now the scale is unbalanced.

To rebalance the scale, take away 14 from the other side.

Taking away 14 from both sides of the scale is the same as subtracting 14 from both sides of the equation.

$$\begin{array}{rcr} h + 14 = & & 82 \\ -\,14 & & -\,14 \\ \hline h \quad = & & 68 \end{array}$$

A surfer using an 82-inch surfboard should be 68 inches tall.

Inverse operations undo each other. Addition and subtraction are inverse operations. If an equation contains addition, solve it by subtracting from both sides to "undo" the addition.

[Video] **Lesson Tutorials Online** my.hrw.com

Buzz Pictures/SuperStock

EXAMPLE 1 Solving Addition Equations

Interactivities Online ▶

Solve each equation. Check your answers.

A $x + 62 = 93$

$x + 62 = 93$	*62 is added to x.*
$\underline{-62 \quad -62}$	*Subtract 62 from both sides to undo*
$x = 31$	*the addition.*

Check $x + 62 = 93$

$31 + 62 \overset{?}{=} 93$ *Substitute 31 for x in the equation.*

$93 \overset{?}{=} 93$ ✔ *31 is the solution.*

B $81 = 17 + y$

$81 = 17 + y$	*17 is added to y.*
$\underline{-17 \quad -17}$	*Subtract 17 from both sides to undo*
$64 = y$	*the addition.*

Check $81 = 17 + y$

$81 \overset{?}{=} 17 + 64$ *Substitute 64 for y in the equation.*

$81 \overset{?}{=} 81$ ✔ *64 is the solution.*

EXAMPLE 2 *Social Studies Application*

Tulsa, Oklahoma City, and Lawton are located in Oklahoma, as shown on the map. Find the distance d between Oklahoma City and Tulsa.

distance between Tulsa and Lawton	=	distance between Oklahoma City and Lawton	+	distance between Oklahoma City and Tulsa
175	=	75	+	d

$175 = 75 + d$	*75 is added to d.*
$\underline{-75 \quad -75}$	*Subtract 75 from both sides to undo*
$100 = d$	*the addition.*

The distance between Oklahoma City and Tulsa is 100 miles.

MATHEMATICAL PRACTICES

Think and Discuss

1. **Tell** whether the solution of $c + 4 = 21$ will be less than 21 or greater than 21. Explain.

2. **Describe** how you could check your answer in Example 2.

Exercises

Learn It Online
Homework Help Online
Exercises 1–17, 21, 23, 25, 27, 29, 31, 33

GUIDED PRACTICE

See Example 1 Solve each equation. Check your answers.

1. $x + 54 = 90$ **2.** $49 = 12 + y$ **3.** $n + 27 = 46$

4. $22 + t = 91$ **5.** $31 = p + 13$ **6.** $c + 38 = 54$

See Example 2 **7.** Lou, Michael, and Georgette live on Mulberry Street, as shown on the map. Lou lives 10 blocks from Georgette. Georgette lives 4 blocks from Michael. How many blocks does Michael live from Lou?

Mulberry Street

Lou's block   Michael's block   Georgette's block

INDEPENDENT PRACTICE

See Example 1 Solve each equation. Check your answers.

8. $x + 19 = 24$ **9.** $10 = r + 3$ **10.** $s + 11 = 50$

11. $b + 17 = 42$ **12.** $12 + m = 28$ **13.** $z + 68 = 77$

14. $72 = n + 51$ **15.** $g + 28 = 44$ **16.** $27 = 15 + y$

See Example 2 **17.** What is the length of a killer whale?

21 m

Fin whale

Gray whale

Killer whale

15 m   ?

PRACTICE AND PROBLEM SOLVING

Extra Practice
See Extra Practice for more exercises.

Solve each equation.

18. $x + 12 = 16$ **19.** $n + 32 = 39$ **20.** $23 + q = 34$

21. $52 + y = 71$ **22.** $73 = c + 35$ **23.** $93 = h + 15$

24. $125 = n + 85$ **25.** $87 = b + 18$ **26.** $12 + y = 50$

27. $t + 17 = 43$ **28.** $k + 9 = 56$ **29.** $25 + m = 47$

Physical Science

This ice sculpture, called Ice Dragon, was carved by Steve Rose and David Patterson as part of the First Night celebrations in Boston, Massachusetts.

Write an equation for each statement.

30. The number of eggs e increased by 3 equals 14.

31. The number of new photos taken p added to 20 equals 36.

32. Physical Science Temperature can be measured in degrees Fahrenheit, degrees Celsius, or kelvins. To convert from degrees Celsius to kelvins, add 273 to the Celsius temperature. Complete the table.

	Kelvins (K)	°C + 273 = K	Celsius (°C)
Water Freezes	273	°C + 273 = 273	▦
Body Temperature	310	▦	▦
Water Boils	373	▦	▦

33. History In 1520, the explorer Ferdinand Magellan tried to measure the depth of the ocean. He weighted a 370 m rope and lowered it into the ocean. This rope was not long enough to reach the ocean floor. Suppose the depth at this location was 1,250 m. How much longer would Magellan's rope have to have been to reach the ocean floor?

34. Write a Problem Use data from your science book to write a problem that can be solved using an addition equation. Solve your problem.

35. Write About It Why are addition and subtraction called inverse operations?

36. Challenge In the magic square at right, each row, column, and diagonal has the same sum. Find the values of x, y, and z.

7	61	x
y	37	1
31	z	67

Test Prep

37. Multiple Choice Pauline hit 6 more home runs than Danielle. Pauline hit 18 home runs. How many home runs did Danielle hit?

    Ⓐ 3   Ⓑ 12   Ⓒ 18   Ⓓ 24

38. Multiple Choice Which is the solution to the equation $79 + r = 118$?

    Ⓕ $r = 39$ Ⓖ $r = 52$ Ⓗ $r = 79$ Ⓙ $r = 197$

2-6 Subtraction Equations

COMMON CORE

CC.6.EE.6 Use variables to represent numbers and write expressions when solving a real-world or mathematical problem; understand that a variable can represent an unknown number, or, depending on the purpose at hand, any number in a specified set

When Theodore Roosevelt became president of the United States, he was 42 years old. He was 27 years younger than Ronald Reagan was when Reagan became president. How old was Reagan when he became president?

Let *a* represent Ronald Reagan's age.

Ronald Reagan's age	−	27	=	Theodore Roosevelt's age
a	−	27	=	42

Recall that addition and subtraction are inverse operations. When an equation contains subtraction, use addition to "undo" the subtraction. Remember to add the same amount to both sides of the equation.

$$
\begin{array}{rcl}
a - 27 &=& 42 \\
+\,27 & & +\,27 \\
\hline
a &=& 69
\end{array}
$$

Ronald Reagan was 69 years old when he became president.

EXAMPLE 1 Solving Subtraction Equations

Interactivities Online ▶

Solve each equation. Check your answers.

A $p - 2 = 5$

$$
\begin{array}{rcl}
p - 2 &=& 5 \\
+\,2 & & +\,2 \\
\hline
p &=& 7
\end{array}
$$

2 is subtracted from *p*.
Add 2 to both sides to undo the subtraction.

Check $p - 2 = 5$

$7 - 2 \overset{?}{=} 5$ Substitute 7 for *p* in the equation.

$5 \overset{?}{=} 5$ ✔   7 is the solution.

Video **Lesson Tutorials Online** my.hrw.com

(tr) Bettmann/CORBIS; (tc) Photodisc/Getty Images; (cl) Wally McNamee/CORBIS

Solve each equation. Check your answers.

B $40 = x - 11$

$$
\begin{array}{rl}
40 = & x - 11 \\
\underline{+\,11} & \underline{+\,11} \\
51 = & x
\end{array}
$$

11 is subtracted from x.

Add 11 to both sides to undo the subtraction.

Check $40 = x - 11$

$40 \overset{?}{=} 51 - 11$ *Substitute 51 for x in the equation.*

$40 \overset{?}{=} 40$ ✔ *51 is the solution.*

C $x - 56 = 19$

$$
\begin{array}{rl}
x - 56 = & 19 \\
\underline{+\,56} & \underline{+\,56} \\
x \quad\;\; = & 75
\end{array}
$$

56 is subtracted from x.

Add 56 to both sides to undo the subtraction.

Check $x - 56 = 19$

$75 - 56 \overset{?}{=} 19$ *Substitute 75 for x in the equation.*

$19 \overset{?}{=} 19$ ✔ *75 is the solution.*

Think and Discuss

1. **Tell** whether the solution of $b - 14 = 9$ will be less than 9 or greater than 9. Explain.

2. **Explain** how you know what number to add to both sides of an equation containing subtraction.

Exercises

Learn It Online
Homework Help Online
Exercises 1–15, 17, 19, 21, 23, 25, 27, 29

GUIDED PRACTICE

See Example **1** Solve each equation. Check your answers.

1. $p - 8 = 9$ **2.** $3 = x - 16$ **3.** $a - 13 = 18$

4. $15 = y - 7$ **5.** $n - 24 = 9$ **6.** $39 = d - 2$

INDEPENDENT PRACTICE

See Example **1** Solve each equation. Check your answers.

7. $y - 18 = 7$ **8.** $8 = n - 5$ **9.** $a - 34 = 4$

10. $c - 21 = 45$ **11.** $a - 40 = 57$ **12.** $31 = x - 14$

13. $28 = p - 5$ **14.** $z - 42 = 7$ **15.** $s - 19 = 12$

Practice

Practice for more exercises.

Solve each equation.

16. $r - 57 = 7$ **17.** $11 = x - 25$ **18.** $8 = y - 96$

19. $a - 6 = 15$ **20.** $q - 14 = 22$ **21.** $f - 12 = 2$

22. $18 = j - 19$ **23.** $109 = r - 45$ **24.** $d - 8 = 29$

25. $g - 71 = 72$ **26.** $p - 13 = 111$ **27.** $13 = m - 5$

28. Geography Mt. Rainier, in Washington, has a higher elevation than Mt. Shasta. The difference between their elevations is 248 feet. What is the elevation of Mt. Rainier? Write an equation and solve.

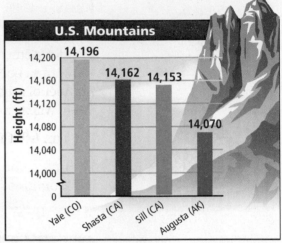

U.S. Mountains

Height (ft): 14,196 (Yale (CO)), 14,162 (Shasta (CA)), 14,153 (Sill (CA)), 14,070 (Augusta (AK))

29. Social Studies In 2004, the population of New York City was 5 million less than the population of Shanghai, China. The population of New York City was 8 million. Solve the equation $8 = s - 5$ to find the population of Shanghai.

 30. Write About It Suppose $n - 15$ is a whole number. What do you know about the value of n? Explain.

31. What's the Error? Look at the student paper at right. What did the student do wrong? What is the correct answer?

32. Challenge Write "the difference between n and 16 is 5" as an algebraic equation. Then find the solution.

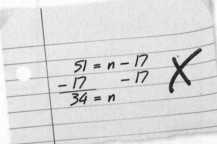

$$51 = n - 17$$
$$-17 \quad\quad -17$$
$$\overline{34 = n}$$
✗

Test Prep

33. Multiple Choice Which is a solution to the equation $j - 39 = 93$?

　Ⓐ $j = 54$　　　Ⓑ $j = 66$　　　Ⓒ $j = 93$　　　Ⓓ $j = 132$

34. Short Response When 17 is subtracted from a number, the result is 64. Write an equation that can be used to find the original number. Then find the original number.

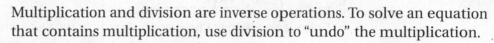

COMMON CORE

CC.6.EE.7 Solve real-world and mathematical problems by writing and solving equations of the form $x + p = q$ and $px = q$ for cases in which p, q and x are all nonnegative rational numbers *Also CC.6.EE.6*

Nine-banded armadillos are always born in groups of 4. If you count 32 babies, what is the number of mother armadillos?

To put together equal groups of 4, multiply. Let m represent the number of mother armadillos. There will be m equal groups of 4.

You can use the equation $4m = 32$.

Multiplication and division are inverse operations. To solve an equation that contains multiplication, use division to "undo" the multiplication.

Caution! //////

$4m$ means "$4 \times m$."

$$4m = 32$$
$$\frac{4m}{4} = \frac{32}{4}$$ There are 8 mother armadillos.
$$m = 8$$

EXAMPLE 1 **Solving Multiplication Equations**

Interactivities Online ▶

Solve each equation. Check your answers.

A $3x = 12$

$3x = 12$	*x is multiplied by 3.*
$\dfrac{3x}{3} = \dfrac{12}{3}$	*Divide both sides by 3 to undo the multiplication.*
$x = 4$	

Check $3x = 12$

$3(4) \overset{?}{=} 12$	*Substitute 4 for x in the equation.*
$12 \overset{?}{=} 12$ ✔	*4 is the solution.*

B $8 = 4w$

$8 = 4w$	*w is multiplied by 4.*
$\dfrac{8}{4} = \dfrac{4w}{4}$	*Divide both sides by 4 to undo the multiplication.*
$2 = w$	

Check $8 = 4w$

$8 \overset{?}{=} 4(2)$	*Substitute 2 for w in the equation.*
$8 \overset{?}{=} 8$ ✔	*2 is the solution.*

Bianca Lavies/National Geographic Image Collection

EXAMPLE **2** **PROBLEM SOLVING APPLICATION**

The area of a rectangle is 36 square inches. Its length is 9 inches. What is its width?

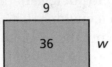

Make sense of problems and persevere in solving them.

1 **Understand the Problem**

The **answer** will be the width of the rectangle in inches.

List the **important information:**
- The area of the rectangle is 36 square inches.
- The length of the rectangle is 9 inches.

Draw a diagram to represent this information.

9

36   *w*

2 **Make a Plan**

You can write and solve an equation using the formula for area. To find the area of a rectangle, multiply its length by its width.

$A = \ell w$
$36 = 9w$ *w*

ℓ

3 **Solve**

$36 = 9w$ *w is multiplied by 9.*

$\frac{36}{9} = \frac{9w}{9}$ *Divide both sides by 9 to undo the multiplication.*

$4 = w$

So the width of the rectangle is 4 inches.

4 **Look Back**

Arrange 36 identical squares in a rectangle. The length is 9, so line up the squares in rows of 9. You can make 4 rows of 9, so the width of the rectangle is 4.

MATHEMATICAL PRACTICES

Think and Discuss

1. Tell what number you would use to divide both sides of the equation $15x = 60$.

2. Tell whether the solution of $10c = 90$ will be less than 90 or greater than 90. Explain.

Multiplication Equations

CC.6.EE.7 Solve real-world and mathematical problems by writing and solving equations of the form $x + p = q$ and $px = q$ for cases in which p, q and x are all nonnegative rational numbers **Also CC.6.EE.6**

Nine-banded armadillos are always born in groups of 4. If you count 32 babies, what is the number of mother armadillos?

To put together equal groups of 4, multiply. Let m represent the number of mother armadillos. There will be m equal groups of 4.

You can use the equation $4m = 32$.

Multiplication and division are inverse operations. To solve an equation that contains multiplication, use division to "undo" the multiplication.

Caution!

$4m$ means "$4 \times m$."

$$4m = 32$$
$$\frac{4m}{4} = \frac{32}{4}$$ There are 8 mother armadillos.
$$m = 8$$

EXAMPLE 1 **Solving Multiplication Equations**

Interactivities Online ▶

Solve each equation. Check your answers.

A $3x = 12$

$3x = 12$ *x is multiplied by 3.*

$\dfrac{3x}{3} = \dfrac{12}{3}$ *Divide both sides by 3 to undo the multiplication.*

$x = 4$

Check $3x = 12$

$3(4) \overset{?}{=} 12$ *Substitute 4 for x in the equation.*

$12 \overset{?}{=} 12$ ✔   *4 is the solution.*

B $8 = 4w$

$8 = 4w$ *w is multiplied by 4.*

$\dfrac{8}{4} = \dfrac{4w}{4}$ *Divide both sides by 4 to undo the multiplication.*

$2 = w$

Check $8 = 4w$

$8 \overset{?}{=} 4(2)$ *Substitute 2 for w in the equation.*

$8 \overset{?}{=} 8$ ✔   *2 is the solution.*

EXAMPLE 2 **PROBLEM SOLVING APPLICATION**

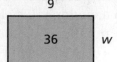
Make sense of problems and persevere in solving them.

The area of a rectangle is 36 square inches. Its length is 9 inches. What is its width?

1 Understand the Problem

The **answer** will be the width of the rectangle in inches.

List the **important information:**
- The area of the rectangle is 36 square inches.
- The length of the rectangle is 9 inches.

Draw a diagram to represent this information.

9

36 w

2 Make a Plan

You can write and solve an equation using the formula for area. To find the area of a rectangle, multiply its length by its width.

$A = \ell w$
$36 = 9w$

w

ℓ

3 Solve

$36 = 9w$ *w is multiplied by 9.*

$\frac{36}{9} = \frac{9w}{9}$ *Divide both sides by 9 to undo the multiplication.*

$4 = w$

So the width of the rectangle is 4 inches.

4 Look Back

Arrange 36 identical squares in a rectangle. The length is 9, so line up the squares in rows of 9. You can make 4 rows of 9, so the width of the rectangle is 4.

Think and Discuss

1. Tell what number you would use to divide both sides of the equation $15x = 60$.

2. Tell whether the solution of $10c = 90$ will be less than 90 or greater than 90. Explain.

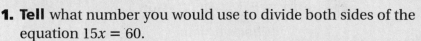

GUIDED PRACTICE

See Example **1** Solve each equation. Check your answers.

1. $7x = 21$ **2.** $27 = 3w$ **3.** $90 = 10a$

4. $56 = 7b$ **5.** $3c = 33$ **6.** $12 = 2n$

See Example **2** **7.** The area of a rectangular deck is 675 square feet. The deck's width is 15 feet. What is its length?

15 ft

INDEPENDENT PRACTICE

See Example **1** Solve each equation. Check your answers.

8. $12p = 36$ **9.** $52 = 13a$ **10.** $64 = 8n$

11. $20 = 5x$ **12.** $6r = 30$ **13.** $77 = 11t$

14. $14s = 98$ **15.** $12m = 132$ **16.** $9z = 135$

See Example **2** **17.** Marcy spreads out a rectangular picnic blanket with an area of 24 square feet. Its width is 4 feet. What is its length?

PRACTICE AND PROBLEM SOLVING

Extra Practice

See Extra Practice for more exercises.

Solve each equation.

18. $5y = 35$ **19.** $18 = 2y$ **20.** $54 = 9y$ **21.** $15y = 120$

22. $4y = 0$ **23.** $22y = 440$ **24.** $3y = 63$ **25.** $z - 6 = 34$

26. $6y = 114$ **27.** $161 = 7y$ **28.** $135 = 3y$ **29.** $y - 15 = 3$

30. $81 = 9y$ **31.** $4 + y = 12$ **32.** $7y = 21$ **33.** $a + 12 = 26$

34. $10x = 120$ **35.** $36 = 12x$ **36.** $s - 2 = 7$ **37.** $15 + t = 21$

38. Estimation Colorado is almost a perfect rectangle on a map. Its border from east to west is about 387 mi, and its area is about 104,247 mi^2. Estimate the length of Colorado's border from north to south. (Area = length × width)

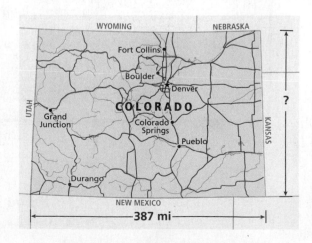

Arthropods make up the largest group of animals on Earth. They include insects, spiders, crabs, and centipedes. Arthropods have segmented bodies. In centipedes and millipedes, all of the segments are identical.

Millipedes kept as pets can live for up to 7 years and grow to be up to 15 inches long.

39. Centipedes have 2 legs per segment. They can have from 30 to 354 legs. Find a range for the number of segments a centipede can have.

40. Millipedes have 4 legs per segment. The record number of legs on a millipede is 752. How many segments did this millipede have?

Many arthropods have compound eyes. Compound eyes are made up of tiny bundles of identical light-sensitive cells.

41. A dragonfly has 7 times as many light-sensitive cells as a housefly. How many of these cells does a housefly have?

42. Find how many times more light-sensitive cells a dragonfly has than a butterfly.

43. **Write About It** A trapdoor spider can pull with a force that is 140 times its own weight. What other information would you need to find the spider's weight? Explain.

44. ⭐ **Challenge** There are about 6 billion humans in the world. Scientists estimate that there are a billion billion arthropods in the world. About how many times larger is the arthropod population than the human population?

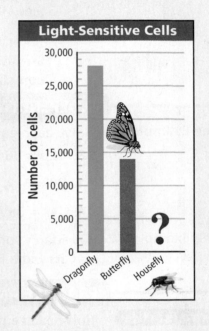

Test Prep

45. **Multiple Choice** Solve the equation $25x = 175$.

   Ⓐ $x = 5$ Ⓑ $x = 6$ Ⓒ $x = 7$ Ⓓ $x = 8$

46. **Multiple Choice** The area of a rectangle is 42 square inches. Its width is 6 inches. What is its length?

   Ⓕ 5 inches   Ⓖ 7 inches   Ⓗ 9 inches   Ⓙ 11 inches

COMMON CORE

CC.6.EE.6 Use variables to represent numbers and write expressions when solving a real-world or mathematical problem; understand that a variable can represent an unknown number, or, depending on the purpose at hand, any number in a specified set

Recreational scuba divers go as deep as 130 feet underwater to view fish and coral. At this depth, the pressure on a diver is much greater than at the water's surface. Water pressure can be described using equations containing division.

Recall that multiplication and division are inverse operations. If an equation contains division, solve it by multiplying on both sides to "undo" the division.

EXAMPLE **1**   **Solving Division Equations**

Interactivities Online ▶

Solve each equation. Check your answers.

A $\frac{y}{5} = 4$

$$\frac{y}{5} = 4 \qquad \text{\textit{y is divided by 5.}}$$

$$5 \cdot \frac{y}{5} = 5 \cdot 4 \qquad \text{\textit{Multiply both sides by 5 to undo the division.}}$$

$$y = 20$$

Check

$$\frac{y}{5} = 4$$

$$\frac{20}{5} \overset{?}{=} 4 \qquad \text{\textit{Substitute 20 for y in the equation.}}$$

$$4 \overset{?}{=} 4 \checkmark \qquad \text{\textit{20 is the solution.}}$$

B $12 = \frac{z}{4}$

$$12 = \frac{z}{4} \qquad \text{\textit{z is divided by 4.}}$$

$$4 \cdot 12 = 4 \cdot \frac{z}{4} \qquad \text{\textit{Multiply both sides by 4 to undo the division.}}$$

$$48 = z$$

Check

$$12 = \frac{z}{4}$$

$$12 \overset{?}{=} \frac{48}{4} \qquad \text{\textit{Substitute 48 for z in the equation.}}$$

$$12 \overset{?}{=} 12 \checkmark \qquad \text{\textit{48 is the solution.}}$$

Stephen Frink/Photographer's Choice RF/Getty Images

EXAMPLE 2 **Physical Science Application**

Pressure is the amount of force exerted on an area. Pressure can be measured in pounds per square inch, or psi.

The pressure at the surface of the water is half the pressure at 30 ft underwater.

$$\text{pressure at surface} = \frac{\text{pressure at 30 ft underwater}}{2}$$

The pressure at the surface is 15 psi. What is the water pressure at 30 ft underwater?

Let p represent the pressure at 30 ft underwater.

$15 = \frac{p}{2}$ *Substitute 15 for pressure at the surface. p is divided by 2.*

$2 \cdot 15 = 2 \cdot \frac{p}{2}$ *Multiply both sides by 2 to undo the division.*

$30 = p$

The water pressure at 30 ft underwater is 30 psi.

Think and Discuss

1. Tell whether the solution of $\frac{c}{10} = 70$ will be less than 70 or greater than 70. Explain.

2. Describe how you would check your answer to Example 2.

3. Explain why $13 \cdot \frac{x}{13} = x$.

2-8 Exercises

Learn It Online
Homework Help Online
Exercises 1–18, 19, 21, 23, 25, 27

GUIDED PRACTICE

See Example **1** Solve each equation. Check your answers.

1. $\frac{y}{4} = 3$ **2.** $14 = \frac{z}{2}$ **3.** $\frac{r}{9} = 7$ **4.** $\frac{s}{10} = \frac{4}{40}$

5. $12 = \frac{j}{3}$ **6.** $9 = \frac{x}{5}$ **7.** $\frac{f}{12} = 5$ **8.** $\frac{g}{2} = 1$

See Example **2** **9.** Irene mowed the lawn and planted flowers. The amount of time she spent mowing the lawn was one-third the amount of time it took her to plant flowers. It took her 30 minutes to mow the lawn. Find the amount of time Irene spent planting flowers.

 **Lesson Tutorials Online** my.hrw.com

See Example 1 Solve each equation. Check your answers.

10. $\frac{d}{3} = 12$ 11. $\frac{c}{2} = 13$ 12. $7 = \frac{m}{7}$ 13. $\frac{g}{7} = 14$

14. $6 = \frac{f}{4}$ 15. $\frac{x}{12} = 12$ 16. $\frac{j}{20} = 10$ 17. $9 = \frac{r}{9}$

See Example 2 18. The area of Danielle's garden is one-twelfth the area of her entire yard. The area of the garden is 10 square feet. Find the area of the yard.

PRACTICE AND PROBLEM SOLVING

Extra Practice
See Extra Practice for more exercises.

Find the value of c in each equation.

19. $\frac{c}{12} = 8$ 20. $4 = \frac{c}{9}$ 21. $\frac{c}{15} = 11$ 22. $c + 21 = 40$

23. $14 = \frac{c}{5}$ 24. $\frac{c}{4} = 12$ 25. $\frac{c}{4} = 15$ 26. $5c = 120$

27. **Multi-Step** The Empire State Building is 381 m tall. At the Grand Canyon's widest point, 76 Empire State Buildings would fit end to end. Write and solve an equation to find the width of the Grand Canyon at this point.

28. **Earth Science** You can estimate the distance of a thunderstorm in kilometers by counting the number of seconds between the lightning flash and the thunder and then dividing this number by 3. If a storm is 5 km away, how many seconds will you count between the lightning flash and the thunder?

 29. **Write a Problem** Write a problem about money that can be solved with a division equation.

 30. **Write About It** Use a numerical example to explain how multiplication and division undo each other.

31. **Challenge** A number halved and then halved again is equal to 2. What was the original number?

Test Prep

32. **Multiple Choice** Carl has n action figures in his collection. He wants to place them in 6 bins with 12 figures in each bin. Solve the equation $\frac{n}{6} = 12$ to determine the number of action figures Carl has.

  (A) $n = 2$ (B) $n = 6$ (C) $n = 18$ (D) $n = 72$

33. **Multiple Choice** Which equation does NOT have $k = 28$ as a solution?

  (F) $\frac{k}{14} = 2$ (G) $\frac{k}{7} = 4$ (H) $\frac{k}{28} = 1$ (J) $\frac{k}{6} = 12$

Quiz for Lessons 4 Through 8

4 Equations and Their Solutions

Determine whether the given value of the variable is a solution.

1. $c - 13 = 54$ for $c = 67$ **2.** $5r = 65$ for $r = 15$ **3.** $48 \div x = 6$ for $x = 8$

4. Brady buys 2 notebooks and should get $3 back in change. The cashier gives him 12 quarters. Determine if Brady was given the correct amount of change.

5 Addition Equations

Solve each equation. Check your answers.

5. $p + 51 = 76$ **6.** $107 = 19 + j$ **7.** $45 = s + 27$

8. A large section of the original Great Wall of China is now in ruins. As measured today, the length of the wall is about 6,350 kilometers. When the length of the section now in ruins is included, the length of the wall is about 6,850 kilometers. Write and solve an equation to find the approximate length of the section of the Great Wall that is now in ruins.

6 Subtraction Equations

Solve each equation. Check your answers.

9. $k - 5 = 17$ **10.** $150 = p - 30$ **11.** $n - 24 = 72$

12. The Kingda Ka roller coaster at Six Flags® Great Adventure in New Jersey is taller than the Top Thrill Dragster located at Cedar Point™ in Ohio. The difference between their heights is 36 feet. The Top Thrill Dragster is 420 feet high. Write and solve an equation to find the height of Kingda Ka.

7 Multiplication Equations

Solve each equation. Check your answers.

13. $6f = 18$ **14.** $105 = 5d$ **15.** $11x = 99$

16. Taryn buys 8 identical glasses. Her total is $48 before tax. Write and solve an equation to find out how much Taryn pays per glass.

8 Division Equations

Solve each equation. Check your answers.

17. $10 = \frac{j}{9}$ **18.** $5 = \frac{t}{6}$ **19.** $\frac{r}{15} = 3$

20. Paula is baking peach pies for a bake sale. Each pie requires 2 pounds of peaches. She bakes 6 pies. Write and solve an equation to find how many pounds of peaches Paula had to buy.

Ready to Go On?

The First Oil Well In 1859, Edwin Drake drilled the world's first oil well, beside Oil Creek near Titusville, Pennsylvania. Almost overnight, towns sprang up in the area and people came from everywhere to be part of the oil boom. Until 1901, Pennsylvania produced half of the world's oil.

PENNSYLVANIA
Titusville

1. Before Drake drilled his well, about 5 gallons of oil could be collected aboveground each day near Oil Creek. Drake's well produced 210 times as much oil each day as could be collected aboveground.

   a. Given that there are 42 gallons in one barrel, find the daily production in barrels of Drake's well.

   b. Let x represent the number of days. Write an expression for the number of barrels of oil produced in x days.

   c. How many days did it take the well to produce 500 barrels of oil? How do you know?

2. In 3 days, Drake's well produced oil worth $1,500. What was the value of the oil produced in one week?

3. The surface of the ground at Drake's well is 1,200 ft above sea level. To reach oil, Drake first drilled through gravel to a point 1,168 ft above sea level. He then drilled an additional 38 ft through shale. What was the total depth of the well?

Ground surface

Gravel

Gravel/shale boundary

Shale

Oil

H. Mark Weidman

Real-World Connections

Game Time

Math Magic

Guess what your friends are thinking with this math magic trick.

Copy the following number charts.

1	10	19
2, 2	11, 11	20, 20
4	13	22
5, 5	14, 14	23, 23
7	16	25
8, 8	17, 17	26, 26

3	12	21
4	13	22
5	14	23
6, 6	15, 15	24, 24
7, 7	16, 16	25, 25
8, 8	17, 17	26, 26

9	15	21, 21
10	16	22, 22
11	17	23, 23
12	18, 18	24, 24
13	19, 19	25, 25
14	20, 20	26, 26

Step 1: Ask a friend to think of a number from 1 to 26.
Example: Your friend thinks of 26.

Step 2: Show your friend the first chart and ask how many times the chosen number appears. Remember the answer.
Your friend says the chosen number appears twice on the first chart.

2

Step 3: Show the second chart and ask the same question. Multiply the answer by 3. Add your result to the answer from step 2. Remember this answer.
Your friend says the chosen number appears twice.
The answer from step 2 is 2.

$3 \cdot 2 = 6$
$6 + 2 = 8$

Step 4: Show the third chart and ask the same question. Multiply the answer by 9. Add your result to the answer from step 3. The answer is your friend's number.
Your friend says the chosen number appears twice.
The answer from step 3 is 8.

$9 \cdot 2 = 18$
$18 + 8 = 26$

↑
Your friend's number

How does it work?

Your friend's number will be the following:

(answer from step 2) + (3 · answer from step 3) + (9 · answer from step 4)

This is an expression with three variables: $a + 3b + 9c$. A number will be on a particular chart 0, 1, or 2 times, so a, b, and c will always be 0, 1, or 2. With these values, you can write expressions for each number from 1 to 26.

a	b	c	a + 3b + 9c
1	0	0	$1 + 3(0) + 9(0) = 1$
2	0	0	$2 + 3(0) + 9(0) = 2$
0	1	0	$0 + 3(1) + 9(0) = 3$

Can you complete the table for 4–26?

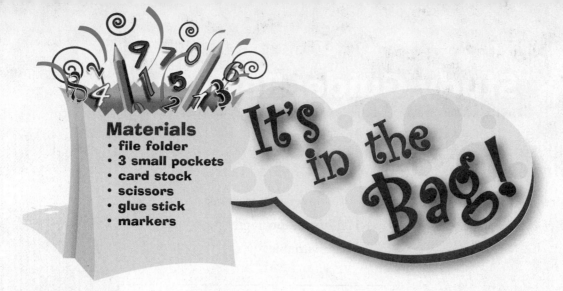

Materials
- file folder
- 3 small pockets
- card stock
- scissors
- glue stick
- markers

It's in the Bag!

PROJECT Tri-Sided Equations

Use a colorful file folder to prepare a three-sided review of algebra!

Directions

1 Close the file folder. Fold one side down to the folded edge. Turn the folder over and fold the other side down to the folded edge. **Figure A**

2 Open the folder. It will be divided into four sections. On the top section, cut off $\frac{1}{4}$ inch from each edge. On the bottom section, make a 1 inch diagonal slit in the top left corner and in the top right corner. **Figure B**

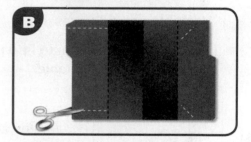

3 Fold the folder so that the corners of the smaller top section fit into the slits. This will create your three-sided holder for notes. **Figure C**

4 Write the definition of an equation on one side of your note holder. Write the order of operations on another side. Write examples of expressions on the third side.

Taking Note of the Math

Glue a small pocket made from construction paper or card stock onto each side of your note holder. On rectangular slips of card stock, write problems that demonstrate your knowledge of equations, order of operations, and expressions. Store the note cards in the appropriate pockets.

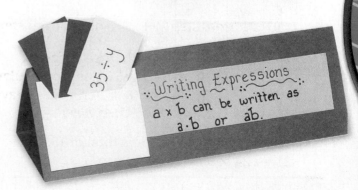

HMH

Study Guide: Review

Vocabulary

algebraic expression

constant

equation

evaluate

inverse operations

solution

variable

Complete the sentences below with vocabulary words from the list above.

1. A(n) ___?___ contains one or more variables.

2. A(n) ___?___ is a mathematical statement that says two quantities are equal.

3. In the equation $12 + t = 22$, t is a ___?___.

EXAMPLES

1 ### Variables and Expressions

■ Evaluate the expression to find the missing values in the table.

n	3n + 4
1	7
2	■
3	■

$n = 1; \quad 3 \times 1 + 4 = 7$

$n = 2; \quad 3 \times 2 + 4 = 10$

$n = 3; \quad 3 \times 3 + 4 = 13$

The missing values are 10 and 13.

■ A rectangle is 3 units wide. How many square units does the rectangle cover if it is 5, 6, 7, or 8 units long?

ℓ	w	ℓ × w
5	3	15
6	3	■
7	3	■
8	3	■

$5 \times 3 = 15$ square units

$6 \times 3 = 18$ square units

$7 \times 3 = 21$ square units

$8 \times 3 = 24$ square units

The rectangle will cover a total of 15, 18, 21, or 24 square units.

EXERCISES

Evaluate each expression to find the missing values in the tables.

4.

y	y ÷ 7
56	8
49	■
42	■

5.

k	k × 4 − 6
2	2
3	■
4	■

6. A rectangle is 9 units long. How many square units does the rectangle cover if it is 1, 2, 3, or 4 units wide?

7. Karen buys 3 bouquets of flowers. How many flowers does she buy if each bouquet contains 10, 11, 12, or 13 flowers?

8. Ron buys 5 bags of marbles. How many marbles does he buy if each bag contains 15, 16, 17, or 18 marbles?

2   Translating Between Words and Math

Write each phrase as a numerical or algebraic expression.

- 617 minus 191

  $617 - 191$

- d multiplied by 5

  $5d$ or $5 \cdot d$ or $(5)(d)$

Write two phrases for each expression.

- $a \div 5$
  - a divided by 5
  - the quotient of a and 5
- $67 + 19$
  - the sum of 67 and 19
  - 19 more than 67

Write each phrase as a numerical or algebraic expression.

9. 15 plus b

10. the product of 6 and 5

11. 9 times t

12. the quotient of g and 9

Write two phrases for each expression.

13. $4z$

14. $15 + x$

15. $54 \div 6$

16. $\frac{m}{20}$

17. $3 - y$

18. $5,100 + 64$

19. $y - 3$

20. $g - 20$

3   Translating Between Tables and Expressions

- Write an expression for the sequence in the table.

Position	1	2	3	4	n
Value of Term	9	18	27	36	

To go from the position to the value of the term, multiply the position by 9. The expression is $9n$.

Write an expression for the sequence in each table.

21.

Position	1	2	3	4	n
Value of Term	4	7	10	13	

22.

Position	1	2	3	4	n
Value of Term	0	1	2	3	

4   Equations and Their Solutions

- Determine whether the given value of the variable is a solution.

  $f + 14 = 50$ for $f = 34$

  $f + 14 = 50$

  $34 + 14 \overset{?}{=} 50$ *Substitute 34 for f.*

  $48 \neq 50$ *Add.*

  34 is not a solution.

Determine whether the given value of the variable is a solution.

23. $28 + n = 39$ for $n = 11$

24. $12t = 74$ for $t = 6$

25. $y - 53 = 27$ for $y = 80$

26. $96 \div w = 32$ for $w = 3$

Study Guide: Review

5 **Addition Equations**

- Solve the equation $x + 18 = 31$.

$$\begin{array}{rcl} x + 18 & = & 31 \\ -18 & & -18 \\ \hline x & = & 13 \end{array}$$

18 is added to x.
Subtract 18 from both
sides to undo the addition.

Solve each equation.

27. $4 + x = 10$ **28.** $n + 10 = 24$

29. $c + 71 = 100$ **30.** $y + 16 = 22$

31. $44 = p + 17$ **32.** $94 + w = 103$

33. Melinda's new HD radio will play 93 channels. This is 26 more channels than her old radio played. How many channels could she listen to with her old radio?

6 **Subtraction Equations**

- Solve the equation $c - 7 = 16$.

$$\begin{array}{rcl} c - 7 & = & 16 \\ +7 & & +7 \\ \hline c & = & 23 \end{array}$$

7 is subtracted from c.
Add 7 to each side to
undo the subtraction.

Solve each equation.

34. $28 = k - 17$ **35.** $d - 8 = 1$

36. $p - 55 = 8$ **37.** $n - 31 = 36$

38. $3 = r - 11$ **39.** $97 = w - 47$

40. There are 14 Winter Olympics sports. This is 17 fewer than the number of Summer Olympics sports. How many Summer sports are there?

7 **Multiplication Equations**

- Solve the equation $6x = 36$.

$$6x = 36$$

$$\frac{6x}{6} = \frac{36}{6}$$

$$x = 6$$

x is multiplied by 6.

Divide both sides by 6 to
undo the multiplication.

Solve each equation.

41. $5v = 40$ **42.** $27 = 3y$

43. $12c = 84$ **44.** $18n = 36$

45. $72 = 9s$ **46.** $11t = 110$

47. The average American eats about 30 pounds of cheese per year. This is $\frac{3}{5}$ the amount eaten by the average French person. How many pounds of cheese does a French person eat in one year?

8 **Division Equations**

- Solve the equation $\frac{k}{4} = 8$.

$$\frac{k}{4} = 8$$

$$4 \cdot \frac{k}{4} = 4 \cdot 8$$

$$k = 32$$

k is divided by 4.

Multiply both sides by 4
to undo the division.

Solve each equation.

48. $\frac{r}{7} = 6$ **49.** $\frac{t}{5} = 3$

50. $6 = \frac{y}{3}$ **51.** $12 = \frac{n}{6}$

52. $\frac{z}{13} = 4$ **53.** $20 = \frac{b}{5}$

Study Guide: Review

Chapter Test

Evaluate each expression to find the missing values in the tables.

1.

a	$a + 18$
10	28
12	▥
14	▥

2.

y	$y \div 6$
18	3
30	▥
42	▥

3.

n	$n \div 5 + 7$
10	9
20	▥
30	▥

4. A van can seat 6 people. How many people can ride in 3, 4, 5, and 6 vans?

5. A rectangle is 5 units wide. How many square units does the rectangle cover if it is 10, 11, 12, or 13 units long?

Write an expression for the missing value in each table.

6.

Packages	Rolls
1	8
2	16
3	24
4	32
p	▥

7.

Students	Groups
5	1
10	2
15	3
20	4
s	▥

Write an expression for the sequence in the table.

8.

Position	1	2	3	4	5	n
Value of Term	4	7	10	13	16	▥

9. There are more reptile species than amphibian species. There are 3,100 living species of amphibians. Write an expression to show how many more reptile species there are than amphibian species.

Write each phrase as a numerical or algebraic expression.

10. 26 more than n **11.** g multiplied by 4   **12.** the quotient of 180 and 15

Write two phrases for each expression.

13. $(14)(16)$ **14.** $n \div 8$ **15.** $p + 11$ **16.** $s - 6$

Determine whether the given value of the variable is a solution.

17. $5d = 70$ for $d = 12$ **18.** $29 = 76 - n$ for $n = 46$

19. $108 \div a = 12$ for $a = 9$ **20.** $15 + m = 27$ for $m = 12$

Solve each equation.

21. $a + 7 = 25$ **22.** $121 = 11d$ **23.** $3 = t - 8$ **24.** $6 = \frac{k}{9}$

25. Air typically has about 4,000 bacteria per cubic meter. If your room is 30 cubic meters, about how many bacteria would there be in the air in your room?

Chapter Test

Cumulative Assessment

Multiple Choice

1. Which is an algebraic expression for the product of 15 and x?

Ⓐ $15 - x$ Ⓒ $x + 15$

Ⓑ $15x$ Ⓓ $15 \div x$

2. Max earned $560 working as a landscaper. If he worked a total of 80 hours, which expression can be used to find how much he earned each hour?

Ⓕ $560 - 80$ Ⓗ $560 + 80$

Ⓖ $560 \div 80$ Ⓙ $560 \cdot 80$

3. Find the expression for the table.

x	
3	9
8	19
11	25
15	33

Ⓐ $3x$ Ⓒ $2x + 3$

Ⓑ $x + 18$ Ⓓ $3x - 5$

4. A rectangular classroom has an area of 252 square feet. The width of the classroom is 14 feet. What is its length?

Ⓕ 14 feet   Ⓗ 18 feet

Ⓖ 16 feet   Ⓙ 20 feet

5. What is the difference between 82,714 and 54,221 rounded to the nearest hundred?

Ⓐ 28,500   Ⓒ 26,900

Ⓑ 27,700   Ⓓ 26,000

6. What is the value of 8^3?

Ⓕ 11   Ⓗ 192

Ⓖ 24   Ⓙ 512

7. Zane biked 23 miles this week. This is 8 miles more than he biked the week before. Solve the equation $x + 8 = 23$ to find how many miles Zane biked last week.

Ⓐ 15 miles   Ⓒ 31 miles

Ⓑ 23 miles   Ⓓ 33 miles

8. Which team sold the most fund-raising products?

Fund-raising Results by Team	
Team	Products Sold
Golf	6,536
Soccer	6,421
Swim	6,879
Track	6,019

Ⓕ Soccer team   Ⓗ Swim team

Ⓖ Golf team   Ⓙ Track team

9. Which equation is an example of the Associative Property?

Ⓐ $3 + (4 + 6) = (3 + 4) + 6$

Ⓑ $(42 + 6) + 18 = (42 + 18) + 6$

Ⓒ $(3 \times 20) + (3 \times 4) = 3 \times 24$

Ⓓ $8(2 \times 6) = (8 \times 2) + (8 \times 6)$

10. Nicole is 15 years old. She is 3 years younger than her sister Jan. Solve the equation $j - 3 = 15$ to find Jan's age.

- Ⓕ 18 years
- Ⓗ 12 years
- Ⓖ 17 years
- Ⓙ 5 years

11. Divide: 3,806 ÷ 22

- Ⓐ 93
- Ⓒ 163
- Ⓑ 112
- Ⓓ 173

Substitute the values given in the answers into an equation to see which value makes the equation true.

Gridded Response

12. Use the table to find the unknown value.

t	$11 \times t + 3$
5	58
8	▨

13. What is the value of $5^2 - (18 \div 6) \times 7$?

14. Scott spends 16 minutes in the pool treading water during swim practice. This is $\frac{1}{3}$ of his practice time. How many total minutes is Scott's swim practice?

15. A case of pencils costs $15. If the academic team spends $135 on pencils for the school tournament, how many cases of pencils did the academic team buy?

16. What value of x will make each of the following expressions equal 12?

$$2x + 4 \qquad 5x - 8$$

17. What is the solution to the equation $8a = 48$?

Short Response

S1. Every week Brandi runs 7 more miles than her sister Jamie.

- **a.** Write an expression for the number of miles that Brandi runs each week. Identify the variable.
- **b.** Evaluate your expression to find the number of miles Brandi runs when Jamie runs 5 miles.

S2. A vacation tour costs $450. Additional outings cost $25 each. The table shows the total cost to go on additional outings.

Outings	1	2	3	n
Total Cost ($)	475	500	525	▨

Write an expression for the cost of n outings. Use the expression to find how much it costs to go on 5 outings.

Extended Response

E1. Chrissy and Kathie are sisters. Chrissy was born on Kathie's birthday and is exactly 8 years younger. Chrissy celebrated her 16th birthday on December 8, 2005.

- **a.** Complete the table to show the ages of the sisters in the years 2005, 2008, and 2011.

Year	Kathie's Age	Chrissy's Age
2005	▨	▨
2008	▨	▨
2011	▨	▨

- **b.** Write an equation that could be used to find Kathie's age in 2011. Identify the variable in the equation.
- **c.** Solve the equation. Show your work. Compare your answer to the value in the table. Are the two solutions the same? Explain your answer.

COMMON CORE

Chapter
- Use common procedures to multiply and divide decimals.
- Evaluate expressions and solve equations with decimals.

Why Learn This?

Most statistics in sports are reported as decimals. In basketball, for example, a player who has made 52 out of 60 free throws would have a "free throw percentage" of 0.867. In this chapter, you will learn about decimals and how to use them to solve problems.

Learn It Online
Chapter Project Online

(a) John Dunstan SMI/CORBIS

 # Are You Ready?

✓ Vocabulary

Choose the best term from the list to complete each sentence.

1. The first place value to the left of the decimal point is the
   ___?___ place, and the place value two places to the
   left of the decimal point is the ___?___ place.

2. In the expression 72 ÷ 9, 72 is the ___?___, and 9 is
   the ___?___.

3. The answer to a subtraction expression is the
   _____?_____.

4. A(n) ___?___ is a mathematical statement that says
   two quantities are equivalent.

difference

dividend

divisor

equation

ones

quotient

tens

Complete these exercises to review skills you will need for this chapter.

✓ Place Value of Whole Numbers

Identify the place value of each underlined digit.

5. 1<u>5</u>2

6. <u>7</u>,903

7. <u>1</u>45,072

8. 4,8<u>9</u>3,025

9. 13,7<u>9</u>6,020

10. 14<u>5</u>,683,032

✓ Add and Subtract Whole Numbers

Find each sum or difference.

11. $425 − $75

12. 532 + 145

13. 160 − 82

✓ Multiply and Divide Whole Numbers

Find each product or quotient.

14. $320 × 5

15. 125 ÷ 5

16. 54 × 3

✓ Exponents

Find each value.

17. 10^3

18. 3^6

19. 10^5

20. 4^5

21. 8^3

22. 2^7

✓ Solve One-Step Equations

Solve each equation.

23. $y + 382 = 743$

24. $n - 150 = 322$

25. $9x = 108$

Study Guide: Preview

Where You've Been

Previously, you

- compared and ordered whole numbers.

- rounded numbers to a given place value.

- used addition, subtraction, multiplication, and division of whole numbers to solve problems.

In This Chapter

You will study

- reading, writing, comparing, and ordering decimals.

- using rounding to estimate answers to problems that involve decimals.

- solving decimal equations.

Where You're Going

You can use the skills learned in this chapter

- to solve two-step decimal equations in higher-level math classes, such as Algebra 1.

- to solve problems involving money in business and financial situations.

Key Vocabulary/Vocabulario

clustering	agrupación
front-end estimation	estimación por partes

Vocabulary Connections

To become familiar with some of the vocabulary terms in the chapter, consider the following. You may refer to the chapter, the glossary, or a dictionary if you like.

1. When you estimate, you approximate the value of something. What part of a decimal do you think you are using to approximate a value when you use **front-end estimation**?

2. A *cluster* is a close grouping of similar items. When do you think **clustering** might be a good method of estimation?

Reading and Writing Math

Writing Strategy: Keep a Math Journal

You can help improve your writing and reasoning skills by keeping a math journal. When you express your thoughts on paper, you can make sense of confusing math concepts.

You can also record your thoughts about each lesson and reflect on what you learned in class. Your journal will become a personal math reference book from which to study.

Journal Entry:
Read the entry Jaime wrote in his math journal about translating between math and words.

> **Journal Entry 2**   October
> Today's lesson was on translating between words and math. I understand that a math expression like 18 x 2 can be written as "18 multiplied by 2." However, I am confused which symbol to use when translating from words to math. My teacher suggested that I make a list in this journal of common terms and their symbols.
>
> | Words | Symbols |
> |---|---|
> | sum, added, plus | + |
> | difference, less than | - |
> | product, times | x or • |
> | divide, quotient | ÷ |
>
> Now I understand!
> This list will help me when I need to know which symbol goes with which word.

Try This

Begin a math journal. Make an entry every day for one week. Use the following ideas to start your journal entries. Be sure to date each entry.

- What I already know about this lesson is . . .

- The skills I used to complete this lesson were . . .

- What problems did I have? How did I deal with these problems?

- What I liked/did not like about this lesson . . .

Reading and Writing Math

3-1 Representing, Comparing, and Ordering Decimals

The smaller the apparent magnitude of a star, the brighter the star appears when viewed from Earth. The magnitudes of some stars are listed in the table as decimal numbers.

Apparent Magnitudes of Stars	
Star	Magnitude
Procyon	0.38
Proxima Centauri	11.0
Wolf 359	13.5
Vega	0.03

Decimal numbers represent combinations of whole numbers and numbers between whole numbers.

Interactivities Online ▶ Place value can help you understand and write and compare decimal numbers.

Place Value

Hundreds	Tens	Ones	Tenths	Hundredths	Thousandths	Ten-Thousandths	Hundred-Thousandths
	2	3 • 0	0	5	0	3	

EXAMPLE 1 Reading and Writing Decimals

Write each decimal in standard form, expanded form, and words.

A 1.05

Expanded form: 1 + 0.05
Word form: one *and* five hundredths

Reading Math
Read the decimal point as "and."

B 0.05 + 0.001 + 0.0007

Standard form: 0.0517
Word form: five hundred seventeen ten-thousandths

C sixteen and nine hundredths

Standard form: 16.09
Expanded form: 10 + 6 + 0.09

You can use place value to compare decimal numbers.

Video LESSON TUTORIALS Online   my.hrw.com

EXAMPLE 2 **Earth Science Application**

Rigel and Betelgeuse are two stars in the constellation Orion. The apparent magnitude of Rigel is 0.12. The apparent magnitude of Betelgeuse is 0.50. Which star has the smaller magnitude? Which star appears brighter?

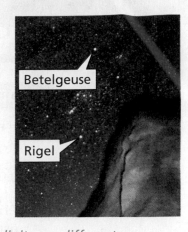

Betelgeuse

Rigel

0.⌐1⌐2   *Line up the decimal points.*
          Start from the left and compare
          the digits.

0.⌐5⌐0   *Look for the first place where the digits are different.*

1 is less than 5.
0.12 < 0.50

Rigel has a smaller apparent magnitude than Betelgeuse.
The star with the smaller magnitude appears brighter. When seen from Earth, Rigel appears brighter than Betelgeuse.

EXAMPLE 3 **Comparing and Ordering Decimals**

Order the decimals from least to greatest.
14.35, 14.3, 14.05

Helpful Hint
Writing zeros at the end of a decimal does not change the value of the decimal.
0.3 = 0.30 = 0.300

14.35
14.30   14.30 < 14.35   *Compare two of the numbers at a time.*
                            Write 14.3 as "14.30."

14.35
14.05   14.05 < 14.35   *Start at the left and compare the digits.*

14.30
14.05   14.05 < 14.30   *Look for the first place where the digits are different.*

Graph the numbers on a number line.

```
        14.05       14.30  14.35
    ←┼──●──┼───┼───┼─●──●┼───┼───┼───┼───┼───┼───┼──→
     14   14.1 14.2 14.3 14.4 14.5 14.6 14.7 14.8 14.9  15
```

The numbers are ordered when you read the number line from left to right. The numbers in order from least to greatest are 14.05, 14.3, and 14.35.

MATHEMATICAL PRACTICES

Think and Discuss

1. **Explain** why 0.5 is greater than 0.29 even though 29 is greater than 5.

2. **Name** the decimal with the least value: 0.29, 2.09, 2.009, 0.029

3. **Name** three numbers between 1.5 and 1.6.

Jerry Schad/Photo Researchers, Inc.

Learn It Online
Homework Help Online
Exercises 1–16, 19, 23, 27, 29, 31, 37, 41

GUIDED PRACTICE

See Example **1** Write each decimal in standard form, expanded form, and words.

1. 1.98

2. ten and forty-one thousandths

3. 0.07 + 0.006 + 0.0005

4. 0.0472

See Example **2** **5. Physical Science** Osmium and iridium are precious metals. The density of osmium is 22.58 g/cm^3, and the density of iridium is 22.56 g/cm^3. Which metal is denser?

See Example **3** Order the decimals from least to greatest.

6. 9.5, 9.35, 9.65

7. 4.18, 4.1, 4.09

8. 12.39, 12.09, 12.92

INDEPENDENT PRACTICE

See Example **1** Write each decimal in standard form, expanded form, and words.

9. 7.0893

10. 12 + 0.2 + 0.005

11. seven and fifteen hundredths

12. 3 + 0.1 + 0.006

See Example **2** **13. Astronomy** Two meteorites landed in Mexico. The one found in Bacuberito weighed 24.3 tons, and the one found in Chupaderos weighed 26.7 tons. Which meteorite weighed more?

See Example **3** Order the decimals from least to greatest.

14. 15.25, 15.2, 15.5

15. 1.56, 1.62, 1.5

16. 6.7, 6.07, 6.23

PRACTICE AND PROBLEM SOLVING

Extra Practice
See Extra Practice for more exercises.

Write each number in words.

17. 9.007

18. 5 + 0.08 + 0.004

19. 10.022

20. 4.28

21. 142.6541

22. 0.001 + 0.0007

23. 0.92755

24. 1.02

Compare. Write <, >, or =.

25. 8.04 ■ 8.403

26. 0.907 ■ 0.6801

27. 1.246 ■ 1.29

28. one and fifty-two ten-thousandths ■ 1.0052

29. ten and one hundredth ■ 10.100

Write the value of the red digit in each number.

30. 3.026

31. 17.53703

32. 0.000598

33. 425.1055

Order the numbers from greatest to least.

34. 32.525, 32.5254, 31.6257

35. 0.34, 1.43, 4.034, 1.043, 1.424

36. 1.01, 1.1001, 1.101, 1.0001

37. 652.12, 65.213, 65.135, 61.53

Proxima Centauri, the closest star to Earth other than the Sun, was discovered in 1913. It would take about 115,000 years for a spaceship traveling from Earth at 25,000 mi/h to reach Proxima Centauri.

NEXT EXITS	
MOON	238,855 mi
SUN	92,000,000 mi
PLUTO	2,700,000,000 mi
PROXIMA CENTAURI	24,000,000,000,000 mi

Use the table for Exercises 38–44.

38. Order the stars Sirius, Luyten 726-8, and Lalande 21185 from closest to farthest from Earth.

39. Which star in the table is farthest from Earth?

40. How far in light-years is Ross 154 from Earth? Write the answer in words and expanded form.

41. List the stars that are less than 5 light-years from Earth.

42. **? What's the Error?** A student wrote the distance of Proxima Centauri from Earth as "four hundred and twenty-two hundredths." Explain the error. Write the correct answer.

43. **✏ Write About It** Which star is closer to Earth, Alpha Centauri or Proxima Centauri? Explain how you can compare the distances of these stars. Then answer the question.

44. **★ Challenge** Wolf 359 is located 7.75 light-years from Earth. If the stars in the table were listed in order from closest to farthest from Earth, between which two stars would Wolf 359 be located?

Distance of Stars from Earth	
Star	**Distance (light-years)**
Alpha Centauri	4.35
Barnard's Star	5.98
Lalande 21185	8.22
Luyten 726-8	8.43
Proxima Centauri	4.22
Ross 154	9.45
Sirius	8.65

Test Prep

45. Multiple Choice What is the standard form of "five and three hundred twenty-one hundred-thousandths"?

Ⓐ 5.321 Ⓑ 5.0321 Ⓒ 5.00321 Ⓓ 5.000321

46. Gridded Response Write $30 + 2 + 0.8 + 0.009$ in standard form.

Billy's health class is learning about fitness and nutrition. The table shows the approximate number of calories burned by someone who weighs 90 pounds.

Vocabulary

clustering

front-end estimation

Activity (45 min)	Calories Burned (Approx.)
Cycling	198.45
Playing ice hockey	210.6
Rowing	324
Water skiing	194.4

When numbers are about the same value, you can use *clustering* to estimate.
Clustering means rounding the numbers to the same value.

EXAMPLE **1** *Health Application*

Billy wants to cycle, play ice hockey, and water ski. If Billy weighs 90 pounds and spends 45 minutes doing each activity, *about* how many calories will he burn in all?

198.45 →	200	*The addends cluster around 200.*
210.6 →	200	*To estimate the total number of calories,*
+ 194.4 →	+ 200	*round each addend to 200.*
	600	*Add.*

Billy will burn about 600 calories.

EXAMPLE **2** **Rounding Decimals to Estimate Sums and Differences**

Estimate by rounding to the indicated place value.

Caution!

Look at the digit to the right of the place to which you are rounding.
• If it is *5 or greater*, round *up*.
• If it is *less than 5*, round *down*.
See the Skills Bank.

A 3.92 + 6.48; ones

$$3.92 + 6.48$$ *Round to the nearest whole number.*

$$4 + 6 = 10$$ *The sum is about 10.*

B 8.6355 − 5.039; hundredths

8.6355	8.64	*Round to the hundredths.*
− 5.039	− 5.04	*Align the decimals.*
	3.60	*Subtract.*

Video **Lesson Tutorials Online** my.hrw.com

David Deas/DK Stock/Getty Images

EXAMPLE 3 Using Compatible Numbers to Estimate Products and Quotients

Estimate each product or quotient.

A 26.76 × 2.93

$$25 \times 3 = 75$$ *25 and 3 are compatible.*

So 26.76 × 2.93 is about 75.

B 42.64 ÷ 16.51

$$45 \div 15 = 3$$ *45 and 15 are compatible.*

So 42.64 ÷ 16.51 is about 3.

You can also use *front-end estimation* to estimate with decimals. **Front-end estimation** means to use only the whole-number part of the decimal.

EXAMPLE 4 Using Front-End Estimation

Estimate a range for the sum.

9.99 + 22.89 + 8.3

Use front-end estimation.

$$
\begin{array}{r}
9.99 \rightarrow 9 \\
22.89 \rightarrow 22 \\
+8.30 \rightarrow +8 \\
\hline
\text{at least } 39
\end{array}
$$

Add the whole numbers only.

The whole-number values of the decimals are less than the actual numbers, so the answer is an underestimate.

The exact answer of 9.99 + 22.89 + 8.3 is greater than 39.

You can estimate a range for the sum by adjusting the decimal part of the numbers. Round the decimals to 0.5 or 1.

$$
\begin{array}{r}
0.99 \rightarrow 1.00 \\
0.89 \rightarrow 1.00 \\
+0.30 \rightarrow +0.50 \\
\hline
2.50
\end{array}
$$

$$39.00 + 2.50 = 41.50$$

Add the adjusted decimal part of the numbers.

Add the whole-number estimate and this sum.

The adjusted decimals are greater than the actual decimals, so 41.50 is an overestimate.

The estimated range for the sum is between 39.00 and 41.50.

Think and Discuss

1. Tell what number the following decimals cluster around: 34.5, 36.78, and 35.234.

2. Determine whether a front-end estimation without adjustment is always an overestimation or an underestimation.

GUIDED PRACTICE

See Example 1

1. Elba runs every Monday, Wednesday, and Friday. Last week she ran 3.62 miles on Monday, 3.8 miles on Wednesday, and 4.3 miles on Friday. About how many miles did she run last week?

See Example 2

Estimate by rounding to the indicated place value.

2. 2.746 − 0.866; tenths

3. 6.735 + 4.9528; ones

4. 10.8071 + 5.392; hundredths

5. 5.9821 − 0.48329; ten-thousandths

See Example 3

Estimate each product or quotient.

6. 38.92 ÷ 4.06

7. 14.51 × 7.89

8. 22.47 ÷ 3.22

See Example 4

Estimate a range for each sum.

9. 7.8 + 31.39 + 6.95

10. 14.27 + 5.4 + 21.86

INDEPENDENT PRACTICE

See Example 1

11. **Multi-Step** Before Mike's trip, the odometer in his car read 146.8 miles. He drove 167.5 miles to a friend's house and 153.9 miles to the beach. About how many miles did the odometer read when he arrived at the beach?

12. The rainfall in July, August, and September was 16.76 cm, 13.97 cm, and 15.24 cm, respectively. About how many total centimeters of rain fell during those three months?

See Example 2

Estimate by rounding to the indicated place value.

13. 2.0993 + 1.256; tenths

14. 7.504 − 2.3792; hundredths

15. 0.6271 + 4.53027; thousandths

16. 13.274 − 8.5590; tenths

See Example 3

Estimate each product or quotient.

17. 9.64 × 1.769

18. 11.509 ÷ 4.258

19. 19.03 ÷ 2.705

See Example 4

Estimate a range for each sum.

20. 17.563 + 4.5 + 2.31

21. 1.620 + 10.8 + 3.71

PRACTICE AND PROBLEM SOLVING

Extra Practice
See Extra Practice for more exercises.

Estimate by rounding to the nearest whole number.

22. 8.456 + 7.903

23. 12.43 × 3.72

24. 1,576.2 − 150.50

25. Estimate the quotient of 67.55 and 3.83.

26. Estimate $84.85 divided by 17.

Use the table for Exercises 27–31.

27. **Money** Round each cost in the table to the nearest cent. Write your answer using a dollar sign and decimal point.

28. About how much does it cost to phone someone in Russia and talk for 8 minutes?

29. About how much more does it cost to make a 12-minute call to Japan than to make an 18-minute call within the United States?

Long-Distance Costs for Callers in the United States	
Country	**Cost per Minute (¢)**
Venezuela	22
Russia	9.9
Japan	7.9
United States	3.7

30. Will the cost of a 30-minute call to someone within the United States be greater or less than $1.20? Explain.

31. **Multi-Step** Kim is in New York. She calls her grandmother in Venezuela and speaks for 20 minutes, then calls a friend in Japan and talks for 15 minutes, and finally calls her mother in San Francisco and talks for 30 minutes. Estimate the total cost of all her calls.

32. **Health** The recommended daily allowance (RDA) for iron is 15 mg/day for teenage girls. Julie eats a hamburger that contains 3.88 mg of iron. About how many more milligrams of iron does she need to meet the RDA?

33. **Write a Problem** Write a problem with three decimal numbers that have a total sum between 30 and 32.5.

34. **Write About It** How do you adjust a front-end estimation? Why is this done?

35. **Challenge** Place a decimal point in each number so that the sum of the numbers is between 124 and 127: 1059 + 725 + 815 + 1263.

Test Prep

36. **Multiple Choice** Which is the estimated difference of 34.45 − 24.71 by rounding to the nearest whole number?

Ⓐ 11   Ⓑ 10   Ⓒ 9   Ⓓ 8

37. **Short Response** The average rainfall in Oklahoma City is 2.8 inches in April, 5.3 inches in May, and 4.3 inches in June. A weather forecaster predicts that the rainfall one year will double the average in April and May and half the average in June. Estimate the predicted rainfall each month to the nearest inch.

Hands-on LAB

Explore Decimal Addition and Subtraction

Use with Adding and Subtracting Decimals

 Learn It Online
Lab Resources Online

 **Use appropriate tools strategically.**

CC.6.NS.3 Fluently add, subtract, multiply, and divide multi-digit decimals using the standard algorithm for each operation

KEY

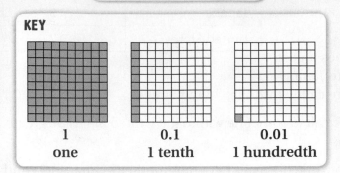

| 1 | 0.1 | 0.01 |
| one | 1 tenth | 1 hundredth |

You can model addition and subtraction of decimals with decimal grids.

Activity 1

Use decimal grids to find each sum.

a. 0.24 + 0.32

To represent 0.24, shade 24 squares.

To represent 0.32, shade 32 squares in another color.

There are 56 shaded squares.

0.24 + 0.32 = 0.56

b. 1.56 + 0.4

To represent 1.56, shade a whole grid and 56 squares of another.

To represent 0.4, shade 4 columns in another color.

One whole grid and 96 squares are shaded.

1.56 + 0.4 = 1.96

c. 0.75 + 0.68

To represent 0.75, shade 75 squares.

To represent 0.68, shade 68 squares in another color. You will need to use another grid.

One whole grid and 43 squares are shaded.

0.75 + 0.68 = 1.43

1. How would you shade a decimal grid to represent 0.2 + 0.18?

Try This

Use decimal grids to find each sum.

1. 0.2 + 0.6   **2.** 1.07 + 0.03   **3.** 1.62 + 0.08

4. 0.45 + 0.29   **5.** 0.88 + 0.12   **6.** 1.29 + 0.67

7. 0.07 + 0.41   **8.** 0.51 + 0.51   **9.** 1.01 + 0.23

Activity 2

Use a decimal grid to find each difference.

a. 0.6 − 0.38

To represent 0.6, shade 6 columns.

Subtract 0.38 by removing 38 squares.

There are 22 remaining squares.

0.6 − 0.38 = 0.22

b. 1.22 − 0.41

To represent 1.22, shade an entire decimal grid and 22 squares of another.

Subtract 0.41 by removing 41 squares.

There are 81 remaining squares.

1.22 − 0.41 = 0.81

Think and Discuss

1. How would you shade a decimal grid to represent 1.3 − 0.6?

Try This

Use decimal grids to find each difference.

1. 0.9 − 0.3   **2.** 1.2 − 0.98   **3.** 0.6 − 0.41

4. 1.6 − 0.07   **5.** 0.35 − 0.03   **6.** 2.12 − 0.23

7. 2.0 − 0.86   **8.** 0.78 − 0.76   **9.** 1.06 − 0.55

Adding and Subtracting Decimals

COMMON CORE

CC.6.EE.7 Solve real-world and mathematical problems by writing and solving equations of the form $x + p = q$ and $px = q$ for cases in which p, q and x are all nonnegative rational numbers **Also CC.6.NS.3**

At the 2004 U.S. Gymnastics Championships, Carly Patterson and Courtney Kupets tied for the All-Around title.

Carly Patterson's Preliminary Scores	
Event	**Points**
Floor exercise	9.7
Balance beam	9.7
Vault	9.3
Uneven bars	9.45

To find the total number of points, you can add all of the scores.

Carly Patterson also won a gold medal in the Women's Individual All-Around in the 2004 Olympic Games.

EXAMPLE 1 · Sports Application

Interactivities Online ▶

Helpful Hint

Estimating before you add or subtract will help you check whether your answer is reasonable.

A **What was Carly Patterson's preliminary total score in the 2004 U.S. Championships?**

First estimate the sum of 9.7, 9.7, 9.3, and 9.45.

$$9.7 + 9.7 + 9.3 + 9.45$$
$$\downarrow \qquad \downarrow \qquad \downarrow \qquad \downarrow$$
$$10 + 10 + 9 + 9 = 38$$

Estimate by rounding to the nearest whole number.

The total is about 38 points.

Then add.

$$\begin{array}{r} 9.70 \\ 9.70 \\ 9.30 \\ + 9.45 \\ \hline 38.15 \end{array}$$

Align the decimal points.

Use zeros as placeholders.

Add. Then place the decimal point.

Since 38.15 is close to the estimate of 38, the answer is reasonable. Patterson's total preliminary score was 38.15 points.

B **How many more points did Patterson need on the uneven bars to have a perfect score of 10?**

Find the difference between 10 and 9.45.

$$\begin{array}{r} 10.00 \\ - 9.45 \\ \hline 0.55 \end{array}$$

Align the decimal points.

Use zeros as placeholders.

Subtract. Then place the decimal point.

Patterson needed another 0.55 points to have a perfect score.

Video **Lesson Tutorials Online** my.hrw.com

EXAMPLE **2** Using Mental Math to Add and Subtract Decimals

Find each sum or difference.

A $1.6 + 0.4$

$1.6 + 0.4$ *Think: 0.6 + 0.4 = 1*

$1.6 + 0.4 = 2$

B $3 - 0.8$

$3 - 0.8$ *Think: 0.8 + 0.2 = 1,*

$3 - 0.8 = 2.2$ *so 1 − 0.8 = 0.2.*

EXAMPLE **3** Evaluating Decimal Expressions

Evaluate $7.52 - s$ for each value of s.

A $s = 2.9$

$7.52 - s$	
$7.52 - 2.9$	*Substitute 2.9 for s.*
$\begin{array}{r} 7.52 \\ -\ 2.90 \\ \hline 4.62 \end{array}$	*Align the decimal points.* *Use a zero as a placeholder.* *Subtract.* *Place the decimal point.*

> **Remember!**
>
> You can place any number of zeros at the end of a decimal number without changing its value.

B $s = 4.5367$

$7.52 - s$	
$7.52 - 4.5367$	*Substitute 4.5367 for s.*
$\begin{array}{r} 7.5200 \\ -\ 4.5367 \\ \hline 2.9833 \end{array}$	*Align the decimal points.* *Use zeros as placeholders.* *Subtract.* *Place the decimal point.*

Think and Discuss

1. **Show** how you would write $2.678 + 124.5$ to find the sum.

2. **Tell** why it is a good idea to estimate the answer before you add and subtract.

3. **Explain** how you can use mental math to find how many more points Carly Patterson would have needed to have scored a perfect 10 on the floor exercise.

GUIDED PRACTICE

See Example **1** Use the table for Exercises 1–3.

Rea's Triathlon Training	
Sport	**Distance (mi)**
Cycling	14.25
Running	4.35
Swimming	1.6

1. How many miles in all is Rea's triathlon training?

2. How many miles did Rea run and swim in all?

3. How much farther did Rea cycle than swim?

See Example **2** Find each sum or difference.

4. $2.7 + 0.3$ 5. $6 - 0.4$ 6. $5.2 + 2.8$ 7. $8.9 - 4$

See Example **3** Evaluate $5.35 - m$ for each value of m.

8. $m = 2.37$ 9. $m = 1.8$ 10. $m = 4.7612$ 11. $m = 0.402$

INDEPENDENT PRACTICE

See Example **1**

12. **Sports** During a diving competition, Phil performed two reverse dives and two dives from a handstand position. He received the following scores: 8.765, 9.45, 9.875, and 8.025. What was Phil's total score?

13. Brad works after school at a local grocery store. How much did he earn in all for the month of October?

Brad's Earnings for October				
Week	1	2	3	4
Earnings	$123.48	$165.18	$137.80	$140.92

See Example **2** Find each sum or difference.

14. $7.2 + 1.8$ 15. $8.5 - 7$ 16. $3.3 + 0.7$ 17. $15.9 + 2.1$

18. $7 - 0.6$ 19. $7.55 - 3.25$ 20. $21.4 + 3.6$ 21. $5 - 2.7$

See Example **3** Evaluate $9.67 - x$ for each value of x.

22. $x = 1.52$ 23. $x = 3.8$ 24. $x = 7.21$ 25. $x = 0.635$

26. $x = 6.9$ 27. $x = 1.001$ 28. $x = 8$ 29. $x = 9.527$

PRACTICE AND PROBLEM SOLVING

Extra Practice
See Extra Practice for more exercises.

Add or subtract.

30. $5.62 + 4.19$ 31. $10.508 - 6.73$ 32. $13.009 + 12.83$

33. Find the sum of 0.0679 and 3.75.   34. Subtract 3.0042 from 7.435.

35. **Sports** Terin Humphrey was ranked third at the 2004 U.S. Gymnastics Championships with a score of 75.45. What was the difference between her score and Courtney Kupet's and Carly Patterson's score of 76.45?

Evaluate each expression.

36. $8.09 - a$ for $a = 4.5$

37. $7.03 + 33.8 + n$ for $n = 12.006$

38. $b + (5.68 - 3.007)$ for $b = 6.134$

39. $(2 \times 14) - a + 1.438$ for $a = 0.062$

40. $5^2 - w$ for $w = 3.5$

41. $100 - p$ for $p = 15.034$

42. Career A fire helmet must be sturdy enough to protect the firefighter's head from dangerous objects and extremely hot temperatures while still being as lightweight as possible. One fire helmet weighs 1.616 kg, and another fire helmet weighs 1.403 kg. What is the difference in weights?

43. Multi-Step Logan wants to buy a new bike that costs $135.00. He started with $14.83 in his savings account. Last week, he deposited $15.35 into his account. Today, he deposited $32.40. How much more money does he need to buy the bike?

44. Swimming With a time of 60.35 seconds, Martina Moracova broke Jennifer Thompson's world record time in the women's 100-meter medley. How much faster was Thompson than Moracova when, in the next heat, she reclaimed the record with a time of 59.30 seconds?

45. Sports The highest career batting average ever achieved by a professional baseball player is 0.366. Bill Bergen finished with a career 0.170 average. How much lower is Bergen's career average than the highest career average?

46. What's the Question? A cup of rice contains 0.8 mg of iron, and a cup of lima beans contains 4.4 mg of iron. If the answer is 6 mg, what is the question?

47. Write About It Why is it important to align the decimal points before adding or subtracting decimal numbers?

48. Challenge Evaluate $(5.7 + a) \times (9.75 - b)$ for $a = 2.3$ and $b = 7.25$.

Test Prep

49. Multiple Choice What is the sum of 24.91 and 35.8?

(A) 28.49   (B) 59.99   (C) 60.71   (D) 60.99

50. Multiple Choice Lead has an atomic weight of 207.19. Mercury has an atomic weight of 200.6. How much greater is the atomic weight of lead than mercury?

(F) 6.59   (G) 7.41   (H) 7.59   (J) 187.13

Ready To Go On?

Quiz for Lessons 1 Through 3

 1 **Representing, Comparing, and Ordering Decimals**

Write each decimal in standard form, expanded form, and words.

1. 4.012

2. ten and fifty-four thousandths

3. On Monday Jamie ran 3.54 miles. On Wednesday he ran 3.6 miles. On which day did he run farther?

Order the decimals from least to greatest.

4. 3.406, 30.08, 3.6

5. 10.10, 10.01, 101.1

6. 16.782, 16.59, 16.79

7. 62.0581, 62.148, 62.0741

8. 123.05745, 132.05628, 123.05749

 2 **Estimating Decimals**

9. Matt drove 106.8 miles on Monday, 98.3 miles on Tuesday, and 103.5 miles on Wednesday. About how many miles did he drive in all?

Estimate.

10. $8.345 - 0.6051$; round to the hundredths

11. $16.492 - 2.613$; round to the tenths

12. 18.79×4.68

13. $71.378 \div 8.13$

14. 52.055×7.18

Estimate a range for each sum.

15. $7.42 + 13.87 + 101.2$

16. $1.79 + 3.45 + 7.92$

 3 **Adding and Subtracting Decimals**

17. Greg's scores at four gymnastic meets were 9.65, 8.758, 9.884, and 9.500. What was his total score for all four meets?

18. Mrs. Henry buys groceries each week and uses a spreadsheet to keep track of how much she spends. How much did she spend in all for the month of December?

Grocery Spending for December				
Week	1	2	3	4
Amount Spent ($)	52.35	77.97	90.10	42.58

19. Sally walked 1.2 miles on Monday, 1.6 miles on Wednesday, and 2.1 miles on Friday. How many miles did she walk in all?

Find each sum or difference.

20. $0.47 + 0.03$

21. $8 - 0.6$

22. $2.2 + 1.8$

Evaluate $8.67 - s$ for each value of s.

23. $s = 3.4$

24. $s = 2.0871$

25. $s = 7.205$

Focus on Problem Solving

MATHEMATICAL PRACTICES

Make sense of problems and persevere in solving them.

Solve

• **Write an equation**

Read the whole problem before you try to solve it. Sometimes you need to solve the problem in more than one step.

Read the problem. Determine the steps needed to solve the problem.

Brian buys erasers and pens for himself and 4 students in his class. The erasers cost $0.79 each, and the pens cost $2.95 each. What is the total amount that Brian spends on the erasers and pens?

Here is one way to solve the problem.

5 erasers cost	5 pens cost
5 · $0.79	5 · $2.95

$$(5 \cdot \$0.79) + (5 \cdot \$2.95)$$

Read each problem. Decide whether you need more than one step to solve the problem. List the possible steps. Then choose an equation with which to solve the problem.

1 Joan is making some costumes. She cuts 3 pieces of fabric, each 3.5 m long. She has 5 m of fabric left. Which equation can you use to find f, the amount of fabric she had to start with?

Ⓐ $(3 \cdot 3.5) + 5 = f$

Ⓑ $3 + 3.5 + 5 = f$

Ⓒ $(5 \times 3.5) \div 3 = f$

Ⓓ $5 - (3 \cdot 3.5) = f$

2 Mario buys 4 chairs and a table. He spends $245.99 in all. If each chair costs $38.95, which equation can you use to find T, the cost of the table?

Ⓕ $4 + \$245.99 + \$38.95 = T$

Ⓖ $(4 \cdot \$38.95) + \$245.99 = T$

Ⓗ $\$245.99 - (4 \cdot \$38.95) = T$

Ⓙ $\$245.99 \div (4 \cdot \$38.95) = T$

3 Mya skis down Ego Bowl three times and down Fantastic twice. Ego Bowl is 5.85 km long, and Fantastic is 8.35 km long. Which equation can you use to estimate d, the distance Mya skis in all?

Ⓐ $(6 \cdot 3) + (8 \cdot 2) = d$

Ⓑ $(6 + 8) + (3 + 2) = d$

Ⓒ $3(6 + 8) = d$

Ⓓ $(6 \div 3) + (8 \div 2) = d$

(all) Peter Van Steen/HMH

Explore Decimal Multiplication and Division

Use with Multiplying and Dividing Decimals

Learn It Online
Lab Resources Online

MATHEMATICAL PRACTICES Use appropriate tools strategically.

CC.6.NS.3 Fluently add, subtract, multiply, and divide multi-digit decimals using the standard algorithm for each operation

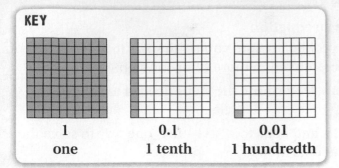

KEY

1	0.1	0.01
one	1 tenth	1 hundredth

You can use decimal grids to model multiplication and division of decimals.

Activity 1

Use decimal grids to find each product.

a. 3 · 0.32

$3 \cdot 0.32 = 0.96$

To represent 3 · 0.32, shade 32 small squares three times.

Use a different color to shade a different group of 32 small squares each time.

There are 96 shaded squares.

b. 0.3 · 0.5

$0.3 \cdot 0.5 = 0.15$

To represent 0.3, shade 3 columns.

To represent 0.5, shade 5 rows in another color.

There are 15 squares in the area where the shading overlaps.

Think and Discuss

1. How is multiplying a decimal by a decimal different from multiplying a decimal by a whole number?

2. Why can you shade 5 rows to represent 0.5?

Try This

Use decimal grids to find each product.

1. 3 · 0.14	**2.** 5 · 0.18	**3.** 0.7 · 0.5	**4.** 0.6 · 0.4
5. 4 · 0.25	**6.** 0.2 · 0.9	**7.** 9 · 0.07	**8.** 8 · 0.15

Activity 2

Use decimal grids to find each quotient.

a. 3.66 ÷ 3

Shade 3 grids and 66 small squares of a fourth grid to represent 3.66.

Divide the shaded wholes into 3 equal groups. Use scissors to divide the 66 hundredths into 3 equal groups.

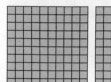 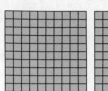 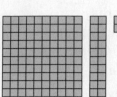

3.66 ÷ 3 = 1.22   *One whole grid and 22 small squares are in each group.*

b. 3.6 ÷ 1.2

Shade 3 grids and 6 columns of a fourth grid to represent 3.6. Cut apart the 6 tenths.

Divide the grids and tenths into equal groups of 1.2.

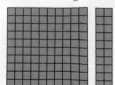 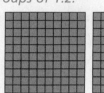

3.6 ÷ 1.2 = 3   *There are 3 equal groups of 1.2.*

Think and Discuss

1. Find 36 ÷ 12. How does this problem and its quotient compare to 3.6 ÷ 1.2?

Try This

Use decimal grids to find each quotient.

1. 4.04 ÷ 4   **2.** 3.25 ÷ 5   **3.** 7.8 ÷ 1.3   **4.** 5.6 ÷ 0.8

5. 6.24 ÷ 2   **6.** 5.1 ÷ 1.7   **7.** 5.7 ÷ 3   **8.** 5.4 ÷ 0.9

Multiplying Decimals

COMMON CORE

CC.6.EE.7 Solve real-world and mathematical problems by writing and solving equations of the form $x + p = q$ and $px = q$ for cases in which p, q and x are all nonnegative rational numbers **Also CC.6.NS.3**

Because the Moon has less mass than Earth, it has a smaller gravitational effect. An object that weighs 1 pound on Earth weighs only 0.17 pound on the Moon.

You can multiply the weight of an object on Earth by 0.17 to find its weight on the Moon.

Gravity on Earth is about six times the gravity on the surface of the Moon.

You can multiply decimals by first multiplying as you would whole numbers. Then place the decimal point by finding the total of the number of decimal places in the factors. The product will have the same number of decimal places.

EXAMPLE 1 | *Science Application*

A flag weighs 3 pounds on Earth. What is the weight of the flag on the Moon?

Multiply 3 by 0.17, since 1 pound on Earth is 0.17 pound on the Moon.

$$\begin{array}{r} 17 \\ \times\ 3 \\ \hline 51 \end{array}$$ *Multiply as you would with whole numbers.*

Place the decimal point by adding the number of decimal places in the numbers multiplied.

$$\begin{array}{r} 0.17 \\ \times\ \ \ 3 \\ \hline 0.51 \end{array}$$ 2 decimal places
   + 0 decimal places
   2 decimal places

A 3 lb flag on Earth weighs 0.51 lb on the Moon.

EXAMPLE 2 | **Multiplying a Decimal by a Decimal**

Helpful Hint

You can use a decimal grid to model multiplication of decimals.

Find each product.

A 0.2×0.6

$$\begin{array}{r} 0.2 \\ \times\ 0.6 \\ \hline 0.12 \end{array}$$

Multiply. Then place the decimal point.
   1 decimal place
   + 1 decimal place
   2 decimal places

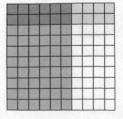

[Video] **Lesson Tutorials Online** my.hrw.com

Find each product.

B 3.25 × 4.8

$3 × 5 = 15$ *Estimate the product. Round each factor to the nearest whole number.*

         3.25   *Multiply. Then place the decimal point.*
      × 4.8
      ‾‾‾‾‾‾
       2600
    13000
   ‾‾‾‾‾‾‾
   15.600   *2 + 1 = 3 decimal places*

15.600 is close to the estimate of 15. The answer is reasonable.

C 0.05 × 0.9

$0.05 × 1 = 0.05$ *Estimate the product. 0.9 is close to 1.*

                         Multiply. Then place the decimal point.

       0.05   *2 decimal places*
     × 0.9   *+ 1 decimal place*
    ‾‾‾‾‾‾‾
     0.045   *3 decimal places; use a placeholder zero.*

0.045 is close to the estimate of 0.05. The answer is reasonable.

EXAMPLE **3**   **Evaluating Decimal Expressions**

Evaluate 3x for each value of *x*.

> **Remember!**
>
> These notations all mean multiply 3 times *x*.
>
> $3 \cdot x$ $3x$ $3(x)$

A $x = 4.047$

$3x = 3(4.047)$ *Substitute 4.047 for x.*

      4.047   *3 decimal places*
   ×   3   *+ 0 decimal places*
   ‾‾‾‾‾‾‾
   12.141   *3 decimal places*

B $x = 2.95$

$3x = 3(2.95)$ *Substitute 2.95 for x.*

       2.95   *2 decimal places*
    ×   3   *+ 0 decimal places*
   ‾‾‾‾‾‾‾
     8.85   *2 decimal places*

MATHEMATICAL PRACTICES

Think and Discuss

1. Tell how many decimal places are in the product of 235.2 and 0.24.

2. Show how to use the Distributive Property to find 1.7 × 2.

3. Describe how the products of 0.3 × 0.5 and 3 × 5 are similar. How are they different?

GUIDED PRACTICE

See Example **1**

1. Each can of cat food costs $0.28. How much will 6 cans of cat food cost?

2. Jorge buys 8 baseballs for $9.29 each. How much does he spend in all?

See Example **2** **Find each product.**

3. 0.6
   × 0.4

4. 0.008
   ×   0.5

5.   3.0
   × 0.07

6. 0.12
   × 0.6

See Example **3** **Evaluate $5x$ for each value of x.**

7. $x = 3.304$

8. $x = 4.58$

9. $x = 7.126$

10. $x = 1.9$

INDEPENDENT PRACTICE

See Example **1**

11. Gwenyth walks her dog each morning. If she walks 0.37 kilometers each morning, how many kilometers will she have walked in 7 days?

12. Consumer Math Apples are on sale for $0.49 per pound. What is the price for 4 pounds of apples?

See Example **2** **Find each product.**

13. 0.9
   × 0.03

14. 4.5
   × 0.5

15. 0.31
   × 0.7

16.   1.6
   × 0.08

17. 0.007×0.06

18. 0.04×3.0

19. 2.0×0.006

20. 0.005×0.003

See Example **3** **Evaluate $7x$ for each value of x.**

21. $x = 1.903$

22. $x = 2.461$

23. $x = 3.72$

24. $x = 4.05$

25. $x = 0.164$

26. $x = 5.89$

27. $x = 0.3702$

28. $x = 1.82$

PRACTICE AND PROBLEM SOLVING

Extra Practice
See Extra Practice for more exercises.

Multiply.

29. 0.3×0.03

30. 1.4×0.21

31. 0.06×1.02

32. 8.2×4.1

33. 12.6×2.1

34. 3.04×0.6

35. 0.66×2.52

36. 3.08×0.7

37. $0.2 \times 0.94 \times 1.3$

38. $1.54 \times 3.05 \times 2.6$

39. $1.98 \times 0.4 \times 5.2$

40. $1.7 \times 2.41 \times 0.5$

41. $2.5 \times 1.52 \times 3.7$

42. $6.5 \times 0.15 \times 3.8$

Evaluate.

43. $6n$ for $n = 6.23$

44. $5t + 0.462$ for $t = 3.04$

45. $8^2 - 2b$ for $b = 0.95$

46. $4^3 + 5c$ for $c = 1.9$

47. $3h - 15 + h$ for $h = 5.2$

48. $5^2 + 6j + j$ for $j = 0.27$

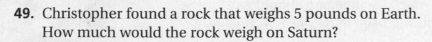

Physical Science LINK

Saturn is the second-largest planet in the solar system. Saturn is covered by thick clouds. Saturn's density is very low. Suppose you weigh 180 pounds on Earth. If you were able to stand on Saturn, you would weigh only 165 pounds. To find the weight of an object on another planet, multiply its weight on Earth by the gravitational pull listed in the table.

49. Christopher found a rock that weighs 5 pounds on Earth. How much would the rock weigh on Saturn?

50. On which two planets would the weight of an object be the same?

51. **Multi-Step** An object weighs 9 pounds on Earth. How much more would this object weigh on Neptune than on Mars?

52. ✏ **Write a Problem** Use the data in the table to write a word problem that can be answered by evaluating an expression with multiplication. Solve your problem.

53. ？ **What's the Error?** A student said that his new baby brother, who weighs 10 pounds, would weigh 120 pounds on Neptune. What is the error? Write the correct answer.

54. ★ **Challenge** An object weighs between 2.79 lb and 5.58 lb on Saturn. Give a range for the object's weight on Earth.

Gravitational Pull of Planets (Compared with Earth)	
Planet	**Gravitational Pull**
Mercury	0.38
Venus	0.91
Mars	0.38
Jupiter	2.54
Saturn	0.93
Neptune	1.2

Galileo Galilei was the first person to look at Saturn through a telescope. He thought there were groups of stars on each side of the planet, but it was later determined that he had seen Saturn's rings.

Test Prep

55. Multiple Choice Max uses 1.6 liters of gasoline each hour mowing lawns. How much gas does he use in 5.8 hours?

   Ⓐ 7.4 liters   Ⓑ 9.28 liters   Ⓒ 92.8 liters   Ⓓ 928 liters

56. Multiple Choice What is the value of $5x$ when $x = 3.2$?

   Ⓕ 16   Ⓖ 1.6   Ⓗ 0.16   Ⓙ 8.2

3-5 Dividing Decimals by Whole Numbers

COMMON CORE

CC.6.NS.3 Fluently add, subtract, multiply, and divide multi-digit decimals using the standard algorithm for each operation

Emily and two of her friends are going to share equally the cost of making pottery for the art fair.

To find how much each person should pay for the materials, you will need to divide a decimal by a whole number.

EXAMPLE 1 Dividing a Decimal by a Whole Number

Find each quotient.

Remember!

Quotient
↓
0.15
5)0.75
↑   ↑
Divisor Dividend
For more on dividing with whole numbers, see the Skills Bank.

A 0.75 ÷ 5

$$
\begin{array}{r}
0.15 \\
5)\overline{0.75} \\
-5\downarrow \\
\hline
25 \\
-25 \\
\hline
0
\end{array}
$$

Place a decimal point in the quotient directly above the decimal point in the dividend.

Divide as you would with whole numbers.

B 2.52 ÷ 3

$$
\begin{array}{r}
0.84 \\
3)\overline{2.52} \\
-24\downarrow \\
\hline
12 \\
-12 \\
\hline
0
\end{array}
$$

Place a decimal point in the quotient directly above the decimal point in the dividend.

Divide as you would with whole numbers.

EXAMPLE 2 Evaluating Decimal Expressions

Evaluate 0.435 ÷ x for each given value of x.

A $x = 3$

$0.435 \div x$

$0.435 \div 3$ *Substitute 3 for x.*

$$
\begin{array}{r}
0.145 \\
3)\overline{0.435} \\
-3\downarrow \\
\hline
13 \\
-12\downarrow \\
\hline
15 \\
-15 \\
\hline
0
\end{array}
$$

Divide as you would with whole numbers.

B $x = 15$

$0.435 \div x$

$0.435 \div 15$ *Substitute 15 for x.*

$$
\begin{array}{r}
0.029 \\
15)\overline{0.435} \\
-0\downarrow \\
\hline
43 \\
-30\downarrow \\
\hline
135 \\
-135 \\
\hline
0
\end{array}
$$

Sometimes you need to use a zero as a placeholder.

15 > 4, so place a zero in the quotient and divide 15 into 43.

Video LESSON Tutorials Online my.hrw.com

Digital Vision/Alamy

EXAMPLE 3 **Consumer Math Application**

Emily and two of her friends are making pottery using clay, glaze, and paint. The materials cost $11.61. If they share the cost equally, how much should each person pay?

$11.61 should be divided into three equal groups.
Divide $11.61 by 3.

$$
\begin{array}{r}
3.87 \\
3\overline{)11.61} \\
-9 \\
\hline
2\,6 \\
-2\,4 \\
\hline
21 \\
-21 \\
\hline
0
\end{array}
$$

Place a decimal point in the quotient directly above the decimal point in the dividend.

Divide as you would with whole numbers.

Remember!

Multiplication can "undo" division. To check your answer to a division problem, multiply the divisor by the quotient.

Check

$3.87 \times 3 = 11.61$

Each person should pay $3.87.

Think and Discuss

1. **Tell** how you know where to place the decimal point in the quotient.

2. **Explain** why you can use multiplication to check your answer to a division problem.

3-5

Exercises

Learn It Online
Homework Help Online
Exercises 1–18, 19, 21, 23

GUIDED PRACTICE

See Example 1   **Find each quotient.**

1. $1.38 \div 6$ 2. $0.96 \div 8$ 3. $1.75 \div 5$ 4. $0.72 \div 4$

See Example 2   **Evaluate $0.312 \div x$ for each given value of x.**

5. $x = 4$ 6. $x = 6$ 7. $x = 3$ 8. $x = 12$

See Example 3   9. **Consumer Math** Mr. Richards purchased 8 T-shirts for the volleyball team. The total cost of the T-shirts was $70.56. How much did each shirt cost?

See Example **1** Find each quotient.

10. $0.91 \div 7$ **11.** $1.32 \div 6$ **12.** $4.68 \div 9$ **13.** $0.81 \div 3$

See Example **2** Evaluate $0.684 \div x$ for each given value of x.

14. $x = 3$ **15.** $x = 4$ **16.** $x = 18$ **17.** $x = 9$

See Example **3** **18. Consumer Math** Charles, Kate, and Kim eat lunch in a restaurant. The bill is $27.12. If they share the bill equally, how much will each person pay?

PRACTICE AND PROBLEM SOLVING

Extra Practice

See Extra Practice for more exercises.

Find the value of each expression.

19. $(0.49 + 0.045) \div 5$ **20.** $(4.9 - 3.125) \div 5$ **21.** $(13.28 - 7.9) \div 4$

Evaluate the expression $x \div 4$ for each value of x.

22. $x = 0.504$ **23.** $x = 0.944$ **24.** $x = 57.484$ **25.** $x = 1.648$

26. Multi-Step At the grocery store, a 6 lb bag of oranges costs $2.04. Is this more or less expensive than the price shown at the farmers' market?

27. Critical Thinking How could you use rounding to check your answer to the problem $5.58 \div 6$?

? **28. Choose a Strategy** Sarah had $1.19 in coins. Jeff asked her for change for a dollar, but she did not have the correct change. What coins did she have?

29. Write About It When do you use a placeholder zero in the quotient?

★ **30. Challenge** Evaluate the expression $x \div 2$ for the following values of $x = 520$, 52, and 5.2. Try to predict the value of the same expression for $x = 0.52$.

Test Prep

31. Multiple Choice What is the value of $0.98 \div x$ when $x = 2$?

(A) 49   (B) 4.9   (C) 0.49   (D) 0.049

32. Gridded Response Danika spent $89.24 on two pairs of shoes. Each pair of shoes cost the same amount. How much, in dollars, did each pair cost?

Dividing by Decimals

COMMON CORE

CC.6.NS.3 Fluently add, subtract, multiply, and divide multi-digit decimals using the standard algorithm for each operation

Julie and her family traveled to the Grand Canyon. They stopped to refill their gas tank with 13.4 gallons of gasoline after they had driven 368.5 miles.

To find the miles that they drove per gallon, you will need to divide a decimal by a decimal.

EXAMPLE **1** **Dividing a Decimal by a Decimal**

Find each quotient.

Helpful Hint

Multiplying the divisor and the dividend by the same number does not change the quotient.

$$42 \div 6 = 7$$
$$\times 10 \downarrow \quad \times 10 \downarrow$$
$$420 \div 60 = 7$$

$$42 \div 6 = 7$$
$$\times 100 \downarrow \quad \times 100 \downarrow$$
$$4{,}200 \div 600 = 7$$

A $3.6 \div 1.2$

$$1.2\overline{)3.6}$$

Multiply the divisor by 10^1, or 10, to make it a whole number. Multiply the dividend by the same power of 10.

$$\begin{array}{r} 3 \\ 12\overline{)36} \\ -36 \\ \hline 0 \end{array}$$

There is one decimal place in the divisor. Multiply by 10^1, or 10.
Think: $1.2 \times 10 = 12$ $3.6 \times 10 = 36$
Divide as with whole numbers.

$$3.6 \div 1.2 = 3$$

B $42.3 \div 0.12$

$$0.12\overline{)42.3}$$

Multiply the divisor by 10^2, or 100, to make it a whole number. Multiply the dividend by the same power of 10.
Think: $0.12 \times 100 = 12$ $42.3 \times 100 = 4{,}230$

$$\begin{array}{r} 352.5 \\ 12\overline{)4230.0} \\ -36 \downarrow \\ \hline 63 \\ -60 \downarrow \\ \hline 30 \\ -24 \downarrow \\ \hline 60 \\ -60 \\ \hline 0 \end{array}$$

Place the decimal point in the quotient. Divide as with whole numbers.

When there is a remainder, place a zero after the decimal point in the dividend and continue to divide.

$$42.3 \div 0.12 = 352.5$$

EXAMPLE **2** **PROBLEM SOLVING APPLICATION**

MATHEMATICAL PRACTICES Make sense of problems and persevere in solving them.

After driving 368.5 miles, Julie and her family refilled the tank of their car with 13.4 gallons of gasoline. On average, how many miles did they drive per gallon of gas?

1 Understand the Problem

The **answer** will be the average number of miles per gallon.

List the **important information:**

• They drove 368.5 miles.   • They used 13.4 gallons of gas.

2 Make a Plan

Solve a simpler problem by replacing the decimals in the problem with whole numbers.

If they drove 10 miles using 2 gallons of gas, they averaged 5 miles per gallon. You need to divide miles by gallons to solve the problem.

3 Solve

First estimate the answer. You can use compatible numbers.
$368.5 \div 13.4 \longrightarrow 360 \div 12 = 30$

$$13.4\overline{)368.5}$$

Multiply the divisor and the dividend by 10.
Think: $13.4 \times 10 = 134$ $368.5 \times 10 = 3,685$

$$
\begin{array}{r}
27.5 \\
134\overline{)3685.0} \\
-268 \\
\hline
1005 \\
-938 \\
\hline
67\,0 \\
-67\,0 \\
\hline
0
\end{array}
$$

Place the decimal point in the quotient.
Divide as with whole numbers.

Julie and her family averaged 27.5 miles per gallon.

4 Look Back

The answer is reasonable, since 27.5 is close to the estimate of 30.

MATHEMATICAL PRACTICES

Think and Discuss

1. Tell how the quotient of $48 \div 12$ is similar to the quotient of $4.8 \div 1.2$. How is it different?

     Lesson Tutorials Online   my.hrw.com

GUIDED PRACTICE

See Example 1 **Find each quotient.**

1. $6.5 \div 1.3$ **2.** $20.7 \div 0.6$ **3.** $25.5 \div 1.5$

4. $5.4 \div 0.9$ **5.** $13.2 \div 2.2$ **6.** $63.39 \div 0.24$

See Example 2 **7.** Marcus drove 354.9 miles in 6.5 hours. On average, how many miles per hour did he drive?

8. Consumer Math Anthony spends $87.75 on shrimp. The shrimp cost $9.75 per pound. How many pounds of shrimp does Anthony buy?

INDEPENDENT PRACTICE

See Example 1 **Find each quotient.**

9. $3.6 \div 0.6$ **10.** $8.2 \div 0.5$ **11.** $18.4 \div 2.3$

12. $4.8 \div 1.2$ **13.** $52.2 \div 0.24$ **14.** $32.5 \div 2.6$

15. $49.5 \div 4.5$ **16.** $96.6 \div 0.42$ **17.** $6.5 \div 1.3$

See Example 2 **18.** Jen spends $5.98 on ribbon. Ribbon costs $0.92 per meter. How many meters of ribbon does Jen buy?

19. Kyle's family drove 329.44 miles. Kyle calculated that the car averaged 28.4 miles per gallon of gas. How many gallons of gas did the car use?

20. Consumer Math Peter is saving $4.95 each week to buy a DVD that costs $24.75, including tax. For how many weeks will he have to save?

PRACTICE AND PROBLEM SOLVING

Extra Practice
See Extra Practice for more exercises.

Divide.

21. $2.52 \div 0.4$ **22.** $12.586 \div 0.35$ **23.** $0.5733 \div 0.003$

24. $10.875 \div 1.2$ **25.** $92.37 \div 0.5$ **26.** $8.43 \div 0.12$

Evaluate.

27. $0.732 \div n$ for $n = 0.06$ **28.** $73.814 \div c$ for $c = 1.3$

29. $b \div 0.52$ for $b = 6.344$ **30.** $r \div 4.17$ for $r = 10.5918$

Find the value of each expression.

31. $6.35 \times 10^2 \div 0.5$ **32.** $8.1 \times 10^2 \div 0.9$ **33.** $4.5 \times 10^3 \div 4$

34. $20.1 \times 10^3 \div 0.1$ **35.** $2.76 \times 10^2 \div 0.3$ **36.** $6.2 \times 10^3 \div 8$

37. Multi-Step Find the value of $6.45 \times 10^6 \div 0.3$. Write your answer in scientific notation.

History

The U.S. Mint was established by the Coinage Act in 1792. The first coins were copper and were made in Philadelphia.

38. Earth Science A planet's year is the time it takes that planet to revolve around the Sun. A Mars year is 1.88 Earth years. If you are 13 years old in Earth years, about how old would you be in Mars years?

39. History The U.S. Treasury first printed paper money in 1862. The paper money we use today is 0.0043 inch thick. Estimate the number of bills you would need to stack to make a pile that is 1 inch thick. If you stacked $20 bills, what would be the total value of the money in the pile?

Use the map for Exercises 40 and 41.

40. Multi-Step Bill drove from Washington, D.C., to Charlotte in 6.5 hours. What was his average speed in miles per hour?

41. Estimation Betty drove a truck from Richmond to Washington, D.C. It took her about 2.5 hours. Estimate the average speed she was driving.

 42. What's the Error? A student incorrectly answered the division problem below. Explain the error and write the correct quotient.

$$0.004\overline{)53.824} \quad 13.456$$

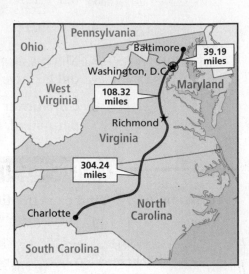

 43. Write About It Explain how you know where to place the decimal point in the quotient when you divide by a decimal number.

44. Challenge Find the value of a in the division problem.

$$4a3\overline{)0417.13} \quad 1.01$$

Test Prep

45. Multiple Choice Nick bought 2.5 pounds of popcorn for $8.35. How much did he pay for each pound of popcorn?

   Ⓐ $20.88   Ⓑ $3.43   Ⓒ $3.34   Ⓓ $33.40

46. Extended Response In the 2006–2007 NBA season, Kevin Garnett earned a salary of $21,000,000. He played in 76 games and averaged 39.4 minutes per game. How much money did Kevin Garnett earn each minute he played? Round your answer to the nearest dollar. Explain how you solved the problem.

COMMON CORE

CC.6.NS.3 Fluently add, subtract, multiply, and divide multi-digit decimals using the standard algorithm for each operation

In science lab, Ken learned to make slime from corn starch, water, and food coloring. He has 0.87 kg of corn starch, and the recipe for one bag of slime calls for 0.15 kg. To find the number of bags of slime Ken can make, you need to divide.

EXAMPLE 1 · *Measurement Application*

Ken will use 0.87 kg of corn starch to make gift bags of slime for his friends. If each bag requires 0.15 kg of corn starch, how many bags of slime can he make?

The question asks how many whole bags of slime can be made when the corn starch is divided into groups of 0.15 kg.

$0.87 \div 0.15 = ?$
$87 \div 15 = 5.8$

> **Remember!**
>
> To divide decimals, first write the divisor as a whole number. Multiply the divisor and dividend by the same power of ten.

Think: The quotient shows that there is not enough to make 6 bags of slime that are 0.15 kg each. There is only enough for 5 bags. The decimal part of the quotient will not be used in the answer.

Ken can make **5** gift bags of slime.

EXAMPLE 2 · *Photography Application*

There are 246 students in the sixth grade. If Ms. Lee buys rolls of film with 24 exposures each, how many rolls will she need to take every student's picture?

The question asks how many whole rolls are needed to take a picture of every one of the students.

$246 \div 24 = ?$

$246 \div 24 = 10.25$

 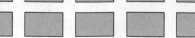

Think: Ten rolls of film will not be enough to take every student's picture. Ms. Lee will need to buy another roll of film. The quotient must be rounded up to the next highest whole number.

Ms. Lee will need 11 rolls of film.

Sam Dudgeon/HMH

EXAMPLE 3

Social Studies Application

Marissa is drawing a time line of the Stone Age. She plans for 6 equal sections, two each for the Paleolithic, Mesolithic, and Neolithic periods. If she has 7.8 meters of paper, how long is each section?

The question asks exactly how long each section will be when the paper is divided into 6 sections.

$7.8 \div 6 = 1.3$ *Think: The question asks for an exact answer, so do not estimate. Use the entire quotient.*

Each section will be **1.3** meters long.

When the question asks	→ You should
How many whole groups can be made when you divide?	→ Drop the decimal part of the quotient.
How many whole groups are needed to put all items from the dividend into a group?	→ Round the quotient up to the next highest whole number.
What is the exact number when you divide?	→ Use the entire quotient as the answer.

Think and Discuss

1. **Tell** how you would interpret the quotient: A group of 27 students will ride in vans that carry 12 students each. How many vans are needed?

3-7 Exercises

Learn It Online
Homework Help Online
Exercises 1–6, 7, 13

GUIDED PRACTICE

See Example 1. Kay is making beaded belts for her friends from 6.5 meters of cord. One belt uses 0.625 meter of cord. How many belts can she make?

See Example 2. Julius is supplying cups for a party of 136 people. If cups are sold in packs of 24, how many packs of cups will he need?

See Example 3. Miranda is decorating for a party. She has 13 balloons and 29.25 meters of ribbon. She wants to tie the same length of ribbon on each balloon. How long will each ribbon be?

　　　　Video **Lesson Tutorials Online** my.hrw.com

See Example **1**   **4.** There are 0.454 kg of corn starch in a container. How many 0.028 kg portions are in one container?

See Example **2**   **5.** Tina needs 36 flowers for her next project. The flowers are sold in bunches of 5. How many bunches will she need?

See Example **3**   **6.** Bobby's goal is to run 27 miles a week. If he runs the same distance 6 days a week, how many miles would he have to run each day?

PRACTICE AND PROBLEM SOLVING

Extra Practice
See Extra Practice for more exercises.

7. Nick wants to write thank-you notes to 15 of his friends. The cards are sold in packs of 6. How many packs does Nick need to buy?

8. Multi-Step The science teacher has 7 packs of seeds and 36 students. If the students should each plant the same number of seeds, how many can each student plant?

9. Critical Thinking How do you know when to round your answer up to the next whole number?

 10. Write a Problem Create a problem that is solved by interpreting the quotient.

 11. Write About It Explain how a calculator shows the remainder when you divide 145 by 8.

 12. Challenge Leonard wants to place a fence on both sides of a 10-meter walkway. If he puts a post at both ends and at every 2.5 meters in between, how many posts does he use?

Test Prep

13. Multiple Choice There are 375 students going on a field trip. Each bus holds 65 students. How many buses are needed for the field trip?

   Ⓐ 4   Ⓑ 5   Ⓒ 6   Ⓓ 7

14. Multiple Choice Mrs. Neal has 127 stickers. She wants to give each of the 22 students in her class the same number of stickers. Which expression can be used to find how many stickers each student will get?

   Ⓕ 127 − 22   Ⓖ 127 ÷ 22   Ⓗ 127 + 22   Ⓙ 127 × 22

3-8 Solving Decimal Equations

CC.6.EE.7 Solve real-world and mathematical problems by writing and solving equations of the form $x + p = q$ and $px = q$ for cases in which p, q and x are all nonnegative rational numbers *Also CC.6.EE.6*

Interactivities Online ▶

Felipe has earned $45.20 by mowing lawns for his neighbors. He wants to buy inline skates that cost $69.95. Write and solve an equation to find how much more money Felipe must earn to buy the skates.

Let m be the amount of money Felipe needs. $45.20 + m = 69.95$

You can solve equations with decimals using inverse operations just as you solved equations with whole numbers.

$$\begin{array}{r} \$45.20 + m = \$69.95 \\ -\ \$45.20 \qquad -\ \$45.20 \\ \hline m = \$24.75 \end{array}$$

Felipe needs $24.75 more to buy the inline skates.

E X A M P L E **1** **Solving One-Step Equations with Decimals**

Solve each equation. Check your answer.

> **Remember!**
> Use inverse operations to get the variable alone on one side of the equation.

A $g - 3.1 = 4.5$

$$\begin{array}{rl} g - 3.1 = & 4.5 \qquad \text{\textit{3.1 is subtracted from g.}} \\ +\ 3.1 & +\ 3.1 \qquad \text{\textit{Add 3.1 to both sides to undo the subtraction.}} \\ \hline g = & 7.6 \end{array}$$

Check

$$g - 3.1 = 4.5$$
$$7.6 - 3.1 \overset{?}{=} 4.5 \qquad \text{\textit{Substitute 7.6 for g in the equation.}}$$
$$4.5 \overset{?}{=} 4.5 \checkmark \qquad \text{\textit{7.6 is the solution.}}$$

B $3k = 8.1$

$$3k = 8.1 \qquad \text{\textit{k is multiplied by 3.}}$$
$$\frac{3k}{3} = \frac{8.1}{3} \qquad \text{\textit{Divide both sides by 3 to undo the}}$$
$$k = 2.7 \qquad \text{\textit{multiplication.}}$$

Check

$$3k = 8.1$$
$$3(2.7) \overset{?}{=} 8.1 \qquad \text{\textit{Substitute 2.7 for k in the equation.}}$$
$$8.1 \overset{?}{=} 8.1 \checkmark \qquad \text{\textit{2.7 is the solution.}}$$

Video **Lesson Tutorials Online** my.hrw.com

Solve each equation. Check your answer.

C $\dfrac{m}{5} = 1.5$

$\dfrac{m}{5} = 1.5$ *m is divided by 5.*

$\dfrac{m}{5} \cdot 5 = 1.5 \cdot 5$ *Multiply both sides by 5 to undo the division.*

$m = 7.5$

Check

$\dfrac{m}{5} = 1.5$

$\dfrac{7.5}{5} \overset{?}{=} 1.5$ *Substitute 7.5 for m in the equation.*

$1.5 \overset{?}{=} 1.5$ ✔   *7.5 is the solution.*

E X A M P L E 2   *Measurement Application*

Remember!

The area of a rectangle is its length times its width.

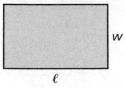

ℓ

$A = \ell w$

A The area of the floor in Jonah's bedroom is 28 square meters. If its length is 3.5 meters, what is the width of the bedroom?

area	=	length	·	width
28	=	3.5	·	*w*

$28 = 3.5w$ *Write the equation for the problem. Let w be the width of the room. w is multiplied by 3.5.*

$\dfrac{28}{3.5} = \dfrac{3.5w}{3.5}$ *Divide both sides by 3.5 to undo the multiplication.*

$8 = w$

The width of Jonah's bedroom is 8 meters.

B Jonah is carpeting his bedroom. The carpet costs $22.50 per square meter. What is the total cost to carpet the bedroom?

total cost = area · cost of carpet per square meter

$C = 28 \cdot 22.50$ *Let C be the total cost. Write the equation for the problem.*

$C = 630$ *Multiply.*

The cost of carpeting the bedroom is $630.

MATHEMATICAL PRACTICES

Think and Discuss

1. Explain whether the value of *m* will be less than or greater than 1 when you solve $5m = 4.5$.

2. Tell how you can check the answer in Example 2A.

Exercises

Learn It Online
Homework Help Online
Exercises 1–19, 21, 23, 25, 27, 29, 31, 33

GUIDED PRACTICE

See Example 1 | Solve each equation. Check your answer.

1. $a - 2.3 = 4.8$

2. $6n = 8.4$

3. $\frac{c}{4} = 3.2$

4. $8.5 = 2.49 + x$

5. $\frac{d}{3.2} = 1.09$

6. $1.6 = m \cdot 4$

See Example 2

7. The length of a window is 10.5 meters, and the width is 5.75 meters. Solve the equation $a \div 10.5 = 5.75$ to find the area of the window.

8. Gretchen wants to add a wallpaper border along the top of the walls of her square room. The distance around her room is 20.4 meters.

    a. What is the length of each wall of Gretchen's room?

    b. The price of wallpaper border is $1.25 per meter. What is the total cost to add the border to her room?

INDEPENDENT PRACTICE

See Example 1 | Solve each equation. Check your answer.

9. $b - 5.6 = 3.7$

10. $1.6 = \frac{p}{7}$

11. $3r = 62.4$

12. $9.5 = 5x$

13. $a - 4.8 = 5.9$

14. $\frac{n}{8} = 0.8$

15. $8 + f = 14.56$

16. $5.2s = 10.4$

17. $1.95 = z - 2.05$

See Example 2 | **18.** **Geometry** The area of a rectangle is 65.8 square units. The length is 7 units. Solve the equation $7 \cdot w = 65.8$ to find the width of the rectangle.

19. Ken wants to fence his square garden. He will need 6.4 meters of fence to enclose all four sides of the garden.

    a. How long is each side of his garden?

    b. The price of fencing is $2.25 per meter. What is the total cost to fence Ken's garden?

PRACTICE AND PROBLEM SOLVING

Extra Practice
See Extra Practice for more exercises.

Solve each equation and check your answer.

20. $9.8 = t - 42.1$

21. $q \div 2.6 = 9.5$

22. $45.36 = 5.6 \cdot m$

23. $1.3b = 5.46$

24. $4.93 = 0.563 + m$

25. $\frac{a}{5} = 2.78$

26. $w - 64.99 = 13.044$

27. $6.205z = 80.665$

28. $74.2 = 38.06 + c$

29. **Geometry** The shortest side of the triangle is 10 units long.

    a. What are the lengths of the other two sides of the triangle?

    b. What is the perimeter of the triangle?

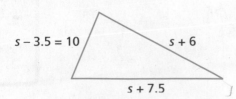

$s - 3.5 = 10$ $s + 6$

$s + 7.5$

The London Eye is the world's largest Ferris wheel. Use the table for Exercises 30–32.

30. Write the height of the wheel in kilometers.

31. **Multi-Step** There are 1,000 kilograms in a metric ton. What is the weight of the wheel in kilograms written in scientific notation?

32. a. How many seconds does it take for the wheel to make one revolution?

    b. The wheel moves at a rate of 0.26 meters per second. Use the equation $d \div 0.26 = 1,800$ to find the distance of one revolution.

33. Each capsule can hold 25 passengers. How many capsules are needed to hold 210 passengers?

Weight of wheel	1,900 metric tons
Time to revolve	30 minutes
Height of wheel	135 meters

34. In 2007, 15 standard flight adult tickets for the London Eye cost £217.50 (about $432.43). What is the cost for one ticket? Give the answer in both pounds sterling (£) and U.S. dollars.

35. **What's the Error?** When solving the equation $b - 12.98 = 5.03$, a student said that $b = 7.95$. Describe the error. What is the correct value for b?

36. **Write About It** Explain how you solve for the variable in a multiplication equation such as $2.3a = 4.6$.

37. **Challenge** Solve $1.45n \times 3.2 = 23.942 + 4.13$.

Test Prep

38. **Multiple Choice** Solve the equation $d \div 4 = 6.7$ for d.

    (A) $d = 26.8$ (B) $d = 10.7$ (C) $d = 2.7$ (D) $d = 1.675$

39. **Multiple Choice** Kelly bought 2.8 pounds of beef for $5.04. How much did she pay for each pound of beef?

    (F) $18.00 (G) $7.84 (H) $1.80 (J) $0.18

Ready To Go On?

Learn It Online
Resources Online

Ready to Go On?

Quiz for Lessons 4 Through 8

4 Multiplying Decimals

Evaluate $5x$ for each value of x.

1. $x = 1.025$ **2.** $x = 6.2$ **3.** $x = 2.64$

4. Neptune has a gravitational pull 1.2 times that of Earth. If an object weighs 15 pounds on Earth, how much would it weigh on Neptune?

5 Dividing Decimals by Whole Numbers

Find each quotient.

5. $17.5 \div 5$ **6.** $11.6 \div 8$ **7.** $23.4 \div 6$ **8.** $35.5 \div 5$

9. Five apples cost $4.90. How much does each apple cost?

6 Dividing by Decimals

Find each quotient.

10. $2.226 \div 0.42$ **11.** $13.49 \div 7.1$ **12.** $35.34 \div 6.2$ **13.** $178.64 \div 81.2$

14. Peri spent $21.89 on material to make a skirt. The material cost $3.98 per yard. How many yards did Peri buy?

7 Interpreting the Quotient

15. There are 352 students graduating from high school. The photographer takes one picture of each student as the student receives his or her diploma. If the photographer has 36 exposures on each roll of film, how many rolls will she have to buy to take each student's picture?

8 Solving Decimal Equations

Solve each equation.

16. $t - 6.3 = 8.9$ **17.** $4h = 20.4$ **18.** $\frac{p}{7} = 4.6$ **19.** $d + 2.8 = 9.5$

20. A customer at a deli orders 3.25 lb of turkey breast. She asks if the meat can be evenly distributed into 5 bags. How much turkey breast will be in each bag?

Puget Sound Ferries Puget Sound is an arm of the Pacific Ocean with about 2,000 miles of coastline. Not surprisingly, ferries play an important role for Washington residents who live near Puget Sound. The sound's state-run ferry system is the largest in the United States.

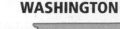

WASHINGTON

1. Estimate the total length of the five ferry routes shown on the map.

2. Which route is longer, Kingston-Edmonds or Southworth-Fauntleroy?

3. How much longer is the Seattle-Bremerton route than the Seattle-Bainbridge Island route?

4. The Anacortes-Orcas route (not shown on the map) is 8.5 times as long as the Tahlequah-Pt. Defiance route. Find the length of the Anacortes-Orcas route.

5. A one-way trip on the Southworth-Fauntleroy ferry takes 0.75 hours.

   a. How many one-way trips can the ferry make in 12 hours? (Assume the ferry departs immediately after reaching its destination.) Explain which operation you used to solve this problem.

   b. What is the total distance that the ferry travels while making these one-way trips?

WASHINGTON

5.15 mi — Kingston — Edmonds

Bainbridge Island

7.9 mi

17.8 mi

Bremerton — Seattle

Southworth — Fauntleroy

5.2 mi

1.7 mi — Tahlequah

Pt. Defiance

Real-World Connections

Greg Probst/Corbis

Game Time

Jumbles

Do you know what eleven plus two equals?

Use your calculator to evaluate each expression. Keep the letters under the expressions with the answers you get. Then order the answers from least to greatest, and write down the letters in that order. You will spell the answer to the riddle.

$4 - 1.893$	$0.21 \div 0.3$	$0.443 - 0.0042$	$4.509 - 3.526$	$3.14 \cdot 2.44$	$1.56 \cdot 3.678$
E	**L**	**E**	**V**	**E**	**N**

$6.34 \div 2.56$	$1.19 + 1.293$	$8.25 \div 2.5$	$7.4 - 2.356$
P	**L**	**U**	**S**

$0.0003 + 0.003$	$0.3 \cdot 0.04$	$2.17 + 3.42$
T	**W**	**O**

Make A Buck

The object of the game is to win the most points by adding decimal numbers to make a sum close to but not over $1.00.

Most cards have a decimal number on them representing an amount of money. Others are wild cards: The person who receives a wild card decides its value.

The dealer gives each player four cards. Taking turns, players add the numbers in their hand. If the sum is less than $1.00, a player can either draw a card from the top of the deck or pass.

Learn It Online
Game Time Extra

When each player has taken a turn or passed, the player whose sum is closest to but not over $1.00 scores a point. If players tie for the closest sum, each of those players scores a point. All cards are then discarded and four new cards are dealt to each player.

When all of the cards have been dealt, the player with the most points wins.

A complete copy of the rules and game pieces are available online.

Jenny Thomas/HMH

Materials
- 2 plastic slide holders
- squares of card stock
- clear tape
- permanent marker

PROJECT ▸ **Project E Z 2 C Decimals**

Practice reading decimals by making this see-through decimal holder.

Directions

❶ Cut out about 40 small squares of colored card stock. Remove ten of the squares. On these squares, write "Ones," "Tens," "Hundreds," "Thousands," "Ten-Thousands," "Tenths," "Hundredths," "Thousandths," "Ten-Thousandths," and "Hundred-Thousandths." **Figure A**

❷ On each of the remaining squares, write a number from 0 to 9.

❸ Tape the two slide holders together. Using a permanent marker, draw decimal points down the middle where the holders are taped together. **Figure B**

❹ Put the squares with the names of the place values in the correct slots along the top row.

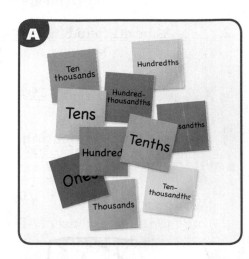

A

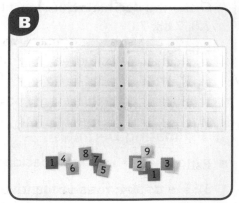

B

Putting the Math into Action

Put numbered squares in the remaining slots. Work with a partner to practice reading the resulting decimals. Mix up the numbered squares and repeat the process several more times, sometimes using all of the slots in a row and sometimes making shorter decimals.

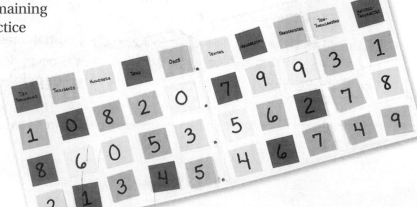

HMH

Study Guide: Review

Vocabulary

clustering   front-end estimation

Complete the sentences below with vocabulary words from the list above.

1. When you estimate a sum by using only the whole-number part of the decimals, you are using ___?___.

2. ___?___ means rounding all the numbers to the same value.

EXAMPLES

EXERCISES

1 Representing, Comparing, and Ordering Decimals

■ Write 4.025 in expanded form and words.

Expanded form: $4 + 0.02 + 0.005$

Word form: four and twenty-five thousandths

Write each in expanded form and words.

3. 5.68   **4.** 1.0076

5. 1.203   **6.** 23.005

7. 71.038   **8.** 99.9999

■ Order the decimals from least to greatest.
7.8, 7.83, 7.08

$7.08 < 7.80 < 7.83$ *Compare the numbers.*
7.08, 7.8, 7.83   *Then order the numbers.*

Order the decimals from least to greatest.

9. 1.2, 1.3, 1.12   **10.** 11.17, 11.7, 11.07

11. 0.3, 0.303, 0.033   **12.** 5.009, 5.950, 5.5

13. 101.52, 101.25, 101.025

---

2 Estimating Decimals

■ Estimate.

5.35 − 0.7904; round to tenths

$$\begin{array}{r} 5.4 \\ -\,0.8 \\ \hline 4.6 \end{array}$$ *Align the decimals.*
Subtract.

Estimate.

14. 8.0954 + 3.218; round to the hundredths

15. 6.8356 − 4.507; round to the tenths

16. 9.258 + 4.97; round to the ones

■ Estimate 49.67 × 2.88.

49.67×2.88
$50 \times 3 = 150$

Estimate each product or quotient.

17. 21.19 × 4.23

18. 53.98 ÷ 5.97

19. 102.89 × 19.95

EXAMPLES

EXERCISES

3 Adding and Subtracting Decimals

■ **Find the sum.**

7.62 + 0.563

7.620	*Align the decimal points.*
+ 0.563	*Use zeros as placeholders.*
8.183	*Add. Place the decimal point.*

■ **Find the difference.**

18 − 11.45

18.00	*Align the decimal points.*
− 11.45	*Use zeros as placeholders.*
6.55	*Subtract. Place the decimal point.*

Find each sum or difference.

20. 7.08 + 4.5 + 13.27 **21.** 6 − 0.7

22. 6.21 + 5.8 + 21.01 **23.** 7.001 − 2.0785

Evaluate 6.48 − s for each value of s.

24. $s = 3.9$ **25.** $s = 3.6082$

26. $s = 5.01$ **27.** $s = 0.057$

28. Rodney bought a new book for $15.75 and two new CDs for $12.99 each. How much did Rodney spend?

4 Multiplying Decimals

■ **Find the product.**

0.3	*1 decimal place*
× 0.08	*+ 2 decimal places*
0.024	*3 decimal places*

Find each product.

29. 4 × 2.36   **30.** 0.5 × 1.73

31. 0.6 × 0.012   **32.** 8 × 3.052

33. 1.2 × 0.45   **34.** 9.7 × 1.084

Evaluate.

35. $3w − 2.45$ for $w = 1.5$

36. $10 + 3.3x$ for $x = 5$

37. An object on the surface of the Sun would weigh around 28 times as much as it weighs on Earth. How much would a 202.8-pound man weigh on the Sun?

5 Dividing Decimals by Whole Numbers

■ Find the quotient.

0.95 ÷ 5

Place a decimal point directly above the decimal point in the dividend. Then divide.

$$\begin{array}{r} 0.19 \\ 5\overline{)0.95} \end{array}$$

Find each quotient.

38. 6.18 ÷ 6

39. 2.16 ÷ 3

40. 34.65 ÷ 9

41. 20.72 ÷ 8

42. If four people equally share a bill for $14.56, how much should each person pay?

6 Dividing by Decimals

■ Find the quotient.

9.65 ÷ 0.5

Make the divisor a whole number.

Place the decimal point in the quotient.

$$\begin{array}{r} 19.3 \\ 5\overline{)96.5} \end{array}$$

Find each quotient.

43. 4.86 ÷ 0.6

44. 1.85 ÷ 0.3

45. 34.89 ÷ 9

46. 62.73 ÷ 1.2

47. Ana cuts some wood that is 3.75 meters long into 5 pieces of equal length. How long is each piece?

7 Interpreting the Quotient

■ Ms. Ald needs 26 stickers for her preschool class. Stickers are sold in packs of 8. How many packs should she buy?

26 ÷ 8 = 3.25

3.25 is between 3 and 4.

3 packs will not be enough.

Ms. Ald should buy 4 packs of stickers.

48. Billy has 3.6 liters of juice. How many 0.25 L containers can he fill?

49. There are 34 people going on a field trip. If each car holds 4 people, how many cars will they need for the field trip?

50. Mr. Paxton has 16.5 feet of twine. If he is wrapping 3 packages, how much twine can he use on each package?

8 Solving Decimal Equations

■ Solve $4x = 20.8$.

$4x = 20.8$ *x is multiplied by 4.*

$\dfrac{4x}{4} = \dfrac{20.8}{4}$ *Divide both sides by 4.*

$x = 5.2$

Solve each equation.

51. $a - 6.2 = 7.18$

52. $3y = 7.86$

53. $n + 4.09 = 6.38$

54. $\dfrac{p}{7} = 8.6$

55. Jasmine buys 2.25 kg of apples for $11.25. How much does 1 kg of apples cost?

1. The New York Philharmonic Orchestra performs at Avery Fisher Hall in New York City. It seats 2,738 people. The Boston Symphony Orchestra performs at Symphony Hall in Boston, Massachusetts. It seats 2,625 people. Which hall seats more people?

Order the decimals from least to greatest.

2. 12.6, 12.07, 12.67

3. 3.5, 3.25, 3.08

4. 0.10301, 0.10318, 0.10325

Estimate by rounding to the indicated place value.

5. 6.178 − 0.2805; hundredths

6. 7.528 + 6.075; ones

Estimate.

7. 21.35 × 3.18

8. 98.547 ÷ 4.93

9. 11.855 × 8.45

Estimate a range for each sum.

10. 3.89 + 42.71 + 12.32

11. 20.751 + 2.55 + 17.4

12. 4.987 + 28.27 + 0.098

13. Britney wants to exercise in a step aerobics class. The class uses the 4-inch step for 15 minutes and the 6-inch step for 15 minutes. About how many calories will she burn in all?

Step Height (in.)	Calories Burned in 15 minutes
4	67.61
6	82.2
8	96

Evaluate.

14. 0.76 + 2.24

15. 7 − 0.4

16. 0.12 × 0.006

17. 5.85 ÷ 3.9

Solve each equation.

18. $b - 4.7 = 2.1$

19. $5a = 4.75$

20. $\frac{y}{6} = 7.2$

21. $c + 1.9 = 26.04$

22. The school band is going to a competition. There are 165 students in the band. If each bus holds 25 students, how many buses will be needed?

23. Marisol bought six sweaters on sale for a total of $126.24. How much did each sweater cost if they were all marked down to the same price?

Chapter Test

STANDARDIZED TEST STRATEGIES

Short Response: Write Short Responses

Short-response test items require a solution to the problem and the reasoning or work used to get that solution. Short-response test items are scored according to a 2-point scoring rubric. A sample scoring rubric is provided below.

EXAMPLE 1

Short Response Coach Mott needs to order jackets for the boys' basketball team. Each jacket costs $28.75. The team has $125 from their fund-raiser to go toward the total cost of the jackets. If there are 10 players on the team, how much money will each player need to give to Coach Mott for a jacket so he can place the order? Explain.

2-point response:

> Cost of one jacket: $28.75
> Total cost for team jackets (10 players):
> $28.75 × 10 = $287.50
>
> Subtract the money the team already has from the total cost.
> $287.50 − $125 = $162.50
>
> Divide the remaining cost by the number of players on the team.
> $162.50 ÷ 10 = $16.25
>
> Each player needs to give Coach Mott $16.25 so he can place the order for the jackets.

1-point response:

> ($287.50 − $125) ÷ $10 = $16.25
>
> He will need $16.25 from each player.

0-point response:

> $16.25

Scoring Rubric

2 points: The student correctly answers the question, shows all work, and provides a complete and correct explanation.

1 point: The student correctly answers the question but does not show all work or does not provide a complete explanation; or the student makes minor errors resulting in an incorrect solution but shows all work and provides a complete explanation.

0 points: The student gives an incorrect answer and shows no work or explanation, or the student gives no response.

The student correctly solved the problem but did not show all of his or her work or did not provide an explanation.

The student gave a correct answer but did not show any work or give an explanation.

Read each test item and answer the questions that follow by using the scoring rubric below.

Item A
Short Response Write two equations that each have a solution of 12. You cannot use the same mathematical operation for both equations. Explain how to solve both equations.

Student's Answer

One equation that has a solution of 12 is $\frac{x}{6} = 2$. To solve this equation, I must undo the division by multiplying by 6 on both sides.

$$\frac{x}{6} = 2$$

$$6 \cdot \left(\frac{x}{6}\right) = 6 \cdot 2$$

$$x = 12$$

Another equation with a solution of 12 is $x - 8 = 20$.

To solve this equation, I must add the opposite of 8 to both sides.

$$x - 8 = 20$$
$$\underline{-8 = -8}$$
$$x = 12$$

1. The student's answer will not receive full credit. Find the error in the student's answer.

2. Rewrite the student's answer so that it receives full credit.

Item B
Short Response June is 8 years older than her cousin Liv. Write an expression to find June's age. Identify the variable and list three possible solutions showing the ages of June and Liv.

Student's Answer

Let x = Liv's age. Since June is 8 years older, the expression x + 8 can be used to find June's age.
Three possible solutions for Liv and June follow:
x = 3, 3 + 8 = 11; Liv: 3, June: 11
x = 8, 8 + 8 = 16; Liv: 8, June: 16
x = 11, 11 + 8 = 19; Liv: 11, June: 19

3. What score should the student's answer receive? Explain your reasoning.

4. What additional information, if any, should the student's answer include in order to receive full credit?

Item C
Short Response Write an equation to represent the following situation. Define the variable. Solve the problem. *Sam has two kittens. The larger kitten weighs 3.2 kg. The other kitten needs to gain 1.9 kg to weigh as much as the larger kitten. How much does the smaller kitten weigh?*

Student's Answer

Let x = the weight of the smaller kitten.
x + 1.9 = 3.2
3.2 + 1.9 = 5.1

5. How would you score the student's response? Explain.

6. Rewrite the response so that it receives full credit.

Standardized Test Prep

Learn It Online
State Test Practice

Cumulative Assessment

Multiple Choice

1. Which of the following is the standard form for six and eighty-six thousandths?

   (A) 6.860

   (B) 6.086

   (C) 6.0086

   (D) 6.00086

2. The weights of three backpacks are 15.8 pounds, 18.1 pounds, and 16.7 pounds. About how many pounds do the backpacks weigh all together?

   (F) 30 pounds

   (G) 40 pounds

   (H) 50 pounds

   (J) 60 pounds

3. For which equation is $c = 8$ NOT a solution?

   (A) $\frac{c}{4} = 2$

   (B) $c + 4 = 12$

   (C) $4c = 28$

   (D) $c - 5 = 3$

4. Jerah scored 15 more points in a basketball game than his brother Jim did. Jim scored 7 points. Which expression can be used to find the number of points Jerah scored?

   (F) $15 - 7$

   (G) 15×7

   (H) $15 \div 7$

   (J) $15 + 7$

5. Find the sum of 1.4 and 0.9.

   (A) 0.1

   (B) 0.5

   (C) 1.3

   (D) 2.3

6. Which number is the greatest?

   (F) 18.095

   (G) 18.9

   (H) 18.907

   (J) 18.75

7. The heights of four different plants are listed below. Which statement is supported by the data?

Plant Height (in.)				
Plant	T	S	U	W
Week 1	15.9	23.6	17.1	12.5
Week 2	21.4	27.4	22.9	16.4

   (A) Plant T was the shortest during week 1.

   (B) Plant S grew more than 4 inches between week 1 and week 2.

   (C) Plant U grew the most between week 1 and week 2.

   (D) Plant W is the tallest.

8. What is the value of 3^4?

   (F) 7

   (G) 12

   (H) 81

   (J) 96

9. A gallon of water weighs about 8.35 pounds. A 5-gal water bottle weighs 0.5 pound. What is the weight of the bottle when full of water?

   (A) 9.175 pounds

   (B) 13.35 pounds

   (C) 20.875 pounds

   (D) 42.25 pounds

10. Tomas needs 42 cups for a party. The cups are sold in packages of 5. How many packages should he buy?

    (F) 10 packages

    (G) 9 packages

    (H) 8 packages

    (J) 7 packages

11. What is $7.89 \div 3$?

    (A) 263

    (B) 26.3

    (C) 0.263

    (D) 2.63

12. Which set of numbers is in order from least to greatest?

- Ⓕ 23.7, 23.07, 23.13, 23.89
- Ⓖ 21.4, 21.45, 21.79, 21.8
- Ⓗ 22, 22.09, 21.9, 22.1
- Ⓙ 25.4, 25.09, 25.6, 25.7

13. Megan is beginning an exercise routine. She plans to walk 1 mile on day 1 and increase her distance each day by 0.25 mile. How many miles will she be walking on day 10?

- Ⓐ 2.5 miles
- Ⓒ 4.75 miles
- Ⓑ 3.25 miles
- Ⓓ 6.0 miles

 HOT TIP! Estimate your answer before solving the question. Use your estimate to check the reasonableness of your answer.

Gridded Response

14. What is the value of c in the equation $\frac{c}{6} = 3.4$?

15. What is the missing term in the following sequence?

5, 12, 26, 47, ▆, 110, . . .

16. Sam has 10 boxes full of computer games. Each box holds 13 games. How many games does Sam own?

17. Cindy bought 3 bunches of daisies and 4 bunches of carnations. There are 6 daisies and 10 carnations in a bunch. How many flowers does she have in all?

18. Bart and his 2 friends buy lunch. The total is $13.74. If they share the cost equally, how much, in dollars, should each person pay?

19. Daisy buys a shirt that costs $21.64 after tax. She gives the cashier $25. How much, in dollars, does she get back in change?

Short Response

S1. Kevin buys 5 steaks for $43.75. Let b equal the cost of one steak. Write and solve the equation to find the cost of one steak.

S2. Ms. Maier has 8 packs of pencils to give out to students taking a state test. Each pack has 8 pencils. There are 200 students taking the test who need pencils.

- **a.** How many more packs of pencils does Ms. Maier need to buy? Explain your answer and show your work.
- **b.** If each pack of pencils costs $0.79, how much money will Ms. Maier need to spend to buy the extra pencils? Show your work.

Extended Response

E1. Admission to the Children's Museum is listed below. Use the chart to answer the following questions.

Admission Costs ($)	
Adult	7.50
Child	5.75

- **a.** Write an expression to find the cost of admission for 2 adults and c children.
- **b.** Use your expression to find the total cost for Mr. and Mrs. Chu and their 8-year-old triplets. Show your work.
- **c.** If Mr. Chu pays for admission using a $50 bill, how much change does he get back? Show your work.
- **d.** On the Chu's next visit, Mrs. Chu plans to use a coupon and will only pay $28.50 for the family. How much will she save using the coupon?

Number Theory and Fractions

COMMON CORE

Chapter
- Know that a fraction can be viewed as parts of a whole.
- Use multiplication and division to determine equivalent fractions.

Why Learn This?

Recipes often list quantities of ingredients as fractions and mixed numbers. Professional chefs must be able to work with these numbers in order to follow recipes.

Learn It Online
Chapter Project Online

(all) Design Pics Inc./Alamy

Are You Ready?

Learn It Online
Resources Online

✓ Vocabulary

Choose the best term from the list to complete each sentence.

1. To find the sum of two numbers, you should ___?___.
2. Fractions are written as a ___?___ over a ___?___.
3. In the equation 4 · 3 = 12, 12 is the ___?___.
4. The ___?___ of 18 and 10 is 8.
5. The numbers 18, 27, and 72 are ___?___ of 9.

add
denominator
difference
multiples
numerator
product
quotient

Complete these exercises to review skills you will need for this chapter.

✓ Write and Read Decimals

Write each decimal in word form.

6. 0.5   7. 2.78   8. 0.125
9. 12.8   10. 125.49   11. 8.024

✓ Multiples

List the first four multiples of each number.

12. 6   13. 8   14. 5   15. 12
16. 7   17. 20   18. 14   19. 9

✓ Evaluate Expressions

Evaluate each expression for the given value of the variable.

20. $y + 4.3$ for $y = 3.2$ 21. $\frac{x}{5}$ for $x = 6.4$
22. $3c$ for $c = 0.75$ 23. $a + 4 \div 8$ for $a = 3.75$
24. $27.8 - d$ for $d = 9.25$ 25. $2.5b$ for $b = 8.4$

✓ Factors

Find all the whole-number factors of each number.

26. 8   27. 12   28. 24   29. 30
30. 45   31. 52   32. 75   33. 150

Where You've Been

Previously, you

- identified a number as prime or composite.
- identified common factors of a set of whole numbers.
- generated equivalent fractions.
- compared two fractions with common denominators.

In This Chapter

You will study

- writing the prime factorization of a number.
- finding the greatest common factor (GCF) of a set of whole numbers.
- generating equivalent forms of numbers, including whole numbers, fractions, and decimals.
- comparing and ordering fractions, decimals, and whole numbers.

Where You're Going

You can use the skills learned in this chapter

- to determine whether you have enough of an ingredient when cooking.
- to compare two measurements when one has a fraction part and the other a decimal part.

Key Vocabulary/Vocabulario

coefficient	coeficiente
common denominator	denominador común
equivalent fractions	fracciones equivalentes
factor	factor
greatest common factor (GCF)	máximo común divisor (MCD)
improper fraction	fracción impropia
prime factorization	factorización prima
term	término
terminating decimal	decimal cerrado

Vocabulary Connections

To become familiar with some of the vocabulary terms in the chapter, consider the following. You may refer to the chapter, the glossary, or a dictionary if you like.

1. The word *equivalent* means "equal in value." What do you think **equivalent fractions** are?

2. To *terminate* something means to bring it to an end. If a decimal is a **terminating decimal**, what do you think happens to it? Explain.

3. When people have something in *common*, they have something that they share. What do you think **common denominators** share?

4. If something is *improper*, it is not right. In fractions, it is *improper* to have the numerator be greater than the denominator. How would you expect an **improper fraction** to look?

Reading Strategy: Read a Lesson for Understanding

Reading ahead will prepare you for new ideas and concepts presented in class. As you read a lesson, make notes. Write down the main points of the lesson, math terms that you do not understand, examples that need more explanation, and questions you can ask during class.

Solving Decimal Equations

The title of a lesson can tell you the main idea, or objective, of the lesson.

Work through the examples and write down any questions you have.

Solving One-Step Equations with Decimals

Solve each equation. Check your answer.

A $g - 3.1 = 4.5$

$$
\begin{array}{rl}
g - 3.1 = & 4.5 \\
\underline{+\ 3.1 \quad +\ 3.1} & \\
g = & 7.6
\end{array}
$$

    3.1 is subtracted from g.

    Add 3.1 to both sides to undo the subtraction.

Check

$$g - 3.1 = 4.5$$
$$7.6 - 3.1 \overset{?}{=} 4.5 \qquad \text{\textit{Substitute 7.6 for g in the equation.}}$$
$$4.5 \overset{?}{=} 4.5 \ ✔ \qquad \text{\textit{7.6 is the solution.}}$$

Questions:
• *How do I know what operation to use?*
• *What should I do if I check my answer and the two sides are not equal?*

Write down questions you have as you read the lesson.

Read the first lesson of this chapter before your next class and answer the following questions.

1. What is the objective of the lesson?

2. Are there new vocabulary terms, formulas, or symbols? If so, what are they?

Mastering *the* Standards

for Mathematical Practice

The topics described in the Standards for Mathematical Content will vary from year to year. However, the *way* in which you learn, study, and think about mathematics will not. The Standards for Mathematical Practice describe skills that you will use in all of your math courses.

Mathematical Practices

1. *Make sense of problems and persevere in solving them.*
2. *Reason abstractly and quantitatively.*
3. *Construct viable arguments and critique the reasoning of others.*
4. *Model with mathematics.*
5. *Use appropriate tools strategically.*
6. *Attend to precision.*
7. *Look for and make use of structure.*
8. *Look for and express regularity in repeated reasoning.*

① Make sense of problems and persevere in solving them.

Mathematically proficient students start by explaining to themselves the meaning of a problem... They analyze givens, constraints, relationships, and goals. They make conjectures about the form... of the solution and plan a solution pathway...

In your book

Focus on Problem Solving describes a four-step plan for problem solving. The plan is introduced at the beginning of your book, and practice with the plan appears throughout the book.

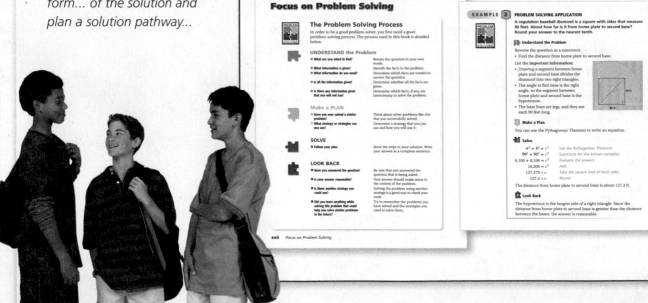

Factors and Prime Factorization

Whole numbers that are multiplied to find a product are called **factors** of that product. A number is divisible by its factors.

$$2 \cdot 3 = 6 \qquad 6 \div 3 = 2$$

$$6 \div 2 = 3$$

6 is divisible by 3 and 2.

Factors   Product

Vocabulary

factor

prime factorization

EXAMPLE 1 Finding Factors

Interactivities Online ▶

List all of the factors of each number.

A 18

Begin listing factors in pairs.

$18 = 1 \cdot 18$ *1 is a factor.*

$18 = 2 \cdot 9$ *2 is a factor.*

$18 = 3 \cdot 6$ *3 is a factor.*

4 and 5 are not factors.

$18 = 6 \cdot 3$ *6 and 3 have already been listed, so stop here.*

1   2   3   6   9   18

You can draw a diagram to illustrate the factor pairs.

The factors of 18 are 1, 2, 3, 6, 9, and 18.

B 13

$13 = 1 \cdot 13$

Begin listing factors in pairs. 13 is not divisible by any other whole numbers.

The factors of 13 are 1 and 13.

> **Helpful Hint**
>
> When the pairs of factors begin to repeat, then you have found all of the factors of the number you are factoring.

You can use factors to write a number in different ways.

Factorization of 12			
$1 \cdot 12$	$2 \cdot 6$	$3 \cdot 4$	$3 \cdot 2 \cdot 2$

◄── Notice that these factors are all prime.

The **prime factorization** of a number is the number written as the product of its prime factors.

EXAMPLE **2** **Writing Prime Factorizations**

Write the prime factorization of each number.

A 36

Method 1: Use a factor tree.

Choose any two factors of 36 to begin. Keep finding factors until each branch ends at a prime factor.

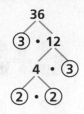

$$36 = 3 \cdot 2 \cdot 2 \cdot 3 \qquad\qquad 36 = 2 \cdot 3 \cdot 3 \cdot 2$$

The prime factorization of 36 is $2 \cdot 2 \cdot 3 \cdot 3$, or $2^2 \cdot 3^2$.

B 54

Method 2: Use a ladder diagram.

Choose a prime factor of 54 to begin. Keep dividing by prime factors until the quotient is 1.

2	54
3	27
3	9
3	3
	1

3	54
3	18
2	6
3	3
	1

$$54 = 2 \cdot 3 \cdot 3 \cdot 3 \qquad\qquad 54 = 3 \cdot 3 \cdot 2 \cdot 3$$

The prime factorization of 54 is $2 \cdot 3 \cdot 3 \cdot 3$, or $2 \cdot 3^3$.

> **Helpful Hint**
>
> You can use exponents to write prime factorizations. Remember that an exponent tells you how many times the base is a factor.

In Example 2, notice that the prime factors may be written in a different order, but they are still the same factors. Except for changes in the order, there is only one way to write the prime factorization of a number.

Think and Discuss MATHEMATICAL PRACTICES

1. **Tell** how you know when you have found all of the factors of a number.

2. **Tell** how you know when you have found the prime factorization of a number.

3. **Explain** the difference between factors of a number and prime factors of a number.

 Lesson Tutorials Online my.hrw.com

GUIDED PRACTICE

See Example **1** **List all of the factors of each number.**

1. 12   **2.** 21   **3.** 52   **4.** 75

See Example **2** **Write the prime factorization of each number.**

5. 48   **6.** 20   **7.** 66   **8.** 34

INDEPENDENT PRACTICE

See Example **1** **List all of the factors of each number.**

9. 24   **10.** 37   **11.** 42   **12.** 56

13. 67   **14.** 72   **15.** 85   **16.** 92

See Example **2** **Write the prime factorization of each number.**

17. 49   **18.** 38   **19.** 76   **20.** 60

21. 81   **22.** 132   **23.** 140   **24.** 87

PRACTICE AND PROBLEM SOLVING

Extra Practice
See Extra Practice for
more exercises.

Write each number as a product in two different ways.

25. 34   **26.** 82   **27.** 88   **28.** 50

29. 15   **30.** 78   **31.** 94   **32.** 35

33. Sports Little League Baseball began in 1939 in Pennsylvania. When it first started, there were 45 boys on 3 teams.

  a. If the teams were equally sized, how many boys were on each team?

  b. Name another way the boys could have been divided into equally sized teams. (Remember that a baseball team must have at least 9 players.)

34. Critical Thinking Use the divisibility rules to list the factors of 171. Explain how you determined the factors.

Find the prime factorization of each number.

35. 99   **36.** 249   **37.** 284   **38.** 620

39. 840   **40.** 150   **41.** 740   **42.** 402

43. The prime factorization of 50 is $2 \cdot 5^2$. Without dividing or using a diagram, find the prime factorization of 100.

44. Geometry The area of a rectangle is the product of its length and width. Suppose the area of a rectangle is 24 in². What are the possible whole number measurements of its length and width?

45. Physical Science The speed of sound at sea level at 20 °C is 343 meters per second. Write the prime factorization of 343.

Climate changes, habitat destruction, and overhunting can cause animals and plants to die in large numbers. When the entire population of a species begins to die out, the species is considered endangered.

The graph shows the number of endangered species in each category of animal.

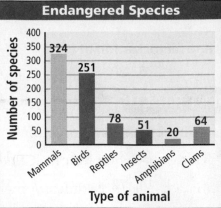

Endangered Species

Number of species vs. Type of animal

- Mammals: 324
- Birds: 251
- Reptiles: 78
- Insects: 51
- Amphibians: 20
- Clams: 64

Most white tigers are found in zoos or sanctuaries for big cats. They are very rarely seen in the wild.

46. How many species of mammals are endangered? Write this number as the product of prime factors.

47. Which category of animal has a prime number of endangered species?

48. How many species of reptiles and amphibians combined are endangered? Write the answer as the product of prime factors.

49. **? What's the Error?** When asked to write the prime factorization of the number of endangered amphibian species, a student wrote 4 × 5. Explain the error and write the correct answer.

50. **✐ Write About It** A team of five scientists is going to study endangered insect species. The scientists want to divide the species evenly among them. Will they be able to do this? Why or why not?

51. **★ Challenge** Add the number of endangered mammal species to the number of endangered bird species. Find the prime factorization of this number.

Test Prep

52. **Multiple Choice** Which expression shows the prime factorization of 50?

   Ⓐ 2×5^2 Ⓑ 2×5^{10} Ⓒ 10^5 Ⓓ 5×10

53. **Gridded Response** What number has a prime factorization of $2 \times 2 \times 3 \times 5$?

CC.6.NS.4 Find the greatest common factor of two whole numbers less than or equal to 100... Use the distributive property to express a sum of two whole numbers 1–100 with a common factor as a multiple of a sum of two whole numbers with no common factor

Factors shared by two or more whole numbers are called common factors. The largest of the common factors is called the **greatest common factor**, or **GCF**.

Factors of 24: 1, 2, 3, 4, 6, 8, 12, 24

Factors of 36: 1, 2, 3, 4, 6, 9, 12, 18, 36

Common factors: 1, 2, 3, 4, 6, (12)

The greatest common factor (GCF) of 24 and 36 is 12.

Example 1 shows three different methods for finding the GCF.

EXAMPLE 1 Finding the GCF

Find the GCF of each set of numbers.

A 16 and 24
Method 1: List the factors.
factors of 16: 1, 2, 4, (8), 16   *List all the factors.*
factors of 24: 1, 2, 3, 4, 6, (8), 12, 24   *Circle the GCF.*

The GCF of 16 and 24 is 8.

B 12, 24, and 32
Method 2: Use prime factorization.
$12 = \boxed{2} \cdot \boxed{2} \cdot 3$ *Write the prime factorization of each number.*
$24 = \boxed{2} \cdot \boxed{2} \cdot 2 \cdot 3$
$32 = \boxed{2} \cdot \boxed{2} \cdot 2 \cdot 2 \cdot 2$ *Find the common prime factors.*

$2 \cdot 2 = 4$ *Find the prime factors common to all the numbers.*

The GCF of 12, 24, and 32 is 4.

C 12, 18, and 60
Method 3: Use a ladder diagram.

2	12	18	60
3	6	9	30
	2	3	10

Begin with a factor that divides into each number. Keep dividing until the three numbers have no common factors.

$2 \cdot 3 = 6$ *Find the product of the numbers you divided by.*

The GCF is 6.

Vocabulary
greatest common factor (GCF)

EXAMPLE 2

PROBLEM SOLVING APPLICATION

Make sense of problems and persevere in solving them.

There are 12 boys and 18 girls in Ms. Ruiz's science class. The students must form lab groups. Each group must have the same number of boys and the same number of girls. What is the greatest number of groups Ms. Ruiz can make if every student must be in a group?

1 Understand the Problem

The **answer** will be the *greatest* number of groups 12 boys and 18 girls can form so that each group has the same number of boys, and each group has the same number of girls.

2 Make a Plan

You can make an organized list of the possible groups.

3 Solve

There are more girls than boys in the class, so there will be more girls than boys in each group.

Helpful Hint

If more students are put in each group, there will be fewer groups. You need the most groups possible, so put the smallest possible number of students in each team. Start with 1 boy in each group.

Boys	Girls	Groups
1	2	(B GG) (B GG) (B GG) (B GG) (B GG) (B GG) (B GG) (B GG) (B GG) 9 boys, 18 girls: There are 3 boys not in groups. ✗
2	3	(BB GGG) (BB GGG) (BB GGG) (BB GGG) (BB GGG) (BB GGG) 12 boys, 18 girls: Every student is in a group. ✓

The greatest number of groups is 6.

4 Look Back

The number of groups will be a common factor of the number of boys and the number of girls. To form the largest number of groups, find the GCF of 12 and 18.

factors of 12: 1, 2, 3, 4, ⑥, 12   factors of 18: 1, 2, 3, ⑥, 9, 18

The GCF of 12 and 18 is 6.

Think and Discuss

1. Explain what the GCF of two prime numbers is.

2. Tell what the least common factor of a group of numbers would be.

Somos Images LLC/Alamy

GUIDED PRACTICE

See Example 1 **Find the GCF of each set of numbers.**

1. 18 and 27   **2.** 32 and 72   **3.** 21, 42, and 56

4. 15, 30, and 60   **5.** 18, 24, and 36   **6.** 9, 36, and 81

See Example 2 **7.** Kim is making flower arrangements. She has 16 red roses and 20 pink roses. Each arrangement must have the same number of red roses and the same number of pink roses. What is the greatest number of arrangements Kim can make if every flower is used?

INDEPENDENT PRACTICE

See Example 1 **Find the GCF of each set of numbers.**

8. 10 and 35   **9.** 28 and 70   **10.** 36 and 72

11. 26, 48, and 62   **12.** 16, 40, and 88   **13.** 12, 60, and 68

14. 30, 45, and 75   **15.** 24, 48, and 84   **16.** 16, 48, and 72

See Example 2 **17.** The local recreation center held a scavenger hunt. There were 15 boys and 9 girls at the event. The group was divided into the greatest number of teams possible with the same number of boys on each team and the same number of girls on each team. How many teams were made if each person was on a team?

18. Ms. Kline makes balloon arrangements. She has 32 blue balloons, 24 yellow balloons, and 16 white balloons. Each arrangement must have the same number of each color. What is the greatest number of arrangements that Ms. Kline can make if every balloon is used?

PRACTICE AND PROBLEM SOLVING

Extra Practice
See Extra Practice for more exercises.

Write the GCF of each set of numbers.

19. 60 and 84   **20.** 14 and 17   **21.** 10, 35, and 110

22. 21 and 306   **23.** 630 and 712   **24.** 16, 24, and 40

25. 75, 225, and 150   **26.** 42, 112, and 105   **27.** 12, 16, 20, and 24

28. Jared has 12 jars of grape jam, 16 jars of strawberry jam, and 24 jars of raspberry jam. He wants to place the jam into the greatest possible number of boxes so that each box has the same number of jars of each kind of jam. How many boxes does he need?

29. Pam is making fruit baskets. She has 30 apples, 24 bananas, and 12 oranges. What is the greatest number of baskets she can make if each type of fruit is distributed equally among the baskets?

30. Critical Thinking Write a set of three different numbers that have a GCF of 9. Explain your method.

Write the GCF of each set of numbers.

31. 16, 24, 30, and 42   **32.** 25, 90, 45, and 100   **33.** 27, 90, 135, and 72

34. $2 \times 2 \times 3$ and 2×2 **35.** $2 \times 3^2 \times 7$ and $2^2 \times 3$ **36.** $3^2 \times 7$ and $2 \times 3 \times 5^2$

37. Mr. Chu is planting 4 types of flowers in his garden. He wants each row to contain the same number of each type of flower. What is the greatest number of rows Mr. Chu can plant if every bulb is used?

Flower Types

38. In a parade, one school band will march directly behind another school band. All rows must have the same number of students. The first band has 36 students, and the second band has 60 students. What is the greatest number of students who can be in each row?

39. **Social Studies** Branches of the U.S. Mint in Denver and Philadelphia make all U.S. coins for circulation. A tiny *D* or *P* on the coin tells you where the coin was minted. Suppose you have 32 *D* quarters and 36 *P* quarters. What is the greatest number of groups you can make with the same number of *D* quarters in each group and the same number of *P* quarters in each group so that every quarter is placed in a group?

40. **What's the Error?** Mike says if $12 = 2^2 \cdot 3$ and $24 = 2^3 \cdot 3$, then the GCF of 12 and 24 is $2 \cdot 3$, or 6. Explain Mike's error.

41. **Write About It** What method do you like best for finding the GCF? Why?

42. **Challenge** The GCF of three numbers is 9. The sum of the numbers is 90. Find the three numbers.

Test Prep

43. **Multiple Choice** For which set of numbers is 16 the GCF?

Ⓐ 16, 32, 48   Ⓑ 12, 24, 32   Ⓒ 24, 48, 60   Ⓓ 8, 80, 100

44. **Multiple Choice** Mrs. Lyndon is making baskets of muffins. She has 48 lemon muffins, 120 blueberry muffins, and 112 banana nut muffins. How many baskets can Mrs. Lyndon make with each type of muffin distributed evenly?

Ⓕ 4   Ⓖ 6   Ⓗ 8   Ⓙ 12

Technology LAB

Greatest Common Factor

Use with Greatest Common Factor

Use appropriate tools strategically.
CC.6.NS.4 Find the greatest common factor of two whole numbers less than or equal to 100…

You can use a graphing calculator to quickly find the greatest common factor (GCF) of two or more numbers. A calculator is particularly useful when you need to find the GCF of large numbers.

Activity

Find the GCF of 504 and 3,150.

The GCF is also known as the *greatest common divisor,* or GCD. The GCD function is found on the **MATH** menu.

To find the GCD on a graphing calculator, press **MATH**. Press ▶ to highlight **NUM**, and then use ▼ to scroll down and highlight **9:**.

Press **ENTER** 504 **,** 3150 **)** **ENTER** .

The greatest common factor of 504 and 3,150 is 126.

Think and Discuss

1. Suppose your calculator will not allow you to enter three numbers into the GCD function. How could you still use your calculator to find the GCF of the three following numbers: 4,896; 2,364; and 656? Explain your strategy and why it works.

2. Would you use your calculator to find the GCF of 6 and 18? Why or why not?

Try This

Find the GCF of each set of numbers.

1. 14, 48   2. 18, 54   3. 99, 121   4. 144, 196

5. 200, 136   6. 246, 137   7. 72, 860   8. 55, 141, 91

COMMON CORE

CC.6.EE.4 Identify when two expressions are equivalent (i.e., when the two expressions name the same number regardless of which value is substituted into them)

Vocabulary

term

coefficient

equivalent expressions

A rhino weighed 140 pounds at birth and gained about 4 pounds each day. The expression $140 + 4x$ represents the rhino's weight after x days.

The **terms** of an expression are the parts of the expression that are added or subtracted. The terms of the expression $140 + 4x$ are 140 and $4x$.

Image Source/Alamy

In the term $4x$, 4 is called the *coefficient*. A **coefficient** is a number that is multiplied by a variable in an algebraic expression.

You can use the greatest common factor (GCF) and the Distributive Property to factor numerical expressions.

EXAMPLE 1   **Factoring Numerical Expressions**

Factor the sum of terms as a product of the GCF and a sum.

$20 + 56$

$20 + 56$	*The terms are 20 and 56.*
$2 \cdot 2 \cdot 5 + 2 \cdot 2 \cdot 2 \cdot 7$	*The GCF of the terms is 2 · 2.*
$4 \cdot 5 + 4 \cdot 14$	*Rewrite each term as a product with the GCF.*
$4(5 + 14)$	*Apply the Distributive Property.*

Remember!

The greatest common factor (GCF) is the largest common factor of two or more given numbers.

You can also use the GCF and the Distributive Property to factor algebraic expressions.

EXAMPLE 2   **Factoring Algebraic Expressions**

Factor the sum of terms as a product of the GCF and a sum.

$15x + 18$

$15x + 18$	*The terms are 15x and 18.*
$3 \cdot 5 \cdot x + 2 \cdot 3 \cdot 3$	*The GCF of the terms is 3.*
$3 \cdot 5x + 3 \cdot 6$	*Rewrite each term as a product with the GCF.*
$3(5x + 6)$	*Apply the Distributive Property.*

Equivalent expressions are expressions that have the same value all values of the variables. The expressions $15x + 18$ and $3(5x + 6)$ a equivalent expressions since $15x + 18 = 3(5x + 6)$ for every value of x.

You can use factors and properties of operations to generate many equivalent expressions. All of the expressions shown below are equivalent.

$$52 - 12$$
$$= 4 \cdot 13 - 4 \cdot 3$$
$$= 4(13 - 3)$$
$$= 4 \cdot 10$$
$$= 40$$

$$52 - 12$$
$$= 2 \cdot 26 - 2 \cdot 6$$
$$= 2(26 - 6)$$
$$= 2 \cdot 20$$
$$= 40$$

$$52 - 12$$
$$= 26 \cdot 2 - 6 \cdot 2$$
$$= (26 - 6)2$$
$$= 20 \cdot 2$$
$$= 40$$

EXAMPLE 3 **Writing Equivalent Expressions**

Write four equivalent expressions for each given expression.

$8 + 24$

A | $8 + 24$ | *The terms are 8 and 24.*
| $8 \cdot 1 + 8 \cdot 3$ | *Rewrite each term as a product with the GCF.*
| $8(1 + 3)$ | *Apply the Distributive Property.*
| $8(3 + 1)$ | *Apply the Commutative Property.*
| $2^3(3 + 1)$ | *Write 8 as 2^3.*

Helpful Hint

There are many other ways to write equivalent expressions for each of the expressions in Example 3.

$40y - 30y$

B | $40y - 30y$ | *The terms are 40y and 30y.*
| $20 \cdot 2y - 15 \cdot 2y$ | *Rewrite each term as a product with the common factor 2y.*
| $(20 - 15)\, 2y$ | *Apply the Distributive Property.*
| $5 \cdot 2y$ | *Subtract.*
| $10y$ | *Multiply.*

$3(1 + 27m)$

C | $3(1 + 27m)$
| $3 \cdot 1 + 3 \cdot 27m$ | *Apply the Distributive Property.*
| $3 + 81m$ | *Multiply.*
| $81m + 3$ | *Apply the Commutative Property.*
| $3^4 m + 3$ | *Write the coefficient of 81m as 3^4.*

Think and Discuss

1. Describe different ways to write an equivalent expression.

2. Explain why the expressions $5x + 1$ and $5(x + 1)$ are *not* equivalent.

Exercises

GUIDED PRACTICE

See Example **1**   Factor the sum of terms as a product of the GCF and a sum.

1. $16 + 12$ **2.** $21 + 9$ **3.** $15 + 20$

4. $14 + 18$ **5.** $70 + 42$ **6.** $22 + 99$

See Example **2**   **7.** $6y + 8$ **8.** $25 + 15x$ **9.** $36n + 24$

10. $100p + 70$ **11.** $32w + 8$ **12.** $3 + 18x$

See Example **3**   Write four equivalent expressions for each given expression.

13. $16 + 30$ **14.** $34 - 4$ **15.** $18x - 12x$

16. $20m - 10m$ **17.** $8(z + 1)$ **18.** $4(2 + 4c)$

INDEPENDENT PRACTICE

See Example **1**   Factor the sum of terms as a product of the GCF and a sum.

19. $48 + 32$ **20.** $49 + 77$ **21.** $60 + 42$

22. $72 + 60$ **23.** $32 + 34$ **24.** $64 + 100$

See Example **2**   **25.** $7x + 28$ **26.** $12 + 30k$ **27.** $52v + 39$

28. $90 + 54s$ **29.** $48c + 64$ **30.** $72m + 69$

See Example **3**   Write four equivalent expressions for each given expression.

31. $40 - 12$ **32.** $2 \cdot 4 + 2 \cdot 5$ **33.** $9x - 7x$

34. $15y - 15y$ **35.** $3(2p + 2)$ **36.** $6 \cdot 4 + 6 \cdot w$

PRACTICE AND PROBLEM SOLVING

Extra Practice
See Extra Practice for more exercises.

Determine whether the two expressions in each pair are equivalent.

37. $7(x + 2); 7x + 14$ **38.** $9(n + 1); 9n + 1$ **39.** $20v + 15; 5(4v + 3)$

40. $2^2(1 + x); 4 + 4x$ **41.** $18 - 3y; 3y - 18$ **42.** $5 \cdot 2 + 4y; 5 \cdot 6y$

43. In Mr. Chen's science class, there are g girls and 15 boys. Write two equivalent expressions for the total number of students in the class.

44. Andrea bought n notebooks for \$2 each. She also bought a stapler for \$6. Write three equivalent expressions for the total amount Andrea spent.

45. Recreation The table shows the cost of renting a kayak.
   a. Write two different expressions that can be used to find the cost of renting a kayak for h hours.
   b. How much does it cost to rent a kayak for 6 hours?

Clear Lake Kayak Rentals				
Number of Hours	1	2	3	4
Total Cost ($)	15	20	25	30

Write an expression that matches the given description.

46. The expression has three terms.

47. The expression is a difference of two terms. One of the terms has a coefficient of 6.

48. The expression is a product of a whole number and a sum. The sum has two terms.

49. The expression is a product. Each factor of the product is a whole number.

Architecture

Octagonal houses were popular in the 1850s. They were considered easier to heat than rectangular homes.

50. Architecture Octagon House in Watertown, Wisconsin, has 8 sides of equal length.
a. Let *s* represent the length of one side of the house. Write two different expressions that represent the total distance around the house.

b. Each side of Octagon House is 21 feet long. Use one of your expressions to find the total distance around the house.

c. Explain how you decided which expression to use in part **b**.

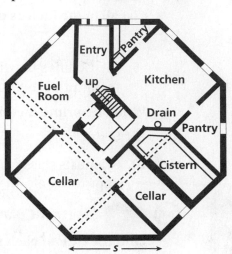

51. What's the Error? A student was asked to write two equivalent expressions for $26 - 4$. Explain the error the student made. What are the correct expressions?

$$26 - 4$$
$$= 2(13 - 4)$$
$$= 2 \cdot 9$$

52. Write About It Write a sum of two terms and then explain the steps for writing it as a product of the GCF and a sum.

53. Challenge Write $24xy - 30y$ as a product of the GCF and a difference.

Test Prep

54. Multiple Choice Which expression is equivalent to $9x + 24$?

Ⓐ $3(3x + 24)$ Ⓑ $3(3x + 8)$ Ⓒ $9(x + 24)$ Ⓓ $9(x + 3)$

55. Short Response During a basketball game, Kyra scored 6 points on free throws. She also scored 2 points for each field goal she made. Kyra made *f* field goals during the game. Write three equivalent expressions for the total number of points Kyra scored.

Ready To Go On?

Learn It Online
Resources Online

Quiz for Lessons 1 Through 3

 1 Factors and Prime Factorization

List all of the factors of each number.

1. 26   **2.** 32   **3.** 39   **4.** 84

5. Mr. Collins's bowling league has 48 members. If the league splits into teams of 12 members each, how many equally sized teams will there be?

Write the prime factorization of each number.

6. 96   **7.** 50   **8.** 104   **9.** 63

10. Scientists classify many sunflowers in the genus *Helianthus.* There are approximately 67 species of *Helianthus.* Write the prime factorization of 67.

2 Greatest Common Factor

Find the GCF of each set of numbers.

11. 16 and 36   **12.** 22 and 88   **13.** 65 and 91   **14.** 20, 55, and 85

15. There are 36 sixth-graders and 40 seventh-graders. What is the greatest number of teams that the students can form if each team has the same number of sixth-graders and the same number of seventh-graders and every student must be on a team?

16. There are 14 girls and 21 boys in Mrs. Sutter's gym class. To play a certain game, the students must form teams. Each team must have the same number of girls and the same number of boys. What is the greatest number of teams Mrs. Sutter can make if every student is on a team?

17. Mrs. Young, an art teacher, is organizing the art supplies. She has 76 red markers, 52 blue markers, and 80 black markers. She wants to divide the markers into boxes with the same number of red, the same number of blue, and the same number of black markers in each box. What is the greatest number of boxes she can have if every marker is placed in a box?

3 Equivalent Expressions

Factor the sum of terms as a product of the GCF and a sum.

18. $28 + 35$ **19.** $36 + 27$ **20.** $4x + 22$ **21.** $28 + 12k$

Write four equivalent expressions for each expression.

22. $32 + 48$ **23.** $36 - 9$ **24.** $5(25z + 1)$ **25.** $100k - 25k$

Focus on Problem Solving

Understand

Understand the Problem

• Interpret unfamiliar words

You must understand the words in a problem in order to solve it. If there is a word you do not know, try to use context clues to figure out its meaning. Suppose there is a problem about red, green, blue, and chartreuse fabric. You may not know the word *chartreuse*, but you can guess that it is probably a color. To make the problem easier to understand, you could replace *chartreuse* with the name of a familiar color, like *white*.

In some problems, the name of a person, place, or thing might be difficult to pronounce, such as *Mr. Joubert*. When you see a proper noun that you do not know how to pronounce, you can use another proper noun or a pronoun in its place. You could replace *Mr. Joubert* with *he*. You could replace *Koenisburg Street* with *K Street*.

Copy each problem. Underline any words that you do not understand. Then replace each word with a more familiar word.

1 Grace is making flower bouquets. She has 18 chrysanthemums and 42 roses. She wants to arrange them in groups that each have the same number of chrysanthemums and the same number of roses. What is the fewest number of flowers that Grace can have in each group? How many chrysanthemums and how many roses will be in each group?

2 Most marbles are made from glass. The glass is liquefied in a furnace and poured. It is then cut into cylinders that are rounded off and cooled. Suppose 1,200 cooled marbles are put into packages of 8. How many packages could be made? Would there be any marbles left over?

3 In ancient times, many civilizations used calendars that divided the year into months of 30 days. A year has 365 days. How many whole months were in these ancient calendars? Were there any days left over? If so, how many?

4 Mrs. LeFeubre is tiling her garden walkway. It is a rectangle that is 4 feet wide and 20 feet long. Mrs. LeFeubre wants to use square tiles, and she does not want to have to cut any tiles. What is the size of the largest square tile that Mrs. LeFeubre can use?

Hands-on LAB

Explore Decimals and Fractions

Use with Decimals and Fractions

KEY

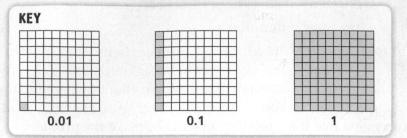

| 0.01 | 0.1 | 1 |

MATHEMATICAL PRACTICES **Use appropriate tools strategically.**

You can use decimal grids to show the relationship between fractions and decimals.

Activity

Write the number represented on each grid as a fraction and as a decimal.

 1

Seven hundredths squares are shaded → 0.07

How many squares are shaded? $\dfrac{7}{100}$ ← numerator

How many squares are in the whole?   ← denominator

$0.07 = \dfrac{7}{100}$

 2

Three tenths columns are shaded →   0.3

How many complete columns are shaded? $\dfrac{3}{10}$

How many columns are in the whole?

$0.3 = \dfrac{3}{10}$

Think and Discuss

1. Is 0.09 the same as $\dfrac{9}{10}$? Use decimal grids to support your answer.

Try This

Use decimal grids to represent each number.

1. 0.8   **2.** $\dfrac{37}{100}$ **3.** 0.53   **4.** $\dfrac{1}{10}$ **5.** $\dfrac{67}{100}$

6. For 1–5, write each decimal as a fraction and each fraction as a decimal.

Decimals and Fractions

Decimals and fractions can often be used to represent the same number.

For example, a baseball player's or baseball team's batting average can be represented as a fraction:

$$\frac{\text{number of hits}}{\text{number of times at bat}}$$

The Oregon State University baseball team won the College World Series in 2006 and 2007.

In 2007, the Oregon State University baseball team won its second College World Series title. During that season, the team had 659 hits and 2,297 at bats. The team's batting average was $\frac{659}{2,297}$.

$$659 \div 2,297 = 0.2868959512\ldots$$

The 2007 batting average for the Oregon State baseball team is reported as .287.

Interactivities Online ▶

Decimals can be written as fractions or mixed numbers. A number that contains both a whole number greater than 0 and a fraction, such as $1\frac{3}{4}$, is called a **mixed number**.

Vocabulary

mixed number

terminating decimal

repeating decimal

Mixed numbers

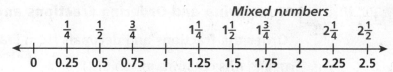

$\frac{1}{4}$	$\frac{1}{2}$	$\frac{3}{4}$	$1\frac{1}{4}$	$1\frac{1}{2}$	$1\frac{3}{4}$	$2\frac{1}{4}$	$2\frac{1}{2}$	

0   0.25   0.5   0.75   1   1.25   1.5   1.75   2   2.25   2.5

EXAMPLE 1   Writing Decimals as Fractions or Mixed Numbers

Write each decimal as a fraction or mixed number.

A 0.23

0.23   *Identify the place value of the digit farthest to the right.*

$\frac{23}{100}$ *The 3 is in the **hundred**ths place, so use **100** as the denominator.*

B 1.7

1.7   *Identify the place value of the digit farthest to the right.*

$1\frac{7}{10}$ *Write the whole number, 1. The 7 is in the **ten**ths place, so use **10** as the denominator.*

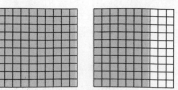

Remember!

Place Value

Ones	Tenths	Hundredths	Thousandths

Dcug Pensinger/Getty Images

EXAMPLE 2 **Writing Fractions as Decimals**

Write each fraction or mixed number as a decimal.

A $\frac{3}{4}$

$$
\begin{array}{r}
0.75 \\
4\overline{)3.00} \\
-28 \\
\hline
20 \\
-20 \\
\hline
0
\end{array}
$$

Divide 3 by 4.
Add zeros after the decimal point.
The remainder is 0.

$\frac{3}{4} = 0.75$

B $5\frac{2}{3}$

$$
\begin{array}{r}
0.666 \\
3\overline{)2.000} \\
-18 \\
\hline
20 \\
-18 \\
\hline
20 \\
-18 \\
\hline
2
\end{array}
$$

Divide 2 by 3.
Add zeros after the decimal point.
The 6 repeats in the quotient.

$5\frac{2}{3} = 5.666... = 5.\overline{6}$

Writing Math

To write a repeating decimal, you can show three dots or draw a bar over the repeating part: $0.666... = 0.\overline{6}$

A **terminating decimal**, such as 0.75, has a finite number of decimal places. A **repeating decimal**, such as 0.666..., has a block of one or more digits that repeat without end.

Common Fractions and Equivalent Decimals								
$\frac{1}{5}$	$\frac{1}{4}$	$\frac{1}{3}$	$\frac{2}{5}$	$\frac{1}{2}$	$\frac{3}{5}$	$\frac{2}{3}$	$\frac{3}{4}$	$\frac{4}{5}$
0.2	0.25	$0.\overline{3}$	0.4	0.5	0.6	$0.\overline{6}$	0.75	0.8

EXAMPLE 3 **Comparing and Ordering Fractions and Decimals**

Order the fractions and decimals from least to greatest.

$0.5, \frac{1}{5}, 0.37$

First rewrite the fraction as a decimal. $\frac{1}{5} = 0.2$
Order the three decimals.

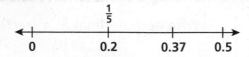

The numbers in order from least to greatest are $\frac{1}{5}$, 0.37, and 0.5.

MATHEMATICAL PRACTICES

Think and Discuss

1. Tell how reading the decimal 6.9 as "six and nine tenths" helps you to write 6.9 as a mixed number.

2. Look at the decimal 0.121122111222.... If the pattern continues, is this a repeating decimal? Why or why not?

Video **Lesson Tutorials Online** my.hrw.com

Exercises

GUIDED PRACTICE

See Example 1 Write each decimal as a fraction or mixed number.

1. 0.15   **2.** 1.25   **3.** 0.43   **4.** 2.6

See Example 2 Write each fraction or mixed number as a decimal.

5. $\frac{2}{5}$ **6.** $2\frac{7}{8}$ **7.** $\frac{1}{8}$ **8.** $4\frac{1}{10}$

See Example 3 Order the fractions and decimals from least to greatest.

9. $\frac{2}{3}$, 0.78, 0.21   **10.** $\frac{5}{16}$, 0.67, $\frac{1}{6}$ **11.** 0.52, $\frac{1}{9}$, 0.3

INDEPENDENT PRACTICE

See Example 1 Write each decimal as a fraction or mixed number.

12. 0.31   **13.** 5.71   **14.** 0.13   **15.** 3.23

16. 0.5   **17.** 2.7   **18.** 0.19   **19.** 6.3

See Example 2 Write each fraction or mixed number as a decimal.

20. $\frac{1}{9}$ **21.** $1\frac{3}{5}$ **22.** $\frac{8}{9}$ **23.** $3\frac{11}{40}$

24. $2\frac{5}{6}$ **25.** $\frac{3}{8}$ **26.** $4\frac{4}{5}$ **27.** $\frac{5}{8}$

See Example 3 Order the fractions and decimals from least to greatest.

28. 0.49, 0.82, $\frac{1}{2}$ **29.** $\frac{3}{8}$, 0.29, $\frac{1}{9}$ **30.** 0.94, $\frac{4}{5}$, 0.6

31. 0.11, $\frac{1}{10}$, 0.13   **32.** $\frac{2}{3}$, 0.42, $\frac{2}{5}$ **33.** $\frac{3}{7}$, 0.76, 0.31

PRACTICE AND PROBLEM SOLVING

Extra Practice
See Extra Practice for
more exercises.

Write each decimal in expanded form and use a whole number or fraction for each place value.

34. 0.81   **35.** 92.3   **36.** 13.29   **37.** 107.17

Write each fraction as a decimal. Tell whether the decimal terminates or repeats.

38. $\frac{7}{9}$ **39.** $\frac{1}{6}$ **40.** $\frac{17}{20}$ **41.** $\frac{5}{12}$ **42.** $\frac{7}{8}$

43. $\frac{4}{5}$ **44.** $\frac{9}{5}$ **45.** $\frac{15}{18}$ **46.** $\frac{7}{3}$ **47.** $\frac{11}{12}$

Compare. Write < , >, or =.

48. 0.75 ▦ $\frac{3}{4}$ **49.** $\frac{5}{8}$ ▦ 0.5   **50.** 0.78 ▦ $\frac{7}{9}$ **51.** $\frac{1}{3}$ ▦ 0.35

52. $\frac{2}{5}$ ▦ 0.4   **53.** 0.75 ▦ $\frac{4}{5}$ **54.** $\frac{3}{8}$ ▦ 0.25   **55.** 0.8 ▦ $\frac{5}{6}$

56. Multi-Step Peter walked $1\frac{3}{5}$ miles on a treadmill. Sally walked 1.5 miles on the treadmill. Who walked farther? Explain.

Order the mixed numbers and decimals from greatest to least.

57. $4.48, 3.92, 4\frac{1}{2}$ **58.** $10\frac{5}{9}, 10.5, 10\frac{1}{5}$ **59.** $125.205, 125.25, 125\frac{1}{5}$

Sports The table shows batting averages for two baseball seasons. Use the table for Exercises 60–62.

Player	Season 1	Season 2
Pedro	0.360	$\frac{3}{10}$
Jill	0.380	$\frac{3}{8}$
Lamar	0.290	$\frac{1}{3}$
Britney	0.190	$\frac{3}{20}$

60. Which players had higher batting averages in season 1 than they had in season 2?

61. Who had the highest batting average in either season?

62. **Multi-Step** Whose batting average changed the most between season 1 and season 2?

63. **Life Science** Most people with color deficiency (often called color blindness) have trouble distinguishing shades of red and green. About 0.05 of men in the world have color deficiency. What fraction of men have color deficiency?

64. **What's the Error?** A student found the decimal equivalent of $\frac{7}{18}$ to be $0.\overline{38}$. Explain the error. What is the correct answer?

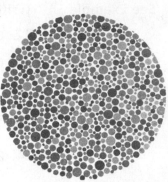

People with normal color vision will see "7" in this color-blindness test.

65. **Write About It** The decimal for $\frac{1}{25}$ is 0.04, and the decimal for $\frac{2}{25}$ is 0.08. Without dividing, find the decimal for $\frac{6}{25}$. Explain how you found your answer.

66. **Challenge** Write $\frac{1}{999}$ as a decimal.

Test Prep

67. Multiple Choice Which numbers are listed from least to greatest?

Ⓐ $0.65, 0.81, \frac{4}{5}$ Ⓑ $0.81, 0.65, \frac{4}{5}$ Ⓒ $\frac{4}{5}, 0.81, 0.65$ Ⓓ $0.65, \frac{4}{5}, 0.81$

68. Gridded Response Write $5\frac{1}{8}$ as a decimal.

Model Equivalent Fractions

Use with Equivalent Fractions

 MATHEMATICAL PRACTICES   Use appropriate tools strategically.

 **Learn It Online**
Lab Resources Online

KEY

 = 1   = $\frac{1}{2}$ = $\frac{1}{4}$ = $\frac{1}{6}$ = $\frac{1}{12}$

Pattern blocks can be used to model equivalent fractions. To find a fraction that is equivalent to $\frac{1}{2}$, first choose the pattern block that represents $\frac{1}{2}$. Then find all the pieces of one color that will fit evenly on the $\frac{1}{2}$ block. Count these pieces to find the equivalent fraction. You may be able to find more than one equivalent fraction.

$\frac{1}{2}$ = $\frac{2}{4}$ = $\frac{3}{6}$ = $\frac{6}{12}$

Activity

Use pattern blocks to find an equivalent fraction for $\frac{8}{12}$.

   *First show $\frac{8}{12}$.*   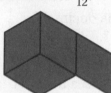   *You can cover $\frac{8}{12}$ with four of the $\frac{1}{6}$ pieces.*

$\frac{8}{12} = \frac{4}{6}$

Think and Discuss

1. Can you find a combination of pattern blocks for $\frac{1}{3}$? Find an equivalent fraction for $\frac{1}{3}$.

2. Are $\frac{9}{12}$ and $\frac{3}{6}$ equivalent? Use pattern blocks to support your answer.

Try This

Write the fraction that is modeled. Then find an equivalent fraction.

1.

2.

Hands-On Lab   **167**

Rulers often have marks for inches, $\frac{1}{2}$, $\frac{1}{4}$, and $\frac{1}{8}$ inches.

Notice that $\frac{1}{2}$ in., $\frac{2}{4}$ in., and $\frac{4}{8}$ in. all name the same length. Fractions that represent the same value are **equivalent fractions**. So $\frac{1}{2}$, $\frac{2}{4}$, and $\frac{4}{8}$ are equivalent fractions.

Vocabulary

equivalent fractions

simplest form

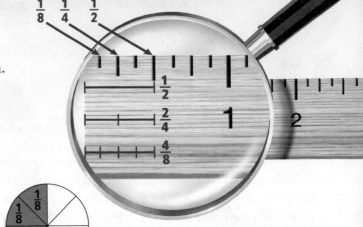

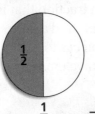

$$\frac{1}{2} = \frac{2}{4} = \frac{4}{8}$$

EXAMPLE 1 Finding Equivalent Fractions

Interactivities Online ▶

Find two equivalent fractions for $\frac{6}{8}$.

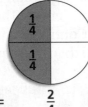

$$\frac{6}{8} = \frac{9}{12} = \frac{3}{4}$$

The same area is shaded when the rectangle is divided into 8 parts, 12 parts, and 4 parts.

So $\frac{6}{8}$, $\frac{9}{12}$, and $\frac{3}{4}$ are all equivalent fractions.

EXAMPLE 2 Multiplying and Dividing to Find Equivalent Fractions

Find the missing number that makes the fractions equivalent.

Ⓐ $\frac{2}{3} = \frac{\blacksquare}{18}$

$\frac{2 \cdot 6}{3 \cdot 6} = \frac{12}{18}$ *In the denominator, 3 is multiplied by 6 to get 18. Multiply the numerator, 2, by the same number, 6.*

So $\frac{2}{3}$ is equivalent to $\frac{12}{18}$.

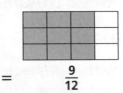 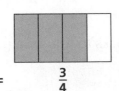

$$\frac{2}{3} = \frac{12}{18}$$

Video **Lesson Tutorials Online** my.hrw.com

Find the missing number that makes the fractions equivalent.

B $\dfrac{70}{100} = \dfrac{7}{\blacksquare}$

$\dfrac{70 \div 10}{100 \div 10} = \dfrac{7}{10}$ *In the numerator, 70 is divided by 10 to get 7. Divide the denominator by the same number, 10.*

So $\dfrac{70}{100}$ is equivalent to $\dfrac{7}{10}$.

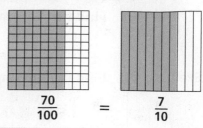

$\dfrac{70}{100} = \dfrac{7}{10}$

Every fraction has one equivalent fraction that is called the simplest form of the fraction. A fraction is in **simplest form** when the GCF of the numerator and the denominator is 1.

Example 3 shows two methods for writing a fraction in simplest form.

EXAMPLE 3 **Writing Fractions in Simplest Form**

Write each fraction in simplest form.

A $\dfrac{18}{24}$

The GCF of 18 and 24 is 6, so $\dfrac{18}{24}$ is not in simplest form.

Method 1: Use the GCF.

$\dfrac{18 \div 6}{24 \div 6} = \dfrac{3}{4}$ *Divide 18 and 24 by their GCF, 6.*

Method 2: Use prime factorization.

$\dfrac{18}{24} = \dfrac{2 \cdot 3 \cdot 3}{2 \cdot 2 \cdot 2 \cdot 3} = \dfrac{3}{4}$ *Write the prime factors of 18 and 24. Simplify.*

So $\dfrac{18}{24}$ written in simplest form is $\dfrac{3}{4}$.

B $\dfrac{8}{9}$

The GCF of 8 and 9 is 1, so $\dfrac{8}{9}$ is already in simplest form.

> **Helpful Hint**
>
> Method 2 is useful when you know that the numerator and denominator have common factors, but you are not sure what the GCF is.

Think and Discuss

1. Explain whether a fraction is equivalent to itself.

2. Tell which of the following fractions are in simplest form: $\dfrac{9}{21}$, $\dfrac{20}{25}$, and $\dfrac{5}{13}$. Explain.

3. Explain how you know that $\dfrac{7}{16}$ is in simplest form.

Exercises

Learn It Online
Homework Help Online
Exercises 1–36, 37, 39, 41, 43, 47

GUIDED PRACTICE

See Example **1**   Find two equivalent fractions for each fraction.

1. $\frac{4}{6}$ **2.** $\frac{3}{12}$ **3.** $\frac{3}{6}$ **4.** $\frac{6}{16}$

See Example **2**   Find the missing numbers that make the fractions equivalent.

5. $\frac{2}{5} = \frac{10}{\blacksquare}$ **6.** $\frac{7}{21} = \frac{1}{\blacksquare}$ **7.** $\frac{3}{4} = \frac{\blacksquare}{28}$ **8.** $\frac{8}{12} = \frac{\blacksquare}{3}$

See Example **3**   Write each fraction in simplest form.

9. $\frac{2}{10}$ **10.** $\frac{6}{18}$ **11.** $\frac{4}{16}$ **12.** $\frac{9}{15}$

INDEPENDENT PRACTICE

See Example **1**   Find two equivalent fractions for each fraction.

13. $\frac{3}{9}$ **14.** $\frac{2}{10}$ **15.** $\frac{3}{21}$ **16.** $\frac{3}{18}$

17. $\frac{12}{15}$ **18.** $\frac{4}{10}$ **19.** $\frac{10}{12}$ **20.** $\frac{6}{10}$

See Example **2**   Find the missing numbers that make the fractions equivalent.

21. $\frac{3}{7} = \frac{\blacksquare}{35}$ **22.** $\frac{6}{48} = \frac{1}{\blacksquare}$ **23.** $\frac{2}{5} = \frac{28}{\blacksquare}$ **24.** $\frac{12}{18} = \frac{\blacksquare}{3}$

25. $\frac{2}{7} = \frac{\blacksquare}{21}$ **26.** $\frac{8}{32} = \frac{\blacksquare}{4}$ **27.** $\frac{2}{7} = \frac{40}{\blacksquare}$ **28.** $\frac{3}{5} = \frac{21}{\blacksquare}$

See Example **3**   Write each fraction in simplest form.

29. $\frac{2}{8}$ **30.** $\frac{10}{15}$ **31.** $\frac{6}{30}$ **32.** $\frac{6}{14}$

33. $\frac{12}{16}$ **34.** $\frac{4}{28}$ **35.** $\frac{4}{8}$ **36.** $\frac{10}{35}$

PRACTICE AND PROBLEM SOLVING

Extra Practice

See Extra Practice for
more exercises.

Write the equivalent fractions represented by each picture.

37. 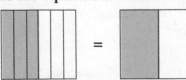   **38.**

39. 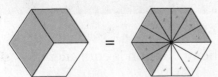   **40.**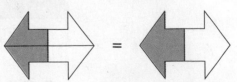

Write each fraction in simplest form. Show two ways to simplify.

41. $\frac{10}{40}$ **42.** $\frac{4}{52}$ **43.** $\frac{28}{70}$ **44.** $\frac{112}{220}$

The Old City Market is a public market in Charleston, South Carolina. Local artists, craftspeople, and vendors display and sell their goods in open-sided booths.

45. You can buy food, such as southern sesame seed cookies, at $\frac{1}{10}$ of the booths. Write two equivalent fractions for $\frac{1}{10}$.

46. Handwoven sweetgrass baskets are a regional specialty. About 8 out of every 10 baskets sold are woven at the market. Write a fraction for "8 out of 10." Then write this fraction in simplest form.

47. Suppose the circle graph shows the number of each kind of craft booth at the Old City Market. For each type of booth, tell what fraction it represents of the total number of craft booths. Write these fractions in simplest form.

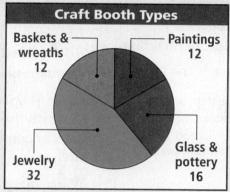

Craft Booth Types

Baskets & wreaths 12 — Paintings 12 — Jewelry 32 — Glass & pottery 16

48. Customers can buy packages of dried rice and black-eyed peas, which can be made into black-eyed pea soup. One recipe for black-eyed pea soup calls for $\frac{1}{2}$ tsp of basil. How could you measure the basil if you had only a $\frac{1}{4}$ tsp measuring spoon? What if you had only a $\frac{1}{8}$ tsp measuring spoon?

49. **Write About It** The recipe for soup also calls for $\frac{1}{4}$ tsp of pepper. How many fractions are equivalent to $\frac{1}{4}$? Explain.

50. **Challenge** Silver jewelry is a popular item at the market. Suppose there are 28 bracelets at one jeweler's booth and that $\frac{3}{7}$ of these bracelets have red stones. How many bracelets have red stones?

Test Prep

51. Multiple Choice Which fraction is NOT equivalent to $\frac{1}{6}$?

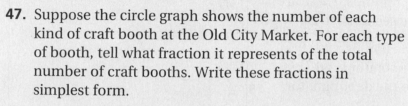

Ⓐ $\frac{2}{12}$ Ⓑ $\frac{6}{1}$ Ⓒ $\frac{3}{18}$ Ⓓ $\frac{6}{36}$

52. Multiple Choice Which denominator makes the fractions $\frac{7}{28}$ and $\frac{21}{\blacksquare}$ equivalent?

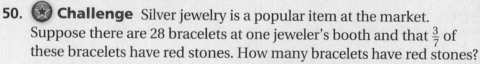

Ⓕ 3   Ⓖ 4   Ⓗ 84   Ⓙ 112

4-6 Mixed Numbers and Improper Fractions

Vocabulary
improper fraction
proper fraction

Reading Math

$\frac{11}{4}$ is read as "eleven-fourths."

Have you ever witnessed a total eclipse of the sun? It occurs when the sun's light is completely blocked out. A total eclipse is rare—only three have been visible in the continental United States since 1963.

The graph shows that the eclipse in 2017 will last $2\frac{3}{4}$ minutes. There are eleven $\frac{1}{4}$-minute sections, so $2\frac{3}{4} = \frac{11}{4}$.

An **improper fraction** is a fraction in which the numerator is greater than or equal to the denominator, such as $\frac{11}{4}$.

Approximate Length of U.S. Total Solar Eclipses

1963	
1970	
1979	
2017	

$\blacktriangle = \frac{1}{4}$ minute

Whole numbers can be written as improper fractions. The whole number is the numerator, and the denominator is 1. For example, $7 = \frac{7}{1}$.

Interactivities Online ▶ When the numerator is less than the denominator, the fraction is called a **proper fraction**.

Improper and Proper Fractions		
Improper Fractions		
• Numerator equals denominator → fraction is equal to 1	$\frac{3}{3} = 1$	$\frac{102}{102} = 1$
• Numerator greater than denominator → fraction is greater than 1	$\frac{9}{5} > 1$	$\frac{13}{1} > 1$
Proper Fractions		
• Numerator less than denominator → fraction is less than 1	$\frac{2}{5} < 1$	$\frac{102}{351} < 1$

You can write an improper fraction as a mixed number.

EXAMPLE 1 *Astronomy Application*

The longest total solar eclipse in the next 200 years will take place in 2186. It will last about $\frac{15}{2}$ minutes. Write $\frac{15}{2}$ as a mixed number.

Method 1: Use a model.

Draw squares divided into half sections. Shade 15 of the half sections.

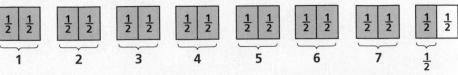

There are 7 whole squares and 1 half square, or $7\frac{1}{2}$ squares, shaded.

Video **Lesson Tutorials Online** my.hrw.com

Frank Zullo/Photo Researchers, Inc.

Method 2: Use division.

$$7\tfrac{1}{2}$$
$$2\overline{)15}$$
$$\underline{-14}$$
$$1$$

Divide the numerator by the denominator.

To form the fraction part of the quotient, use the remainder as the numerator and the divisor as the denominator.

The 2186 eclipse will last about $7\tfrac{1}{2}$ minutes.

Mixed numbers can be written as improper fractions.

 E X A M P L E 2 **Writing Mixed Numbers as Improper Fractions**

Write $2\tfrac{1}{5}$ as an improper fraction.

Method 1: Use a model.
You can draw a diagram to illustrate the whole and fractional parts.

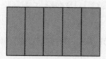 

There are 11 fifths, or $\tfrac{11}{5}$.   *Count the fifths in the diagram.*

Method 2: Use multiplication and addition.
When you are changing a mixed number to an improper fraction, spiral clockwise as shown in the picture. The order of operations will help you remember to multiply before you add.

 **Then add.**

First multiply.

$2\tfrac{1}{5} = \dfrac{(5 \cdot 2) + 1}{5}$

$= \dfrac{10 + 1}{5}$

$= \dfrac{11}{5}$

Multiply the whole number by the denominator and add the numerator. Keep the same denominator.

 MATHEMATICAL PRACTICES

Think and Discuss

1. **Read** each improper fraction: $\dfrac{10}{7}, \dfrac{25}{9}, \dfrac{31}{16}$.

2. **Tell** whether each fraction is less than 1, equal to 1, or greater than 1: $\dfrac{21}{21}, \dfrac{54}{103}, \dfrac{9}{11}, \dfrac{7}{3}$.

3. **Explain** why any mixed number written as a fraction will be improper.

GUIDED PRACTICE

See Example **1**   1. The fifth largest meteorite found in the United States is named the Navajo. The Navajo weighs $\frac{12}{5}$ tons. Write $\frac{12}{5}$ as a mixed number.

See Example **2**   Write each mixed number as an improper fraction.

2. $1\frac{1}{4}$ 3. $2\frac{2}{3}$ 4. $1\frac{2}{7}$ 5. $2\frac{2}{5}$

INDEPENDENT PRACTICE

See Example **1**   6. **Astronomy** Saturn is the sixth planet from the Sun. It takes Saturn $\frac{59}{2}$ years to revolve around the Sun. Write $\frac{59}{2}$ as a mixed number.

7. **Astronomy** Pluto has low surface gravity. A person who weighs 143 pounds on Earth weighs $\frac{43}{5}$ pounds on Pluto. Write $\frac{43}{5}$ as a mixed number.

See Example **2**   Write each mixed number as an improper fraction.

8. $1\frac{3}{5}$ 9. $2\frac{2}{9}$ 10. $3\frac{1}{7}$ 11. $4\frac{1}{3}$

12. $2\frac{3}{8}$ 13. $4\frac{1}{6}$ 14. $1\frac{4}{9}$ 15. $3\frac{4}{5}$

PRACTICE AND PROBLEM SOLVING

Extra Practice
See Extra Practice for more exercises.

Write each improper fraction as a mixed number or whole number. Tell whether your answer is a mixed number or whole number.

16. $\frac{21}{4}$ 17. $\frac{32}{8}$ 18. $\frac{20}{3}$ 19. $\frac{43}{5}$

20. $\frac{108}{9}$ 21. $\frac{87}{10}$ 22. $\frac{98}{11}$ 23. $\frac{105}{7}$

Write each mixed number as an improper fraction.

24. $9\frac{1}{4}$ 25. $4\frac{9}{11}$ 26. $11\frac{4}{9}$ 27. $18\frac{3}{5}$

28. **Measurement** The actual dimensions of a piece of lumber called a 2-by-4 are $1\frac{1}{2}$ inches and $3\frac{1}{2}$ inches. Write these numbers as improper fractions.

Replace each shape with a number that will make the equation correct.

29. $\blacksquare\frac{2}{5} = \frac{17}{\bullet}$ 30. $\blacksquare\frac{6}{11} = \frac{83}{\bullet}$ 31. $\blacksquare\frac{1}{9} = \frac{118}{\bullet}$

32. $\blacksquare\frac{6}{7} = \frac{55}{\bullet}$ 33. $\blacksquare\frac{9}{10} = \frac{29}{\bullet}$ 34. $\blacksquare\frac{1}{3} = \frac{55}{\bullet}$

35. Daniel is a costume designer for movies and music videos. He recently purchased $\frac{256}{9}$ yards of metallic fabric for space-suit costumes. Write a mixed number to represent the number of yards of fabric Daniel purchased.

Write the improper fraction as a decimal. Then use <, >, or = to compare.

36. $\frac{7}{5}$ $\blacksquare$ 1.8   37. 6.875 $\blacksquare$ $\frac{55}{8}$ 38. $\frac{27}{2}$ $\blacksquare$ 13   39. $\frac{20}{5}$ $\blacksquare$ 4.25

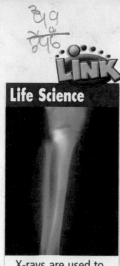

Life Science

X-rays are used to produce images of bones.

Life Science The table lists the lengths of the longest bones in the human body. Use the table for Exercises 40–42.

Longest Human Bones	
Fibula (outer lower leg)	$\frac{81}{2}$ cm
Ulna (inner lower arm)	$28\frac{1}{5}$ cm
Femur (upper leg)	$\frac{101}{2}$ cm
Humerus (upper arm)	$36\frac{1}{2}$ cm
Tibia (inner lower leg)	43 cm

40. Write the length of the ulna as an improper fraction. Then do the same for the length of the humerus.

41. Write the length of the fibula as a mixed number. Then do the same for the length of the femur.

42. Use the mixed-number form of each length. Compare the whole-number part of each length to write the bones in order from longest to shortest.

43. **Social Studies** The European country of Monaco, with an area of only $1\frac{4}{5}$ km², is one of the smallest countries in the world. Write $1\frac{4}{5}$ as an improper fraction.

44. For a disc to be approved by the Professional Disc Golf Association, it must not weigh more than $8\frac{3}{10}$ gram for each centimeter of its diameter. Write $8\frac{3}{10}$ as an improper fraction.

45. **What's the Question?** The lengths of Victor's three favorite movies are $\frac{11}{4}$ hours, $\frac{9}{4}$ hours, and $\frac{7}{4}$ hours. The answer is $2\frac{1}{4}$ hours. What is the question?

46. **Write About It** Draw models representing $\frac{4}{4}$, $\frac{5}{5}$, and $\frac{9}{9}$. Use your models to explain why a fraction whose numerator is the same as its denominator is equal to 1.

47. **Challenge** Write $\frac{65}{12}$ as a decimal.

Test Prep

48. **Multiple Choice** What is $3\frac{2}{11}$ written as an improper fraction?

  (A) $\frac{35}{11}$ (B) $\frac{35}{3}$ (C) $\frac{33}{22}$ (D) $\frac{70}{11}$

49. **Multiple Choice** It takes $\frac{24}{5}$ new pencils placed end to end to be the same length as one yardstick. What is this improper fraction written as a mixed number?

  (F) $3\frac{4}{5}$ (G) $4\frac{1}{4}$ (H) $4\frac{1}{5}$ (J) $4\frac{4}{5}$

Comparing and Ordering Fractions

Potstickers

3/4 cup ground pork
1 1/2 cup chopped cabbage
1/3 cup chopped green onion
1 tablespoon minced garlic
2 tablespoons minced ginger
1/2 cup soy sauce
48 dumpling wrappers

COMMON CORE

CC.6.NS.7 Understand ordering and absolute value of rational numbers

Rachel and Hannah are making a kind of dumpling called a *potsticker*. They have $\frac{1}{2}$ cup of green onion, but the recipe requires $\frac{1}{3}$ cup.

To determine if they have enough for the recipe, they need to compare the fractions $\frac{1}{2}$ and $\frac{1}{3}$.

Vocabulary

like fractions

unlike fractions

common denominator

When you are comparing fractions, first check their denominators. When fractions have the same denominator, they are called **like fractions**. For example, $\frac{1}{8}$ and $\frac{5}{8}$ are like fractions. When two fractions have different denominators, they are called **unlike fractions**. For example, $\frac{7}{10}$ and $\frac{1}{2}$ are unlike fractions.

EXAMPLE 1 **Comparing Fractions**

Compare. Write <, >, or =.

Helpful Hint

When two fractions have the same denominator, the one with the larger numerator is greater.

$\frac{2}{5} < \frac{3}{5}$ $\frac{3}{8} > \frac{1}{8}$

A $\frac{1}{8}$ ▢ $\frac{5}{8}$

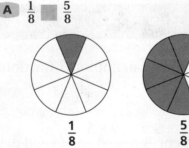

$\frac{1}{8}$ $\frac{5}{8}$

Model $\frac{1}{8}$ and $\frac{5}{8}$.

From the model, $\frac{1}{8} < \frac{5}{8}$.

B $\frac{7}{10}$ ▢ $\frac{1}{2}$

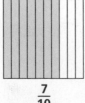   

$\frac{7}{10}$ $\frac{1}{2}$

Model $\frac{7}{10}$ and $\frac{1}{2}$.

From the model, $\frac{7}{10} > \frac{1}{2}$.

Video **Lesson Tutorials Online**   my.hrw.com

Craig Lovell/Eagle Visions Photography/Alamy

To compare unlike fractions without models, first rename the fractions so they have the same denominator. This is called finding a **common denominator**. This method can be used to compare mixed numbers as well.

EXAMPLE 2 **Cooking Application**

Rachel and Hannah have $1\frac{2}{3}$ cups of cabbage. They need $1\frac{1}{2}$ cups to make potstickers. Do they have enough for the recipe?

Compare $1\frac{2}{3}$ and $1\frac{1}{2}$.

Compare the whole-number parts of the numbers.
$1 = 1$ The whole-number parts are equal.

Compare the fractional parts. Find a common denominator by multiplying the denominators. $2 \cdot 3 = 6$

Find equivalent fractions with 6 as the denominator.

$$\frac{2}{3} = \frac{}{6} \qquad\qquad \frac{1}{2} = \frac{}{6}$$

$$\frac{2 \cdot 2}{3 \cdot 2} = \frac{4}{6} \qquad\qquad \frac{1 \cdot 3}{2 \cdot 3} = \frac{3}{6}$$

$$\frac{2}{3} = \frac{4}{6} \qquad\qquad \frac{1}{2} = \frac{3}{6}$$

Compare the like fractions. $\frac{4}{6} > \frac{3}{6}$, so $\frac{2}{3} > \frac{1}{2}$.

Therefore, $1\frac{2}{3}$ is greater than $1\frac{1}{2}$.

Since $1\frac{2}{3}$ cups is more than $1\frac{1}{2}$ cups, they have enough cabbage.

EXAMPLE 3 **Ordering Fractions**

Order $\frac{3}{7}$, $\frac{3}{4}$, and $\frac{1}{4}$ from least to greatest.

$$\frac{3 \cdot 4}{7 \cdot 4} = \frac{12}{28} \qquad \frac{3 \cdot 7}{4 \cdot 7} = \frac{21}{28} \qquad \frac{1 \cdot 7}{4 \cdot 7} = \frac{7}{28} \qquad$$ *Rename with like denominators.*

> **Remember!**
>
> Numbers increase in value as you move from left to right on a number line.

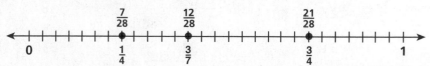

The fractions in order from least to greatest are $\frac{1}{4}, \frac{3}{7}, \frac{3}{4}$.

> MATHEMATICAL PRACTICES
>
> ## Think and Discuss
>
> **1. Tell** whether the values of the fractions change when you rename two fractions so that they have common denominators.
>
> **2. Explain** how to compare $\frac{2}{5}$ and $\frac{4}{5}$.

Exercises

Learn It Online
Homework Help Online
Exercises 1–26, 27, 29, 39, 41, 43, 45, 47

GUIDED PRACTICE

See Example 1   Compare. Write <, >, or =.

1. $\frac{3}{5}$ ▢ $\frac{2}{5}$ 2. $\frac{1}{9}$ ▢ $\frac{2}{9}$ 3. $\frac{6}{8}$ ▢ $\frac{3}{4}$ 4. $\frac{3}{7}$ ▢ $\frac{6}{7}$

See Example 2   5. Arsenio has $\frac{2}{3}$ cup of brown sugar. The recipe he is using requires $\frac{1}{4}$ cup of brown sugar. Does he have enough brown sugar for the recipe? Explain.

See Example 3   Order the fractions from least to greatest.

6. $\frac{3}{8}, \frac{1}{5}, \frac{2}{3}$ 7. $\frac{1}{4}, \frac{2}{5}, \frac{1}{3}$ 8. $\frac{5}{9}, \frac{1}{8}, \frac{2}{7}$ 9. $\frac{1}{2}, \frac{1}{6}, \frac{2}{3}$

INDEPENDENT PRACTICE

See Example 1   Compare. Write <, >, or =.

10. $\frac{2}{5}$ ▢ $\frac{4}{5}$ 11. $\frac{1}{10}$ ▢ $\frac{3}{10}$ 12. $\frac{3}{4}$ ▢ $\frac{3}{8}$ 13. $\frac{5}{6}$ ▢ $\frac{4}{6}$

14. $\frac{4}{5}$ ▢ $\frac{5}{5}$ 15. $\frac{2}{4}$ ▢ $\frac{1}{2}$ 16. $\frac{4}{8}$ ▢ $\frac{16}{24}$ 17. $\frac{11}{16}$ ▢ $\frac{9}{16}$

See Example 2   18. Kelly needs $\frac{2}{3}$ gallon of paint to finish painting her deck. She has $\frac{5}{8}$ gallon of paint. Does she have enough paint to finish her deck? Explain.

See Example 3   Order the fractions from least to greatest.

19. $\frac{1}{2}, \frac{3}{5}, \frac{3}{7}$ 20. $\frac{1}{6}, \frac{2}{5}, \frac{1}{4}$ 21. $\frac{4}{9}, \frac{3}{8}, \frac{1}{3}$ 22. $\frac{1}{4}, \frac{5}{6}, \frac{5}{9}$

23. $\frac{3}{4}, \frac{7}{10}, \frac{2}{3}$ 24. $\frac{13}{18}, \frac{5}{9}, \frac{5}{6}$ 25. $\frac{3}{8}, \frac{1}{4}, \frac{2}{3}$ 26. $\frac{3}{10}, \frac{2}{3}, \frac{5}{11}$

PRACTICE AND PROBLEM SOLVING

Extra Practice
See Extra Practice for more exercises.

Compare. Write <, >, or =.

27. $\frac{4}{15}$ ▢ $\frac{3}{10}$ 28. $\frac{7}{12}$ ▢ $\frac{13}{30}$ 29. $\frac{5}{9}$ ▢ $\frac{4}{11}$ 30. $\frac{8}{14}$ ▢ $\frac{8}{9}$

31. $\frac{3}{5}$ ▢ $\frac{26}{65}$ 32. $\frac{3}{5}$ ▢ $\frac{2}{21}$ 33. $\frac{24}{41}$ ▢ $\frac{2}{7}$ 34. $\frac{10}{38}$ ▢ $\frac{1}{4}$

Order the fractions from least to greatest.

35. $\frac{2}{5}, \frac{1}{2}, \frac{3}{10}$ 36. $\frac{3}{4}, \frac{3}{5}, \frac{7}{10}$ 37. $\frac{7}{15}, \frac{2}{3}, \frac{1}{5}$ 38. $\frac{3}{4}, \frac{1}{3}, \frac{8}{15}$

39. $\frac{2}{5}, \frac{4}{9}, \frac{11}{15}$ 40. $\frac{7}{12}, \frac{5}{8}, \frac{1}{2}$ 41. $\frac{5}{8}, \frac{3}{4}, \frac{5}{12}$ 42. $\frac{2}{3}, \frac{7}{8}, \frac{7}{15}$

43. Laura and Kim receive the same amount of allowance each week. Laura spends $\frac{3}{5}$ of it on going to the movies. Kim spends $\frac{4}{7}$ of it on a CD. Which girl spent more of her allowance? Explain.

44. Kyle operates a hot dog cart in a large city. He spends $\frac{2}{5}$ of his budget on supplies, $\frac{1}{12}$ on advertising, and $\frac{2}{25}$ on taxes and fees. Does Kyle spend more on advertising or more on taxes and fees?

Agriculture

There are over 3,500 different uses for corn products, from ethanol fuel and industrial products to the household items you see above.

Order the numbers from least to greatest.

45. $1\frac{2}{5}$, $1\frac{1}{8}$, $3\frac{4}{5}$, 3, $3\frac{2}{5}$

46. $7\frac{1}{2}$, $9\frac{4}{7}$, $9\frac{1}{2}$, 8, $8\frac{3}{4}$

47. $\frac{1}{2}$, $3\frac{1}{5}$, $3\frac{1}{10}$, $\frac{3}{4}$, $3\frac{1}{15}$

48. $2\frac{1}{5}$, $2\frac{5}{6}$, $1\frac{1}{4}$, 2, $\frac{7}{8}$

49. $4\frac{3}{4}$, 5, $3\frac{5}{7}$, $4\frac{2}{3}$, $5\frac{1}{3}$

50. $6\frac{1}{3}$, $5\frac{1}{4}$, $5\frac{7}{8}$, 6, $5\frac{1}{2}$

51. Agriculture The table shows the fraction of the world's total corn each country produces.

a. List the countries in order from the country that produces the most corn to the country that produces the least corn.

World's Corn Production	
United States	$\frac{39}{100}$
China	$\frac{1}{5}$
Canada	$\frac{7}{500}$

b. Brazil produces $\frac{1}{10}$ of the world's corn. Tell whether Brazil's corn production is more than or less than Canada's corn production.

52. Multi-Step The Dixon Dragons must win at least $\frac{3}{7}$ of their remaining games to qualify for their district playoffs. If they have 15 games left and they win 7 of them, will the Dragons compete in the playoffs? Explain.

53. Write a Problem Write a problem that involves comparing two fractions with different denominators.

54. Write About It Compare the fractions below. What do you notice about two fractions that have the same numerator but different denominators? Which one is greater?

$\frac{1}{2}$ ▨ $\frac{1}{4}$ $\frac{2}{3}$ ▨ $\frac{2}{5}$ $\frac{3}{4}$ ▨ $\frac{3}{7}$ $\frac{4}{5}$ ▨ $\frac{4}{9}$

55. Challenge Name a fraction that would make the inequality true.

$$\frac{1}{4} > \blacksquare > \frac{1}{5}$$

Test Prep

56. Multiple Choice Which fraction has the least value?

Ⓐ $\frac{1}{5}$ Ⓑ $\frac{3}{11}$ Ⓒ $\frac{2}{15}$ Ⓓ $\frac{4}{18}$

57. Extended Response Kevin is making potato soup. The recipe shows that he needs $\frac{1}{2}$ gallon of milk and 3.5 pounds of potatoes. He has $\frac{2}{5}$ gallon of milk and $\frac{21}{5}$ pounds of potatoes. Does Kevin have enough milk and potatoes to make the soup? Show your work and explain your answer.

Quiz for Lessons 4 Through 7

4 Decimals and Fractions

Write each decimal as a fraction. Write each fraction as a decimal.

1. 0.67 **2.** 0.9 **3.** $\frac{1}{6}$

Compare. Write <, >, or =.

4. $\frac{7}{10}$ ▢ 0.9 **5.** 0.4 ▢ $\frac{2}{5}$ **6.** $\frac{3}{5}$ ▢ 0.5

5 Equivalent Fractions

Write two equivalent fractions for each fraction.

7. $\frac{9}{12}$ **8.** $\frac{18}{42}$ **9.** $\frac{25}{30}$

Write each fraction in simplest form.

10. $\frac{20}{24}$ **11.** $\frac{14}{49}$ **12.** $\frac{12}{28}$

13. Mandy ate $\frac{1}{6}$ of a pizza. Write two equivalent fractions for $\frac{1}{6}$.

6 Mixed Numbers and Improper Fractions

Replace each shape with a number that will make the equation correct.

14. $\dfrac{\blacksquare\,2}{7} = \dfrac{9}{\bullet}$ **15.** $6\dfrac{\blacksquare}{8} = \dfrac{49}{\bullet}$ **16.** $\dfrac{\blacksquare\,4}{9} = \dfrac{157}{\bullet}$

Use the table for Exercises 17–19.

17. Write the lengths of *1900* and *Empire* as mixed numbers in simplest form.

18. Write the lengths of *Fanny and Alexander* and *War and Peace* as improper fractions.

19. Write the movies in order from longest to shortest.

20. The proboscis bat, with a length of $\frac{19}{5}$ cm, is one of the smallest bats. Write $\frac{19}{5}$ as a mixed number.

World's Longest Movies	
Title	Length (h)
1900	$\frac{318}{60}$
Empire	$\frac{480}{60}$
Fanny and Alexander	$5\frac{1}{5}$
War and Peace	$8\frac{31}{60}$

7 Comparing and Ordering Fractions

Compare. Write <, >, or =.

21. $\frac{3}{4}$ ▢ $\frac{2}{3}$ **22.** $\frac{7}{9}$ ▢ $\frac{5}{6}$ **23.** $\frac{4}{9}$ ▢ $\frac{4}{7}$ **24.** $\frac{5}{11}$ ▢ $\frac{3}{5}$

Order the fractions from least to greatest.

25. $\frac{5}{8}, \frac{1}{2}, \frac{3}{4}$ **26.** $\frac{3}{4}, \frac{3}{5}, \frac{7}{10}$ **27.** $\frac{1}{3}, \frac{3}{8}, \frac{1}{4}$ **28.** $\frac{2}{5}, \frac{4}{9}, \frac{11}{15}$

Real-World CONNECTIONS

 Reason abstractly and quantitatively.

CHAPTER 4

Glacier National Park Glacier National Park stretches across nearly 1,600 square miles of northwestern Montana. With more than 130 lakes, 1,000 species of plants, and 700 miles of hiking trails, the park offers something for everyone who loves the outdoors.

MONTANA
Glacier National Park

1. A visitor to the park plans to hike either Snyder Lake Trail or Ptarmigan Lake Trail. She wants to choose the longer of the two trails. Which trail should she choose?

2. List the following four trails from shortest to longest: Ptarmigan Lake, Iceberg Lake, Trout Lake, Mt. Brown Lookout.

3. a. Write the length of Swiftcurrent Pass Trail as a mixed number.

   b. A visitor hikes Swiftcurrent Pass Trail one day and Snyder Lake Trail the next day. Find the total distance he hikes.

4. Write the length of Grinnell Lake Trail as a decimal.

5. A family plans to hike Iceberg Lake Trail and Grinnell Lake Trail.

   a. Estimate the total distance the family will hike.

   b. The family can usually hike one mile in 30 minutes. About how long will it take them to hike the two trails?

Trails at Glacier National Park	
Trail Name	**Length (mi)**
Snyder Lake	$4\frac{2}{5}$
Ptarmigan Lake	$4\frac{3}{10}$
Iceberg Lake	4.7
Trout Lake	$4\frac{1}{5}$
Mt. Brown Lookout	5.4
Swiftcurrent Pass	6.6
Grinnell Lake	$3\frac{2}{5}$

Real-World Connections

James Randklev/Corbis

Game Time

Riddle Me This

"When you go from there to here,
you'll find I disappear.
Go from here to there, and then
you'll see me again.
What am I?"

To solve this riddle, copy the square below. If 3 is a factor of a number, color that box red. If 3 is not a factor of a number, color that box blue.

102	981	210	6,015	72
79	1,204	576	10,019	1,771
548	3,416	12,300	904	1,330
217	2,662	1,746	3,506	15,025
34,351	725	2,352	5,675	6,001

On a Roll

The object is to be the first person to fill in all the squares on your game board.

On your turn, roll a number cube and record the number rolled in any blank square on your game board. Once you have placed a number in a square, you cannot move that number. If you cannot place the number in a square, then your turn is over. The winner is the first player to complete their game board correctly.

Learn It Online
Game Time Extra

A complete copy of the rules and game pieces are available online.

Randall Hyman/HMH

Materials

- tan card stock
- scissors
- reinforcements
- hole punch
- wire ring
- markers

It's in the Bag!

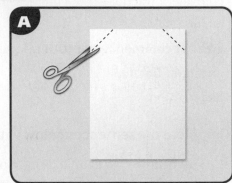

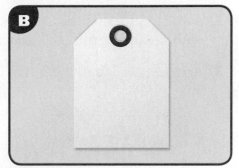

PROJECT ## Spec-Tag-Ular Number Theory

Tags will help you keep notes about number theory and fractions on an easy-to-use reference ring.

Directions

❶ Make tags by cutting ten rectangles from card stock, each approximately $2\frac{3}{4}$ inches by $1\frac{1}{2}$ inches.

❷ Use scissors to clip off two corners at the end of each tag. **Figure A**

❸ Punch a hole between the clipped corners of each tag. Put a reinforcement around the hole on both sides of the tag. **Figure B**

❹ Hook all of the tags together on a wire ring. On one of the tags, write the number and name of the chapter. **Figure C**

Taking Note of the Math

On each tag, write an important fact about fractions.

HMH

Vocabulary

common denominator	mixed number
coefficient	prime factorization
equivalent expressions	proper fraction
equivalent fractions	repeating decimal
factor	simplest form
greatest common factor (GCF)	term
improper fraction	terminating decimal
like fractions	unlike fractions

Complete the sentences below with vocabulary words from the list above.

1. The number $\frac{11}{9}$ is an example of a(n) ___?___, and $3\frac{1}{6}$ is an example of a(n) ___?___.

2. A(n) ___?___, such as 0.3333…, has a block of one or more digits that repeat without end. A(n) ___?___, such as 0.25, has a finite number of decimal places.

3. A(n) ___?___ is a number that is multiplied by a variable in an algebraic expression.

EXAMPLES

EXERCISES

1 Factors and Prime Factorization

■ List all the factors of 10.

$10 = 1 \cdot 10$ $\qquad$ $10 = 2 \cdot 5$

The factors of 10 are 1, 2, 5, and 10.

■ Write the prime factorization of 30.

$30 = 2 \cdot 3 \cdot 5$

List all the factors of each number.

4. 60 $\qquad$ **5.** 72

6. 29 $\qquad$ **7.** 56

8. 85 $\qquad$ **9.** 71

Write the prime factorization of each number.

10. 65	**11.** 94	**12.** 110
13. 81	**14.** 99	**15.** 76
16. 77	**17.** 55	**18.** 46

2 Greatest Common Factor

■ **Find the GCF of 35 and 50.**

factors of 35: 1, ⑤, 7, 35
factors of 50: 1, 2, ⑤, 10, 25, 50

The GCF of 35 and 50 is 5.

Find the GCF of each set of numbers.

19. 36 and 60

20. 50, 75, and 125

21. 45, 81, and 99

22. Mr. Rojo needs to put 12 trumpets and 8 trombones in groups with the same number of each instrument in each group. What is the greatest number of groups he can make?

3 Equivalent Expressions

■ **Factor the sum of terms 44 + 66 as a product of the GCF and a sum.**

$44 + 66$
$2 \cdot 2 \cdot 11 + 2 \cdot 3 \cdot 11$
$22 \cdot 2 + 22 \cdot 3$
$22(2 + 3)$

■ **Factor the sum of terms $10z + 26$ as a product of the GCF and a sum.**

$10z + 26$
$2 \cdot 5 \cdot z + 2 \cdot 13$
$2 \cdot 5z + 2 \cdot 13$
$2(5z + 13)$

Factor the sum of terms as a product of the GCF and a sum.

23. $20 + 64$ **24.** $65 + 13$

25. $35 + 28$ **26.** $120 + 25$

27. $15 + 50$ **28.** $24 + 27$

29. $30n + 18$ **30.** $9b + 21$

31. $30y + 20$ **32.** $49m + 14$

33. $24t + 45$ **34.** $39 + 15x$

4 Decimals and Fractions

■ **Write 1.29 as a mixed number.**

$1.29 = 1\frac{29}{100}$

■ **Write $\frac{3}{5}$ as a decimal.**

$$\frac{0.6}{5)\overline{3.0}} \qquad \frac{3}{5} = 0.6$$

Write as a fraction or mixed number.

35. 0.37   **36.** 1.8   **37.** 0.4

Write as a decimal.

38. $\frac{7}{8}$ **39.** $\frac{2}{5}$ **40.** $\frac{7}{9}$

Study Guide: Review

5 **Equivalent Fractions**

■ Find an equivalent fraction for $\frac{4}{5}$.

$$\frac{4}{5} = \frac{\blacksquare}{15} \qquad \frac{4 \cdot 3}{5 \cdot 3} = \frac{12}{15}$$

■ Write $\frac{8}{12}$ in simplest form.

$$\frac{8 \div 4}{12 \div 4} = \frac{2}{3}$$

Find two equivalent fractions.

41. $\frac{4}{6}$ **42.** $\frac{4}{5}$ **43.** $\frac{3}{12}$

Write each fraction in simplest form.

44. $\frac{14}{16}$ **45.** $\frac{9}{30}$ **46.** $\frac{7}{10}$

6 **Mixed Numbers and Improper Fractions**

■ Write $3\frac{5}{6}$ as an improper fraction.

$$3\frac{5}{6} = \frac{(3 \cdot 6) + 5}{6} = \frac{18 + 5}{6} = \frac{23}{6}$$

■ Write $\frac{19}{4}$ as a mixed number.

$$4\overline{)19} \;\; {}^{4R3} \qquad \frac{19}{4} = 4\frac{3}{4}$$

Write as an improper fraction.

47. $3\frac{7}{9}$ **48.** $2\frac{5}{12}$ **49.** $5\frac{2}{7}$

Write as a mixed number.

50. $\frac{23}{6}$ **51.** $\frac{17}{5}$ **52.** $\frac{41}{8}$

53. Katie gathered all her leftover clay and found that she had $\frac{15}{4}$ blocks of clay. Write $\frac{15}{4}$ as a mixed number.

7 **Comparing and Ordering Fractions**

■ Order from least to greatest.

$\frac{3}{5}, \frac{2}{3}, \frac{1}{3}$ *Rename with like denominators.*

$$\frac{3 \cdot 3}{5 \cdot 3} = \frac{9}{15} \qquad \frac{2 \cdot 5}{3 \cdot 5} = \frac{10}{15} \qquad \frac{1 \cdot 5}{3 \cdot 5} = \frac{5}{15}$$

$\frac{1}{3}, \frac{3}{5}, \frac{2}{3}$

Compare. Write $<$, $>$, or $=$.

54. $\frac{6}{8}$ ▢ $\frac{3}{6}$ **55.** $\frac{7}{9}$ ▢ $\frac{2}{3}$

56. $\frac{4}{5}$ ▢ $\frac{8}{10}$ **57.** $\frac{2}{5}$ ▢ $\frac{2}{3}$

Order from least to greatest.

58. $\frac{3}{8}, \frac{2}{3}, \frac{7}{8}$ **59.** $\frac{4}{6}, \frac{3}{12}, \frac{1}{3}$

60. $\frac{1}{2}, \frac{3}{8}, \frac{1}{3}$ **61.** $\frac{5}{6}, \frac{9}{10}, \frac{7}{8}$

Study Guide: Review

Chapter Test

List all the factors of each number.

1. 98

2. 40

3. 45

Write the prime factorization of each number.

4. 64

5. 130

6. 49

Find the GCF of each set of numbers.

7. 24 and 108

8. 45, 18, and 39

9. 49, 77, and 84

10. Ms. Arrington is making supply boxes for her students. She has 63 pencils, 42 pens, and 21 packs of markers. Each type of supply must be evenly distributed. What is the greatest number of supply boxes she can make if every supply is used?

Factor the sum of terms as a product of the GCF and a sum.

11. $21 + 99$

12. $88 + 20$

13. $34n + 12$

Write four equivalent expressions for each given expression.

14. $50 + 225$

15. $6(y - 1)$

16. $64x + 80$

Write each decimal as a fraction or mixed number.

17. 0.37

18. 1.9

19. 0.92

Write each fraction or mixed number as a decimal.

20. $\frac{3}{8}$

21. $9\frac{3}{5}$

22. $\frac{2}{3}$

Write each fraction in simplest form.

23. $\frac{4}{12}$

24. $\frac{6}{9}$

25. $\frac{3}{15}$

Write each mixed number as an improper fraction.

26. $4\frac{7}{8}$

27. $7\frac{5}{12}$

28. $3\frac{5}{7}$

Compare. Write $<$, $>$, or $=$.

29. $\frac{5}{6}$ ■ $\frac{3}{6}$

30. $\frac{3}{4}$ ■ $\frac{7}{8}$

31. $\frac{4}{5}$ ■ $\frac{7}{10}$

Order the fractions and decimals from least to greatest.

32. $2.17, 2.3, 2\frac{1}{9}$

33. $0.1, \frac{3}{8}, 0.3$

34. $0.9, \frac{2}{8}, 0.35$

Cumulative Assessment

Multiple Choice

1. Of which of the following numbers are 3, 4, and 8 factors?

   Ⓐ 12   Ⓒ 20
   Ⓑ 16   Ⓓ 24

2. When June sits down today to read, she notices she is on page 20 of a 200-page book. She decides to read 4 pages of this book every day until she is finished. If this pattern continues, what page of the book will June be on in 10 more days?

   Ⓕ 24   Ⓗ 60
   Ⓖ 44   Ⓙ 120

3. Alice is using three different colors of beads to make necklaces. She has 48 blue beads, 56 pink beads, and 32 white beads. She wants to use the same number of pink, same number of blue, and same number of white beads on each necklace. What is the greatest number of necklaces she can make if she uses all of the beads?

   Ⓐ 16   Ⓒ 8
   Ⓑ 12   Ⓓ 4

4. A writer spends $144.75 on 5 ink cartridges. Which equation can be used to find the cost c of one ink cartridge?

   Ⓕ $5c = 144.75$

   Ⓖ $\frac{c}{144.75} = 5$

   Ⓗ $5 + c = 144.75$

   Ⓙ $144.75 - c = 5$

5. Which fraction is equal to 0.25?

   Ⓐ $\frac{1}{3}$ Ⓒ $\frac{2}{5}$
   Ⓑ $\frac{1}{4}$ Ⓓ $\frac{1}{25}$

6. Which fraction is NOT equivalent to $\frac{4}{6}$?

   Ⓕ $\frac{2}{3}$ Ⓗ $\frac{8}{12}$
   Ⓖ $\frac{10}{15}$ Ⓙ $\frac{16}{18}$

7. Which fraction is equivalent to the shaded area of the model?

   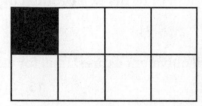

   Ⓐ $\frac{2}{4}$ Ⓒ $\frac{6}{32}$
   Ⓑ $\frac{3}{24}$ Ⓓ $\frac{4}{40}$

8. Steve bought a movie ticket for $6.25, a box of popcorn for $2.25, and a large drink for $4.75. How much money did he spend at the movie?

   Ⓕ $12.00   Ⓗ $13.25
   Ⓖ $12.75   Ⓙ $13.50

9. Four boys each order their own small pizza. William eats $\frac{2}{3}$ of his pizza. Mike eats $\frac{2}{5}$ of his pizza. Julio eats $\frac{1}{2}$ of his pizza. Lee eats $\frac{3}{8}$ of his pizza. Who ate the least amount of pizza?

   Ⓐ Lee

   Ⓑ Mike

   Ⓒ Julio

   Ⓓ William

10. There are 78 students going on a field trip to the state capitol. The students are in groups of 4. Each group must have an adult leader. How many adult leaders are needed for each student group to have an adult leader?

   Ⓕ 15   Ⓗ 20

   Ⓖ 19   Ⓙ 22

11. Which of the following is equivalent to 2.52?

   Ⓐ $2\frac{52}{100}$ Ⓒ $\frac{52}{200}$

   Ⓑ $2\frac{52}{10}$ Ⓓ $\frac{2}{52}$

HOT TIP! You can answer some problems without doing many calculations. Use mental math, estimation, or logical reasoning to eliminate answer choices and save time.

Gridded Response

12. What prime number is greater than 90 but less than 100?

13. Find the least common multiple of 4 and 6.

14. Suppose you are making fruit baskets that contain 6 bananas, 4 oranges, and 5 apples each. If you need to make 100 fruit baskets, how many apples do you need?

15. What is the solution to the equation $97.56 + x = 143.07$?

16. The prime factorization of a number is $2^3 \times 3 \times 5$. What is the number?

17. The table below shows the number of days it rained each month. How many total days did it rain during the 3-month period?

Month	Rainy Days
January	6
February	5
March	7

Short Response

S1. Stacie has $16\frac{3}{8}$ yards of material. She uses $7\frac{1}{8}$ yards for a skirt. How much material does she have left? Write your answer as a mixed number in simplest form. Then give three other equivalent answers, including one decimal.

S2. Maggie says that 2, 4, and 8 are factors of 348. Is she correct? Give any other number that is a factor of 348. Explain.

S3. Write the numbers 315 and 225 as products of prime factors. Then list all the factors of each number and find the GCF. Are 315 and 225 prime or composite? Explain.

S4. Suzanne has 317 flyers to mail. Each flyer requires 1 stamp. If she buys books of stamps that contain 20 stamps each, how many books will she need to mail the flyers?

Extended Response

E1. Mr. Peters needs to build a rectangular pig pen $14\frac{4}{5}$ meters long and $5\frac{1}{5}$ meters wide.

   a. How much fencing does Mr. Peters need to buy? Show how you found your answer. Write your answer in simplest form.

   b. Mr. Peters's pig pen will need 6 meters more fencing than the rectangular pig pen his neighbor is building. Write and solve an equation to find how much fencing his neighbor needs to buy. Show your work.

   c. If the neighbor's pig pen is going to be 4 meters wide, how long will it be? Show your work.

CHAPTER 5

Fraction Operations

Why Learn This?

Fractions are a very important part of music. Musical notes even have fractional names, which tell you how long each note is. For example, an eighth note is held for one eighth the length of a four-beat measure.

Learn It Online
Chapter Project Online

Chapter
• Understand the procedures for multiplying and dividing fractions.

• Evaluate expressions and solve equations with fractions.

(tr) Michelle Pedone/zefa/Corbis

Are You Ready?

Learn It Online
Resources Online

✓ Vocabulary

Choose the best term from the list to complete each sentence.

denominator

factors

improper fraction

like fractions

multiples

numerator

proper fraction

simplest form

unlike fractions

1. The first five ___?___ of 6 are 6, 12, 18, 24, and 30. The ___?___ of 6 are 1, 2, 3, and 6.

2. Fractions with the same denominator are called ___?___.

3. A fraction is in ___?___ when the GCF of the numerator and the denominator is 1.

4. The fraction $\frac{13}{9}$ is a(n) ___?___ because the ___?___ is greater than the ___?___.

Complete these exercises to review skills you will need for this chapter.

✓ Simplify Fractions

Write each fraction in simplest form.

5. $\frac{6}{10}$ 6. $\frac{5}{15}$ 7. $\frac{14}{8}$ 8. $\frac{8}{12}$

9. $\frac{10}{100}$ 10. $\frac{12}{144}$ 11. $\frac{33}{121}$ 12. $\frac{15}{17}$

✓ Write a Mixed Number as an Improper Fraction

Write each mixed number as an improper fraction.

13. $1\frac{1}{8}$ 14. $2\frac{3}{4}$ 15. $2\frac{4}{5}$ 16. $1\frac{7}{9}$

17. $3\frac{1}{5}$ 18. $5\frac{2}{3}$ 19. $4\frac{4}{7}$ 20. $3\frac{11}{12}$

✓ Add and Subtract Like Fractions

Add or subtract. Write each answer in simplest form.

21. $\frac{5}{8} + \frac{1}{8}$ 22. $\frac{3}{7} + \frac{5}{7}$ 23. $\frac{9}{10} - \frac{3}{10}$ 24. $\frac{5}{9} - \frac{2}{9}$

25. $\frac{1}{2} + \frac{1}{2}$ 26. $\frac{7}{12} - \frac{5}{12}$ 27. $\frac{3}{5} + \frac{4}{5}$ 28. $\frac{4}{15} - \frac{1}{15}$

✓ Multiplication Facts

Multiply.

29. 8×11 30. 7×8 31. 4×12 32. 12×7

33. 10×13 34. 9×7 35. 6×8 36. 11×12

Where You've Been

Previously, you

- added and subtracted fractions with like denominators.
- estimated sums and differences of whole numbers.
- wrote equivalent fractions.

In This Chapter

You will study

- modeling addition and subtraction situations involving fractions.
- estimating sums and differences of mixed numbers.
- adding, subtracting, multiplying, and dividing fractions and mixed numbers with unlike denominators.
- solving equations with fractions.

Where You're Going

You can use the skills learned in this chapter

- to solve measurement problems that involve fractions and mixed numbers.
- to calculate sums and differences between distances that involve fractions.

Key Vocabulary/Vocabulario

least common denominator (LCD)	mínimo común denominador (m.c.d.)
least common multiple (LCM)	mínimo común múltiplo (m.c.m.)
reciprocal	recíproco

Vocabulary Connections

To become familiar with some of the vocabulary terms in the chapter, consider the following. You may refer to the chapter, the glossary, or a dictionary if you like.

1. The word *reciprocal* means "inversely related or opposite." What do you think the **reciprocal** of a fraction will look like?

2. When people have something in *common*, they have something that they share. What do you think two numbers with a common multiple share? What do you think the **least common multiple** of two numbers is?

3. Fractions with the same denominator have a common denominator. What do you think the **least common denominator** of two fractions is?

Study Strategy: Make Flash Cards

Create flash cards to help you learn a sequence of steps, vocabulary, math symbols, formulas, or mathematical rules. Study your flash cards often.

Use these suggestions to make flash cards.

- Use examples or exercises from your book for each topic.

- Write the name of the formula, term, or rule on one side of the card, and the meaning or an example on the other side of the card.

- Write definitions using your own words.

Life Science Application

Sophie plants a young oak tree in her backyard. The distance around the trunk grows at a rate of $\frac{1}{8}$ inch per month. Use pictures to model how much this distance will increase in two months, then write your answer in simplest form.

$\frac{1}{8} + \frac{1}{8}$

$\frac{1}{8} + \frac{1}{8} = \frac{2}{8}$ *Add the numerators. Keep the same denominator.*

$\quad\quad = \frac{1}{4}$ *Write your answer in simplest form.*

The distance around the trunk will increase by $\frac{1}{4}$ inch.

Sample Flash Card

Adding and Subtracting Fractions with Like Denominators

Front

		$\frac{1}{8} + \frac{1}{8}$
Keep the denominators.	$\frac{1}{8} + \frac{1}{8} = \frac{}{8}$	
Add the numerators.	$\frac{1}{8} + \frac{1}{8} = \frac{2}{8}$	
Write in simplest form.	$\frac{1}{4}$	

Back

Try This

1. Use Example 2 in Lesson 1 of this chapter to make flash cards for the rules for the different methods for finding a least common multiple.

Least Common Multiple

CC.6.NS.4 Find... the least common multiple of two whole numbers less than or equal to 12...

Vocabulary

least common multiple (LCM)

After games in Lydia's basketball league, one player's family brings snacks for both teams to share. This week Lydia's family will provide juice boxes and granola bars for 24 players.

You can make a model to help you find the least number of juice and granola packs Lydia's family should buy. Use colored counters, drawings, or pictures to illustrate the problem.

E X A M P L E **1** **Consumer Application**

Remember!

A multiple of a number is the product of the number and any nonzero whole number. See the Skills Bank.

Juice comes in packs of 6, and granola bars in packs of 8. If there are 24 players, what is the least number of packs needed so that each player has a drink and granola bar and there are none left over?

Draw juice boxes in groups of 6. Draw granola bars in groups of 8. Stop when you have drawn the same number of each.

There are 24 juice boxes and 24 granola bars.

Lydia's family should buy 4 packs of juice and 3 packs of granola bars.

The smallest number that is a multiple of two or more numbers is the **least common multiple (LCM)**. In Example 1, the LCM of 6 and 8 is 24.

Video Lesson Tutorials Online my.hrw.com

EXAMPLE 2 Using Multiples to Find the LCM

Find the least common multiple (LCM).

Method 1: Use a number line.

A 6 and 9

Use a number line to skip count by 6 and 9.

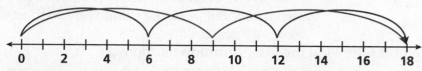

The least common multiple (LCM) of 6 and 9 is 18.

Method 2: Use a list.

B 3, 5, and 6

3: 3, 6, 9, 12, 15, 18, 21, 24, 27, 30, 33, . . .

5: 5, 10, 15, 20, 25, 30, 35, . . .

6: 6, 12, 18, 24, 30, 36, . . .

List multiples of 3, 5, and 6.

Find the smallest number that is in all the lists.

LCM: 30

Method 3: Use prime factorization.

> **Remember!**
>
> The prime factorization of a number is the number written as a product of its prime factors.

C 8 and 12

$8 = 2 \cdot 2 \cdot 2$

$12 = 2 \cdot 2 \cdot \quad 3$

$2 \cdot 2 \cdot 2 \cdot 3$

$2 \cdot 2 \cdot 2 \cdot 3 = 24$

Write the prime factorization of each number. Line up the common factors.

To find the LCM, multiply one number from each column.

LCM: 24

D 12, 10, and 15

$12 = 2^2 \cdot 3$

$10 = 2 \cdot \quad 5$

$15 = \quad 3 \cdot 5$

$2^2 \cdot 3 \cdot 5$

$2^2 \cdot 3 \cdot 5 = 60$

Write the prime factorization of each number in exponential form.

To find the LCM, multiply each prime factor once with the greatest exponent used in any of the prime factorizations.

LCM: 60

MATHEMATICAL PRACTICES

Think and Discuss

1. Explain why you cannot find a greatest common multiple for a group of numbers.

2. Tell whether the LCM of a set of numbers can ever be smaller than any of the numbers in the set.

GUIDED PRACTICE

See Example **1**

1. Pencils are sold in packs of 12, and erasers in packs of 9. Mr. Joplin wants to give each of 36 students a pencil and an eraser. What is the least number of packs he should buy so there are none left over?

See Example **2** **Find the least common multiple (LCM).**

2. 3 and 5   **3.** 4 and 9   **4.** 2, 3, and 6   **5.** 2, 4, and 5

6. 4 and 12   **7.** 6 and 16   **8.** 4, 6, and 8   **9.** 2, 5, and 8

10. 6 and 10   **11.** 21 and 63   **12.** 3, 5, and 9   **13.** 5, 6, and 25

INDEPENDENT PRACTICE

See Example **1**

14. String-cheese sticks are sold in packs of 10, and celery sticks in packs of 15. Ms. Sobrino wants to give each of 30 students one string-cheese stick and one celery stick. What is the least number of packs she should buy so there are none left over?

See Example **2** **Find the least common multiple (LCM).**

15. 2 and 8   **16.** 3 and 7   **17.** 4 and 10   **18.** 3 and 9

19. 3, 6, and 9   **20.** 4, 8, and 10   **21.** 4, 6, and 12   **22.** 4, 6, and 7

23. 3, 8, and 12   **24.** 3, 7, and 10   **25.** 2, 6, and 11   **26.** 2, 3, 6, and 9

27. 2, 4, 5, and 6   **28.** 10 and 11   **29.** 4, 5, and 7   **30.** 2, 3, 6, and 8

PRACTICE AND PROBLEM SOLVING

Extra Practice
See Extra Practice for more exercises.

31. What is the LCM of 6 and 12?   **32.** What is the LCM of 5 and 11?

33. The diagram at right is a Venn diagram. The numbers in the red circle are multiples of 4. The numbers in the blue circle are multiples of 6. The numbers in the purple section are multiples of both 4 and 6.

Multiples of 4   **Multiples of 6**

a   c   6

4   24

d   b

Find the missing numbers in the Venn diagram.

a. a two-digit multiple of 4 that is not a multiple of 6

b. a two-digit multiple of 6 that is not a multiple of 4

c. the LCM of 4 and 6

d. a three-digit common multiple of 4 and 6

Find a pair of numbers that has the given characteristics.

34. The LCM of the two numbers is 26. One number is even and one is odd.

35. The LCM of the two numbers is 48. The sum of the numbers is 28.

36. The LCM of the two numbers is 60. The difference of the two numbers is 3.

37. During its grand opening weekend, a restaurant offered the specials shown in order to attract new customers.

GRAND OPENING SPECIALS

Every 8th customer:
FREE APPETIZER!

Every 12th customer:
FREE BEVERAGE!

Every 15th customer:
FREE DESSERT!

   a. Which customer was the first to receive all three free items?

   b. Which customer was the first to receive a free appetizer and frozen yogurt?

   c. If the restaurant served 500 customers that weekend, how many of those customers received all three free items?

38. Choose a Strategy Sophia gave $\frac{1}{2}$ of her semi-precious-rock collection to her son. She gave $\frac{1}{2}$ of what she had left to her grandson. Then she gave $\frac{1}{2}$ of what she had left to her great-grandson. She kept 10 rocks for herself. How many rocks did she have in the beginning?

   (A) 40   (B) 80   (C) 100   (D) 160

39. Write About It Explain the steps you can use to find the LCM of two numbers. Choose two numbers to show an example of your method.

40. Challenge Find the LCM of each pair of numbers.

   a. 4 and 6   **b.** 8 and 9   **c.** 5 and 7   **d.** 8 and 10

   When is the LCM of two numbers equal to the product of the two numbers?

Test Prep

41. Multiple Choice Cheese cubes are sold in packs of 60. Crackers are sold in packs of 12. To make 60 snacks of 2 cheese cubes and 1 cracker, what is the least number of packs of each type needed?

   (A) 2 cheese, 1 cracker   (C) 2 cheese, 2 cracker

   (B) 2 cheese, 5 cracker   (D) 5 cheese, 2 cracker

42. Multiple Choice What is the least common multiple of 5 and 8?

   (F) 40   (G) 20   (H) 80   (J) 60

Adding and Subtracting with Unlike Denominators

The Pacific Ocean covers $\frac{1}{3}$ of Earth's surface. The Atlantic Ocean covers $\frac{1}{5}$ of Earth's surface. To find the fraction of Earth's surface that is covered by both oceans, you can add $\frac{1}{3}$ and $\frac{1}{5}$, which are unlike fractions.

Vocabulary

least common denominator (LCD)

Fractions that represent the same value are equivalent.

To add or subtract unlike fractions, first rewrite them as equivalent fractions with a common denominator.

EXAMPLE 1 **Social Studies Application**

What fraction of Earth's surface is covered by the Atlantic and Pacific Oceans? Add $\frac{1}{3}$ and $\frac{1}{5}$.

$$\begin{array}{r} \frac{1}{3} \\ + \frac{1}{5} \\ \hline \end{array}$$

Find a common denominator for 3 and 5: 3 × 5 = 15.

$\frac{1}{3} \rightarrow \frac{5}{15}$

Write equivalent fractions with 15 as the common denominator.

$$+ \frac{1}{5} \rightarrow \frac{3}{15}$$

$$\frac{8}{15}$$

Add the numerators. Keep the common denominator.

The Pacific and Atlantic Oceans cover $\frac{8}{15}$ of Earth's surface.

You can use *any* common denominator or the *least common denominator* to add and subtract unlike fractions. The **least common denominator (LCD)** is the least common multiple of the denominators.

Video **Lesson Tutorials Online** my.hrw.com

EXAMPLE **2** **Adding and Subtracting Unlike Fractions**

Add or subtract. Write each answer in simplest form.

Method 1: Multiply the denominators.

A $\dfrac{9}{10} - \dfrac{7}{8}$

$\dfrac{9}{10} - \dfrac{7}{8}$	*Multiply the denominators. $10 \cdot 8 = 80$*
$\dfrac{72}{80} - \dfrac{70}{80}$	*Write equivalent fractions with a common denominator.*
$\dfrac{2}{80}$	*Subtract.*
$\dfrac{1}{40}$	*Write the answer in simplest form.*

Method 2: Use the LCD.

B $\dfrac{9}{10} - \dfrac{7}{8}$

$\dfrac{9}{10} - \dfrac{7}{8}$	*Multiples of 10: 10, 20, 30, 40, . . .*
$\dfrac{9}{10} - \dfrac{7}{8}$	*Multiples of 8: 8, 16, 24, 32, 40, . . . The LCD is 40.*
$\dfrac{36}{40} - \dfrac{35}{40}$	*Write equivalent fractions with a common denominator.*
$\dfrac{1}{40}$	*Subtract.*

Method 3: Use mental math.

C $\dfrac{5}{12} + \dfrac{1}{6}$

$\dfrac{5}{12} + \dfrac{1}{6}$	*Think: 12 is a multiple of 6, so the LCD is 12.*
$\dfrac{5}{12} + \dfrac{2}{12}$	*Rewrite $\frac{1}{6}$ with a denominator of 12.*
$\dfrac{7}{12}$	*Add.*

D $\dfrac{1}{3} - \dfrac{2}{9}$

$\dfrac{1}{3} - \dfrac{2}{9}$	*Think: 9 is a multiple of 3, so the LCD is 9.*
$\dfrac{3}{9} - \dfrac{2}{9}$	*Rewrite $\frac{1}{3}$ with a denominator of 9.*
$\dfrac{1}{9}$	*Subtract.*

MATHEMATICAL
PRACTICES

Think and Discuss

1. **Explain** an advantage of using the least common denominator (LCD) when adding unlike fractions.

2. **Tell** when the least common denominator (LCD) of two fractions is the product of their denominators.

3. **Explain** how you can use mental math to subtract $\frac{1}{12}$ from $\frac{3}{4}$.

GUIDED PRACTICE

See Example **1**
1. A trailer hauling wood weighs $\frac{2}{3}$ ton. The trailer weighs $\frac{1}{4}$ ton without the wood. What is the weight of the wood?

See Example **2** Add or subtract. Write each answer in simplest form.

2. $\frac{1}{3} + \frac{1}{9}$
3. $\frac{7}{10} - \frac{2}{5}$
4. $\frac{2}{3} - \frac{2}{5}$
5. $\frac{1}{2} + \frac{3}{7}$

INDEPENDENT PRACTICE

See Example **1**
6. **Social Studies** Approximately $\frac{1}{5}$ of the world's population lives in China. The people of India make up about $\frac{1}{6}$ of the world's population. What fraction of the world's people live in either China or India?

7. Cedric is making an Italian dish using a recipe that calls for $\frac{2}{3}$ cup of grated mozarella cheese. If Cedric has grated $\frac{1}{2}$ cup of mozarella cheese, how much more does he need to grate?

See Example **2** Add or subtract. Write each answer in simplest form.

8. $\frac{3}{4} - \frac{1}{2}$
9. $\frac{1}{6} + \frac{5}{12}$
10. $\frac{5}{6} - \frac{3}{4}$
11. $\frac{1}{5} + \frac{1}{4}$

12. $\frac{7}{10} + \frac{1}{8}$
13. $\frac{1}{3} + \frac{4}{5}$
14. $\frac{8}{9} - \frac{2}{3}$
15. $\frac{5}{8} + \frac{1}{2}$

PRACTICE AND PROBLEM SOLVING

Extra Practice

See Extra Practice for more exercises.

Find each sum or difference. Write your answer in simplest form.

16. $\frac{3}{10} + \frac{1}{2}$
17. $\frac{4}{5} - \frac{1}{3}$
18. $\frac{5}{8} - \frac{1}{6}$
19. $\frac{1}{6} + \frac{2}{9}$

20. $\frac{2}{7} + \frac{2}{5}$
21. $\frac{7}{12} - \frac{1}{4}$
22. $\frac{7}{8} - \frac{2}{3}$
23. $\frac{2}{11} + \frac{2}{3}$

Evaluate each expression for $b = \frac{1}{2}$. Write your answer in simplest form.

24. $b + \frac{1}{3}$
25. $\frac{8}{9} - b$
26. $b - \frac{2}{11}$
27. $\frac{7}{10} - b$

28. $\frac{2}{7} + b$
29. $b + b$
30. $b - b$
31. $b + \frac{5}{8}$

Evaluate. Write each answer in simplest form.

32. $\frac{1}{3} + \frac{1}{9} + \frac{1}{3}$
33. $\frac{9}{10} - \frac{2}{10} - \frac{1}{5}$
34. $\frac{1}{2} + \frac{1}{4} - \frac{1}{8}$
35. $\frac{3}{7} + \frac{1}{14} + \frac{2}{28}$

36. $\frac{5}{6} - \frac{2}{3} + \frac{7}{12}$
37. $\frac{2}{3} + \frac{1}{4} - \frac{1}{6}$
38. $\frac{2}{9} + \frac{1}{6} + \frac{1}{3}$
39. $\frac{1}{2} - \frac{1}{4} + \frac{5}{8}$

40. Bailey spent $\frac{2}{3}$ of his monthly allowance at the movies and $\frac{1}{5}$ of it on baseball cards. What fraction of Bailey's allowance is left?

41. **Multi-Step** Betty is making punch for a party. She needs a total of $\frac{9}{10}$ gallon of water to add to fruit juice. In one container she has $\frac{1}{3}$ gallon water, and in another she has $\frac{2}{5}$ gallon. How much more water does she need?

Life Science

The red lorikeet, galah cockatoo, and green-cheeked Amazon are three very colorful birds. The African grey parrot is known for its ability to mimic sounds it hears. In fact, one African grey named Prudle had a vocabulary of almost 1,000 words.

42. Which bird weighs more, the green-cheeked Amazon or the red lorikeet?

43. What is the difference in weights between the green-cheeked Amazon and the red lorikeet?

44. Does the red lorikeet weigh more or less than $\frac{1}{2}$ lb? Explain.

45. ? **What's the Error?** A student found the difference in weight between the African grey parrot and the galah cockatoo to be 1 lb. Explain the error. Then find the correct difference between the weights of these birds.

46. ✏ **Write About It** Explain how you find the difference in weight between the galah cockatoo and green-cheeked Amazon.

47. ★ **Challenge** Find the average weight of the birds.

Red lorikeet, $\frac{3}{8}$ lb, $11\frac{2}{5}$ in.

Galah cockatoo, $\frac{3}{4}$ lb, $13\frac{9}{10}$ in.

Green-cheeked Amazon, $\frac{3}{5}$ lb, $13\frac{1}{5}$ in.

African grey parrot, $\frac{7}{8}$ lb, 13 in.

Test Prep

48. Multiple Choice One apple weighs $\frac{1}{4}$ lb and another apple weighs $\frac{3}{16}$ lb. Find the difference in their weights.

Ⓐ $\frac{1}{16}$ lb   Ⓑ $\frac{1}{6}$ lb   Ⓒ $\frac{1}{4}$ lb   Ⓓ $\frac{7}{16}$ lb

49. Short Response Wanda walked $\frac{7}{24}$ mile more than Lori. Lori walked $\frac{5}{6}$ mile less than Jack. Wanda walked $\frac{3}{8}$ mile. How many miles did Jack walk? Give your answer in simplest form. Explain how you solved the problem.

Regrouping to Subtract Mixed Numbers

Jimmy and his mother planted a tree when it was $1\frac{3}{4}$ ft tall. Now the tree is $2\frac{1}{4}$ ft tall. How much has the tree grown since it was planted?

The difference in the heights can be represented by the expression $2\frac{1}{4} - 1\frac{3}{4}$.

You will need to regroup $2\frac{1}{4}$ because the fraction in $1\frac{3}{4}$ is greater than $\frac{1}{4}$.

Divide *one whole* of $2\frac{1}{4}$ into fourths.

1	1	$\frac{1}{4}$
1	$\frac{1}{4}$ $\frac{1}{4}$ $\frac{1}{4}$ $\frac{1}{4}$ $\frac{1}{4}$	

Regroup $2\frac{1}{4}$ as $1\frac{5}{4}$.

$$
\begin{array}{r}
2\frac{1}{4} \rightarrow \quad 1\frac{5}{4} \\
- 1\frac{3}{4} \rightarrow - 1\frac{3}{4} \\
\hline
\frac{2}{4} = \frac{1}{2}
\end{array}
$$

1	$\frac{1}{4}$ $\frac{1}{4}$ $\frac{1}{4}$ $\frac{1}{4}$ $\frac{1}{4}$

Remove $1\frac{3}{4}$.

The tree has grown $\frac{1}{2}$ ft since it was planted.

EXAMPLE 1 **Regrouping Mixed Numbers**

Subtract. Write each answer in simplest form.

A $6\frac{5}{12} - 2\frac{7}{12}$

$6 - 3 = 3$ *Estimate the difference.*

$$
\begin{array}{r}
6\frac{5}{12} \longrightarrow 5\frac{17}{12} \\
- 2\frac{7}{12} \longrightarrow - 2\frac{7}{12} \\
\hline
3\frac{10}{12}
\end{array}
$$

Regroup $6\frac{5}{12}$ as $5 + 1\frac{5}{12} = 5 + \frac{12}{12} + \frac{5}{12}$. Subtract the fractions and then the whole numbers.

$= 3\frac{5}{6}$ *Write the answer in simplest form.*

$3\frac{5}{6}$ is close to the estimate of 3. The answer is reasonable.

Video **Lesson Tutorials Online** my.hrw.com

JUPITERIMAGES/Liquid Library Value/Alamy

Subtract. Write each answer in simplest form.

B $8 - 5\frac{3}{4}$

$8 - 6 = 2$ *Estimate the difference.*

$$8 \longrightarrow 7\frac{4}{4}$$
$$-5\frac{3}{4} \longrightarrow -5\frac{3}{4}$$
$$\overline{\phantom{-5\frac{3}{4}}}\quad\overline{2\frac{1}{4}}$$

Write 8 as a mixed number with a denominator of 4. Regroup 8 as $7 + \frac{4}{4}$.

Subtract the fractions and then the whole numbers.

$2\frac{1}{4}$ is close to the estimate of 2. The answer is reasonable.

EXAMPLE 2   *Measurement Application*

Dave is re-covering an old couch and cushions. He determines that he needs 17 yards of fabric for the job.

A Dave has $1\frac{2}{3}$ yards of fabric. How many more yards does he need?

$$17 \longrightarrow 16\frac{3}{3}$$
$$-1\frac{2}{3} \longrightarrow -1\frac{2}{3}$$
$$\overline{\phantom{-1\frac{2}{3}}}\quad\overline{15\frac{1}{3}}$$

Write 17 as a mixed number with a denominator of 3. Regroup 17 as $16 + \frac{3}{3}$.

Subtract the fractions and then the whole numbers.

Dave needs another $15\frac{1}{3}$ yards of material.

B If Dave uses $9\frac{5}{6}$ yards of fabric to cover the couch frame, how much of the 17 yards will he have left?

$$17 \longrightarrow 16\frac{6}{6}$$
$$-9\frac{5}{6} \longrightarrow -9\frac{5}{6}$$
$$\overline{\phantom{-9\frac{5}{6}}}\quad\overline{7\frac{1}{6}}$$

Write 17 as a mixed number with a denominator of 6. Regroup 17 as $16 + \frac{6}{6}$.

Subtract the fractions and then the whole numbers.

Dave will have $7\frac{1}{6}$ yards of material left.

MATHEMATICAL PRACTICES

Think and Discuss

1. **Explain** why you regroup 2 as $1\frac{8}{8}$ instead of $1\frac{3}{3}$ when you find $2 - 1\frac{3}{8}$.

2. **Give an example** of a subtraction expression in which you would need to regroup the first mixed number to subtract.

3. **Explain** whether you would need to regroup to simplify the expression $7\frac{7}{8} - 2\frac{5}{8} - 1\frac{3}{8}$.

GUIDED PRACTICE

See Example **1** Subtract. Write each answer in simplest form.

1. $2\frac{1}{2} - 1\frac{3}{4}$

2. $8\frac{2}{9} - 2\frac{7}{9}$

3. $3\frac{2}{6} - 1\frac{2}{3}$

4. $7\frac{1}{4} - 4\frac{11}{12}$

See Example **2** **5.** Mr. Jones purchased a 4-pound bag of flour. He used $1\frac{2}{5}$ pounds of flour to make bread. How many pounds of flour are left?

INDEPENDENT PRACTICE

See Example **1** Subtract. Write each answer in simplest form.

6. $6\frac{3}{11} - 3\frac{10}{11}$

7. $9\frac{2}{5} - 5\frac{3}{5}$

8. $4\frac{3}{10} - 3\frac{3}{5}$

9. $10\frac{1}{2} - 2\frac{5}{8}$

10. $11\frac{1}{4} - 9\frac{3}{8}$

11. $7\frac{5}{9} - 2\frac{5}{6}$

12. $6 - 2\frac{2}{3}$

13. $5\frac{3}{10} - 3\frac{1}{2}$

See Example **2** **14.** **Measurement** A standard piece of notebook paper has a length of 11 inches and a width of $8\frac{1}{2}$ inches. What is the difference between these two measures?

15. Chad opened a 10-pound bag of birdseed to refill his feeders. He used $3\frac{1}{3}$ pounds to fill them. How many pounds of birdseed were left?

PRACTICE AND PROBLEM SOLVING

Extra Practice

See Extra Practice for more exercises.

Find each difference. Write the answer in simplest form.

16. $8 - 6\frac{4}{7}$

17. $13\frac{1}{9} - 11\frac{2}{3}$

18. $10\frac{3}{4} - 6\frac{1}{2}$

19. $13 - 4\frac{2}{11}$

20. $15\frac{2}{5} - 12\frac{3}{4}$

21. $17\frac{5}{9} - 6\frac{1}{3}$

22. $18\frac{1}{4} - 14\frac{3}{8}$

23. $20\frac{1}{6} - 7\frac{4}{9}$

24. **Economics** A single share of stock in a company cost $23\frac{2}{5}$ on Monday. By Tuesday, the cost of a share in the company had fallen to $19\frac{1}{5}$. By how much did the price of a share fall?

25. Jasmine is $62\frac{1}{2}$ inches tall. Her brother, Antoine, is $69\frac{3}{4}$ inches tall. What is the difference, in inches, in their heights?

Simplify each expression. Write the answer in simplest form.

26. $4\frac{2}{3} + 5\frac{1}{3} - 7\frac{1}{8}$

27. $12\frac{5}{9} - 6\frac{2}{3} + 1\frac{4}{9}$

28. $7\frac{7}{8} - 4\frac{1}{8} + 1\frac{1}{4}$

29. $7\frac{4}{11} - 2\frac{8}{11} - \frac{10}{11}$

30. $8\frac{1}{3} - 5\frac{8}{9} + 8\frac{1}{2}$

31. $5\frac{2}{7} - 2\frac{1}{14} + 8\frac{5}{14}$

32. **Multi-Step** Octavio used a brand new 6-hour tape to record some television shows. He recorded a movie that is $1\frac{1}{2}$ hours long and a cooking show that is $1\frac{1}{4}$ hours long. How much time is left on the tape?

Evaluate each expression for $a = 6\frac{2}{3}$, $b = 8\frac{1}{2}$, and $c = 1\frac{3}{4}$. Write the answer in simplest form.

33. $a - c$ **34.** $b - c$ **35.** $b - a$ **36.** $10 - b$

37. $b - (a + c)$ **38.** $c + (b - a)$ **39.** $(a + b) - c$ **40.** $(10 - c) - a$

Use the table for Exercises 41–44.

41. Gustavo is working at a gift wrap center. He has 2 yd² of wrapping paper to wrap a small box. How much wrapping paper will be left after he wraps the gift?

42. Gustavo must now wrap two extra-large boxes. If he has 6 yd² of wrapping paper, how much more wrapping paper will he need to wrap the two gifts?

43. To wrap a large box, Gustavo used $\frac{3}{4}$ yd² less wrapping paper than the amount listed in the table. How many square yards did he use to wrap the gift?

Gustavo's Gift Wrap Table	
Gift Size	Paper Needed (yd²)
Small	$\frac{11}{12}$
Medium	$1\frac{5}{9}$
Large	$2\frac{2}{3}$
X-large	$3\frac{1}{9}$

44. What's the Error? Gustavo calculated the difference between the amount needed to wrap an extra-large box and the amount needed to wrap a medium box to be $2\frac{4}{9}$ yd². Explain his error and find the correct answer.

45. Write About It Explain why you write equivalent fractions before you regroup them. Explain why you do not regroup them first.

46. Challenge Fill in the box with a mixed number that makes the inequality true.

$$12\frac{1}{2} - 8\frac{3}{4} > 10 - \blacksquare$$

47. Multiple Choice Find the difference of $5 - \frac{4}{9}$.

(A) $5\frac{5}{9}$ (B) $5\frac{1}{9}$ (C) $4\frac{5}{9}$ (D) $4\frac{1}{9}$

48. Gridded Response Tami worked 4 hours on Saturday at the city pool. She spent $1\frac{3}{4}$ hours cleaning the pool and the remaining time working as a lifeguard. How many hours did Tami spend working as a lifeguard?

Solving Fraction Equations: Addition and Subtraction

COMMON CORE

CC.6.EE.7 Solve real-world and mathematical problems by writing and solving equations of the form $x + p = q$ and $px = q$ for cases in which p, q and x are all nonnegative rational numbers

Sugarcane is the main source of the sugar we use to sweeten our foods. It grows in tropical areas, such as Costa Rica and Brazil.

In one year, the average person in Costa Rica consumes $24\frac{1}{4}$ lb less sugar than the average person in the United States consumes.

EXAMPLE **1** **Solving Equations by Adding and Subtracting**

Solve each equation. Write the solution in simplest form.

Interactivities Online ▶

A $x + 6\frac{2}{3} = 11$

$$x + 6\frac{2}{3} = 11$$
$$\underline{- 6\frac{2}{3} \qquad - 6\frac{2}{3}}$$ *Subtract $6\frac{2}{3}$ from both sides to undo the addition.*

$$x = 10\frac{3}{3} - 6\frac{2}{3}$$ *Regroup 11 as $10\frac{3}{3}$.*

$$x = 4\frac{1}{3}$$ *Subtract.*

B $2\frac{1}{4} = x - 3\frac{1}{2}$

$$2\frac{1}{4} = x - 3\frac{1}{2}$$
$$\underline{+ 3\frac{1}{2} \qquad + 3\frac{1}{2}}$$ *Add $3\frac{1}{2}$ to both sides to undo the subtraction.*

$$2\frac{1}{4} + 3\frac{2}{4} = x$$ *Find a common denominator. $3\frac{1}{2} = 3\frac{2}{4}$*

$$5\frac{3}{4} = x$$ *Add.*

C $5\frac{3}{5} = m + \frac{7}{10}$

$$5\frac{3}{5} = m + \frac{7}{10}$$
$$\underline{- \frac{7}{10} \qquad - \frac{7}{10}}$$ *Subtract $\frac{7}{10}$ from both sides to undo the addition.*

$$5\frac{6}{10} - \frac{7}{10} = m$$ *Find a common denominator. $5\frac{3}{5} = 5\frac{6}{10}$*

$$4\frac{16}{10} - \frac{7}{10} = m$$ *Regroup $5\frac{6}{10}$ as $4\frac{10}{10} + \frac{6}{10}$.*

$$4\frac{9}{10} = m$$ *Subtract.*

Video **Lesson Tutorials Online** my.hrw.com

Paulo Fridman/Corbis

Solve each equation. Write the solution in simplest form.

D $w - \frac{1}{2} = 2\frac{3}{4}$

$$w - \frac{1}{2} = 2\frac{3}{4}$$

$$\underline{+\frac{1}{2} \quad +\frac{1}{2}}$$ *Add $\frac{1}{2}$ to both sides to undo the subtraction.*

$$w = 2\frac{3}{4} + \frac{1}{2}$$

$$w = 2\frac{3}{4} + \frac{2}{4}$$ *Find a common denominator. $\frac{1}{2} = \frac{2}{4}$*

$$w = 2\frac{5}{4}$$ *Add.*

$$w = 3\frac{1}{4}$$ *Regroup: $2\frac{5}{4} = 2 + 1\frac{1}{4}$*

EXAMPLE 2   *Social Studies Application*

On average, a person in Costa Rica consumes $132\frac{1}{4}$ lb of sugar per year. If the average person in Costa Rica consumes $24\frac{1}{4}$ lb less than the average person in the U.S., what is the average sugar consumption per year by a person in the U.S.?

Costa Rica

$$u - 24\frac{1}{4} = 132\frac{1}{4}$$ *Let u represent the average amount of sugar consumed in the U.S.*

$$\underline{+24\frac{1}{4} \quad +24\frac{1}{4}}$$ *Add $24\frac{1}{4}$ to both sides to undo the subtraction.*

$$u = 156\frac{2}{4} = 156\frac{1}{2}$$ *Simplify.*

Check

$$u - 24\frac{1}{4} = 132\frac{1}{4}$$

$$156\frac{1}{2} - 24\frac{1}{4} \stackrel{?}{=} 132\frac{1}{4}$$ *Substitute $156\frac{1}{2}$ for u.*

$$156\frac{2}{4} - 24\frac{1}{4} \stackrel{?}{=} 132\frac{1}{4}$$ *Find a common denominator.*

$$132\frac{1}{4} \stackrel{?}{=} 132\frac{1}{4} \checkmark$$ *$156\frac{1}{2}$ is the solution.*

On average, a person in the U.S. consumes $156\frac{1}{2}$ lb of sugar per year.

MATHEMATICAL PRACTICES

Think and Discuss

1. **Explain** how regrouping a mixed number when subtracting is similar to regrouping when subtracting whole numbers.

2. **Give an example** of an addition equation with a solution that is a fraction between 3 and 4.

GUIDED PRACTICE

See Example **1** Solve each equation. Write the solution in simplest form.

1. $x + 2\frac{1}{2} = 7$ **2.** $3\frac{1}{3} = x - 5\frac{1}{9}$ **3.** $9\frac{3}{4} = x + 4\frac{1}{8}$

4. $x + 1\frac{1}{5} = 5\frac{3}{10}$ **5.** $3\frac{2}{5} + x = 7\frac{1}{2}$ **6.** $8\frac{7}{10} = x - 4\frac{1}{4}$

See Example **2** **7.** A tailor increased the length of a robe by $2\frac{1}{4}$ inches. The new length of the robe is 60 inches. What was the original length?

INDEPENDENT PRACTICE

See Example **1** Solve each equation. Write the solution in simplest form.

8. $x - 4\frac{3}{4} = 1\frac{1}{12}$ **9.** $x + 5\frac{3}{8} = 9$ **10.** $3\frac{1}{2} = 1\frac{3}{10} + x$

11. $4\frac{2}{3} = x - \frac{1}{6}$ **12.** $6\frac{3}{4} + x = 9\frac{1}{8}$ **13.** $x - 3\frac{7}{9} = 5$

See Example **2** **14.** Robert is taking a movie-making class in school. He edited his short video and cut $3\frac{2}{5}$ minutes. The new length of the video is $12\frac{1}{10}$ minutes. How long was his video before he cut it?

15. An extension for a table increased its length by $2\frac{1}{2}$ feet. The new length of the table is $8\frac{3}{4}$ feet. What was the original length?

PRACTICE AND PROBLEM SOLVING

Extra Practice

See Extra Practice for more exercises.

Find the solution to each equation. Check your answers.

16. $y + 8\frac{2}{4} = 10$ **17.** $p - 1\frac{2}{5} = 3\frac{7}{10}$ **18.** $6\frac{2}{3} + n = 7\frac{5}{6}$

19. $5\frac{3}{5} = s - 2\frac{3}{10}$ **20.** $k - 8\frac{1}{4} = 1\frac{1}{3}$ **21.** $\frac{23}{24} = c + \frac{5}{8}$

22. The difference between Cristina's and Erin's heights is $\frac{1}{2}$ foot. Erin's height is $4\frac{1}{4}$ feet, and she is shorter than Cristina. How tall is Cristina?

23. **Measurement** Lori used $2\frac{5}{8}$ ounces of shampoo to wash her dog. When she was finished, the bottle contained $13\frac{3}{8}$ ounces of shampoo. How many ounces of shampoo were in the bottle before Lori washed her dog?

24. **Sports** Jack decreased his best time in the 400-meter race by $1\frac{3}{10}$ seconds. His new best time is $52\frac{3}{5}$ seconds. What was Jack's old time in the 400-meter race?

25. **Crafts** Juan makes bracelets to sell at his mother's gift shop. He alternates between green and blue beads.

What is the length of the green bead?

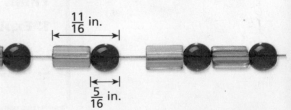

$\frac{11}{16}$ in.

$\frac{5}{16}$ in.

Find the solution to each equation. Check your answers.

26. $m + 4 = 6\frac{3}{8} - 1\frac{1}{4}$ **27.** $3\frac{2}{9} - 1\frac{1}{3} = p - 5\frac{1}{2}$ **28.** $q - 4\frac{1}{4} = 1\frac{1}{6} + 1\frac{1}{2}$

29. $a + 5\frac{1}{4} + 2\frac{1}{2} = 13\frac{1}{6}$ **30.** $11\frac{2}{7} = w + 3\frac{1}{2} - 1\frac{1}{7}$ **31.** $9 - 5\frac{7}{8} = x - 1\frac{1}{8}$

32. Music A string quartet is performing Antonio Vivaldi's *The Four Seasons*. The concert is scheduled to last 45 minutes.

   a. After playing "Spring," "Summer," and "Autumn," how much time will be left in the concert?

   b. Is the concert long enough to play the four movements and another piece that is $6\frac{1}{2}$ minutes long? Explain.

33. Write a Problem Use the pictograph to write a subtraction problem with two mixed numbers.

34. Choose a Strategy How can you draw a line that is 5 inches long using only one sheet of $8\frac{1}{2}$ in. × 11 in. notebook paper?

35. Write About It Explain how you know whether to add a number to or subtract a number from both sides of an equation in order to solve the equation.

36. Challenge Use the numbers 1, 2, 3, 4, 5, and 6 to write a subtraction problem with two mixed numbers that have a difference of $4\frac{13}{20}$.

Test Prep

37. Multiple Choice Solve $4\frac{1}{2} + x = 6\frac{1}{6}$ for x.

  Ⓐ $x = 1\frac{1}{4}$ Ⓑ $x = 1\frac{2}{3}$ Ⓒ $x = 2\frac{1}{4}$ Ⓓ $x = 2\frac{2}{3}$

38. Multiple Choice Ambra's hair was $7\frac{2}{3}$ inches long. After she got her hair cut, the length of her hair was $5\frac{4}{5}$ inches. How many inches of hair were cut?

  Ⓕ $1\frac{13}{15}$ Ⓖ $2\frac{2}{5}$ Ⓗ $2\frac{2}{3}$ Ⓙ $2\frac{13}{15}$

Ready To Go On?

Quiz for Lessons 1 Through 4

 1 **Least Common Multiple**

1. Markers are sold in packs of 8, and crayons are sold in packs of 16. If there are 32 students in Mrs. Reading's art class, what is the least number of packs needed so that each student can have one marker and one crayon and none will be left over?

2. Cans of soup are sold in packs of 24, and packets of crackers are sold in groups of 4. If there are 120 people to be fed and each will get one can of soup and one packet of crackers, what is the least number of packs needed to feed everyone such that no crackers or soup are left over?

Find the least common multiple (LCM).

   3. 4 and 6   **4.** 2 and 15   **5.** 3, 5, and 9   **6.** 4, 6, and 10

2 **Adding and Subtracting with Unlike Denominators**

Add or subtract. Write each answer in simplest form.

   7. $\frac{5}{7} - \frac{3}{14}$ **8.** $\frac{7}{8} + \frac{1}{24}$ **9.** $\frac{8}{9} - \frac{1}{10}$ **10.** $\frac{1}{6} + \frac{1}{2}$

11. Alexia needs to add $\frac{2}{3}$ cup of sugar for the recipe she is making. She has added $\frac{1}{2}$ cup already. How much more sugar does she need to add?

3 **Regrouping to Subtract Mixed Numbers**

Subtract. Write each answer in simplest form.

   12. $2\frac{1}{13} - 1\frac{1}{26}$ **13.** $7\frac{1}{3} - 5\frac{7}{9}$ **14.** $3\frac{3}{10} - 1\frac{4}{5}$ **15.** $10\frac{1}{2} - 5\frac{2}{3}$

16. Mary Ann buys $4\frac{2}{5}$ pounds of bananas. She uses $1\frac{1}{2}$ pounds making banana bread. How many pounds of bananas does she have left?

4 **Solving Fraction Equations: Addition and Subtraction**

Solve each equation. Write the solution in simplest form.

   17. $t + 2\frac{5}{8} = 9$ **18.** $5\frac{1}{6} = x - \frac{7}{8}$ **19.** $g + \frac{1}{4} = 2\frac{9}{10}$ **20.** $a + \frac{3}{5} = 1\frac{7}{10}$

21. Bryn bought $5\frac{1}{8}$ yards of material. She used $3\frac{7}{9}$ yards to make a dress. How much material does she have left?

Focus on Problem Solving

Solve

Solve
• **Choose the operation: multiplication or division**

Read the whole problem before you try to solve it. Determine what action is taking place in the problem. Then decide whether you need to multiply or divide in order to solve the problem.

If you are asked to combine equal groups, you need to multiply. If you are asked to share something equally or to separate something into equal groups, you need to divide.

Action	Operation	
Combining equal groups	Multiplication	
Sharing things equally or separating into equal groups	Division	

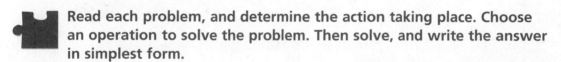

Read each problem, and determine the action taking place. Choose an operation to solve the problem. Then solve, and write the answer in simplest form.

1 Jason picked 30 cups of raspberries. He put them in giant freezer bags with 5 cups in each bag. How many bags does he have?

2 When the cranberry flowers start to open in June, cranberry growers usually bring in about $2\frac{1}{2}$ beehives per acre of cranberries to pollinate the flowers. A grower has 36 acres of cranberries. About how many beehives does she need?

3 A recipe that makes 3 cranberry banana loaves calls for 4 cups of cranberries. Linh wants to make only 1 loaf. How many cups of cranberries does she need?

4 Clay wants to double a recipe for blueberry muffins that calls for 1 cup of blueberries. How many blueberries will he need?

Ingram Publishing/SuperStock

Multiplying Mixed Numbers

Janice and Carla are making homemade pasta from a recipe that calls for $1\frac{1}{2}$ cups of flour. They want to make $\frac{1}{3}$ of the recipe.

You can find $\frac{1}{3}$ of $1\frac{1}{2}$, or multiply $\frac{1}{3}$ by $1\frac{1}{2}$, to find how much flour Janice and Carla need.

EXAMPLE 1   Multiplying Fractions and Mixed Numbers

Multiply. Write each answer in simplest form.

Interactivities Online ▶

> **Remember!**
>
> To write a mixed number as an improper fraction, start with the denominator, multiply by the whole number, and add the numerator. Use the same denominator.
>
> $1\frac{1}{5} = \frac{1 \cdot 5 + 1}{5} = \frac{6}{5}$

A $\frac{1}{3} \cdot 1\frac{1}{2}$

$\frac{1}{3} \cdot \frac{3}{2}$ *Write $1\frac{1}{2}$ as an improper fraction. $1\frac{1}{2} = \frac{3}{2}$*

$\frac{1 \cdot 3}{3 \cdot 2}$ *Multiply numerators. Multiply denominators.*

$\frac{3}{6}$

$\frac{1}{2}$ *Write the answer in simplest form.*

B $1\frac{1}{5} \cdot \frac{2}{3}$

$\frac{6}{5} \cdot \frac{2}{3}$ *Write $1\frac{1}{5}$ as an improper fraction. $1\frac{1}{5} = \frac{6}{5}$*

$\frac{6 \cdot 2}{5 \cdot 3}$ *Multiply numerators. Multiply denominators.*

$\frac{12}{15}$

$\frac{4}{5}$ *Write the answer in simplest form.*

C $\frac{3}{4} \cdot 2\frac{1}{3}$

$\frac{3}{4} \cdot \frac{7}{3}$ *Write $2\frac{1}{3}$ as an improper fraction. $2\frac{1}{3} = \frac{7}{3}$*

$\frac{\overset{1}{\cancel{3}}}{4} \cdot \frac{7}{\underset{1}{\cancel{3}}}$ *Use the GCF to simplify before multiplying.*

$\frac{1 \cdot 7}{4 \cdot 1}$

$\frac{7}{4} = 1\frac{3}{4}$ *You can write the answer as a mixed number.*

    Video **Lesson Tutorials Online** my.hrw.com

David Young-Wolff/Photographer's Choice/Getty Images

EXAMPLE 2 **Multiplying Mixed Numbers**

Find each product. Write the answer in simplest form.

Remember!

You can estimate the product to see whether your answer is reasonable.

A $2\frac{1}{2} \cdot 1\frac{1}{3}$

$\frac{5}{2} \cdot \frac{4}{3}$ *Write the mixed numbers as improper fractions.* $2\frac{1}{2} = \frac{5}{2}$ $1\frac{1}{3} = \frac{4}{3}$

$\frac{5 \cdot 4}{2 \cdot 3}$ *Multiply numerators.*
Multiply denominators.

$\frac{20}{6}$

$3\frac{2}{6}$ *Write the improper fraction as a mixed number.*

$3\frac{1}{3}$ *Simplify.*

B $1\frac{1}{4} \cdot 1\frac{1}{3}$

$\frac{5}{4} \cdot \frac{4}{3}$ *Write the mixed numbers as improper fractions.* $1\frac{1}{4} = \frac{5}{4}$ $1\frac{1}{3} = \frac{4}{3}$

$\frac{5}{\underset{1}{4}} \cdot \frac{\overset{1}{4}}{3}$ *Use the GCF to simplify before multiplying.*

$\frac{5 \cdot 1}{1 \cdot 3}$ *Multiply numerators. Multiply denominators.*

$\frac{5}{3}$

$1\frac{2}{3}$ *Write the answer as a mixed number.*

C $5 \cdot 3\frac{2}{11}$

$5 \cdot 3\frac{2}{11}$

$5 \cdot \left(3 + \frac{2}{11}\right)$

$(5 \cdot 3) + \left(5 \cdot \frac{2}{11}\right)$ *Use the Distributive Property.*

$(5 \cdot 3) + \left(\frac{5}{1} \cdot \frac{2}{11}\right)$

$15 + \frac{10}{11}$ *Multiply.*

$15\frac{10}{11}$ *Add.*

MATHEMATICAL PRACTICES

Think and Discuss

1. **Tell** how you multiply a mixed number by a mixed number.

2. **Explain** two ways you would multiply a mixed number by a whole number.

3. **Explain** whether the product of a proper fraction and a mixed number is less than, between, or greater than the two factors.

GUIDED PRACTICE

See Example **1** Multiply. Write each answer in simplest form.

1. $1\frac{1}{4} \cdot \frac{2}{3}$ **2.** $2\frac{2}{3} \cdot \frac{1}{4}$ **3.** $\frac{3}{7} \cdot 1\frac{5}{6}$

4. $1\frac{1}{3} \cdot \frac{6}{7}$ **5.** $\frac{2}{3} \cdot 1\frac{3}{10}$ **6.** $2\frac{6}{11} \cdot \frac{2}{7}$

See Example **2** Find each product. Write the answer in simplest form.

7. $1\frac{5}{6} \cdot 1\frac{1}{8}$ **8.** $2\frac{2}{5} \cdot 1\frac{1}{12}$ **9.** $4 \cdot 5\frac{3}{7}$

10. $2\frac{3}{4} \cdot 1\frac{5}{6}$ **11.** $2\frac{3}{8} \cdot 5\frac{1}{5}$ **12.** $10\frac{1}{2} \cdot 1\frac{1}{4}$

INDEPENDENT PRACTICE

See Example **1** Multiply. Write each answer in simplest form.

13. $1\frac{1}{4} \cdot \frac{3}{4}$ **14.** $\frac{4}{7} \cdot 1\frac{1}{4}$ **15.** $1\frac{1}{6} \cdot \frac{2}{5}$ **16.** $2\frac{1}{6} \cdot \frac{3}{7}$

17. $\frac{5}{9} \cdot 1\frac{9}{10}$ **18.** $2\frac{2}{9} \cdot \frac{3}{5}$ **19.** $1\frac{3}{10} \cdot \frac{5}{7}$ **20.** $\frac{3}{4} \cdot 1\frac{2}{5}$

See Example **2** Find each product. Write the answer in simplest form.

21. $1\frac{1}{3} \cdot 1\frac{5}{7}$ **22.** $1\frac{2}{3} \cdot 2\frac{3}{10}$ **23.** $4 \cdot 3\frac{7}{8}$ **24.** $6 \cdot 2\frac{1}{3}$

25. $5 \cdot 4\frac{7}{10}$ **26.** $2\frac{2}{3} \cdot 3\frac{5}{8}$ **27.** $1\frac{1}{2} \cdot 2\frac{2}{5}$ **28.** $3\frac{5}{6} \cdot 2\frac{3}{4}$

PRACTICE AND PROBLEM SOLVING

Extra Practice
See Extra Practice for more exercises.

Write each product in simplest form.

29. $1\frac{2}{3} \cdot \frac{2}{9}$ **30.** $3\frac{1}{3} \cdot \frac{7}{10}$ **31.** $2 \cdot \frac{5}{8}$ **32.** $2\frac{8}{11} \cdot \frac{3}{10}$

33. $\frac{3}{8} \cdot \frac{4}{9}$ **34.** $2\frac{1}{12} \cdot 1\frac{3}{5}$ **35.** $3\frac{3}{10} \cdot 4\frac{1}{6}$ **36.** $2\frac{1}{4} \cdot 1\frac{2}{9}$

37. $2 \cdot \frac{4}{5} \cdot 1\frac{2}{3}$ **38.** $3\frac{5}{6} \cdot \frac{9}{10} \cdot 4\frac{2}{3}$ **39.** $1\frac{7}{8} \cdot 2\frac{1}{3} \cdot 4$ **40.** $1\frac{2}{7} \cdot 3 \cdot 2\frac{5}{8}$

41. Multi-Step Jared used $1\frac{2}{5}$ bags of soil for his garden. He is digging another garden that will need $\frac{1}{5}$ as much soil as the original. How much will he use total?

42. Milo is making $1\frac{1}{2}$ batches of muffins. If one batch calls for $1\frac{3}{4}$ cups flour, how much flour will he need?

43. Critical Thinking Is the product of two mixed numbers less than, between, or greater than the two factors?

Evaluate each expression.

44. $\frac{1}{2} \cdot c$ for $c = 4\frac{2}{5}$ **45.** $1\frac{5}{7} \cdot x$ for $x = \frac{5}{6}$ **46.** $1\frac{3}{4} \cdot b$ for $b = 1\frac{1}{7}$

47. $1\frac{5}{9} \cdot n$ for $n = 18$ **48.** $2\frac{5}{9} \cdot t$ for $t = 4$ **49.** $3\frac{3}{4} \cdot p$ for $p = \frac{1}{2}$

50. $\frac{4}{5} \cdot m$ for $m = 2\frac{2}{3}$ **51.** $6y$ for $y = 3\frac{5}{8}$ **52.** $2\frac{3}{5} \cdot c$ for $c = 1\frac{1}{5}$

Muffins probably started out as a form of cake, or possibly as a variety of cornbread. Early muffins didn't have nearly as much variety as is available today.

Fresh Fruit Muffins

1 3/4 cups all-purpose flour
1/3 cup granulated sugar
2 1/2 teaspoons baking powder
1/2 teaspoon salt
3/4 cup milk
1 egg
1/3 cup butter, melted
1 cup fresh fruit

In a large bowl, whisk together dry ingredients. Add milk, egg, and butter, and mix until ingredients are moistened – do not over-beat. Stir in fruit and pour into greased muffin cups. Bake at 400°F for 20-25 minutes, or until tops spring back when lightly touched. Makes 12 muffins.

Use the recipe for Exercises 53–57.

53. How much flour and baking powder would you need if you doubled the recipe?

54. How much baking powder is needed for half of the recipe?

55. Raquel is baking muffins for a bake sale at school. She plans on multiplying the recipe by $3\frac{1}{2}$.

   a. How much flour will she need?

   b. How much sugar will she need?

   c. How much salt will she need?

56. Each muffin contains $22\frac{1}{5}$ grams of carbohydrates. How many grams of carbohydrates are contained in 12 muffins?

57. ⭐ **Challenge** What is the smallest number by which you could multiply the entire recipe so that the amount of each ingredient would be a whole number?

Test Prep

58. **Multiple Choice** A chef uses $2\frac{1}{4}$ cups of water for a recipe. The chef doubled the recipe. How much water did the chef use?

   Ⓐ 4 cups   Ⓑ $4\frac{1}{4}$ cups   Ⓒ $4\frac{1}{2}$ cups   Ⓓ $4\frac{3}{4}$ cups

59. **Gridded Response** Keith ate $\frac{1}{3}$ pound of grapes last week. Jamal ate five times as many grapes as Keith last week. How many pounds of grapes did Jamal eat?

60. **Short Response** Josh is training to run in a half-marathon. So far this week, he has run $6\frac{3}{8}$ miles on each of three days. What is the total distance Josh has run this week?

Model Fraction Division

Use with Dividing Fractions and Mixed Numbers

 **Learn It Online**
Lab Resources Online

 MATHEMATICAL PRACTICES **Use appropriate tools strategically.**
CC.6.NS.1 Interpret and compute quotients of fractions… by using visual fraction models and equations…

You can use grids to help you understand division of fractions.

Activity 1

Find $4\frac{1}{2} \div 3$.

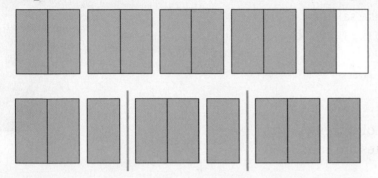

Think of $4\frac{1}{2} \div 3$ as dividing $4\frac{1}{2}$ into 3 equal groups.

Shade $4\frac{1}{2}$ squares.

Divide the shaded parts into 3 equal groups.

Look at one of the shaded groups.

What fraction is this?

$$4\frac{1}{2} \div 3 = 1\frac{1}{2}$$

Think and Discuss

1. Explain how you know the number of groups into which you must divide the squares.

Try This

Write the division expression modeled on each grid.

1.

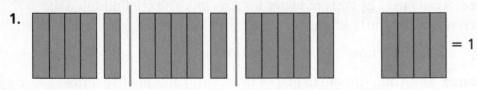 = 1

Draw a model for each division expression. Then find the value of the expression.

2. $9\frac{1}{3} \div 4$ 3. $3\frac{3}{4} \div 5$ 4. $4\frac{2}{3} \div 2$ 5. $4\frac{1}{5} \div 3$

Activity 2

1 Find $2\frac{2}{3} \div \frac{2}{3}$.

Shade $2\frac{2}{3}$ squares.

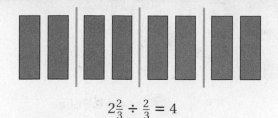

Divide the shaded squares and shaded thirds into equal groups of $\frac{2}{3}$.

There are 4 groups of $\frac{2}{3}$ in $2\frac{2}{3}$.

$$2\frac{2}{3} \div \frac{2}{3} = 4$$

2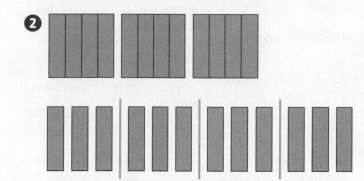

To find $3 \div \frac{3}{4}$, think, "How many groups of $\frac{3}{4}$ are in 3?"

Shade 3 squares. Then divide the squares into fourths because the denominator of $\frac{3}{4}$ is 4.

Divide the shaded squares into equal groups of $\frac{3}{4}$.

There are 4 groups of $\frac{3}{4}$ in 3.

$$3 \div \frac{3}{4} = 4$$

Think and Discuss

1. Explain what prediction you can make about the value of $6 \div \frac{3}{4}$ if you know that $3 \div \frac{3}{4}$ is 4.

Try This

Write the division expression modeled by each grid.

1.  = 1

2. 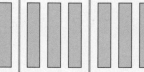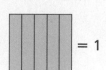 = 1

Draw a model for each division expression. Then find the value of the expression.

3. $4 \div 1\frac{1}{3}$

4. $3\frac{3}{4} \div \frac{3}{4}$

5. $5\frac{1}{3} \div \frac{2}{3}$

6. $6\frac{2}{3} \div 1\frac{2}{3}$

Model Fraction Division in Context

Use with Dividing Fractions and Mixed Numbers

Learn It Online
Lab Resources Online

MATHEMATICAL PRACTICES

Use appropriate tools strategically.
CC.6.NS.1 …solve word problems involving division of fractions by fractions, e.g., by using visual fraction models and equations to represent the problem

You can use fraction bars to model the division of fractions in word problems.

Activity 1

Vera makes 2 cups of cookie batter. She uses $\frac{1}{8}$ cup of batter to make each cookie. How many cookies can Vera make in all?

a. Use fraction bars to model the problem. Vera has 2 cups of cookie batter, so use 2 whole fraction bars to represent the batter. Use $\frac{1}{8}$ fraction bars to represent the amount of batter used to make each cookie.

b. You want to find $2 \div \frac{1}{8}$, or the number of eighths in 2 wholes. See how many $\frac{1}{8}$ fraction bars are equal to 2 whole fraction bars. This models the quotient.

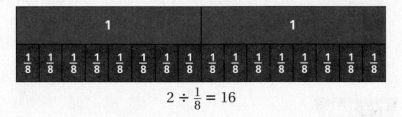

$$2 \div \frac{1}{8} = 16$$

The model shows that sixteen $\frac{1}{8}$ fraction bars are equal to 2 whole fraction bars. Therefore, 2 divided by $\frac{1}{8}$ is equal to 16. Vera can make 16 cookies from her batter.

Think and Discuss

1. How do you know that you need to divide 2 by $\frac{1}{8}$?

Try This

1. Jordan has 4 yards of ribbon to use for a craft project. She needs to cut the ribbon into pieces that are $\frac{1}{3}$ yard long. How many pieces of ribbon will Jordan have?

Activity 2

Slater wants to divide a $\frac{3}{4}$-pound box of trail mix into small bags. Each of the bags will hold $\frac{1}{6}$ pound of trail mix. How many bags of trail mix can Slater fill?

a. Represent the $\frac{3}{4}$-pound box using a unit fraction with the least common denominator of $\frac{3}{4}$ and $\frac{1}{6}$, which is 12. (The least common denominator is the least common multiple of two or more denominators.) So, represent the $\frac{3}{4}$-pound box using $\frac{1}{12}$ fraction bars.

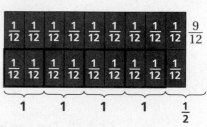

b. Next, represent each $\frac{1}{6}$-pound bag using $\frac{1}{12}$ fraction bars.

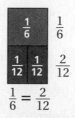

c. You want to find $\frac{3}{4} \div \frac{1}{6}$, or the number of sixths in three-fourths. Place the two $\frac{1}{12}$ fraction bars that represent each $\frac{1}{6}$ below the nine $\frac{1}{12}$ fraction bars that represent $\frac{3}{4}$. This models the quotient.

The model shows that $\frac{3}{4} \div \frac{1}{6} = 4\frac{1}{2}$. Slater could fill $4\frac{1}{2}$ bags with trail mix.

Think and Discuss

1. Can you think of any limitations to using fraction bars to solve word problems?

Try This

1. If one honeybee makes $\frac{1}{12}$ teaspoon of honey during its lifetime, how many honeybees are needed to make $\frac{1}{2}$ teaspoon of honey?

2. Liv is making sandwiches for a picnic. She wants each sandwich to have $\frac{1}{5}$ pound of meat. If Liv has $\frac{3}{4}$ pound of turkey, does she have enough meat to make 4 sandwiches? Explain.

Dividing Fractions and Mixed Numbers

CC.6.NS.1 Interpret and compute quotients of fractions, and solve word problems involving division of fractions by fractions, e.g., by using visual fraction models and equations to represent the problem

Vocabulary

reciprocal

multiplicative inverse

Curtis is making sushi rolls. First, he will place a sheet of seaweed, called *nori*, on the sushi rolling mat. Then, he will use the mat to roll up rice, cucumber, avocado, and crabmeat. Finally, he will slice the roll into smaller pieces.

Curtis has 2 cups of rice and will use $\frac{1}{3}$ cup for each sushi roll. How many sushi rolls can he make?

Think: How many $\frac{1}{3}$ pieces equal 2 wholes?

There are six $\frac{1}{3}$ pieces in 2 wholes, so Curtis can make 6 sushi rolls.

Reciprocals can help you divide by fractions. Two numbers are **reciprocals** or *multiplicative inverses*, if their product is 1.

Multiplicative Inverse Property	
Words	**Numbers**
The product of a nonzero number and its reciprocal, or **multiplicative inverse**, is 1.	$\frac{3}{4} \cdot \frac{4}{3} = 1$

EXAMPLE **1** **Finding Reciprocals**

Find the reciprocal.

A $\frac{1}{5}$

$\frac{1}{5} \cdot \blacksquare = 1$ *Think: $\frac{1}{5}$ of what number is 1?*

$\frac{1}{5} \cdot 5 = 1$ *$\frac{1}{5}$ of $\frac{5}{1}$ is 1.*

The reciprocal of $\frac{1}{5}$ is 5.

B $2\frac{1}{3}$

$\frac{7}{3} \cdot \blacksquare = 1$ *Write $2\frac{1}{3}$ as $\frac{7}{3}$.*

$\frac{7}{3} \cdot \frac{3}{7} = \frac{21}{21} = 1$ *$\frac{7}{3}$ of $\frac{3}{7}$ is 1.*

The reciprocal of $\frac{7}{3}$ is $\frac{3}{7}$.

[Video] **Lesson Tutorials Online**   my.hrw.com

Victoria Smith/HMH

Look at the relationship between the fractions $\frac{3}{4}$ and $\frac{4}{3}$. If you switch the numerator and denominator of a fraction, you will find its reciprocal. Dividing by a number is the same as multiplying by its reciprocal.

$$24 \div 4 = 6 \qquad 24 \cdot \frac{1}{4} = 6$$

EXAMPLE **2** **Using Reciprocals to Divide Fractions and Mixed Numbers**

Divide. Write each answer in simplest form.

A $\frac{4}{5} \div 5$

$\frac{4}{5} \div 5 = \frac{4}{5} \cdot \frac{1}{5}$ *Rewrite as multiplication using the reciprocal of 5, $\frac{1}{5}$.*

$= \frac{4 \cdot 1}{5 \cdot 5}$ *Multiply by the reciprocal.*

$= \frac{4}{25}$ *The answer is in simplest form.*

B $\frac{3}{4} \div \frac{1}{2}$

$\frac{3}{4} \div \frac{1}{2} = \frac{3}{4} \cdot \frac{2}{1}$ *Rewrite as multiplication using the reciprocal of $\frac{1}{2}$, $\frac{2}{1}$.*

$= \frac{3 \cdot \overset{1}{\cancel{2}}}{\underset{2}{\cancel{4}} \cdot 1}$ *Simplify before multiplying.*

$= \frac{3}{2}$ *Multiply.*

$= 1\frac{1}{2}$ *You can write the answer as a mixed number.*

C $2\frac{2}{3} \div 1\frac{1}{6}$

$2\frac{2}{3} \div 1\frac{1}{6} = \frac{8}{3} \div \frac{7}{6}$ *Write the mixed numbers as improper fractions. $2\frac{2}{3} = \frac{8}{3}$ and $1\frac{1}{6} = \frac{7}{6}$*

$= \frac{8}{3} \cdot \frac{6}{7}$ *Rewrite as multiplication.*

$= \frac{8 \cdot \overset{2}{\cancel{6}}}{\underset{1}{\cancel{3}} \cdot 7}$ *Simplify before multiplying.*

$= \frac{16}{7}$ *Multiply.*

$= 2\frac{2}{7}$ *You can write the answer as a mixed number.*

Caution!

When you divide by a proper fraction, the quotient will be greater than the dividend. For example, since there are 8 halves in 4, $4 \div \frac{1}{2} = 8$.

MATHEMATICAL PRACTICES

Think and Discuss

1. **Explain** how you can use mental math to find the value of n in the equation $\frac{5}{8} \cdot n = 1$.

2. **Explain** how to find the reciprocal of $3\frac{6}{11}$.

Learn It Online
Homework Help Online
Exercises 1–35, 37, 39, 43, 45, 49, 55, 61

GUIDED PRACTICE

See Example **1**   Find the reciprocal.

1. $\frac{2}{7}$ **2.** $\frac{5}{9}$ **3.** $\frac{1}{9}$ **4.** $\frac{3}{11}$ **5.** $2\frac{3}{5}$

See Example **2**   Divide. Write each answer in simplest form.

6. $\frac{5}{6} \div 3$ **7.** $2\frac{1}{7} \div 1\frac{1}{4}$ **8.** $\frac{5}{12} \div 5$ **9.** $1\frac{5}{8} \div \frac{3}{4}$

10. $\frac{2}{3} \div \frac{1}{6}$ **11.** $\frac{3}{10} \div 1\frac{2}{3}$ **12.** $\frac{4}{7} \div 1\frac{1}{7}$ **13.** $4 \div \frac{7}{8}$

INDEPENDENT PRACTICE

See Example **1**   Find the reciprocal.

14. $\frac{7}{8}$ **15.** $\frac{1}{10}$ **16.** $\frac{3}{8}$ **17.** $\frac{11}{12}$ **18.** $2\frac{5}{8}$

19. $\frac{8}{11}$ **20.** $\frac{5}{6}$ **21.** $\frac{6}{7}$ **22.** $\frac{2}{9}$ **23.** $5\frac{1}{4}$

See Example **2**   Divide. Write each answer in simplest form.

24. $\frac{7}{8} \div 4$ **25.** $2\frac{3}{8} \div 1\frac{3}{4}$ **26.** $\frac{8}{9} \div 12$ **27.** $9 \div \frac{3}{4}$

28. $3\frac{5}{6} \div 1\frac{5}{9}$ **29.** $\frac{9}{10} \div 3$ **30.** $2\frac{4}{5} \div 1\frac{5}{7}$ **31.** $3\frac{1}{5} \div 1\frac{2}{7}$

32. $\frac{5}{8} \div \frac{1}{2}$ **33.** $1\frac{1}{2} \div 2\frac{1}{4}$ **34.** $\frac{7}{12} \div 2\frac{5}{8}$ **35.** $\frac{1}{8} \div 5$

PRACTICE AND PROBLEM SOLVING

Extra Practice
See Extra Practice for more exercises.

Multiply or divide. Write each answer in simplest form.

36. $2\frac{3}{4} \div 2\frac{1}{5}$ **37.** $4\frac{4}{5} \div 2\frac{6}{7}$ **38.** $\frac{3}{8} \cdot \frac{5}{12}$

39. $6 \cdot \frac{7}{9}$ **40.** $3\frac{1}{7} \div 5$ **41.** $\frac{9}{14} \cdot \frac{1}{6}$

42. At Lina's restaurant, one serving of chili is $1\frac{1}{2}$ cups. The chef makes 48 cups of chili each night. How many servings of chili are in 48 cups?

43. Rhula bought 12 lb of raisins. She packed them into freezer bags so that each bag weighs $\frac{3}{4}$ lb. How many freezer bags did she pack?

Decide whether the fractions in each pair are reciprocals. If not, write the reciprocal of each fraction.

44. $\frac{1}{2}, 2$ **45.** $\frac{3}{8}, \frac{16}{6}$ **46.** $\frac{7}{9}, \frac{21}{27}$ **47.** $\frac{5}{6}, \frac{12}{10}$

48. $1\frac{1}{2}, \frac{2}{3}$ **49.** $\frac{2}{5}, \frac{4}{25}$ **50.** $\frac{3}{7}, 2\frac{1}{3}$ **51.** $5, \frac{5}{1}$

52. Lisa had some wood that was $12\frac{1}{2}$ feet long. She cut it into 5 pieces that are equal in length. How long is each piece of wood?

53. Critical Thinking How can you recognize the reciprocal of a fraction?

Multiply or divide. Write each answer in simplest form.

54. $\frac{11}{12} \cdot \frac{9}{10} \div 1\frac{1}{4}$

55. $2\frac{3}{4} \cdot 1\frac{2}{3} \div 5$

56. $1\frac{1}{2} \div \frac{3}{4} \cdot \frac{2}{5}$

57. $\frac{3}{4} \cdot \left(\frac{5}{7} \div \frac{1}{2}\right)$

58. $4\frac{2}{3} \div \left(6 \cdot \frac{3}{5}\right)$

59. $5\frac{1}{5} \cdot \left(3\frac{2}{5} \cdot 2\frac{1}{3}\right)$

Life Science The bar graph shows the lengths of some species of snakes found in the United States. Use the bar graph for Exercises 60–62.

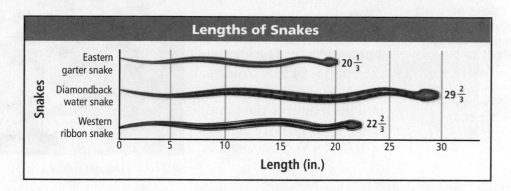

60. Is the length of the eastern garter snake greater than or less than $\frac{1}{2}$ yd? Explain.

61. What is the average length of all the snakes?

62. Jim measured the length of a rough green snake. It was $27\frac{1}{3}$ in. long. What would the average length of the snakes be if Jim's measure of a rough green snake were added?

63. **What's the Error?** A student said the reciprocal of $6\frac{2}{3}$ is $6\frac{3}{2}$. Explain the error. Then write the correct reciprocal.

64. **Write About It** Explain how to divide fractions to find $\frac{3}{4} \div 2\frac{1}{3}$.

65. **Challenge** Evaluate the expression $\frac{(6-3)}{4} \div \frac{1}{8} \cdot 5$.

Test Prep

66. Multiple Choice A piece of wood was 12 feet long. Gene cut the wood into pieces $\frac{2}{3}$ foot long. How many pieces did Gene have?

(A) 4   (B) 8   (C) 16   (D) 18

67. Multiple Choice Which product is NOT equal to 1?

(F) $\frac{2}{3} \cdot \frac{3}{2}$ (G) $8 \cdot \frac{1}{8}$ (H) $\frac{1}{9} \cdot \frac{9}{3}$ (J) $\frac{2}{13} \cdot \frac{13}{2}$

Solving Fraction Equations: Multiplication and Division

CC.6.EE.7 Solve real-world and mathematical problems by writing and solving equations of the form $x + p = q$ and $px = q$ for cases in which p, q and x are all nonnegative rational numbers **Also CC.6.NS.1**

Josef is building a fish pond for koi in his backyard. He makes the width of the pond $\frac{2}{3}$ of the length. The width of the pond is 14 feet. You can use the equation $\frac{2}{3}\ell = 14$ to find the length of the pond.

Small koi in a backyard pond usually grow 2 to 4 inches per year.

E X A M P L E 1 Solving Equations by Multiplying and Dividing

Solve each equation. Write the answer in simplest form.

Interactivities Online ▶

Remember!

Dividing by a number is the same as multiplying by its reciprocal.

A $\frac{2}{3}\ell = 14$

$$\frac{2}{3}\ell = 14$$

$$\frac{2}{3}\ell \div \frac{2}{3} = 14 \div \frac{2}{3}$$ *Divide both sides of the equation by $\frac{2}{3}$.*

$$\frac{2}{3}\ell \cdot \frac{3}{2} = 14 \cdot \frac{3}{2}$$ *Multiply by $\frac{3}{2}$, the reciprocal of $\frac{2}{3}$.*

$$\ell = 14 \cdot \frac{3}{2}$$

$$\ell = \frac{14 \cdot 3}{1 \cdot 2}$$

$$\ell = \frac{42}{2}, \text{ or } 21$$

B $2x = \frac{1}{3}$

$$2x = \frac{1}{3}$$

$$\frac{2x}{1} \cdot \frac{1}{2} = \frac{1}{3} \cdot \frac{1}{2}$$ *Multiply both sides by the reciprocal of 2.*

$$x = \frac{1 \cdot 1}{3 \cdot 2}$$

$$x = \frac{1}{6}$$ *The answer is in simplest form.*

C $\frac{5x}{6} = 4$

$$\frac{5x}{6} = 4$$

$$\frac{5x}{6} \div \frac{5}{6} = \frac{4}{1} \div \frac{5}{6}$$ *Divide both sides by $\frac{5}{6}$.*

$$\frac{5x}{6} \cdot \frac{6}{5} = \frac{4}{1} \cdot \frac{6}{5}$$ *Multiply by the reciprocal of $\frac{5}{6}$.*

$$x = \frac{24}{5}, \text{ or } 4\frac{4}{5}$$

EXAMPLE 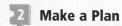 2

EXAMPLE 2 | **PROBLEM SOLVING APPLICATION**

MATHEMATICAL PRACTICES Make sense of problems and persevere in solving them.

Pets

No more than $\frac{1}{10}$ of a dog's diet should consist of treats and biscuits.

Dexter makes dog biscuits for the animal shelter. He makes $\frac{3}{4}$ of a recipe and uses 15 cups of powdered milk. How many cups of powdered milk are in the recipe?

1. **Understand the Problem**

The **answer** will be the number of cups of powdered milk in the recipe.

List the **important information:**

- He makes $\frac{3}{4}$ of the recipe.
- He uses 15 cups of powdered milk.

2 **Make a Plan**

You can write and solve an equation. Let x represent the number of cups in the recipe.

He uses 15 cups, which is three-fourths of the amount in the recipe.
$15 = \frac{3}{4}x$

3 **Solve**

$$15 = \frac{3}{4}x$$

$$15 \cdot \frac{4}{3} = \frac{3}{4}x \cdot \frac{4}{3}$$ *Multiply both sides by $\frac{4}{3}$, the reciprocal of $\frac{3}{4}$.*

$$\frac{\overset{5}{\cancel{15}}}{1} \cdot \frac{4}{\underset{1}{\cancel{3}}} = x$$ *Simplify. Then multiply.*

$$20 = x$$

There are 20 cups of powdered milk in the recipe.

4 **Look Back**

Check $\quad 15 = \frac{3}{4}x$

$\qquad 15 \overset{?}{=} \frac{3}{4}(20)$ *Substitute 20 for x.*

$\qquad 15 \overset{?}{=} \frac{\overset{15}{\cancel{60}}}{\underset{1}{\cancel{4}}}$ *Multiply and simplify.*

$\qquad 15 \overset{?}{=} 15 \checkmark$ *20 is the solution.*

MATHEMATICAL PRACTICES

Think and Discuss

1. **Explain** whether $\frac{2}{3}x = 4$ is the same as $\frac{2}{3} = 4x$.

2. **Tell** how you know which numbers to divide by in the following equations: $\frac{2}{3}x = 4$ and $\frac{4}{5} = 8x$.

Exercises

GUIDED PRACTICE

See Example 1 Solve each equation. Write the answer in simplest form.

1. $\frac{3}{4}z = 12$ **2.** $4n = \frac{3}{5}$ **3.** $\frac{2x}{3} = 5$ **4.** $2c = \frac{9}{10}$

See Example 2 **5. School** In PE class, $\frac{3}{8}$ of the students want to play volleyball. If 9 students want to play volleyball, how many students are in the class?

INDEPENDENT PRACTICE

See Example 1 Solve each equation. Write the answer in simplest form.

6. $3t = \frac{2}{7}$ **7.** $\frac{1}{3}x = 3$ **8.** $\frac{3r}{5} = 9$ **9.** $8t = \frac{4}{5}$

10. $\frac{4}{5}a = 1$ **11.** $\frac{y}{4} = 5$ **12.** $2b = \frac{6}{7}$ **13.** $\frac{7}{9}j = 10$

See Example 2 **14.** Jason uses 2 cans of paint to paint $\frac{1}{2}$ of his room. How many cans of paint will he use to paint the whole room?

15. Cassandra baby-sits for $\frac{4}{5}$ of an hour and earns $8. What is her hourly rate?

PRACTICE AND PROBLEM SOLVING

Extra Practice
See Extra Practice for more exercises.

Solve each equation. Write the answer in simplest form.

16. $m = \frac{3}{8} \cdot 4$ **17.** $\frac{3y}{5} = 6$ **18.** $4z = \frac{7}{10}$ **19.** $t = \frac{4}{5} \cdot 20$

20. $\frac{3}{5}a = \frac{3}{5}$ **21.** $\frac{1}{6}b = 2\frac{1}{3}$ **22.** $5c = \frac{2}{3} \div \frac{2}{3}$ **23.** $\frac{3}{4}x = 7$

24. $\frac{1}{2} = \frac{w}{4}$ **25.** $8 = \frac{2n}{3}$ **26.** $\frac{1}{4} \cdot \frac{1}{2} = 4d$ **27.** $2y = \frac{4}{5} \div \frac{3}{5}$

Write each equation. Then solve, and check the solution.

28. A number n is divided by 4 and the quotient is $\frac{1}{2}$.

29. A number n is multiplied by $1\frac{1}{2}$ and the product is 9.

30. A recipe for a loaf of bread calls for $\frac{3}{4}$ cup of oatmeal.

   a. How much oatmeal do you need if you make half the recipe?

   b. How much oatmeal do you need if you double the recipe?

31. Entertainment Connie rode the roller coaster at the amusement park. After 3 minutes, the ride was $\frac{3}{4}$ complete. How long did the entire ride take?

32. Zac moved $\frac{1}{5}$ of the things from his old bedroom to his new dorm room in $32\frac{1}{2}$ minutes. How long will it take in minutes for him to move all of his things to his new dorm room?

33. A dress pattern requires $3\frac{1}{8}$ yards of fabric. Jody wants to make matching dresses for the girls in her sewing club so she purchased $34\frac{3}{8}$ yards of fabric. How many dresses can Jody make using this pattern?

Life Science

The northwest corner of Madagascar is home to black lemurs. These primates live in groups of 7–10, and they have an average life span of 20–25 years.

34. Multi-Step Alder cut 3 pieces of fabric from a roll. Each piece of fabric she cut is $1\frac{1}{2}$ yd long. She has 2 yards of fabric left on the roll. How much fabric was on the roll before she cut it?

35. Life Science Sasha's book report is about animals in Madagascar. She writes 10 pages, which represents $\frac{1}{3}$ of her report, about lemurs. How many more pages does Sasha have to write to complete her book report?

36. Critical Thinking How can you tell, without solving the equation $\frac{1}{2}x = 4\frac{7}{8}$, that x is greater that $4\frac{7}{8}$?

Use the circle graph for Exercises 37 and 38.

37. The circle graph shows the results of a survey of people who were asked to choose their favorite kind of bagel.

a. One hundred people chose plain bagels as their favorite kind of bagel. How many people were surveyed in all?

b. One-fifth of the people who chose sesame bagels also chose plain cream cheese as their favorite spread. How many people chose plain cream cheese? (*Hint*: Use the answer to part **a** to help you solve this problem.)

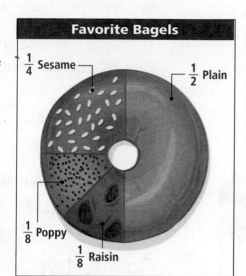

Favorite Bagels

$\frac{1}{4}$ Sesame

$\frac{1}{2}$ Plain

$\frac{1}{8}$ Poppy

$\frac{1}{8}$ Raisin

38. What's the Question? If the answer is 25 people, what is the question?

39. Write About It Explain how to solve $\frac{3}{5}x = 4$.

40. Challenge Solve $2\frac{3}{4}n = \frac{11}{12}$

Ready To Go On?

Quiz for Lessons 5 Through 7

 5 **Multiplying Mixed Numbers**

Multiply. Write each answer in simplest form.

1. $\frac{1}{4} \cdot 2\frac{1}{3}$

2. $1\frac{1}{6} \cdot \frac{2}{3}$

3. $\frac{7}{8} \cdot 2\frac{2}{3}$

Find each product. Write the answer in simplest form.

4. $2\frac{1}{4} \cdot 1\frac{1}{6}$

5. $1\frac{2}{3} \cdot 2\frac{1}{5}$

6. $3 \cdot 4\frac{2}{7}$

7. Robert is making trail mix. The recipe calls for $1\frac{2}{3}$ cups of raisins for each batch. Robert plans to make $2\frac{1}{2}$ batches. How many cups of raisins does he need?

 6 **Dividing Fractions and Mixed Numbers**

Find the reciprocal.

8. $\frac{2}{7}$

9. $\frac{5}{12}$

10. $\frac{3}{5}$

Divide. Write each answer in simplest form.

11. $\frac{3}{5} \div 4$

12. $1\frac{3}{10} \div 3\frac{1}{4}$

13. $1\frac{1}{5} \div 2\frac{1}{3}$

14. Sophia has $10\frac{1}{2}$ yards of fabric to make banners for a school track meet. She needs $1\frac{3}{4}$ yards for each banner. How many banners can she make?

7 **Solving Fraction Equations: Multiplication and Division**

Solve each equation.

15. $\frac{2y}{3} = 10$

16. $6p = \frac{3}{4}$

17. $\frac{2x}{3} = 9$

18. Michael has a black cat and a gray kitten. The black cat weighs 12 pounds. The gray kitten weighs $\frac{3}{5}$ the weight of the black cat. How much does the gray kitten weigh?

The American Royal Barbecue Since 1980, Kansas City has hosted one of the "hottest" events of the year. The annual American Royal Barbecue is the world's largest barbecue contest, with nearly 500 grilling teams from around the world. Each year, 70,000 visitors sample barbecued ribs, chicken, turkey, and much more.

MISSOURI

Kansas City

1. Anne's team is using the recipe for barbecue sauce shown here. She starts by stirring together the steak sauce and the hot pepper sauce. How many tablespoons of this mixture will she have?

Kansas City Barbecue Sauce

2 cups apple cider vinegar
4 ounces tomato paste
1 1/2 tablespoons sugar
1 1/2 tablespoons peanut oil
1 1/2 tablespoons salt
3/4 tablespoon steak sauce
3/4 tablespoon Worcestershire sauce
1/2 tablespoon hot pepper sauce

Mix ingredients together in a saucepan. Simmer for 10 minutes. Makes 3 1/2 cups.

2. Miguel's team uses a different recipe for barbecue sauce. It makes $3\frac{3}{4}$ cups of sauce.

   a. How much more sauce does Miguel's recipe make than the recipe shown here?

   b. Miguel's recipe calls for $\frac{2}{3}$ of the amount of peanut oil that is in the recipe shown here. How much peanut oil is in Miguel's recipe?

3. Ray's team uses the recipe shown here to make a large amount of barbecue sauce for the contest. He multiplies all the quantities in the recipe by 5.

   a. How many cups of sauce will Ray make?

   b. Ray plans to divide the sauce equally among 7 storage containers. How much sauce will be in each container?

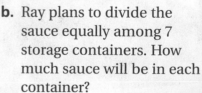

Real-World Connections

Game Time

Fraction Riddles

1 What is the value of one-half of two-thirds of three-fourths of four-fifths of five-sixths of six-sevenths of seven-eighths of eight-ninths of nine-tenths of one thousand?

2 What is the next fraction in the sequence below?

$$\frac{1}{12}, \frac{1}{6}, \frac{1}{4}, \frac{1}{3}, \cdots$$

3 I am a three-digit number. My hundreds digit is one-third of my tens digit. My tens digit is one-third of my ones digit. What number am I?

4 A *splorg* costs three-fourths of a dollar plus three-fourths of a *splorg*. How much does a *splorg* cost?

5 How many cubic inches of dirt are in a hole that measures $\frac{1}{3}$ feet by $\frac{1}{4}$ feet by $\frac{1}{2}$ feet?

Fraction Bingo

The object is to be the first player to cover five squares in a row horizontally, vertically, or diagonally.

One person is the caller. On each of the caller's cards, there is an expression containing fractions. When the caller draws a card, he or she reads the expression aloud for the players.

The players must find the value of the expression. If a square on the player's card has that value or a fraction equivalent to that value, they cover the square.

The first player to cover five squares in a row is the winner. Take turns being the caller. A variation can be played in which the winner is the first person to cover all their squares.

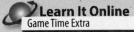

Learn It Online
Game Time Extra

A complete copy of the rules and game pieces are available online.

Ken Karp/HMH

Materials
- file folder
- scissors
- white paper
- hole punch
- chenille stem
- surveyor's flagging tape
- tape

It's in the Bag!

PROJECT **Flipping over Fractions**

Make a flip-flop book to take notes and work sample problems related to fraction operations.

Directions

❶ Cut the folder in half from the fold to the edge. Then cut out a flip-flop shape, with the "toe" of the flip-flop along the folded edge. **Figure A**

❷ Cut about ten flip-flop shapes out of the white paper. They should be slightly smaller than the flip-flop you cut out of the file folder.

❸ Put the white flip-flops inside the file-folder flip-flop. Punch a hole at the top through all the layers. Also punch holes at the sides of the flip-flip cover. These side holes should go through only the cover. **Figure B**

❹ Insert the chenille stem into the hole at the top, make a loop, and trim. Insert the surveyor's flagging tape through the loop, and insert the ends into the holes at the sides of the flip-flop. Tape the surveyor's flagging tape to the back of the cover to hold it in place. **Figure C**

Taking Note of the Math

Write the chapter number and title on the flip-flop. Then use the inside pages to work problems from the chapter. Choose problems that will help you remember the most important concepts.

A

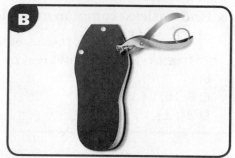

B

C

FLIPPING OVER FRACTIONS

Study Guide: Review

Vocabulary

least common denominator (LCD)   reciprocals

least common multiple (LCM)   multiplicative inverse

Complete the sentences below with vocabulary words from the list above.

1. Two numbers are ___?___ if their product is 1.

2. The ___?___ is the smallest number that is a common multiple of two or more denominators.

EXAMPLES

EXERCISES

1 ⃞ Least Common Multiple

■ Find the least common multiple (LCM) of 4, 6, and 8.

4: 4, 8, 12, 16, 20, 24, 28, . . .
6: 6, 12, 18, 24, 30, . . .
8: 8, 16, 24, 32, . . .
LCM: 24

Find the least common multiple (LCM).

3. 3, 5, and 10   **4.** 6, 8, and 16

5. 3, 9, and 27   **6.** 4, 12, and 30

7. 25 and 45   **8.** 12, 22, and 30

2 ⃞ Adding and Subtracting with Unlike Denominators

■ Add. Write the answer in simplest form.

$\frac{7}{9} + \frac{2}{3}$

$\frac{7}{9} + \frac{2}{3}$ *Write equivalent fractions. Add.*

$\frac{7}{9} + \frac{6}{9} = \frac{13}{9} = 1\frac{4}{9}$

Add or subtract. Write each answer in simplest form.

9. $\frac{1}{5} + \frac{5}{8}$ **10.** $\frac{1}{6} + \frac{7}{12}$

11. $\frac{13}{15} - \frac{4}{5}$ **12.** $\frac{7}{8} - \frac{2}{3}$

3 **Regrouping to Subtract Mixed Numbers**

- Subtract. Write the answer in simplest form.

$$4\frac{7}{10} - 2\frac{9}{10}$$

$$3\frac{17}{10} - 2\frac{9}{10} \qquad \textit{Regroup } 4\frac{7}{10}. \textit{ Subtract.}$$

$$1\frac{8}{10}$$

$$1\frac{4}{5}$$

Subtract. Write each answer in simplest form.

13. $7\frac{2}{9} - 3\frac{5}{9}$ **14.** $3\frac{1}{5} - 1\frac{7}{10}$

15. $8\frac{7}{12} - 2\frac{11}{12}$ **16.** $5\frac{3}{8} - 2\frac{3}{4}$

17. $11\frac{6}{7} - 4\frac{13}{14}$ **18.** $10 - 8\frac{7}{8}$

19. Georgette needs 8 feet of ribbon to decorate gifts. She has $3\frac{1}{4}$ feet of ribbon. How many more feet of ribbon does Georgette need?

4 **Solving Fraction Equations: Addition and Subtraction**

- Solve $n + 2\frac{5}{7} = 8$. Write the solution in simplest form.

$$n + 2\frac{5}{7} - 2\frac{5}{7} = 8 - 2\frac{5}{7}$$

$$n = 8 - 2\frac{5}{7}$$

$$n = 7\frac{7}{7} - 2\frac{5}{7}$$

$$n = 5\frac{2}{7}$$

Solve each equation. Write the solution in simplest form.

20. $x - 12\frac{3}{4} = 17\frac{2}{5}$ **21.** $t + 6\frac{11}{12} = 21\frac{5}{6}$

22. $3\frac{2}{3} = m - 1\frac{3}{4}$ **23.** $5\frac{2}{3} = p + 2\frac{2}{9}$

24. $y - 1\frac{2}{3} = 3\frac{4}{5}$ **25.** $4\frac{2}{5} + j = 7\frac{7}{10}$

26. Jon poured $1\frac{1}{2}$ oz of lemon juice onto a salad. He has $5\frac{1}{2}$ oz lemon juice left in the bottle. How many ounces of lemon juice were in the bottle before Jon poured some on the salad?

27. Abigail is walking to her grandparents' house. If she has walked $1\frac{1}{3}$ miles and her grandparents live 3 miles away, how much farther does Abigail have to walk?

Study Guide: Review

Video **Lesson Tutorials Online** my.hrw.com

5 Multiplying Mixed Numbers

■ Multiply. Write the answer in simplest form.

$\frac{2}{5} \cdot 1\frac{2}{3} = \frac{2}{5} \cdot \frac{5}{3} = \frac{10}{15} = \frac{2}{3}$

Multiply. Write each answer in simplest form.

28. $\frac{2}{5} \cdot 2\frac{1}{4}$ **29.** $\frac{3}{4} \cdot 1\frac{2}{3}$ **30.** $3\frac{1}{3} \cdot \frac{3}{5}$

6 Dividing Fractions and Mixed Numbers

■ Divide. Write the answer in simplest form.

$\frac{3}{4} \div 6 = \frac{3 \cdot 1}{4 \cdot 6} = \frac{3}{24} = \frac{1}{8}$

Divide. Write each answer in simplest form.

31. $\frac{4}{7} \div 3$ **32.** $\frac{3}{10} \div 2$ **33.** $1\frac{1}{3} \div 2\frac{2}{5}$

34. Beverly needs to measure $2\frac{2}{3}$ cups of bread crumbs. She has a $\frac{1}{3}$ cup measuring scoop. How many times must she fill the $\frac{1}{3}$ cup measuring scoop to get $2\frac{2}{3}$ cups of bread crumbs?

7 Solving Fraction Equations: Multiplication and Division

■ Solve the equation.

$\frac{4}{5}n = 12$

$\frac{4}{5}n \div \frac{4}{5} = 12 \div \frac{4}{5}$ *Divide both sides by $\frac{4}{5}$.*

$\frac{4}{5}n \cdot \frac{5}{4} = 12 \cdot \frac{5}{4}$ *Multiply by the reciprocal.*

$n = \frac{60}{4} = 15$

Solve each equation.

35. $4a = \frac{1}{2}$ **36.** $\frac{3b}{4} = 1\frac{1}{2}$

37. $\frac{2m}{7} = 5$ **38.** $6g = \frac{4}{5}$

39. $\frac{5}{6}r = 9$ **40.** $\frac{s}{8} = 6\frac{1}{4}$

41. $6p = \frac{2}{3}$ **42.** $\frac{8j}{9} = 1\frac{5}{8}$

43. Marcus is $66\frac{2}{3}$ inches tall. If Marcus is $\frac{5}{6}$ as tall as his father, how tall is Marcus's father?

Study Guide: Review

Chapter Test

Find the least common multiple (LCM).

1. 10 and 15 **2.** 4, 6, and 18 **3.** 9, 10, and 12 **4.** 6, 15, and 20

Add or subtract. Write the answer in simplest form.

5. $4\frac{1}{9} - 2\frac{4}{9}$ **6.** $1\frac{7}{10} + 3\frac{3}{4}$ **7.** $\frac{2}{3} - \frac{3}{8}$ **8.** $2\frac{1}{3} - \frac{5}{6}$

9. $4\frac{1}{5} - 2\frac{1}{2}$ **10.** $\frac{1}{12} + \frac{5}{6}$ **11.** $\frac{3}{8} + \frac{3}{4}$ **12.** $\frac{5}{6} - \frac{2}{3}$

13. On Saturday, Cecelia ran $3\frac{3}{7}$ miles. On Sunday, she ran $4\frac{5}{6}$ miles. How much farther did Cecelia run on Sunday than on Saturday?

14. Michael studied social studies for $\frac{3}{4}$ of an hour, Spanish for $1\frac{1}{2}$ hours, and math for $1\frac{1}{4}$ hours. How many hours did Michael spend studying all three subjects?

15. Quincy needs $6\frac{1}{3}$ feet of rope to tie down the things he is hauling in his truck. He finds a 9 foot long rope in his garage. How much extra rope does Quincy have?

Find the reciprocal.

16. $\frac{3}{5}$ **17.** $\frac{7}{11}$ **18.** $\frac{5}{9}$ **19.** $\frac{1}{8}$

Multiply or divide. Write the answer in simplest form.

20. $1\frac{2}{7} \cdot \frac{4}{9}$ **21.** $1\frac{3}{8} \cdot \frac{6}{11}$ **22.** $2\frac{1}{4} \cdot 2\frac{2}{3}$ **23.** $\frac{7}{8} \div 2$

24. $3\frac{1}{3} \div 1\frac{5}{12}$ **25.** $\frac{4}{5} \cdot 1\frac{1}{3}$ **26.** $3\frac{1}{8} \div 1\frac{1}{4}$ **27.** $\frac{3}{8} \cdot \frac{2}{3}$

Evaluate the expression $n \cdot \frac{1}{4}$ for each value of n. Write the answer in simplest form.

28. $n = \frac{7}{8}$ **29.** $n = \frac{2}{5}$ **30.** $n = \frac{8}{9}$ **31.** $n = \frac{4}{11}$

32. A recipe for granola bars require $1\frac{1}{2}$ cups of flour. How much flour is needed to make a triple batch of granola bars?

Solve each equation. Write the solution in simplest form.

33. $3r = \frac{9}{10}$ **34.** $n + 3\frac{1}{6} = 12$ **35.** $5\frac{5}{6} = x - 3\frac{1}{4}$

36. $\frac{2}{5}t = 9$ **37.** $\frac{4}{5}m = 7$ **38.** $y - 15\frac{3}{5} = 2\frac{1}{3}$

39. Jessica purchased a bag of cat food. She feeds her cat 1 cup of cat food each day. After 7 days, she has fed her cat $\frac{2}{3}$ of the food in the bag. How many cups of food were in the bag of cat food when Jessica bought it?

Test Tackler
STANDARDIZED TEST STRATEGIES

Gridded Response: Write Gridded Responses

When responding to a test item that has an answer grid, you must fill out the grid correctly, or the item will be marked as incorrect.

EXAMPLE 1

Gridded Response: Simplify the expression $(8 \times 3) - 5 \times (6 - 3)$.

$(8 \times 3) - 5 \times (6 - 3)$		
$24 - 5 \times 3$		*Perform operations within parentheses.*
$24 - 15$		*Multiply.*
9		*Subtract.*

The expression simplifies to 9.

- Use a pencil to write your answer in the answer boxes at the top of the grid.

- The answer can be entered starting in the far left column, or in the far right column, but not in the middle.

- Write only one digit in each box. Do not leave a blank box in the middle of an answer.

- Shade the correct bubble below your written digit.

EXAMPLE 2

Gridded Response: Evaluate $2\frac{1}{4} + 1\frac{1}{4} + 3\frac{3}{4}$.

$$2\frac{1}{4} + 1\frac{1}{4} + 3\frac{3}{4}$$

$$6\frac{5}{4} \qquad \textit{Add the fractions and then add the whole numbers.}$$

$$6\frac{5}{4} = 6 + 1\frac{1}{4} = 7\frac{1}{4} \text{ or } 7.25 \text{ or } \frac{29}{4} \qquad \textit{Simplify.}$$

- You cannot fill in mixed numbers. You must fill in the answer as an improper fraction or a decimal.

- Use a pencil to write your answer in the answer boxes at the top of the grid.

- Write only one digit or symbol in each box. On some grids, the fraction bar and the decimal point have a special box. If so, write your fraction or decimal around it correctly. Do not leave a blank box in the middle of an answer.

- Shade the correct bubble below your written digit.

When filling out a grid be sure to use a pencil and completely fill in the bubbles directly below each digit or symbol you wrote.

Read each sample and then answer the questions that follow.

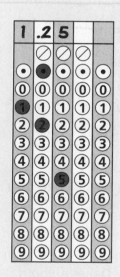

Sample A
A student divided two fractions and got $\frac{4}{25}$ as a result. Then the student filled in the grid as shown.

1. What error did the student make when filling in the grid?

2. Explain how to fill in the answer correctly.

Sample B
A student solved the equation $x + 2.1 = 5$, and found that $x = 2.9$. This answer is displayed in the grid as shown.

3. What error did the student make when filling in the grid?

4. Explain how to fill in the answer correctly.

Sample C
A student correctly simplified the expression $6\frac{7}{8} + 1\frac{3}{8} - 2\frac{5}{8}$. Then the student filled in the grid as shown.

5. What answer does the grid show?

6. Explain why you cannot grid a mixed number.

7. Write the answer $5\frac{5}{8}$ in two forms that could be entered in the grid correctly.

Sample D
A student wrote the standard form of the decimal one and twenty-five hundredths and then filled in the grid as shown.

8. What error did the student make when filling in the grid?

9. Explain how to fill in the answer correctly.

Test Tackler

Standardized Test Prep

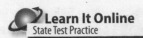
Cumulative Assessment
Multiple Choice

1. Which number is less than $\frac{3}{4}$?

  (A) $\frac{2}{3}$ (C) $\frac{5}{6}$

  (B) $\frac{4}{5}$ (D) $\frac{9}{10}$

2. Mr. Ledden's briefcase has a mass of 9.4 kilograms on Earth. How much would his briefcase weigh on Jupiter?

Gravitational Pull of Planets (Compared with Earth)	
Planet	**Gravitational Pull**
Mercury	0.38
Venus	0.91
Mars	0.38
Jupiter	2.54
Saturn	0.93
Neptune	1.2

  (F) 8.554 kg   (H) 11.94 kg

  (G) 11.28 kg   (J) 23.876 kg

3. Brandon's family is planning a trip from Dallas to San Antonio. Dallas is about 272 miles from San Antonio. If Brandon's dad drives an average of 60 miles per hour, about how long will the trip take?

  (A) 3 hours   (C) 6 hours

  (B) 5 hours   (D) 7 hours

4. What is the value of 5^4?

  (F) 9   (H) 625

  (G) 20   (J) 1,000

5. A recipe calls for $\frac{1}{4}$ cup of sugar and $\frac{2}{3}$ cup of flour. How much more flour than sugar is needed for this recipe?

  (A) $\frac{1}{7}$ cup   (C) $\frac{1}{2}$ cup

  (B) $\frac{5}{12}$ cup   (D) $\frac{3}{4}$ cup

6. Maggie needs $15\frac{3}{8}$ yards of blue rope, $24\frac{1}{3}$ yards of white rope, and $8\frac{3}{4}$ yards of red rope. About how many yards of rope does she need in all?

  (F) 38 yards   (H) 48 yards

  (G) 45 yards   (J) 55 yards

7. Let d represent the number of dogs that Max walks in 1 day. Which expression shows the number of dogs Max walks in 7 days?

  (A) $7 + d$ (C) $7d$

  (B) $d - 7$ (D) $\frac{d}{7}$

8. Charlie eats $\frac{5}{8}$ of a pizza. One-fifth of the pizza he eats is covered with mushrooms. How much of Charlie's pizza is covered with mushrooms?

  (F) $\frac{1}{8}$ pizza   (H) $\frac{1}{5}$ pizza

  (G) $\frac{5}{13}$ pizza   (J) $3\frac{1}{8}$ pizza

9. Which of the following sets of decimals is ordered from least to greatest?

  (A) 3.8, 3.89, 3.08, 3.9

  (B) 3.89, 3.8, 3.9, 3.08

  (C) 3.08, 3.89, 3.8, 3.9

  (D) 3.08, 3.8, 3.89, 3.9

10. Samantha gets to choose a number for her soccer jersey. She picks a number that is divisible by 3, 5, and 9, but not by 2, 4, or 6. Which of the following can be Samantha's jersey number?

F 15　　　　H 30

G 27　　　　J 45

11. A theater has 145 rows of seats. There are 12 seats in each row. The sixth grade class from Brookpark Middle School has 168 students and 15 chaperones that are attending a play next week. How many rows will they need to reserve for the upcoming play?

A 14 rows　　　C 16 rows

B 15 rows　　　D 17 rows

HOT TIP! Underline key words given in the test question so you know for certain what the question is asking.

Gridded Response

12. What is the least common denominator for the following fractions: $\frac{4}{5}$, $\frac{3}{4}$, and $\frac{1}{10}$?

13. During a walk-a-thon, Brian walks $3\frac{1}{4}$ kilometers, and Stacey walks $2\frac{7}{8}$ kilometers. How many more kilometers does Brian walk than Stacy?

14. What is the reciprocal of $6\frac{1}{7}$?

15. Ying caught a fish that measured 62.5 centimeters. This fish measured 8.2 centimeters less than the fish Ying caught yesterday. How many centimeters did the fish Ying caught yesterday measure?

16. Name the decimal that is equivalent to $\frac{3}{5}$.

17. Natalie lives $\frac{1}{6}$ mile from school. Peter lives $\frac{3}{10}$ mile from school. How many miles further does Peter live from the school than Natalie?

Short Response

S1. Jane is building a tank for her pet snake. The tank's minimum length should equal two-thirds of the snake's length, and the tank's width should be equal to half the snake's length. Jane's snake is $2\frac{1}{2}$ feet long. Calculate and explain how to find the dimensions of the tank.

S2. Lucy has $\frac{5}{6}$ yard of ribbon to wrap gifts for her friends. The bow on each gift requires $\frac{1}{6}$ yard of ribbon. Write an equation to determine how many b bows Lucy can make. Solve and interpret your answer.

Extended Response

E1. Garrett attends a summer day camp for 6 hours each day. The circle graph below shows what fraction of each day he spends doing different activities.

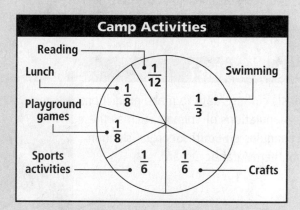

Camp Activities

a. How long does Garrett spend doing each activity? Write the activities in order from longest to shortest.

b. Sports activities and playground games are all held on the camp fields. What fraction of the day does Garrett spend on the fields? Write your answer in simplest form.

c. Lunch and crafts are held in the cafeteria. How many hours does Garrett spend in the cafeteria during a 5-day week at day camp? Write your answer in simplest form, and show the work necessary to determine the correct answer.

Why Learn This?

Scientists can use data to make predictions about populations of animals such as these King penguins on South Georgia Island in the southern Atlantic Ocean.

Learn It Online
Chapter Project Online

Chapter
• Use mean, median, mode, and range to summarize data sets.
• Make and interpret a variety of graphs.

(bkgd) Eastcott Momatiuk/Getty Images

Are You Ready?

 **Learn It Online**
Resources Online

✓ Vocabulary

Choose the best term from the list to complete each sentence.

1. The answer to an addition problem is called the ___?___.

2. The ___?___ of the 6 in 5,672 is hundreds.

3. When you move ___?___, you move left or right.
   When you move ___?___, you move up or down.

horizontally

place value

quotients

sum

vertically

Complete these exercises to review skills you will need for this chapter.

✓ Place Value of Whole Numbers

Write the digit in the tens place of each number.

4. 718   **5.** 989   **6.** 55   **7.** 7,709

✓ Compare and Order Whole Numbers

Order the numbers from least to greatest.

8. 40, 32, 51, 78, 26, 43, 27   **9.** 132, 150, 218, 176, 166

10. 92, 91, 84, 92, 87, 90   **11.** 23, 19, 33, 27, 31, 31, 28, 18

Find the greatest number in each set.

12. 452, 426, 502, 467, 530, 512   **13.** 711, 765, 723, 778, 704, 781

14. 143, 122, 125, 137, 140, 118, 139   **15.** 1,053; 1,106; 1,043; 1,210; 1,039; 1,122

✓ Write Fractions as Decimals

Write each fraction as a decimal.

16. $\frac{1}{4}$ **17.** $\frac{5}{8}$ **18.** $\frac{1}{6}$ **19.** $\frac{2}{5}$

20. $\frac{5}{6}$ **21.** $\frac{1}{2}$ **22.** $\frac{3}{4}$ **23.** $\frac{9}{11}$

✓ Locate Points on a Number Line

Name the point on the number line that corresponds to each given value.

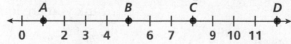

24. 5   **25.** 12   **26.** 8   **27.** 1

Where You've Been

Previously, you

- described characteristics of data such as the shape of the data and the middle number.
- graphed a given set of data using an appropriate graphical representation.

In This Chapter

You will study

- using mean, median, mode, and range to describe data.
- solving problems by collecting, organizing, and analyzing data.
- describing distributions of data.

Where You're Going

You can use the skills learned in this chapter

- to recognize misuses of graphical information and evaluate conclusions based on data analysis.
- to display distributions of data correctly for projects in social studies and science.

Key Vocabulary/Vocabulario

box-and-whisker plot	gráfica de mediana y rango
frequency table	tabla de frecuencia
interquartile range	rango entre cuartiles
mean	media
median	mediana
mode	moda
outlier	valor atípico
quartile	cuartil
range	rango (en estadística)

Vocabulary Connections

To become familiar with some of the vocabulary terms in the chapter, consider the following. You may refer to the chapter, the glossary, or a dictionary if you like.

1. A *box* often has a rectangular shape. The *whiskers* on an animal stick out to the side of the animal's cheeks. How do you think a **box-and-whisker plot** looks?

2. *Frequency* is a measure of how often an event occurs or the number of like objects that are in a group. What do you think a **frequency table** shows?

3. The word *quartile* is closely related to *quarter*. What might make up a **quartile** of a data set?

4. A *range* can mean the distance between possible extremes. If you are looking for the **range** of a set of numbers, what do you think you are looking for?

Reading and Writing Math

Reading Strategy: Read and Interpret Graphics

Figures, diagrams, charts, and graphs are used to illustrate data. Knowing how to understand these visual aids will help you learn the important facts and details of a problem.

Chart

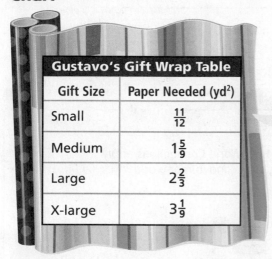

Gustavo's Gift Wrap Table	
Gift Size	**Paper Needed (yd²)**
Small	$\frac{11}{12}$
Medium	$1\frac{5}{9}$
Large	$2\frac{2}{3}$
X-large	$3\frac{1}{9}$

Read and understand each column head and each row head.

- **Title:** Gustavo's Gift Wrap Table
- **Gift Size:** Small, Medium, Large, and X-large
- **Paper Needed (yd²):** Tells how much paper is needed to wrap the given gift size.

Graph

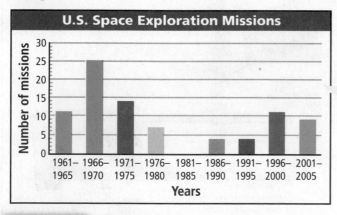

The titles of the graph describe what information is being graphed. Read the label on each axis.

- **Title:** U.S. Space Exploration Missions
- **x-axis:** Years (given as 5-year intervals)
- **y-axis:** Number of missions

Reading and Writing Math

Try This

Use the graph above to answer the following questions.

1. How many space missions were flown between 1966–1970?

2. Which ranges of years had fewer than 5 space missions?

Mastering the Standards

for Mathematical Practice

The topics described in the Standards for Mathematical Content will vary from year to year. However, the *way* in which you learn, study, and think about mathematics will not. The Standards for Mathematical Practice describe skills that you will use in all of your math courses.

Mathematical Practices

1. Make sense of problems and persevere in solving them.
2. Reason abstractly and quantitatively.
3. Construct viable arguments and critique the reasoning of others.
4. Model with mathematics.
5. Use appropriate tools strategically.
6. Attend to precision.
7. Look for and make use of structure.
8. Look for and express regularity in repeated reasoning.

(4) Model with mathematics.

Mathematically proficient students can apply... mathematics... to... problems... in everyday life, society, and the workplace...

In your book

Application exercises and **Real-World Connections** apply mathematics to other disciplines and in real-world scenarios.

Real-World CONNECTIONS CHAPTER 3

Civil Rights in Education Heritage Trail The roots of free public education in the United States can be traced to southern Virginia. A self-guided driving tour of the area takes visitors to more than 40 schools, libraries, and other sites that played a key role in the story of civil rights in education.

The Wilson family is driving the Civil Rights in Education Heritage Trail. Use the map to solve these problems about their trip.

1. The Wilsons drive from Appomattox to Petersburg on the first day of their trip. How many miles do they drive?

2. On the second day of the trip, they drive from Petersburg to South Hill. How much farther do they drive on the first day than on the second day?

3. The distance from South Boston to Halifax is $\frac{1}{3}$ of the distance from Farmville to Nottoway. What is the distance from South Boston to Halifax?

4. The entire trip from Appomattox to Halifax is 202.1 miles. The Wilsons' car gets 21.5 miles to the gallon. How many gallons of gas will they use for the trip?

5. Gas costs $3.65 per gallon. How much will gas cost for the entire trip?

Life Science LINK

The map shows the number of critically endangered animal species in each country in South America. A species is critically endangered when it faces a very high risk of extinction in the wild in the near future.

11. Which country has the fewest critically endangered species? Which has the most?

12. Make a cumulative frequency table of the data. How many countries have fewer than 20 critically endangered species?

13. Make a stem-and-leaf plot of the data.

14. **Write About It** Explain how changing the size of the intervals you used in Exercise 12 affects your cumulative frequency table.

15. **Challenge** In a recent year, the number of endangered animal species in the United States was 190. Show how to represent this number on a stem-and-leaf plot.

Golden Lion Tamarin

Numbers of Critically Endangered Animal Species in South America

Venezuela 30 — Guyana 7
Colombia 74 — Suriname 7
Ecuador 74 — French Guiana 8
Peru 35
Bolivia 9 — Brazil 60
— Paraguay 5
Chile 15 — Uruguay 6
— Argentina 11

Source: International Union for Conservation of Nature and Natural Resources

PhotoDisc/Getty Images

Collect Data to Explore Mean

Use with Mean, Median, Mode, and Range

Learn It Online
Lab Resources Online

 MATHEMATICAL PRACTICES **Use appropriate tools strategically.**

CC.6.SP.2 Understand that a set of data... has a distribution which can be described by its center, spread, and overall shape

You can use counters to find a single number that describes an entire set of data. Consider the set of data in the table.

| 2 | 5 | 4 | 3 | 6 |

First use counters to make stacks that match the data.

Now move some of the counters so that all of the stacks are the same height.

All of the stacks have 4 counters. The set of data can be described by the number 4. It is the *mean* (average) of the set of data.

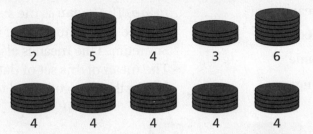

Activity

❶ Ella surveys five people to find out how many brothers and sisters they have.

❷ She collects the data and records the results.

❸ Use counters to show the data.

❹ Move counters so that all of the stacks are the same height. The mean is 2.

Number of Siblings				
2	3	1	1	3

Think and Discuss

1. Suppose one of the people surveyed had 8 brothers and sisters instead of 3. How would this change the mean?

2. All of the students in a classroom have 3 textbooks. What is the mean of the set of data? How do you know?

Try This

1. Collect data by surveying four friends to find out how many pets they have. Use counters to find the mean of the set of data.

Mean, Median, Mode, and Range

COMMON CORE

CC.6.SP.3 Recognize that a measure of center for a numerical data set summarizes all of its values with a single number... *Also CC.6.SP.2*

Vocabulary

mean

median

mode

range

Players on a volleyball team measured how high they could jump. The results in inches are recorded in the table.

| 13 | 23 | 21 | 20 | 21 | 24 | 18 |

One way to describe this data set is to find the *mean*. The **mean** is the sum of all the items divided by the number of items in the set. Sometimes the mean is also called the *average*. The mean of this set of data is the average height that the volleyball team could jump.

EXAMPLE 1

Finding the Mean of a Data Set

Find the mean of each data set.

A

Heights of Vertical Jumps (in.)						
13	23	21	20	21	24	18

$13 + 23 + 21 + 20 + 21 + 24 + 18 = 140$ *Add all values.*
$140 \div 7 = 20$ *Divide the sum by the number of items.*

The mean is 20 inches.

B

Numbers of Pets Owned				
2	4	1	1	2

$2 + 4 + 1 + 1 + 2 = 10$ *Add all values.*
$10 \div 5 = 2$ *Divide the sum by the number of items.*

The mean is 2. The average number of pets that these five people own is 2.

Check

Use counters to make stacks that match the data.

2   4   1   1   2

Move the chips so that each stack has the same number.

Each stack has 2 counters. The mean is 2.

Video **Lesson Tutorials Online** my.hrw.com

Some other descriptions of a set of data are called the *median, mode,* and *range.*

- The **median** is the middle value when the data are in numerical order, or the mean of the two middle values if there are an even number of items.

- The **mode** is the value or values that occur most often. There may be more than one mode for a data set. When all values occur an equal number of times, the data set has no mode.

- The **range** is the difference between the greatest and least values in the set.

E X A M P L E **2** **Finding the Mean, Median, Mode, and Range of a Data Set**

Find the mean, median, mode, and range of each data set.

NFL Career Touchdowns			
Marcus Allen	145	Franco Harris	100
Jim Brown	126	Walter Payton	125

mean: $\dfrac{145 + 126 + 100 + 125}{4}$

$= 124$

Add all values. Divide the sum by the number of items.

Write the data in numerical order: 100, 125, 126, 145

median: 100, (125, 126) 145

$\dfrac{125 + 126}{2} = 125.5$

mode: none

range: $145 - 100 = 45$

There are an even number of items, so find the mean of the two middle values.
No value occurs most often.
Subtract least value from greatest value.

The mean is 124 touchdowns; the median is 125.5 touchdowns; there is no mode; and the range is 45 touchdowns.

MATHEMATICAL PRACTICES

Think and Discuss

1. Describe what you can say about the values in a data set if the set has a small range.

2. Tell how many modes are in the following data set. Explain your answer. 15, 12, 13, 15, 12, 11

3. Describe how adding 20 inches to the data set in Example 1A would affect the mean.

GUIDED PRACTICE

See Example **1** Find the mean of the data set.

1.

Number of Petals	13	24	35	18	15	27

See Example **2** Find the mean, median, mode, and range of the data set.

2.

Heights of Students (in.)	51	67	63	52	49	48	48

INDEPENDENT PRACTICE

See Example **1** Find the mean of the data set.

3.

Numbers of Books Read	6	4	10	5	6	8

See Example **2** Find the mean, median, mode, and range of each data set.

4.

Ages of Students (yr)	14	16	15	17	16	12

5.

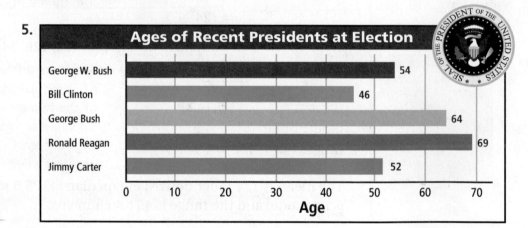

Ages of Recent Presidents at Election

George W. Bush — 54
Bill Clinton — 46
George Bush — 64
Ronald Reagan — 69
Jimmy Carter — 52

PRACTICE AND PROBLEM SOLVING

Extra Practice

See Extra Practice for more exercises.

6. Frank has 3 nickels, 5 dimes, and 2 quarters. Find the range, mean, median, and mode of the values of Frank's coins.

7. **Education** For the six New England states, the mean scores on the math section of the SAT one year were as follows: Connecticut, 509; Maine, 500; Massachusetts, 513; New Hampshire, 519; Rhode Island, 500; and Vermont, 508. Create a table using this data. Then find the range, mean, median, and mode.

8. **Critical Thinking** Gina spent $4, $5, $7, $7, and $6 over the past 5 days buying lunch. Is the mean, median, mode, or range the most useful way to describe this data set? Explain.

Find each missing value.

9. 3, 5, 7, 9, ▪ ; mean: 7

10. 15, 17, ▪ , 28, 30; mean: 23

11. 10, 9, ▪ , 4, 8, 8, 4, 7; mode: 4

12. 7, 2, ▪ , 15, 20, 8, 14, 29; median: 13

13. 50, 100, 75, 60, ▪ , 25, 105, 40; median: 65

14. 14, 8, 17, 21, ▪ , 11, 3, 13; range: 20

15. **Critical Thinking** Find the set of 5 items of data that has a range of 9, a mean of 11, a median of 12, and a mode of 15.

16. **What's the Error?** Joey says that the mean of the set of data is 23.5. Describe Joey's error.

Numbers of Flowers in Bouquets	25	20	21	22	25	25

17. **What's the Question?** On an exam, three students scored 75, four students scored 82, three students scored 88, four students scored 93, and one student scored 99. If the answer is 88, what is the question?

18. **Challenge** In the Super Bowls from 2002 to 2007, the winning team won by a mean of $9\frac{5}{6}$ points. By how many points did the New England Patriots win in 2002?

Year	Super Bowl Champion	Points Won By
2007	Indianapolis Colts	12
2006	Pittsburgh Steelers	11
2005	New England Patriots	3
2004	New England Patriots	3
2003	Tampa Bay Buccaneers	27
2002	New England Patriots	▪

Test Prep

19. **Multiple Choice** Over 5 days, Pedro jogged 6.5 miles, 5 miles, 2 miles, 2 miles, and 4.5 miles. Find the mean distance that Pedro jogged.

Ⓐ 2 miles   Ⓑ 3.5 miles   Ⓒ 4 miles   Ⓓ 4.75 miles

20. **Multiple Choice** Which value is NOT always a number in the data set it represents?

Ⓕ Mode   Ⓖ Mean   Ⓗ Least value   Ⓙ Greatest value

21. **Gridded Response** The mean of 12, 15, 20 and x is 18. Find the value of x.

6-2 Additional Data and Outliers

COMMON CORE

CC.6.SP.3 Recognize that a measure of center for a numerical data set summarizes all of its values with a single number, while a measure of variation describes how its values vary with a single number

The mean, median, and mode may change when you add data to a data set.

USA's Shani Davis at the 2007 ISU World Single Distances Speed Skating Championships.

EXAMPLE **1** *Sports Application*

Vocabulary

outlier

A **Find the mean, median, and mode of the data in the table.**

U.S. Winter Olympic Medals Won							
Year	2006	2002	1998	1994	1992	1988	1984	1980
Medals	25	34	13	13	11	6	8	12

mean = 15.25   mode = 13   median = 12.5

B **The United States also won 10 medals in 1976 and 8 medals in 1972. Add this data to the data in the table and find the mean, median, and mode.**

mean = 14   *The mean decreased by 1.25.*

modes = 8, 13   *There is an additional mode.*

median = 11.5   *The median decreased by 1.*

Interactivities Online ▶ An **outlier** is a value in a set that is very different from the other values.

EXAMPLE **2** *Social Studies Application*

In 2001, 64-year-old Sherman Bull became the oldest American to reach the top of Mount Everest. Other climbers to reach the summit that day were 33, 31, 31, 32, 33, and 28 years old. Find the mean, median, and mode without and with Bull's age, and explain the changes.

Data without Bull's age: mean ≈ 31.3   modes = 31, 33   median = 31.5

Data with Bull's age: mean = 36   modes = 31, 33   median = 32

When you add Bull's age, the mean increases by 4.7, the modes stay the same, and the median increases by 0.5. The mean is the most affected by the outlier.

Helpful Hint

In Example 2, Sherman Bull's age is an outlier because he is much older than the others in the group.

Doug Pensinger/Getty Images

Video **Lesson Tutorials Online**   my.hrw.com

Sometimes one or two data values can greatly affect the mean, median, or mode. When one of these values is affected like this, you should choose a different value to best describe the data set.

EXAMPLE 3 **Describing a Data Set**

The Seawells are shopping for a DVD player. They found ten DVD players with the following prices:

$175, $180, $130, $150, $180, $500, $160, $180, $150, $160

What are the mean, median, and mode of this data set? Which one best describes the data set?

mean:

$$\frac{175 + 180 + 130 + 150 + 180 + 500 + 160 + 180 + 150 + 160}{10} = \frac{1965}{10}$$
$$= 196.50$$

The mean is $196.50.

Most of the DVD players cost less than $200, so the mean does not describe the data set best.

median:

130, 150, 150, 160, ⟨160, 175⟩ 180, 180, 180, 500

$$\frac{160 + 175}{2} = 167.50$$

The median is $167.50.

The median best describes the data set because a majority of the data is clustered around the value $167.50.

mode:

The value $180 occurs 3 times, more than any other value. The mode is $180.

The mode represents only 3 of the 10 values. The mode does not describe the entire data set.

Some data sets, such as {red, blue, red}, do not contain numbers. In this case, the only way to describe the data set is with the mode.

Think and Discuss

1. **Explain** how an outlier with a large value will affect the mean of a data set. What is the effect of a small outlier value?

2. **Explain** why the mean would not be a good description of the following high temperatures that occurred over 7 days: 72°F, 73°F, 70°F, 68°F, 70°F, 71°F, and 39°F.

GUIDED PRACTICE

See Example 1

1. **Sports** The graph shows how many times some countries have won the Davis Cup in tennis from 1900 to 2000.

   a. Find the mean, median, and mode of the data.

   b. The United States won 31 Davis Cups between 1900 and 2000. Add this number to the data in the graph and find the mean, median, and mode.

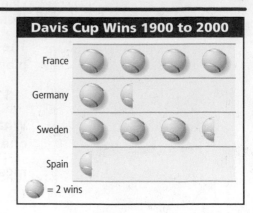

Davis Cup Wins 1900 to 2000

France
Germany
Sweden
Spain

= 2 wins

See Example 2

2. In 1998, 77-year-old John Glenn became the oldest person to travel into space. Other astronauts traveling on that same mission were 43, 37, 38, 46, 35, and 42 years old. Find the mean, median, and mode of all their ages with and without Glenn's age, and explain the changes.

See Example 3

3. Kate read books that were 240, 450, 180, 160, 195, 170, 240, and 165 pages long. What are the mean, median, and mode of this data set? Which one best describes the data set?

INDEPENDENT PRACTICE

See Example 1

4. **History** The table shows the ages of the 10 youngest signers of the Declaration of Independence.

   a. Find the mean, median, and mode of the data.

   b. Benjamin Franklin was 70 years old when he signed the Declaration of Independence. Add his age to the data in the table and find the mean, median, and mode.

Ages of 10 Youngest Signers of Declaration of Independence						
Age	26	29	30	31	33	34
Number Of Signers	//	/	/	/	///	//

See Example 2

5. **Geography** The map shows the population densities of several states along the Atlantic coast. Find the mean, median, and mode of the data with and without Maine's population density, and explain the changes.

See Example 3

6. The passengers in a van are 16, 19, 17, 18, 15, 14, 32, 32, and 41 years old. What are the mean, median, and mode of this data set? Which one best describes the data set?

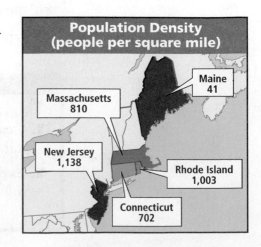

Population Density (people per square mile)

Maine 41
Massachusetts 810
New Jersey 1,138
Rhode Island 1,003
Connecticut 702

Extra Practice
See Extra Practice for more exercises.

On September 13, 1922, the temperature in El Azizia, Libya, reached 136°F, the record high for the planet. (*Source: The World Almanac and Book of Facts*)

7. What are the mean, median, and mode of the highest recorded temperatures on each continent?

8. a. Which temperature is an outlier?

b. What are the mean, median, and mode of the temperatures if the outlier is not included?

Continent	Highest Temperature (°F)
Africa	136
Antarctica	59
Asia	129
Australia	128
Europe	122
North America	134
South America	120

Erg Murzuq Dunes in the Libyan Desert

9. **?** **What's the Error?** A student stated that the median temperature would rise to 120.6°F if a new record high of 75°F were recorded in Antarctica. Explain the error. How would the median temperature actually be affected if a high of 75°F were recorded in Antarctica?

10. **Write About It** Is the data in the table best described by the mean, median, or mode? Explain.

11. **★** **Challenge** Suppose a new high temperature were recorded in Europe, and the new mean temperature became 120°F. What is Europe's new high temperature?

Test Prep

12. Multiple Choice Which value will change the most when 5 is added to the data set 0, 1, 4, 0, 3, 4, 2, and 1?

A Range   **B** Median   **C** Mode   **D** Mean

13. Gridded Response The table shows the speeds, in miles per hour, of certain animals. Which speed is an outlier?

Animal	House cat	Rabbit	Cheetah	Reindeer	Zebra	Elk	Elephant
Speed (mi/h)	30	35	70	32	40	45	25

6-3 Measures of Variation

COMMON CORE

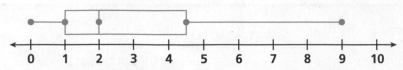

CC.6.SP.1 Recognize a statistical question as one that anticipates variability in the data related to the question and accounts for it in the answers *Also CC.6.SP.3, CC.6.SP.4*

Vocabulary

box-and-whisker plot

quartiles

variation

interquartile range (IQR)

Ms. Snow asks some of her students how many pets they have. The responses are 9, 0, 4, 1, 1, 2, 3, 5, and 2 pets.

You can display this data using a box-and-whisker plot. A **box-and-whisker plot** or *box plot* is a data display that shows how data are distributed by using the median, *quartiles*, least value, and greatest value. **Quartiles** are three values, one of which is the median, that divide a data set into fourths. Each quartile contains one-fourth, or 25%, of the data.

PhotoDisc/Getty Images

EXAMPLE **1** **Making a Box-and-Whisker Plot**

The numbers of pets that several students in Ms. Snow's class own are given. Use the data to make a box-and-whisker plot.

$$9, 0, 4, 1, 1, 2, 3, 5, 2$$

Step 1: Order the data from least to greatest.

$$0, 1, 1, 2, 2, 3, 4, 5, 9$$

Step 2: Find the least and greatest values, the median, and the first and third quartiles.

Reading Math

The first quartile is the median of the lower half of the data, and the third quartile is the median of the upper half of the data.

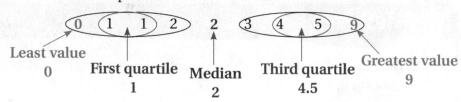

Least value
0

First quartile
1

Median
2

Third quartile
4.5

Greatest value
9

The first quartile is the mean of 1 and 1. The third quartile is the mean of 4 and 5.

Step 3: Draw a number line, and plot a point above each of the five values you just identified. Draw a box through the first and third quartiles and a vertical line through the median. Draw lines from the box to the least value and the greatest value. (These are the whiskers.)

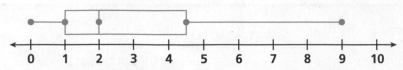

A box-and-whisker plot can be used to show how the values in a data set are distributed. **Variation** (*variability*) is the spread of the values.

The **interquartile range (IQR)** is the difference between the first and third quartiles. It is a measure of the spread of the middle 50% of the data. A small interquartile range means that the data in the middle of the set are close in value. A large interquartile range means that the data in the middle are spread out.

EXAMPLE 2 Finding the Interquartile Range

Reading Math

The first quartile is sometimes called the lower quartile, or Q1. The third quartile is sometimes called the upper quartile, or Q3.

Find the interquartile range for the data set 12, 14, 11, 10, 9, 10, 9.

9, 9, 10, 10, 11, 12, 14   *Order the data from least to greatest.*

9, 9, 10, 10, 11, 12, 14   *Find the median and quartiles.*

$IQR = 12 - 9 = 3$ *Find the difference between the first quartile (9) and the third quartile (12).*

The interquartile range is 3.

Another measure of variation is the *mean absolute deviation*. This is the mean amount that data values differ from the mean of data values.

EXAMPLE 3 Finding Mean Absolute Deviation

Sandy enters her dog in a jumping contest. Her dog, Tee, makes the following jumps (in feet): 18.6, 19.3, 17.7, 20.0. What is the mean absolute deviation of Tee's jumps, to the nearest tenth?

$$\frac{18.6 + 19.3 + 17.7 + 20.0}{4} = 18.9$$ *Find the mean.*

18.6 is **0.3 unit** from 18.9.   *Find the distance on a number line each data value is from the mean.*
19.3 is **0.4 unit** from 18.9.
17.7 is **1.2 units** from 18.9.
20.0 is **1.1 units** from 18.9.

$$\frac{0.3 + 0.4 + 1.2 + 1.1}{4} = 0.75$$ *Find the mean of the distances.*

The mean absolute deviation of Tee's jumps is 0.75 feet. So, on average Tee's jumps were within 0.75 feet of the mean, 18.9 feet.

Think and Discuss

1. **Explain** what is shown in a box-and-whisker plot.

2. **Discuss** what the mean absolute deviation shows about a set of data.

Exercises

GUIDED PRACTICE

See Example **1**

1. A solution used to kill bacteria is tested. The solution kills the following percentages of bacteria in six trials: 85, 84, 87, 86, 90, 80. Use the data to make a box-and-whisker plot.

See Example **2**

Find the interquartile range for each data set. Round your answers to the nearest tenth, if necessary.

2. 4, 5, 3, 7, 4, 5, 6

3. 12, 15, 15, 10, 23

4. 2, 2, 1, 8

5. 4, 5, 7, 6, 5, 4, 8, 6

See Example **3**

6. There are 7 animal shelters in the local area. The number of cats in each is 4, 6, 3, 7, 4, 5, and 20. What is the mean absolute deviation for the number of cats in shelters, to the nearest tenth?

INDEPENDENT PRACTICE

See Example **1**

7. A new song was rated by eight students on a scale from 1 to 10 (1 being the lowest rating and 10 the highest). The song was rated: 2, 8, 9, 3, 10, 9, 2, 3. Use the data to make a box-and-whisker plot.

See Example **2**

Find the interquartile range for each data set. Round your answers to the nearest tenth, if necessary.

8. 5, 2, 4, 7, 4, 4, 1

9. 14, 3, 9, 13, 5, 12

10. 6, 7, 5, 9, 10, 9, 9

11. 20, 15, 15, 10, 32

See Example **3**

12. The number of points Maggie has scored in each of the first 5 games of the basketball season are 14, 17, 17, 13, and 34. What is the mean absolute deviation for the number of points for Maggie's first 5 games?

13. The ages (in weeks) at which 6 infants learned to crawl are 23, 37, 33, 39, 29, and 31. What is the mean absolute deviation for the age at which the infants learned to crawl, to the nearest tenth?

PRACTICE AND PROBLEM SOLVING

Extra Practice
See Extra Practice for more exercises.

14. Dennis wants to find out people's opinions on a new game system. He surveys 10 people to rate the new system from 1 to 10. In his survey, 1 means the system is extremely uncool and 10 means the system is the coolest. The survey shows the following ratings: 9, 7, 7, 8, 7, 9, 9, 3, 10, and 8.
   a. What is the interquartile range of the ratings?
   b. What is the mean absolute deviation of the ratings?
   c. What do these measures of variation indicate about the ratings for the game system?

Find the interquartile range for each data set.

15. Number of minutes that 8 students wait for a bus: 1, 5, 12, 4, 10, 5, 8, 2

16. Number of players on each of 7 teams in a soccer league: 13, 18, 15, 17, 13, 16, 17

17. Life Science The weights, in pounds, of seven blue marlin caught in Maui are 55, 70, 250, 400, 100, 260, and 300. Find the interquartile range.

18. Multi-Step The number of pounds each member of a weight loss club lost in the first week was 1, 1, 2, 3, 0, 4, 0, 1, and 3. The second week the losses in pounds were 3, 3, 1, 1, 5, 2, 2, 4, and 4.
 a. Make a box-and-whisker plot of the data for each week.
 b. Find the interquartile range of the data for each week.
 c. Compare the box-and-whisker plots and the interquartile ranges. On average, during which week did the members lose more weight?

19. Tim and Tony each ran 6 days last week. The distances in miles Tim ran were 4, 5, 4, 7, 8, and 7. Tony's distances were 5, 6, 10, 3, 10, and 4 miles.
 a. Find the mean absolute deviation for both runners.
 b. Use the mean absolute deviations to determine which runner is more consistent in the number of miles he runs each day. Explain your answer.

20. What's the Error? A student found the first quartile of the data set 1, 9, 14, 8, 3, 13, 5, 7, and 8 to be 5. What error did the student make?

21. Write About It Describe how dramatically increasing one number in a data set affects the IQR and the mean absolute deviation. Explain which measure would be most affected by unusually large or small numbers in a data set.

22. Challenge Create a data set with eight numbers that has an interquartile range of 4 and a median of 20.

Test Prep

23. Multiple Choice A data set has numbers: 3, 5, 5, 6, 4, 3, 1, 7. Which is the interquartile range?

 Ⓐ 2.0 Ⓑ 2.5 Ⓒ 3.5 Ⓓ 4.0

24. Multiple Choice A data set has numbers: 2, 1, 3, 1, 2. Which is the mean absolute deviation?

 Ⓐ 0.64 Ⓑ 1.3 Ⓒ 1.5 Ⓓ 1.7

 **Ready To Go On?**

Quiz for Lessons 1 Through 3

1   Mean, Median, Mode, and Range

Find the mean, median, mode, and range of each data set.

1.

Distance (mi)					
5	6	4	7	3	5

2.

Test Scores				
78	80	85	92	90

3.

Ages of Students (yr)							
11	13	12	12	12	13	9	14

4.

Number of Pages in Each Book						
145	119	156	158	125	128	135

2   Additional Data and Outliers

5. The table shows the number of people who attended each monthly meeting from January to May.

Number of People Attending				
Jan	Feb	Mar	Apr	May
27	26	32	30	30

   a. Find the mean, median, and mode of the attendances.

   b. In June, 39 people attended the meeting, and in July, 26 people attended the meeting. Add this data to the table and find the mean, median, and mode with the new data.

6. The four states with the longest coastlines are Alaska, Florida, California, and Hawaii. Alaska's coastline is 6,640 miles. Florida's coastline is 1,350 miles. California's coastline is 840 miles, and Hawaii's coastline is 750 miles. Find the mean, median, and mode of the lengths with and without Alaska's, and explain the changes.

7. The daily snowfall amounts for the first ten days of December are listed below.

   2 in., 5 in., 0 in., 0 in., 15 in., 1 in., 0 in., 3 in., 1 in., 4 in.

   What are the mean, median, and mode of this data set? Which one best describes the data set?

3   Measures of Variation

8. The number of minutes it takes Will to complete each of 5 crossword puzzles is 18, 22, 21, 27, 19. What is the mean absolute deviation for the time needed to complete the puzzles, to the nearest tenth?

Focus on Problem Solving

Make sense of problems and persevere in solving them.

Make a Plan

• Prioritize and sequence information

Some problems give you a lot of information. Read the entire problem carefully to be sure you understand all of the facts. You may need to read it over several times, perhaps aloud so that you can hear yourself say the words.

Then decide which information is most important (prioritize). Is there any information that is absolutely necessary to solve the problem? This information is important.

Finally, put the information in order (sequence). Use comparison words like *before, after, longer, shorter,* and so on to help you. Write the sequence down before you try to solve the problem.

Read the problems below and answer the questions that follow.

1 The portable MP3 player appeared 300 years after the piano. The tape recorder was invented in 1898. Thomas Edison invented the phonograph 21 years before the tape recorder and 122 years before the portable MP3 player. What is the date of each invention?

a. Which invention's date can you use to find the dates of all the others?

b. Can you solve the problem without this date? Explain.

c. List the inventions in order from earliest invention to latest invention.

2 Jon recorded the heights of his family members. There are 4 people in Jon's family, including Jon. Jon's mother is 2 inches taller than Jon's father. Jon is 56 inches tall. Jon's sister is 4 inches taller than Jon and 5 inches shorter than Jon's father. What are the heights of Jon and his family members?

a. Whose height can you use to find the heights of all the others?

b. Can you solve the problem without this height? Explain.

c. List Jon's family members in order from shortest to tallest.

?

1898

?

?

6-4 Line Plots, Frequency Tables, and Histograms

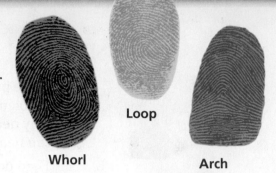

COMMON CORE

CC.6.SP.4 Display numerical data in plots on a number line, including dot plots, histograms, and box plots

Vocabulary

frequency

frequency table

line plot

histogram

Your fingerprints are unlike anyone else's. Even identical twins have slightly different fingerprint patterns.

All fingerprints have one of three patterns: whorl, loop, or arch.

Loop

Whorl

Arch

The **frequency** of a data value is the number of times it occurs.

A **frequency table** tells the number of items an event, category, or group occurs.

EXAMPLE 1 **Using Tally Marks to Make a Frequency Table**

Each student in Mrs. Choe's class recorded their fingerprint pattern. Which type is most common in Mrs. Choe's class?

| whorl | loop | loop | loop | loop | arch | loop |
| whorl | arch | loop | arch | loop | arch | whorl |

Make a table to show each type of fingerprint.

Step 1: For each fingerprint, make a tally mark in the appropriate row.

Step 2: Count the number of tally marks for each pattern. This is the frequency.

Reading Math

A group of four tally marks with a line through it means five.

卌 = 5

卌 卌 = 10

Fingerprint Patterns

Pattern	Tallies	Frequency
Whorl	///	3
Arch	////	4
Loop	卌 //	7

The loop pattern is the most common in Mrs. Choe's class.

A **line plot** uses a number line and x's or other symbols to show frequencies of values.

EXAMPLE 2 **Making a Line Plot**

Students in Mr. Lee's class each ran several miles in a week. Make a line plot of the data.

Step 1: Draw a number line.

Step 2: For each student, use an x on the number line to represent how many miles he or she ran.

Number of Miles Run
8 3 5 6 7 8 5 5 3 6 10 7 5

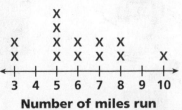

(l) Leonard Lessin/Peter Arnold/Photolibrary; (c) Peter Miller/Stone/Getty Images; (r) Federal Bureau of Investigation

Video **Lesson Tutorials Online** my.hrw.com

EXAMPLE **3** **Making a Frequency Table with Intervals**

Use the data in the table to make a frequency table with intervals.

Number of Representatives per State in the U.S. House of Representatives												
7	1	6	4	52	6	6	1	1	23	11	2	2
20	10	5	4	6	7	2	8	10	16	8	5	9
1	3	2	2	13	3	31	12	1	19	6	5	21
2	6	1	9	30	3	1	11	9	3	9		

Step 1: Choose equal intervals.

Step 2: Find the number of data values in each interval. Write these numbers in the "Frequency" row.

Number of Representatives per State in the U.S. House of Representatives									
Number	0–5	6–11	12–17	18–23	24–29	30–35	36–41	42–47	48–53
Frequency	22	18	3	4	0	2	0	0	1

This table shows that 22 states have between 0 and 5 representatives, 18 states have between 6 and 11 representatives, and so on.

A **histogram** is a bar graph that shows the number of data items that occur within each interval.

EXAMPLE **4** **Making a Histogram**

Use the frequency table in Example 3 to make a histogram.

Step 1: Choose an appropriate scale and interval.

Step 2: Draw a bar for the number of states in each interval. The bars should touch but not overlap.

Step 3: Title the graph and label the axes.

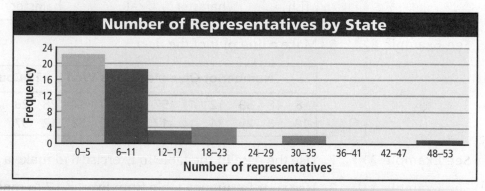

Think and Discuss

MATHEMATICAL PRACTICES

1. Describe a data set that can appropriately be displayed using a histogram.

GUIDED PRACTICE

See Example 1

1. Each student in the band recorded the type of instrument he or she plays. The results are shown in the box. Make a frequency table to organize the data. Which instrument do the fewest students play?

trumpet	tuba	French horn	drums	trombone
drums	trombone	trombone	trumpet	trumpet
trumpet	French horn	trumpet	French horn	French horn

See Example 2

2. Make a line plot of the data.

Length of Each U.S. Presidency (yr)										
8	4	8	8	8	4	8	4	0	4	4	1	3	4	4	4	4	8	4	0	4
4	4	4	4	8	4	8	2	6	4	12	8	8	2	6	5	3	4	8	4	8

See Example 3

3. Use the data in the table in Exercise 2 to make a frequency table with intervals.

See Example 4

4. Use your frequency table from Exercise 3 to make a histogram.

INDEPENDENT PRACTICE

See Example 1

5. Students recorded the type of pet they own. The results are shown in the box. Make a frequency table. Which type of pet do most students own?

cat	cat	bird	dog	dog
dog	bird	dog	bird	fish
bird	cat	fish	dog	cat
fish	hamster	cat	hamster	dog

See Example 2

6. Make a line plot of the data.

Number of Olympic Medals Won by 27 Countries													
8	88	59	12	11	57	38	17	14	28	28	26	25	23
18	8	29	34	14	17	13	13	58	12	97	10	9	

See Example 3

7. Use the data in the table in Exercise 6 to make a frequency table with intervals.

See Example 4

8. Use your frequency table from Exercise 7 to make a histogram.

PRACTICE AND PROBLEM SOLVING

Extra Practice
See Extra Practice for more exercises.

9. **Critical Thinking** Would a bar graph or a histogram be more appropriate to display the state test scores for an entire sixth grade class? Explain.

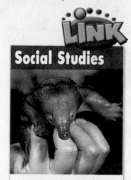

Social Studies

Echidnas are egg-laying mammals found only in Australia and New Guinea. A baby echidna is called a puggle.

10. **Multi-Step** Gather data on the number of pairs of shoes your classmates own. Make two line plots of the data, one for the boys and one for the girls. Compare the data.

11. **Social Studies** The map shows the populations of Australia's states and territories. Use the data to make a frequency table with intervals.

Northern Territory 187,100
Queensland 3,401,200
AUSTRALIA
New South Wales 6,274,400
Australian Capital Territory 309,800
Western Australia 1,798,100
South Australia 1,479,800
Victoria 4,605,100
Tasmania 473,500

12. **Social Studies** Use your frequency table from Exercise 11 to make a histogram.

13. **Critical Thinking** Can a frequency table have intervals of 0–5, 5–10, and 10–15? Why or why not?

14. **What's the Error?** Reading from the line plot, Kathryn says that there are 10 campers who are three years old. What is Kathryn's error?

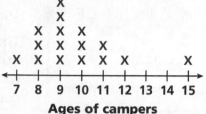

Ages of campers

15. **Write About It** Choose one of the histograms you made for this lesson and redraw it using different intervals. How did the histogram change? Explain.

16. **Challenge** Can you find the mean, median, and mode price using this frequency table? If so, find them. If not, explain why not.

Cost of Video Game Rentals at Different Stores			
Price	$2.00–$2.99	$3.00–$3.99	$4.00–$4.99	$5.00–$5.99
Frequency	5	12	8	5

Test Prep

17. **Multiple Choice** Emily is making a histogram for the data 12, 24, 56, 7, 34, 75, 34, 86, 34, 78, and 96. Which is the most appropriate first interval?

   Ⓐ 0–5   Ⓑ 0–10   Ⓒ 0–50   Ⓓ 0–100

18. **Short Response** Use the data in the table to make a frequency table with three-goal intervals. How many times were 6–8 goals scored?

Number of Goals Scored Each Game
3 5 2 5 4 7 1 0 6 4 8 5 3 2 4 5 9

Roland Seitre/Peter Arnold, Inc.

6-4 Line Plots, Frequency Tables, and Histograms **263**

Frequency Distribution

CC.6.SP.5 Summarize
numerical data sets in
relation to their context
Also CC.6.SP.2

In the previous lesson you learned how to make frequency tables and histograms. These represent the *frequency distribution* of a data set. **Frequency distribution** describes the number of values in a data set that fall into each interval. The shape of a histogram may also help you find the median and any outliers.

EXAMPLE 1 Describing Frequency Distribution

Vocabulary

frequency distribution

cumulative frequency

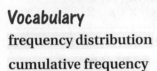

Reading Math

In this data set, most of the values are near the lower part of the range.

The histogram shows the number of students who have given numbers of first cousins in their family.

A **Around what value(s) does the data cluster?**

The data clusters around the values 3–6.

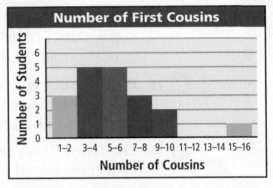

B **Explain whether the histogram shows the median or outliers of the data set.**

There are 19 values shown in the histogram, so the 10th value is the median. The median falls in the interval 5–6. The histogram does not show whether 5 or 6 is the median.

One data value is in the interval 15–16. It is an outlier because it is very different from the other values.

Recall that a frequency table shows the number of times a category or group occurs. If you add a third column to a frequency table, you can make a *cumulative frequency* table. **Cumulative frequency** is the frequency of all data values that are less than or equal to a given value.

EXAMPLE 2 Making a Cumulative Frequency Table

The best jumps in inches in a high-jump contest are given below.

60, 54, 63, 56, 45, 62, 58, 60, 61, 60, 54, 62

A **Use the data to make a cumulative frequency table.**

Step 1 Title the table.

Step 2 Choose intervals for the first column of the table.

Step 3 Put the frequency of each interval in the second column.

Step 4 Add the frequency of each interval to the frequencies of all the intervals above it. Put the sum in the third column.

Best High Jumps		
Height (in.)	Frequency	Cumulative Frequency
45–50	1	1
51–55	2	3
56–60	5	8
61–65	4	12

B **How many of the jumps are less than 61 inches?**

All jumps below 61 in. are in the top three rows. The cumulative frequency in the third row is 8, so 8 of the jumps are below 61 in.

C **Make a histogram and a line graph of the data in the cumulative frequency table in part A.**

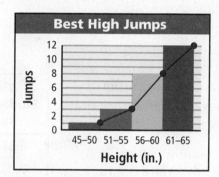

To make a histogram, draw a bar for the cumulative frequency for each interval.

To make a line graph, place points in the upper right corner of each bar. Then connect those points with line segments, as shown.

EXTENSION

Exercises

The histogram shows the number of times Jaime deposits given amounts of money in his account.

1. Around what value(s) does the data cluster?

2. Does the histogram show the median or any outliers? Explain.

3. Make a cumulative frequency table of the data set.

4. **What's the Error** Explain the error in the table.

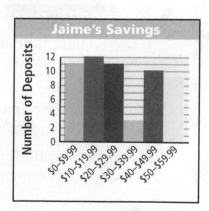

CDs Sold		
Price ($)	Frequency	Cumulative Frequency
6–9	5	12
10–13	7	19
14–17	4	23
18–20	2	25

Use a Survey to Collect Data

Use with Line Plots, Frequency Tables, and Histograms

Learn It Online
Lab Resources Online

MATHEMATICAL PRACTICES **Use appropriate tools strategically.**

CC.6.SP.5 Summarize numerical data sets in relation to their context

You can use a survey to collect data. In this lab, you will split into teams and ask your classmates how long it takes them to get to school.

Work in teams of 2 or 3 students. Each team will survey students as they arrive at school, but the teams will work in different locations:

- Half the teams should survey students outside as they get off the school buses.

- The other teams should survey students as they enter their homerooms.

Each team should follow the steps below for their survey.

Activity

1 Ask students if they have been surveyed by any other team. If not, ask them what time they left their house that morning. Try to get 10 to 15 responses.

2 After you've finished surveying, calculate the time between when each student left the house and the time that first period of school starts. Record your data in a table like the one at right.

3 Calculate the mean travel time for the students you surveyed.

Time Student Left Home	Total Time Spent Getting to First Period (min)
6:57 A.M.	33
7:05 A.M.	25
■	■
■	■

Think and Discuss

1. Do you think the mean times will be longer for the bus teams or for the homeroom teams? Explain why.

2. As a class, find the mean time of all the students surveyed by the bus teams. Then find the mean time of all the students surveyed by the homeroom teams. Do the results match your prediction from problem **1**?

3. Do you think the bus mean or the homeroom mean is a more accurate estimate of the average time students take to get to school? Why?

Try This

1. Draw a histogram to display your team's data.

2. Think of something you'd like to know about the students in your school and write a survey question to find the answer. Explain how you would conduct the survey to get accurate results.

CC.6.SP.5 Summarize numerical data sets in relation to their context *Also CC.6.SP.2, CC.6.SP.3, CC.6.SP.4*

Recall that a frequency distribution is a display that shows how many times data values fall into categories of quantity. Frequency distributions are categorized by their general shape.

Shapes of a Distribution	
Skewed	**Normal**
Data are not symmetric about the center.	Data are symmetric about the center.
The measures of center may not be equal.	The measures of center are equal.

EXAMPLE **1** **Displaying Distributions on Dot Plots**

A The data set and dot plot display the grades of Ms. Lee's students. Describe the shape of the data distribution.

82	95	84	87	85	92	85	78	87	84	83
86	80	86	85	75	83	90	86	84	88	85

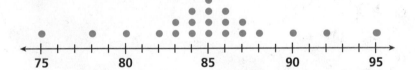

The data is symmetrical about the center. It shows a normal shape of distribution. The mean, median, and mode of the data set are 85.

B The data set and dot plot display the number of siblings that 20 students have. Describe the shape of the data distribution.

1	2	3	0	1	4	2	2	1	3
3	4	2	2	6	1	3	4	1	1

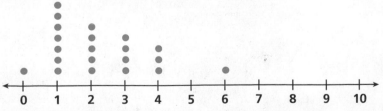

The data is skewed. The mean, median, and mode are varied.

EXAMPLE 2 Displaying Distributions on Box-and-Whisker Plots

The data set and box-and-whisker plot display the heights in inches of players on a basketball team. Describe the shape of the data distribution.

81	72	76	83	81	74
80	85	82	82	71	79

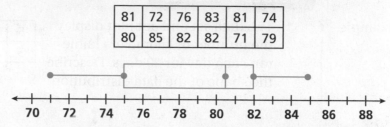

The data is skewed. The mean, median, and mode are varied.

A box-and-whisker plot shows the center, spread, and shape of a data distribution clearly. Therefore, you can use box-and-whisker plots to compare data distributions.

EXAMPLE 3 Comparing Distributions Using Box-and-Whisker Plots

The box-and-whisker plots show the distribution of the low temperatures in Tallahassee, Florida, and Tampa, Florida, during one month. What conclusions can you make about the temperatures?

Low Temperatures During One Month

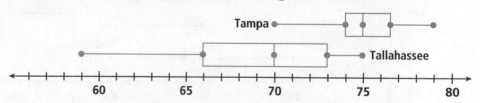

Helpful Hint

Another word to describe the range of values from the least to the greatest value is the "spread."

In general, the low temperatures in Tampa are higher than the low temperatures in Tallahassee. The spread of the data is greater for Tallahassee, which means that there is more variation in the data. The temperature in Tampa is more predictable than the temperature in Tallahassee.

MATHEMATICAL PRACTICES

Think and Discuss

1. **Explain** how a box-and-whisker plot gives information that is hard to see by just looking at the numbers.

2. **Describe** the benefits of displaying data using a dot plot as opposed to a box-and-whisker plot.

GUIDED PRACTICE

See Example 1

1. The data set and dot plot display the number of kilometers Jaime ran each day for 20 days. Describe the shape of the data distribution.

5	2	5	9	5	4	6	5	1	7
3	7	4	8	5	6	3	5	4	6

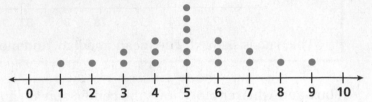

See Example 2

2. Ira hit a number of home runs over the 14 years he played on the baseball team. His results are displayed in the data set and box-and-whisker plot. Describe the shape of the data distribution.

7	11	18	14	13
16	14	8	10	13
1	14	7	9	

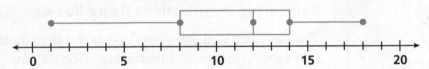

See Example 3

3. What conclusions can you make about the test scores?

Amy and Jackson's First Semester Test Scores

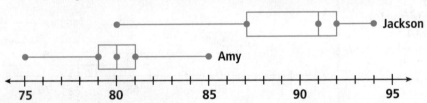

INDEPENDENT PRACTICE

See Example 1

4. The dot plot shows the approximate heights of 14 buildings in meters. Describe the shape of the data distribution.

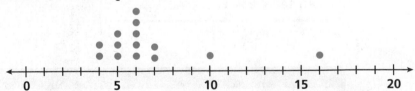

See Example 2

5. The box-and-whisker plot shows the ages of the 20 boys and girls at Ella's birthday party. Describe the shape of the data distribution.

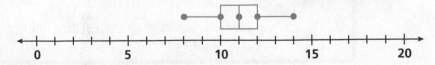

6. What conclusions can you make about the amount of sugar in each drink?

Comparison of Grams of Sugar in Juice and Soda

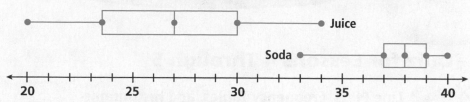

PRACTICE AND PROBLEM SOLVING

7. Life Science A veterinarian monitored 18 pregnant cats in a year. The number of kittens per litter were: 4, 2, 5, 6, 3, 5, 1, 4, 3, 6, 4, 3, 7, 2, 3, 9, 5, and 2. What conclusions can you make about the data?

8. What's the Error? A student created the following box-and-whisker plot from the data set {2, 3, 5, 6, 10, 10, 14, 15}. Explain the error that the student made. Then draw the correct box-and-whisker plot.

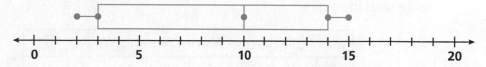

9. Write About It Two box-and-whisker plots look identical, but they represent different sets of data. What must the data sets have in common? What do you NOT know that the data sets have in common?

10. Challenge Describe a set of data in which there is only one whisker in its box-and-whisker plot.

Life Science

An average female cat gives birth to 1 to 8 kittens per litter.

Test Prep

11. Multiple Choice A box-and-whisker plot shows that the third quartile is the same as the median. Which data set could represent the data in the box-and-whisker plot?

Ⓐ 0, 0, 0, 0, 0, 1, 1, 1, 1

Ⓒ 11, 15, 15, 15, 15, 16, 16

Ⓑ 0, 10, 20, 30, 40, 50, 60, 70

Ⓓ 8, 8, 8, 26, 26, 26, 55

12. Short Response A manager of a retirement home tracks the ages of each of the residents. She creates a dot plot with a number line from 0 to 100. Describe the most likely shape of the distribution of the manager's data, and explain why it will have that shape.

Ready To Go On?

Quiz for Lessons 4 Through 5

✓ **4** Line Plots, Frequency Tables, and Histograms

Shoppers leaving Midtown Mall were each asked to give their age. Use the line plot to answer each question.

Shoppers at Midtown Mall

```
                          X
          X               X       X
          X               X   X   X
  X   X       X   X   X   X   X
  ←─┼───┼───┼───┼───┼───┼───┼───┼─→
   15  16  17  18  19  20  21  22
```

Ages of shoppers

1. What are the range and mode of the data?

2. How many of the shoppers surveyed were older than 20?

3. The table below shows the results of a survey about the number of movies a group of people saw last year. Use the data in the table to make a frequency table with intervals.

Number of Movies Seen Last Year							
3	18	22	5	9	10	8	12
6	20	15	17	13	11	9	16

✓ **5** Describing Distributions

4. The data set and dot plot show the shot put throw distances (in meters) at a track meet. Describe the shape of the data distribution.

20.80	19.82	21.63	18.42	20.20	20.68	20.32	20.80
21.16	18.86	19.24	19.91	20.68	18.75	20.90	19.63

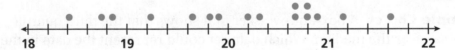

5. The box-and-whisker plots show the distribution of passengers on two bus routes each day in a month. What conclusions can you make about the data?

Passengers on Green Street and City Avenue Bus Routes

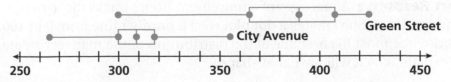

Real-World CONNECTIONS

MATHEMATICAL PRACTICES Reason abstractly and quantitatively.

Tornado Alley Oklahoma lies at the heart of Tornado Alley, the region of the central United States where tornadoes are most likely to occur. The state has survived some of the world's most powerful tornadoes, including a 1999 twister with the greatest wind speeds ever recorded on earth—318 mi/h!

OKLAHOMA

1. The table shows the number of tornadoes in Oklahoma from 2000 to 2007. What is the mode of the data?

Tornadoes in Oklahoma								
Year	2000	2001	2002	2003	2004	2005	2006	2007
Number of Tornadoes	44	61	18	78	62	27	27	49

2. Find the mean number of tornadoes per year.

3. Find the median number of tornadoes per year.

4. Make a box-and-whisker plot of the data. What is the interquartile range for the data set?

5. In 1999, there were 145 tornadoes in Oklahoma. Suppose this value is included in the data set shown in the table.

   a. Find the mean, median, and mode when the 1999 data is included.

   b. Explain how the mean, median, and mode change when the 1999 data is included.

   c. Does the mean, median, or mode best describe the data set when the 1999 data is included? Why?

Real-World Connections

Real-World Connections

Game Time

A Thousand Words

Did you ever hear the saying "A picture is worth a thousand words"?
A graph can be worth a thousand words too!

Each of the graphs below tells a story about a student's trip to school.
Read each story and think about what each graph is showing. Can you
match each graph with its story?

Kyla:
I rode my bike to
school at a steady pace.
I had to stop and wait
for the light to change at
two intersections.

Tom:
I walked to my bus stop
and waited there for the
bus. After I boarded the
bus, it was driven straight
to school.

Megan:
On my way to school, I
stopped at my friend's
house. She wasn't ready
yet, so I waited for her.
Then we walked to school.

Graph A

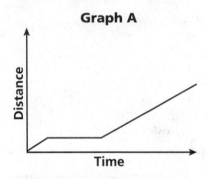

Graph B

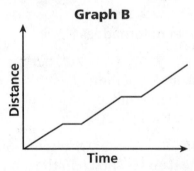

Graph C

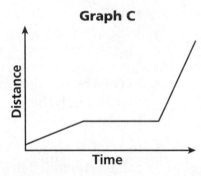

Spinnermeania

Round 1: On your turn, spin the spinner four
times and record the results. After everyone has
had a turn, find the mean, median, and mode
of your results. For every category in which you
have the highest number, you get one point. If
there is a tie in a category, each player with that
number gets a point. If your data set has more
than one mode, use the greatest one.

Spin five times in round 2, eight times
in round 3, ten times in round 4, and
twelve times in round 5. The player with
the highest score at the end of five rounds
is the winner.

Learn It Online
Game Time Extra

A complete copy of the rules and
game pieces are available online.

Materials
- 2 pieces of card stock
- 6 sandwich-size zipper bags
- clear packaging tape
- graph paper
- scissors

It's in the Bag!

PROJECT | **Graphing According to Me**

Create different types of graphs and make a zippered accordion book to hold them all.

Directions

❶ Place one piece of card stock that is $6\frac{1}{2}$ inches by 7 inches next to one of the bags. The opening of the bag should be at the top, and there should be a small space between the card stock and the bag. Tape the card stock and bag together on the front and back sides. **Figure A**

❷ Lay another bag down next to the first, keeping a small space between them. Tape them together, front and back. **Figure B**

❸ Continue with the rest of the bags. At the end of the chain, tape a second piece of card stock that is $6\frac{1}{2}$ inches by 7 inches to the last bag. **Figure C**

❹ Fold the bags accordion-style, back and forth, with the two card stock covers on the front and back.

❺ Cut out squares of graph paper so they will fit in the bags.

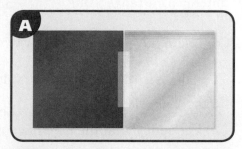

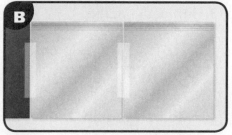

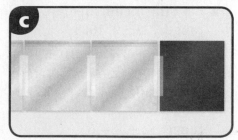

Taking Note of the Math

Write a title for your book on the cover. On each piece of graph paper, draw and label an example of one type of data distribution you have seen. Store the graphs in the bags.

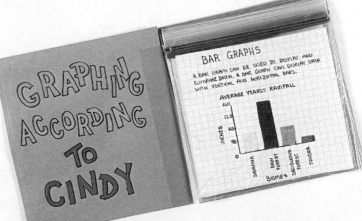

HMH

Vocabulary

box-and-whisker plot	line plot	quartiles
frequency	mean	range
frequency table	median	variation
histogram	mode	
interquartile range (IQR)	outlier	

Complete the sentences below with vocabulary words from the list above.

1. ___?___ is the spread of the values in a data set.

2. A(n) ___?___ lists items together according to the number of times, or frequency, that the items occur.

3. In a data set, the ___?___ is the value or values that occur most often.

EXAMPLES

EXERCISES

1 | Mean, Median, Mode, and Range

■ Find the mean, median, mode, and range. 7, 8, 12, 10, 8

mean: $7 + 8 + 8 + 10 + 12 = 45$
$\qquad 45 \div 5 = 9$
median: 8
mode: 8
range: $12 - 7 = 5$

Find the mean, median, mode, and range.

4.

Hours Worked Each Week						
32	39	39	38	36	39	36

5.

Amount Saved Each Month ($)							
50	120	75	30	40	50	35	100

2 Additional Data and Outliers

■ **Find the mean, median, and mode with and without the outlier.**

10, 4, 7, 8, 34, 7, 7, 12, 5, 8   *The outlier is 34.*

With: **mean** = 10.2,
       mode = 7,
       median = 7.5
Without: **mean** ≈ 7.555,
         mode = 7,
         median = 7

Find the mean, median, and mode of each data set with and without the outlier.

6. 12, 11, 9, 38, 10, 8, 12

7. 34, 12, 32, 45, 32

8. 16, 12, 15, 52, 10, 13

9. The table below shows a student's test scores for four classes. The student also received a score of 82 on a project for Art class. Find the mean, median, mode, and range of the data, with and without the Art score, and explain the changes.

Test	Math	English	History	Science
Grade	95	85	90	80

3 Measures of Variation

■ **Find the interquartile range for the data set.**

8, 20, 14, 11, 18, 15

8, 11, 14, 15, 18, 20   *Order the data.*

(8, 11, 14) (15, 18, 20)   *Find the median and quartiles.*

$IQR = 18 - 11 = 7$ *Find the difference between the first and third quartiles.*

The interquartile range is 7.

Use the box-and-whisker plot for Exercises 10 and 11.

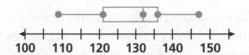

10. What are the least value, first quartile, median, third quartile, and greatest value for the data set?

11. What is the interquartile range for the data set?

12. A group of employees compared the distances they travel from home to work. The distances in miles are listed below.

15.6, 7.2, 17.4, 16, 11.3

What is the mean absolute deviation of the travel distances, to the nearest tenth?

Study Guide: Review

4 Line Plots, Frequency Tables, and Histograms

■ **Make a frequency table with intervals.**

Ages of people at Irene's birthday party: 37, 39, 18, 15, 13

Ages of People at Irene's Birthday Party				
Ages	13–19	20–26	27–33	34–40
Frequency	3	0	0	2

13. Each student on a class trip recorded how many fish he or she recognized at the City Aquarium. Make a line plot of the data.

Number of Fish Identified						
7	10	16	9	13	18	8
10	11	13	17	10	8	11
13	10	9	8	10	11	15

14. Make a frequency table with intervals.

Points Scored					
6	4	5	4	7	10

15. Use the frequency table from Exercise 14 to make a histogram.

5 Describing Distributions

■ **The box-and-whisker plots show the distribution of movie running times for movies showing now at two different theaters. What conclusions can you make about the movie running times?**

Movie Running Times (minutes)

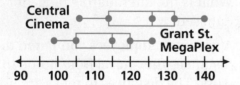

Half of the movies at Central Cinema run longer than all of the movies at Grant St. MegaPlex. There is a greater spread in the movie running times at Central Cinema than at Grant St. MegaPlex.

The data set and dot plot display the cost of tickets at a number of movie theaters. Use this information for Exercises 16 and 17.

8	12	9	12	11	12	10
11	9	16	14	13	14	12

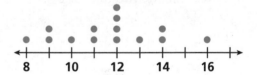

16. What is the shape of the distribution?

17. What can you conclude about the measures of center for the data set?

Chapter Test

Use the bar graph for Exercises 1–4.

1. Find the mean, median, mode, and range of the rainfall amounts.

2. Which month had the lowest average rainfall?

3. Which months had rainfall amounts greater than 2 inches?

4. The rainfall in August was 0.5 inch. How is the mean rainfall amount affected when this data value is included?

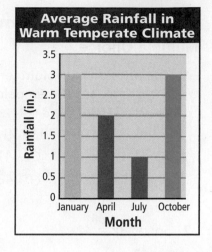

Use the table for Exercises 5 and 6.

Number of Push-ups Performed						
35	33	25	45	52	21	18
41	27	35	40	53	24	38

5. Make a box-and-whisker plot of the push-up data.

6. Find the interquartile range for the data set.

7. The number of goals scored by five hockey teams in a tournament were 4, 5, 7, 2, and 6. What is the mean absolute deviation for the number of goals scored?

8. The table shows the number of strawberries picked by customers at a pick-your-own strawberry patch. Organize the data in a line plot.

Number of Strawberries Picked							
28	33	35	27	35	28	35	29
30	27	30	35	28	27	31	32

9. The data set and dot plot display the numbers of people attending each session in a lecture series at a museum. Describe the shape of the data distribution.

42	50	43	39	42	54	42	40
44	51	49	41	40	45	39	40

Standardized Test Prep

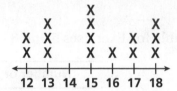
Cumulative Assessment

Multiple Choice

1. The ages of the volunteers at a local food bank are shown below.
16, 22, 23, 30, 31, 34, 41, 44, 48
What is the median of this set of data?

(A) 31   (C) 41

(B) 32.1   (D) 48

2. Solve: $3x = 42$

(F) 12

(G) 14

(H) 39

(J) 126

3. Harrison spends $3\frac{1}{2}$ hours a week working in his yard. He spends $1\frac{1}{3}$ hours pulling weeds. He spends the rest of the time mowing the yard. How much time does he spend mowing the yard?

(A) $1\frac{1}{6}$ hours   (C) $2\frac{1}{3}$ hours

(B) $2\frac{1}{6}$ hours   (D) $3\frac{1}{3}$ hours

4. Which value is equivalent to 4^4?

(F) 8   (H) 64

(G) 16   (J) 256

5. Jamie is making a fruit salad. She needs $2\frac{1}{4}$ cups of crushed pineapple, $3\frac{3}{4}$ cups of sliced apples, $1\frac{1}{3}$ cups of mandarin oranges, and $2\frac{2}{3}$ cups of red grapes. How many cups total of fruit does she need for the fruit salad?

(A) 6 cups   (C) 10 cups

(B) 8 cups   (D) 12 cups

6. The line plot shows the ages of the number of participants in a science fair. Which of the following statements is NOT supported by the line plot?

Ages of Science Fair Participants

```
                    X
        X       X           X
    X   X       X       X   X
    X   X       X   X   X   X
   ←─┼───┼───┼───┼───┼───┼───┼─→
    12  13  14  15  16  17  18
```

(F) The range is 6.

(G) The mean age of the participants in the science fair is 15.1.

(H) The mode of the ages of the participants in the science fair is 16.

(J) The median age of the participants in the science fair is 15.

7. What is the mode of the following data? 17, 13, 14, 13, 21, 18, 16, 19

(A) 13   (C) 16.5

(B) 16   (D) 16.375

8. The heights (in inches) of 8 students are 48, 51, 50, 66, 52, 47, 53, and 49. What is the mean if the outlier is removed from the data?

(F) 48

(G) 50

(H) 52

(J) 66

9. Which equation has a solution of 8?

Ⓐ $2x = 18$ Ⓒ $x + 6 = 24$

Ⓑ $x - 4 = 12$ Ⓓ $\frac{x}{4} = 2$

 HOT TIP! Read graphs and diagrams carefully. Look at the labels for important information.

Gridded Response

Use the following data set for items 10 and 11.

4, 13, 7, 26, 6, 7, 3, 4, 2, 8, 10, 9

10. Which number in the data set is an outlier?

11. What is the mean of the data set?

12. Greg is separating his marbles into sets. He has 16 green marbles and 20 red marbles. Each set must have the same number of green marbles and the same number of red marbles. What is the greatest number of marble sets that Greg can make if he wants to use every marble?

13. What is the least common multiple of 5, 6, and 8?

14. Miguel has a piece of lumber that is 48.6 centimeters long. How many centimeters does he need to cut off if he wants the piece of lumber to measure 32.8 centimeters?

15. Write $4\frac{3}{8}$ as a decimal.

Short Response

S1. Look at the bar graph of favorite flavors of frozen fruit bars. Can you determine the mean, median, or mode of the data? Explain.

S2. The data set and dot plot display the ages of people in line at the bank one morning.

21	35	23	55	55
55	32	26	40	43
39	32	32		

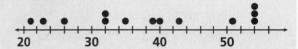

a. Find the range, mean, median, and mode of the data.

b. How does adding 82, 18, and 42 to the data change the range, mean, median, and mode?

Extended Response

E1. The high temperature on Monday was 54°F. On Tuesday, it was 62°F. On Wednesday, it was 65°F. On Thursday, it was 60°F. On Friday, it was 62°F.

a. Organize this data in a table. Find the range, mean, median, and mode of the data.

b. Which graph would be more appropriate to show the data—a bar graph or a line graph? Explain.

c. Make a graph of the data.

Proportional Relationships

Chapter
- Use tables to determine whether quantities are in equivalent ratios.
- Use proportional reasoning to solve rate and ratio problems.

Why Learn This?

Scale models use proportional relationships to make smaller versions of large objects and larger versions of small objects. This scale model of Shanghai, China, is $\frac{1}{2,000}$ the size of the actual city.

Learn It Online
Chapter Project Online

Ryan Pyle/None/Corbis

Are You Ready?

✓ Vocabulary

Choose the best term from the list to complete each sentence.

divide

denominator

equivalent

fraction

multiply

numerator

1. To solve the equation $\frac{1}{4}x = 24$, you can ___?___ both sides of the equation by 4.

2. A(n) ___?___ is used to name a part of a whole.

3. When two numbers have the same value, they are said to be ___?___.

4. When writing 0.25 as a fraction, 25 is the ___?___ and 100 is the ___?___.

Complete these exercises to review skills you will need for this chapter.

✓ Simplify Fractions

Write each fraction in simplest form.

5. $\frac{6}{10}$ 6. $\frac{9}{12}$ 7. $\frac{8}{6}$

✓ Write Equivalent Fractions

Write three equivalent fractions for each given fraction.

8. $\frac{4}{16}$ 9. $\frac{5}{10}$ 10. $\frac{5}{6}$

✓ Compare Fractions

Compare. Write >, <, or =.

11. $\frac{3}{10}$ ▪ $\frac{2}{5}$ 12. $1\frac{3}{4}$ ▪ $1\frac{5}{7}$ 13. $\frac{5}{8}$ ▪ $\frac{1}{2}$ 14. $2\frac{11}{12}$ ▪ $\frac{35}{12}$

✓ Write Fractions as Decimals

Write each fraction as a decimal.

15. $\frac{1}{2}$ 16. $\frac{7}{20}$ 17. $\frac{2}{25}$ 18. $\frac{3}{25}$

✓ Multiply Decimals

Multiply.

19. $0.42 \cdot 10$ 20. $0.3 \cdot 52$ 21. $20.5 \cdot 0.25$ 22. $6.75 \cdot 0.40$

23. $9.8 \cdot 0.2$ 24. $0.8 \cdot 7.4$ 25. $0.52 \cdot 0.64$ 26. $0.75 \cdot 8.9$

Where You've Been

Previously, you

- used fractions to represent situations involving division.
- generated equivalent fractions and decimals.
- used multiplication and division to find equivalent fractions.

In This Chapter

You will study

- using ratios to describe proportional situations.
- representing ratios and percents with concrete models, fractions, and decimals.
- using multiplication and division to solve problems involving equivalent ratios and rates.

Where You're Going

You can use the skills learned in this chapter

- to find sales tax on retail items at stores.
- to convert between fractions, decimals, and percents.

Key Vocabulary/Vocabulario

coordinate grid	cuadrícula de coordenadas
equivalent ratios	razones equivalentes
ordered pair	par ordenado
percent	porcentaje
proportion	proporción
rate	tasa
ratio	razón
unit rate	tasa unitaria

Vocabulary Connections

To become familiar with some of the vocabulary terms in the chapter, consider the following. You may refer to the chapter, the glossary, or a dictionary if you like.

1. A *grid* is a network of uniformly spaced horizontal and perpendicular lines. What do you think a **coordinate grid** looks like?

2. *Equivalent* can mean "equal in value." How do you think **equivalent ratios** are related?

3. *Ordered* means "to be arranged." The word *pair* can mean "two things designed for use together." What do you think an **ordered pair** is made up of?

4. *Percent* comes from *per* and the Latin word *centum,* meaning "hundred." What do you think **percent** means?

5. *Ratio* can mean "the relationship in quantity, amount, or size between two things." How many numbers do you think a **ratio** will have?

Reading and Writing Math

Writing Strategy: Write a Convincing Explanation

You will see the Write About It icons throughout the book. These icons show exercises that require you to write a convincing explanation.

A convincing explanation should include

- a restatement of the question or problem.

- a complete solution to the problem.

- any work, definitions, diagrams, or charts needed to answer the problem.

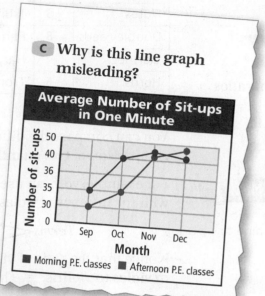

C Why is this line graph misleading?

Average Number of Sit-ups in One Minute

Number of sit-ups: 50, 40, 36, 35, 30, 0

Month: Sep, Oct, Nov, Dec

■ Morning P.E. classes   ■ Afternoon P.E. classes

Step 1 **Restate the question.**
The graph is misleading because the scale does not have equal intervals.

Step 2 **Provide a complete solution to the problem with facts and an explanation.**
For example, an increase from 35 sit-ups to 40 sit-ups appears greater than an increase from 30 sit-ups to 35 sit-ups. By reading the scale, you know that this is incorrect. Therefore, the graph is misleading.

Try This

Use your textbook.

1. Write a convincing explanation to explain why there are two modes in the data set 4, 6, 1, 0, 4, 8, 9, 0.

2. Look at one of your previous Write About It exercises. Does your answer follow the method outlined above? If so, label the items that should be included. If not, rewrite the explanation.

7-1 Ratios and Rates

COMMON CORE

CC.6.RP.2 Understand the concept of a unit rate *a/b* associated with a ratio *a : b* with *b ≠ 0*, and use rate language in the context of a ratio relationship.

Vocabulary

ratio

equivalent ratios

rate

unit rate

For a time, a local symphony orchestra was made up of 95 musicians.

Violins	29	Violas	12
Cellos	10	Basses	9
Flutes	5	Trumpets	3
Double reeds	8	Percussion	5
Clarinets	4	Harp	1
Horns	6	Trombones	3

You can compare the different groups by using ratios. A **ratio** is a comparison of two quantities using division.

For example, you can use a ratio to compare the number of violins with the number of violas. This ratio can be written in three ways.

Reading Math

Read the ratio $\frac{29}{12}$ as "twenty-nine to twelve."

$$Terms \!\!\!<\begin{array}{c} \\ \\ \end{array}\!\!\! \frac{29}{12} \qquad 29 \text{ to } 12 \qquad 29{:}12$$

Notice that the ratio of **violins** to **violas**, $\frac{29}{12}$, is different from the ratio of **violas** to **violins**, $\frac{12}{29}$. The order of the terms is important.

Ratios can be written to compare a part to a part, a part to the whole, or the whole to a part.

EXAMPLE **1** **Writing Ratios**

Use the table above to write each ratio.

A **flutes to clarinets**

$\frac{5}{4}$ *or* 5 to 4 *or* 5:4   *Part to part*

B **trumpets to total instruments**

$\frac{3}{95}$ *or* 3 to 95 *or* 3:95   *Part to whole*

C **total instruments to basses**

$\frac{95}{9}$ *or* 95 to 9 *or* 95:9   *Whole to part*

Equivalent ratios are ratios that name the same comparison. You can find an equivalent ratio by multiplying or dividing both terms of a ratio by the same number.

MIKE THEILER/AFP/Getty Images

Video **Lesson Tutorials Online** my.hrw.com

EXAMPLE 2 Writing Equivalent Ratios

Write three equivalent ratios to compare the number of stars with the number of moons in the pattern.

$$\frac{\text{number of stars}}{\text{number of moons}} = \frac{4}{6} \qquad \textit{There are 4 stars and 6 moons.}$$

$$\frac{4}{6} = \frac{4 \div 2}{6 \div 2} = \frac{2}{3} \qquad \textit{There are 2 stars for every 3 moons.}$$

$$\frac{4}{6} = \frac{4 \cdot 2}{6 \cdot 2} = \frac{8}{12} \qquad \textit{If you double the pattern, there will be 8 stars and 12 moons.}$$

So $\frac{4}{6}$, $\frac{2}{3}$, and $\frac{8}{12}$ are equivalent ratios.

Interactivities Online ▶ A **rate** compares two quantities that have different units of measure.

Suppose a 2-liter bottle of soda costs $1.98.

$$\text{rate} = \frac{\text{price}}{\text{number of liters}} = \frac{\$1.98}{2 \text{ liters}} \qquad \$1.98 \text{ for 2 liters}$$

When the comparison is to one unit, the rate is called a **unit rate**.

Divide both terms by the second term to find the unit rate.

$$\text{unit rate} = \frac{\$1.98}{2} = \frac{\$1.98 \div 2}{2 \div 2} = \frac{\$0.99}{1} \qquad \$0.99 \text{ for 1 liter}$$

When the prices of two or more items are compared, the item with the lowest unit rate is the best deal.

EXAMPLE 3 *Consumer Math Application*

A 2-liter bottle of soda costs $2.02. A 3-liter bottle of the same soda costs $2.79. Which is the better deal?

2-liter bottle

$$\frac{\$2.02}{2 \text{ liters}} \qquad \textit{Write the rate.}$$

$$\frac{\$2.02 \div 2}{2 \text{ liters} \div 2} \qquad \textit{Divide both terms by 2.}$$

$$\frac{\$1.01}{1 \text{ liter}} \qquad \textit{\$1.01 for 1 liter}$$

3-liter bottle

$$\frac{\$2.79}{3 \text{ liters}} \qquad \textit{Write the rate.}$$

$$\frac{\$2.79 \div 3}{3 \text{ liters} \div 3} \qquad \textit{Divide both terms by 3.}$$

$$\frac{\$0.93}{1 \text{ liter}} \qquad \textit{\$0.93 for 1 liter}$$

The 3-liter bottle is the better deal.

MATHEMATICAL PRACTICES

Think and Discuss

1. Explain why the ratio 2:5 is different from the ratio 5:2.

2. Tell whether the ratios $\frac{4}{5}$ and $\frac{16}{25}$ are equivalent. If they are not, give a ratio that is equivalent to $\frac{4}{5}$.

Exercises

Learn It Online
Homework Help Online
Exercises 1–11, 13, 15, 17, 19, 27

GUIDED PRACTICE

See Example **1** **Use the table to write each ratio.**

1. music programs to art programs

2. arcade games to entire collection

3. entire collection to educational games

Jacqueline's Software Collection	
Educational games	16
Word processing	2
Art programs	10
Arcade games	10
Music programs	3

See Example **2** 4. Write three equivalent ratios to compare the number of red hearts in the picture with the total number of hearts.

See Example **3** 5. **Consumer Math** An 8-ounce bag of sunflower seeds costs $1.68. A 4-ounce bag of sunflower seeds costs $0.88. Which is the better deal?

INDEPENDENT PRACTICE

See Example **1** **Use the table to write each ratio.**

6. Redbirds to Blue Socks

7. right-handed Blue Socks to left-handed Blue Socks

	Redbirds	Blue Socks
Left-Handed Batters	8	3
Right-Handed Batters	11	19

8. left-handed Redbirds to total Redbirds

See Example **2** 9. Write three equivalent ratios to compare the number of stars in the picture with the number of stripes.

See Example **3** 10. Gina charges $28 for 3 hours of swimming lessons. Hector charges $18 for 2 hours of swimming lessons. Which instructor offers a better deal?

11. **Consumer Math** A 12-pound bag of dog food costs $12.36. A 15-pound bag of dog food costs $15.30. Which is the better deal?

PRACTICE AND PROBLEM SOLVING

Extra Practice
See Extra Practice for more exercises.

Write each ratio two different ways.

12. 10 to 7

13. $\frac{24}{11}$

14. 4 to 30

15. $\frac{7}{10}$

16. 16 to 20

17. $\frac{5}{9}$

18. 50 to 79

19. 100 to 101

20. A florist can create 16 bouquets during an 8-hour work day. How many bouquets can the florist create per hour?

Use the diagram of an oxygen atom and a boron atom for Exercises 21–24. Find each ratio. Then give two equivalent ratios.

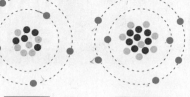

21. oxygen protons to boron protons

22. boron neutrons to boron protons

23. boron electrons to oxygen electrons

24. oxygen electrons to oxygen protons

Boron   Oxygen

25. A lifeguard received 16 hours of first aid training and 8 hours of cardiopulmonary resuscitation (CPR) training. Write the ratio of hours of CPR training to hours of first aid training.

26. **Critical Thinking** Cassandra has three pictures on her desk. The pictures measure 4 in. long by 6 in. wide, 24 mm long by 36 mm wide, and 6 cm long by 7 cm wide. Which photos have a length-to-width ratio equivalent to 2:3?

27. **Multi-Step** On which day did Alfonso run faster?

Day	Distance (m)	Time (min)
Monday	1,020	6
Wednesday	1,554	9

28. **Earth Science** Water rushes over Niagara Falls at the rate of 180 million cubic feet every 30 minutes. How much water goes over the falls in 1 minute?

29. **What's the Question?** The ratio of total students in Mr. Avalon's class to students in the class who have a blue backpack is 3 to 1. The answer is 1:2. What is the question?

30. **Write About It** How are equivalent ratios like equivalent fractions?

31. **Challenge** There are 36 performers in a dance recital. The ratio of men to women is 2:7. How many men are in the dance recital?

Test Prep

32. **Multiple Choice** Which ratio is equivalent to $\frac{1}{20}$?

ⓐ 9:180   ⓑ 180 to 9   ⓒ 4 to 100   ⓓ 100:4

33. **Short Response** A 24-ounce box of raisins costs $4.56. A 15-ounce box of raisins costs $3.15. Which is the better deal? Explain.

Using Tables to Explore Equivalent Ratios and Rates

COMMON CORE

CC.6.RP.3 Use ratio and rate reasoning to solve real-world and mathematical problems, e.g., by reasoning about tables of equivalent ratios, tape diagrams, double number line diagrams, or equations

Mrs. Kennedy's students are painting a mural in their classroom. They mixed yellow and blue paints for a green background and found that the ratio of the amount of yellow to the amount of blue is 3 to 2.

Now they need to make more green paint, using the same ratio as before.

Use a table to find ratios equivalent to 3 to 2.

Reading Math

Finding equivalent ratios is sometimes referred to as "scaling up" or "scaling down."

Original ratio → 3·2   3·3   3·4

Pints of yellow	3	6	9	12
Pints of blue	2	4	6	8

2·2   2·3   2·4

You can increase amounts but keep them in the same ratio by multiplying both the numerator and denominator of the ratio by the same number.

The ratios 3 to 2, 6 to 4, 9 to 6, and 12 to 8 are equivalent.

You can also decrease amounts in the same ratio by dividing the numerator and denominator by the same number.

EXAMPLE 1   **Making a Table to Find Equivalent Ratios**

Use a table to find three equivalent ratios.

Helpful Hint

Multiplying the ratio in Example 1A by 2, 3, and 4 will give you three equivalent ratios, but there are many other equivalent ratios that are correct.

A $\dfrac{8}{3}$

Original ratio → 8·2   8·3   8·4

8	16	24	32
3	6	9	12

3·2   3·3   3·4

Multiply the numerator and the denominator by 2, 3, and 4.

The ratios $\dfrac{8}{3}$, $\dfrac{16}{6}$, $\dfrac{24}{9}$, and $\dfrac{32}{12}$ are equivalent.

  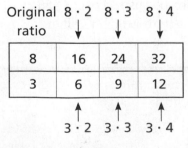 Video   **Lesson Tutorials Online**   my.hrw.com

Use a table to find three equivalent ratios.

B 4 to 7

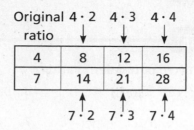

Original ratio: 4 · 2, 4 · 3, 4 · 4

4	8	12	16
7	14	21	28

7 · 2, 7 · 3, 7 · 4

Multiply the numerator and the denominator by 2, 3, and 4.

The ratios 4 to 7, 8 to 14, 12 to 21, and 16 to 28 are equivalent.

C 40:16

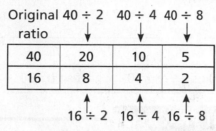

Original ratio: 40 ÷ 2, 40 ÷ 4, 40 ÷ 8

40	20	10	5
16	8	4	2

16 ÷ 2, 16 ÷ 4, 16 ÷ 8

Divide the numerator and the denominator by 2.

The ratios 40:16, 20:8, 10:4, and 5:2 are equivalent.

Ratios in tables can be used to make estimates or predictions.

EXAMPLE 2 *Entertainment Application*

A group of 10 friends is in line to see a movie. The table shows how much different groups will pay in all. Predict how much the group of 10 will pay.

Number in Group	3	5	6	12
Amount Paid ($)	15	25	30	60

6 < 10 < 12; therefore, the group will pay between $30 and $60.

Use the amount paid by the group of 5.   *The only factor of 10 in the table is 5.*

2 · 5 = 10   *Multiply the numerator and*
2 · $25 = $50   *denominator by the same factor, 2.*

A group of 10 friends would pay $50.00.

Think and Discuss

1. **Explain** how you can be sure that all the ratios you have written are correct when you have multiplied or divided a ratio to find equivalent ratios.

2. **Explain** how you can be sure that you have written the numerator and denominator in the correct order when rewriting ratios that have colons as fractions.

GUIDED PRACTICE

See Example **1** Use a table to find three equivalent ratios.

1. $\frac{2}{7}$ 2. 7 to 12   3. 96:48   4. $\frac{3}{5}$

5. 5 to 8   6. $\frac{9}{4}$ 7. 24 to 16   8. 25:26

See Example **2** 9. **Sports** Leo runs laps around a track. The table shows how long it takes him to run different numbers of laps. Predict how long it will take Leo to run 7 laps.

Number of Laps	2	4	6	8	10
Time (min)	10	20	30	40	50

INDEPENDENT PRACTICE

See Example **1** Use a table to find three equivalent ratios.

10. 6:5   11. 8 to 15   12. $\frac{12}{4}$ 13. 6 to 7

14. $\frac{13}{20}$ 15. 11:25   16. 5 to 18   17. $\frac{51}{75}$

See Example **2** 18. Lee Middle School orders 15 textbooks for every 12 students. The table shows how many textbooks the school orders for certain numbers of students. Predict the number of textbooks that the school would order for 72 students.

Students	12	24	48	96	192
Textbooks	15	30	60	120	240

PRACTICE AND PROBLEM SOLVING

Extra Practice

See Extra Practice for more exercises.

19. **Biology** Brown bats vary in length from 3 to 6 inches and have wing spans from 8 to 16 inches. Write a ratio in simplest form of a bat's wing span to the bat's body length.

20. Buy-A-Lot Market has tomatoes on sale. The table shows some sale prices. Predict how much a restaurant owner will pay for 25 pounds of tomatoes at the rate shown in the table.

Amount (lb)	30	20	15	10	5
Cost ($)	11.70	7.80	5.85	3.90	1.95

Complete each table to find the missing ratios.

21.

6	12	18	
5	10		20

22.

96	48	24	
48	24		6

President Lyndon Baines Johnson, often referred to as LBJ, was born in Stillwater, Texas, in 1908. President Johnson had no vice president from November 1963 to January 1965.

Multiply and divide each ratio to find two equivalent ratios.

23. 36:48

24. $\frac{4}{60}$

25. $\frac{128}{48}$

26. 15:100

27. **Multi-Step** Lyndon Johnson was elected president in 1964. The ratio of the number of votes he received to the number of votes that Barry Goldwater received was about 19:12. About how many votes were cast for both candiates?

Candidates	Number of Votes
Lyndon Johnson	43,121,085
Barry Goldwater	

28. **What's the Error?** A student said that 3:4 is equivalent to 9:16 and 18:64. What did the student do wrong? Correct the ratios so they are equivalent.

29. **Write About It** If Daniel drives the same distance each day, will he be able to complete a 4,500-mile trip in 2 weeks? Explain how you solved the problem.

Days	Distance (mi)
3	1,020
5	1,700
9	3,060

30. **Challenge** The table shows the regular and sale prices of CDs at Bargain Blast. How much money will you save if you buy 10 CDs on sale?

Number of CDs	Regular Price ($)	Sale Price ($)
2	17.00	14.40
3	25.50	21.60
6	51.00	43.20

Test Prep

31. **Multiple Choice** Which ratio is NOT equivalent to 3 to 7?

Ⓐ 9:21　　　Ⓑ 36:77　　　Ⓒ 45:105　　　Ⓓ 54:126

32. **Short Response** The table shows the distances traveled and the numbers of gallons of gas used on four automobile trips. Predict the number of gallons of gas that would be used for a trip of 483 miles.

Distance (mi)	552	414	276	138
Gas Used (gal)	24	18	12	6

Mastering *the* Standards

for Mathematical Practice

The topics described in the Standards for Mathematical Content will vary from year to year. However, the *way* in which you learn, study, and think about mathematics will not. The Standards for Mathematical Practice describe skills that you will use in all of your math courses.

Mathematical Practices

1. Make sense of problems and persevere in solving them.
2. Reason abstractly and quantitatively.
3. Construct viable arguments and critique the reasoning of others.
4. Model with mathematics.
5. Use appropriate tools strategically.
6. Attend to precision.
7. Look for and make use of structure.
8. Look for and express regularity in repeated reasoning.

5 Use appropriate tools strategically.

Mathematically proficient students consider the available tools when solving a... problem... [and] are... able to use technological tools to explore and deepen their understanding...

In your book

Hands-on Labs and **Technology Labs** use concrete and technological tools to explore mathematical concepts.

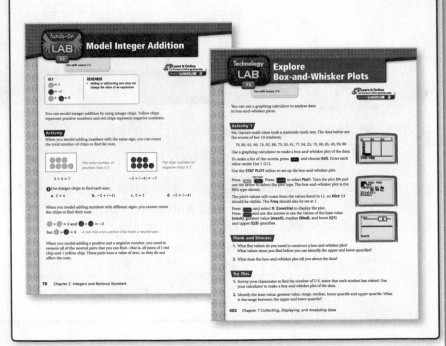

San Diego, CA. Image courtesy of spaceimaging.com.

CC.6.NS.6 ...Extend number line diagrams and coordinate axes familiar from previous grades to represent points on the line and in the plane with negative number coordinates *Also CC.6.NS.6c*

Vocabulary

coordinate grid

ordered pair

Interactivities Online ▶

Cities, towns, and neighborhoods are often laid out on a grid. This makes it easier to map and find locations.

A **coordinate grid** is formed by horizontal and vertical lines and is used to locate points.

Each point on a coordinate grid can be located by using an **ordered pair** of numbers, such as (4, 6). The starting point is (0, 0).

- The first number tells how far to move horizontally from (0, 0).
- The second number tells how far to move vertically.

EXAMPLE 1

Identifying Ordered Pairs

Name the ordered pair for each location.

A library

Start at (0, 0). Move right 2 units and then up 3 units.

The library is located at (2, 3).

B school

Start at (0, 0). Move right 6 units and then up 5 units.

The school is located at (6, 5).

C pool

Start at (0, 0). Move right 12 units and up 1 unit.

The pool is located at (12, 1).

Image courtesy of spaceimaging.com

EXAMPLE 1 Graphing Ordered Pairs

Graph and label each point on a coordinate grid.

A $Q\left(4\frac{1}{2}, 6\right)$ *Start at (0, 0).*
Move right $4\frac{1}{2}$ units.
Move up 6 units.

B $S(0, 4)$ *Start at (0, 0).*
Move right 0 units.
Move up 4 units.

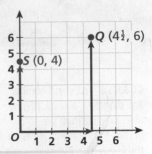

Think and Discuss

1. **Tell** what point is the starting location when you are graphing on a coordinate grid.

2. **Describe** how to graph $(2\frac{1}{2}, 8)$ on a coordinate grid.

7-3 Exercises

Learn It Online
Homework Help Online
Exercises 1–22, 23, 25, 27, 29, 31, 33

GUIDED PRACTICE

See Example 1 **Name the ordered pair for each location.**

1. school
2. store
3. hospital
4. mall
5. office
6. hotel

See Example 2 **Graph and label each point on a coordinate grid.**

7. $T\left(3\frac{1}{2}, 4\right)$
8. $S(2, 8)$
9. $U(5, 5)$
10. $V\left(4\frac{1}{2}, 1\right)$

INDEPENDENT PRACTICE

See Example 1 **Name the ordered pair for each location.**

11. diner
12. library
13. store
14. bank
15. theater
16. town hall

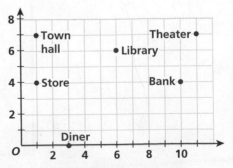

Video **Lesson Tutorials Online** my.hrw.com

Graph and label each point on a coordinate grid.

17. $P\left(5\frac{1}{2}, 1\right)$ **18.** $R(2, 4)$ **19.** $Q\left(3\frac{1}{2}, 2\right)$

20. $V(6, 5)$ **21.** $X\left(1\frac{1}{2}, 3\right)$ **22.** $Y(7, 4)$

PRACTICE AND PROBLEM SOLVING

Extra Practice
See Extra Practice for more exercises.

Use the coordinate grid for Exercises 23–35.
Name the point found at each location.

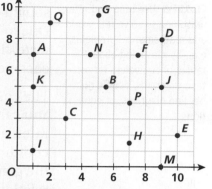

23. $(1, 7)$ **24.** $\left(5, 9\frac{1}{2}\right)$ **25.** $(3, 3)$

26. $\left(4\frac{1}{2}, 7\right)$ **27.** $(7, 4)$ **28.** $\left(7\frac{1}{2}, 7\right)$

Give the ordered pair for each point.

29. D **30.** H **31.** K

32. Q **33.** M **34.** B

35. Multi-Step The coordinates of points B, J, and M in the coordinate grid above form three of the corners of a rectangle. What are the coordinates of the fourth corner? Explain how you found your answer.

36. Write About It Explain the difference between the points $(3, 2)$ and $(2, 3)$.

37. What's the Question? If the answer is "Start at $(0, 0)$ and move 3 units to the right," what is the question?

38. Challenge Locate and graph points that can be connected to form your initials. What are the ordered pairs for these points?

Test Prep

Use the coordinate grid for Exercises 39 and 40.

39. Multiple Choice At which ordered pair is the airport located?

Ⓐ $(7, 9)$ Ⓑ $(3, 4)$ Ⓒ $(6, 3)$ Ⓓ $(9, 7)$

40. Multiple Choice Which location is at $(1, 2)$?

Ⓕ Airport Ⓗ Supermarket

Ⓖ Library Ⓙ Train station

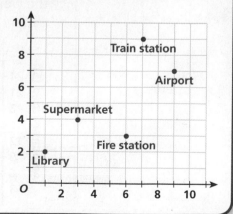

Graphing Equivalent Ratios and Rates

COMMON CORE

CC.6.RP.3 Use ratio and rate reasoning to solve real-world and mathematical problems, e.g., by reasoning about tables of equivalent ratios, tape diagrams, double number line diagrams, or equations

King crabs are one of the most sought-after shellfish in the ocean. Due to their large size and sweet taste, fisherman can earn $4 for each pound of king crab caught.

The cost of $4 per pound is a rate. You can use a table to find equivalent rates, and then graph the data on a coordinate plane. The pattern on the graph can help illustrate relationships in the data.

EXAMPLE **1** **Graphing Equivalent Ratios and Rates**

Make a table that shows 5 equivalent ratios for the rate $\frac{\$4}{lb}$. Plot the points on the coordinate plane, and describe the pattern.

For every pound that the crab weighs, the amount earned will be 4 times greater.

Original ratio

Weight (lb)	1	2	3	4	5	6
Amount Earned ($)	4	8	12	16	20	24

Since the amount earned *depends* on the weight, use x for the weight and y for the amount earned to write ordered pairs: (1, 4), (2, 8), (3, 12), (4, 16), (5, 20), and (6, 24).

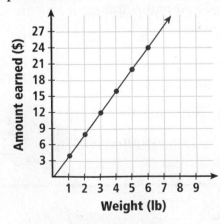

Graph the ordered pairs, and connect the points.

The amount earned (y-axis) increases by $4 for each pound (x-axis).

Because the points can be connected with a straight line, the pattern is "linear."

You can also use a graph to find equivalent ratios and the unit rate.

EXAMPLE 2 **Using a Graph to Find Equivalent Ratios**

Use the graph to find 3 equivalent ratios. Then identify the unit rate.

To find 3 equivalent ratios, choose any 3 points on the graph: (2, 4), (3, 6), (4, 8).

Possible ratios: $\frac{4}{2}, \frac{6}{3}, \frac{8}{4}$ *Write ratios in the form $\frac{distance}{time}$.*

The unit rate is a comparison where one of the measurements has a value of 1. In this case, set the time equal to 1 minute.

$\frac{8}{4} = \frac{x}{1}$ *Make a proportion with an existing ratio.*

$4x = 8$ *Cross multiply.*

$x = 2$ *Isolate the variable, x.*

The unit rate is 2 kilometers per 1 minute.

EXTENSION

Exercises

1. A satellite orbits Earth every 1.5 hours.

   a. Create a table with 6 equivalent ratios.

   b. Plot your points on a coordinate graph.

   ? c. **What's the Error?** Jasmine determines that a satellite orbits Earth 15 times every 10 hours. What error did Jasmine make?

Use the graph for Exercises 2 and 3.

2. List 3 equivalent ratios from the graph.

3. What is the unit rate?

4. Complete the table to find the missing ratios.

Teachers	1	3	7	
Students	18	54		180

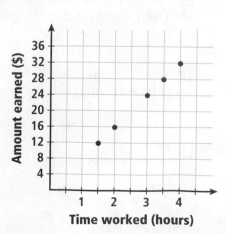

Explore Proportions

Use with Proportions

Learn It Online
Lab Resources Online

You can use counters to model equivalent ratios.

 Use appropriate tools strategically.
CC.6.RP.1 Understand the concept of a ratio and use ratio language to describe a ratio relationship between two quantities

Activity 1

Find three ratios that are equivalent to $\frac{6}{12}$.

1 Show 6 red counters and 12 yellow counters.

2 Separate the red counters into two equal groups. Then separate the yellow counters into two equal groups.

3 Write the ratio of red counters in each group to yellow counters in each group.

$$\frac{3 \text{ red counters}}{6 \text{ yellow counters}} = \frac{3}{6}$$

4 Now separate the red counters into three equal groups. Then separate the yellow counters into three equal groups.

5 Write the ratio of red counters in each group to yellow counters in each group.

$$\frac{2 \text{ red counters}}{4 \text{ yellow counters}} = \frac{2}{4}$$

6 Now separate the red counters into six equal groups. Then separate the yellow counters into six equal groups.

7 Write the ratio of red counters in each group to yellow counters in each group.

$$\frac{1 \text{ red counter}}{2 \text{ yellow counters}} = \frac{1}{2}$$

The three ratios you wrote are equivalent to $\frac{6}{12}$.

$$\frac{6}{12} = \frac{3}{6} = \frac{2}{4} = \frac{1}{2}$$

When you write an equation showing equivalent ratios, that equation is called a *proportion*.

1. How do the models show that the ratios are equivalent?

Try This

Use models to determine whether the ratios form a proportion.

1. $\frac{1}{3}$ and $\frac{4}{12}$ 2. $\frac{3}{4}$ and $\frac{6}{9}$ 3. $\frac{4}{10}$ and $\frac{2}{5}$

Activity 2

Write a proportion in which one of the ratios is $\frac{1}{3}$.

1 You must find a ratio that is equivalent to $\frac{1}{3}$. First show one red counter and three yellow counters.

2 Show one more group of one red counter and three yellow counters.

3 Write the ratio of red counters to yellow counters for the two groups.

$$\frac{2 \text{ red counters}}{6 \text{ yellow counters}} = \frac{2}{6}$$

4 The two ratios are equivalent. Write the proportion $\frac{1}{3} = \frac{2}{6}$.

You can find more equivalent ratios by adding more groups of one red counter and three yellow counters. Use your models to write proportions.

$$\frac{3 \text{ red counters}}{9 \text{ yellow counters}} = \frac{3}{9}$$

$$\frac{3}{9} = \frac{1}{3}$$

$$\frac{4 \text{ red counters}}{12 \text{ yellow counters}} = \frac{4}{12}$$

$$\frac{4}{12} = \frac{1}{3}$$

Think and Discuss

1. The models above show that $\frac{1}{3}$, $\frac{2}{6}$, $\frac{3}{9}$, and $\frac{4}{12}$ are equivalent ratios. Do you see a pattern in this list of ratios?

2. Use counters to find another ratio that is equivalent to $\frac{1}{3}$.

Try This

Use counters to write a proportion containing each given ratio.

1. $\frac{1}{4}$ 2. $\frac{1}{5}$ 3. $\frac{3}{7}$ 4. $\frac{1}{6}$ 5. $\frac{4}{9}$

CC.6.RP.1 Understand the concept of a ratio and use ratio language to describe a ratio relationship between two quantities

Vocabulary

proportion

Have you ever heard water called H_2O? H_2O is the scientific formula for water. One molecule of water contains two hydrogen atoms (H_2) and one oxygen atom (O). No matter how many molecules of water you have, hydrogen and oxygen will always be in the ratio 2 to 1.

"Remember everybody this is planet Earth So whatever you do, don't drink the water

© Cartoon Stock

Water Molecules	1	2	3	4
Hydrogen atoms / Oxygen atoms	$\frac{2}{1}$	$\frac{4}{2}$	$\frac{6}{3}$	$\frac{8}{4}$

Reading Math

Read the proportion $\frac{2}{1} = \frac{4}{2}$ as "two is to one as four is to two."

Notice that $\frac{2}{1}$, $\frac{4}{2}$, $\frac{6}{3}$, and $\frac{8}{4}$ are equivalent ratios.

A **proportion** is an equation that shows two equivalent ratios.

$$\frac{2}{1} = \frac{4}{2} \qquad \frac{4}{2} = \frac{8}{4} \qquad \frac{2}{1} = \frac{6}{3}$$

EXAMPLE 1 **Modeling Proportions**

Write a proportion for the model.

First write the ratio of triangles to circles.

$$\frac{\text{number of triangles}}{\text{number of circles}} = \frac{4}{2}$$

Next separate the triangles and the circles into two equal groups.

Now write the ratio of triangles to circles in each group.

$$\frac{\text{number of triangles in each group}}{\text{number of circles in each group}} = \frac{2}{1}$$

A proportion shown by the model is $\frac{4}{2} = \frac{2}{1}$.

Video **Lesson Tutorials Online** my.hrw.com

CROSS PRODUCTS

Cross products in proportions are equal.

$\frac{4}{8} \bowtie \frac{2}{4}$	$\frac{3}{5} \bowtie \frac{9}{15}$	$\frac{9}{6} \bowtie \frac{3}{2}$	$\frac{14}{7} \bowtie \frac{2}{1}$
$8 \cdot 2 = 4 \cdot 4$	$5 \cdot 9 = 3 \cdot 15$	$6 \cdot 3 = 9 \cdot 2$	$7 \cdot 2 = 14 \cdot 1$
$16 = 16$	$45 = 45$	$18 = 18$	$14 = 14$

Interactivities Online ▶

EXAMPLE 2

Using Cross Products to Complete Proportions

Find the missing value in the proportion $\frac{3}{4} = \frac{n}{16}$.

$\frac{3}{4} \bowtie \frac{n}{16}$ *Find the cross products.*

$4 \cdot n = 3 \cdot 16$ *The cross products are equal.*

$4n = 48$ *n is multiplied by 4.*

$\frac{4n}{4} = \frac{48}{4}$ *Divide both sides by 4 to undo the multiplication.*

$n = 12$

EXAMPLE 3

Measurement Application

The label from a bottle of pet vitamins shows recommended dosages. What dosage would you give an adult dog that weighs 15 lb?

$\frac{1 \text{ tsp}}{20 \text{ lb}} = \frac{v}{15 \text{ lb}}$ *Let v be the amount of vitamins for a 15 lb dog.*

$\frac{1 \text{ tsp}}{20 \text{ lb}} \bowtie \frac{v}{15 \text{ lb}}$ *Write a proportion.*

$20 \cdot v = 1 \cdot 15$ *The cross products are equal.*

$20v = 15$ *v is multiplied by 20.*

$\frac{20v}{20} = \frac{15}{20}$ *Divide both sides by 20 to undo the multiplication.*

$v = \frac{3}{4} \text{ tsp}$ *Write your answer in simplest form.*

You should give $\frac{3}{4}$ tsp of vitamins to a 15 lb dog.

> **Caution!**
>
> In a proportion, the units must be in the same order in both ratios.
>
> $\frac{\text{tsp}}{\text{lb}} = \frac{\text{tsp}}{\text{lb}}$
>
> or $\frac{\text{lb}}{\text{tsp}} = \frac{\text{lb}}{\text{tsp}}$

> **Pet Vitamins**
>
> • **Adult dogs:**
>   1 tsp per 20 lb body weight
> • **Puppies, pregnant dogs, or nursing dogs:**
>   1 tsp per 10 lb body weight
> • **Cats:**
>   1 tsp per 12 lb body weight

MATHEMATICAL PRACTICES

Think and Discuss

1. **Tell** whether $\frac{7}{8} = \frac{4}{14}$ is a proportion. How do you know?
2. **Give an example** of a proportion. Tell how you know that it is a proportion.

GUIDED PRACTICE

See Example 1   **1.** Write a proportion for the model.

See Example 2   **Find the missing value in each proportion.**

2. $\frac{12}{9} = \frac{n}{3}$ **3.** $\frac{t}{5} = \frac{28}{20}$ **4.** $\frac{1}{c} = \frac{6}{12}$ **5.** $\frac{6}{7} = \frac{30}{b}$

See Example 3   **6.** Ursula is entering a bicycle race for charity. Her mother pledges $0.75 for every 0.5 mile she bikes. If Ursula bikes 17.5 miles, how much will her mother donate?

INDEPENDENT PRACTICE

See Example 1   **7.** Write a proportion for the model.

See Example 2   **Find the missing value in each proportion.**

8. $\frac{3}{2} = \frac{24}{d}$ **9.** $\frac{p}{40} = \frac{3}{8}$ **10.** $\frac{6}{14} = \frac{x}{7}$ **11.** $\frac{5}{p} = \frac{7}{77}$

See Example 3   **12.** According to Ty's study guidelines, how many minutes of science reading should he do if his science class is 90 minutes long?

Ty's Study Guidelines	
Class	**Reading Time**
Literature	35 minutes for every 50 minutes of class time
Science	20 minutes for every 60 minutes of class time
History	30 minutes for every 55 minutes of class time

PRACTICE AND PROBLEM SOLVING

Extra Practice
See Extra Practice for more exercises.

Find the value of p in each proportion.

13. $\frac{18}{6} = \frac{6}{p}$ **14.** $\frac{4}{p} = \frac{48}{60}$ **15.** $\frac{p}{10} = \frac{15}{50}$ **16.** $\frac{3}{5} = \frac{12}{p}$

17. $\frac{21}{15} = \frac{p}{5}$ **18.** $\frac{3}{6} = \frac{p}{8}$ **19.** $\frac{15}{5} = \frac{9}{p}$ **20.** $\frac{6}{p} = \frac{4}{28}$

21. Patterns Given that the first term in a sequence is $\frac{7}{2}$, the second term is $\frac{14}{4}$, the fourth term is $\frac{28}{8}$, and the fifth term is $\frac{35}{10}$, find the value of the third term.

The value of the U.S. dollar as compared to the values of currencies from other countries changes every day. The graph shows recent values of various currencies compared to the U.S. dollar. Use the graph for Exercises 22–26.

22. What is the value of 9.72 European euros in U.S. dollars?

23. Multi-Step You have $100 in U.S. dollars. Determine how much money this is in euros, Canadian dollars, yuan, shekels, and Mexican pesos.

24. **?** **What's the Error?** A student set up the proportion $\frac{1}{7.52} = \frac{x}{30}$ to determine the value of 30 U.S. dollars in China. Why is this proportion incorrect? Write the correct proportion, and find the missing value.

25. **Write About It** Which is worth more: five U.S. dollars or five Canadian dollars? Why?

26. **Challenge** A dime is worth about how many Mexican pesos?

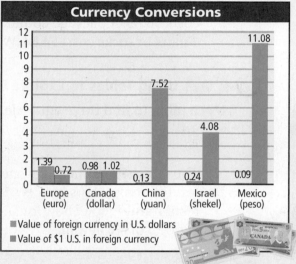

Currency Conversions

- Value of foreign currency in U.S. dollars
- Value of $1 U.S. in foreign currency

	Europe (euro)	Canada (dollar)	China (yuan)	Israel (shekel)	Mexico (peso)
Foreign in U.S.	1.39	0.98	0.13	0.24	0.09
$1 U.S.	0.72	1.02	7.52	4.08	11.08

Test Prep

27. Multiple Choice A recipe calls for 4 cups of sugar and 16 cups of water. If the recipe is reduced, how many cups of water should be used with 1 cup of sugar?

   (A) 0.25 cups   (B) 1.6 cups   (C) 4 cups   (D) 16 cups

28. Multiple Choice Li mixes 3 units of red paint with 8 units of white paint to get pink. How many units of red paint should she mix with 12 units of white paint to get the same pink shade?

   (F) $2\frac{3}{4}$ (G) 3   (H) $3\frac{1}{4}$ (J) $4\frac{1}{2}$

CHAPTER

7

SECTION A

Ready To Go On?

Learn It Online
Resources Online

Ready to Go On?

Quiz for Lessons 1 Through 4

✓ 1 Ratios and Rates

Use the table to write each ratio.

1. classical CDs to rock CDs

2. country to total CDs

Types of CDs in Mark's Music Collection			
Classical	4	Jazz	3
Country	9	Pop	14
Dance	8	Rock	10

3. A package containing 6 pairs of socks costs $6.89. A package containing 4 pairs of socks costs $4.64. Which is the better deal?

✓ 2 Using Tables to Explore Equivalent Ratios and Rates

Use a table to find three equivalent ratios.

4. $\frac{21}{30}$ **5.** 15:6   **6.** 3 to 101

7. The table shows the wait time for different groups at a restaurant. Predict how long a group of 8 will wait.

Number in Group	1	2	5	7	10
Wait Time (min)	3	6	15	21	30

✓ 3 Ordered Pairs

Graph and label each point on a coordinate grid.

8. $A\,(4, 5)$ **9.** $B\left(0, 3\frac{1}{2}\right)$

✓ 4 Proportions

Find the missing value in each proportion.

10. $\frac{1}{4} = \frac{n}{12}$ **11.** $\frac{3}{n} = \frac{15}{25}$ **12.** $\frac{n}{4} = \frac{18}{6}$ **13.** $\frac{10}{4} = \frac{5}{n}$

Focus on Problem Solving

Plan

Make a Plan

• **Estimate or find an exact answer**

Sometimes an estimate is all you need to solve a problem, and sometimes you need to find an exact answer.

One way to decide whether you can estimate is to see if you can rewrite the problem using the words *at most, at least,* or *about*. For example, suppose Laura has $30. Then she could spend *at most* $30. She would not have to spend *exactly* $30. Or, if you know it takes 15 minutes to get to school, you must leave your house *at least* (not exactly) 15 minutes before school starts.

 Read the problems below. Decide whether you can estimate or whether you must find the exact answer. How do you know?

1 Alex is a radio station disc jockey. He is making a list of songs that should last no longer than 30 minutes total when played in a row. His list of songs and their playing times are given in the table. Does Alex have the right amount of music?

Song Title	Length (min)
Color Me Blue	4.5
Hittin' the Road	7.2
Stand Up, Shout	2.6
Top Dog	3.6
Kelso Blues	4.3
Smile on Me	5.7
A Long Time Ago	6.4

2 For every 10 minutes of music, Alex has to play 1.5 minutes of commercials. If Alex plays the songs on the list, how much time does he need to allow for commercials?

3 If Alex must play the songs on the list and the commercials in 30 minutes, how much music time does he need to cut to allow for commercials?

Model Percents

Use with Percents

Learn It Online
Lab Resources Online

A *percent* shows the ratio of a number to 100. You can model percents by using a 10-by-10 grid on graph paper.

MATHEMATICAL PRACTICES
Use appropriate tools strategically.
CC.6.RP.3c Find a percent of a quantity as a rate per 100…

Activity

1 Model 55% on a 10-by-10 grid.

Write 55% as a ratio comparing 55 to 100.

$55\% = \frac{55}{100}$

Since there are 100 squares in a 10 × 10 grid, shade in 55 squares.

$\frac{\text{number of squares shaded}}{\text{total number of squares}} = \frac{55}{100} = 55\%$

The model represents 55%.

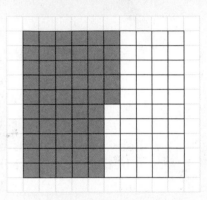

2 What percent of grid A is shaded?

Find the number of squares shaded in grid A. Compare it with the total number of squares.

$\frac{\text{number of squares shaded}}{\text{total number of squares}} = \frac{42}{100}$

Since 42 out of 100 squares are shaded, the grid models 42%.

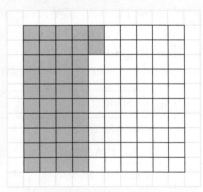

Grid A

Think and Discuss

1. Shade in $\frac{3}{4}$ of a 10-by-10 grid. What percent of the grid is shaded? Explain.

2. How can equivalent ratios help you find your answer to **1**?

3. How would you model 105%? 0.5%? Explain your answer.

Try This

Model each percent on a 10-by-10 grid.

1. 50%   **2.** 68%   **3.** 4%   **4.** 91%   **5.** 100%

CC.6.RP.3c Find a percent of a quantity as a rate per 100…

Vocabulary

percent

Most states charge sales tax on items you purchase. Sales tax is a percent of the item's price. A **percent** is a ratio of a number to 100.

You can remember that *percent* means "per hundred." For example, 8% means "8 per hundred," or "8 out of 100."

If a sales tax rate is 8%, the following statements are true:

At a sales tax rate of 8%, the tax on this wakeskate would be $12.80.

- For every $1.00 you spend, you pay $0.08 in sales tax.

- For every $10.00 you spend, you pay $0.80 in sales tax.

- For every $100 you spend, you pay $8 in sales tax.

Because *percent* means "per hundred," 100% means "100 out of 100." This is why 100% is often used to mean "all" or "the whole thing."

EXAMPLE 1 **Modeling Percents**

Interactivities Online ▶

Use a 10-by-10-square grid to model 8%.

A 10-by-10-square grid has 100 squares.

8% means "8 out of 100," or $\frac{8}{100}$.

Shade 8 squares out of 100 squares.

EXAMPLE 2 **Writing Percents as Fractions**

Write 40% as a fraction in simplest form.

$40\% = \frac{40}{100}$ *Write the percent as a fraction with a denominator of 100.*

$\frac{40 \div 20}{100 \div 20} = \frac{2}{5}$ *Write the fraction in simplest form.*

Written as a fraction, 40% is $\frac{2}{5}$.

Victoria Smith/HMH

Video **Lesson Tutorials Online** my.hrw.com

EXAMPLE 3 *Life Science Application*

Up to 55% of the heat lost by your body can be lost through your head. Write 55% as a fraction in simplest form.

$55\% = \dfrac{55}{100}$ *Write the percent as a fraction with a denominator of 100.*

$\dfrac{55 \div 5}{100 \div 5} = \dfrac{11}{20}$ *Write the fraction in simplest form.*

Written as a fraction, 55% is $\dfrac{11}{20}$.

EXAMPLE 4 **Writing Percents as Decimals**

Write 24% as a decimal.

$24\% = \dfrac{24}{100}$ *Write the percent as a fraction with a denominator of 100.*

Write the fraction as a decimal.

$$\begin{array}{r} 0.24 \\ 100\overline{)24.00} \\ -200 \\ \hline 400 \\ -400 \\ \hline 0 \end{array}$$

Written as a decimal, 24% is 0.24.

> **Remember!**
>
> To divide by 100, move the decimal point two places to the left.
>
> $24 \div 100 = 0.24$

EXAMPLE 5 *Earth Science Application*

The water frozen in glaciers makes up almost 75% of the world's fresh water supply. Write 75% as a decimal.

$75\% = \dfrac{75}{100}$ *Write the percent as a fraction with a denominator of 100.*

$75 \div 100 = 0.75$ *Write the fraction as a decimal.*

Written as a decimal, 75% is 0.75.

MATHEMATICAL PRACTICES

Think and Discuss

1. **Give an example** of a situation in which you have seen percents.

2. **Tell** how much sales tax you would have to pay on $1, $10, and $100 if your state had a 5% sales tax rate.

3. **Explain** how to write a percent as a fraction.

4. **Write** 100% as a decimal and as a fraction.

Video **Lesson Tutorials Online** my.hrw.com

Exercises

Learn It Online
Homework Help Online
Exercises 1–33, 35, 37, 39, 41, 43, 45, 47

GUIDED PRACTICE

See Example **1** **Use a 10-by-10-square grid to model each percent.**

    1. 45%   **2.** 3%   **3.** 61%

See Example **2** **Write each percent as a fraction in simplest form.**

    4. 25%   **5.** 80%   **6.** 54%

See Example **3** **7. Social Studies** Belize is a country in Central America. Of the land in Belize, 92% is made up of forests and woodlands. Write 92% as a fraction in simplest form.

See Example **4** **Write each percent as a decimal.**

    8. 72%   **9.** 4%   **10.** 90%

See Example **5** **11.** About 64% of the runways at airports in the United States are not paved. Write 64% as a decimal.

INDEPENDENT PRACTICE

See Example **1** **Use a 10-by-10-square grid to model each percent.**

    12. 14%   **13.** 98%   **14.** 36%   **15.** 28%

See Example **2** **Write each percent as a fraction in simplest form.**

    16. 20%   **17.** 75%   **18.** 11%   **19.** 72%

    20. 5%   **21.** 64%   **22.** 31%   **23.** 85%

See Example **3** **24.** Nikki must answer 80% of the questions on her final exam correctly to pass her class. Write 80% as a fraction in simplest form.

See Example **4** **Write each percent as a decimal.**

    25. 44%   **26.** 13%   **27.** 29%   **28.** 51%

    29. 60%   **30.** 92%   **31.** 7%   **32.** 87%

See Example **5** **33.** Brett was absent 2% of the school year. Write 2% as a decimal.

PRACTICE AND PROBLEM SOLVING

Extra Practice
See Extra Practice for more exercises.

Write each percent as a fraction in simplest form and as a decimal.

    34. 23%   **35.** 1%   **36.** 49%   **37.** 70%   **38.** 10%

    39. 37%   **40.** 85%   **41.** 8%   **42.** 63%   **43.** 75%

    44. 94%   **45.** 100%   **46.** 0%   **47.** 52%   **48.** 12%

    49. Model 15%, 52%, 71%, and 100% using different 10-by-10 grids. Then write each percent as a fraction in simplest form.

The circle graph shows the percent of radio stations around the world that play each type of music listed. Use the graph for Exercises 50–57.

50. What fraction of the radio stations play easy listening music? Write this fraction in simplest form.

51. Use a 10-by-10-square grid to model the percent of radio stations that play country music. Then write this percent as a decimal.

52. Which type of music makes up $\frac{1}{20}$ of the graph?

53. Someone reading the graph said, "More than $\frac{1}{10}$ of the radio stations play top 40 music." Do you agree with this statement? Why or why not?

54. Suppose you converted all of the percents in the graph to decimals and added them. Without actually doing this, tell what the sum would be. Explain.

55. 🖊 **Write a Problem** Write a question about the circle graph that involves changing a percent to a fraction. Then answer your question.

56. 🖊 **Write About It** How does the percent of radio stations that play Spanish music compare with the fraction $\frac{1}{6}$? Explain.

57. ⭐ **Challenge** Name a fraction that is greater than the percent of radio stations that play Spanish music but less than the percent of radio stations that play urban/rap music.

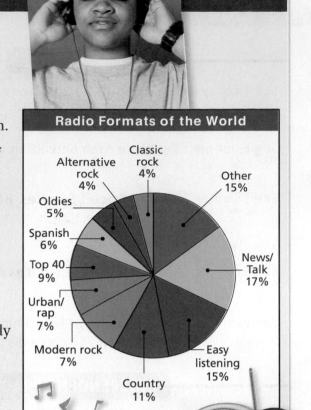

Radio Formats of the World

Classic rock 4%
Alternative rock 4%
Oldies 5%
Spanish 6%
Top 40 9%
Urban/rap 7%
Modern rock 7%
Country 11%
Easy listening 15%
News/Talk 17%
Other 15%

Source: Scholastic Kid's Almanac for the 21st Century

Test Prep

58. **Multiple Choice** Which decimal is equivalent to 85%?

Ⓐ 85.0   Ⓑ 8.5   Ⓒ 0.85   Ⓓ 0.085

59. **Multiple Choice** Which term best describes a number compared to 100?

Ⓕ Rate   Ⓖ Unit Rate   Ⓗ Percent   Ⓙ Proportion

Percents, Decimals, and Fractions

COMMON CORE

CC.6.RP.3c Find a percent of a quantity as a rate per 100 (e.g., 30% of a quantity means 30/100 times the quantity); solve problems involving finding the whole, given a part and the percent.

Percents, decimals, and fractions appear in newspapers, on television, and on the Internet. To fully understand the data you see in your everyday life, you should be able to change from one number form to another.

In Lesson 7, you learned how to write a percent as a fraction or as a decimal. You can also express decimals and fractions as percents.

$$\frac{1}{2} = 0.5 = 50\%$$

EXAMPLE 1

Interactivities Online ▶

Writing Decimals as Percents

Write each decimal as a percent.

Method 1: Use place value.

A 0.3

$0.3 = \frac{3}{10}$ *Write the decimal as a fraction.*

$\frac{3 \cdot 10}{10 \cdot 10} = \frac{30}{100}$ *Write an equivalent fraction with 100 as the denominator.*

$\frac{30}{100} = 30\%$ *Write the numerator with a percent symbol.*

B 0.43

$0.43 = \frac{43}{100}$ *Write the decimal as a fraction.*

$\frac{43}{100} = 43\%$ *Write the numerator with a percent symbol.*

Method 2: Multiply by 100.

C 0.7431

$0.7431 \cdot 100$ *Multiply by 100.*

74.31% *Add the percent symbol.*

D 0.023

$0.023 \cdot 100$ *Multiply by 100.*

2.3% *Add the percent symbol.*

EXAMPLE 2 Writing Fractions as Percents

Write each fraction as a percent.

Method 1: Write an equivalent fraction with a denominator of 100.

A $\frac{4}{5}$

$$\frac{4 \cdot 20}{5 \cdot 20} = \frac{80}{100}$$ *Write an equivalent fraction with a denominator of 100.*

$$\frac{80}{100} = 80\%$$ *Write the numerator with a percent symbol.*

Method 2: Use division to write the fraction as a decimal.

B $\frac{3}{8}$

$$\begin{array}{r} 0.375 \\ 8\overline{)3.000} \end{array}$$ *Divide the numerator by the denominator.*

$0.375 = 37.5\%$ *Multiply by 100 by moving the decimal point right two places. Add the percent symbol.*

> **Helpful Hint**
>
> When the denominator is a factor of 100, it is often easier to use method 1. When the denominator is not a factor of 100, it is usually easier to use method 2.

EXAMPLE 3 *Earth Science Application*

About $\frac{39}{50}$ of Earth's atmosphere is made up of nitrogen. About what percent of the atmosphere is nitrogen?

$$\frac{39}{50}$$

$$\frac{39 \cdot 2}{50 \cdot 2} = \frac{78}{100}$$ *Write an equivalent fraction with a denominator of 100.*

$$\frac{78}{100} = 78\%$$ *Write the numerator with a percent symbol.*

About 78% of Earth's atmosphere is made up of nitrogen.

The number line below shows common equivalent fractions, decimals, and percents.

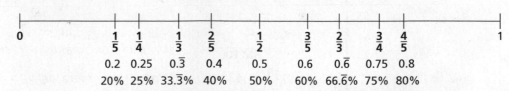

Think and Discuss

1. **Tell** which method you prefer for converting decimals to percents—using equivalent fractions or multiplying by 100. Why?

2. **Give** two different ways to write three-tenths.

3. **Explain** how to write fractions as percents using two different methods.

     Video **Lesson Tutorials Online** my.hrw.com

GUIDED PRACTICE

See Example **1** **Write each decimal as a percent.**

1. 0.39   **2.** 0.125   **3.** 0.8   **4.** 0.112

See Example **2** **Write each fraction as a percent.**

5. $\frac{11}{25}$ **6.** $\frac{7}{8}$ **7.** $\frac{7}{10}$ **8.** $\frac{1}{2}$ **9.** $\frac{9}{15}$

See Example **3** **10.** Patti spent $\frac{3}{4}$ of her allowance on a new backpack. What percent of her allowance did she spend?

INDEPENDENT PRACTICE

See Example **1** **Write each decimal as a percent.**

11. 0.6   **12.** 0.55   **13.** 0.34   **14.** 0.308   **15.** 0.62

See Example **2** **Write each fraction as a percent.**

16. $\frac{3}{5}$ **17.** $\frac{3}{10}$ **18.** $\frac{24}{25}$ **19.** $\frac{9}{20}$ **20.** $\frac{17}{20}$

21. $\frac{1}{8}$ **22.** $\frac{11}{16}$ **23.** $\frac{37}{50}$ **24.** $\frac{2}{5}$ **25.** $\frac{18}{45}$

See Example **3** **26.** About $\frac{1}{125}$ of the people in the United States have the last name *Johnson*. What percent of people in the United States have this last name?

PRACTICE AND PROBLEM SOLVING

Extra Practice

See Extra Practice for more exercises.

Write each decimal as a percent and a fraction.

27. 0.04   **28.** 0.32   **29.** 0.45   **30.** 0.59   **31.** 0.01

32. 0.81   **33.** 0.6   **34.** 0.39   **35.** 0.14   **36.** 0.62

Write each fraction as a percent and as a decimal. Round to the nearest hundredth, if necessary.

37. $\frac{4}{5}$ **38.** $\frac{1}{3}$ **39.** $\frac{5}{6}$ **40.** $\frac{7}{12}$ **41.** $\frac{17}{50}$

42. $\frac{2}{30}$ **43.** $\frac{1}{25}$ **44.** $\frac{8}{11}$ **45.** $\frac{4}{15}$ **46.** $\frac{22}{35}$

Compare. Write <, >, or =.

47. 70% ▮ $\frac{3}{4}$ **48.** $\frac{5}{8}$ ▮ 6.25%   **49.** 0.2 ▮ $\frac{1}{5}$ **50.** 1.25 ▮ $\frac{1}{8}$

51. 0.7 ▮ 7%   **52.** $\frac{9}{10}$ ▮ 0.3   **53.** 37% ▮ $\frac{3}{7}$ **54.** $\frac{17}{20}$ ▮ 0.85

55. Language Arts The longest word in all of Shakespeare's plays is *honorificabilitudinitatibus*. About what percent of the letters in this word are vowels? About what percent of the letters are consonants?

LINK

Entertainment

The Recording Industry Association of America awards gold records to artists who sell at least 500,000 copies of an album.

Order the numbers from least to greatest.

56. 45%, $\frac{21}{50}$, 0.43, 89% **57.** $\frac{7}{8}$, 90%, 0.098 **58.** 0.7, 26%, $\frac{1}{4}$, 34%

59. 38%, $\frac{7}{25}$, 0.21 **60.** $\frac{9}{20}$, 14%, 0.125, 24% **61.** 0.605, 17%, $\frac{5}{9}$

62. Entertainment A record-company official estimates that 3 out of every 100 albums released become hits. What percent of albums do not become hits?

63. Multi-Step About 97 million households in the United States have at least one television. Use the table below to answer the questions that follow.

Television in the United States	
Fraction of households with at least one television	$\frac{49}{50}$
Percent of households with three televisions	38%
Fraction of television owners with basic cable	$\frac{2}{3}$

   a. About what percent of television owners have basic cable?

   b. Write a decimal to express the percent of television owners who have three televisions.

64. What's the Question? Out of 25 students, 12 prefer to take their test on Monday, and 5 prefer to take their test on Tuesday. The answer is 32%. What is the question?

65. Write About It Explain why 0.8 is equal to 80% and not 8%.

66. Challenge The dimensions of a rectangle are 0.5 yard and 24% of a yard. What is the area of the rectangle? Write your answer as a fraction in simplest form.

Test Prep

67. Multiple Choice Which expression is NOT equal to half of n?

   (A) $0.5n$ (B) $\frac{n}{2}$ (C) $n \div 2$ (D) 5% of n

68. Multiple Choice Approximately $\frac{2}{3}$ of U.S. homeowners own a cell phone. What percent of homeowners do NOT own a cell phone?

   (F) 0.67%   (G) 2.3%   (H) 33.3%   (J) 66.7%

Mastering *the* Standards

for Mathematical Practice

The topics described in the Standards for Mathematical Content will vary from year to year. However, the *way* in which you learn, study, and think about mathematics will not. The Standards for Mathematical Practice describe skills that you will use in all of your math courses.

Mathematical Practices

1. *Make sense of problems and persevere in solving them.*
2. *Reason abstractly and quantitatively.*
3. *Construct viable arguments and critique the reasoning of others.*
4. *Model with mathematics.*
5. *Use appropriate tools strategically.*
6. *Attend to precision.*
7. *Look for and make use of structure.*
8. *Look for and express regularity in repeated reasoning.*

① Make sense of problems and persevere in solving them.

Mathematically proficient students start by explaining to themselves the meaning of a problem... They analyze givens, constraints, relationships, and goals. They make conjectures about the form... of the solution and plan a solution pathway...

In your book

Focus on Problem Solving describes a four-step plan for problem solving. The plan is introduced at the beginning of your book, and practice with the plan appears throughout the book.

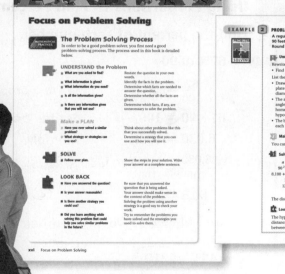

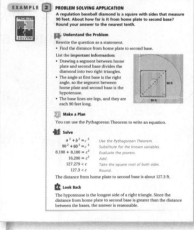

Percent of a Number

COMMON CORE

CC.6.RP.3 Use ratio and rate reasoning to solve real-world and mathematical problems, e.g., by reasoning about tables of equivalent ratios, tape diagrams, double number line diagrams, or equations **Also** **CC.6.RP.3c**

The human body is made up mostly of water. In fact, about 67% of a person's total (100%) body weight is water. If Cameron weighs 90 pounds, about how much of his weight is water?

Recall that a percent is a part of 100. Since you want to know the part of Cameron's body that is water, you can set up and solve a proportion to find the answer.

Interactivities Online ▶

Part → $\frac{67}{100} = \frac{n}{90}$ ← Part
Whole → $\phantom{\frac{67}{100}}$ ← Whole

EXAMPLE **1** **Using Proportions to Find Percents of Numbers**

Find the percent of each number.

A 67% of 90

$$\frac{67}{100} = \frac{n}{90}$$ *Write a proportion.*

$67 \cdot 90 = 100 \cdot n$ *Set the cross products equal.*

$6{,}030 = 100n$ *Multiply.*

$\frac{6{,}030}{100} = \frac{100n}{100}$ *Divide each side by 100 to isolate the variable.*

$60.3 = n$

67% of 90 is 60.3.

B 145% of 210

$$\frac{145}{100} = \frac{n}{210}$$ *Write a proportion.*

$145 \cdot 210 = 100 \cdot n$ *Set the cross products equal.*

$30{,}450 = 100n$ *Multiply.*

$\frac{30{,}450}{100} = \frac{100n}{100}$ *Divide each side by 100 to isolate the variable.*

$304.5 = n$

145% of 210 is 304.5.

Helpful Hint

When solving a problem with a percent greater than 100%, the *part* will be greater than the *whole*.

In addition to using proportions, you can find the percent of a number by using decimal equivalents.

EXAMPLE 2

Using Decimal Equivalents to Find Percents of Numbers

Find the percent of each number. Check whether your answer is reasonable.

A 8% of 50

$8\% \text{ of } 50 = 0.08 \cdot 50$ *Write the percent as a decimal.*
$\qquad = 4$ *Multiply.*

Model

Since 10% of 50 is 5, a reasonable answer for 8% of 50 is 4.

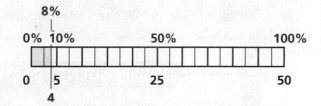

B 0.5% of 36

$0.5\% \text{ of } 36 = 0.005 \cdot 36$ *Write the percent as a decimal.*
$\qquad = 0.18$ *Multiply.*

Estimate

1% of 40 = 0.4, so 0.5% of 40 is half of 0.4, or 0.2. Thus 0.18 is a reasonable answer.

EXAMPLE 3

Geography Application

Earth's total land area is about 57,308,738 mi². The land area of Asia is about 30% of this total. What is the approximate land area of Asia to the nearest square mile?

Find 30% of 57,308,738.

$0.30 \cdot 57{,}308{,}738$ *Write the percent as a decimal.*
$= 17{,}192{,}621.4$ *Multiply.*

The land area of Asia is about 17,192,621 mi².

Think and Discuss

1. Explain how to set up a proportion to find 150% of a number.

2. Describe a situation in which you might need to find a percent of a number.

GUIDED PRACTICE

See Example **1** **Find the percent of each number.**

1. 30% of 80 **2.** 38% of 400 **3.** 200% of 10 **4.** 180% of 90

See Example **2** **Find the percent of each number. Check whether your answer is reasonable.**

5. 16% of 50 **6.** 7% of 200 **7.** 47% of 900 **8.** 40% of 75

See Example **3** **9.** Of the 450 students at Miller Middle School, 38% ride the bus to school. How many students ride the bus to school?

INDEPENDENT PRACTICE

See Example **1** **Find the percent of each number.**

10. 80% of 35 **11.** 16% of 70 **12.** 150% of 80 **13.** 118% of 3,000

14. 5% of 58 **15.** 1% of 4 **16.** 103% of 50 **17.** 225% of 8

See Example **2** **Find the percent of each number. Check whether your answer is reasonable.**

18. 9% of 40 **19.** 20% of 65 **20.** 36% of 50 **21.** 2.9% of 60

22. 5% of 12 **23.** 220% of 18 **24.** 0.2% of 160 **25.** 155% of 8

See Example **3** **26.** In 2004, there were 19,396 bulldogs registered by the American Kennel Club. Approximately 86% of this number were registered in 2003. About how many bulldogs were registered in 2003?

PRACTICE AND PROBLEM SOLVING

Extra Practice

See Extra Practice for more exercises.

Solve.

27. 60% of 10 is what number? **28.** What number is 25% of 160?

29. What number is 15% of 30? **30.** 10% of 84 is what number?

31. 25% of 47 is what number? **32.** What number is 59% of 20?

33. What number is 125% of 4,100? **34.** 150% of 150 is what number?

Find the percent of each number. If necessary, round to the nearest tenth.

35. 160% of 50 **36.** 350% of 20 **37.** 480% of 25 **38.** 115% of 200

39. 18% of 3.4 **40.** 0.9% of 43 **41.** 98% of 4.3 **42.** 1.22% of 56

43. **Consumer Math** Fun Tees is offering a 30% discount on all merchandise. Find the amount of discount on a T-shirt that was originally priced at $15.99.

44. **Multi-Step** Shoe Style is discounting everything in the store by 25%. What is the sale price of a pair of flip-flops that was originally priced at $10?

45. **Nutrition** The United States Department of Agriculture recommends that women should eat 25 g of fiber each day. A granola bar provides 9% of that amount. How many grams of fiber does it contain?

46. **Physical Science** The percent of pure gold in 14-karat gold is about 58.3%. A 14-karat gold ring weighs 5.6 grams. About how many grams of pure gold are in the ring?

47. **Earth Science** The apparent magnitude of the star Mimosa is 1.25. Spica, another star, has an apparent magnitude that is 78.4% of Mimosa's. What is Spica's apparent magnitude?

48. **Multi-Step** Trahn purchased a pair of slacks for $39.95 and a jacket for $64.00. The sales tax rate on his purchases was 5.5%. Find the total cost of Trahn's purchases, including sales tax.

49. The graph shows the results of a student survey about computers. Use the graph to predict how many students in your class have a computer at home.

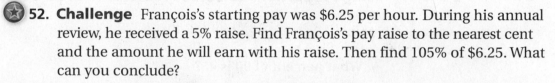

Student Survey Results

Have a computer at home	69
Have Internet access at home	45
Use a computer at school	29

Percent of students

50. **What's the Error?** A student used the proportion $\frac{n}{100} = \frac{5}{26}$ to find 5% of 26. What did the student do wrong?

51. **Write About It** Describe two ways to find 18% of 40.

52. **Challenge** François's starting pay was $6.25 per hour. During his annual review, he received a 5% raise. Find François's pay raise to the nearest cent and the amount he will earn with his raise. Then find 105% of $6.25. What can you conclude?

Test Prep

53. **Multiple Choice** Of the 875 students enrolled at Sycamore Valley Middle School, 48% are boys. How many of the students are boys?

Ⓐ 250 　　 Ⓑ 310 　　 Ⓒ 420 　　 Ⓓ 440

54. **Gridded Response** A children's multivitamin has 80% of the recommended daily allowance of zinc. The recommended daily allowance is 15 mg. How many milligrams of zinc does the vitamin provide?

7-8 Solving Percent Problems

COMMON CORE

CC.6.RP.3 Use ratio and rate reasoning to solve real-world and mathematical problems, e.g., by reasoning about tables of equivalent ratios, tape diagrams, double number line diagrams, or equations

Sloths may seem lazy, but their extremely slow movement helps them seem almost invisible to predators. Sloths sleep an average of 16.5 hours per day. To find out what percent of a 24-hour day 16.5 hours is, you can use a proportion or an equation.

Proportion method

$$\text{Part} \rightarrow \frac{n}{100} = \frac{16.5}{24} \leftarrow \text{Part} \atop \text{Whole}$$
Whole $\rightarrow$

$$n \cdot 24 = 100 \cdot 16.5$$
$$24n = 1{,}650$$
$$n = 68.75$$

Equation method

What **percent** of **24** is **16.5**?

$$n \quad \cdot 24 = 16.5$$
$$n = \frac{16.5}{24}$$
$$n = 0.6875$$

Sloths spend about **69%** of the day sleeping!

EXAMPLE **Using Proportions to Solve Problems with Percents**

Solve.

A **What percent of 90 is 45?**

$$\frac{n}{100} = \frac{45}{90} \qquad \textit{Write a proportion.}$$

$$n \cdot 90 = 100 \cdot 45 \qquad \textit{Set the cross products equal.}$$

$$90n = 4{,}500 \qquad \textit{Multiply.}$$

$$\frac{90n}{90} = \frac{4{,}500}{90} \qquad \textit{Divide each side by 90 to isolate the variable.}$$

$$n = 50$$

50% of 90 is 45.

B **12 is 8% of what number?**

$$\frac{8}{100} = \frac{12}{n} \qquad \textit{Write a proportion.}$$

$$8 \cdot n = 100 \cdot 12 \qquad \textit{Set the cross products equal.}$$

$$8n = 1{,}200 \qquad \textit{Multiply.}$$

$$\frac{8n}{8} = \frac{1{,}200}{8} \qquad \textit{Divide each side by 8 to isolate the variable.}$$

$$n = 150$$

12 is 8% of 150.

Video **Lesson Tutorials Online** my.hrw.com

EXAMPLE **2** **Using Equations to Solve Problems with Percents**

Solve.

A **What percent of 75 is 105?**

$n \cdot 75 = 105$ *Write an equation.*

$\dfrac{n \cdot 75}{75} = \dfrac{105}{75}$ *Divide each side by 75 to isolate the variable.*

$n = 1.4$

$n = 140\%$ *Write the decimal as a percent.*

140% of 75 is 105.

B **48 is 20% of what number?**

$48 = 20\% \cdot n$ *Write an equation.*

$48 = 0.2 \cdot n$ *Write 20% as a decimal.*

$\dfrac{48}{0.2} = \dfrac{0.2 \cdot n}{0.2}$ *Divide each side by 0.2 to isolate the variable.*

$240 = n$

48 is 20% of 240.

EXAMPLE **3** **Finding Sales Tax**

Helpful Hint

The *sales tax rate* is the percent used to calculate sales tax.

Ravi bought a T-shirt with a retail sales price of $12 and paid $0.99 sales tax. What is the sales tax rate where Ravi bought the T-shirt?

Restate the question: What percent of $12 is $0.99?

$\dfrac{n}{100} = \dfrac{0.99}{12}$ *Write a proportion.*

$n \cdot 12 = 100 \cdot 0.99$ *Set the cross products equal.*

$12n = 99$ *Multiply.*

$\dfrac{12n}{12} = \dfrac{99}{12}$ *Divide each side by 12.*

$n = 8.25$

8.25% of $12 is $0.99. The sales tax rate where Ravi bought the T-shirt is 8.25%.

Think and Discuss

1. **Describe** two methods for solving percent problems.

2. **Explain** whether you prefer to use the proportion method or the equation method when solving percent problems.

3. **Tell** what the first step is in solving a sales tax problem.

GUIDED PRACTICE

Solve.

See Example **1**

1. What percent of 100 is 25?

2. What percent of 5 is 4?

3. 6 is 10% of what number?

4. 8 is 20% of what number?

See Example **2**

5. What percent of 50 is 9?

6. What percent of 30 is 27?

7. 7 is 14% of what number?

8. 30 is 15% of what number?

See Example **3**

9. The sales tax on a $120 skateboard at Surf 'n' Skate is $9.60. What is the sales tax rate?

INDEPENDENT PRACTICE

Solve.

See Example **1**

10. What percent of 60 is 40?

11. What percent of 48 is 16?

12. What percent of 45 is 9?

13. What percent of 6 is 18?

14. 56 is 140% of what number?

15. 45 is 20% of what number?

See Example **2**

16. What percent of 80 is 10?

17. What percent of 12.4 is 12.4?

18. 18 is 15% of what number?

19. 9 is 30% of what number?

20. 210% of what number is 147?

21. 8.8 is 40% of what number?

See Example **3**

22. A 12-pack of cinnamon-scented pencils sells for $3.00 at a school booster club sale. What is the sales tax rate if the total cost of the pencils is $3.21?

PRACTICE AND PROBLEM SOLVING

Extra Practice

See Extra Practice for more exercises.

Solve. Round to the nearest tenth, if necessary.

23. 5 is what percent of 9?

24. What is 45% of 39?

25. 55 is 80% of what number?

26. 12 is what percent of 19?

27. What is 155% of 50?

28. 5.8 is 0.9% of what number?

29. 36% of what number is 57?

30. What percent of 64 is 40?

31. Multi-Step The advertised cost of admission to a water park in a nearby city is $25 per student. A student paid $30 for admission and received $3.75 in change. What is the sales tax rate in that city?

32. Consumer Math The table shows the cost of sunscreen purchased in Beach City and Desert City with and without sales tax. Which city has a greater sales tax rate? Give the sales tax rate for each city.

	Cost	Cost + Tax
Beach City	$10	$10.83
Desert City	$5	$5.42

The viola family is made up of the cello, violin, and viola. Of the three instruments, the cello is the largest.

33. Critical Thinking What number is always used when you set up a proportion to solve a percent problem? Explain.

34. Health The circle graph shows the approximate distribution of blood types among people in the United States.

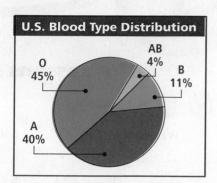

U.S. Blood Type Distribution

O 45%
AB 4%
B 11%
A 40%

a. In a survey, 126 people had type O blood. Predict how many people were surveyed.

b. How many of the people surveyed had type AB blood?

35. Music Beethoven wrote 9 trios for the piano, violin, and cello. These trios make up 20% of the chamber music pieces Beethoven wrote. How many pieces of chamber music did he write?

36. History The length of Abraham Lincoln's first inaugural speech was 3,635 words. The length of his second inaugural speech was about 19.3% of the length of his first speech. About how long was Lincoln's second speech?

37. What's the Question? The first lap of an auto race is 2,500 m. This is 10% of the total race distance. The answer is 10. What is the question?

38. Write About It If 35 is 110% of a number, is the number greater than or less than 35? Explain.

39. Challenge Kayleen has been offered two jobs. The first job offers an annual salary of $32,000. The second job offers an annual salary of $10,000 plus 8% commission on all of her sales. How much money per month would Kayleen need to make in sales to earn enough commission to make more money at the second job?

Test Prep

40. Multiple Choice Thirty children from an after-school club went to the matinee. This is 20% of the children in the club. How many children are in the club?

(A) 6   (B) 67   (C) 150   (D) 600

41. Gridded Response Jason saves 30% of his monthly paycheck for college. He earned $250 last month. How many dollars did he save for college?

Quiz for Lessons 5 Through 8

 5 **Percents**

Write each percent as a fraction in simplest form.

1. 60%   **2.** 15%   **3.** 75%

Write each percent as a decimal.

4. 34%   **5.** 77%   **6.** 6%

7. About 71% of Earth's surface is covered with water. Write 71% as a decimal.

 6 **Percents, Decimals, and Fractions**

Write each fraction as a percent.

8. $\frac{9}{20}$ **9.** $\frac{2}{3}$ **10.** $\frac{21}{50}$

Write each decimal as a percent.

11. 0.28   **12.** 0.9   **13.** 0.02

14. Mike's baseball team won $\frac{17}{20}$ of its games. What percent of the games did Mike's baseball team win?

 7 **Percent of a Number**

Find the percent of each number.

15. 25% of 84   **16.** 52% of 300   **17.** 0.5% of 40   **18.** 160% of 450

19. 41% of 122   **20.** 178% of 35   **21.** 29% of 88   **22.** 80% of 176

23. Students get a 15% discount off the original prices at the Everything Fluorescent store during its back-to-school sale. Find the amount of discount on fluorescent notebooks originally priced at $7.99.

 8 **Solving Percent Problems**

Solve. Round to the nearest tenth, if necessary.

24. 14 is 44% of what number?   **25.** 22 is what percent of 900?

26. 99 is what percent of 396?   **27.** 75 is 24% of what number?

28. The sales tax on a $105 digital camera is $7.15. What is the sales tax rate?

Real-World CONNECTIONS

MATHEMATICAL PRACTICES — Reason abstractly and quantitatively.

Greenfield Village Greenfield Village in Dearborn, Michigan, is the largest outdoor museum in the country. Visitors to the village travel back in time to see how Americans have lived and worked. To create the village, nearly 100 historic buildings were moved to the site from their original locations.

MICHIGAN

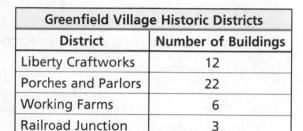

Dearborn

Greenfield Village consists of seven historic districts. The table gives information on five of the districts. Use the table for Exercises 1–2.

1. What is the ratio of buildings at Railroad Junction to buildings at Liberty Craftworks?

2. The ratio of buildings in the Main Street district to buildings at Liberty Craftworks is 3:2.

   a. Write and solve a proportion to find the number of buildings in the Main Street district.

   b. In the Main Street district, the ratio of stores to other types of buildings is 1:2. How many stores are there in the district?

Greenfield Village Historic Districts	
District	**Number of Buildings**
Liberty Craftworks	12
Porches and Parlors	22
Working Farms	6
Railroad Junction	3
Edison at Work	7

3. Greenfield Village is spread across 240 acres of land. Only 37% of the land is used for the exhibits, while the rest of the land consists of forests, rivers, and pastures. How many acres are used for exhibits?

4. The village has a special walking tour with a garden theme. Six of the stops on the tour are at historic homes. This is 30% of the tour stops. How many stops are on the tour?

Real-World Connections

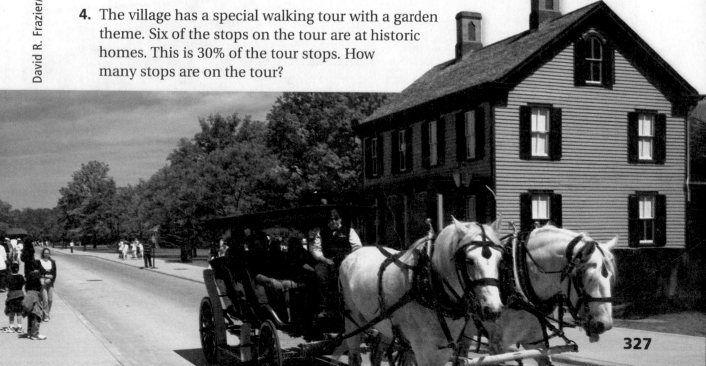

Game Time

The Golden Rectangle

Which rectangle do you find most visually pleasing?

Did you choose rectangle 3? If so, you agree with artists and architects throughout history. Rectangle 3 is a golden rectangle. Golden rectangles are said to be the most pleasing to the human eye.

In a golden rectangle, the ratio of the length of the longer side to the length of the shorter side is approximately equal to 1.6. In other words,

$$\frac{\text{length of long er side}}{\text{length of shorter side}} \approx \frac{1.6}{1}$$

Measure the length and width of each rectangle below. Which could be golden rectangles? Are they the most pleasing to your eye?

Triple Play

Number of players: 3–5

Deal five cards to each player. Place the remaining cards in a pile facedown. At any time, you may remove *triples* from your hand. A *triple* is a fraction card, a decimal card, and a percent card that are all equivalent.

On your turn, ask any other player for a specific card. For example, if you have the $\frac{3}{5}$ card, you might ask another player if he or she has the 60% card. If so, he or she must give it to you, and you repeat your turn. If not, take the top card from the deck, and your turn is over.

The first player to get rid of his or her cards is the winner.

🪐 **Learn It Online**
Game Time Extra

A complete copy of the rules and game pieces are available online.

Materials
- construction paper
- $\frac{1}{4}$ in. graph paper
- glue
- scissors
- markers

It's in the Bag!

PROJECT **Double-Door Fractions, Decimals, and Percents**

Open the door to fractions, decimals, and percents by making this handy converter.

Directions

1 Cut the construction paper to $6\frac{1}{2}$ inches by $8\frac{1}{2}$ inches. Fold it in half lengthwise and then unfold it. Fold the top and bottom edges to the middle crease to make a double door. **Figure A**

2 Cut a strip of graph paper that is 2 inches wide by $8\frac{1}{2}$ inches long. Make a percent number line along the middle of the strip. Include 0%, 5%, 10%, and so on, up to 100%. **Figure B**

3 Cut two 1-by-$8\frac{1}{2}$-inch strips of graph paper. On one strip, make a fraction number line that includes $\frac{0}{20}$, $\frac{1}{20}$, and so on, up to $\frac{20}{20}$. Write the fractions in simplest form. On the other strip, make a decimal number line that includes 0.0, 0.05, 0.1, and so on, up to 1. **Figure C**

4 Glue the percent number line along the center fold of the construction paper. **Figure D**

5 Close the double doors. Glue the remaining number lines to the outside of the doors, making sure the number lines match up.

Putting the Math into Action

Team up with a classmate. Use your double-door converters to quiz each other on equivalent fractions, decimals, and percents.

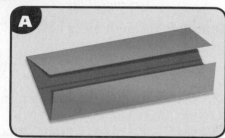

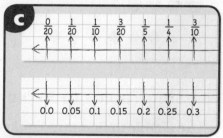

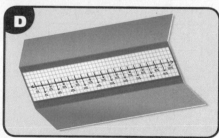

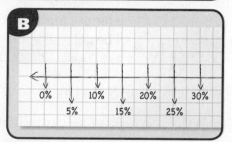

Study Guide: Review

Study Guide: Review

Vocabulary

coordinate grid

equivalent ratios

ordered pair

percent

proportion

rate

ratio

unit rate

Complete the sentences below with vocabulary words from the list above.

1. A(n) ___?___ of numbers can be used to locate points on a coordinate grid.

2. A(n) ___?___ is a ratio of a number to 100.

3. A(n) ___?___ is a comparison of two quantities using division.

EXAMPLES

EXERCISES

1 Ratios and Rates

■ Write the ratio of hearts to diamonds.

$$\frac{\text{hearts}}{\text{diamonds}} = \frac{4}{8}$$

4. Write three equivalent ratios for 4:8.

5. Which is the better deal—an 8 oz package of pretzels for $1.92 or a 12 oz package of pretzels for $2.64?

2 Using Tables to Explore Equivalent Ratios and Rates

■ Use a table to find three ratios equivalent to 6:7.

6	12	18	24
7	14	21	28

Multiply the numerator and denominator by 2, 3, and 4.

The ratios 6:7, 12:14, 18:21, and 24:28 are equivalent.

Use a table to find three equivalent ratios.

6. $\frac{3}{10}$ 7. 5 to 21   8. 15:7

9. The table below shows the cost of canoeing for different-sized groups. Predict how much a group of 9 will pay.

Number in Group	2	4	8	10
Cost ($)	10.50	21	42	52.50

3 Ordered Pairs

■ Name the ordered pair for *A*.

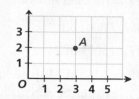

A is at (3, 2).

Name the ordered pair for each location.

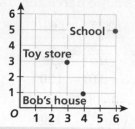

10. Bob's house

11. toy store

4 Proportions

■ Find the value of *n* in $\frac{5}{6} = \frac{n}{12}$.

$6 \cdot n = 5 \cdot 12$ *Cross products are equal.*

$\frac{6n}{6} = \frac{60}{6}$ *Divide both sides by 6.*

$n = 10$

Find the value of *n* in each proportion.

12. $\frac{3}{5} = \frac{n}{15}$ **13.** $\frac{1}{n} = \frac{3}{9}$

14. $\frac{7}{8} = \frac{n}{16}$ **15.** $\frac{n}{4} = \frac{8}{16}$

16. A fruit salad recipe calls for 2 cups of bananas for every 3 cups of apples. If Shannon is using 9 cups of apples to make fruit salad for a party, how many cups of bananas does she need?

5 Percents

■ Write 48% as a fraction in simplest form.

$48\% = \frac{48}{100}$ $\frac{48 \div 4}{100 \div 4} = \frac{12}{25}$

■ Write 16% as a decimal.

$16\% = \frac{16}{100}$ $16 \div 100 = 0.16$

Write each as a fraction in simplest form.

17. 75%   **18.** 6%   **19.** 30%

Write each percent as a decimal.

20. 8%   **21.** 65%   **22.** 20%

6 Percents, Decimals, and Fractions

■ Write 0.365 as a percent.

$0.365 = 36.5\%$ *Multiply by 100.*

■ Write $\frac{3}{5}$ as a percent.

$\frac{3 \cdot 20}{5 \cdot 20} = \frac{60}{100} = 60\%$

Write each decimal or fraction as a percent.

23. 0.896   **24.** 0.70   **25.** 0.057

26. 0.12   **27.** $\frac{7}{10}$ **28.** $\frac{3}{12}$

29. $\frac{7}{8}$ **30.** $\frac{4}{5}$ **31.** $\frac{1}{16}$

32. Water constitutes approximately $\frac{13}{20}$ of the body of an average adult male. About what percent of the average adult male body is made of water?

Study Guide: Review

Study Guide: Review

7 **Percent of a Number**

■ Find the percent of the number.

125% of 610

$\dfrac{125}{100} = \dfrac{n}{610}$ *Write a proportion.*

$125 \cdot 610 = 100 \cdot n$ *Cross products*

$76{,}250 = 100n$ *Multiply.*

$\dfrac{76{,}250}{100} = \dfrac{100n}{100}$ *Divide each side by 100.*

$762.5 = n$

125% of 610 is 762.5.

Find the percent of each number.

33. 16% of 425   **34.** 48% of 50

35. 7% of 63   **36.** 96% of 125

37. 130% of 21   **38.** 72% of 75

39. Canyon Middle School has 1,247 students. About 38% of the students are in the seventh grade. About how many seventh-graders currently attend Canyon Middle School?

8 **Solving Percent Problems**

■ Solve.

80 is 32% of what number?

$80 = 32\% \cdot n$ *Write an equation.*

$80 = 0.32 \cdot n$ *Write 32% as a decimal.*

$\dfrac{80}{0.32} = \dfrac{0.32 \cdot n}{0.32}$ *Divide each side by 0.32.*

$250 = n$

80 is 32% of 250.

Solve.

40. 20% of what number is 25?

41. 4 is what percent of 50?

42. 30 is 250% of what number?

43. What percent of 96 is 36?

44. 6 is 75% of what number?

45. 200 is what percent of 720?

46. The sales tax on a $25 shirt purchased at a store in Oak Park is $1.99. What is the sales tax rate in Oak Park?

47. Jaclyn paid a sales tax of $10.03 on a camera. The tax rate in her state is 8%. About how much did the camera cost?

Chapter Test

Use the table to write each ratio.

1. three equivalent ratios to compare dramas to documentaries

2. documentaries to total videos

3. music videos to exercise videos

4. Which is a better deal—5 videos for $29.50 or 3 videos for $17.25?

Types of Videos in Richard's Collection			
Comedy	5	Cartoon	7
Drama	6	Exercise	3
Music	3	Documentary	2

Find the value of n in each proportion.

5. $\frac{5}{6} = \frac{n}{24}$

6. $\frac{8}{n} = \frac{12}{3}$

7. $\frac{n}{10} = \frac{3}{6}$

8. $\frac{3}{9} = \frac{4}{n}$

9. The table shows the time it takes Jenny to swim laps. Predict how long it will take her to swim 14 laps.

Number of Laps	4	8	12	16
Time (min)	3	6	9	12

Name the ordered pair for each point on the grid.

10. A

11. B

12. C

13. D

14. E

15. F

16. G

17. H

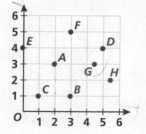

Graph and label each point on a coordinate grid.

18. $T(3, 4)$

19. $M\left(\frac{1}{2}, 6\right)$

20. $P(5, 1)$

21. $S\left(3\frac{1}{2}, 2\right)$

Write each percent as a fraction in simplest form and as a decimal.

22. 66%

23. 90%

24. 5%

25. 18%

Write each decimal or fraction as a percent.

26. 0.546

27. 0.092

28. $\frac{14}{25}$

29. $\frac{1}{8}$

Find the percent of each number.

30. 35% of 210

31. 16% of 85

32. 250% of 30

Solve.

33. 36 is what percent of 150?

34. 51 is what percent of 340?

35. 36 is 40% of what number?

36. Hampton Middle School is expecting 376 seventh-graders next year. This is 40% of the expected school enrollment. How many students are expected to enroll in the school next year?

Chapter Test

Test Tackler
STANDARDIZED TEST STRATEGIES

Extended Response: Write Extended Responses

When you answer an extended-response test item, you need to explain your reasoning clearly. Extended-response items are scored using a 4-point scoring rubric like the one shown below.

EXAMPLE

Extended Response Amber tracks her math test scores. Her goal is to have a 92% average. Her 10 test scores are 94, 76, 90, 98, 91, 93, 88, 90, 89, and 85. Find the range, mean, median, and mode of the data set. If her lowest score is dropped, will she meet her goal? Explain your answer.

Here is an example of a 4-point response according to the scoring rubric at right.

Scoring Rubric

4 points: The student correctly answers all parts of the question, shows all work, and provides a complete and correct explanation.

3 points: The student answers all parts of the question, shows all work, and provides a complete explanation that demonstrates understanding, but the student makes minor errors in computation.

2 points: The student does not answer all parts of the question but shows all work and provides a complete and correct explanation for the parts answered, or the student correctly answers all parts of the question but does not show all work or does not provide an explanation.

1 point: The student gives incorrect answers and shows little or no work or explanation, or the student does not follow directions.

0 points: The student gives no response.

4-point response:

Range: $98 - 76 = 22$
The range is 22.
Mean:
$$\frac{94 + 76 + 90 + 98 + 91 + 93 + 88 + 90 + 89 + 85}{10} = \frac{894}{10} = 89.4$$

The mean is 89.4.

Median: There are an even number of values in this set. The two middle numbers are 90 and 90. The median is 90.

Mode: The value that occurs most often is 90. The mode is 90.

When the lowest score, 76, is dropped, the average is
$$\frac{894 - 76}{9} = \frac{818}{9} = 90.9.$$ This value is less than 92. Even if the lowest score is dropped, Amber will not meet her goal.

The student correctly calculates and shows how to find the range, mean, median, and mode of this data set.

The student correctly answers the questions and shows how the answer is calculated.

Once you have answered an extended-response test item, double-check to make sure that you answered all of the different parts.

Read each test item and use the scoring rubric to answer the questions that follow.

Item A
Extended Response Use the table below to identify a pattern and find the next three terms. Is this sequence arithmetic? Explain.

Position	Value of Term
1	4
2	7
3	10
4	13
5	16
n	▣

1. What needs to be included in a response that would receive 4 points?

2. Write a response that would receive full credit.

Item B
Extended Response Draw a polygon that has three congruent sides. What is true about the measures of the angles of this polygon? Find the measurement of each angle. Classify the type of polygon you drew. Explain your answer.

Kim wrote this response:

Each angle measures 60°.
This is an equilateral triangle.

3. Score Kim's response. Explain your scoring decision.

4. Rewrite Kim's response so that it receives full credit.

Item C
Extended Response Look at the graph. Why is this graph misleading? Explain your answer. What might someone believe from this graph? What changes would you make to the graph so it is not misleading?

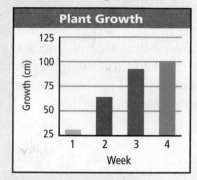

5. What needs to be included in a response that would receive 4 points?

6. Write a response that would receive full credit.

Item D
Extended Response The ages of the employees at a discount store are shown below. Find the mean, median, and mode of the data set. Which one bests describes the data set? Explain your answer.

68	32	16	23	21
17	28	20	39	38
21	22	17	23	37

7. Should the response shown receive a score of 4 points? Why or why not?

The mean is 28.
The modes are 17 and 23.
The median is 22.
The best descriptor is the mode because there is more than one.

8. Correct or add any information, if necessary, for the response to receive full credit.

Cumulative Assessment

Multiple Choice

1. Janet has a flower garden with 6 rose bushes, 7 lilac bushes, and 5 azaleas. Which of the following shows the ratio of lilac bushes to the total number of plants in Janet's garden?

   (A) 7:11   (C) 11:18

   (B) 7:18   (D) 18:5

2. Carina rode her exercise bike 30 minutes on Monday, 45 minutes on Tuesday, 30 minutes on Wednesday, 60 minutes on Thursday, and 50 minutes on Friday. Find the mean amount of time that Carina rode her bike in these 5 days.

   (F) 30 minutes   (H) 45 minutes

   (G) 43 minutes   (J) 215 minutes

3. The sixth grade chorus is going to a competition. There are 116 students in the sixth grade chorus. If each bus holds 35 students, how many buses will be needed to take the students to the competition?

   (A) 5 buses   (C) 3 buses

   (B) 4 buses   (D) 2 buses

4. Which of the following is NOT an example of a proportion?

   (F) $\frac{3}{4} = \frac{9}{12}$ (H) $\frac{1}{3} = \frac{15}{42}$

   (G) $\frac{5}{9} = \frac{45}{81}$ (J) $\frac{7}{8} = \frac{35}{40}$

5. On the map the distance between point R and point T is 1.125 inches. Find the actual distance between point R and point T.

   Scale: 1 in:10 mi

   (A) 10 miles   (C) 12.5 miles

   (B) 11.25 miles   (D) 15 miles

6. Esperanza has a puppy that weighs $3\frac{1}{4}$ pounds. In 3 months, the puppy should weigh 3 times as much as it weighs now. How much weight should the puppy gain in the next 3 months?

   (F) $6\frac{1}{2}$ pounds

   (G) $6\frac{3}{4}$ pounds

   (H) $8\frac{1}{4}$ pounds

   (J) $9\frac{3}{4}$ pounds

7. Which value is greatest?

   (A) $\frac{5}{6}$ (C) 80%

   (B) 0.7   (D) $\frac{6}{7}$

8. Max earns $7.25 per hour working for a florist. His weekly paycheck is $108.75 before taxes. If h equals the number of hours worked, which equation can be used to find the number of hours Max works each week?

    Ⓕ $7.25 + h = 108.75$

    Ⓖ $\frac{7.25}{h} = 108.75$

    Ⓗ $108.75 - h = 7.25$

    Ⓙ $7.25h = 108.75$

 HOT TIP! Estimate your answer before solving the problem. You can often use your estimate to eliminate some of the answer choices.

Gridded Response

9. A school band is putting together music kits for the local music fair. They have 72 recorders, 96 kazoos, and 60 whistles. If each kit has the same number of each instrument, what is the greatest number of kits that can be made if the band uses all the instruments?

10. Find the value of $40 \div (3 + 5) \times 2$.

11. Rylee has a collection of music boxes. Of the 36 music boxes she owns, 25% of them have parts that move when the music plays. How many of her music boxes have moving parts?

12. What is $2\frac{3}{4} + \frac{1}{3}$ written as an improper fraction?

13. Ms. Chavez is ordering art supplies. She orders enough pencils for every student and then adds 20% more for extras. If she has 210 students, how many pencils does she need to order?

Short Response

S1. Chrissy is shopping for T-shirts for the pep club. Package A is 10 shirts for $15.50. Package B is 15 shirts for $20.50. Package C is 20 shirts for $25.50. Find the unit price for each package. Which T-shirt package is the best deal? Explain your reasoning and show your work.

S2. A computer is marked 30% off the original price. The computer originally cost $685. Find the amount of the discount and the sale price of the computer.

Extended Response

E1. Two rectangles A and B are called *similar* if the widths and lengths of the rectangles are in proportion. That is, $\frac{\text{width of } A}{\text{width of } B} = \frac{\text{length of } A}{\text{length of } B}$. A small purple rectangle is 8 millimeters wide and 18 millimeters long. A larger purple rectangle is 18 millimeters wide and 25 millimeters long.

    a. Are the two purple rectangles similar? Explain your answer.

    b. A third rectangle is similar to the smaller purple rectangle. The width of the third rectangle is 14 millimeters. Let x represent the length of the third rectangle. Write an equation that could be used to find x.

    c. Find the height of the third rectangle. Show your work.

Measurement and Geometry

COMMON CORE

Chapter
- Solve problems that involve lengths, areas, and volumes.
- Use fractions and decimals to solve measurement problems.

Why Learn This?

Different three-dimensional figures can be seen in various architectural structures. Many buildings are simple rectangular prisms while others are in the shape of pyramids or cylinders.

Learn It Online
Chapter Project Online

Are You Ready?

✓ Vocabulary

Choose the best term from the list to complete each sentence.

1. A(n) ___?___ is a quadrilateral with opposite sides that are parallel and congruent.

2. Some customary units of length are ___?___ and ___?___. Some metric units of length are ___?___ and ___?___.

3. A(n) ___?___ is a quadrilateral with side lengths that are all congruent and four right angles.

4. A(n) ___?___ is a polygon with six sides.

centimeters
cube
feet
hexagon
inches
liters
meters
parallelogram
square
trapezoid

Complete these exercises to review skills you will need for this chapter.

✓ Add and Multiply Whole Numbers, Fractions, and Decimals

Find each sum or product.

5. $1.5 + 2.4 + 3.6 + 2.5$

6. $2 \cdot 3.5 \cdot 4$

7. $\frac{22}{7} \cdot 21$

8. $\frac{1}{2} \cdot 5 \cdot 4$

9. $3.2 \cdot 5.6$

10. $\frac{1}{2} \cdot 10 \cdot 3$

11. $(2 \cdot 5) + (6 \cdot 8)$

12. $2(3.5) + 2(1.5)$

13. $9(20 + 7)$

✓ Measure with Metric Units

Use a centimeter ruler to measure each line to the nearest centimeter.

14. _____

15. _____

✓ Identify Polygons

Name each polygon. Determine whether it appears to be regular or not regular.

16.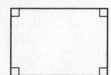

17.

18.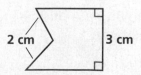

Where You've Been

Previously, you

- selected appropriate units to measure perimeter, area, and volume.
- classified polygons.
- identified three-dimensional figures.

In This Chapter

You will study

- solving problems involving area.
- identifying, drawing, and building three-dimensional figures.
- finding the surface area of prisms, pyramids, and cylinders.
- finding the volume of prisms.

Where You're Going

You can use the skills learned in this chapter

- to find the volume of pyramids, cones, and spheres.
- to find the surface area of spheres.

Key Vocabulary/Vocabulario

area	área
surface area	área total
volume	volumen

Vocabulary Connections

To become familiar with some of the vocabulary terms in the chapter, consider the following. You may refer to the chapter, the glossary, or a dictionary if you like.

1. The Egyptian pyramids are huge stone structures whose outside walls, in the form of four triangles, meet in a point at the top. What shapes do you think make up a **pyramid**?

2. You may have heard the expression "pump up the volume!" How can this help to remember what **volume** means in terms of three-dimensional figures?

Reading and Writing Math

Reading Strategy: Learn Math Vocabulary

Many new math terms fill the pages of your textbook. By learning these new terms and their meanings when they are introduced, you will be able to apply this knowledge to different concepts throughout your math classes.

Some ways that may help you learn vocabulary include the following:

- Try to find the meaning of the new term by its context.
- Use the prefix or suffix to figure out the meaning of the term.
- Relate the new term to familiar everyday words or situations.

Vocabulary Word	Definition	Study Tip
Origin	The point (0, 0) where the *x*-axis and *y*-axis intersect on the coordinate plane	The word begins with an "O" which can remind you that the coordinates of the origin are (0, 0).
Quadrants	The *x*- and *y*- axis divide the coordinate plane into four regions. Each region is called a quadrant.	The prefix *quad* means "four." A *quadrilateral* is a four-sided figure, for example.
Coordinate	One of the numbers of an ordered pair that locate a point on a coordinate graph	*Think: x* coordinates with *y*.

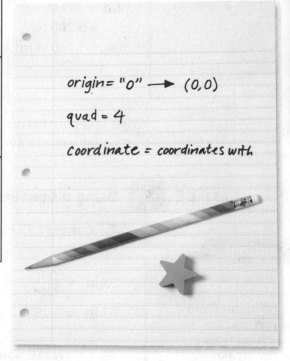

origin = "o" → (0,0)

quad = 4

coordinate = coordinates with

Try This

Complete the table as you work through the chapter to help you learn the vocabulary words.

	Vocabulary Word	Definition	Study Tip
1.	Area	■	■
2.	■	■	■
3.	■	■	■

Converting Customary Units

COMMON
CORE

CC.6.RP.3d Use ratio reasoning to convert measurement units; manipulate and transform units appropriately when multiplying or dividing quantities

Jacques Freitag is the first athlete to win gold medals at the International Association of Athletic Federations (IAAF) Youth, Junior, and Senior Championships. His personal best in the high jump is over 93 inches. How many feet is this?

You can use the information in the table below to convert one customary unit to another.

Common Customary Measurements		
Length	**Weight**	**Capacity**
1 foot = 12 inches	1 pound = 16 ounces	1 cup = 8 fluid ounces
1 yard = 36 inches	1 ton = 2,000 pounds	1 pint = 2 cups
1 yard = 3 feet		1 quart = 2 pints
1 mile = 5,280 feet		1 quart = 4 cups
1 mile = 1,760 yards		1 gallon = 4 quarts
		1 gallon = 16 cups
		1 gallon = 128 fluid ounces

When you convert one unit of measure to another, you can multiply by a conversion factor.

EXAMPLE 1 Using a Conversion Factor

A Convert 93 inches to feet.

Set up a conversion factor.

$$93 \text{ in.} \times \frac{1 \text{ ft}}{12 \text{ in.}}$$

$$93 \text{ in.} = 7.75 \text{ ft}$$

Think: inches to feet—1 ft = 12 in., so use $\frac{1 \text{ ft}}{12 \text{ in.}}$. Multiply 93 in. by the conversion factor.
Cancel the common unit, in.

Caution!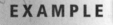

Write the unit you are converting *to* in the numerator and the unit you are converting *from* in the denominator.

B Convert 2 pounds to ounces.

Set up a conversion factor.

$$2 \text{ lb} \times \frac{16 \text{ oz}}{1 \text{ lb}} = 32 \text{ oz}$$

$$2 \text{ lb} = 32 \text{ oz}$$

Think: ounces to pounds—16 oz = 1 lb, so use $\frac{16 \text{ oz}}{1 \text{ lb}}$. Multiply 2 lb by the conversion factor.
Cancel the common unit, lb.

Another way to convert units is to use proportions.

[Video] **Lesson Tutorials Online** my.hrw.com

Michael Steele/Getty Images

EXAMPLE 2

Converting Units of Measure by Using Proportions

Remember!

A proportion shows that two ratios are equivalent. Use a conversion factor for one of the ratios.

Convert 48 quarts to gallons.

48 qt = ▮ gal

$$\frac{4 \text{ qt}}{1 \text{ gal}} = \frac{48 \text{ qt}}{x \text{ gal}}$$ *1 gallon is 4 quarts. Write a proportion. Use a variable for the value you are trying to find.*

$4 \cdot x = 1 \cdot 48$ *The cross products are equal.*

$4x = 48$ *Divide both sides by 4 to undo the multiplication.*

$x = 12$

48 qt = 12 gal

EXAMPLE 3

 Make sense of problems and persevere in solving them.

PROBLEM SOLVING APPLICATION

The Washington Monument is about 185 yards tall. This height is almost equal to the length of two football fields. About how many feet is this?

1 Understand the Problem

The **answer** will be the height of the Washington Monument in feet.

List the **important information:**

• The height of the Washington Monument is about 185 yards.

2 Make a Plan

Make a table from the information to show the number of feet in 1, 2, and 3 yards. Then find the number of feet in *n* yards.

3 Solve

Yards	Feet
1	3
2	6
3	9
n	3n

Look for a pattern.

$1 \cdot 3 = 3$
$2 \cdot 3 = 6$
$3 \cdot 3 = 9$
$n \cdot 3 = 3n$

$185 \cdot 3 = 555$ so, the Washington Monument is about 555 ft tall.

4 Look Back

Round 185 to 200. Then multiply by 3.

$200 \cdot 3 = 600$

The answer is reasonable because 555 is close to 600.

MATHEMATICAL PRACTICES

Think and Discuss

1. Explain how to set up a proportion to convert miles to yards.

GUIDED PRACTICE

See Example 1 Convert.

1. 9 ft = ▩ in.
2. 10 pt = ▩ qt
3. 14,000 lb = ▩ T
4. 5 yd = ▩ ft
5. 24 fl oz = ▩ c
6. 4 lb = ▩ oz

See Example 2
7. 32 qt = ▩ gal
8. 9 lb = ▩ oz
9. 36 in. = ▩ ft
10. 2 yd = ▩ in.
11. 11 qt = ▩ pt
12. 6 T = ▩ lb

See Example 3
13. **Biology** An adult male of average size normally has about 6 quarts of blood in his body. Approximately how many cups of blood does the average adult male have in his body?

INDEPENDENT PRACTICE

See Example 1 Convert.

14. 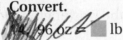96 oz = ▩ lb
15. 6 c = ▩ fl oz
16. 3 mi = ▩ ft
17. 4,000 lb = ▩ T
18. 6 lb = ▩ oz
19. 3,520 yd = ▩ mi

See Example 2
20. 27 ft = ▩ yd
21. 3 T = ▩ lb
22. 16 qt = ▩ gal
23. 48 oz = ▩ lb
24. 3 yd = ▩ in.
25. 10 pt = ▩ c

See Example 3
26. **Architecture** The steel used to make the Statue of Liberty weighs about 125 tons. About how many pounds of steel were used to make the Statue of Liberty?

PRACTICE AND PROBLEM SOLVING

Extra Practice
See Extra Practice for more exercises.

Compare. Use <, >, or =.

27. 18 ft ▩ 220 in.
28. 24 lb ▩ 388 oz
29. $\frac{1}{2}$ pt ▩ 1 c

30. 2 mi ▩ 10,000 ft
31. 12 pt ▩ 3 gal
32. 72 ft ▩ 24 yd

33. 9 c ▩ 72 fl oz
34. 30 yd ▩ 93 ft
35. 145 in. ▩ 4 yd

36. Linda cut off $1\frac{1}{2}$ feet of her hair to donate to an organization that makes wigs for children with cancer. How many inches of hair did Linda cut off?

37. **Geography** Lake Superior is about 1,302 feet deep at its deepest point. What is this depth in yards?

38. **Multi-Step** A company produces 3 tons of cereal each week. How many 12-ounce cereal boxes can be filled each week?

39. **Sports** The width of a singles tennis court is 27 feet.

   a. How many yards wide is a singles tennis court?

   b. How many inches wide is a singles tennis court?

Art

Long-Term Parking is 65 feet tall and stands in front of a parking lot in Paris.

Convert.

40. 108 in. = ▮ ft = ▮ yd

41. 10,560 ft = ▮ yd = ▮ mi

42. 12 qt = ▮ c = ▮ fl oz

43. 2 gal = ▮ qt = ▮ pt

44. **Art** In Paris, the sculpture *Long-Term Parking,* created by Armand Fernandez, contains 60 cars embedded in 3.5 million pounds of concrete. How many tons of concrete is this?

45. **Multi-Step** If a half-gallon of milk sells for $1.60, what is the cost of a fluid ounce of milk? (Round your answer to the nearest cent.)

46. **Critical Thinking** Make a table to convert ounces to pounds. Write an expression for the number of pounds in *n* ounces. Then write an expression for the number of ounces in *n* pounds.

47. **Multi-Step** If you drink 14 quarts of water per week, on average, how many pints do you drink per day?

48. **What's the Error?** Sari said that she walked a total of 8,800 feet in a 5-mile walk-a-thon. Explain Sari's error.

49. **Write About It** Explain how to compare a length given in inches to a length given in feet.

50. **Challenge** In 1942, there were 15,000 troops on the ship *Queen Mary.* Each soldier was given 2 quarts of fresh water for the entire journey.

 a. How many gallons of fresh water did the soldiers have in all?

 b. **Estimation** If the journey took 5 days, about how many fluid ounces of fresh water should a soldier have rationed himself each day?

Test Prep

51. **Multiple Choice** Which of the following amounts is NOT equivalent to 1 gal?

 (A) 64 fl oz   (B) 16 c   (C) 8 pt   (D) 4 qt

52. **Multiple Choice** The world's largest ice cream sundae weighed about 55,000 pounds. How many tons did it weigh?

 (F) 2.7 T   (G) 27.5 T   (H) 275 T   (J) 2,750 T

Converting Metric Units

COMMON CORE

CC.6.RP.3d Use ratio reasoning to convert measurement units; manipulate and transform units appropriately when multiplying or dividing quantities

The first Tour de France was in 1903 and was 2,428 km long. It had only 6 stages. Compare that to the 2005 Tour de France, which had 21 stages and covered 3,607 km.

During the 2005 Tour de France, Lance Armstrong was the stage winner from Tours to Blois, which has a distance of 67.5 km. How many meters is this distance?

In the metric system, the value of each place is 10 times greater than the value of the place to its right. When you convert one unit of measure to another, you can multiply or divide by a power of 10.

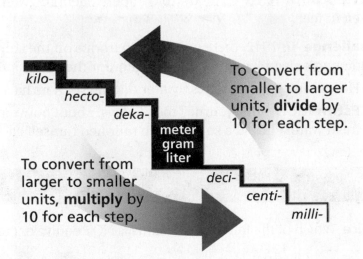

To convert from smaller to larger units, **divide** by 10 for each step.

To convert from larger to smaller units, **multiply** by 10 for each step.

kilo-
hecto-
deka-
meter gram liter
deci-
centi-
milli-

EXAMPLE 1 *Sports Application*

Helpful Hint

To multiply by a power of 10, move the decimal to the right; to divide by a power of 10, move the decimal to the left.

During the 2005 Tour de France, Lance Armstrong was the stage winner from Tours to Blois, which has a distance of 67.5 km. How many meters is this distance?

67.5 km = ⬛ m

Think: Kilometer to meter is going from a bigger unit to a smaller unit. A meter is 3 places to the right of a kilometer in the chart, so $10 \cdot 10 \cdot 10$ or $10^3 = 1,000$.

67.5 km = $(67.5 \cdot 1,000)$ m

1 km $= 1,000$ m. You are converting a bigger unit to a smaller unit, so multiply by 1,000.

67.5 km = 67,500 m

Move the decimal point 3 places to the right.

Video **Lesson Tutorials Online** my.hrw.com

EXAMPLE 2 Using Powers of Ten to Convert Metric Units of Measure

Caution!
Make sure you are multiplying or dividing by the correct power of ten.

Convert.

A The width of a book is about 22 cm. 22 cm = ■ mm

22 cm = (22 · 10) mm   *1 cm = 10 mm, bigger unit to smaller unit, so multiply by 10.*

22 cm = 220 mm   *Move the decimal point 1 place right.*

B A backpack has a mass of about 6 kg. 6 kg = ■ g

6 kg = (6 · 1,000) g   *1 kg = 1,000 g, bigger unit to smaller unit, so multiply by 1,000.*

6 kg = 6,000 g   *Move the decimal point 3 places right.*

C A water bottle holds about 400 mL. 400 mL = ■ L

400 mL = (400 ÷ 1,000) L   *1,000 mL = 1 L, smaller unit to bigger unit, so divide by 1,000.*

400 mL = 0.4 L   *Move the decimal point 3 places left.*

Metric Measurements		
Distance	**Mass**	**Capacity**
1 km = 1,000 m	1 kg = 1,000 g	1 L = 1,000 mL
1 m = 100 cm	1 g = 1,000 mg	
1 cm = 10 mm		

Convert metric measures by using a conversion factor or using proportions.

EXAMPLE 3 Converting Metric Units of Measure

Convert.

A Method 1: Use a conversion factor.

11 m = ■ cm   *Think: 100 cm = 1 m so use $\frac{100\ cm}{1\ m}$.*

11 m · $\frac{100\ cm}{1\ m}$ = 1,100 cm   *Multiply 11 m by the conversion factor. Cancel the common unit, m.*

B Method 2: Use proportions.

190 mL = ■ L

$\frac{190\ mL}{x\ L} = \frac{1000\ mL}{1\ L}$ *Write a proportion.*

1,000x = 190   *The cross products are equal. Divide both sides by 1,000 to undo the multiplication.*

x = 0.19 L

MATHEMATICAL PRACTICES

Think and Discuss

1. Describe how to convert 825 cm to mm.

GUIDED PRACTICE

See Example **1**   **1.** The length of a school hallway is 115 meters. How many kilometers long is the hallway?

See Example **2**   Convert.

     2. The diameter of a ceiling fan is about 95 cm. 95 cm = ◼ m

     3. A rock has a mass of about 852 g. 852 g = ◼ kg

     4. A vase holds about 1.25 L of water. 1.25 L = ◼ mL

     5. A sheet of paper has a mass of about 3.5 g. 3.5 g = ◼ mg

See Example **3**   **6.** 3 kg = ◼ g   **7.** 4.4 L = ◼ mL   **8.** 1 kg = ◼ mg

     9. 50 mm = ◼ m   **10.** 21 km = ◼ cm   **11.** 6 ml = ◼ L

INDEPENDENT PRACTICE

See Example **1**   **12.** A juice container holds 300 milliliters. How many liters of juice are in the container?

See Example **2**   Convert.

     13. A teacup holds about 110 mL. 110 mL = ◼ L

     14. The distance around a school is about 825 m. 825 m = ◼ km

     15. A chair has a mass of about 22.5 kg. 22.5 kg = ◼ g

     16. A gas tank holds about 85 L. 85 L = ◼ mL

See Example **3**   **17.** 2,460 m = ◼ km   **18.** 842 mm = ◼ cm   **19.** 9,680 mg = ◼ g

     20. 25 cm = ◼ mm   **21.** 782 g = ◼ kg   **22.** 1.2 km = ◼ m

PRACTICE AND PROBLEM SOLVING

Extra Practice

See Extra Practice for more exercises.

23. Multi-Step There are 28 L of soup in a pot. Marshall serves 400 mL in each bowl. If he fills 16 bowls, how much soup is left in the pot? Write your answer two ways: as a number of liters and as a number of milliliters.

24. Multi-Step Joanie wants to frame a rectangular picture that is 1.7 m by 0.9 m. Joanie has 500 cm of wood to use for a frame. Does Joanie have enough wood to frame the picture? Explain.

Convert.

25. $\dfrac{23{,}850 \text{ cm}}{x \text{ km}} = \dfrac{100{,}000 \text{ cm}}{1 \text{ km}}$

26. $\dfrac{350 \text{ L}}{x \text{ mL}} = \dfrac{1 \text{ L}}{1{,}000 \text{ mL}}$

27. $7 \text{ km} \cdot \dfrac{1{,}000 \text{ m}}{\text{km}} = $ ◼ m

28. $9.5 \text{ L} \cdot \dfrac{1{,}000 \text{ mL}}{\text{L}} = $ ◼ mL

Compare. Use <, >, or =.

29. 1,000 mm ▊ 1 m   **30.** 5.2 kg ▊ 60 g   **31.** 3 L ▊ 6,000 mL

32. 2 g ▊ 20,000 mg   **33.** 0.0065 m ▊ 6.5 mm   **34.** 0.1 km ▊ 10 mm

35. Multi-Step The St. Louis Gateway Arch in Missouri is about 19,200 centimeters tall. The San Jacinto Monument, outside of Houston, Texas, is about 174 m tall. Which structure is taller? by how much? Give your answer in meters.

St. Louis Gateway Arch   San Jacinto Monument

36. Critical Thinking A *millimicron* is equal to one-billionth of a meter. How many millimicrons are there in 2.5 meters?

37. What's the Error? Edgar wanted to know the mass of a package of cereal in kilograms. The label on the box says 672 g. Edgar said that the mass is 672,000 kg. Explain Edgar's error and give the correct answer.

38. Write About It Amy ran a 1,000-meter race. Explain how to find the number of centimeters in 1,000 meters.

39. Challenge The lemonade cooler at the class picnic holds 12.5 L. One liter is approximately equal to 0.26 gallons. Each plastic cup holds 7.5 fl oz. Estimate the number of cups that can be filled from the cooler.

Test Prep

40. Multiple Choice Complete the statement with the most reasonable metric unit. A snail might crawl at a rate of about 0.01 ___?___ per hour.

ⓐ mm   ⓑ m   ⓒ mL   ⓓ km

41. Extended Response Liza, Toni, and Kim used a metric scale to weigh some shells they collected at the beach. The masses of the shells were 29 g, 52 g, 18 g, 103 g, 154 g, and 96 g. What was the combined mass of the shells in kilograms? in milligrams? What is the difference in kilograms between the heaviest and lightest shells?

Area of Rectangles and Parallelograms

CC.6.G.1 Find the area of... special quadrilaterals, and polygons by composing into rectangles... apply these techniques in the context of solving real-world and mathematical problems
Also CC.6.EE.2c

Vocabulary

area

When colonists settled the land that would become the United States, ownership boundaries were sometimes natural landmarks such as rivers, trees, and hills. Landowners who wanted to know the size of their property needed to estimate the area of their land.

The **area** of a figure is the amount of surface it covers. We measure area in square units.

THE UNITED STATES
At the Close of the Revolution
Showing Western Land Claims of States
and the Boundaries fixed by Treaty of 1783
See also Table of Boundaries

EXAMPLE 1 **Estimating the Area of an Irregular Figure**

Estimate the area of the figure.

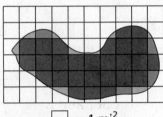

$\square$ = 1 mi^2

Count full squares: 16 red squares.

Count almost-full squares: 11 blue squares.

Count squares that are about half-full:
4 green squares ≈ 2 full squares.

Do not count almost empty yellow squares.

Add. **16 + 11 + 2 = 29**

The area of the figure is about 29 mi^2.

AREA OF A RECTANGLE

To find the area of a rectangle, multiply the length by the width.

$$A = \ell w$$
$$A = 4 \cdot 3 = 12$$

The area of the rectangle is 12 square units.

EXAMPLE 2 **Finding the Area of a Rectangle**

Find the area of the rectangle.

13 m
8 m

$A = \ell w$ *Write the formula.*
$A = 13 \cdot 8$ *Substitute 13 for ℓ and 8 for w.*
$A = 104$ *Multiply.*

The area is 104 m^2.

Video **Lesson Tutorials Online** my.hrw.com

You can use the formula for the area of a rectangle to write a formula for the area of a parallelogram. Imagine cutting off the triangle drawn in the parallelogram and sliding it to the right to form a rectangle.

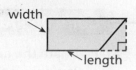

The area of a parallelogram = *bh*.   The area of a rectangle = *ℓw*.

The **base** of the parallelogram is the **length** of the rectangle.
The **height** of the parallelogram is the **width** of the rectangle.

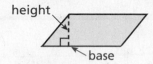 **EXAMPLE** **3** **Finding the Area of a Parallelogram**

Find the area of the parallelogram.

$3\frac{1}{2}$ in.

$2\frac{1}{3}$ in.

$A = bh$	*Write the formula.*
$A = 2\frac{1}{3} \cdot 3\frac{1}{2}$	*Substitute $2\frac{1}{3}$ for b and $3\frac{1}{2}$ for h.*
$A = \frac{7}{3} \cdot \frac{7}{2}$	*Multiply.*
$A = \frac{49}{6}$, or $8\frac{1}{6}$	*The area is $8\frac{1}{6}$ in².*

EXAMPLE **4** *Recreation Application*

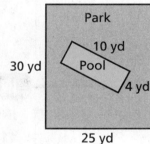

A rectangular park is made up of a rectangular spring-fed pool and a limestone picnic ground that surrounds it. The rectangular park is 30 yd by 25 yd, and the pool is 10 yd by 4 yd. What is the area of the limestone picnic ground?

To find the area of the picnic ground, subtract the area of the pool from the area of the park.

park area	–	pool area	=	picnic ground area	
(30 · 25)	–	(10 · 4)	=	*n*	*Substitute for ℓ and w in A = ℓw.*
750	–	40	=	710	*Use the order of operations.*

The area of the limestone picnic ground is 710 yd².

Think and Discuss

1. Explain how the area of a parallelogram and the area of a rectangle that have the same base and the same height are related.

2. Give a formula for the area of a square.

Learn It Online
Homework Help Online
Exercises 1–20, 25

GUIDED PRACTICE

See Example 1 — **Estimate the area of each figure.**

1.

2.

3.

See Example 2 — **Find the area of each rectangle.**

4. 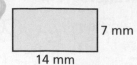 7 mm / 14 mm

5. 13 in. / 7.7 in.

6. 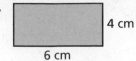 4 cm / 6 cm

See Example 3 — **Find the area of each parallelogram.**

7. 4 ft / 12 ft

8. $2\frac{1}{3}$ cm 9 cm

9. 2.5 in. / 4 in.

See Example 4 — 10. Mindy is designing a rectangular fountain in a courtyard. The rest of the courtyard will be covered with stone. The rectangular courtyard is 12 ft by 15 ft. What is the area of the courtyard that will be covered with stone?

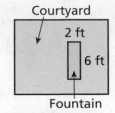
Courtyard / 2 ft / 6 ft / Fountain

INDEPENDENT PRACTICE

See Example 1 — **Estimate the area of each figure.**

11.

12.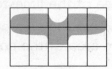

13.

See Example 2 — **Find the area of each rectangle.**

14. 5 mi / 25 mi

15. 1.5 m / 8.5 m

16. 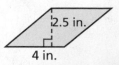 2 cm / 12 cm

See Example 3 — **Find the area of each parallelogram.**

17. 13 ft / 20 ft

18. 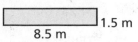 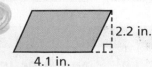 2.2 in. / 4.1 in.

19. 0.5 cm / 1.5 cm

See Example 4 — 20. Bob is planting in a rectangular container. In the center of the container, he places a smaller rectangular tub with mint. The tub is 8 in. by 3 in. He plants flowers around the tub. What is the area of the container planted with flowers?

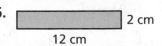
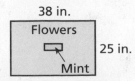
38 in. / Flowers / 25 in. / Mint

Extra Practice

See Extra Practice for more exercises.

Iceland has many active volcanoes and frequent earthquakes. There are more hot springs in Iceland than in any other country in the world.

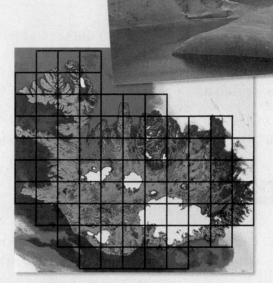

Use the map for Exercises 21 and 22.

21. **Choose a Strategy** One square on the map represents 1,700 km². Which is a reasonable estimate for the area of Iceland?

   Ⓐ Less than 65,000 km²

   Ⓑ Between 90,000 and 105,000 km²

   Ⓒ Between 120,000 and 135,000 km²

   Ⓓ Greater than 150,000 km²

22. **Estimation** About 10% of the area of Iceland is covered with glaciers. Estimate the area covered by glaciers.

23. **Write About It** The House is Iceland's oldest building. When it was built in 1765, the builders measured length in *ells*. The base of the House is 14 ells wide and 20 ells long. Explain how to find the area in ells of the House.

24. **Challenge** The length of one ell varied from country to country. In England, one ell was equal to $1\frac{1}{4}$ yd. Suppose the House were measured in English ells. Find the area in yards of the House.

Test Prep

25. **Multiple Choice** A small square is inside a larger square. The larger square is 14 feet long. The smaller square is 2 feet long. What is the area of the shaded region?

   14 ft

   ☐ 2 ft

   Ⓐ 52 ft²   Ⓑ 192 ft²   Ⓒ 196 ft²   Ⓓ 200 ft²

26. **Multiple Choice** Find the area of a rectangle with length 3 in. and width 12 in.

   Ⓕ 9 in²   Ⓖ 18 in²   Ⓗ 36 in²   Ⓙ 144 in²

Hands-on LAB

Squares and Square Roots

Use with Area of Rectangles and Parallelograms

Learn It Online
Lab Resources Online

MATHEMATICAL PRACTICES Use appropriate tools strategically.

VOCABULARY
• perfect square
• square root

WHAT YOU NEED
• grid paper

When a number is raised to the second power, or multiplied by itself, we say that it is squared. Because the length of any two sides of a square are equal, the area of any square can be written as $x \cdot x$, or x^2.

You can use grid paper to model the relationship between the area of a square and the length of its sides.

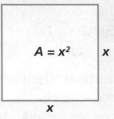

$A = x^2$

Activity

➊ Use grid paper to copy the figures below. When you have copied these figures, continue the pattern until you have drawn 10 figures.

Figure 1   Figure 2   Figure 3

➋ Use your drawings to complete the table.

Area of Figure (units²)	Side Length of Figure (units)
1	1
4	2
9	
16	
25	
36	

The numbers 1, 4, 9, 16, 25, and 36 are called *perfect squares*. A perfect square is the square of a whole number.

3 When the area of a square is 4, the side length is 2. Because $2^2 = 4$, we call 2 a *square root* of 4. This is written as $\sqrt{4}$.
Use your drawings to find $\sqrt{49}$, $\sqrt{64}$, $\sqrt{81}$, and $\sqrt{100}$. Record your results in the table.

Number	Square Root
49	■
64	■
81	■
100	■

Think and Discuss

1. Why do you think squaring 3 and finding $\sqrt{9}$ are called inverse operations?
2. Explain why the square root of 12 is not a whole number.
3. Can the area of any rectangle be found by squaring one of the sides? Explain.

Try This

Find the side length of each square. Explain how you found your answer.

1.
Area = 121 units^2

2.
Area = 144 units^2

3.
Area = 196 units^2

4.
Area = 225 units^2

5.
Area = 361 units^2

6.
Area = 400 units^2

Complete each equation.

7. $\sqrt{■} = 13$ 8. $\sqrt{■} = 16$ 9. $\sqrt{■} = 18$

10. Find two perfect squares whose sum is 100.

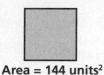

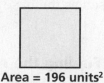

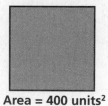

Area of Triangles and Trapezoids

COMMON CORE

CC.6.G.1 Find the area of right triangles, other triangles, special quadrilaterals, and polygons by composing into rectangles or decomposing into triangles and other shapes; apply these techniques in the context of solving real-world and mathematical problems

The Flatiron Building in New York City was built in 1902. Many people consider it to be New York's first skyscraper. The foundation of the building is shaped like a triangle. You can find the area of the triangle to find how much land the building occupies.

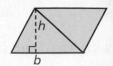

You can divide any parallelogram into two congruent triangles. The area of each triangle is half the area of the parallelogram.

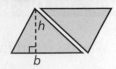

AREA OF A TRIANGLE

The area A of a triangle is half the product of its base b and its height h.

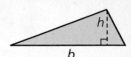

$A = \frac{1}{2}bh$

When the legs of a triangle meet at a 90° angle, the lengths of the legs can be used as the base and height.

EXAMPLE 1 Finding the Area of a Triangle

Find the area of each triangle.

Reading Math

An altitude of a triangle is a perpendicular segment from one vertex to the line containing the opposite side. The length of the altitude is the height.

A

8 cm

12 cm

$A = \frac{1}{2}bh$	Write the formula.
$A = \frac{1}{2}(12 \cdot 8)$	Substitute 12 for b. Substitute 8 for h.
$A = \frac{1}{2}(96)$	Multiply.
$A = 48$	

The area is 48 cm².

B

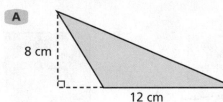

$4\frac{1}{2}$ yd

6 yd

$A = \frac{1}{2}bh$	Write the formula.
$A = \frac{1}{2}\left(6 \cdot 4\frac{1}{2}\right)$	Substitute 6 for b. Substitute $4\frac{1}{2}$ for h.
$A = \frac{1}{2}(27)$	Multiply.
$A = 13\frac{1}{2}$	

The area is $13\frac{1}{2}$ yd².

Raymond Patrick/Taxi/Getty Images

EXAMPLE 2

Architecture Application

The diagram shows the outline of the foundation of the Flatiron Building. What is the area of the foundation?

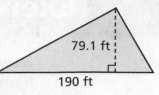

79.1 ft

190 ft

$A = \frac{1}{2}bh$ *Write the formula.*

$A = \frac{1}{2}(190 \cdot 79.1)$ *Substitute 190 for b. Substitute 79.1 for h.*

$A = \frac{1}{2}(15{,}029) = 7{,}514.5$ *Multiply.*

The area of the foundation is 7,514.5 ft².

You can divide a parallelogram into two congruent trapezoids. The area of each trapezoid is half the area of the parallelogram.

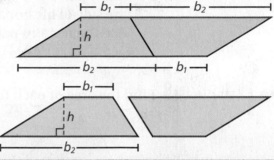

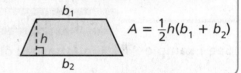

AREA OF A TRAPEZOID

The area A of a trapezoid is half the product of its height h and the sum of its bases b_1 and b_2.

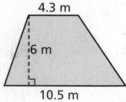

$$A = \frac{1}{2}h(b_1 + b_2)$$

EXAMPLE 3

Finding the Area of a Trapezoid

Find the area of the trapezoid.

4.3 m

6 m

10.5 m

$A = \frac{1}{2}h(b_1 + b_2)$ *Write the formula.*

$A = \frac{1}{2}(6)(4.3 + 10.5)$ *Substitute 6 for h, 4.3 for b_1, and 10.5 for b_2.*

$A = \frac{1}{2}(6)(14.8) = 44.4$ *Multiply.*

The area is 44.4 m².

MATHEMATICAL PRACTICES

Think and Discuss

1. **Explain** how the areas of a triangle and a parallelogram with the same base and height are related.

2. **Explain** whether this is correct: To find the area of a trapezoid, multiply the height by the top base and the height by the bottom base. Then add the two numbers together and divide the sum by 2.

GUIDED PRACTICE

See Example **1** Find the area of each triangle.

1.

2 yd
3 yd

2.

11 cm
6 cm

3.
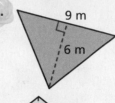
9 m
6 m

See Example **2** **4.** Harry plans to paint the triangular portion of the side of his house. How many square feet does he need to paint?

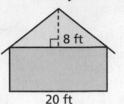
8 ft
20 ft

See Example **3** Find the area of each trapezoid.

5.
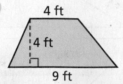
4 ft
4 ft
9 ft

6.
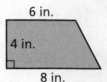
6 in.
4 in.
8 in.

7.

15 cm
8 cm
7 cm

INDEPENDENT PRACTICE

See Example **1** Find the area of each triangle.

8.

8 m
9.25 m

9.
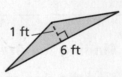
1 ft
6 ft

10.

5 yd
6 yd

See Example **2** **11.** Sean is making pennants for the school football team. How many square inches of felt does he use for one pennant?

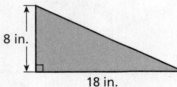
8 in.
18 in.

12. Erin has a triangular garden plot that is 5 meters long and 3 meters tall. What is the area of the plot?

See Example **3** Find the area of each trapezoid.

13.

2 yd
4 yd
6 yd

14.

16 in.
12 in.
21 in.

15.
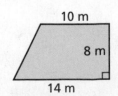
10 m
8 m
14 m

PRACTICE AND PROBLEM SOLVING

Extra Practice
See Extra Practice for more exercises.

16. The water in a drainage canal is 4 feet deep. What is the area of a cross section of the water in the ditch, which is shaped like a trapezoid?

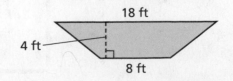
18 ft
4 ft
8 ft

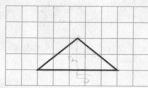

Social Studies

Nevada has many ghost towns scattered around the state. Many were once boom-towns built during the gold and silver mining rush.

For Exercises 17–21, find the area of each figure.

17.

18.

19.

20. triangle: $b = 2\frac{1}{2}$ in.; $h = 1\frac{3}{4}$ in. 21. trapezoid: $b_1 = 18$ m; $b_2 = 27$ m; $h = 15.4$ m

22. **Social Studies** The shape of the state of Nevada is similar to a trapezoid with the measurements shown. Estimate the area of the state in square miles.

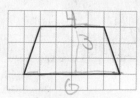

320 mi
198 mi
490 mi

23. **Critical Thinking** The areas and heights of a triangle and a rectangle are the same. How do the lengths of their bases compare?

Find the missing measurement for each figure.

24. Area = 16 in²

3 in.
h
5 in.

25. Area = 5 cm²

2 cm
b

26. Area = 18 m²

h
6 m

27. **Write a Problem** Write a problem about a trapezoid with bases 12 ft and 18 ft and height 10 ft.

28. **Write About It** Two triangles have the same base. The height of one triangle is half the height of the other. How do the areas of the triangles compare?

29. **Challenge** Find the area of the unshaded portion of the trapezoid.

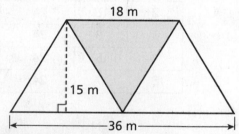

18 m
15 m
36 m

Test Prep

30. **Multiple Choice** A building sign in the shape of a trapezoid has the measurements shown. Which expression can be used to find the area of the sign?

10 ft
11 ft
18 ft

Ⓐ $\frac{1}{2}(11)(10 + 18)$ Ⓑ $\frac{1}{2}(18)(10)$ Ⓒ $\frac{1}{2}(11)(10)(18)$ Ⓓ $(11)(10 + 18)$

31. **Short Response** Find the area of a right triangle with legs measuring 14 cm and 25 cm.

Hands-on LAB

Explore Perimeter and Area

Use with Area of Triangles and Trapezoids

Learn It Online
Lab Resources Online

Use appropriate tools strategically.

WHAT YOU NEED:
- 1-inch grid paper
- corkboard
- 30-inch piece of string
- 4 push pins

REMEMBER

$P = 2l + 2w$

$A = lw$

Attach 1-inch grid paper to a piece of corkboard. Then use string and push pins to model the relationship between perimeters and areas.

Activity

1 Set push pins at grid intersections to model the first rectangle in the table below.

2 Use the string to measure the perimeter. Multiply to find the area of the rectangle. Model each of the rectangles in the table below and record its perimeter and area.

Length	Width	Perimeter (in.)	Area (in²)
2	10	24	20
3	9	24	27
4	8	24	32
5	7	24	35

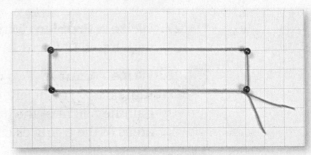

3 Use push pins to model rectangles with the dimensions in the table below. Use the string to measure the perimeters. Multiply to find the areas. Record your results in the table below.

Length	Width	Perimeter (in.)	Area (in²)
1	12	26	12
2	6	16	12
3	4	14	12

Think and Discuss

1. Compare the perimeters and areas of each rectangle in the first table.

2. Compare the perimeters and areas of each rectangle in the second table.

Try This

1. List all the whole-number dimensions of rectangles with a perimeter of 16 inches.

2. List all the whole-number dimensions of rectangles with an area of 18 square inches.

Victoria Smith/HMH

8-5 Area of Composite Figures

CC.6.G.1 Find the area of… polygons by… decomposing into… other shapes

You can find the areas of irregular polygons by breaking them apart into rectangles, parallelograms, and triangles.

EXAMPLE 1 Finding Areas of Composite Figures

Find the area of each polygon.

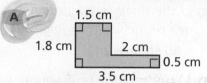

Think: Break the polygon apart into rectangles.

Helpful Hint

In Example 1A, the figure could be broken apart as follows.

1.5 cm
1.3 cm
0.5 cm
3.5 cm

The area is the same.

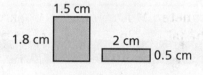

Find the area of each rectangle.

$A = \ell w$ $A = \ell w$ *Write the formula for the area of a rectangle.*

$A = 1.8 \cdot 1.5$ $A = 2 \cdot 0.5$

$A = 2.7$ $A = 1$

$2.7 + 1 = 3.7$ *Add to find the total area.*

The area of the polygon is 3.7 cm^2.

B

13 cm
8 cm
10 cm

Think: Break the figure apart into a triangle and a rectangle.

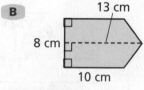

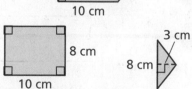

$A = \ell w$ $A = \frac{1}{2}bh$ *Find the area of each polygon.*

$A = 8 \cdot 10$ $A = \frac{1}{2} \cdot 8 \cdot 3$

$A = 80$ $A = 12$

$80 + 12 = 92$ *Add to find the total area of the figure.*

The area of the figure is 92 cm^2.

EXAMPLE 2

Art Application

Helpful Hint

You can also count the squares and multiply by the area of one square.
1 square = 4 square units
17 · 4 = 68 square units

Stan made a wall hanging. Use the coordinate grid to find its area.

Think: Divide the wall hanging into rectangles.

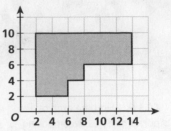

Find the area of each rectangle.

Rectangle 1
$\ell = 8$, $w = 4$; $A = 8 \cdot 4 = 32$

Rectangle 2
$\ell = 6$, $w = 2$; $A = 6 \cdot 2 = 12$

Rectangle 3
$\ell = 4$, $w = 6$; $A = 4 \cdot 6 = 24$

Add the areas of the three rectangles to find the total area of the wall hanging.

$32 + 12 + 24 = 68$ square units

The area of the wall hanging is 68 square units.

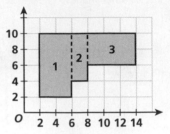

MATHEMATICAL PRACTICES

Think and Discuss

1. Explain how you can find the area of a regular octagon by breaking it apart into congruent triangles, if you know the area of one triangle.

2. Explain another way that you can divide the wall hanging in Example 2.

8-5 Exercises

Learn It Online
Homework Help Online
Exercises 1–6, 11

GUIDED PRACTICE

See Example **1** **Find the area of each polygon.**

1.
20 m
70 m
50 m
90 m

2. 10.2 cm
1 cm
1.8 cm
1 cm
5.4 cm

See Example **2** **3.** Gina used tiles to create a design. Use the coordinate grid to find the area of Gina's design.

Video **Lesson Tutorials Online** my.hrw.com

See Example **1** **Find the area of each polygon.**

4.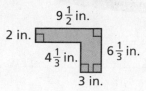
9½ in.
2 in.
4⅓ in.
6⅓ in.
3 in.

5.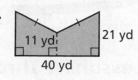
11 yd   21 yd
40 yd

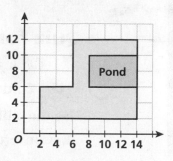
12
10
8   Pond
6
4
2
O   2 4 6 8 10 12 14

See Example **2** **6.** Edgar plants daffodils around a rectangular pond. The yellow part of the diagram shows where the daffodils are planted. Use the coordinate grid to find the area of the yellow part of the diagram.

Extra Practice

See Extra Practice for more exercises.

7. Social Studies The map shows the approximate dimensions of the state of South Australia, outlined in red.

a. Estimate the area of the state of South Australia.

b. The total area of Australia is about 7.7 million km². About what fraction of the total area of Australia is the area of the state of South Australia?

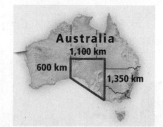
Australia
1,100 km
600 km
1,350 km

8. Write About It Draw a figure that can be broken up into two rectangles. Label the lengths of each side. Explain how you can find the area of the figure. Then find the area.

9. Challenge The perimeter of the figure is 42.5 cm. Find the area of this figure.

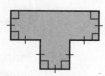

Test Prep

10. Multiple Choice What is the area of the polygon?

(F) 40 cm²   (G) 65 cm²   (H) 45 cm²   (J) 90 cm²

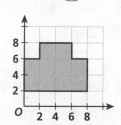
9 cm
4 cm
10 cm

11. Gridded Response Use the coordinate grid to find the area, in square units, of the polygon.

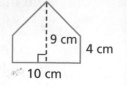
8
6
4
2
O   2 4 6 8

Ready To Go On?

Learn It Online
Resources Online

Quiz for Lessons 1 Through 5

✓ **1** **Converting Customary Units**

Use the table for Exercises 1 and 2.

1. Convert Ty's length to feet and inches.

2. How many ounces does Ty weigh?

Baby Ty Rodriguez	
Birth Date	July 8, 2005, 11:50 P.M.
Weight	9 lb 8 oz
Length	$21\frac{1}{2}$ in.

✓ **2** **Converting Metric Units**

Convert.

3. 8 m = ⬛ cm

4. 12 kg = ⬛ g

5. 2,000 mL = ⬛ L

✓ **3** **Area of Rectangles and Parallelograms**

Find the area of each figure.

6.
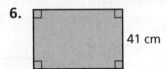
41 cm
62 cm

7.
$2\frac{1}{4}$ ft
$5\frac{1}{3}$ ft

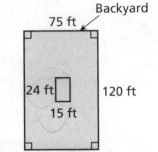
Backyard
75 ft
24 ft 120 ft
15 ft

8. Mark is making a rectangular vegetable garden in his backyard. The rest of the backyard is covered with gravel. What is the area of the backyard that is covered with gravel?

✓ **4** **Area of Triangles and Trapezoids**

Find the area of each figure.

9.
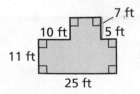
2 cm
3 cm

10.
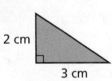
4.5 ft
3 ft
7.5 ft

11.
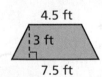
5.8 m
8 m

✓ **5** **Area of Composite Figures**

12. Find the area of the polygon.

7 ft
10 ft 5 ft
11 ft
25 ft

13. Using the approximate dimensions, estimate the area of the state of Oklahoma.

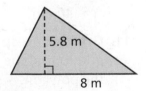
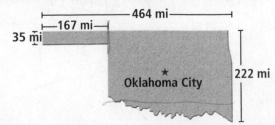
464 mi
167 mi
35 mi
222 mi
Oklahoma City

Focus on Problem Solving

Solve

• **Choose the operation**

Read the whole problem before you try to solve it. Determine what action is taking place in the problem. Then decide whether you need to add, subtract, multiply, or divide in order to solve the problem.

Action	Operation
Combining or putting together	Add
Removing or taking away Comparing or finding the difference	Subtract
Combining equal groups	Multiply
Sharing equally or separating into equal groups	Divide

 Read each problem and determine the action taking place. Choose an operation, and then solve the problem.

❶ There are 3 lily ponds in the botanical gardens. They are identical in size and shape. The total area of the ponds is 165 ft². What is the area of each lily pond?

❷ The greenhouse is made up of 6 rectangular rooms with an area of 4,800 ft² each. What is the total area of the greenhouse?

❸ A shady area with 17 different varieties of magnolia trees, which bloom from March to June, surrounds the plaza in Magnolia Park. In the center of the plaza, there is a circular bed of shrubs as shown in the chart. If the total area of the park is 625 ft², what is the area of the plaza?

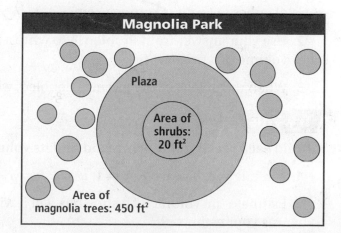

Magnolia Park

Plaza

Area of shrubs: 20 ft²

Area of magnolia trees: 450 ft²

Hands-on LAB — Explore Volume of Prisms

Use with Volume of Prisms

REMEMBER
- Volume is the number of cubic units needed to fill a space.

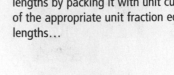

Use appropriate tools strategically.

CC.6.G.2 Find the volume of a right rectangular prism with fractional edge lengths by packing it with unit cubes of the appropriate unit fraction edge lengths…

You can use centimeter cubes to help you find the volume of a *prism*.

Activity 1

Use the steps and diagrams below to fill in the table.

	Length (ℓ)	Width (w)	Height (h)	Total Number of Cubes (V)
Figure A	⬛	⬛	⬛	⬛
Figure B	⬛	⬛	⬛	⬛
Figure C	⬛	⬛	⬛	⬛

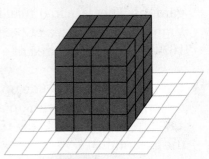

Figure A

Figure B

Figure C

❶ Draw a 4 × 3 rectangle on centimeter graph paper. Place centimeter cubes on the rectangle *(Figure A)*. How many cubes did you use? What is the height of this prism?

❷ Make a prism that is 2 units tall *(Figure B)*. How many cubes did you use?

❸ Make a prism that is 5 units tall *(Figure C)*. How many cubes did you use?

Think and Discuss

1. How can you use the length, width, and height of a prism to find the total number of cubes without counting them?

2. Use your answer from Problem 1 to write a formula for the volume of a prism.

3. When the height of the prism is doubled, what happens to the volume?

Try This

Build each rectangular prism and find its volume.

1. ℓ = 4; w = 2; h = 3   2. ℓ = 1; w = 4; h = 5   3. ℓ = 3; w = 3; h = 3   4. ℓ = 5; w = 10; h = 2

5. Estimate the volume of a shoe box. Fill it with centimeter cubes. How close was your estimate?

You can use centimeter cubes to help you find the volume of a prism with fractional edge lengths.

Activity 2

1 Use a centimeter cube to represent a cube with edge length $\frac{1}{3}$ meter. Calculate the volume of the cube in cubic meters (m³) by multiplying the length, width, and height.

$\frac{1}{3}$ m
$\frac{1}{3}$ m
$\frac{1}{3}$ m

Length (ℓ)	Width (w)	Height (h)	Volume (V)
$\frac{1}{3}$ m	$\frac{1}{3}$ m	$\frac{1}{3}$ m	▮ m³

2 Use the $\frac{1}{3}$-m cubes to build a prism that is 3 cubes by 4 cubes by 5 cubes. How many cubes are in this prism?

3 Find the volume of the prism in cubic meters by multiplying the number of cubes by the volume of one cube.

Number of Cubes	Volume of Cube	Volume of Prism
▮	▮ m³	▮ m³

4 Is the volume of the prism that you found in Step 3 equal to the length, width, and height multiplied together? Complete the table to find out.

Length (ℓ)	Width (w)	Height (h)	Volume (V)
$3 \times \frac{1}{3}$-m cube	$4 \times \frac{1}{3}$-m cube	$5 \times \frac{1}{3}$-m cube	ℓwh
▮ m	▮ m	▮ m	▮ m³

Think and Discuss

1. Does the formula for the volume of a prism work when the edges of the prism have fractional lengths? Discuss.

2. How many cubes of edge length $\frac{1}{2}$ meter will fit into a cube of edge length 1 meter?

Try This

Find the volume of the prism from its length (ℓ), width (w), and height (h).

1. $\ell = 1$ unit, $w = \frac{1}{2}$ unit, $h = 3\frac{1}{2}$ units

2. $\ell = 4.5$ m, $w = 2.8$ m, $h = 3.9$ m

3. $\ell = 8\frac{1}{3}$ cm, $w = 2$ cm, $h = \frac{1}{3}$ cm

COMMON CORE

CC.6.G.2 ...Apply the formulas $V = lwh$ and $V = bh$ to find volumes of right rectangular prisms with fractional edge lengths in the context of solving real-world and mathematical problems **Also CC.6.EE.2c**

Interactivities Online ▶

Vocabulary

volume

Volume is the number of cubic units needed to fill a space.

You need 10, or 5 · 2, centimeter cubes to cover the bottom of this rectangular prism.

You need 3 layers of 10 cubes each to fill the prism. It takes 30, or 5 · 2 · 3, cubes.

Volume is expressed in cubic units, so the volume of the prism is 5 cm · 2 cm · 3 cm = 30 cubic centimeters, or 30 cm³.

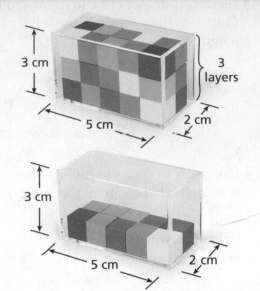

EXAMPLE 1 **Finding the Volume of a Rectangular Prism**

Find the volume of the rectangular prism.

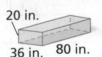

20 in.
36 in.   80 in.

$V = \ell wh$	*Write the formula.*
$V = 80 \cdot 36 \cdot 20$	$\ell = 80; w = 36; h = 20$
$V = 57{,}600 \text{ in}^3$	*Multiply.*

To find the volume of any prism, you can use the formula $V = Bh$, where B is the area of the base, and h is the prism's height.

EXAMPLE 2 **Finding the Volume of a Triangular Prism**

Find the volume of each triangular prism.

A

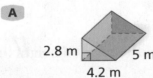

2.8 m   5 m
4.2 m

$V = Bh$	*Write the formula.*
$V = \left(\frac{1}{2} \cdot 2.8 \cdot 4.2\right) \cdot 5$	$B = \frac{1}{2} \cdot 2.8 \cdot 4.2; h = 5$
$V = 29.4 \text{ m}^3$	*Multiply.*

Caution!

The bases of a prism are always two congruent, parallel polygons.

B

4.3 ft
9 ft   8.2 ft

$V = Bh$	*Write the formula.*
$V = \left(\frac{1}{2} \cdot 8.2 \cdot 4.3\right) \cdot 9$	$B = \frac{1}{2} \cdot 8.2 \cdot 4.3; h = 9$
$V = 158.67 \text{ ft}^3$	*Multiply.*

EXAMPLE 3 **PROBLEM SOLVING APPLICATION**

A toy maker ships 12 alphabet blocks in a box. What are the possible dimensions for a box of the alphabet blocks?

MATHEMATICAL PRACTICES Make sense of problems and persevere in solving them.

1 Understand the Problem

The **answer** will be all possible dimensions for a box of 12 cubic blocks.

List the **important information:**

- There are 12 blocks in a box.
- The blocks are cubic, or square prisms.

2 Make a Plan

You can make models using cubes to find the possible dimensions for a box of 12 blocks.

3 Solve

Make different arrangements of 12 cubes.

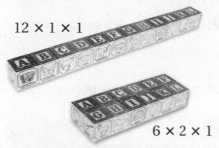

12 × 1 × 1

6 × 2 × 1

4 × 3 × 1

3 × 2 × 2

The possible dimensions for a box of 12 alphabet blocks are the following: 12 × 1 × 1, 4 × 3 × 1, 6 × 2 × 1, and 3 × 2 × 2.

4 Look Back

Notice that each dimension is a factor of 12. Also, the product of the dimensions (length · width · height) is 12, showing that the volume of each case is 12 cubes.

MATHEMATICAL PRACTICES

Think and Discuss

1. **Explain** how to find the height of a rectangular prism if you know its length, width, and volume.

2. **Describe** the difference between the units used to measure perimeter, area, and volume.

(all) Victoria Smith/HMH

GUIDED PRACTICE

See Example **1** Find the volume of each rectangular prism.

1.
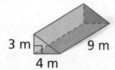
2 cm, 9 cm, 9 cm

2.
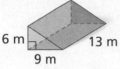
4 in., 4 in., 4 in.

3.
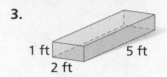
1 ft, 5 ft, 2 ft

See Example **2** Find the volume of each triangular prism.

4.
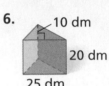
6 m, 13 m, 9 m

5.
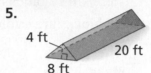
4 ft, 20 ft, 8 ft

6.
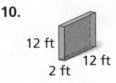
10 dm, 20 dm, 25 dm

See Example **3** **7.** A toy company packs 10 cubic boxes of toys in a case. What are the possible dimensions for a case of toys?

INDEPENDENT PRACTICE

See Example **1** Find the volume of each rectangular prism.

8.
$2\frac{1}{2}$ in., 8 in., $2\frac{1}{2}$ in.

9.
3.2 in., 7.75 in., 3.2 in.

10.
12 ft, 12 ft, 2 ft

See Example **2** Find the volume of each triangular prism.

11.
3 m, 9 m, 4 m

12.
$2\frac{1}{2}$ cm, 8 cm, $8\frac{3}{4}$ cm

13.
4.5 ft, 3.75 ft, 8.5 ft

See Example **3** **14.** A printing company packs 18 cubic boxes of business cards in a larger shipping box. What are the possible dimensions for the shipping box?

PRACTICE AND PROBLEM SOLVING

Extra Practice
See Extra Practice for more exercises.

Find the volume of each figure.

15.
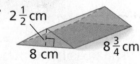
8 in., 6 in., 10 in.

16.
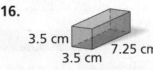
3.5 cm, 3.5 cm, 7.25 cm

17.

7.5 km, 11.5 km, 11 km

Find the missing measurement for each prism.

18. $\ell = \underline{\quad?\quad}$; $w = 25$ m; $h = 4$ m; $V = 300$ m^3

19. $\ell = 9$ ft; $w = \underline{\quad?\quad}$; $h = 5$ ft; $V = 900$ ft^3

20. $B = 9.28$ in.; $h = \underline{\quad?\quad}$; $V = 55.68$ in^3

The density of a substance is a measure of its mass per unit of volume. The density of a particular substance is always the same. The formula for density D is the mass m of a substance divided by its volume V, or $D = \frac{m}{V}$.

21. Find the volume of each substance in the table.

22. Calculate the density of each substance.

23. Water has a density of 1 g/cm³. A substance whose density is less than that of water will float. Which of the substances in the table will float in water?

24. A fresh egg has a density of approximately 1.2 g/cm³. A spoiled egg has a density of about 0.9 g/cm³. How can you tell whether an egg is fresh without cracking it open?

25. **Multi-Step** Alicia has a solid rectangular prism of a substance she believes is gold. The dimensions of the prism are 2 cm by 1 cm by 2 cm, and the mass is 20.08 g. Is the substance that Alicia has gold? Explain.

26. ✐ **Write About It** In a science lab, you are given a prism of copper. You determine that its dimensions are 4 cm, 2 cm, and 6 cm. Without weighing the prism, how can you determine its mass? Explain your answer.

27. ⭐ **Challenge** A solid rectangular prism of silver has a mass of 84 g. What are some possible dimensions of the prism?

Rectangular Prisms				
Substance	Length (cm)	Width (cm)	Height (cm)	Mass (g)
Copper	2	1	5	89.6
Gold	$\frac{2}{3}$	$\frac{3}{4}$	2	19.32
Iron pyrite	0.25	2	7	17.57
Pine	10	10	3	120
Silver	2.5	4	2	210

Test Prep

28. **Multiple Choice** A rectangular prism has a volume of 1,080 ft³. The height of the prism is 8 ft, and the width is 9 ft. What is the length of the prism?

    Ⓐ 15 ft   Ⓑ 120 ft   Ⓒ 135 ft   Ⓓ 77,760 ft

29. **Gridded Response** The dimensions of a rectangular prism are 4.3 inches, 12 inches, and 1.5 inches. What is the volume, in cubic inches, of the prism?

Model Three-Dimensional Figures

Use with Surface Area

You can build a solid figure by cutting its faces from paper, taping them together, and then folding them to form the solid. A pattern of shapes that can be folded to form a solid figure is called a *net*.

MATHEMATICAL PRACTICES **Use appropriate tools strategically.**
CC.6.G.4 Represent three-dimensional figures using nets made up of rectangles and triangles, and use the nets to find the surface area of these figures...

Activity

1 To make a pattern for a rectangular prism follow the steps below.

   a. Draw the following rectangles and cut them out:

   Two 2 in. × 3 in. rectangles

   Two 1 in. × 3 in. rectangles

   Two 1 in. × 2 in. rectangles

   b. Tape the pieces together to form the prism.

   c. Remove the tape from some of the edges so that the pattern lies flat.

2 Create a net for a cylinder.

   Think: What shapes can make a cylinder?

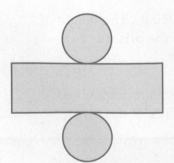

   If a cylinder is "unfolded," the bases of the cylinder are circles, and the curved surface is a rectangle.

The net is made up of two circles and a rectangle.

3 Create a net for a square pyramid.

Think: What shapes can make a square pyramid?

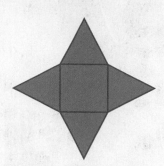

If the square pyramid is "unfolded," the base is a square, and the lateral faces are triangles.

The net is made up of a square and four triangles.

Think and Discuss

1. Compare the nets for a rectangular prism and a cube.

2. Tell what shapes will always appear in a net for a triangular pyramid.

3. Tell what shapes will always appear in a net for a hexagonal prism.

Try This

Tell whether each net can be folded to form a cube. If not, explain.

1.

2.

3.

4.

Name the three-dimensional figure that can be formed from each net.

5.

6.

7. Create a net for a cone.

Surface Area

CC.6.G.4 Represent three-dimensional figures using nets… and use the nets to find the surface area of these figures. Apply these techniques in the context of solving real-world and mathematical problems

Vocabulary

surface area

net

The amount of wrapping paper needed to cover a present depends on the surface area of the present.

The **surface area** of a three-dimensional figure is the sum of the areas of its surfaces. To help you see all the surfaces of a three-dimensional figure, you can use a *net*. A **net** is the pattern made when the surface of a three-dimensional figure is layed out flat showing each face of the figure.

EXAMPLE 1

Interactivities Online ▶

Finding the Surface Area of a Prism

Find the surface area *S* of each prism.

A Method 1: Use a net.

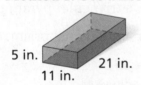

5 in.
11 in.
21 in.

Draw a net to help you see each face of the prism.

Use the formula $A = \ell w$ to find the area of each face.

A: $A = 11 \times 5 = 55$
B: $A = 21 \times 11 = 231$
C: $A = 21 \times 5 = 105$
D: $A = 21 \times 11 = 231$
E: $A = 21 \times 5 = 105$
F: $A = 11 \times 5 = 55$

$S = 55 + 231 + 105 + 231 + 105 + 55 = 782$ *Add the areas of each face.*

The surface area is 782 in².

B Method 2: Use a three-dimensional drawing.

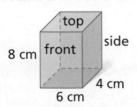

top
front
side
8 cm
4 cm
6 cm

Find the area of the front, top, and side, and multiply each by 2 to include the opposite faces.

Front: $6 \times 8 = 48 \longrightarrow 48 \times 2 = 96$
Top: $6 \times 4 = 24 \longrightarrow 24 \times 2 = 48$
Side: $4 \times 8 = 32 \longrightarrow 32 \times 2 = 64$

$S = 96 + 48 + 64 = 208$ *Add the areas of the faces.*

The surface area is 208 cm².

Video **Lesson Tutorials Online** my.hrw.com

The surface area of a pyramid equals the sum of the area of the base and the areas of the triangular faces. To find the surface area of a pyramid, think of its net.

EXAMPLE 2

Finding the Surface Area of a Pyramid

Find the surface area S of the pyramid.

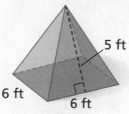

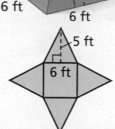

$S =$ area of square $+ 4 \times$ (area of triangular face)

$S = s^2 + 4 \times \left(\frac{1}{2}bh\right)$

$S = 6^2 + 4 \times \left(\frac{1}{2} \times 6 \times 5\right)$ *Substitute.*

$S = 36 + 4 \times 15$

$S = 36 + 60$

$S = 96$

The surface area is 96 ft².

The surface area of a cylinder equals the sum of the area of its bases and the area of its curved surface.

EXAMPLE 3

Finding the Surface Area of a Cylinder

Find the surface area S of the cylinder. Use 3.14 for π, and round to the nearest hundredth.

Helpful Hint

To find the area of the curved surface of a cylinder, multiply its height by the circumference of the base.

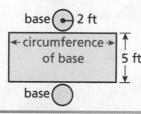

$S =$ area of curved surface $+ 2 \times$ (area of each base)

$S = h \times (2\pi r) + 2 \times (\pi r^2)$

$S = 5 \times (2 \times \pi \times 2) + 2 \times (\pi \times 2^2)$ *Substitute.*

$S = 5 \times 4\pi + 2 \times 4\pi$

$S \approx 5 \times 4(3.14) + 2 \times 4(3.14)$ *Use 3.14 for π.*

$S \approx 5 \times 12.56 + 2 \times 12.56$

$S \approx 62.8 + 25.12$

$S \approx 87.92$

The surface area is about 87.92 ft².

Think and Discuss

1. Describe how to find the surface area of a pentagonal prism.

2. Tell how to find the surface area of a cube if you know the area of one face.

GUIDED PRACTICE

See Example 1   Find the surface area *S* of each prism.

1.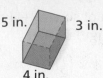
5 in.   3 in.
4 in.

2.
4 m
8 m
2 m

3.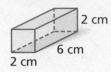
2 cm
6 cm
2 cm

See Example 2   Find the surface area *S* of each pyramid.

4.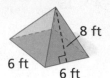
8 ft
6 ft   6 ft

5.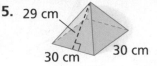
29 cm
30 cm
30 cm

6.
3 m
2 m
2 m

See Example 3   Find the surface area *S* of each cylinder. Use 3.14 for π, and round to the nearest hundredth.

7.
4 ft
9 ft

8.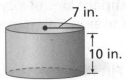
7 in.
10 in.

9.
6 m
4 m

INDEPENDENT PRACTICE

See Example 1   Find the surface area *S* of each prism.

10.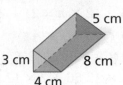
5 cm
3 cm   8 cm
4 cm

11.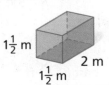
$1\frac{1}{2}$ m
2 m
$1\frac{1}{2}$ m

12.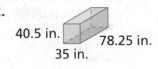
40.5 in.   78.25 in.
35 in.

See Example 2   Find the surface area *S* of each pyramid.

13.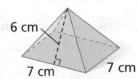
6 cm
7 cm   7 cm

14.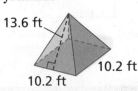
13.6 ft
10.2 ft
10.2 ft

15.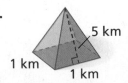
5 km
1 km   1 km

See Example 3   Find the surface area *S* of each cylinder. Use 3.14 for π, and round to the nearest hundredth.

16.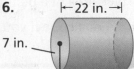
|← 22 in. →|
7 in.

17.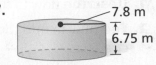
7.8 m
6.75 m

18.
$1\frac{3}{4}$ in.
$9\frac{3}{4}$ in.

Architecture

I. M. Pei is the architect of the pyramid-shaped addition to the Louvre in Paris, France.

19. You are designing a container for oatmeal. Your first design is a rectangular prism with a height of 12 in., a width of 8 in., and a depth of 3 in.

   a. What is the surface area of the package?

   b. You redesign the package as a cylinder with the same surface area as the prism from part **a**. If the radius of the cylinder is 2 in., what is the height of the cylinder? Round to the nearest tenth of an inch.

20. Architecture The entrance to the Louvre Museum is a glass-paned square pyramid. The width of the base is 34.2 m, and the height of the triangular sides is 27 m. What is the surface area of the glass?

Estimation Estimate the surface area of each figure.

21.

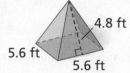

4.8 ft

5.6 ft

5.6 ft

22. 3 m

7 m

23.

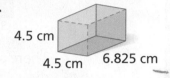

4.5 cm

4.5 cm   6.825 cm

24. What's the Question? The surface area of a cube is 150 cm². The answer is 5 cm. What is the question?

25. Write About It How is finding the surface area of a rectangular pyramid different from finding the surface area of a triangular prism?

26. Challenge This cube is made of 27 smaller cubes whose sides measure 1 in.

   a. What is the surface area of the large cube?

   b. Remove one small cube from each of the eight corners of the larger cube. What is the surface area of the solid formed?

Test Prep

27. Multiple Choice Find the surface area of a cube with a side length of 9.4 yd.

  Ⓐ 56.4 yd²   Ⓑ 88.36 yd²   Ⓒ 338.4 yd²   Ⓓ 530.16 yd²

28. Gridded Response Find the surface area, in square meters, of a cylinder with a radius of 7 m and a height of 6 m. Use 3.14 for π and round to the nearest hundredth.

Ready To Go On?

Quiz for Lessons 6 and 7

6 Volume of Prisms

Find the volume of each prism.

1.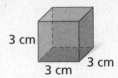
3 cm
3 cm   3 cm

2.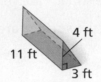
4 ft
11 ft
3 ft

3.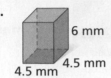
6 mm
4.5 mm   4.5 mm

4. There are 16 cubic boxes of erasers in a case. What are all the possible dimensions for a case of erasers?

7 Surface Area

Find the surface area *S* of each figure. Use 3.14 for *π*, and round to the nearest hundredth.

5.
8 m
4 m   5 m

6.
5 ft
3 ft   3 ft

7.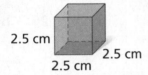
2.5 cm
2.5 cm   2.5 cm

8. Which cylinder has the greater surface area?

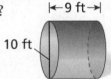
|←9 ft→|
10 ft

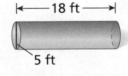
|← 18 ft →|
5 ft

9. A company sells oats in a cylindrical container with dimensions as shown. A rectangular label gets glued around the lateral surface of the container. What is the area of the label? Round your answer to the nearest square inch.

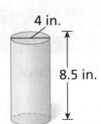
4 in.
8.5 in.

Real-World CONNECTIONS

MATHEMATICAL PRACTICES · Reason abstractly and quantitatively.

CHAPTER 8

Marble House In the late 1800s, some of America's wealthiest families built mansions in the coastal town of Newport, Rhode Island. Marble House is one of the most extravagant examples. Marble House got its name from the approximately 500,000 cubic feet of marble used in its construction.

RHODE ISLAND

Newport

1. A block of marble with a volume of 1 cubic foot weighs approximately 160 pounds. How much does all of the marble in Marble House weigh?

2. A block of marble is in the shape of a rectangular prism. The dimensions are 2 ft wide, 1 foot deep, and 18 inches high.

   a. What is the volume of the block of marble in cubic feet?

   b. Set up and solve a proportion to find out how much this block of marble weighs.

3. The Gold Ballroom in Marble House can be rented for private parties and corporate events. The room is 28 feet long by 46 feet wide.

   a. What is the area of the Gold Ballroom?

   b. A private party wants to fill the Gold Ballroom with rows of round tables. The tables are 4 feet in diameter, and each table must be 5 feet from any walls or other tables. How many tables can fit in the Ballroom?

   c. How much of the floor space will *not* be covered by tables? Round to the nearest square foot.

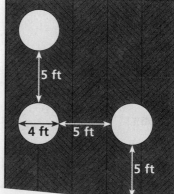

Real-World Connections

(all) Photo by John Corbett/Courtesy of The Preservation Society of Newport County

Game Time

Polygon Hide-and-Seek

Use the figure to name each polygon described.

1. an obtuse scalene triangle
2. a right isosceles triangle
3. a parallelogram with no right angles
4. a trapezoid with two congruent sides
5. a pentagon with three congruent sides

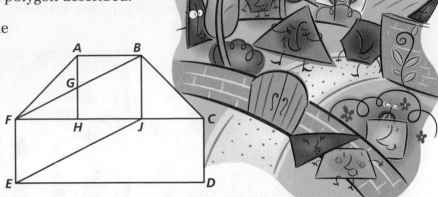

Poly-Cross Puzzle

You will use the names of the figures below to complete a crossword puzzle.

A copy of the crossword puzzle is available online.

Learn It Online
Game Time Extra

ACROSS

1.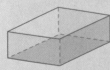

2.

3.

4.

5.

6.

DOWN

1.

7.

8.

Tim Davis/HMH Photo

Materials
- colored file folder
- scissors
- 8 library pockets
- glue stick
- index cards
- black construction paper
- markers
- tag
- string

It's in the Bag!

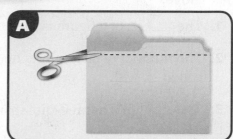

A

PROJECT **Area and Volume Suitcase**

Carry your notes with you as you travel through this chapter.

Directions

❶ Cut the tabs off a colored file folder to form a rectangular folder with straight sides.
Figure A

❷ Open the folder. Glue library pockets inside the folder so that there are four on each side. Place an index card in each pocket.
Figure B

B

❸ Cut out "handles" from the construction paper. Glue these to the folder as shown.
Figure C

❹ Use a piece of string to attach a tag to one of the handles. Write your name and the name of your class on the tag. Write the name and number of the chapter on the front of the folder.

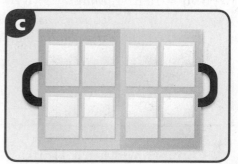

C

Taking Note of the Math

Write the names of a chapter's lessons on the library pockets. Then take notes on each lesson on the appropriate index card.

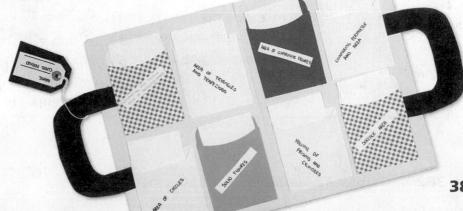

Vocabulary

area   surface area

net   volume

Complete the sentences below with vocabulary words from the list above.

1. The ___?___ of a figure is the amount of surface it covers.

2. The number of cubic units needed to fill a space is called ___?___.

3. The ___?___ of a three-dimensional figure is the sum of the areas of its surfaces.

EXAMPLES

EXERCISES

1 Converting Customary Units

■ **Convert 5 yards to feet.**

Set up a conversion factor.

$5 \, \text{yd} \times \dfrac{3 \, \text{ft}}{1 \, \text{yd}}$ *Think: yards to feet—3 ft = 1 yd, so use $\frac{3 \, ft}{yd}$.*

$5 \, \text{yd} = 15 \, \text{ft}$ *Multiply 5 yd by the conversion factor. Cancel the common unit, yd.*

Convert.

4. 3 mi to feet
5. 18 ft to yards
6. 3 qt to cups
7. 48 c to gal
8. 128 oz to pounds
9. 8,000 lb to tons
10. $\dfrac{64 \, \text{oz}}{x \, \text{lb}} = \dfrac{16 \, \text{oz}}{1 \, \text{lb}}$
11. $\dfrac{12 \, \text{ft}}{x \, \text{in.}} = \dfrac{1 \, \text{ft}}{12 \, \text{in.}}$
12. $\dfrac{8 \, \text{pt}}{x \, \text{qt}} = \dfrac{2 \, \text{pt}}{1 \, \text{qt}}$
13. $\dfrac{3 \, \text{ft}}{1 \, \text{yd}} = \dfrac{x \, \text{ft}}{33 \, \text{yd}}$

14. The Golden Gate Bridge, in San Francisco, has a tower height of 750 ft. How many yards tall is this?

2 Converting Metric Units

■ **Convert.**

$29 \, \text{cm} = \blacksquare \, \text{m}$

$29 \, \text{cm} \cdot \dfrac{1 \, \text{m}}{100 \, \text{cm}} = 0.29 \, \text{m}$ *Cancel the common unit, cm.*

Convert.

15. $3.2 \, \text{L} = \blacksquare \, \text{mL}$
16. $7 \, \text{mL} = \blacksquare \, \text{L}$
17. $342 \, \text{m} = \blacksquare \, \text{km}$
18. $42 \, \text{g} = \blacksquare \, \text{kg}$
19. $51 \, \text{mm} = \blacksquare \, \text{m}$
20. $71 \, \text{km} = \blacksquare \, \text{m}$

21. The heaviest pumpkin ever grown weighed approximately 681.296 kilograms. How many grams is this?

3 Area of Rectangles and Parallelograms

■ Find the area of the rectangle.

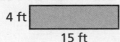
4 ft

15 ft

$A = \ell w$
$A = 15 \cdot 4 = 60$
The area is 60 ft^2

■ Find the area of the parallelogram.

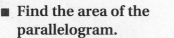
7 mm
10 mm

$A = bh$
$A = 10 \cdot 7 = 70$
The area is 70 mm^2.

Find the area of each rectangle.

22.
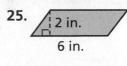
3 ft

6 ft

23.
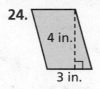
1 m

7 m

Find the area of each parallelogram.

24.
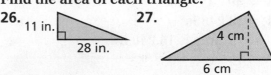
4 in.

3 in.

25.
2 in.

6 in.

4 Area of Triangles and Trapezoids

■ Find the area of the trapezoid.

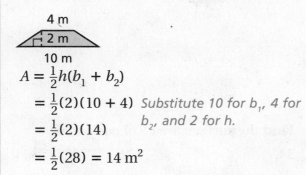
4 m
2 m
10 m

$A = \frac{1}{2}h(b_1 + b_2)$
$= \frac{1}{2}(2)(10 + 4)$ *Substitute 10 for b_1, 4 for b_2, and 2 for h.*
$= \frac{1}{2}(2)(14)$
$= \frac{1}{2}(28) = 14 \text{ m}^2$

Find the area of each triangle.

26. 11 in.

28 in.

27.
4 cm

6 cm

Find the area of each trapezoid.

28.   8 cm

5 cm

4 cm

29.   3.5 ft

3 ft

4.5 ft

Study Guide: Review

EXAMPLES

EXERCISES

5 Area of Composite Figures

■ Find the area of the polygon.

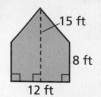 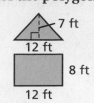

$A_1 = 12 \cdot 8 = 96$

$A_2 = \frac{1}{2} \cdot 12 \cdot 7 = 42$

$42 \text{ ft}^2 + 96 \text{ ft}^2 = 138 \text{ ft}^2$

Find the area of each polygon.

30.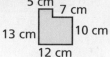

31.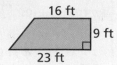

6 Volume of Prisms

■ Find the volume of the rectangular prism.

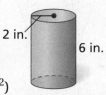

$V = \ell w h$

$V = 48 \cdot 12 \cdot 23$

$V = 13{,}248 \text{ in}^3$

The volume is 13,248 in³.

Find the volume of each prism.

32.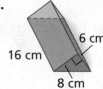

33.

7 Surface Area

■ Find the surface area S of the cylinder.

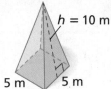

2 in.

6 in.

$S = h \cdot (2\pi r) + 2 \cdot (\pi r^2)$

$S \approx 6 \cdot (2 \cdot 3.14 \cdot 2) + 2 \cdot (3.14 \cdot 2^2)$

$S \approx 100.48 \text{ in}^2$

The surface area is about 100.48 in².

Find the surface area S of each solid.

34.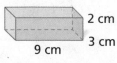

35.

Chapter Test

Convert.

1. 85 mm = ▮ cm

2. 6 fl oz = ▮ c

3. 3,000 km = ▮ m

4. 9 yd = ▮ in.

5. 15,840 ft = ▮ mi

6. 1.5 T = ▮ lb

7. **Baking** One stick of butter is equivalent to $\frac{1}{2}$ cup of butter. A recipe calls for 2 tablespoons of butter. There are 16 tablespoons in a cup. How much of a stick of butter should you use?

Find the area of each figure.

8.
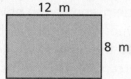
12 m
8 m

9.
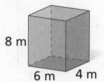

10.
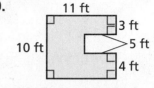
11 ft
3 ft
10 ft
5 ft
4 ft

11. A patio is in the shape of a trapezoid. What is the area of the patio?
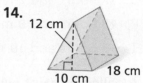
A   24 ft   B
D 6 ft
    32 ft   C

Find the volume V of each three-dimensional figure.

12.
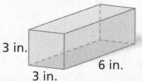
8 m
6 m   4 m

13.
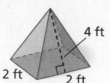
5 in.
11 in.   21 in.

14.
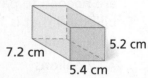
12 cm
10 cm   18 cm

Find the surface area S of each three-dimensional figure.

15.
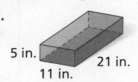
3 in.
3 in.   6 in.

16.
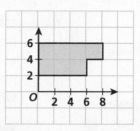
4 ft
2 ft   2 ft

17.
5.2 cm
7.2 cm
5.4 cm

18. A pizza box is just big enough to fit a large pizza, which has a diameter of 15 in. If the box is 1.5 in. tall, what is the surface area of the box?

Cumulative Assessment

Multiple Choice

1. What is the surface area of the figure?

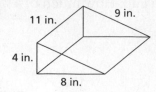

11 in.   9 in.

4 in.

8 in.

Ⓐ 176 in²   Ⓒ 263 in²

Ⓑ 219 in²   Ⓓ 295 in²

2. On May 1, 2005, in Galveston, Texas, the sun rose at 6:37 A.M. The sun set at 7:56 P.M. How much time elapsed from sunrise to sunset?

Ⓕ 1 hour and 39 minutes

Ⓖ 12 hours and 29 minutes

Ⓗ 13 hours and 9 minutes

Ⓙ 13 hours and 19 minutes

3. A gallon of paint will cover 250 square feet. About how many gallons of paint are needed to paint a rectangular billboard that is 120 feet long and 85 feet tall?

Ⓐ 2 gallons   Ⓒ 22 gallons

Ⓑ 10 gallons   Ⓓ 41 gallons

4. Justin has 3 cups of sugar in a canister. He uses $\frac{1}{3}$ cup of sugar in a cookie recipe. He uses $\frac{3}{4}$ of what is remaining in the canister to make a pitcher of lemonade. How much sugar is left?

Ⓕ $\frac{2}{3}$ cup   Ⓗ $1\frac{11}{12}$ cups

Ⓖ 1 cup   Ⓙ 2 cups

5. What is the prime factorization of 324?

Ⓐ $2^2 \times 3^4$ Ⓒ $2^2 \times 3^2 \times 27$

Ⓑ $2^2 \times 9^2$ Ⓓ $2^2 \times 81$

6. Maysville Middle School is hosting a craft fair. The circle graph shows how many different types of booths will be at the craft fair. To the nearest whole number, what percent of the booths will be selling jewelry?

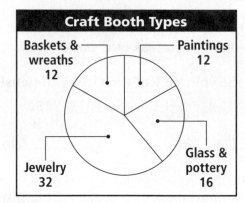

Ⓕ 80%   Ⓗ 44%

Ⓖ 55%   Ⓙ 33%

7. An antique round tabletop has a diameter of 3 feet. It is 2 inches thick. What is the volume of the tabletop? Round to the nearest tenth.

Ⓐ 1.2 ft³   Ⓒ 7.1 ft³

Ⓑ 2.1 ft³   Ⓓ 14.1 ft³

8. The scale on a map is 1 in:50 mi. If Cincinnati, Ohio, is about 300 miles from Chicago, Illinois, about how far apart are the two cities on the map?

Ⓕ 5 in.   Ⓗ 7 in.

Ⓖ 6 in.   Ⓙ 8 in.

9. In March of 2005, Steve Fossett became the first man to complete the first solo, nonstop flight around the world. He did not even stop to refuel. The 36,818-kilometer voyage took 67 hours and 2 minutes. How many kilometers did he travel per minute? Round to the nearest kilometer.

Ⓐ 5 km/min   Ⓒ 23 km/min

Ⓑ 9 km/min   Ⓓ 26 km/min

 HOT TIP! Pay attention to the units used in problems. If the units used in a problem do not match the units used in the answer choices, you will need to convert from one unit to another.

Gridded Response

The table shows the number of people who attended the Super Bowl from 1967 to 1971. Use the table for items 10 and 11.

10. What was the mean attendance? Round to the nearest whole number.

Superbowl Attendance					
Year	1967	1968	1969	1970	1971
Number of People	61,946	75,546	75,389	80,562	79,204

11. How many more people attended the Super Bowl in 1971 than in 1967? Round your answer to the nearest thousand.

12. The area of a triangle is 57.12 cm². If the height of the triangle is 8.4 cm, how many centimeters long is the base?

13. Solve the equation $\frac{2}{7}k = \frac{1}{6}$ for k.

14. Marcia is weighing her produce. A watermelon weighs 2.89 kg. How many grams are in 2.89 kg?

Short Response

S1. Triangle WXY is isosceles. The two short sides have a length of 18 mm. The other side has as length of 30 mm.
   a. Draw a triangle that is similar to triangle WXY.
   b. Write a proportion to prove that the two triangles are similar.

S2. A company's rectangular parking lot is 35 m long and 60 m wide. The company is planning on expanding the area. If the dimensions are doubled, how many times greater will the area of the new parking lot be compared to the area of the original parking lot? Explain how you found your answer.

S3. Carole has a piece of fabric that is 2 yards long. She wants to cut the fabric into 2.4-inch strips. Let s equal one of the fabric strips. Write and solve an equation to find how many 2.4-inch strips Carole can cut from the piece of fabric.

Extended Response

E1. There are 3 pools in Marcie's neighborhood where she can go swimming. The dimensions are listed below. Pool 2 is a circular pool.

Pool	Length (ft)	Depth (ft)	Width (ft)
1	25	5	8
2	–	6	18
3	15	4	9

   a. Find the volume of each pool. Which pool has the greatest volume? Show your work. Use 3.14 for π.
   b. What is the circumference of pool 2?
   c. Samantha's pool has the same volume as pool 1. However, her pool is in the shape of a cube. What are the dimensions of Samantha's pool?

CHAPTER
9

Integers and the Coordinate Plane

COMMON CORE

Chapter
- Use negative numbers in everyday contexts.
- Draw and transform figures in the coordinate plane.

Why Learn This?

Integers are useful in finding and comparing distances both above and below ground level, such as what you encounter in caves and the countryside surrounding them.

Learn It Online
Chapter Project Online

China Tourism Press/The Image Bank/Getty Images;

 # Are You Ready?

Learn It Online
Resources Online

✓ Vocabulary

Choose the best term from the list to complete each sentence.

1. When you ___?___ a numerical expression, you find its value.

2. ___?___ are the set of numbers 0, 1, 2, 3, 4, ...

3. A(n) ___?___ is an exact location in space.

4. A(n) ___?___ is a mathematical statement that two quantities are equal.

equation
evaluate
exponents
less than
point
whole numbers

Complete these exercises to review skills you will need for this chapter.

✓ Compare Whole Numbers

Write <, >, or = to compare the numbers.

5. 9 ▢ 2   6. 4 ▢ 5   7. 8 ▢ 1   8. 3 ▢ 3

9. 412 ▢ 214   10. 1,076 ▢ 1,074 11. 502 ▢ 520   12. 9,123 ▢ 9,001

✓ Whole-Number Operations

Add, subtract, multiply, or divide.

13. $7 + 6$ 14. $15 - 8$ 15. $6 \cdot 7$ 16. $25 \div 5$

17. $129 + 30$ 18. $32 - 25$ 19. $119 \cdot 5$ 20. $156 \div 6$

✓ Solve One-Step Equations

Solve each equation.

21. $4t = 32$ 22. $b - 4 = 12$ 23. $24 = 6r$

24. $3x = 72$ 25. $8 = 4a$ 26. $m + 3 = 63$

✓ Graph Ordered Pairs

Graph each ordered pair.

27. $(1, 3)$ 28. $(0, 5)$ 29. $(3, 2)$ 30. $(4, 0)$

31. $(6, 4)$ 32. $(2, 5)$ 33. $(0, 1)$ 34. $(1, 0)$

Integers and the Coordinate Plane   **389**

Study Guide: Preview

Where You've Been

Previously, you

- graphed and located ordered pairs of whole numbers on a coordinate grid.

- compared and ordered whole numbers, decimals, and fractions.

In This Chapter

You will study

- using integers to represent real-life situations.

- graphing and locating ordered pairs on four quadrants of a coordinate plane.

- using transformations to change the positions of figures in the coordinate plane.

Where You're Going

You can use the skills learned in this chapter

- to interpret graphs of functions that represent real-world situations.

- to solve multi-step equations with integers and positive and negative fractions and decimals.

Key Vocabulary/Vocabulario

coordinates	coordenadas
integer	entero
opposites	opuestos
origin	origen
quadrants	cuadrante

Vocabulary Connections

To become familiar with some of the vocabulary terms in the chapter, consider the following. You may refer to the chapter, the glossary, or a dictionary if you like.

1. The word *opposite* can mean "across from." Where do you think **opposites** will lie on a number line?

2. The word *origin* can mean "the point at which something begins." At what coordinates do you think the **origin** is?

3. The word *quadrant* comes from the Latin *quattuor*, meaning "four." How many **quadrants** do you think a coordinate plane has?

Reading and Writing Math

Writing Strategy:
Write a Convincing Argument

Being able to write a convincing argument about a math concept proves that you have a solid understanding of the concept.

A good argument should include

- an answer.
- support to prove the statement (including examples if necessary).
- a summary statement.

> **6. Critical Thinking** If George enlarges a 3 in. × 4 in. photo so that it is 12 in. × 16 in., how will its area change?

Step 1 **Answer statement:**
The area of the new photo will be 16 times as great as that of the original photo.

Step 2 **Support:**
The dimensions of the 3 in. × 4 in. photo are multiplied by 4 to be enlarged to 12 in. × 16 in.

The area of the new photo is 16 times as great as that of the original photo.

area of original = $3 \times 4 = 12 \text{ in}^2$

area of enlarged = $12 \times 16 = 192 \text{ in}^2$

area of original: area of enlarged

12:192

1:16

16 in.

4 in.

Original photo | 3 in.

12 in.

Enlarged photo

Step 3 **Summary Statement:**
Therefore, to find the area of the enlarged photo, multiply the original area by 4^2, or 16.

Try This

Write a convincing argument to show whether or not a rectangle with whole-number dimensions can have an area of 15 m² and a perimeter of 15 m.

Reading and Writing Math

Integers and Absolute Value

COMMON CORE

CC.6.NS.5 Understand that positive and negative numbers are used together to describe quantities having opposite directions or values… use positive and negative numbers to represent quantities in real-world contexts, explaining the meaning of 0 in each situation

The highest temperature recorded in the United States is 134 °F, in Death Valley, California. The lowest recorded temperature is 80° below 0 °F, in Prospect Creek, Alaska.

Positive numbers are greater than 0. They may be written with a positive sign (+), but they are usually written without it. So, the highest temperature can be written as +134 °F or 134 °F.

Negative numbers are less than 0. They are always written with a negative sign (−). So, the lowest temperature is written as −80 °F.

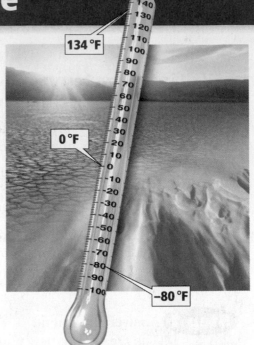

134 °F

0 °F

−80 °F

EXAMPLE **1** **Identifying Positive and Negative Numbers in the Real World**

Name a positive or negative number to represent each situation.

Vocabulary

positive number

negative number

opposites

integer

absolute value

A **a gain of 20 yards in football**

Positive numbers can represent *gains* or *increases*.

+20

B **spending $75**

Negative numbers can represent *losses* or *decreases*.

−75

C **10 feet below sea level**

Negative numbers can represent values *below* or *less than* a certain value.

−10

You can graph positive and negative numbers on a number line.

Remember!

The set of whole numbers includes zero and the counting numbers. {0, 1, 2, 3, 4, …}

On a number line, **opposites** are the same distance from 0 but on different sides of 0. Zero is its own opposite.

Integers are the set of all whole numbers and their opposites.

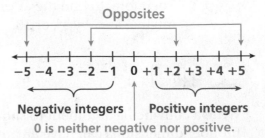

Opposites

−5 −4 −3 −2 −1 0 +1 +2 +3 +4 +5

Negative integers   Positive integers

0 is neither negative nor positive.

Video **Lesson Tutorials Online** my.hrw.com

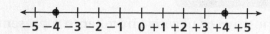

EXAMPLE **2** **Graphing Integers**

Graph each integer and its opposite on a number line.

A −4

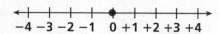

+4 is the same distance from 0 as −4.

B 3

−3 is the same distance from 0 as 3.

C 0

Zero is its own opposite.

The **absolute value** of an integer is its distance from 0 on a number line. The symbol for absolute value is | |.

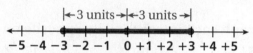

Reading Math

Read | 3 | as "the absolute value of 3."

Read | −3 | as "the absolute value of negative 3."

$|-3| = 3$ $|3| = 3$

- Absolute values are never negative.
- Opposite integers have the same absolute value.
- $|0| = 0$

EXAMPLE **3** **Finding Absolute Value**

Use the number line to find the absolute value of each integer.

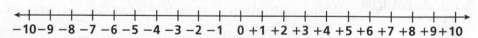

A $|5|$

5   *5 is 5 units from 0, so $|5| = 5$.*

B $|-7|$

7   *−7 is 7 units from 0, so $|-7| = 7$.*

MATHEMATICAL PRACTICES

Think and Discuss

1. Tell whether −3.2 is an integer. Why or why not?

2. Give the opposite of 14. What is the opposite of −11?

3. Name all the integers with an absolute value of 12.

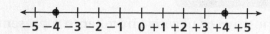

GUIDED PRACTICE

See Example 1 **Name a positive or negative number to represent each situation.**

1. an increase of 5 points
2. a loss of 15 yards

See Example 2 **Graph each integer and its opposite on a number line.**

3. −2   4. 1   5. −6   6. 9

See Example 3 **Use the number line to find the absolute value of each integer.**

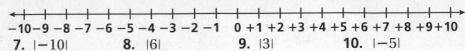

7. |−10| 8. |6| 9. |3| 10. |−5|

INDEPENDENT PRACTICE

See Example 1 **Name a positive or negative number to represent each situation.**

11. earning $50   12. 20° below zero

13. 7 feet above sea level   14. a decrease of 39 points

See Example 2 **Graph each integer and its opposite on a number line.**

15. −5   16. 6   17. 2   18. −3   19. 9

See Example 3 **Use the number line to find the absolute value of each integer.**

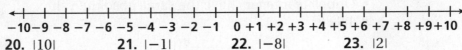

20. |10| 21. |−1| 22. |−8| 23. |2|

PRACTICE AND PROBLEM SOLVING

Extra Practice
See Extra Practice for more exercises.

Write a situation that each integer could represent.

24. +49   25. −83   26. −7   27. +15   28. −2

Write the opposite of each integer.

29. −92   30. +75   31. −25   32. +1,001   33. 0

Write the absolute value of each integer.

34. |−27| 35. |105| 36. |18| 37. |−55| 38. |−1,000|

39. **Astronomy** Use the table to graph the average surface temperatures of the given planets on a number line.

Planet	Earth	Mars	Jupiter
Average Surface Temperature (°C)	15	−65	−110

40. A certain stock dropped 3 points in the stock market. Another stock gained 5 points. Write an integer to represent each stock's gain or loss.

Order the integers in each set from least to greatest.

B −2, 0, 2, −5

Graph the integers on the same number line.

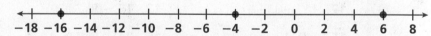

-5 -4 -3 -2 -1 0 1 2 3 4 5

Then read the numbers from left to right: −5, −2, 0, 2.

EXAMPLE 3 **PROBLEM SOLVING APPLICATION**

At a golf tournament, David scored +6, Celia scored −16, and Xavier scored −4. One of these three players was the winner of the tournament. Who won the tournament?

1 Understand the Problem

The **answer** will be the player with the *lowest* score.
List the **important information:**

- David scored +6.
- Celia scored −16.
- Xavier scored −4.

2 Make a Plan

You can draw a diagram to order the scores from least to greatest.

3 Solve

Draw a number line and graph each player's score on it.

-18 -16 -14 -12 -10 -8 -6 -4 -2 0 2 4 6 8

Celia's score, −16, is farthest to the left, so it is the lowest score. Celia won this tournament.

4 Look Back

Negative integers are always less than positive integers, so David cannot be the winner. Since Celia's score of −16 is less than Xavier's score of −4, Celia won.

> **MATHEMATICAL PRACTICES**
> Make sense of problems and persevere in solving them.

Sports

In golf, *par* is the standard number of strokes needed to hit the ball into the hole. A score of −12 means "12 strokes under par." A score of +2 means "2 strokes over par."

MATHEMATICAL PRACTICES

Think and Discuss

1. Tell which is greater, a negative or a positive integer. Explain.

2. Tell which is greater, 0 or a negative integer. Explain.

3. Explain how to tell which of two negative integers is greater.

Alfo/Corbis

Exercises

GUIDED PRACTICE

See Example 1 Use the number line to compare each pair of integers. Write < or >.

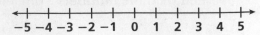

1. −4 ⬜ −5   **2.** −2 ⬜ 0   **3.** −1 ⬜ 3

See Example 2 Order the integers in each set from least to greatest.

4. 9, 0, −2   **5.** 7, −4, 3, −5   **6.** 8, −6, −1, 10

See Example 3 **7.** Use the table.

     a. At what time was the temperature the lowest?

     b. What was the highest temperature?

Time	Temperature (°F)
10:00 P.M.	1
Midnight	−4
3:30 A.M.	−6
6:00 A.M.	1

INDEPENDENT PRACTICE

See Example 1 Use the number line to compare each pair of integers. Write < or >.

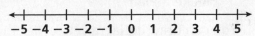

8. 0 ⬜ 2   **9.** 4 ⬜ −4   **10.** −3 ⬜ −1   **11.** −5 ⬜ 2

See Example 2 Order the integers in each set from least to greatest.

12. 11, −6, −3   **13.** 15, −8, 7   **14.** 5, −12, 0, 1

15. −9, 13, −1, −16   **16.** 24, −6, 7, −10, 4   **17.** 22, 0, −19, 8, −3

See Example 3 **18. Geography** Use the table, which shows the depths of the world's three largest oceans.

     a. Which ocean is the deepest?

     b. Which oceans are less than 35,000 feet deep?

Ocean	Depth (ft)
Pacific	−36,200
Atlantic	−30,246
Indian	−24,442

PRACTICE AND PROBLEM SOLVING

Extra Practice

See Extra Practice for more exercises.

Compare. Write < or >.

19. −30 ⬜ 25   **20.** 0 ⬜ −49   **21.** −16 ⬜ −51   **22.** −17 ⬜ 17

23. −64 ⬜ −15   **24.** 77 ⬜ 300   **25.** −28 ⬜ 1   **26.** 25 ⬜ −30

Order the integers in each set from least to greatest.

27. −39, 14, 21   **28.** −18, −9, −31   **29.** 0, −26, 43, −12

30. 15, −25, −4, 31   **31.** −67, 82, −73, −10, 20   **32.** 42, −27, 69, −50, 38

33. Which set of integers is written in order from greatest to least?

- Ⓐ 0, −4, −3, −1
- Ⓑ 2, −4, 8, −16
- Ⓒ 9, −9, −10, −15
- Ⓓ −8, −7, −6, −5

34. Earth Science The normal high temperature in January for Barrow, Alaska, is −7 °F. The normal high temperature in January for Los Angeles is 68 °F. Compare the two temperatures using < or >.

35. Geography The table shows elevations for several natural features. Write the features in order from the least elevation to the greatest elevation.

Elevations of Natural Features	
Mt. Everest	29,022 ft
Mt. Rainier	14,410 ft
Kilimanjaro	19,000 ft
San Augustin Cave	−2,189 ft
Dead Sea	−1,296 ft

36. What's the Error? Your classmate says that 0 < −91. Explain why this is incorrect.

37. Write About It Explain how you would order from least to greatest three numbers that include a positive number, a negative number, and zero.

38. Challenge There is a missing integer from the list below. The missing integer is both the median and the mode. What is the integer? (*Hint:* There could be more than one correct answer.) 2, −10, 7, −7, 5, −5

Test Prep

39. Multiple Choice Which set of integers is written in order from greatest to least?

- Ⓐ −3, −9, −6
- Ⓑ −3, 2, 5
- Ⓒ 2, −1, −3
- Ⓓ 4, 10, 12

40. Short Response The table shows the elevations relative to sea level of several cities. Order the cities from the least elevation to the greatest elevation.

City	Boston	Cincinnati	Death Valley	Salt Lake City	San Antonio
Elevation (ft)	16	483	−282	4,226	807

Negative Rational Numbers

CC.6.NS.6 Understand a rational number as a point on the number line. Extend number line diagrams and coordinate axes familiar from previous grades to represent points on the line and in the plane with negative number coordinates
Also CC.6.NS.6c

Whole numbers, decimals, fractions, percents, and integers belong to the set of *rational numbers*. A **rational number** is a number that can be written as a ratio, with any integer as the numerator, and any integer except 0 as the denominator.

rational numbers
$0.2, \frac{1}{2}, 75\%$
integers
..., −1, 0, 1, ...
whole numbers
0, 1, 2, ...

EXAMPLE **1**   **Comparing Negative Rational Numbers**

Use <, >, or = to compare each pair of numbers.

Vocabulary
rational number

A $-\frac{2}{3} \blacksquare -\frac{1}{2}$

$-\frac{2}{3} \cdot \frac{2}{2} = -\frac{2 \cdot 2}{3 \cdot 2} = -\frac{4}{6}$

$-\frac{1}{2} \cdot \frac{3}{3} = -\frac{1 \cdot 3}{2 \cdot 3} = -\frac{3}{6}$

$-\frac{4}{6} < -\frac{3}{6}$

$-\frac{2}{3} < -\frac{1}{2}$

Write the fractions using a common denominator.

Compare.

Helpful Hint

Integers are rational numbers because they can be written using 1 as the denominator.
$-2 = \frac{-2}{1}$

B $-0.2 \blacksquare -2$

−0.2

−2.0

0 is greater than −2.

$-0.2 > -2$

Line up the decimal points and compare from left to right.

C $-\frac{2}{5} \blacksquare -0.4$

$-0.4 = -\frac{4}{10} = -\frac{2}{5}$

$-\frac{2}{5} = -\frac{2}{5}$

$-\frac{2}{5} = -0.4$

Write −0.4 as a fraction in simplest form.

Compare.

A number line can be used to place rational numbers in order.

EXAMPLE **2** **Ordering Rational Numbers**

Use a number line to write the numbers in order from least to greatest.

$-3\frac{1}{2}, 2, -1.7, -1, \frac{1}{2}$

Graph the numbers on a number line; $-3\frac{1}{2}$ is between -3 and -4, and -1.7 is between -1 and -2.

$-3\frac{1}{2}, -1.7, -1, \frac{1}{2}, 2$

EXTENSION

Exercises

Use <, >, or = to compare each pair of numbers.

1. $-\frac{4}{5}$ ▢ $-\frac{5}{6}$

2. -0.8 ▢ -0.3

3. $-\frac{8}{9}$ ▢ $-\frac{5}{6}$

4. -0.85 ▢ -0.98

5. $-\frac{1}{7}$ ▢ $-\frac{1}{8}$

6. -0.99 ▢ -1

7. -1.7 ▢ $-1\frac{7}{9}$

8. $-\frac{3}{5}$ ▢ -0.6

9. -5.2 ▢ $-5\frac{1}{2}$

10. -2 ▢ -1.98

11. $-2\frac{3}{5}$ ▢ -3

12. $-\frac{1}{10}$ ▢ 0

Write the numbers in order from least to greatest.

13. $0.21, -2\frac{7}{10}, 0, -7\frac{3}{4}$

14. $2\frac{7}{20}, -5, -5\frac{3}{5}, 3.6$

15. $2.25, -4\frac{1}{10}, -3, 4\frac{3}{5}$

16. $-1\frac{12}{25}, -6.8, 3, 3.15$

17. $0.09, -2.7, -3\frac{1}{2}, \frac{4}{5}$

18. $-4.4, 0.61, -3\frac{1}{2}, -6\frac{1}{6}$

19. $2\frac{2}{5}, -8.5, -7\frac{1}{4}, 1.25$

20. $6\frac{3}{5}, -3, -3\frac{9}{10}, -3\frac{1}{3}$

21. $-2.5, -7, 4\frac{1}{5}, -8.25$

22. $-8.8, -5, -3\frac{4}{7}, -9\frac{1}{7}$

23. **What's the Error?** A student wrote on a test that $-2\frac{8}{12} > -2\frac{2}{3}$ because $8 > 2$ and $12 > 3$. What error did the student make?

⭐ 24. **Challenge** Find each absolute value.

   a. $|-1.3|$

   b. $\left|-\frac{9}{10}\right|$

   c. $|-8.2|$

   d. $\left|-2\frac{6}{7}\right|$

Ready To Go On?

Quiz for Lessons 1 Through 2

1 Integers and Absolute Value

Name a positive or negative number to represent each situation.

1. a gain of 10 yards

2. 45 feet below sea level

Write the opposite of each integer.

3. 9

4. −17

5. 1

6. −20

Write the absolute value of each integer.

7. |7|

8. |−6|

9. |−8|

10. |−9|

11. A patient's temperature was taken at 7:00, at 8:00, and again at 9:00. The patient's temperature increased by 2 degrees between 7:00 and 8:00, then decreased by 1 degree between 8:00 and 9:00. What integer could you write for an increase of 2 degrees? a decrease of 1 degree?

2 Comparing and Ordering Integers

Compare. Write < or >.

12. 9 ☐ −22

13. −7 ☐ 4

14. −10 ☐ −19

Order the integers in each set from least to greatest.

15. 2, −7, 14

16. 25, −9, 4, −21

17. 10, 0, −23, −17, 8

18. The elevation of Turpan Pendi in China is −154 meters. The elevation of the Qattara Depression in Egypt is −133 meters. Compare the two elevations using < or >.

Focus on Problem Solving

Understand the Problem

• **Restate the question**

After reading a real-world problem (perhaps several times), look at the question in the problem. Rewrite the question as a statement in your own words. For example, if the question is "How much money did the museum earn?" you could write, "Find the amount of money the museum earned."

Now you have a simple sentence telling you what you must do. This can help you understand and remember what the problem is about. This can also help you find the necessary information in the problem.

Read the problems below. Rewrite each question as a statement in your own words.

1 Israel is one of the hottest countries in Asia. A temperature of 129 °F was once recorded there. This is the opposite of the coldest recorded temperature in Antarctica. How cold has it been in Antarctica?

2 The average recorded temperature in Fairbanks, Alaska, in January is about −10 °F. In February, the average temperature is about −4 °F. Is the average temperature lower in January or in February?

3 The south pole on Mars is made of frozen carbon dioxide, which has a temperature of −193 °F. The coldest day recorded on Earth was −129 °F, in Antarctica. Which temperature is lower?

4 The pirate Blackbeard's ship, the *Queen Anne's Revenge*, sank at Beauford Inlet, North Carolina, in 1718. In 1996, divers discovered a shipwreck believed to be the *Queen Anne's Revenge*. The ship's cannons were found 21 feet below the water's surface, and the ship's bell was found 20 feet below the surface. Were the cannons or the bell closer to the surface?

In this photo of Mars, different colors represent different temperature ranges. When the photo was taken, it was summer in the northern hemisphere and winter in the southern hemisphere.

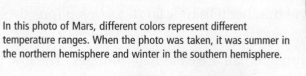

−65 °C   −120 °C

The Coordinate Plane

COMMON CORE

CC.6.NS.6 ...Extend... coordinate axes... to represent points... in the plane with negative number coordinates

Vocabulary

coordinate plane

axes

x-axis

y-axis

quadrants

origin

coordinates

x-coordinate

y-coordinate

A **coordinate plane** is formed by two number lines in a plane that intersect at right angles. The point of intersection is the zero on each number line.

• The two number lines are called the **axes**.

• The horizontal axis is called the **x-axis**.

• The vertical axis is called the **y-axis**.

• The two axes divide the coordinate plane into four **quadrants**.

• The point where the axes intersect is called the **origin**.

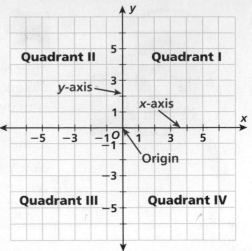

EXAMPLE 1

Identifying Quadrants

Name the quadrant where each point is located.

A *M*

Quadrant I

B *J*

Quadrant IV

C *R*

x-axis

no quadrant

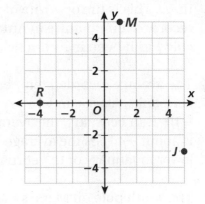

An ordered pair gives the location of a point on a coordinate plane. The first number tells how far to move right (positive) or left (negative) from the origin. The second number tells how far to move up (positive) or down (negative).

Helpful Hint

Points on the axes are not in any quadrant.

The numbers in an ordered pair are called **coordinates**. The first number is called the **x-coordinate**. The second number is called the **y-coordinate**.

The ordered pair for the origin is (0, 0).

EXAMPLE 2

Locating Points on a Coordinate Plane

Give the coordinates of each point.

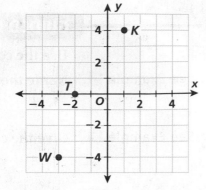

A K

From the origin, K is 1 unit right and 4 units up.

$(1, 4)$

B T

From the origin, T is 2 units left on the x-axis.

$(-2, 0)$

C W

From the origin, W is 3 units left and 4 units down.

$(-3, -4)$

EXAMPLE 3

Graphing Points on a Coordinate Plane

Graph each point on a coordinate plane.

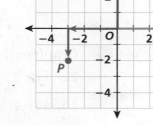

A $P(-3, -2)$

From the origin, move 3 units left and 2 units down.

B $R(0, 4)$

From the origin, move 4 units up.

C $M(3, -4)$

From the origin, move 3 units right and 4 units down.

MATHEMATICAL
PRACTICES

Think and Discuss

1. Tell which number in an ordered pair indicates how far to move left or right from the origin and which number indicates how far to move up or down.

2. Describe how graphing the point (5, 4) is similar to graphing the point (5, −4). How is it different?

3. Tell why it is important to start at the origin when you are graphing points.

Exercises

Learn It Online
Homework Help Online
Exercises 1–27, 31, 33, 35, 37, 45, 47, 49

GUIDED PRACTICE

Use the coordinate plane for Exercises 1–6.

See Example **1** Name the quadrant where each point is located.

1. T **2.** U **3.** B

See Example **2** Give the coordinates of each point.

4. A **5.** B **6.** U

See Example **3** Graph each point on a coordinate plane.

7. $E(4, 2)$ **8.** $F(-1, -4)$ **9.** $G(0, 2)$

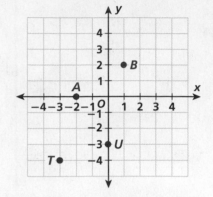

INDEPENDENT PRACTICE

Use the coordinate plane for Exercises 10–21.

See Example **1** Name the quadrant where each point is located.

10. Q **11.** X **12.** H

13. Y **14.** Z **15.** P

See Example **2** Give the coordinates of each point.

16. P **17.** R **18.** Y

19. T **20.** H **21.** Q

See Example **3** Graph each point on a coordinate plane.

22. $L(0, 3)$ **23.** $M(3, -3)$ **24.** $S(2, 0)$

25. $V(-4, 3)$ **26.** $N(-2, -1)$ **27.** $B(4, 3)$

PRACTICE AND PROBLEM SOLVING

Extra Practice

See Extra Practice for more exercises.

Name the quadrant where each ordered pair is located.

28. $(3, -1)$ **29.** $(2, 1)$ **30.** $(-2, 3)$ **31.** $(-4, -3)$

32. $\left(4\frac{1}{2}, -3\right)$ **33.** $\left(10, -7\frac{1}{2}\right)$ **34.** $\left(-6, 2\frac{1}{3}\right)$ **35.** $\left(-8\frac{1}{3}, -\frac{1}{2}\right)$

Graph each ordered pair.

36. $(0, -5)$ **37.** $(-4, -4)$ **38.** $(5, 0)$ **39.** $(3, 2)$

40. $(-2, 2)$ **41.** $(0, -3)$ **42.** $(1, -4)$ **43.** $(0, 0)$

44. $\left(-2\frac{1}{2}, 3\right)$ **45.** $\left(5, 3\frac{1}{2}\right)$ **46.** $\left(-4\frac{1}{3}, 0\right)$ **47.** $\left(0, -\frac{1}{2}\right)$

48. Graph points $A(-1, -1)$, $B(2, 1)$, $C(2, -2)$, and $D(-1, -2)$. Connect the points. What type of quadrilateral do the points form?

We use a coordinate system on Earth to find exact locations. The *equator* is like the *x*-axis, and the *prime meridian* is like the *y*-axis.

The lines that run east-west are *lines of latitude.* They are measured in degrees north and south of the equator.

The lines that run north-south are *lines of longitude.* They are measured in degrees east and west of the prime meridian.

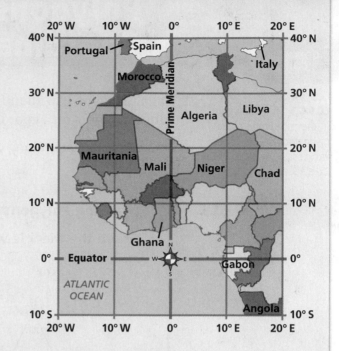

49. In what country is the location 0° latitude, 10° E longitude?

50. Give the coordinates of a location in Algeria.

51. Name two countries that lie along the 30° N line of latitude.

52. Where would you be if you were located at 10° S latitude, 10° W longitude?

53. 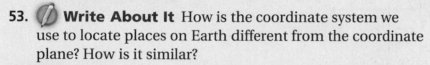 **Write About It** How is the coordinate system we use to locate places on Earth different from the coordinate plane? How is it similar?

54. ⭐ **Challenge** Begin at 10° S latitude, 20° E longitude. Travel 40° north and 20° west. What country would you be in now?

Test Prep

55. **Multiple Choice** In which quadrant is the point (−1, 2) located?

    Ⓐ Quadrant I   Ⓑ Quadrant II   Ⓒ Quadrant III   Ⓓ Quadrant IV

56. **Multiple Choice** Which of the following coordinates is the farthest to the right of the origin on a coordinate plane?

    Ⓕ (−19, 7)   Ⓖ (0, 12)   Ⓗ (4, 15)   Ⓙ (7, 0)

Polygons in the Coordinate Plane

COMMON CORE

CC.6.G.3 Draw polygons in the coordinate plane given coordinates for the vertices… *Also CC.6.NS.6, CC.6.NS.6c, CC.6.NS.8*

On a map, you can identify a location by the intersection of two streets. Finding points on a coordinate plane is like finding a location on a map.

You can also count along the axes to help determine distances in the plane.

EXAMPLE **1** **Drawing Polygons in the Coordinate Plane**

Graph the triangle with vertices $F(-1\frac{1}{2}, -2)$, $G(1, 3)$, and $H(3\frac{1}{2}, -2)$.

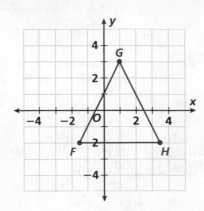

Graph each point on the coordinate plane.

Then connect the points with straight lines to form a polygon.

EXAMPLE **2** **Finding Distance in the Coordinate Plane**

Find the perimeter of the rectangle.

Helpful Hint

Remember that in a rectangle, opposite sides have equal length.

Step 1: Find the length and width.

To find the length of the rectangle, count from left to right along the *x*-axis from −4 to 3. The length is 7 units long. To find the width, count up the *y*-axis from −2 to 4. The width is **6** units long.

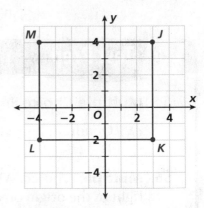

Step 2: Find the perimeter.

Use the formula for the perimeter of a rectangle.

Length of the rectangle = *l*
Width of the rectangle = *w*
Perimeter = $2l + 2w$
$P = 2(7) + 2(6) = 26$

The perimeter of the rectangle is 26 units.

Notice that distance is always measured as a positive number, even though the points have negative coordinates.

EXAMPLE **3** *Social Studies Application*

The streets and avenues of Grid City are arranged in a coordinate plane, where (*x, y*) represents (avenue, street). Stuart lives in Grid City at the corner of 1st Avenue and 2nd Street. One day he walks from his house north to 5th Street, then west to Minus 3rd Avenue, then south to 2nd Street, then east to return home. How far did he walk?

Step 1: Plot the points and draw the rectangle.

Each corner can be plotted as a point on the coordinate plane. The four corners that Stuart visits are:

- 1st Avenue and 2nd Street: (1, 2)

- 1st Avenue and 5th Street: (1, 5)

- Minus 3rd Avenue and 5th Street: (−3, 5)

- Minus 3rd Avenue and 2nd Street: (3, 2)

Plot these points on the coordinate plane and connect them with straight lines.

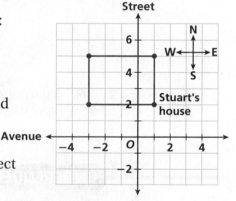

Step 2: Find the length and width of the rectangle.

The width of the rectangle is 3 blocks, and the length is 4 blocks.

Step 3: Find the perimeter.
Perimeter = 2*l* + 2*w*
Perimeter = 2(4) + 2(3) = 14

Stuart walked 14 blocks.

Think and Discuss

1. **Suppose** a skyscraper has one elevator that travels from the lobby to the top floor and a second elevator that travels from the top floor to the lobby. Why do both elevators travel the same distance?

2. **Explain** how the streets and avenues of your town or city are like the coordinate plane. How are they different?

Exercises

GUIDED PRACTICE

See Example 1 · **Graph the polygons with the given vertices.**

1. rectangle: $A(-1, 4\frac{1}{2})$, $B(-1, 2)$, $C(5, 2)$, $D(5, 4\frac{1}{2})$

2. triangle: $R(3, 5)$, $S(-4, 2)$, $T(2, -4)$

See Example 2 · **Find the perimeter of each rectangle.**

3.

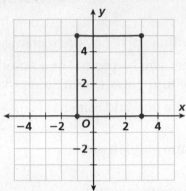

4.

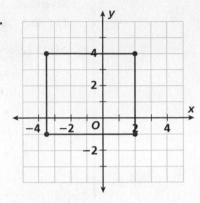

See Example 3 · **5.** A gardener uses string to mark the rectangular border of a garden. On a coordinate plane measured in feet, the corners of the garden are at $(-2, 3)$, $(5, 3)$, $(5, -1)$, and $(-2, -1)$. How much string does the gardener need?

INDEPENDENT PRACTICE

See Example 1 · **Graph the polygons with the given vertices.**

6. triangle: $D(-3\frac{1}{2}, 5\frac{1}{2})$, $E(3, 3)$, $F(-2, -2\frac{1}{2})$

7. quadrilateral: $W(-1, -1)$, $X(5, 3)$, $Y(4, -1)$, $Z(1, -2)$

See Example 2 · **Find the perimeter of each rectangle.**

8.

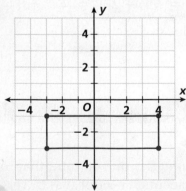

9.

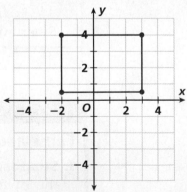

10. Mike draws a model measured in meters of the middle school cafeteria ceiling on a coordinate grid. The corners are located at $(-4, 4)$, $(-4, -3)$, $(8, 4)$, and $(8, -3)$. He will be ordering molding to place along the top of all the walls. What is the length of molding in meters to be placed in the cafeteria?

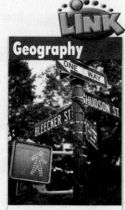

Geography

In most cities, a pair of signs names the intersecting streets at a corner. New York City has over 250,000 street signs.

Thomas Northcut/PhotoDisc/Getty Images

11. A polygon has vertices at (−2, 4), (3, 4), (3, −1), and (−2, −1). What type of polygon is this? What is its perimeter?

12. The points (1, 1), (1, −2), and (5, 1) are three of the four corners of a rectangle. What are the coordinates of the fourth corner? What is the perimeter of the rectangle?

13. Three squares are drawn on the coordinate plane, each with (0, 0) as one of its corners. The first square has its other corners at (1, 0), (1, 1), and (0, 1). The second square has corners at (2, 0), (2, 2), and (0, 2). The third square has corners at (4, 0), (4, 4), and (0, 4). Find the perimeter of each square. When the length of one side of a square is doubled, how does its perimeter change?

14. Geography In many cities, the grid of streets is made of lettered streets that cross numbered streets. The standard length of a block is the same along both lettered and numbered streets. In units of blocks, what is the perimeter of the rectangle described by the street corners C and 13th; C and 19th; H and 13th, and H and 19th?

15. The parallelogram shown has two slanted sides that each have a length of 5 units. What is its perimeter?

16. Write About It Why is the distance between (−3, 4) and (−6, 4) the same as the distance between (3, 4) and (6, 4)?

17. Challenge Can two rectangles have a different shape but the same perimeter? Find examples to support your answer.

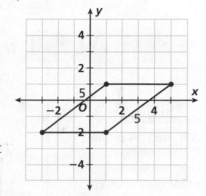

Test Prep

18. Multiple Choice What is the perimeter of the rectangle that has corners at the points (3, 2), (3, 8), (−4, 2), and (−4, 8)?

  Ⓐ 26 units   Ⓑ 22 units   Ⓒ 30 units   Ⓓ 14 units

19. Gridded Response Find the perimeter of the rectangle that has vertices at $(\frac{1}{2}, -2)$, $(\frac{1}{2}, 5)$, $(-3\frac{1}{2}, -2)$, and $(-3\frac{1}{2}, 5)$.

Transformations in the Coordinate Plane

CC.6.NS.8 Solve real-world and mathematical problems by graphing points in all four quadrants of the coordinate plane. Include use of coordinates and absolute value to find distances between points with the same first coordinate or the same second coordinate **Also CC.6.NS.6b, CC.6.NS.6c**

When a marching band moves in formation, it is performing a transformation of any figure it has formed. Recall from Lesson 8-10 that there are three basic transformations. A translation moves a figure along a straight line, a reflection shows a figure's mirror image, and a rotation moves a figure around a fixed point. Remember also that in each of these basic transformations, the figure and its image are congruent.

Transformations can be shown using a coordinate plane.

EXAMPLE 1 **Translating Figures in the Coordinate Plane**

Translate square *ABCD* 6 units left. Give the coordinates of each vertex in the image.

Reading Math

A' is read "*A* prime." Prime notation is used to represent the point on the image that corresponds to the same point on the original figure.

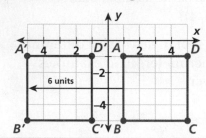

Each vertex is translated 6 units left.

The vertices of the image are *A'*(–5, –1), *B'*(–5, –5), *C'*(–1, –5), and *D'*(–1, –1).

EXAMPLE 2 **Reflecting Figures in the Coordinate Plane**

A Reflect triangle *ABC* across the *y*-axis. Give the coordinates of each vertex in the image.

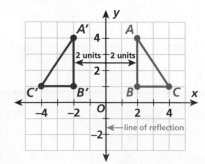

Each vertex of the image is the same distance from the y-axis as the corresponding vertex in the original figure.

The vertices of the image are *A'*(–2, 4), *B'*(–2, 1), and *C'*(–4, 1).

B Reflect triangle *XYZ* across the *x*-axis. Give the coordinates of each vertex in the image.

Helpful Hint

A line of reflection is not limited to the *x*-axis or *y*-axis. Any line can be a line of reflection.

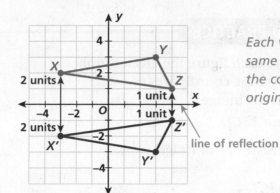

Each vertex of the image is the same distance from the x-axis as the corresponding vertex in the original figure.

The vertices of the image are *X'*(–3, –2), *Y'*(3, –3), and *Z'*(4, –1).

EXAMPLE 3 Rotating Figures in the Coordinate Plane

Rotate rectangle *PQRS* 90° clockwise about the origin. Give the coordinates of each vertex in the image.

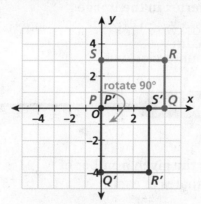

Notice that vertex Q is 4 units to the right of the origin, and vertex Q' is 4 units below the origin.

Similarly, vertex S is 3 units above the origin, and vertex S' is 3 units to the right of the origin.

The vertices of the image are *P'*(0, 0), *Q'*(0, –4), *R'*(3, –4), and *S'*(3, 0).

Think and Discuss

1. Tell how the *x*- and *y*-coordinates change when a figure is translated right *a* units and down *b* units.

2. Explain why the *x*-coordinates of the vertices of a figure do not change when the figure is reflected across the *x*-axis.

3. Predict the coordinates of each vertex in the image of rectangle *PQSR* from Example 3 under a 180° rotation.

GUIDED PRACTICE

See Example 1   **Translate each figure the given number of units. Give the coordinates of each vertex in the image.**

    1. figure *ABCD*; 3 units up

    2. figure *EFG*; 4 units left

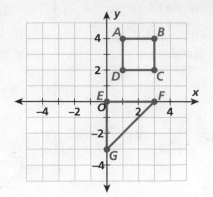

See Example 2   **Reflect each figure across the given axis. Give the coordinates of each vertex in the image.**

    3. figure *ABCD*; *x*-axis

    4. figure *EFG*; *y*-axis

See Example 3   **Rotate each figure the given direction and number of degrees about the origin. Give the coordinates of each vertex in the image.**

    5. figure *EFG*; 90° clockwise

    6. figure *EFG*; 90° counterclockwise

INDEPENDENT PRACTICE

See Example 1   **Translate each figure the given number of units. Give the coordinates of each vertex in the image.**

    7. figure *HJKL*; 2 units left

    8. figure *MNPQ*; 1 unit down

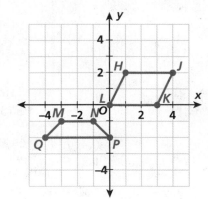

See Example 2   **Reflect each figure across the given axis. Give the coordinates of each vertex in the image.**

    9. figure *HJKL*; *x*-axis

    10. figure *MNPQ*; *y*-axis

See Example 3   **Rotate each figure the given direction and number of degrees about the origin. Give the coordinates of each vertex in the image.**

    11. figure *HJKL*; 180° clockwise

    12. figure *HJKL*; 90° counterclockwise

Extra Practice

See Extra Practice for more exercises.

Describe each transformation.

13.

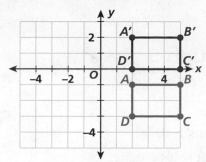

14.

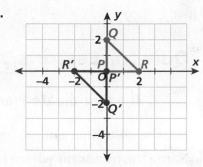

15.

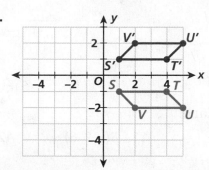

16.

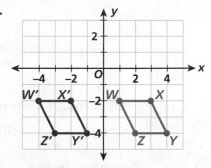

✏️ 17. **Write About It** Will the image of a horizontal line be horizontal after a translation? a reflection over the *x*-axis? a rotation? Explain your answers.

⭐ 18. **Challenge** Lara translated rhombus *MNOP* 2 units right and then rotated it 180° clockwise about the origin. Mike rotated rhombus *MNOP* 180° clockwise about the origin and then translated it 2 units right. Are the coordinates of the vertices of the two images the same? Explain.

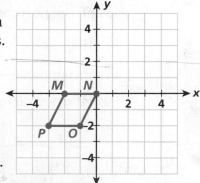

Test Prep

19. **Multiple Choice** The coordinates of the vertices of figure *ABCD* are *A*(−8, 5), *B*(−5, 4), *C*(0, 0), and *D*(−7, 3). The figure is reflected across the *y*-axis. What are the coordinates of *A'*?

　Ⓐ (−8, −5)　　　　Ⓑ (8, −5)　　　　Ⓒ (8, 5)　　　　Ⓓ (5, 4)

20. **Short Response** Figure *ABCD* has vertices *A*(4, −1), *B*(0, 0), *C*(1, −4), and *D*(3, −5). Figure *ABCD* is rotated 180° counterclockwise about the origin. Draw figure *ABCD* and its image.

Quiz for Lessons 3 Through 5

3 **The Coordinate Plane**

Use the coordinate plane for problems 1–8.

Name the quadrant where each point is located.

1. A **2.** Y **3.** J **4.** C

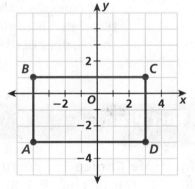

Give the coordinates of each point.

5. H **6.** I **7.** W **8.** B

Graph each point on a coordinate plane.

9. $N(-5, -2)$ **10.** $S(0, 4)$ **11.** $R(-2, 6)$ **12.** $M(2, 2)$

4 **Polygons in the Coordinate Plane**

Graph the polygons with the given vertices.

13. triangle: $J\left(4, 2\frac{1}{2}\right), K\left(-3\frac{1}{2}, 1\right), L(-1, 5)$

14. rectangle: $A(-1, 4), B\left(4\frac{1}{2}, 4\right), C\left(4\frac{1}{2}, 0\right), D(-1, 0)$

Find the perimeter of each rectangle.

15.

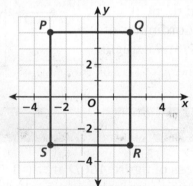

16.

5 **Transformations in the Coordinate Plane**

Use the coordinate plane for problems 17–19.

Perform the given transformation of triangle ABC. Give the coordinates of each vertex in the image.

17. translate 6 units down

18. reflect across the y-axis

19. rotate 90° counterclockwise about point B

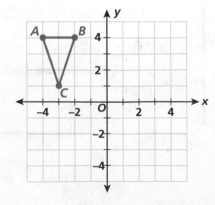

Ready to Go On?

Real-World CONNECTIONS

Shipwreck Diving The ocean floor along the New Jersey coast is dotted with shipwrecks. According to some estimates, there may be as many as 7,000 shipwrecks in the area. This makes the New Jersey coast a favorite spot among scuba divers who enjoy exploring the mysterious remains of sunken ships.

NEW JERSEY

The graph shows the depths of several shipwrecks. Use the graph for Exercise 1.

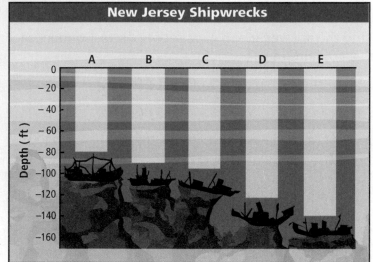

New Jersey Shipwrecks

1. Following are the locations of five shipwrecks: the *Varanger*, 140 feet below sea level, the *S.S. Mohawk*, 80 feet below sea level; the *Tolten*, 95 feet below sea level; the *Resor*, 125 feet below sea level; the *Great Isaac*, 90 feet below sea level. Tell which letter on the graph corresponds to each of the five ships.

2. The *Eureka* is 15 feet closer to the surface of the water than the *Resor* is. Explain how you could use a number line to find the depth of the *Eureka*. Then find the depth of the *Eureka*.

3. Carlos is diving to the *S.S. Mohawk*. Marietta is diving to the *Tolten*. Assuming they descend at the same rate, which dive should take longer? Explain.

Herb Segars-gotosnapshot.com

Real-World Connections

Game Time

A Math Riddle

What coin doubles in value when half is subtracted?

To find the answer, graph each set of points. Connect each pair of points with a straight line.

1. $(-8, 3)$ $(-6, 3)$
2. $(-9, 1)$ $(-7, 5)$
3. $(-7, 5)$ $(-5, 1)$
4. $(-3, 1)$ $(-3, 5)$
5. $(-1, 1)$ $(-1, 5)$
6. $(-3, 3)$ $(-1, 3)$
7. $(1, 1)$ $(3, 5)$
8. $(3, 5)$ $(5, 1)$
9. $(2, 3)$ $(4, 3)$
10. $(6, 1)$ $(6, 5)$
11. $(6, 1)$ $(8, 1)$
12. $(9, 1)$ $(9, 5)$
13. $(9, 5)$ $(11, 5)$
14. $(9, 3)$ $(11, 3)$
15. $(-9, -5)$ $(-9, -1)$
16. $(-9, -1)$ $(-7, -3)$
17. $(-7, -3)$ $(-9, -5)$
18. $(-6, -1)$ $(-6, -5)$
19. $(-6, -5)$ $(-4, -5)$
20. $(-4, -5)(-4, -1)$
21. $(-4, -1)$ $(-6, -1)$
22. $(-3, -1)$ $(-3, -5)$
23. $(-3, -5)$ $(-1, -5)$
24. $(1, -1)$ $(1, -5)$
25. $(1, -5)$ $(3, -5)$
26. $(4, -5)$ $(6, -1)$
27. $(6, -1)$ $(8, -5)$
28. $(5, -3)$ $(7, -3)$
29. $(9, -5)$ $(9, -1)$
30. $(9, -1)$ $(11, -3)$
31. $(11, -3)$ $(9, -3)$
32. $(9, -3)$ $(11, -5)$

Crazy Cubes

This game, called The Great Tantalizer around 1900, was reintroduced in the 1960s as "Instant Insanity™." Make four cubes with paper and tape, numbering each side as shown.

The goal is to line up the cubes so that 1, 2, 3, and 4 can be seen along the top, bottom, front, and back of the row of cubes. They can be in any order, and the numbers do not have to be right-side up.

Jenny Thomas/HMH

Materials
- business-size envelope
- ruler
- scissors
- tape
- hole punch
- chenille stem
- adding-machine tape

It's in the Bag!

A

PROJECT **Positive-Negative Pull-Out**

Pull questions and answers out of the bag to check your knowledge of integers and other rational numbers.

Directions

❶ Seal the envelope. Then cut it in half.

❷ Hold the envelope with the opening at the top. Lightly draw lines $\frac{3}{4}$ inch from the bottom and from each side. Fold the envelope back and forth along these lines until the envelope is flexible and easy to work with. **Figure A**

B

❸ Put your hand into the envelope and push out the sides and bottom to form a bag. There will be two triangular points at the bottom of the bag. Tape these to the bottom so that the bag sits flat. **Figure B**

C

❹ Make a 2-inch slit on the front of the bag about an inch from the bottom. Punch two holes at the top of each side of the bag and insert half of a chenile stem to make handles. **Figure C**

Taking Note of the Math

Starting at the end of the adding-machine tape, write a question about integers and other rational numbers, and then write the answer. After you have written several questions and answers, roll up the tape, place it in the bag, and pull the end through the slit.

HMH

Study Guide: Review

Vocabulary

absolute value

axes

coordinate plane

coordinates

integer

linear equation

negative number

opposites

origin

positive number

quadrants

x-axis

x-coordinate

y-axis

y-coordinate

Complete the sentences below with vocabulary words from the list above.

1. The ___?___ of −12 is 12.

2. The axes separate the ___?___ into four ___?___.

EXAMPLES

EXERCISES

1 Integers and Absolute Value

■ Name a positive or negative number to represent each situation.

15 feet below sea level −15
a bank deposit of $10 +10

■ Graph +4 on a number line.

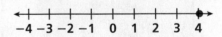

Name a positive or negative number to represent each situation.

3. a raise of $10   **4.** a loss of $50

Graph each integer and its opposite on a number line.

5. −3   **6.** 1   **7.** −9   **8.** 0

Write the absolute value of each integer.

9. |37| **10.** |−14| **11.** |97| **12.** |−13|

2 Comparing and Ordering Integers

■ Compare −2 and 3. Write < or >.

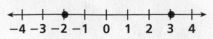

−2 < 3   *−2 is left of 3 on the number line.*

Compare. Write < or >.

13. 3 ▧ 4   **14.** −2 ▧ 5   **15.** 0 ▧ 6

Order the integers in each set from least to greatest.

16. 2, −1, 4   **17.** −3, 0, 4   **18.** −6, −8, 0

3 | The Coordinate Plane

- Give the coordinates of A and name the quadrant where it is located.

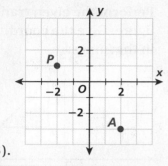

A is in the fourth quadrant with coordinates (2, –3).

Give the coordinates of each point.

19. A **20.** C

Name the quadrant where each point is located.

21. A **22.** B

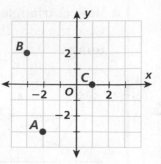

4 | Polygons in the Coordinate Plane

- Graph the triangle with vertices $A\left(-3, 3\frac{1}{2}\right)$, $B(2, 1)$, and $C(-1, -1)$.

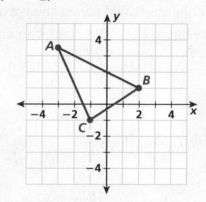

Graph each point on the coordinate plane. Then connect the points with straight lines to form a polygon.

Graph the polygon with the given vertices.

23. triangle: $J(-2, 4)$, $K(3, 3)$, $L(1, -2)$

24. rectangle: $R\left(-2, -1\frac{1}{2}\right)$, $S(-2, 3)$, $T(3, 3)$, $U\left(3, -1\frac{1}{2}\right)$

25. triangle: $D(-2, 3)$, $E\left(3\frac{1}{2}, 5\right)$, $F(2, 1)$

Study Guide: Review

5 | Transformations in the Coordinate Plane

■ Reflect triangle *DEF* across the *x*-axis. Give the coordinates of each vertex in the image.

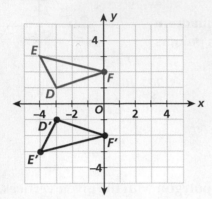

The vertices of the image are *D'* (–3, –1), *E'* (–4, –3), and *F'* (0, –2).

Perform the given transformation on each figure. Give the coordinates of each vertex in the image.

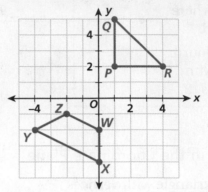

26. translate figure *PRQ* down 3 units

27. reflect figure *WXYZ* across the *y*-axis

28. rotate figure *PQR* 180° clockwise about point *P*.

Chapter Test

Name a positive or negative number to represent each situation.

1. 30° below zero

2. a bank deposit of $75

3. a loss of 5 yards

Write the absolute value of each integer.

4. |99|

5. |−115|

6. |−50|

7. |522|

Compare. Write < or >.

8. −4 ▨ 4

9. 2 ▨ −9

10. −10 ▨ 8

11. −2 ▨ −12

Order each set of integers from least to greatest.

12. 21, −19, 34

13. −16, −2, 13, 46

14. −10, 0, 25, −7, 18

Graph each point on a coordinate plane.

15. A(2, 3)

16. B(3, −2)

17. C(−1, 3)

18. D$\left(-1, 2\frac{1}{2}\right)$

19. E(0, 1)

20. Graph the rectangle with vertices F(−3, 4), G(3, 4), H(3, −1), and J(−3, −1).

Find the perimeter of each rectangle.

21.

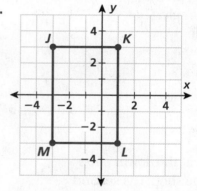

22.

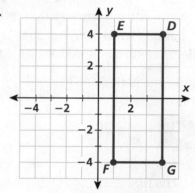

Perform the given transformation of each figure. Give the coordinates for each vertex of the image.

23. rotate figure MNOP 90°
clockwise about the origin.

24. translate figure GHI 4 units up

25. reflect figure MNOP across the y-axis

26. rotate figure GHI 180°
counterclockwise about point I

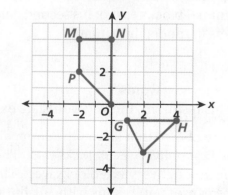

Test Tackler
STANDARDIZED TEST STRATEGIES

Multiple Choice: Identifying Keywords and Context Clues

When reading a test item, pay attention to key words and context clues given in the problem statement. These clues will guide you in providing a correct response.

EXAMPLE 1

Which angle is obtuse?

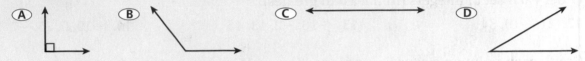

- Look for context clues. Identify what they mean.
- In this test item, **obtuse** is the context clue. It means an angle whose measure is **greater than** 90°.

Find the choice that shows an **obtuse** angle.

A: This angle's measure is 90° because it has a right angle symbol.

B: This angle's measure is greater than 90°. It is an obtuse angle.

C: This angle's measure is 180° because it is a straight angle.

D: This angle's measure is less than 90°. It is an acute angle.

The correct answer is B.

EXAMPLE 2

Kenneth makes flower deliveries along Oak Street. He starts at the flower shop on Oak Street. His first delivery is 8 blocks directly west of the shop. His second delivery takes him 4 blocks directly east of his first delivery. His third delivery takes him 5 blocks east of his second delivery. Write an expression using integers to model this situation.

    (F) $-4 - 5 + 8$ (G) $8 + 4 - 5$ (H) $-8 - 4 - 5$ (J) $-8 + 4 + 5$

- Look for key words.
- In this test item, the key words are **expression** and **integers.**

Find the choice that shows the correct **integer expression** to model the situation.

F: The first delivery is 8 blocks west. This expression does not begin with -8.

G: The first delivery is 8 blocks west. This expression does not begin with -8.

H: The expression begins with -8, but 4 blocks east would be $+4$.

J: This expression's integers correctly correspond to the deliveries.

The correct answer is J.

If you do not understand what a word means, reread the sentences that surround the word and make a logical guess.

Read each test item and answer the questions that follow.

Item A
Multiple Choice Jenny is trimming the edges of a card with ribbon. The rectangular card measures 8 inches by 12 inches. How much ribbon does Jenny need to trim the card?

- (A) 36 inches
- (B) 40 inches
- (C) 64 inches
- (D) 72 inches

1. What are the dimensions of the card?

2. Which words in the problem statement are clues that you need to find the perimeter of the card?

3. When you calculate the perimeter, why are the units not given in square units?

Item B
Multiple Choice Sam has two cylinders. One cylinder has a height of 25 cm and a diameter of 8 cm. The other cylinder has a height of 15 cm and a diameter of 20 cm. What is the difference between the volumes of the two cylinders?

- (F) $400\pi\,cm^3$
- (G) $1,100\pi\,cm^3$
- (H) $1,500\pi\,cm^3$
- (J) $4,400\pi\,cm^3$

4. Make a list of the key words given in the problem statement and link each word to its mathematical meaning.

5. Which choice, if any, can be eliminated? Why?

Item C
Multiple Choice Madeline has 28 daisies and 42 violets. Find the GCF to find the greatest number of wrist corsages that can be made if each corsage has the same number of daisies and the same number of violets.

- (A) 4
- (B) 7
- (C) 14
- (D) 21

6. What is the math term that describes what is being tested?

7. Identify the keywords in this problem statement.

Item D
Multiple Choice An office supply store states that 4 out of 5 customers would recommend the store to another person. Given this information, what percent of customers would NOT recommend the office supply store to someone else?

- (F) 10%
- (G) 20%
- (H) 40%
- (J) 80%

8. What information is needed to solve this problem?

9. Which choice can be eliminated immediately? Why?

10. Write a proportion to find the percent of customers who would recommend the office store to someone else.

11. Describe two different ways to solve this problem.

Standardized Test Prep

Cumulative Assessment

Multiple Choice

1. Marla bought a shirt on sale for $22, which was $\frac{1}{8}$ off the original price. What decimal represents the discount received?

   Ⓐ 0.125   Ⓒ 0.725

   Ⓑ 0.225   Ⓓ 0.825

2. William is bringing small bottles of fruit juice for the company picnic. There are 154 people coming to the company picnic. If the drinks come in packages of 6, how many packages will William need to buy so that each guest can have 3 drinks?

   Ⓕ 20 boxes   Ⓗ 75 boxes

   Ⓖ 26 boxes   Ⓙ 77 boxes

3. Ashlee has 36 basketballs, 48 bean bags, and 60 flying disks. She is making playground sets for the teachers. She wants to put the same number of basketballs, bean bags, and flying disks in each set. What is the greatest number of sets she can make if she uses all of the items?

   Ⓐ 3   Ⓒ 12

   Ⓑ 6   Ⓓ 18

4. At 5:30 P.M., 75% of the people at company A had gone home. What fraction of people had NOT yet gone home?

   Ⓕ $\frac{3}{4}$ Ⓗ $\frac{1}{4}$

   Ⓖ $\frac{1}{2}$ Ⓙ $\frac{1}{25}$

5. What is the ratio of the number of students who play the drums to the number of students who play the trumpet? Give the ratio in simplest form.

School Band	
Instrument	Number of Students
Drums	10
Trombone	14
Trumpet	8
Tuba	3

   Ⓐ 10 to 3   Ⓒ 5 to 7

   Ⓑ 5 to 4   Ⓓ 10 to 27

6. If ∠KHG and ∠JHM are congruent, what is the measure of ∠GHJ?

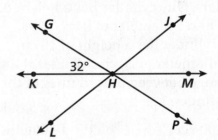

   Ⓕ 148°   Ⓗ 108°

   Ⓖ 116°   Ⓙ 96°

7. What is the reciprocal of $1\frac{3}{5}$?

   Ⓐ $-1\frac{3}{5}$ Ⓒ $\frac{8}{5}$

   Ⓑ $\frac{5}{8}$ Ⓓ 8

8. Find the prime factorization of 80.

   Ⓕ $2 \cdot 5^2$ Ⓗ $2^3 \cdot 10$

   Ⓖ $2^2 \cdot 5$ Ⓙ $2^4 \cdot 5$

9. Louie buys a baseball bat for $125, a catcher's mitt for $55, and a baseball for $3. The tax rate is 5%. If Louie gives the cashier $200, how much change will he get back?

Ⓐ $6.15
Ⓒ $9.25
Ⓑ $7.85
Ⓓ $10.75

10. There are 4 shows a day at the local performing arts theater. The first show starts at 10:15 A.M. Each show lasts 30 minutes, and there is a 1 hour and 30 minute break between shows. What time does the third show end?

Ⓕ 12:15 P.M.
Ⓗ 2:45 P.M.
Ⓖ 12:45 P.M.
Ⓙ 3:15 P.M.

Gridded Response

11. How many feet are in 8 yards?

12. Wyatt has received the following scores on his chapter spelling tests: 92, 98, 90, 97, and 92. What is the mean score of Wyatt's spelling tests?

13. Mrs. Thomas is covering the top of cardboard rectangles with foil to use in a cake display. Each rectangle is 12 in. long by 10 in. wide. How many square inches of foil will she need to cover 5 rectangles?

14. Joshua runs 35% of the way from his house to the gym. If the gym is 5 miles from Joshua's house, how many miles does Joshua run on his way to the gym?

15. What is 65 cm expressed in meters?

Short Response

S1. On Monday, the balance in Graham's checking account was $32. On Tuesday, he wrote three $18 checks. After a deposit on Wednesday, his balance was $15.

a. Find Graham's balance on Tuesday.

b. Write and solve an equation that can be used to find the amount of Graham's deposit. Let d = the amount of Graham's deposit. Show your work.

S2. Find the coordinates of the vertices of the square shown on the grid. Then explain how to find the new coordinates of the square after it is translated 5 units down and 3 units left.

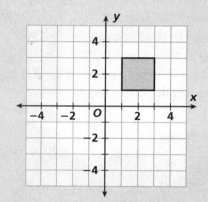

Extended Response

E1. A store sold 44 art masks in September for $528. In October, the store sold 41 art masks for $492. In November, the store sold 38 art masks for $456. All the masks cost the same.

a. Make a table to display the data, and then graph the data. Is the function linear? Explain your answer.

b. Write an equation to represent the function. Tell what each variable represents.

c. In December, the store sold 67 masks. What were the total mask sales in December?

Chapter

- Use equations to describe relationships shown in a table.
- Write inequalities to describe certain situations.

Why Learn This?

Functions, which show how different values are related, can be used in math to describe the real world. With fireworks, a function can show how the length of the fuse is related to the length of time before a shell explodes.

Learn It Online
Chapter Project Online

Learn It Online
Resources Online

Vocabulary

Choose the best term from the list to complete each sentence.

1. ___?___ operations undo each other.

2. A(n) ___?___ is a mathematical statement that two quantities are equivalent.

3. A(n) ___?___ is a ratio that compares two quantities measured in different units.

4. A(n) ___?___ of numbers is used to locate a point on a coordinate plane.

equation

ordered pair

expression

rate

inverse

Complete these exercises to review skills you will need for this chapter.

Words for Operations

Write the operation and algebraic expression for each word expression.

5. the product of 3 and t
6. 9 less than z
7. the quotient of d and 17

8. 28 more than g
9. 101 times k
10. 43 minus x

Inverse Operations

Use the inverse operation to solve each equation.

11. $x + 12 = 31$
12. $8n = 104$
13. $56 \div p = 8$
14. $t - 14 = 33$

15. $a - 82 = 7$
16. $\frac{s}{6} = 5$
17. $b + 22 = 93$
18. $15 = 3n$

Graph Ordered Pairs

Use the coordinate plane. Write the ordered pair for each point.

19. A
20. B
21. C

22. D
23. E
24. F

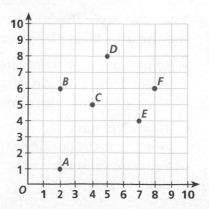

Functions 429

Where You've Been

Previously, you

- created and analyzed different types of graphs.
- graphed ordered pairs on the coordinate plane.
- studied ratios and rates.
- solved algebraic equations by using inverse operations.

In This Chapter

You will study

- special relationships between variables called functions.
- graphing functions on the coordinate plane.
- finding rates of change that describe functions.
- writing inequalities.

Where You're Going

You can use the skills learned in this chapter

- to find the total cost of items or services that charge by the number of units purchased.
- to analyze data and make predictions about linear functions in math and science courses.

Key Vocabulary/Vocabulario

function	función
inequality	desígualdad
input	entrada
linear equation	ecuación lineal
output	salida
rate of change	tasa de cambio
slope	pendiente

Vocabulary Connections

To become familiar with some of the vocabulary terms in the chapter, consider the following. You may refer to the chapter, the glossary, or a dictionary if you like.

1. The prefix *in-* means "not." If two numbers are part of an **inequality**, how do you think they are related to each other?

2. The words *in* and *out* are used all the time. Certain numbers in math are **inputs**, and others are **outputs**. What do you think the difference is?

3. The word *linear* is a form of the word *line*. What do you think a picture of a **linear equation** would look like if you drew it on a coordinate plane?

4. The word *slope* commonly describes something that slants upward or downward like a ski slope. In math, *slope* is used to describe a line. How might a line look different if you changed its **slope**?

Study Strategy: Prepare for Your Final Exam

In your math class, you use skills that you have learned throughout the year, so most final exams cover material from the beginning of the course.

A timeline and checklist like the one shown can help you study for the final exam in an organized way.

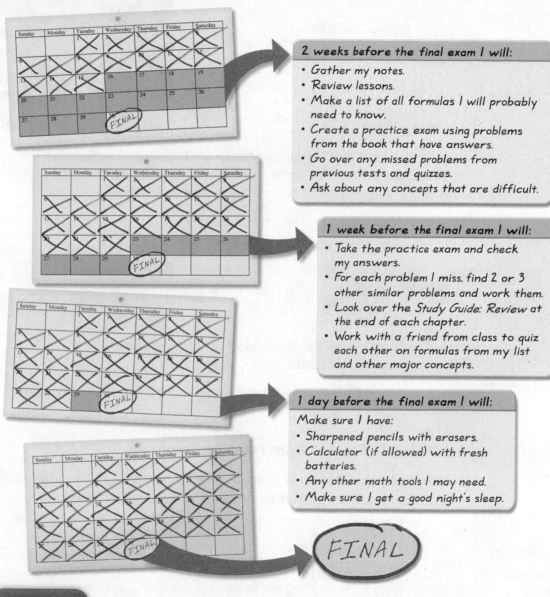

2 weeks before the final exam I will:
- Gather my notes.
- Review lessons.
- Make a list of all formulas I will probably need to know.
- Create a practice exam using problems from the book that have answers.
- Go over any missed problems from previous tests and quizzes.
- Ask about any concepts that are difficult.

1 week before the final exam I will:
- Take the practice exam and check my answers.
- For each problem I miss, find 2 or 3 other similar problems and work them.
- Look over the *Study Guide: Review* at the end of each chapter.
- Work with a friend from class to quiz each other on formulas from my list and other major concepts.

1 day before the final exam I will:
Make sure I have:
- Sharpened pencils with erasers.
- Calculator (if allowed) with fresh batteries.
- Any other math tools I may need.
- Make sure I get a good night's sleep.

Try This

1. Create a timeline and checklist of your own to help you prepare for your final exam.

10-1 Tables and Functions

CC.6.EE.9 Use variables to represent two quantities in a real-world problem that change in relationship to one another; write an equation to express one quantity... in terms of the other quantity...

Vocabulary

function

input

output

A baseball pitch thrown too high, low, or wide is considered outside the strike zone. A pitcher threw a ball 4 inches too low. How far in centimeters was the ball outside the strike zone? Make a table to show how the number of centimeters increases as the number of inches increases.

Lothar Schulz/Getty Images

Inches	Centimeters
1	2.54
2	5.08
3	7.62
4	10.16

+1, +1, +1 (Inches)   +2.54, +2.54, +2.54 (Centimeters)

The number of centimeters is 2.54 times the number of inches. Let x represent the number of inches and y represent the number of centimeters. Then the equation $y = 2.54x$ relates centimeters to inches.

A **function** is a rule that relates two quantities so that each **input** value corresponds exactly to one **output** value.

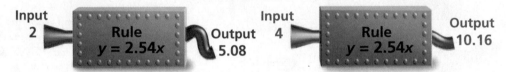

Input 2 → Rule $y = 2.54x$ → Output 5.08   Input 4 → Rule $y = 2.54x$ → Output 10.16

When the input is 4 in., the output is 10.16 cm. So the ball was 10.16 centimeters outside the strike zone.

You can use a function table to show some of the values for a function.

EXAMPLE 1 Writing Equations from Function Tables

Write an equation for a function that gives the values in the table. Use the equation to find the value of y for the indicated value of x.

x	3	4	5	6	7	10
y	6	8	10	12	14	

Helpful Hint

When all the x-values and the y-values are increasing, try using addition and/or multiplication in your equation.

y is 2 times x.   *Compare x and y to find a pattern.*

$y = 2x$ *Use the pattern to write an equation.*

$y = 2(10)$ *Substitute 10 for x.*

$y = 20$ *Use your function rule to find y when $x = 10$.*

Lesson Tutorials Online my.hrw.com

You can write equations for functions that are described in words.

EXAMPLE **2** **Translating Words into Math**

Write an equation for the function. Tell what each variable you use represents.

The length of a rectangle is 5 times its width.

ℓ = length of rectangle   *Choose variables for the equation.*
w = width of rectangle
$\ell = 5w$ *Write an equation.*

EXAMPLE **3** **PROBLEM SOLVING APPLICATION**

 Make sense of problems and persevere in solving them.

Car washers tracked the number of cars they washed and the total amount of money they earned. They charged the same price for each car they washed. They earned $60 for 20 cars, $66 for 22 cars, and $81 for 27 cars. Write an equation for the function.

1 Understand the Problem

The **answer** will be an equation that describes the relationship between the number of cars washed and the money earned.

2 Make a Plan

You can make a table to display the data.

3 Solve

Let c be the number of cars. Let m be the amount of money earned.

c	20	22	27
m	60	66	81

m is equal to 3 times c.   *Compare c and m.*
$m = 3c$ *Write an equation.*

4 Look Back

Substitute the c and m values in the table to check that they are solutions of the equation $m = 3c$.

$m = 3c$ (20, 60) $m = 3c$ (22, 66) $m = 3c$ (27, 81)
$60 \stackrel{?}{=} 3 \cdot 20$ $66 \stackrel{?}{=} 3 \cdot 22$ $81 \stackrel{?}{=} 3 \cdot 27$
$60 \stackrel{?}{=} 60$ ✔ $66 \stackrel{?}{=} 66$ ✔ $81 \stackrel{?}{=} 81$ ✔

MATHEMATICAL PRACTICES

Think and Discuss

1. Explain how you find the y-value when the x-value is 20 for the function $y = 5x$.

GUIDED PRACTICE

See Example **1** Write an equation for a function that gives the values in each table. Use the equation to find the value of *y* for the indicated value of *x*.

1.

x	1	2	3	6	9
y	7	8	9	12	■

2.

x	3	4	5	6	10
y	16	21	26	31	■

See Example **2** Write an equation for the function. Tell what each variable you use represents.

3. Jen is 6 years younger than her brother.

See Example **3** **4.** Brenda sells balloon bouquets. She charges the same price for each balloon in a bouquet. The cost of a bouquet with 6 balloons is $3, with 9 balloons is $4.50, and with 12 balloons is $6. Write an equation for the function.

INDEPENDENT PRACTICE

See Example **1** Write an equation for a function that gives the values in each table. Use the equation to find the value of *y* for the indicated value of *x*.

5.

x	0	1	2	5	7
y	0	4	8	20	■

6.

x	4	5	6	7	12
y	0	2	4	6	■

See Example **2** Write an equation for the function. Tell what each variable you use represents.

7. The cost of a case of bottled juices is $2 less than the cost of twelve individual bottles.

8. The population of New York is twice as large as the population of Michigan.

See Example **3** **9.** Oliver is playing a video game. He earns the same number of points for each prize he captures. He earned 1,050 points for 7 prizes, 1,500 points for 10 prizes, and 2,850 points for 19 prizes. Write an equation for the function.

PRACTICE AND PROBLEM SOLVING

Extra Practice
See Extra Practice for more exercises.

Write an equation for a function that gives the values in each table, and then find the missing terms.

10.

x	−1	0	1	2	5	7
y	■	3.4	4.4	5.4	■	10.4

11.

x	2	3	5	9	11	14
y	−6	−10	−18	−34	−42	■

12.

x	20	24	28	32	36	40
y	−5	−6	−7	■	−9	−10

13.

x	−5	−3	−1	0	1	3
y	−11	−7	■	−1	1	■

14. Multi-Step The height of a triangle is 5 centimeters more than twice the length of its base. Write an equation relating the height of the triangle to the length of its base. Find the height when the base is 20 centimeters long.

Write an equation for each function. Define the variables that you use.

15.

THE NUMERATORS

$125.00 plus $55 per hour

16.

FRED'S Taxi Company

$2.50 plus $0.90 per mile

17. **Multi-Step** Georgia earns $6.50 per hour at a part-time job. She wants to buy a sweater that costs $58.50. Write an equation relating the number of hours she works to the amount of money she earns. Find how many hours Georgia needs to work to buy the sweater.

Use the table for Exercises 18–20.

Width (pixels)	Length (pixels)
30	95
40	125
50	155
60	185

18. **Graphic Design** Margo is designing a Web page displaying rectangles. Use the table to write an equation relating the width of a rectangle to the length of a rectangle. Find the length of a rectangle that has a width of 250 pixels.

19. **What's the Error?** Margo predicted that the length of a rectangle with a width of 100 pixels would be 310 pixels. Explain the error she made. Then find the correct length.

20. **Write About It** Explain how to write an equation for the data in the table.

21. **Challenge** Write an equation that would give the same y-values as $y = 2x + 1$ for $x = 0, 1, 2, 3$.

Test Prep

22. **Multiple Choice** Sunny Lawn Care charges $25 per visit plus $2 per cubic foot. Which equation models this situation?

Ⓐ $y = x + 2$ Ⓑ $y = x + 25$ Ⓒ $y = 25x + 2$ Ⓓ $y = 2x + 25$

23. **Multiple Choice** Which is an equation for the function that gives the values in the table?

x	3	4	5	6	7
y	8	11	14	17	20

Ⓕ $y = 2x + 2$ Ⓗ $y = 2x + 6$

Ⓖ $y = 3x - 1$ Ⓙ $y = 3x + 1$

Graphing Functions

CC.6.EE.9 ...Analyze the relationship between the dependent and independent variables using graphs and tables, and relate these to the equation

Vocabulary

linear equation

Chris is ordering art supplies online. Each canvas costs $16, and the shipping and handling charge is $6 for the whole order.

The total cost y depends on the number of canvasses x. This function is described by the equation $y = 16x + 6$.

To find solutions of an equation with two variables, first choose a replacement value for one variable and then find the value of the other variable.

EXAMPLE 1 **Finding Solutions of Equations with Two Variables**

Use the given x-values to write solutions of the equation $y = 16x + 6$ as ordered pairs.

Make a function table by using the given values for x to find values for y.

Write these solutions as ordered pairs.

x	$16x + 6$	y
1	$16(1) + 6$	22
2	$16(2) + 6$	38
3	$16(3) + 6$	54
4	$16(4) + 6$	70

(x, y)
$(1, 22)$
$(2, 38)$
$(3, 54)$
$(4, 70)$

Check if an ordered pair is a solution of an equation by putting the x and y values into the equation to see if they make it a true statement.

EXAMPLE 2 **Checking Solutions of Equations with Two Variables**

Determine whether the ordered pair is a solution to the given equation.

$(8, 16)$; $y = 2x$

$y = 2x$ *Write the equation.*

$16 \stackrel{?}{=} 2(8)$ *Substitute 8 for x and 16 for y.*

$16 \stackrel{?}{=} 16$ ✔

So $(8, 16)$ is a solution of $y = 2x$.

You can also graph the solutions of an equation on a coordinate plane. When you graph the ordered pairs of some functions, they form a straight line. The equations that express these functions are called **linear equations**.

EXAMPLE 3 **Reading Solutions on Graphs**

Use the graph of the linear function to find the value of *y* for the given value of *x*.

$x = 1$

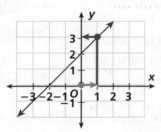

Start at the origin and move 1 unit right. Move up until you reach the graph. Move left to find the y-value on the y-axis.

When $x = 1$, $y = 3$. The ordered pair is (1, 3).

EXAMPLE 4 **Graphing Linear Functions**

Graph the function described by the equation.

$y = 2x + 1$

Make a function table. Substitute different values for x.

Write the solutions as ordered pairs.

x	2x + 1	y
−1	2(−1) + 1	−1
0	2(0) + 1	1
1	2(1) + 1	3

(*x*, *y*)
(−1, −1)
(0, 1)
(1, 3)

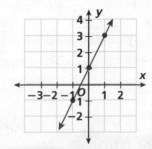

Graph the ordered pairs on a coordinate plane. Draw a line through the points to represent all the values of x you could have chosen and the corresponding values of y.

MATHEMATICAL PRACTICES

Think and Discuss

1. Explain why the points in Example 4 are not the only points on the graph. Name two points that you did not plot.

2. Tell whether the equation $y = 10x - 5$ describes a linear function.

Learn It Online
Homework Help Online
Exercises 1–26, 29, 31, 33

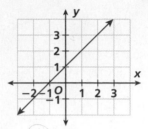

GUIDED PRACTICE

See Example 1 Use the given *x*-values to write solutions of each equation as ordered pairs.

1. $y = 6x + 2$ for $x = 1, 2, 3, 4$

2. $y = -2x$ for $x = 1, 2, 3, 4$

See Example 2 Determine whether each ordered pair is a solution to the given equation.

3. $(2, 12); y = 4x$

4. $(5, 9); y = 2x - 1$

See Example 3 Use the graph of the linear function to find the value of *y* for each given value of *x*.

5. $x = 1$ 6. $x = 0$ 7. $x = -1$

See Example 4 Graph the function described by each equation.

8. $y = x + 3$ 9. $y = 3x - 1$ 10. $y = -2x + 3$

INDEPENDENT PRACTICE

See Example 1 Use the given *x*-values to write solutions of each equation as ordered pairs.

11. $y = -4x + 1$ for $x = 1, 2, 3, 4$

12. $y = 5x - 5$ for $x = 1, 2, 3, 4$

See Example 2 Determine whether each ordered pair is a solution to the given equation.

13. $(3, -10); y = -6x + 8$

14. $(-8, 1); y = 7x - 15$

See Example 3 Use the graph of the linear function to find the value of *y* for each given value of *x*.

15. $x = -2$ 16. $x = 1$ 17. $x = -3$

18. $x = 0$ 19. $x = -1$ 20. $x = 2$

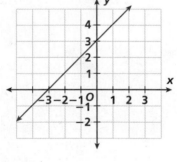

See Example 4 Graph the function described by each equation.

21. $y = 4x + 1$ 22. $y = -x - 2$ 23. $y = x - 2$

24. $y = -2x - 4$ 25. $y = 3x - 2$ 26. $y = -x$

PRACTICE AND PROBLEM SOLVING

Extra Practice
See Extra Practice for more exercises.

Complete each table, and then use the table to graph the function.

27. $y = x - 2$

x	−1	0	1	2
y	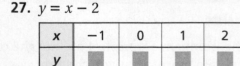			

28. $y = 2x - 4$

x	−1	0	1	2
y				

29. Which of the ordered pairs below is not a solution of $y = 4x + 9$?
    $(1, 14), (0, 9), (-1, 5), (-2, 1), (2, 17)$

Temperature can be expressed according to different scales. The Kelvin scale is divided into units called kelvins, and the Celsius scale is divided into degrees Celsius.

The table shows several temperatures recorded in degrees Celsius and their equivalent measures in kelvins.

30. Write an equation for a function that gives the values in the table. Define the variables that you use.

31. Graph the function described by your equation.

32. Use your graph to find the value of y when x is 0.

Equivalent Temperatures	
Celsius (°C)	Kelvin (K)
−100	173
−50	223
0	273
50	323
100	373

A technician preserves brain cells in this tank of liquid nitrogen, which is at −196 °C, for later research.

33. Use your equation to find the equivalent Kelvin temperature for −54 °C.

34. Use your equation to find the equivalent Celsius temperature for 77 kelvins.

35. ❓ **What's the Question?** The answer is −273 °C. What is the question?

36. ✍ **Write About It** Explain how to use your equation to determine whether 75 °C is equivalent to 345 kelvins. Then determine whether the temperatures are equivalent.

37. ⭐ **Challenge** How many ordered-pair solutions exist for the equation you wrote in Exercise 30?

Test Prep

38. Multiple Choice Which of the ordered pairs is NOT a solution of $y = -5x + 10$?

Ⓐ (−20, 6)   Ⓑ (5, −15)   Ⓒ (4, −10)   Ⓓ (2, 0)

39. Multiple Choice The equation $y = 12x$ shows the number of inches y in x feet. Which ordered pair is on the graph of the equation?

Ⓕ (−2, 24)   Ⓖ (1, 13)   Ⓗ (4, 48)   Ⓙ (12, 1)

Function Notation

Purestock/Alamy

CC.6.EE.9 Use variables to represent two quantities in a real-world problem that change in relationship to one another; write an equation to express one quantity, thought of as the dependent variable, in terms of the other quantity, thought of as the independent variable...

For each child on the merry-go-round, the owner makes $3. The total amount of money changes based on the number of children on the ride.

Many functions representing real-life situations contain two variables. The **independent variable** represents the input of a function. The **dependent variable** represents the output of a function. The value of the dependent variable *depends* on, or is a function of, the value of the independent variable.

EXAMPLE 1 Identifying Independent and Dependent Variables

Identify the independent and dependent variables in each situation.

Vocabulary
independent variable
dependent variable

A A merry-go-round owner earns $3 for every child on the ride.

The **amount of money** earned *depends on* the number of children on the ride.
Dependent: **amount of money**
Independent: number of children

B For every hour Cherise studies, her test score goes up 2 points.

Cherise's **test score** *depends on* the number of hours she studies.
Dependent: **test score**   Independent: number of hours

EXTENSION

Exercises

Identify the independent and dependent variables in each situation.

1. Erica's paycheck is determined by the number of hours she works.

2. The price of the MP3s determines how many Kai will buy.

3. The growth of the grass is a function of the daily amount of rainfall.

4. A salesman's commission depends on how many cars he sells.

Identify the independent and dependent variables. Write a rule in function notation for each situation.

5. Simon charges $10 per hour for yard work.

6. A car can travel 25 miles per gallon of gas.

Focus on Problem Solving

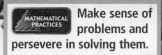

Plan

 Make a Plan

• **Choose a problem-solving strategy**

The following strategies can help you solve problems.

• Use a Venn Diagram
• Draw a Diagram
• Make a Model
• Guess and Test
• Work Backward

• Find a Pattern
• Make a Table
• Solve a Simpler Problem
• Use Logical Reasoning
• Make an Organized List

 Tell which strategy from the list above you would use to solve each problem. Explain your choice. Then solve the problem.

1 The temperature on a winter day is $-6\ °F$ at 8:00 A.M., $-4\ °F$ at 9:00 A.M., and $-2\ °F$ at 10:00 A.M. The temperature continues to change by the same amount each hour. What is the temperature at 2:00 P.M.?

2 Caleb lives in one of the states listed in the table. His home is at an elevation of 600 feet. There is a park in his state at an elevation of 150 feet. Which state does Caleb live in?

State	Lowest Elevation (ft)	Highest Elevation (ft)
California	−282	14,494
Louisiana	−8	535
West Virginia	240	4,861

3 On a map of Nadia's town, the library is located at (2, 3), the museum is located at (1, −2), city hall is located at (−2, −3), and the aquarium is located at (−4, 2). She wants to organize a field trip to the two buildings that are closest to each other. Which two buildings should she choose?

4 In the past month, Ethan's savings account had withdrawals and deposits in the amounts of −$25, +$45, +$15, −$40, and +$60. He wants to check the receipts for one of the withdrawals and one of the deposits. How many different combinations of one withdrawal and one deposit are there?

Slope and Rate of Change

CC.6.RP.3 Use ratio and rate reasoning to solve real-world and mathematical problems, e.g., by reasoning about tables of equivalent ratios, tape diagrams, double number line diagrams, or equations **Also CC.6.RP.3a**

Vocabulary

rate of change

slope

By measuring the height of a plant at the same time each day, you can determine the rate at which the plant is growing. The plant's growth is a *rate of change*.

The **rate of change** of a function is a ratio that compares the difference between two output values to the difference between the corresponding input values.

$$\text{rate of change} = \frac{\text{change in } y\text{-values}}{\text{change in } x\text{-values}}$$

In some functions the rate of change is *constant*, which means that it is the same for all *x*- and *y*-values. In other functions, the rates of change are *variable*, which means they are different for some *x*- and *y*-values.

EXAMPLE **1**   **Using a Table to Identify Rates of Change**

Tell whether the rates of change are constant or variable.

Be careful to put the differences in *y*-values in the numerator and the differences in *x*-values in the denominator when you write a rate of change.

A

x	0	1	3	6	8
y	0	4	8	8	6

+1 +2 +3 +2

x	0	1	3	6	8
y	0	4	8	8	6

+4 +4 +0 −2

Find the differences between consecutive data points.

$\frac{4}{1} = 4$ $\frac{4}{2} = 2$ $\frac{0}{3} = 0$ $\frac{-2}{2} = -1$

Find each ratio of the change in y to the change in x.

The rates of change are variable.

B

x	0	1	4	6	7
y	1	2	5	7	8

+1 +3 +2 +1

x	0	1	4	6	7
y	1	2	5	7	8

+1 +3 +2 +1

Find the differences between consecutive data points.

$\frac{1}{1} = 1$ $\frac{3}{3} = 1$ $\frac{2}{2} = 1$ $\frac{1}{1} = 1$

Find each ratio of the change in y to the change in x.

The rate of change is constant.

Video   **Lesson Tutorials Online**

To show rates of change on a graph, plot the data points and connect them with line segments. This graph shows the data in Example 1B.

When the rate of change is constant, the segments form a straight line. The constant rate of change of a line is its **slope**.

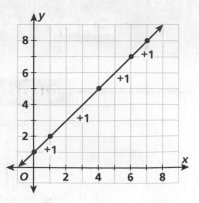

EXAMPLE 2 Gardening Application

Evan planted some new plants in his garden. He measured the height of the same plant each Wednesday for five weeks. The table shows the measurements Evan recorded.

Week	1	2	3	4	5
Height (cm)	3	6	9	12	15

A Determine whether the rates of change are constant or variable.

$$\frac{3}{1} = 3 \quad \frac{3}{1} = 3 \quad \frac{3}{1} = 3 \quad \frac{3}{1} = 3$$

The rate of change is constant.

B Graph the data and connect the points with line segments. If the rate of change is constant, find and interpret the slope.

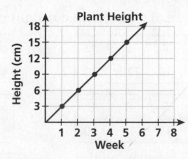

The rate of change between any two points is 3. The slope of the line is 3.

The slope is 3. This means the plant grew 3 cm each week.

Think and Discuss

1. **Explain** how to determine the rate of change from a table of values.

2. **Tell** why rates of change in the real world usually involve two units, such as mi/h.

3. **Give an example** of a constant rate of change and a variable rate of change in the real world.

Learn It Online
Homework Help Online
Exercises 1–10, 11, 15, 17

GUIDED PRACTICE

See Example 1 Tell whether the rates of change are constant or variable.

1.

x	1	3	4	7	10
y	5	15	20	35	50

2.

x	0	4	5	8	9
y	3	7	10	20	23

3.

x	1	2	4	7	12
y	6	12	18	42	54

4.

x	2	3	4	6	8
y	6	9	12	18	24

See Example 2 **5.** McKenzie files documents each day after school for an attorney's office. McKenzie recorded the amount of money she earned for several hours during the past week.

Number of Hours	3	7	10	12	16
Earnings	$25.50	$59.50	$85.00	$102.00	$136.00

a. Determine whether the rates of change are constant or variable.

b. Graph the data and connect the points with line segments. If the rate of change is constant, find and interpret the slope.

INDEPENDENT PRACTICE

See Example 1 Tell whether the rates of change are constant or variable.

6.

x	0	3	4	9	12
y	0	7.5	10	22.5	30

7.

x	0	1	2	5	7
y	0	3	6	15	21

8.

x	0	3	5	6	9
y	11	18	15	16	20

9.

x	2	3	6	7	10
y	0.2	0.3	0.6	0.7	0.1

See Example 2 **10.** Samantha's coach recorded the amount of time it took her to run several miles during her track workout on Thursday.

Miles	1	2	3	4	5
Minutes	6.5	13	19.5	26	32.5

a. Determine whether the rates of change are constant or variable.

b. Graph the data and connect the points with line segments. If the rate of change is constant, find and interpret the slope.

PRACTICE AND PROBLEM SOLVING

Extra Practice
See Extra Practice for more exercises.

Graph each set of points and connect them with line segments. If the rate of change is constant, give the slope of the line containing the points.

11. $(-2, -5), (0, -1), (3, 5), (5, 9)$

12. $(-2, -3), (1, 1.5), (4, 6), (9, 13.5)$

13. $(-2, -8), (-1, -3), (2, 4), (6, 6)$

14. $(-1, 6), (2, 0), (3, -2), (6, -8)$

Economics

George Washington Carver discovered 300 different uses for peanuts, as well as hundreds of other uses for soybeans, pecans, and sweet potatoes.

15. **Transportation** The table shows the number of passengers on a bus at various times during the day. Do the data show a constant rate of change? Explain your answer.

Time	9:00 A.M.	12:00 NOON	5:00 P.M.
Passengers	50	5	49

16. **Economics** The graph shows the cost of peanuts.

   a. Find the rates of change between four consecutive pairs of points.

   b. If the rate of change in part **a** is constant, find and interpret the slope of the line.

17. **What's the Error?** A student says that the rate of change for the data in the table cannot be constant because the y-values do not increase by the same amount. What error did the student make?

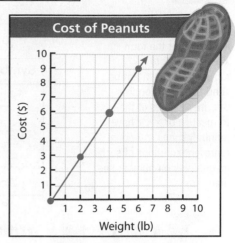

x	0	3	4	9	12
y	0	7.5	10	22.5	30

18. **Critical Thinking** When are the rates of change of a function equal to the slope of the function?

19. **Challenge** Give a situation in which data might show both a constant and a variable rate of change.

Test Prep

20. **Multiple Choice** What is the slope of the line?

   Ⓐ −4   Ⓑ −$\frac{1}{4}$ Ⓒ $\frac{1}{4}$ Ⓓ 4

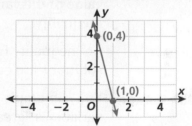

21. **Short Response** Tell whether the rates of change are variable or constant. If the rate of change is constant, find the slope of the line containing the points.

x	0	2	5	7	11
y	0	2.5	6.25	8.75	13.75

Hulton Archive/Getty Images

10-3 Slope and Rate of Change **445**

COMMON CORE

CC.6.EE.8 Write an inequality of the form $x > c$ or $x < c$ to represent a constraint or condition... Recognize that inequalities of the form $x > c$ or $x < c$ have infinitely many solutions; represent solutions of such inequalities on number line diagrams

An **inequality** states that two quantities either are not equal or may not be equal. An inequality uses one of the following symbols:

Symbol	Meaning	Word Phrases
<	Is less than	Fewer than, below
>	Is greater than	More than, above
≤	Is less than or equal to	At most, no more than
≥	Is greater than or equal to	At least, no less than

EXAMPLE 1   **Writing Inequalities**

Vocabulary
inequality

algebraic inequality

solution set

compound inequality

Write an inequality for each situation.

A There are at least 25 students in the auditorium.

number of students ≥ 25   *"At least" means greater than or equal to.*

B No more than 150 people can occupy the room.

room capacity ≤ 150   *"No more than" means less than or equal to.*

An inequality that contains a variable is an **algebraic inequality**. A value of the variable that makes the inequality true is a solution of the inequality.

An inequality may have more than one solution. Together, all of the solutions are called the **solution set**.

Interactivities Online ▶ You can graph the solutions of an inequality on a number line. If the variable is "greater than" or "less than" a number, then that number is indicated with an open circle.

This open circle shows that 5 is not a solution.

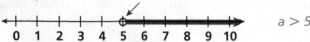

$a > 5$

If the variable is "greater than or equal to" or "less than or equal to" a number, that number is indicated with a closed circle.

This closed circle shows that 3 is a solution.

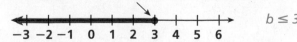

$b ≤ 3$

Video **Lesson Tutorials Online**

EXAMPLE **2** **Graphing Simple Inequalities**

Graph each inequality.

A $x > -2$

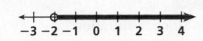

Draw an open circle at −2. The solutions are values of x greater than −2, so shade to the right of −2.

B $-1 \geq y$

Draw a closed circle at −1. The solutions are −1 and values of y less than −1, so shade to the left of −1.

Writing Math

The compound inequality $-2 < y$ and $y < 4$ can be written as $-2 < y < 4$.

A **compound inequality** is the result of combining two inequalities. The words *and* and *or* are used to describe how the two parts are related.

$x > 3$ or $x < -1$

x is either greater than 3 or less than −1.

$-2 < y$ and $y < 4$

y is both greater than −2 and less than 4. y is between −2 and 4.

EXAMPLE 3 **Graphing Compound Inequalities**

Graph each compound inequality.

A $s \geq 0$ or $s < -3$

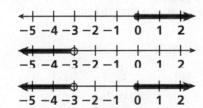

Graph $s \geq 0$.

Graph $s < -3$.

Combine the graphs.

Reading Math

$1 < p$ is the same as $p > 1$.

B $1 < p \leq 5$

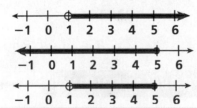

Graph $1 < p$.

Graph $p \leq 5$.

Graph the common solutions.

MATHEMATICAL PRACTICES

Think and Discuss

1. Compare the graphs of the inequalities $y > 2$ and $y \geq 2$.

2. Explain how to graph each type of compound inequality.

Learn It Online
Homework Help Online
Exercises 1–26, 27, 29, 31, 35, 37

GUIDED PRACTICE

See Example 1 **Write an inequality for each situation.**

1. No more than 18 people are allowed in the gallery at one time.

2. There are fewer than 8 fish in the aquarium.

3. The water level is above 45 inches.

See Example 2 **Graph each inequality.**

4. $x < 3$ **5.** $\frac{1}{2} \geq r$ **6.** $2.8 < w$ **7.** $y \geq -4$

See Example 3 **Graph each compound inequality.**

8. $a > 2$ or $a \leq -1$ **9.** $-4 < p \leq 6$ **10.** $-2 \leq n < 0$

INDEPENDENT PRACTICE

See Example 1 **Write an inequality for each situation.**

11. The temperature is below 40 °F.

12. There are at least 24 pictures on the roll of film.

13. No more than 35 tables are in the cafeteria.

14. Fewer than 250 people attended the rally.

See Example 2 **Graph each inequality.**

15. $s \geq -1$ **16.** $y < 0$ **17.** $n \leq -3$

18. $2 < x$ **19.** $-6 \leq b$ **20.** $m < -4$

See Example 3 **Graph each compound inequality.**

21. $p > 3$ or $p < 0$ **22.** $1 \leq x \leq 4$ **23.** $-3 < y < -1$

24. $k > 0$ or $k \leq -2$ **25.** $n \geq 1$ or $n \leq -1$ **26.** $-2 < w \leq 2$

PRACTICE AND PROBLEM SOLVING

Extra Practice
See Extra Practice for more exercises.

Graph each inequality or compound inequality.

27. $z \leq -5$ **28.** $3 > f$ **29.** $m \geq -2$

30. $3 > y$ or $y \geq 6$ **31.** $-9 < p \leq -3$ **32.** $q > 2$ or $-1 > q$

33. **Write About It** Explain how to graph the inequality $13 \geq x$.

34. **Critical Thinking** The *Reflexive Property* states that $x = x$. For which inequality symbols would the Reflexive Property apply? Give examples and explain your answer.

Earth Science LINK

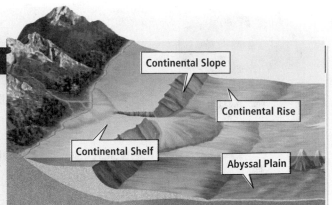

Continental Slope
Continental Rise
Continental Shelf
Abyssal Plain

The portion of the earth's surface that lies beneath the ocean and consists of continental crust is the continental margin. The continental margin is divided into the continental shelf, the continental slope, and the continental rise.

35. The continental shelf begins at the shoreline and slopes toward the open ocean. The depth of the continental shelf can reach 200 meters. Write a compound inequality for the depth of the continental shelf.

36. The continental slope begins at the edge of the continental shelf and continues down to the flattest part of the ocean floor. The depth of the continental slope ranges from about 200 meters to about 4,000 meters. Write a compound inequality for the depth of the continental slope.

37. The bar graph shows the depth of the ocean in various locations as measured by different research vessels. Write a compound inequality that shows the ranges of depth measured by each vessel.

38. ⭐ **Challenge** Water freezes at 32 °F and boils at 212 °F. Write three inequalities to show the ranges of temperatures for which water is a solid, a liquid, and a gas.

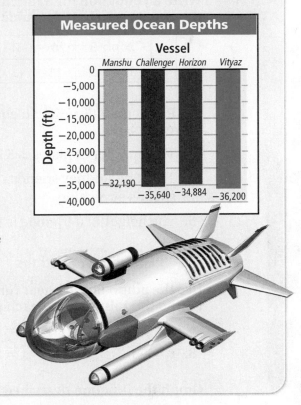

Measured Ocean Depths

Vessel

Manshu Challenger Horizon Vityaz

Depth (ft): 0, −5,000, −10,000, −15,000, −20,000, −25,000, −30,000, −35,000, −40,000

−32,190   −35,640   −34,884   −36,200

Quiz for Lessons 1 Through 4

✓ **1** **Tables and Functions**

Write an equation for a function that gives the values in each table. Use the equation to find the value of *y* for each indicated value of *x*.

1.

x	2	3	4	5	8
y	7	9	11	13	■

2.

x	1	4	5	6	8
y	■	18	23	28	38

For Problems 3–5, write an equation for the function. Tell what each variable you use represents.

3. The number of plates is 5 less than 3 times the number of cups.

4. The time Rodney spends running is 10 minutes more than twice the time he spends stretching.

5. The height of a triangle is twice the length of its base.

✓ **2** **Graphing Functions**

Use the graph of the linear function at right to find the value of *y* for each given value of *x*.

6. $x = 3$ **7.** $x = 0$

8. $x = -1$ **9.** $x = -2$

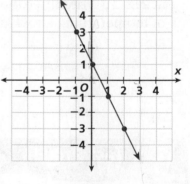

Graph the function described by each equation.

10. $y = x + 5$ **11.** $y = 3x + 2$ **12.** $y = -2x$

✓ **3** **Slope and Rate of Change**

Tell whether the rates of change are constant or variable.

13.

x	0	1	2	3	4	5
y	4	5	6	7	8	9

14.

x	0	3	4	7	8	11
y	5	6	8	11	15	20

✓ **4** **Inequalities**

Write an inequality for each situation.

15. Gray has at least 25 blue T-shirts.   **16.** Capacity: not more than 50 people.

Graph each inequality.

17. $b > -1$ **18.** $5 \leq t$ **19.** $-3 \geq x$

20. $5 \geq p$ and $p > -1$ **21.** $-8 > g$ or $g \geq -1$ **22.** $-4 \leq x < 0$

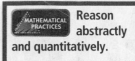 

The Alaska Railroad The Alaska Railroad began in 1903 with just 51 miles of track. Today, the railroad winds through 500 miles of stunning scenery. During the summer months, the railroad is one of Alaska's top tourist attractions.

ALASKA

1. Kayla is taking the Denali Star train to Fairbanks. She gets on at Wasilla, which is 50 miles north of Anchorage. The table shows the time she travels and her distance from Anchorage.

   a. Describe any patterns you see in the table.

   b. Graph the function described by the table.

   c. Does the table show a linear relationship? Why or why not?

   d. Write an equation for a function that gives the values in the table.

   e. Use the equation to find the missing value of y in the table.

Time in hours (x)	0	1	2	3	4
Distance from Anchorage in miles (y)	50	80	110	140	■

2. What is the slope of the graph of the function described by the table? Describe the slope as a rate of change.

3. Suppose you have been on the train for at least 5 hours. A passenger says that the trip to Fairbanks takes 10 hours. Write an inequality that describes in how many more hours h the train will reach Fairbanks.

Real-World Connections

Game Time

Try Angles

Find the greatest integer that makes the inequality true. Then use that value of the variable to decode the answer to the question. The first one has been solved for you.

$i < 14$ **$i = 13$** $z \le -4$

$p < 12$ $f < -8$

$r \le -4.5$ $l < 0$

$h < 1$ $w \le 5$

$s \le 2.5$ $j < 12$

$m < 4$ $e \le 24$

$v < 0$ $r \le 12$

$b < 24$ $a < 8$

$t \le 4$ $o \le 12$

$c < -2$ $x < 9$

$n \le -2$ $g \le 9$

$y \le 6$ $u \le -10$

$d < 11$ $k < 12$

Why did the angle make straight A's?

$\overline{}\ \overline{}\ \overline{}$ $\overline{}\ \overline{}\ \overline{}\ \overline{}\ \overline{}$ $\overline{}\ \overline{}\ \overline{}$ $\overline{}\ \overline{}\ \overline{}\ \overline{}\ \overline{}\ \overline{}$ $\overline{}\ \overset{\text{I}}{\overline{}}\ \overline{}\ \overline{}\ \overline{}$.

 4 0 24   7 −2 9 −1 24   5 7 2   7 −1 5 7 6 2   −5 13 9 0 4

---

24 Points

This traditional Chinese game is played using a deck of 52 cards numbered 1–13, with four of each number. The cards are shuffled, and four cards are placed face up in the center. The winner is the first player who comes up with an expression that equals 24, using each of the numbers on the four cards once.

Learn It Online
Game Time

Complete rules and a set of game cards are available online.

Jenny Thomas/HMH

Materials
- magazine
- glue
- scissors
- index cards

It's in the Bag!

PROJECT **Picture Envelopes**

Make these picture-perfect envelopes in which to store your notes on the lessons of this chapter.

Directions

❶ Flip through a magazine and carefully tear out six pages with full-page pictures that you like.

❷ Lay one of the pages in front of you with the picture face down. Fold the page into thirds as shown, and then unfold the page. **Figure A**

❸ Fold the sides in, about 1 inch, and then unfold. Cut away the four rectangles at the corners of the page. **Figure B**

❹ Fold in the two middle flaps. Then fold up the bottom and glue it onto the flaps. **Figure C**

❺ Cut the corners of the top section at an angle to make a flap. **Figure D**

❻ Repeat the steps to make five more envelopes. Label them so that there is one for each lesson of the chapter.

Taking Note of the Math

Use index cards to take notes on the lessons of the chapter. Store the cards in the appropriate envelopes.

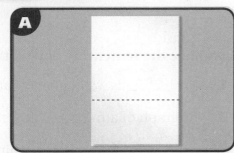

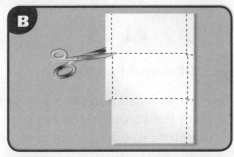

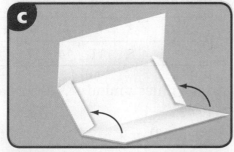

Vocabulary

algebraic inequality	linear equation
compound inequality	output
function	rate of change
inequality	slope
input	solution of an inequality

Complete the sentences below with vocabulary words from the list above.

1. A(n) ___?___ is a statement that two values are not equal.

2. The graph of a(n) ___?___ is a straight line.

3. A(n) ___?___ shows relationships between quantities.

EXAMPLES

1 Tables and Functions

■ Write an equation for a function that gives the values in the table. Use the equation to find the value of y for the indicated value of x.

x	2	3	4	5	6	12
y	5	8	11	14	17	■

y is 3 times x minus 1. *Find a pattern.*

$y = 3x - 1$ *Write an equation.*

$y = 3(12) - 1$ *Substitute 12 for x.*

$y = 36 - 1 = 35$

EXERCISES

Write an equation for a function that gives the values in each table. Use the equation to find the value of y for each indicated value of x.

4.

x	2	3	4	5	6	8
y	6	8	10	12	14	■

Write an equation to describe the function. Tell what each variable you use represents.

5. The length of a rectangle is 4 times its width.

2 Graphing Functions

■ Graph the function described by the equation $y = 3x + 4$.

Make a table.   *Write as ordered pairs.*

x	3x + 4	y
0	3(0) + 4	4
1	3(1) + 4	7
2	3(2) + 4	10

(x, y)

$(0, 0)$

$(1, 7)$

$(2, 10)$

Graph the ordered pairs on a coordinate plane.

Use the given x-values to write solutions of each equation as ordered pairs.

6. $y = 2x + 5$ for $x = 1, 2, 3, 4$

7. $y = x + 7$ for $x = 1, 2, 3, 4$

Determine whether each ordered pair is a solution to the given equation.

8. $(3, 12)$; $y = 5x - 3$

9. $(6, 14)$; $y = x + 7$

3 Slope and Rate of Change

■ Tell whether the rates of change are constant or variable.

x	3	4	5	6
y	2	4	6	8

Find the differences between consecutive data points.

+1 +1 +1

x	3	4	5	6
y	2	4	6	8

+2 +2 +2

Find each ratio of the change in y to the change in x.

$\frac{2}{1} = 2$ $\frac{2}{1} = 2$ $\frac{2}{1} = 2$

The rate of change is constant.

Tell whether the rates of change are constant or variable.

10.

x	4	−5	−3	8
y	10	6	8	9

11.

x	2	10	18	26
y	3	2	1	0

12.

x	6	−7	10	0
y	10	7	4	1

13.

x	−5	1	7	13
y	−1	8	17	26

14. Marco is counting the number of cars that pass through an intersection each time the light turns green. The table shows his data. Determine whether the rates of change are constant or variable.

Time	1:00 P.M.	2:00 P.M.	3:00 P.M.	4:00 P.M.
Number of cars	5	7	4	9

4 Inequalities

Write an inequality for each situation.

- You have to be at least 16 years old to drive a car in New Jersey.
  age of driver ≥ 16

- Graph $x < -1$.

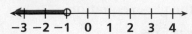

Write an inequality for each situation.

15. A bridge's load limit is at most 9 tons.

16. The large tree in the park is more than 200 years old.

Graph each inequality.

17. $y \geq 3$

18. $-2 \leq k < -1$

19. $-5 < x$

20. $w < 3$ or $w \geq 8$

Study Guide: Review

Chapter Test

Write an equation for a function that gives the values in each table. Use the equation to find the value of y for each indicated value of x.

1.

x	2	3	4	5	6	7
y	▪	8	11	14	17	20

2.

x	1	2	3	4	5	9
y	8	10	12	14	16	▪

Write an equation for the function. Tell what each variable you use represents.

3. The number of buttons on the jacket is 4 more than the number of zippers.

4. The length of a parallelogram is 2 in. more than twice the height.

Use the given x-values to write solutions of each equation as ordered pairs. Then graph the function described by each equation.

5. $y = 5x - 3$ for $x = 1, 2, 3, 4$

6. $y = 2x - 3$ for $x = 0, 1, 2, 3$

Determine whether the rates of change are constant or variable.

7.

x	5	7	9	11
y	1	9	17	25

8.

x	3	8	11	14
y	−3	−1	−5	5

9. Emily is participating in a project for P.E. Every day, she walks a certain distance and keeps track of the total distance she has walked for the entire project. The table shows her data for the first five days.

Day	1	2	3	4	5
Total Distance (mi)	2	4	6	8	10

  a. Determine whether the rates of change are constant or variable.

  b. Graph the data and connect the points with line segments. If the rate of change is constant, find and interpret the slope.

Write an inequality for each situation.

10. You must be more than 4 ft tall to go on the ride.

11. You cannot go more than 65 miles per hour on Route 18.

Graph each inequality.

12. $a < -2$ **13.** $-5 < d$ and $d \leq 2$ **14.** $c > -1$ or $c < -5$ **15.** $b \geq 3$

Test Tackler
STANDARDIZED TEST STRATEGIES

Multiple Choice: Recognize Distracters

In multiple-choice items, the options that are incorrect are called *distracters*. This is an appropriate name, because these incorrect options can distract you from the correct answer.

Test writers create distracters by using common student errors. Beware! Even if the answer you get when you work the problem is one of the options, it may not be the correct answer.

EXAMPLE 1

Simplify the expression $6^2 \div 8 + 15(10 - 3)$.

    (A) 26.5   (C) 109.5

    (B) 106.5   (D) 151.5

Look at each option carefully.

A This is a distracter. You would get this answer if you added 15 to $(10 - 3)$, or 7. Recall that parentheses mean multiplication.

B This is a distracter. You would get this answer if you simplified 6^2 as 12.

C This is the correct answer.

D This is a distracter. You would get this answer if you multiplied 15 by 10 but not by 3.

EXAMPLE 2

What is the value of x in the equation $x + \frac{1}{5} = \frac{3}{5}$?

    (F) 2   (H) $\frac{2}{5}$

    (G) $\frac{4}{5}$ (J) $\frac{1}{5}$

Look at each option carefully.

F This is a distracter. You would get this answer if the original equation was $x + 1 = 3$.

G This is a distracter. You would get this answer if you added $\frac{1}{5}$ to the right side of the equation.

H This is the correct answer.

J This is a distracter. Since $\frac{1}{5}$ is shown on the side of the equation with x, you might think this is the value of x.

When you calculate an answer to a multiple-choice test item, try to solve the problem again with a different method to make sure your answer is correct.

Read each test problem and answer the questions that follow.

Item A
Bob has quiz scores of 89, 70, and 96. What score must he get on his next quiz to increase his quiz average by 2?

Ⓐ 85   Ⓒ 91
Ⓑ 87   Ⓓ 93

1. What common error does choice A represent?

2. What relationship do you notice among the choices?

3. Which is the correct answer?

Item B
Evaluate $1.5x + 2.5$ for $x = 0.5$.

Ⓕ 1   Ⓗ 4.5
Ⓖ 3.25   Ⓙ 10

4. How can you evaluate this algebraic expression?

5. What is a common error when working with decimals?

6. What common error does choice J represent?

7. Which answer is correct?

Item C
The length of a hiking trail is $6\frac{2}{3}$ miles. Along the trail there are 4 exercise stations that are evenly spaced. What is the distance between each exercise station?

Ⓐ $1\frac{1}{2}$ miles   Ⓒ $2\frac{2}{3}$ miles
Ⓑ $1\frac{2}{3}$ miles   Ⓓ $26\frac{2}{3}$ miles

8. Why can choice D be eliminated immediately? What operation was used to get this answer?

9. What error does choice C represent?

10. What operation can you use to find the correct answer?

11. Which is the correct answer?

Item D
What is the area of the composite figure?

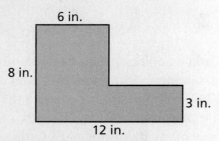

Ⓕ 40 square inches
Ⓖ 66 square inches
Ⓗ 84 square inches
Ⓙ 96 square inches

12. Which answer choice can be eliminated immediately? Why?

13. What common error does choice J represent?

14. Describe how you chose to determine the correct area of the composite figure.

CHAPTER 10

Standardized Test Prep

Learn It Online
State Test Practice

Cumulative Assessment

Multiple Choice

1. Which number line shows the inequality $6 \geq g$?

Ⓐ 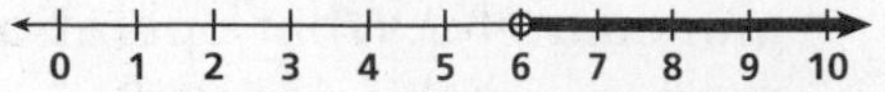

Ⓑ 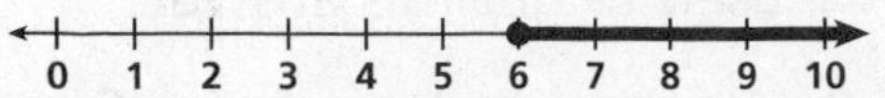

Ⓒ 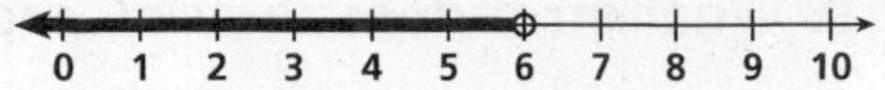

Ⓓ 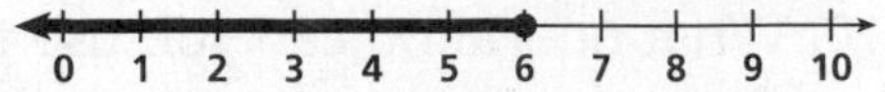

2. Marcus surveyed people to find out how many siblings they had. People who responded to the survey had 0, 2, 4, 3, 1, 1, 2, 11, 3, and 3 siblings. Which number in the data set is an outlier?

Ⓕ 3 Ⓗ 8

Ⓖ 6 Ⓙ 11

3. Carla is selling some of her paintings to raise money for a new bike that costs \$700. She has already raised \$185. If the paintings sell for \$35 each, at least how many paintings must Carla sell to have enough money to buy the bike?

Ⓐ 6 paintings Ⓒ 15 paintings

Ⓑ 9 paintings Ⓓ 20 paintings

4. Convert: 60 ft = ______ yd

Ⓕ 5 Ⓗ 18

Ⓖ 12 Ⓙ 20

5. Simplify: $\sqrt{81}$

Ⓐ 9 Ⓒ 45

Ⓑ 27 Ⓓ 115

6. Solve: $\frac{15}{21} = \frac{x}{7}$

Ⓕ 3 Ⓗ 7

Ⓖ 5 Ⓙ 12

7. A coat has an original price of \$70. A coupon gives the customer a discount of 20%. What is the value of the discount?

Ⓐ \$7 Ⓒ \$12

Ⓑ \$14 Ⓓ \$56

8. For five days, Billy kept track of the number of customers who ate lunch at his new restaurant. If the pattern in the table continues, how many customers will eat lunch at Billy's restaurant on Friday?

Day	Number of Customers
Sunday	12
Monday	25
Tuesday	38
Wednesday	51
Thursday	64
Friday	

Ⓕ 70 Ⓗ 75

Ⓖ 72 Ⓙ 77

9. Which is not equal to 2^5?

Ⓐ $22 + 5(5 - 2) - 5$

Ⓑ $2(2 \times 5) + (32 - 25)$

Ⓒ $15 + 5(5 - 2) + 2$

Ⓓ $5 \times 2 + 22$

10. Jacques collects stamps. Currently he has 124 stamps. If Jacques collects 4 stamps a week, in how many weeks will he have 200 stamps in his collection?

Ⓕ 19 weeks Ⓗ 50 weeks

Ⓖ 31 weeks Ⓙ 81 weeks

11. Shaun wants to raise $350 for his favorite charity. For each mile he runs this month, his sponsors will donate $1. Shaun has already raised $210. If he plans to run 16 more times this month, at least how many miles should he run each time to reach his goal?

Ⓐ 2.5 miles Ⓒ 13.125 miles

Ⓑ 8.75 miles Ⓓ 21.875 miles

Gridded Response

12. In the last 5 days, a bank teller helped the following numbers of customers: 81, 96, 134, 142, and 99. To the nearest whole number, what is the mean number of customers the bank teller helped?

13. How many square feet does the figure cover?

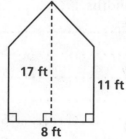

17 ft

11 ft

8 ft

14. Solve $x - 50 = 4$.

15. While hiking in Death Valley, California, Li climbed from a depth of −70 m to the top of Dante's Peak at an elevation of 1,670 m. What was the vertical distance that Li climbed in meters?

Short Response

S1. A new ice cream shop polled several people about their favorite ice cream flavors. The graph below shows the results.

Favorite Ice Cream Flavor

Strawberry 5%

Mint Chocolate Chip 15%

Vanilla 35%

Cookies and Cream 15%

Chocolate 30%

a. If 165 people chose mint chocolate chip as their favorite flavor, how many people chose cookies and cream?

b. What is the total number of people represented in the graph? Explain how you found your answer.

S2. A pizza has 8 slices. Tom buys 4 pizzas for a party. After the party, there was 1 pizza and 3 slices left over. To the nearest percent, how much of the pizzas were eaten?

Extended Response

E1. It cost Sue and Raylene $118.50 to make 19 scarves. They want to sell the scarves for a profit of $100.00.

a. Write and solve an equation to find how much they should charge for each scarf. Show your work.

b. Sue and Raylene each decide to keep one scarf. How much should they charge for each remaining scarf to earn $100.00 in profit?

c. How much more will each scarf cost if they each keep one, rather than selling all 19?

 Student + Handbook ✕ ▬

John Langford/HMH

Extra Practice ... Chapter 1

LESSON 1

Estimate each sum or difference by rounding to the place value indicated.

1. 7,685 + 8,230; thousands

2. 23,218 + 37,518; ten thousands

3. 52,087 − 35,210; ten thousands

4. 292,801 − 156,127; hundred thousands

5. 14,325 + 25,629; hundreds

6. 9,210 − 396; hundreds

7. Mr. Peterson needs topsoil for his garden. His rectangular garden is 78 in. long and 48 in. wide. A bag of topsoil covers an area of 500 square inches. How many bags should Mr. Peterson buy?

8. Natalie's family is having a picnic at an amusement park. The park is 153 miles from Natalie's house. If the family drives 55 mi/h, about how long will it take them to get to the park?

LESSON 2

Find each quotient.

9. 495 ÷ 15

10. 869 ÷ 32

11. 1,675 ÷ 45

12. 12,743 ÷ 60

13. 34,258 ÷ 75

14. 31,752 ÷ 84

15. At the starting line for a marathon, the runners wait in designated areas, often called corrals. The runners are split into the corrals as evenly as possible. The Spring Run Marathon has 1,750 runners and each corral holds 40 runners. How many corrals will be needed?

LESSON 3

Write each expression in exponential form.

16. $5 \times 5 \times 5 \times 5 \times 5 \times 5$

17. $3 \times 3 \times 3 \times 3$

18. $10 \times 10 \times 10 \times 10 \times 10$

19. $2 \times 2 \times 2 \times 2$

20. $7 \times 7 \times 7$

21. 9×9

Find each value.

22. 5^2

23. 5^5

24. 6^3

25. 10^5

26. 9^1

27. 3^6

28. 4^3

29. 2^5

30. A certain colony of bacteria doubles in size every 5 minutes. If the colony began with 2 organisms, how many will there be after 30 minutes?

31. Patricia e-mailed a joke to 4 of her friends. Each of those friends e-mailed the joke to 4 other friends. If this pattern continues, how many people will receive the e-mail on the fifth round of e-mails?

Extra Practice ... Chapter 1

LESSON 4

Simplify each expression.

32. $15 + 7 \times 3$

33. $3 \times 3^2 + 13 - 5$

34. $10 \div (3 + 2) \times 2^3 - 8$

35. $4^2 - 12 \div 3 + (7 - 5)$

36. $10 \times (25 - 11) \div 7 + 6$

37. $(3 + 6) \times 18 \div 2 + 7$

38. The sixth-grade band students sell cases of fruit for a fund-raiser. Emily sold 18 cases of oranges for $12 each, 11 cases of apples for $10 each, and 5 cases of grapefruit for $14 each. Simplify $18 \times 12 + 11 \times 10 + 5 \times 14$ to find how much money she should collect in all.

39. The yearbook committee is selling advertisements in the yearbook for $50 for a 1/4-page ad and $75 for 1/2-page ad. The committee has sold 25 1/4-page ads and 10 1/2-page ads. Simplify $25 \times 50 + 10 \times 75$ to find the amount the committee has earned from the ad sales.

LESSON 5

Simplify.

40. $15 + 7 + 23 + 5$

41. $4 \times 13 \times 5$

42. $34 + 16 + 22 + 18$

Use the Distributive Property to find each product.

43. 5×54

44. 3×32

45. 7×26

46. 9×73

47. A middle school band practices for 80 minutes every day during school. How many minutes do they practice over the course of 3 weeks?

48. A store keeps track of how many people enter the store each hour. On a recent day, 13, 12, 17, and 8 people entered the store during each hour of a four-hour period. How many people entered the store during the 4 hours?

Extra Practice ... Chapter 2

LESSON 1

Evaluate each expression to find the missing values in the tables.

1.

y	23 + y
17	40
27	■
37	■

2.

w	w × 3 + 10
4	22
5	■
6	■

3.

x	x ÷ 8
40	5
48	■
56	■

LESSON 2

4. Earth has a diameter of 7,926 miles. Let d represent the diameter of the Moon, which is smaller than the diameter of Earth. Write an expression to show how much larger the diameter of Earth is than the diameter of the Moon.

Write each phrase as a numerical or algebraic expression.

5. the sum of 322 and 18

6. the product of 7 and 12

7. the quotient of n and 8

8. 14 more than x

Write two phrases for each expression.

9. (23)(6)   **10.** $52 - p$ **11.** $y \div 4$ **12.** $8 + 4$ **13.** $13 \cdot m$

LESSON 3

Write an expression for the missing value in each table.

14.

Albert's Age	Ashley's Age
10	1
14	5
18	9
n	■

15.

Hooves	Horses
16	4
12	3
8	2
n	■

16. A parallelogram has a base of 4 inches. The table shows the area of the parallelogram for different heights. Write an expression that can be used to find the area of the parallelogram when its height is h inches.

Base (in.)	Height (in.)	Area (in²)
4	4	16
4	5	20
4	6	24
4	h	■

Extra Practice ... Chapter 2

LESSON 4

Determine whether the given value of each variable is a solution.

17. $a + 15 = 34$, when $a = 17$

18. $t - 9 = 14$, when $t = 23$

19. Rachel says she is 5 feet tall. Her friend measured her height as 60 inches. Determine if these two measurements are equal.

LESSON 5

Solve each equation. Check your answers.

20. $r + 13 = 36$

21. $52 = 24 + n$

22. $6 + s = 10$

23. Towns A, B, and C are located along Main Road, as shown on the map. Town A is 34 miles from town C. Town B is 12 miles from town C. Find the distance d between town A and town B.

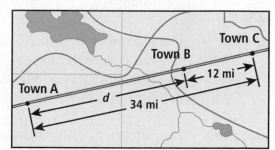

LESSON 6

Solve each equation. Check your answers.

24. $z - 9 = 5$

25. $v - 17 = 14$

26. $24 = w - 6$

27. Reggie withdrew $175 from his bank account to go shopping. After his withdrawal, there was $234 left in Reggie's account. How much money did Reggie have in his account before his withdrawal?

LESSON 7

Solve each equation. Check your answers.

28. $4y = 20$

29. $21 = 3t$

30. $72 = 9g$

31. The area of a rectangle is 54 in². Its width is 6 in. What is its length?

32. A squirrel can run 36 miles in 3 hours. Solve the equation $3m = 36$ to find the number of miles a squirrel can run in 1 hour.

LESSON 8

Solve each equation. Check your answers.

33. $\frac{n}{4} = 6$

34. $7 = \frac{t}{5}$

35. $\frac{a}{8} = 12$

36. Sydney likes to run and ride a bike for exercise. Each day, she runs for one-third the time that she rides her bike. Yesterday, Sydney ran for 15 minutes. How many minutes did she ride her bike?

LESSON 1

Write each decimal in standard form, expanded form, and words.

1. 1.32

2. 0.6 + 0.003 + 0.0008

3. five and three thousandths

4. Joshua ran 1.45 miles, and Jasmine ran 1.5 miles. Who ran farther?

Order the decimals from least to greatest.

5. 3.89, 3.08, 3.8

6. 20.65, 20.09, 20.7

7. 0.053, 0.43, 0.340

LESSON 2

8. The femur is the upper leg bone, and the tibia is one of the lower leg bones. The average length of the femur is 50.5 cm, and the average length of the tibia is 43.03 cm. Estimate the total length of the leg if the bones were placed end to end.

Estimate by rounding to the indicated place value.

9. 5.856 − 1.3497; hundredths

10. 4.7609 + 7.2471; tenths

Estimate each product or quotient.

11. 20.84 ÷ 3.201

12. 31.02 × 4.91

13. 39.76 ÷ 7.94

Estimate a range for the sum.

14. 8.38 + 24.92 + 4.8

15. 38.27 + 2.99 + 15.32

LESSON 3

Find each sum or difference.

16. 1.65 + 4.53 + 3.2

17. 2.2 + 6.8

18. 7 − 0.6

Evaluate 6.35 − s for each value of s.

19. $s = 3.2$

20. $s = 2.108$

21. $s = 5.0421$

22. Brianna is shopping for school clothes and wants to purchase the following items: a shirt for $19.50, shoes for $35.00, a skirt for $12.39, socks for $6.99, and a pair of jeans for $19.95. Not including tax, how much money will Brianna need to purchase these items?

LESSON 4

Find each product.

23. 0.5 × 0.7

24. 0.3 × 0.06

25. 6.12 × 5.9

Evaluate 4x for each value of x.

26. $x = 2.071$ **27.** $x = 5.42$ **28.** $x = 7.85$

29. Each car tire costs $69.99. How much will 4 tires cost?

LESSON 5

Find each quotient.

30. $0.84 \div 6$ **31.** $11.07 \div 9$ **32.** $27.6 \div 12$

Evaluate $0.564 \div x$ for each given value of x.

33. $x = 4$ **34.** $x = 12$ **35.** $x = 2$

36. Marci pays $8.97 at the grocery store for 3 pounds of cherries. How much does each pound cost?

LESSON 6

Find each quotient.

37. $4.5 \div 0.9$ **38.** $59.7 \div 0.4$ **39.** $8.32 \div 8$

40. Lisa paid $13.41 for 4.5 pounds of ground chicken. How much did each pound cost?

LESSON 7

41. Jocelyn has 3.5 yards of ribbon. She needs 0.6 yards of ribbon to make one bow. How many bows can Jocelyn make?

42. Louie has a piece of wood that is 46.8 cm long. If he cuts the piece into 4 equal sections, how long will each section be?

LESSON 8

Solve each equation. Check your answer.

43. $b - 5.2 = 2.6$ **44.** $5t = 24.5$ **45.** $\frac{p}{3} = 1.8$

46. The area of a rectangle is 41 cm². Its length is 8.2 cm. What is its width?

47. The area of Henry's kitchen is 168 ft². The cost of tile is $4.62 per square foot. What is the total cost to tile the kitchen?

Extra Practice ... Chapter 4

LESSON 1

List all of the factors of each number.

1. 28　　　　　**2.** 51　　　　　**3.** 70　　　　　**4.** 24

Write the prime factorization of each number.

5. 48　　　　　**6.** 72　　　　　**7.** 81　　　　　**8.** 150

LESSON 2

Find the GCF of each set of numbers.

9. 15 and 35　　　　　**10.** 16 and 40　　　　　**11.** 22 and 68

12. 6, 36, and 60　　　　　**13.** 27, 36, and 54　　　　　**14.** 14, 28, and 63

15. Alice has 42 red beads and 24 white beads. What is the greatest number of bracelets Alice can make if each bracelet has the same number of red beads and the same number of white beads and if every bead is used?

LESSON 3

Factor the sum of terms as a product of the GCF and a sum.

16. $15 + 39$　　　　**17.** $48 + 36$　　　　**18.** $52y + 13$　　　　**19.** $20k + 16k$

Write four equivalent expressions for each given expression.

20. $90 + 21$　　　　**21.** $100 - 92$　　　　**22.** $80n - 32n$　　　　**23.** $3(12x + 18x)$

LESSON 4

Write each decimal as a fraction or mixed number.

24. 0.31　　　　**25.** 1.9　　　　**26.** 2.53　　　　**27.** 0.07

Write each fraction or mixed number as a decimal.

28. $1\frac{7}{8}$　　　　**29.** $\frac{5}{9}$　　　　**30.** $6\frac{3}{5}$　　　　**31.** $\frac{5}{6}$

Order the fractions and decimals from least to greatest.

32. $0.3, \frac{3}{5}, 0.53$　　　　**33.** $0.8, 0.67, \frac{7}{8}$　　　　**34.** $0.68, \frac{2}{3}, \frac{3}{4}$

Extra Practice ... Chapter 4

LESSON 5

Find the missing numbers that make the fractions equivalent.

35. $\frac{4}{5} = \frac{\blacksquare}{20}$ **36.** $\frac{8}{12} = \frac{2}{\blacksquare}$ **37.** $\frac{6}{7} = \frac{\blacksquare}{28}$ **38.** $\frac{24}{3} = \frac{\blacksquare}{1}$

Write each fraction in simplest form.

39. $\frac{6}{10}$ **40.** $\frac{7}{9}$ **41.** $\frac{4}{16}$ **42.** $\frac{2}{6}$

LESSON 6

Write each mixed number as an improper fraction.

43. $3\frac{1}{4}$ **44.** $6\frac{5}{7}$ **45.** $1\frac{2}{9}$ **46.** $2\frac{7}{10}$

47. Brett's favorite soup recipe calls for $\frac{14}{4}$ cups of chicken broth. Write $\frac{14}{4}$ as a mixed number.

LESSON 7

Compare. Write $<$, $>$, or $=$.

48. $\frac{2}{5}$ $\blacksquare$ $\frac{4}{5}$ **49.** $\frac{5}{6}$ $\blacksquare$ $\frac{7}{8}$ **50.** $\frac{1}{3}$ $\blacksquare$ $\frac{9}{27}$ **51.** $\frac{9}{15}$ $\blacksquare$ $\frac{2}{5}$

52. Natalie lives $\frac{1}{6}$ mile from school. Peter lives $\frac{3}{10}$ mile from school. Who lives closer to the school?

Order the fractions from least to greatest.

53. $\frac{3}{5}, \frac{5}{9}, \frac{4}{5}$ **54.** $\frac{1}{6}, \frac{3}{7}, \frac{1}{3}$ **55.** $\frac{1}{2}, \frac{5}{8}, \frac{7}{12}$

Use the table for Exercises 56 and 57.

56. The table shows the number of hours each day that Michael worked. Did Michael work more hours on Monday or on Friday?

57. Did he work more hours on Tuesday or on Thursday?

Michael's Work Schedule	
Day	**Hours Worked**
Monday	$4\frac{5}{6}$
Tuesday	$5\frac{1}{4}$
Thursday	$5\frac{3}{10}$
Friday	$4\frac{5}{12}$

Extra Practice ... Chapter 5

LESSON 1

1. There are 18 girls on the dance team. Barrettes are sold in packs of 6. Ponytail holders are sold in packs of 2. What is the least number of packs they could buy so that each girl has a barrette and a ponytail holder and none are left over?

Find the least common multiple (LCM).

2. 9 and 15   3. 12 and 16   4. 10 and 12   5. 3, 4, and 5

LESSON 2

Add or subtract. Write each answer in simplest form.

6. $\frac{3}{5} + \frac{2}{3}$ 7. $\frac{7}{8} - \frac{1}{6}$ 8. $\frac{1}{3} + \frac{1}{2}$

9. About $\frac{1}{3}$ of the animals at the zoo are birds. The mammals make up $\frac{2}{5}$ of the zoo's population. What fraction of the zoo's animals are mammals or birds?

LESSON 3

Subtract. Write each answer in simplest form.

10. $4\frac{2}{5} - 2\frac{9}{10}$ 11. $9\frac{1}{6} - 5\frac{5}{6}$ 12. $6 - 1\frac{7}{12}$

13. Adam purchased a 10 lb bag of dog food. His dog ate $7\frac{1}{3}$ lb. of dog food in one week. How many pounds of dog food were left after one week?

LESSON 4

Solve each equation. Write the solution in simplest form.

14. $a + 5\frac{3}{10} = 9$ 15. $1\frac{3}{8} = x - 2\frac{1}{4}$ 16. $6\frac{5}{6} = t + 1\frac{2}{3}$

17. Taylor needs to change a lightbulb that is $12\frac{1}{3}$ feet above the floor. Without a ladder, Taylor can reach $6\frac{1}{2}$ feet. How tall must her ladder be in order for her to reach the lightbulb?

LESSON 5

Multiply. Write each answer in simplest form.

18. $\frac{1}{4} \cdot 1\frac{2}{3}$

19. $2\frac{3}{5} \cdot \frac{1}{3}$

20. $\frac{7}{8} \cdot 1\frac{1}{3}$

Find each product. Write the answer in simplest form.

21. $1\frac{1}{3} \cdot 1\frac{3}{5}$

22. $4 \cdot 2\frac{6}{7}$

23. $\frac{2}{5}$ of $4\frac{1}{2}$

24. An art class has 18 students, and $\frac{1}{3}$ of the students are painting. How many of the students in the class are painting?

LESSON 6

Find the reciprocal.

25. $\frac{7}{9}$

26. $\frac{2}{13}$

27. $\frac{1}{12}$

28. $\frac{8}{5}$

Divide. Write each answer in simplest form.

29. $\frac{1}{6} \div 3$

30. $\frac{4}{7} \div 2$

31. $2\frac{1}{2} \div 1\frac{3}{4}$

32. Debbie bought $8\frac{1}{2}$ lb of ground turkey. She packed the turkey in $\frac{1}{2}$ lb containers and put them in the freezer. How many containers of ground turkey did she pack?

LESSON 7

Solve each equation. Write the answer in simplest form.

33. $\frac{3}{5}a = 12$

34. $6b = \frac{3}{7}$

35. $\frac{3}{8}x = 5$

36. $3s = \frac{7}{9}$

37. $\frac{5}{12}m = 3$

38. $\frac{9}{10}t = 6$

39. Joanie used $\frac{2}{3}$ of a box of invitations to invite friends to her birthday party. If she sent out 12 invitations, how many total invitations were in the box?

Extra Practice ... Chapter 6

LESSON 1

Find the mean, median, mode, and range of each data set.

1.

Points Scored				
16	18	23	13	15

2.

Hours Worked							
37	42	43	38	39	40	45	40

LESSON 2

3. a. The table shows a student's test scores. Find the mean, median, and mode of the test scores.

Test Scores			
78	82	87	95

b. On the next test the student scored a 92. Find the mean, median, and mode with the new test score.

4. The daily temperatures for the first eight days of April were 52 °F, 63 °F, 61°F, 54 °F, 52 °F, 55 °F, 68 °F, and 75 °F. What are the mean, median, and mode of this data set? Which one best describes the data set?

LESSON 3

5. The table shows the number of days with temperatures over 90 °F for six months in a certain city. Use the data to make a box-and-whisker plot.

Number of Days with Temperatures over 90 °F			
May	2	August	14
June	3	September	7
July	5	October	1

6. What is the interquartile range for the temperature data in Exercise 5?

7. The number of years a group of 6 employees have worked at a company are 17, 8, 5, 12, 20, and 2 years. What is the mean absolute deviation for the numbers of years worked, to the nearest tenth?

LESSON 4

8. Use the data of students' heights to make a frequency table with intervals. Then use your frequency table to make a histogram.

Heights of Students (in.)							
63	58	48	60	60	65	56	57
56	62	61	58	59	55	64	50

9. Make a line plot of the data.

Number of Miles Biked																							
14	45	33	34	32	37	44	19	35	36	17	33	35	40	41	38	47	31	44	23	27	20	33	45	27

LESSON 5

10. The data set and dot plot display the time a student spent doing homework for a class over 10 days. Describe the shape of the data distribution.

Time Spent Doing Homework (min)				
15	35	60	65	15
10	35	60	20	35

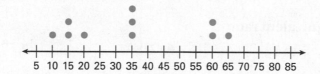

11. The box-and-whisker plots show the costs for the dinner specials at two different restaurants. What conclusions can you make about the data?

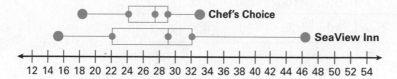

Extra Practice ... Chapter 7

LESSON 1

Use the table to write each ratio.

Types of Books in Doug's Collection			
Reference	10	Comic	7
Mystery	8	Poetry	5
Biography	3	Cooking	4

1. cooking books to poetry books

2. biography books to total books

3. A pack of 12 pens costs $5.52. A pack of 8 pens costs $3.92. Which is the better deal?

LESSON 2

Use a table to find three equivalent ratios.

4. $\frac{2}{5}$ **5.** 5 to 12   **6.** 1:2   **7.** $\frac{6}{7}$

8. The table shows how many pizzas Travis Middle School orders for certain numbers of students. Predict the number of pizzas the school orders for 175 students.

Students	50	100	150	200	250
Pizzas	10	20	30	40	50

LESSON 3

Name the ordered pair for each location on the grid.

9. L **10.** M **11.** R

Graph and label each point on a coordinate grid.

12. $A(0, 3)$ **13.** $B(5\frac{1}{2}, 3)$ **14.** $C(2, 1\frac{1}{2})$

LESSON 4

Find the missing value in each proportion.

15. $\frac{5}{4} = \frac{n}{12}$ **16.** $\frac{2}{9} = \frac{4}{n}$ **17.** $\frac{6}{10} = \frac{n}{5}$ **18.** $\frac{7}{8} = \frac{21}{n}$

19. To make 2 quarts of punch, Jenny adds 16 grams of juice mix to 2 quarts of water. How much mix does Jenny need to make 3 quarts of punch?

LESSON 5

Write each percent as a fraction in simplest form.

20. 50%   **21.** 34%   **22.** 8%   **23.** 12%

24. Michael's baseball team won 85% of its games. Write 85% as a fraction in simplest form.

Write each percent as a decimal.

25. 13%   **26.** 76%   **27.** 5%   **28.** 70%

29. At the toy store, sales increased by 26%. Write 26% as a decimal.

LESSON 6

Write each decimal as a percent.

30. 0.56   **31.** 0.092   **32.** 0.4   **33.** 0.735

Write each fraction as a percent.

34. $\frac{4}{5}$ **35.** $\frac{4}{25}$ **36.** $\frac{7}{16}$ **37.** $\frac{5}{8}$

38. In Mrs. Piper's class, $\frac{17}{20}$ of the students have a pet. What percent of the students in the class have pets?

LESSON 7

Find the percent of each number. Check whether your answer is reasonable.

39. 35% of 80   **40.** 55% of 256   **41.** 75% of 60   **42.** 2% of 68

43. 17% of 51   **44.** 0.5% of 80   **45.** 1% of 8.5   **46.** 1.25% of 48

47. Ryan bought a new CD holder for his car. He can fit only 60 of his CDs in the holder. This represents 60% of his collection. How many CDs does Ryan have?

LESSON 8

Solve.

48. What percent of 150 is 60?   **49.** What percent of 140 is 28?

50. What percent of 120 is 24?   **51.** What percent of 88 is 102?

52. 24 is 60% of what number?   **53.** 9 is 15% of what number?

54. Thomas bought a desk with a retail sales price of $129 and paid $10.32 sales tax. What is the sales tax rate where Thomas bought the desk?

55. The sales tax on a $68 hotel room is $7.48. What is the sales tax rate?

Extra Practice

LESSON 1

Convert.

1. 156 in. = ▇ ft
2. 6 T = ▇ lb
3. 24 qt = ▇ gal
4. 13,200 ft = ▇ mi
5. 8 pt = ▇ qt
6. 33 yd = ▇ ft

7. A marathon is about 26.2 miles. How many feet long is a marathon?

LESSON 2

8. The height of a telephone pole is 15 meters. How many centimeters is this?

Convert.

9. A hat has a mass of about 86 g. 86 g = ▇ kg

10. A rain gauge holds about 0.5 L of water. 0.5 L = ▇ mL

11. 550 g = ▇ kg
12. 88 cm = ▇ mm
13. 1,585 m = ▇ km
14. 5,500 mg = ▇ g
15. 200 mL = ▇ L
16. 2.2 mL = ▇ L

LESSON 3

Find the area of each figure.

17.
7 m
4 m

18.
$1\frac{1}{4}$ cm
$2\frac{1}{2}$ cm

19.
8.5 cm
13.2 cm

LESSON 4

Find the area of each triangle or trapezoid.

20.
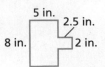
5.5 cm
3 cm

21.

4 cm
2 cm
6 cm

22.

3 cm
4 cm

23. A sailboat's sail is shaped like a triangle with a base of 6 feet and a height of 17 feet. What is the area of the sail?

LESSON 5

Find the area of each polygon.

24.
5 in.
2.5 in.
8 in.
2 in.

25.

9 ft
15 ft
17 ft

LESSON 6

Find the volume of each prism.

26.

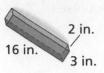

2 in.
16 in.
3 in.

27.

6.1 cm
1.5 cm
3.2 cm

28.

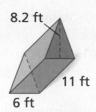

8.2 ft
11 ft
6 ft

29.

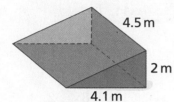

4.5 m
2 m
4.1 m

30.

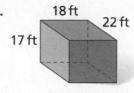

18 ft
22 ft
17 ft

31.

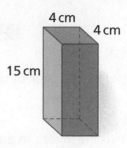

4 cm
4 cm
15 cm

LESSON 7

Find the surface area S of each three-dimensional figure. Use 3.14 for π.

32.

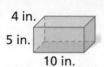

4 in.
5 in.
10 in.

33.

7 ft
3 ft
3 ft

34.

5 in.
12 in.

35. Josef wants to paint the inside and outside of a box. The box is a cube with an edge length of x in., and has no top. Write an expression to represent the surface area that Josef must paint.

Extra Practice

Extra Practice ... Chapter 9

LESSON 1

Name a positive or negative number to represent each situation.

1. 120 feet below sea level   **2.** saving $22   **3.** a decrease of 5°

Graph each integer and its opposite on a number line.

4. +1   **5.** −5   **6.** −3   **7.** +2

Write the absolute value of each integer.

8. |−43| **9.** |82| **10.** |−153| **11.** |39|

LESSON 2

Compare each pair of integers. Write < or >.

12. 15 −19   **13.** −7 ▨ −10   **14.** −3 ▨ 7   **15.** −8 ▨ 2

Order the integers in each set from least to greatest.

16. −6, 5, −2   **17.** 12, −25, 10   **18.** −1, −3, 4, 0

19. On Monday, the temperature was 3 °C. On Tuesday, the temperature was −4 °C. On Wednesday, the temperature was −1 °C. On which day was the temperature the coldest?

LESSON 3

Name the quadrant where each point is located.

20. *A*   **21.** *R*   **22.** *C*   **23.** *T*

Give the coordinates of each point.

24. *B*   **25.** *S*   **26.** *D*   **27.** *U*

Graph each point on a coordinate plane.

28. M(2, −1)   **29.** W(−4, −2)   **30.** A(2, 3)

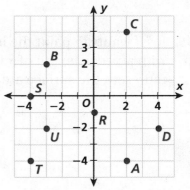

Extra Practice ... Chapter 9

LESSON 4

Graph the polygons with the given vertices.

31. square: $S(3, -1)$, $Q(-1, -1)$, $R(-1, 3)$, $T(3, 3)$

32. triangle: $G(-1\frac{1}{2}, 4)$, $K(3, 1)$, $L(0, -2\frac{1}{2})$

Find the perimeter of each rectangle.

33.

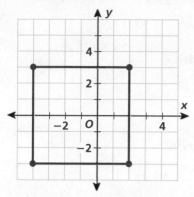

34.

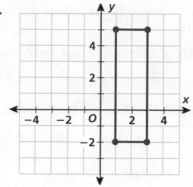

LESSON 5

Perform the given transformation of quadrilateral $ABCD$.
Give the coordinates of each vertex in the image.

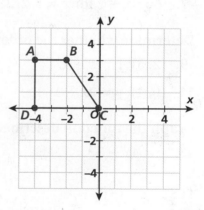

35. translate right 3 units

36. rotate 180° clockwise about the origin

37. reflect across the y-axis

38. translate down 2 units

39. rotate 270° counterclockwise about the origin

40. reflect across the x-axis

Extra Practice ... Chapter 10

LESSON 1

Write an equation for a function that gives the values in each table. Use the equation to find the value of y for the indicated value of x.

1.

x	1	2	3	4	5	10
y	7	9	11	13	15	■

2.

x	3	5	7	9	11	13
y	5	11	17	23	29	■

Write an equation for the function. Tell what each variable you use represents.

3. The length of a rectangle is 4 cm less than 3 times its width.

4. Darren's age is 5 more than 2 times Nicole's age.

5. Madison has 13 more books than Staci.

6. The number of penguins at the zoo is 3 less than 7 times the number of giraffes.

LESSON 2

Use the given x-values to write solutions of each equation as ordered pairs.

7. $y = 6x + 2$ for $x = 1, 2, 3, 4$

8. $y = 5x - 9$ for $x = 2, 3, 4, 5$

Determine whether the ordered pair is a solution to the given equation.

9. $(2, 3)$; $y = x + 1$

10. $(9, 7)$; $y = 3x - 12$

11. $(0, 4)$; $y = 2x - 1$

12. $(1, 1)$; $y = x$

Graph the function described by each equation.

13. $y = 4x - 3$

14. $y = x + 1$

LESSON 3

Determine whether the rates of change are constant or variable.

15.

x	1	3	5	7	9
y	12	14	16	18	20

16.

x	5	8	9	13	17
y	0	3	4	8	12

17.

x	10	20	30	40	50
y	8	15	19	25	31

18.

x	28	26	18	16	8
y	35	33	25	23	15

19. Rico measured the amount of snow that fell during the day. The results are shown. Graph the points. Then find and interpret the slope.

Hour	1	2	3	4	5
Snow (in.)	1	4	7	10	13

LESSON 4

Write an inequality for each situation.

20. The cafeteria could hold no more than 50 people.

21. There were fewer than 20 boats in the marina.

Graph each inequality.

22. $y < -2$ **23.** $f \geq 3$ **24.** $n \leq -1.5$ **25.** $x > 4$

Graph each compound inequality.

26. $1 < s < 4$ **27.** $-1 \leq v < 2$ **28.** $w < 0 \text{ or } w \geq 5$ **29.** $-3.5 \leq y < -2$

Extra Practice

Mastering *the* Standards

for Mathematical Practice

The topics described in the Standards for Mathematical Content will vary from year to year. However, the *way* in which you learn, study, and think about mathematics will not. The Standards for Mathematical Practice describe skills that you will use in all of your math courses.

Mathematical Practices

1. *Make sense of problems and persevere in solving them.*
2. *Reason abstractly and quantitatively.*
3. *Construct viable arguments and critique the reasoning of others.*
4. *Model with mathematics.*
5. *Use appropriate tools strategically.*
6. *Attend to precision.*
7. *Look for and make use of structure.*
8. *Look for and express regularity in repeated reasoning.*

④ Model with mathematics.

Mathematically proficient students can apply... mathematics... to... problems... in everyday life, society, and the workplace...

In your book

Application exercises and **Real-World Connections** apply mathematics to other disciplines and in real-world scenarios.

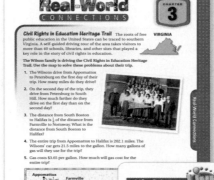

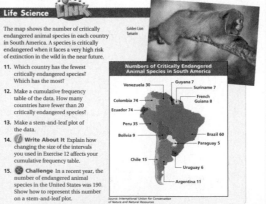

Draw a Diagram

When problems involve objects, distances, or places, you can **draw a diagram** to make the problem easier to understand. You will often be able to use your diagram to solve the problem.

Problem Solving Strategies

Draw a Diagram	Make a Table
Make a Model	Solve a Simpler Problem
Guess and Test	Use Logical Reasoning
Work Backward	Use a Venn Diagram
Find a Pattern	Make an Organized List

All city blocks in Sunnydale are the same size. Tina starts her paper route at the corner of two streets. She travels 8 blocks south, 13 blocks west, 8 blocks north, and 6 blocks east. How far is she from her starting point when she finishes her route?

Understand the Problem	Identify the important information.	

- Each block is the same size.
- You are given Tina's route.

The answer will be the distance from her starting point.

Make a Plan	Use the information in the problem to **draw a diagram** showing Tina's route. Label her starting and ending points.

Solve	The diagram shows that at the end of Tina's route she is $13 - 6$ blocks from her starting point.

$$13 - 6 = 7$$

When Tina finishes, she is 7 blocks from her starting point.

Look Back	Be sure that you have drawn your diagram correctly. Does it match the information given in the problem?

PRACTICE

1. Laurence drives a carpool to school every Monday. He starts at his house and travels 4 miles south to pick up two children. Then he drives 9 miles west to pick up two more children, and then he drives 4 miles north to pick up one more child. Finally, he drives 5 miles east to get to the school. How far does he have to travel to get back home?

2. The roots of a tree reach 12 feet into the ground. A kitten is stuck 5 feet from the top of the tree. From the treetop to the root bottom, the tree measures 32 feet. How far above the ground is the kitten?

Make a Model

Problem Solving Strategies

If a problem involves objects, you can sometimes **make a model** using those objects or similar objects to act out the problem. This can help you understand the problem and find the solution.

Draw a Diagram   Make a Table
Make a Model   Solve a Simpler Problem
Guess and Test   Use Logical Reasoning
Work Backward   Use a Venn Diagram
Find a Pattern   Make an Organized List

Alice has three pieces of ribbon. Their lengths are 7 inches, 10 inches, and 12 inches. Alice does not have a ruler or scissors. How can she use these ribbons to measure a length of 15 inches?

Understand the Problem

Identify the important information.

• The ribbons are 7 inches, 10 inches, and 12 inches long.

The answer will show how to use the ribbons to measure 15 inches.

Make a Plan

Measure and cut three ribbons or strips of paper to **make a model.** One ribbon should be 7 inches long, one should be 10 inches long, and one should be 12 inches long. Try different combinations of the ribbons to form new lengths.

Solve

When you put any two ribbons together end to end, you can form lengths of 17, 19, and 22 inches. All of these are too long.

Try placing the 10-inch ribbon and the 12-inch ribbon end to end to make 22 inches. Now place the 7-inch ribbon above them. The remaining length that is **not** underneath the 7-inch ribbon will measure 15 inches.

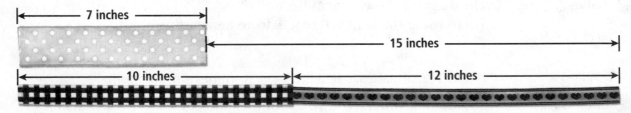

Look Back

Use another strategy. Without using ribbon, you could have **guessed** different ways to add or subtract 7, 10, and 12. Then you could have **tested** to see if any of these gave an answer of 15:

$10 + 12 - 7 = 15$

PRACTICE

1. Find other lengths that you can measure with the three pieces of ribbon.

2. Andy stacks four cubes, one on top of the other, and paints the outside of the stack (not the bottom). How many faces of the cubes are painted?

Guess and Test

If you do not know how to solve a problem, you can always make a **guess**. Then **test** your guess using the information in the problem. Use the result to make a better guess. Repeat until you find the correct answer.

Problem Solving Strategies

Draw a Diagram	Make a Table
Make a Model	Solve a Simpler Problem
Guess and Test	Use Logical Reasoning
Work Backward	Use a Venn Diagram
Find a Pattern	Make an Organized List

There were 25 problems on a test. For each correct answer, 4 points were given. For each incorrect answer, 1 point was subtracted. Tania answered all 25 problems. Her score was 85. How many correct and incorrect answers did she have?

Understand the Problem

Identify the important information.

- There were 25 problems on the test.
- A correct answer received 4 points, and an incorrect answer lost 1 point.
- Tania answered all of the problems and her score was 85.

The answer will be the number of problems that Tania got correct and incorrect.

Make a Plan

Start with a **guess** for the number of correct answers. Then **test** to see whether the total score is 85.

Solve

Make a first guess of 20 correct answers.

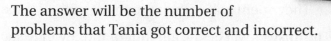

Correct	Incorrect	Score	Result
20	5	$(20 \times 4) - (5 \times 1) = 80 - 5 = 75$	Too low—guess higher
23	2	$(23 \times 4) - (2 \times 1) = 92 - 2 = 90$	Too high—guess lower
22	3	$(22 \times 4) - (3 \times 1) = 88 - 3 = 85$	Correct ✓

Tania had 22 correct answers and 3 incorrect answers.

Look Back

Notice that the guesses made while solving this problem were not just "wild" guesses. Guessing and testing in an organized way will often lead you to the correct answer.

PRACTICE

1. The sum of Joe's age and his younger brother's age is 38. The difference between their ages is 8. How old are Joe and his brother?

2. Amy bought some used books for $4.95. She paid $0.50 each for some books and $0.35 each for the others. She bought fewer than 8 books at each price. How many books did Amy buy? How many cost $0.50?

Work Backward

Problem Solving Strategies

Draw a Diagram   Make a Table
Make a Model   Solve a Simpler Problem
Guess and Test   Use Logical Reasoning
Work Backward   Use a Venn Diagram
Find a Pattern   Make an Organized List

Some problems give you a sequence of information and ask you to find something that happened at the beginning. To solve a problem like this, you may want to start at the end of the problem and **work backward.**

Jaclyn and her twin sister, Bailey, received money for their birthday. They used half of their money to buy a video game. Then they spent half of the money they had left on a pizza. Finally, they spent half of the remaining money to rent a movie. At the end of the day, they had $4.50. How much money did they have to start out with?

 **Understand the Problem**

Identify the important information.

- The girls ended with $4.50.
- They spent half of their money at each of three stops.

The answer will be the amount of money they started with.

Make a Plan

Start with the amount you know the girls have left, $4.50, and **work backward** through the information given in the problem.

Solve

Jaclyn and Bailey had $4.50 at the end of the day.

They had twice that amount before renting a movie. $2 \times \$4.50 = \$9$

They had twice that amount before buying a pizza. $2 \times \$9 = \$18$

They had twice that amount before buying a video game. $2 \times \$18 = \$36$

The girls started with $36.

Look Back

Using the starting amount of $36, work from the beginning of the problem. Find the amount they spent at each location and see whether they are left with $4.50.

Start: $36
Video game: $\$36 \div 2 = \$18$
Pizza: $\$18 \div 2 = \$9$
Movie rental: $\$9 \div 2 = \$4.50$ ✓

PRACTICE

1. Chris is 5 years younger than Mark. Justin is half as old as Chris. Mary, who is 10, is 3 years younger than Justin. How old is Mark?

2. If you divide a mystery number by 4, add 8, and multiply by 3, you get 42. What is the mystery number?

Find a Pattern

In some problems, there is a relationship between different pieces of information. Examine this relationship and try to **find a pattern.** You can then use this pattern to find more information and the solution to the problem.

 Problem Solving Strategies

Draw a Diagram	Make a Table
Make a Model	Solve a Simpler Problem
Guess and Test	Use Logical Reasoning
Work Backward	Use a Venn Diagram
Find a Pattern	Make an Organized List

Students are using the pattern at right to build stairways for a model house. How many blocks are needed to build a stairway with seven steps?

Understand the Problem

The answer will be the total number of blocks in a stairway with seven steps.

Make a Plan

Try to **find a pattern** between the number of steps and the number of blocks needed.

The first step is one block. The second step is two blocks, the third step is three blocks, and the fourth step is four blocks.

Step	Number of Blocks in Step	Total Number of Blocks in Stairway
2	2	$1 + 2 = 3$
3	3	$1 + 2 + 3 = 6$
4	4	$1 + 2 + 3 + 4 = 10$

To find the total number of blocks, add the number of blocks in the first step, the second step, the third step, and so on.

Solve

The seventh step will be made of seven blocks. The total number of blocks will be $1 + 2 + 3 + 4 + 5 + 6 + 7 = 28$.

Look Back

Use another strategy. You can **draw a diagram** of a stairway with 7 steps. Count the number of blocks in your diagram. There are 28 blocks.

PRACTICE

1. A cereal company adds baseball cards to the 3rd box, the 6th box, the 11th box, the 18th box, and so on of each case of cereal. In a case of 40 boxes, how many boxes will have baseball cards?

2. Describe the pattern and find the missing numbers.

1; 4; 16; 64; 256; ▓ ; ▓ ; 16,384

Problem Solving Handbook

(all) Victoria Smith/HMH

Make a Table

When you are given a lot of information in a problem, it may be helpful to organize that information. One way to organize information is to **make a table.**

Problem Solving Strategies

Draw a Diagram	**Make a Table**
Make a Model	Solve a Simpler Problem
Guess and Test	Use Logical Reasoning
Work Backward	Use a Venn Diagram
Find a Pattern	Make an Organized List

Problem Solving Handbook

Mrs. Melo's students scored the following on their math test: 90, 80, 77, 78, 91, 92, 73, 62, 83, 79, 72, 85, 93, 84, 75, 68, 82, 94, 98, and 82. An A is given for 90 to 100 points, a B for 80 to 89 points, a C for 70 to 79 points, a D for 60 to 69 points, and an F for less than 60 points. Find the number of students who scored each letter grade.

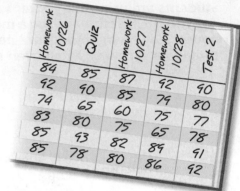

Homework 10/26	Quiz	Homework 10/27	Homework 10/28	Test 2
84	85	87	92	90
92	90	85	79	80
74	65	60	75	77
83	80	75	65	78
85	93	82	84	91
85	78	80	86	92

Understand the Problem

Identify the important information.

• You have been given the list of scores and the letter grades that go with each score.

The answer will be the number of each letter grade.

Make a Plan

Make a table to organize the scores. Use the information in the problem to set up your table. Make one row for each letter grade.

Solve

Read through the list of scores. As you read each score, make a tally in the appropriate place in your table. There are 20 test scores, so be sure you have 20 tallies in all.

Mrs. Melo gave out six A's, six B's, six C's, two D's, and no F's.

Letter Grade	Number
A (90–100)	卌 l
B (80–89)	卌 l
C (70–79)	卌 l
D (60–69)	ll
F (below 60)	

Look Back

Use another strategy. Another way you could solve this problem is to **make an organized list.** Order the scores from least to greatest, and count how many scores are in each range.

62, 68, 72, 73, 75, 77, 78, 79, 80, 82, 82, 83, 84, 85, 90, 91, 92, 93, 94, 98
   D   C   B   A

PRACTICE

1. The debate club has 6 members. Each member will debate each of the other members exactly once. How many total debates will there be?

2. At the library, there are three story-telling sessions. Each one lasts 45 minutes, with 30 minutes between sessions. If the first session begins at 10:00 A.M., what time does the last session end?

Solve a Simpler Problem

Problem Solving Strategies

Sometimes a problem contains large numbers or requires many steps. Try to **solve a simpler problem** that is similar. Solve the simpler problem first, and then try the same steps to solve the original problem.

Draw a Diagram	Make a Table
Make a Model	**Solve a Simpler Problem**
Guess and Test	Use Logical Reasoning
Work Backward	Use a Venn Diagram
Find a Pattern	Make an Organized List

At the end of a soccer game, each player shakes hands with every player on the opposing team. How many handshakes are there at the end of a game between two teams that each have 20 players?

 **Understand the Problem**

Identify the important information.

- There are 20 players on each team.
- Each player will shake hands with every player on the opposing team.

The answer will be the total number of handshakes exchanged.

 **Make a Plan**

Solve a simpler problem. For example, suppose each team had just one player. Then there would only be one handshake between the two players. Expand the number of players to two and then three.

 Solve

When there is 1 player, there is $1 \times 1 = 1$ handshake. For 2 players, there are $2 \times 2 = 4$ handshakes. And for 3 players, there are $3 \times 3 = 9$ handshakes.

Players Per Team	Diagram	Handshakes
1		1
2		4
3		9

If each team has 20 players, there will be $20 \times 20 = 400$ handshakes.

Look Back

If the pattern is correct, for 4 players there will be 16 handshakes and for 5 players there will be 25 handshakes. Complete the next two rows of the table to check these answers.

PRACTICE

1. Martha has 5 pairs of pants and 4 blouses that she can wear to school. How many different outfits can she make?

2. What is the smallest 5-digit number that can be divided by 50 with a remainder of 17?

Problem Solving Handbook

(tr) Cleo Freelance Photography/Painet Inc.

Use Logical Reasoning

Problem Solving Strategies

Sometimes a problem may provide clues and facts that you must use to answer a question. You can **use logical reasoning** to solve this kind of problem.

Draw a Diagram	Make a Table
Make a Model	Solve a Simpler Problem
Guess and Test	**Use Logical Reasoning**
Work Backward	Use a Venn Diagram
Find a Pattern	Make an Organized List

Kevin, Ellie, and Jillian play three different sports. One person plays soccer, one likes to run track, and the other swims. Ellie is the sister of the swimmer. Kevin once went shopping with the swimmer and the track runner. Match each student with his or her sport.

 **Understand the Problem**

Identify the important information.

- There are three people, and each person plays a different sport.
- Ellie is the sister of the swimmer.
- Kevin once went shopping with the swimmer and the track runner.

The answer will tell which student plays each sport.

 **Make a Plan**

Start with clues given in the problem, and **use logical reasoning** to find the answer.

 Solve

Make a table with a column for each sport and a row for each person. Work with the clues one at a time. Write "yes" in a box if the clue applies to that person. Write "no" if the clue does not apply.

	Soccer	Track	Swim
Kevin		no	no
Ellie			no
Jillian			

- Ellie is the sister of the swimmer, so she is not the swimmer.
- Kevin went shopping with the swimmer and the track runner. He is not the swimmer or the track runner.

So Kevin must be the soccer player, and Jillian must be the swimmer. This leaves Ellie as the track runner.

 **Look Back**

Compare your answer to the clues in the problem. Make sure none of your conclusions conflict with the clues.

PRACTICE

1. Karin, Brent, and Lola each ordered a different slice of pizza: pepperoni, plain cheese, and ham-pineapple. Karin is allergic to pepperoni. Lola likes more than one topping. Which kind of pizza did each person order?

2. Leo, Jamal, and Kara are in fourth, fifth, and sixth grades. Kara is not in fourth grade. The sixth-grader is in chorus with Kara and has the same lunch time as Leo. Match the students with their grades.

Problem Solving Handbook

Use a Venn Diagram

You can **use a Venn diagram** to display relationships among sets in a problem. Use ovals, circles, or other shapes to represent individual sets.

Problem Solving Strategies

Draw a Diagram	Make a Table
Make a Model	Solve a Simpler Problem
Guess and Test	Use Logical Reasoning
Work Backward	**Use a Venn Diagram**
Find a Pattern	Make an Organized List

Robert is taking a survey to see what kinds of pets students have. He found that 70 students have dogs, 45 have goldfish, and 60 have birds. Some students have two kinds of pets: 17 students have dogs and fish, 22 students have dogs and birds, and 15 students have birds and goldfish. Five students have all three kinds of pets. How many students in the survey have only birds?

Understand the Problem

List the important information.

- You know that 70 students have dogs, 45 have goldfish, and 60 have birds.

The answer will be the number of students who have only birds.

Make a Plan

Use a Venn diagram to show the sets of students who have dogs, students who have goldfish, and students who have birds.

Solve

Draw and label three overlapping circles. Work from the inside out. Write "5" in the area where all three circles overlap. This represents the number of students who have a dog, a goldfish, and a bird.

Use the information in the problem to fill in other sections of the diagram. You know that 60 students have birds, so the numbers within the bird circle will add to 60.

So 18 students have only pet birds.

Look Back

When your Venn diagram is complete, check it carefully against the information in the problem. Make sure your diagram agrees with the facts given.

PRACTICE

1. How many students have only dogs?

2. How many students have only goldfish?

Make an Organized List

Problem Solving Strategies

Draw a Diagram	Make a Table
Make a Model	Solve a Simpler Problem
Guess and Test	Use Logical Reasoning
Work Backward	Use a Venn Diagram
Find a Pattern	**Make an Organized List**

In some problems, you will need to find how many different ways something can happen. It is often helpful to **make an organized list.** This will help you count the outcomes and be sure that you have included all of them.

In a game at an amusement park, players throw 3 darts at a target to score points and win prizes. If each dart lands within the target area, how many different total scores are possible?

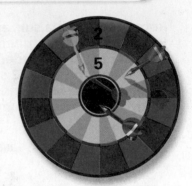

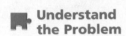 **Understand the Problem**

Identify the important information.

- A player throws three darts at the target.

The answer will be the number of different scores a player could earn.

Make a Plan

Make an organized list to determine all possible outcomes and score totals. List the value of each dart and the point total for all three darts.

Solve

You can organize your list by the number of darts that land in the center. All three darts could hit the center circle. Or, two darts could hit the center circle and the third could hit a different circle. One dart could hit the center circle, or no darts could hit the center circle.

3 Darts Hit Center	2 Darts Hit Center	1 Dart Hits Center	0 Darts Hit Center
10 + 10 + 10 = 30	10 + 10 + 5 = 25	10 + 5 + 5 = 20	5 + 5 + 5 = 15
	10 + 10 + 2 = 22	10 + 5 + 2 = 17	5 + 5 + 2 = 12
		10 + 2 + 2 = 14	5 + 2 + 2 = 9
			2 + 2 + 2 = 6

Count the different outcomes. There are 10 possible scores.

Look Back

You could have listed outcomes in random order, but because your list is organized, you can be sure that you have not missed any possibilities. Check to be sure that every score is different.

PRACTICE

1. A restaurant has three different kinds of pancakes: cinnamon, blueberry, and apple. If you order one of each kind, how many different ways can the three pancakes be stacked?

2. How many ways can you make change for a quarter using dimes, nickels, and pennies?

Skills Bank . . .

Place Value—Trillions Through Thousandths

You can use a place-value chart to read and write numbers.

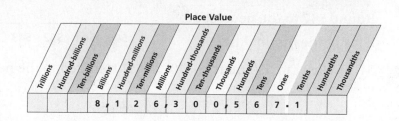

EXAMPLE

What is the place value of the digit 3 in 8,126,300,567.1?

The digit 3 is in the hundred-thousands place.

PRACTICE

Write the place value of the underlined digit.

1. 1<u>4</u>,536,992.1
2. 3<u>4</u>.071
3. 6,<u>1</u>90.05
4. <u>5</u>,027,549,757,202
5. 1<u>0</u>3.526
6. 3.7<u>2</u>1
7. <u>6</u>5,331,040,421
8. 75,983.00<u>9</u>

Compare and Order Whole Numbers

As you read a number line from left to right, the numbers are ordered from least to greatest.

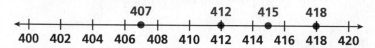

You can use a number line and place value to compare whole numbers. Use the symbols > (is greater than) and < (is less than).

EXAMPLE

Compare. Write <, >, or =.

A 412 ▯ 418
418 is to the right of 412 on a number line.
412 < 418

B 415 ▯ 407
1 ten is greater than 0 tens.
415 > 407

PRACTICE

Compare. Write <, >, or =.

1. 419 ▯ 410
2. 9,161 ▯ 8,957
3. 5,036 ▯ 5,402
4. 617 ▯ 681
5. 700 ▯ 698
6. 1,611 ▯ 1,489

Round Whole Numbers and Decimals

You can use a number line or rounding rules to round whole numbers to the nearest 10, 100, 1,000, or 10,000.

EXAMPLE 1

Round 547 to the nearest 10.

Look at the number line.

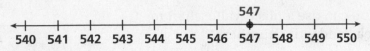

547 is closer to 550 than to 540. So 547 rounded to the nearest 10 is 550.

You can use rounding rules to round whole numbers and decimals to any place value.

ROUNDING RULES

If the digit to the right is 5 or greater, increase the digit in the rounding place by 1.

If the digit to the right is less than 5, keep the digit in the rounding place the same.

EXAMPLE 2

Round each number to the given place value.

A **12,573; thousands**

12,573   *Find the digit in the thousands place.*
   ↑ *Digit is 5 or greater. Add 1.*   *Look at the digit to its right.*

12,573 rounded to the nearest 1,000 is 13,000.

B **5.16; whole number**

   $1 < 5$ So 5.16 rounds to 5.

C **13.45605; ten-thousandth**

   $5 \geq 5$ So 13.45605 rounds to 13.4561.

PRACTICE

Round each number to the given place value.

1. 15,638; hundreds
2. 37,519; thousands
3. 9,298; tens
4. 69,504; ten thousands
5. 852; thousands
6. 33,449; hundreds
7. 3.982; tenth
8. 6.3174; hundredth
9. 1.471; whole number
10. 48.1526; hundredth
11. 5.03654; ten-thousandth
12. 0.083; tenth

Roman Numerals

Instead of using place value, as with the decimal system, combinations of letters are used to represent numbers in the Roman numeral system.

I = 1	V = 5	X = 10
L = 50	C = 100	D = 500
M = 1,000		

No letter can be written more than three times in a row. If a letter is written before a letter that represents a larger value, then subtract the first letter's value from the second letter's value.

EXAMPLE

Write each decimal number as a Roman numeral and each Roman numeral as a decimal number.

A 9

$9 = X - I = IX$

B CLV

$CLV = 100 + 50 + 5 = 155$

PRACTICE

Write each decimal number as a Roman numeral and each Roman numeral as a decimal number.

1. 12   **2.** 25   **3.** 209   **4.** 54

5. VIII   **6.** LXXII   **7.** XIX   **8.** MMIV

Addition

Addition is used to find the total of two or more quantities. The answer to an addition problem is called the *sum*.

EXAMPLE

4,617 + 5,682

Step 1: Add the ones.	**Step 2:** Add the tens.	**Step 3:** Add the hundreds. Regroup.	**Step 4:** Add the thousands.
4,617 + 5,682 9	4,617 + 5,682 99	$\overset{1}{}$4,617 + 5,682 299	$\overset{1}{}$4,617 + 5,682 10,299

The sum is 10,299.

PRACTICE

Find the sum.

1. 711 + 591   **2.** 2,580 + 2,345   **3.** 21,470 + 13,329

4. $165 + $304   **5.** 6,905 + 872   **6.** 47,231 + 3,254

Skills Bank

Subtraction

Subtraction is used to take away one quantity from another quantity. The answer to a subtraction problem is called the *difference*.

780 − 468

Step 1: Regroup. Subtract the ones.	Step 2: Subtract the tens.	Step 3: Subtract the hundreds.
$\begin{array}{r} ^{7}\cancel{8}\,^{10}\cancel{0} \\ 7\ \cancel{8}\ \cancel{0} \\ -\ 4\ 6\ 8 \\ \hline 2 \end{array}$	$\begin{array}{r} ^{7}\cancel{8}\,^{10}\cancel{0} \\ 7\ \cancel{8}\ \cancel{0} \\ -\ 4\ 6\ 8 \\ \hline 1\ 2 \end{array}$	$\begin{array}{r} ^{7}\cancel{8}\,^{10}\cancel{0} \\ 7\ \cancel{8}\ \cancel{0} \\ -\ 4\ 6\ 8 \\ \hline 3\ 1\ 2 \end{array}$

The difference is 312.

PRACTICE

Find the difference.

1. 6,785 − 2,426

2. 3,000 − 1,930

3. 932 − 868

4. 41,003 − 22,500

5. $1,075 − $918

6. 12,035 − 640

Multiply Whole Numbers

Multiplication is used to combine groups of equal amounts. The answer to a multiplication problem is called the *product*.

105 × 214

Step 1: Think of 214 as 2 hundreds, 1 ten, and 4 ones. Multiply by 4 ones.	Step 2: Multiply by 1 ten, or 10.	Step 3: Multiply by 2 hundreds, or 200.	Step 4: Add the partial products.
$\begin{array}{r} ^{2} \\ 105 \\ \times\ 214 \\ \hline 420 \end{array}$ ← 4 × 105	$\begin{array}{r} 105 \\ \times\ 214 \\ \hline 420 \\ 1050 \end{array}$ ← 10 × 105	$\begin{array}{r} ^{1} \\ 105 \\ \times\ 214 \\ \hline 420 \\ 1050 \\ 21000 \end{array}$ ← 200 × 105	$\begin{array}{r} 105 \\ \times\ 214 \\ \hline 420 \\ 1050 \\ +21000 \\ \hline 22,470 \end{array}$

The product is 22,470.

PRACTICE

Find the product.

1. 350 × 112

2. 3,218 × 231

3. 187 × 136

4. 5,028 × 225

5. 642 × 428

6. 2,039 × 570

Divide Whole Numbers

Division is used to separate a quantity into equal groups. The answer to a division problem is known as the *quotient*.

EXAMPLE

$672 \div 16$

| Step 1: Write the first number inside the long division symbol and the second number to the left. Place the first digit of the quotient. $$16\overline{)672}$$ *16 cannot go into 6, so try 67.* | Step 2: Multiply 4 by 16, and place the product under 67. $$\begin{array}{r} 4 \\ 16\overline{)672} \\ -64 \\ \hline 3 \end{array}$$ *Subtract 64 from 67.* | Step 3: Bring down the next digit of the dividend. $$\begin{array}{r} 42 \\ 16\overline{)672} \\ -64\downarrow \\ \hline 32 \\ -32 \\ \hline 0 \end{array}$$ *Divide 32 by 16.* |

The quotient is 42.

PRACTICE

Find the quotient.

1. $578 \div 34$　　　　**2.** $736 \div 8$　　　　**3.** $826 \div 118$

4. $945 \div 45$　　　　**5.** $6{,}312 \div 263$　　　**6.** $5{,}989 \div 53$

Divide with Zeros in the Quotient

Sometimes when dividing, you need to use zeros in the quotient as placeholders.

EXAMPLE

$3{,}648 \div 12$

| Step 1: Divide 36 by 12 because $12 > 3$. $$\begin{array}{r} 3 \\ 12\overline{)3{,}648} \end{array}$$ | Step 2: Place a zero in the quotient because $12 > 4$. $$\begin{array}{r} 30 \\ 12\overline{)3{,}648} \\ -36\downarrow \\ \hline 04 \end{array}$$ | Step 3: Bring down the 8. $$\begin{array}{r} 304 \\ 12\overline{)3{,}648} \\ -36\ \downarrow \\ \hline 048 \\ -48 \\ \hline 0 \end{array}$$ |

The quotient is 304.

PRACTICE

Find the quotient.

1. $424 \div 4$　　　　**2.** $5{,}796 \div 28$　　　**3.** $540 \div 18$

4. $7{,}380 \div 123$　　**5.** $12{,}045 \div 3$　　　**6.** $10{,}626 \div 21$

Multiples

Multiples of a number can be found by multiplying the number by 1, 2, 3, and so on.

Find the first five multiples of 3.

$3 \cdot 1 = 3$ *Multiply 3 times 1.* $3 \cdot 4 = 12$ *Multiply 3 times 4.*
$3 \cdot 2 = 6$ *Multiply 3 times 2.* $3 \cdot 5 = 15$ *Multiply 3 times 5.*
$3 \cdot 3 = 9$ *Multiply 3 times 3.*

The first five multiples of 3 are 3, 6, 9, 12, and 15.

PRACTICE

Find the first five multiples of each number.

1. 9   **2.** 10   **3.** 20   **4.** 15   **5.** 7   **6.** 18

Inverse Properties

Addition and multiplication follow some properties, or laws, such as the Commutative, Associative, and Distributive Properties. Knowing the inverse properties of addition and multiplication can help you evaluate expressions and solve equations.

Inverse Property of Addition	
The sum of any number and its opposite is 0.	$4 + (-4) = 0$

Inverse Property of Multiplication	
For any number except 0, the product of the number and its reciprocal is 1.	$3 \times \frac{1}{3} = 1$

EXAMPLE

Tell whether one of the inverse properties can be used to simplify the expression $3 - 4 + 4$. If so, tell which property.

$3 - 4 + 4$ *−4 and 4 are opposites.*

Yes, the Inverse Property of Addition can be used.

PRACTICE

Tell whether one of the inverse properties can be used to simplify the expression. If so, tell which property.

1. $5 \cdot 6 \cdot \frac{1}{5}$ **2.** $3(6 + (-6))$ **3.** $4 \cdot 3(-4)$

4. $2(6 - 4) + 3$ **5.** $\frac{1}{3}(2 + 1)$ **6.** $5 + 8 \cdot \frac{1}{5}$

Mental Math

You can use mental math to multiply by powers of ten.

EXAMPLE 1

$4,000 \times 100$

Step 1: Look for a basic fact using the nonzero part of the factors.

$$4 \times 1 = 4$$

Step 2: Add the number of zeros in the factors. Place that number of zeros in the product.

$$4,000 \times 100 = 400,000$$

The product is 400,000.

You can use basic facts and place value to solve math problems mentally.

EXAMPLE 2

Solve mentally.

A $300 + 200$

Basic fact: $3 + 2 = 5$ *Think: 3 hundreds + 2 hundreds*

$300 + 200 = 500$

B 200×600

Basic fact: $2 \times 6 = 12$ *Think: There are four zeros in the factors,*

$200 \times 600 = 120,000$ *so place four zeros in the product.*

PRACTICE

Multiply.

1. 600×100
2. $90 \times 1,000$
3. $2,000 \times 10$
4. 400×10
5. $10,000 \times 1,000$
6. $7,100 \times 1,000$

Solve mentally.

7. $500 + 400$
8. $80 - 50$
9. 700×30
10. $2,500 \div 50$
11. $1,200 + 600$
12. $20 \times 9,000$
13. $650 - 300$
14. $320 \div 8$
15. 90×90

Fractional Part of a Region

You can use fractions to name parts of a whole. The denominator tells how many equal parts are in the whole. The numerator tells how many of those parts are being considered.

EXAMPLE

Tell what fraction of each region is shaded.

A
$\frac{1}{2}$

B
$\frac{1}{3}$

C
$\frac{3}{4}$

PRACTICE

Tell what fraction of each region is shaded.

1.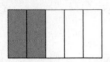

2.

3.

4.

5.

6.

Fractional Part of a Set

You can use fractions to name part of a set. The denominator tells how many items are in the set. The numerator tells how many of those items are being used.

EXAMPLE

Tell what fraction of each set are stars.

A ☐☆☐☆●☆●☐☐☐

3 out of 10 shapes are stars.

$\frac{3}{10}$

B ☆●☆☆●☆☆

5 out of 7 shapes are stars.

$\frac{5}{7}$

PRACTICE

Tell what fraction of each set is shaded.

1. ☆☆☆☆☆☆

2. ■■■■☐

3. ●☆○○☆○

4. ■■■☐☐

5. ●○☐☐

6. ☆⬡■○▯△♡

Like Terms

Terms of an expression are the parts that are added or subtracted. A term can be a number, variable, or a product of numbers and variables. **Like terms** have the same variable raised to the same power.

Like terms often have different *coefficients*. A **coefficient** is a number multiplied by a variable. A variable written without a coefficient has a coefficient of 1. A number written with no variable is a constant. All constants are like terms.

$$\overset{\text{Coefficients}}{\qquad\qquad} \overset{\text{Constant}}{\qquad} $$
$$x^2 - 2y + 3x + 4y + 5$$

You can combine like terms in an expression by adding their coefficients. An expression is said to be simplified if all like terms are combined.

EXAMPLES

Simplify each expression by combining like terms.

A $3x + 6x$

$(3x) + (6x)$ *Identify like terms.*

$9x$ *Add coefficients: 3 + 6 = 9.*

B $3a + 2b + a + 4b$

$(3a) + \boxed{2b} + (a) + \boxed{4b}$ *Identify like terms.*

$3a + a + 2b + 4b$ *Use the Commutative Property to group like terms.*

$4a + 6b$ *Add coefficients: 3 + 1 = 4, 2 + 4 = 6.*

C $6x + 5y + 3 - 4x + 5 - y$

$(6x) + \boxed{5y} + \triangle{3} - (4x) + \triangle{5} - \boxed{y}$ *Identify like terms.*

$6x - 4x + 5y - y + 3 + 5$ *Use the Commutative Property to group like terms.*

       Move the operation in front of each term with that term.

$2x + 4y + 8$ *Combine coefficients: 6 − 4 = 2, 5 − 1 = 4.*

       Combine constants: 3 + 5 = 8.

PRACTICE

Simplify each expression by combining like terms.

1. $5c + 2c$

2. $14d + 5 - 8d$

3. $18p + 3 - 8p - 5$

4. $5m - 15 - 20m + 5$

5. $6x - 12y + 14x + 20y$

6. $9u + 11v - 22u + 12v$

7. $5a + 11b + 5 - 2a - 5b + 6$

8. $16p + 5 + p - 3q + 6 - q$

9. $2u + v + 15u + 6v + 8 - v - 6$

10. $8x + y - 9x + 3z + 2x - 7y + z$

Solve Equations with Variables on Both Sides

You can solve equations with variables on both sides by first collecting the variables on one side of the equation and the constants on the other.

EXAMPLE

Solve each equation.

A $5x + 6 = 3x + 10$

Model the equation using algebra tiles.

You want x-tiles on only one side of the equation. Subtract three tiles from each side.

$$2x + 6 = 10$$

To isolate the x-tiles, subtract six 1-tiles from each side.

$$2x = 4$$

Divide the tiles on each side of the equation so that each x-tile is by itself.

$$x = 2$$

PRACTICE

Solve each equation.

1. $5x + 4 = 4x + 8$

2. $8x - 5 = 6x + 7$

3. $3x - 5 = -2x + 10$

4. $8x + 5 = 7x + 11$

5. $9x - 5 = 4x + 10$

6. $8x + 3 = 5x + 9$

The Pythagorean Theorem

The **legs** of a right triangle are the sides that form the right angle. The side opposite the right angle is the **hypotenuse.**

The Pythagorean Theorem states that the sum of the squares of the lengths of the legs is equal to the square of the length of the hypotenuse. That is, $a^2 + b^2 = c^2$.

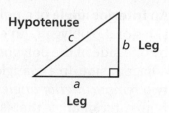

Hypotenuse

EXAMPLE

Find the unknown length.

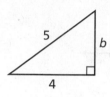

$$a^2 + b^2 = c^2$$
$$4^2 + b^2 = 5^2 \qquad \textit{Substitute 4 for a and 5 for c.}$$
$$16 + b^2 = 25 \qquad \textit{Simplify.}$$
$$\underline{-16 \qquad\quad -16} \qquad \textit{Subtract 16 from both sides.}$$
$$b^2 = 9$$
$$\sqrt{b^2} = \sqrt{9} \qquad \textit{Find the positive square root of both sides.}$$
$$b = 3$$

PRACTICE

Find the unknown length.

1.

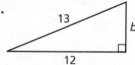

2.

3.

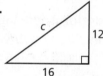

Sectors of Circles

A **sector** of a circle is enclosed by two radii and an arc connecting them. Given a circle of radius r and a central angle that measures $m°$, the area of the sector is $\frac{m}{360}\pi r^2$.

EXAMPLE

Find the area of the sector. Use 3.14 for π.

$$A = \frac{m}{360}\pi r^2$$
$$= \frac{90}{360} \cdot 3.14 \cdot 6^2 = 28.26 \qquad \textit{Substitute 90 for m and 6 for r.}$$

The area of the sector is 28.26 in^2.

PRACTICE

Find the area of each sector. Use 3.14 for π.

1.

2.

3.

Exterior Angles of Polygons

An **interior angle** of a polygon is formed by two sides of the polygon. An **exterior angle** is formed by one side of the polygon and the extension of an adjacent side. In a triangle, each exterior angle has two *remote interior angles*. A **remote interior angle** is an interior angle that is not adjacent to the exterior angle.

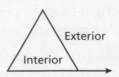

The Exterior Angle Theorem states that the measure of an exterior angle of a triangle is equal to the sum of the measures of its remote interior angles.

$$m\angle 4 = m\angle 1 + m\angle 2$$

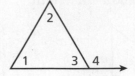

EXAMPLE 1

Find the value of x.

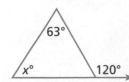

$x° + 63° = 120°$ *Use the Exterior Angle Theorem.*

$x + 63 = 120$

$\underline{-63 \quad -63}$ *Subtract 63 from both sides.*

$x = 57$

The Polygon Exterior Angle Sum Theorem states that the sum of the exterior angle measures, one angle at each vertex, of a convex polygon is 360°.

EXAMPLE 2

Find the value of x.

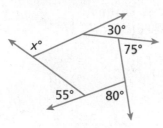

$x° + 30° + 75° + 80° + 55° = 360°$ *Use the Polygon Exterior*

$x + 30 + 75 + 80 + 55 = 360$ *Angle Sum Theorem.*

$x + 240 = 360$ *Simplify.*

$\underline{-240 \quad -240}$ *Subtract 240 from both sides.*

$x = 120$

PRACTICE

Find the value of x.

1.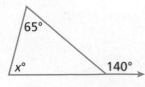

2.

3.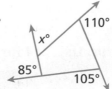

4.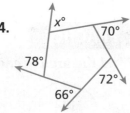

Skills Bank

Relationships Between Planes

Any two unique planes in space either intersect in a line or do not intersect at all. Two planes are parallel if they do not intersect. Two intersecting planes are perpendicular if the angle between them is a right angle.

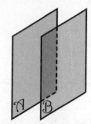

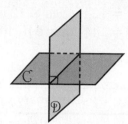

Planes *A* and *B* are parallel.   Planes *C* and *D* are perpendicular.

EXAMPLE

In the diagram, identify all pairs of planes that appear to be parallel to each other, all pairs that appear to be perpendicular to each other, and all pairs that intersect but do not appear perpendicular to each other.

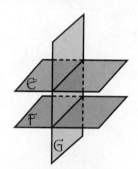

Planes *E* and *F* appear to be parallel to each other.

Planes *E* and *G* appear to be perpendicular to each other.

Planes *F* and *G* appear to be perpendicular to each other.

PRACTICE

In each diagram, identify all pairs of planes that appear to be parallel to each other, all pairs that appear to be perpendicular to each other, and all pairs that intersect but do not appear perpendicular to each other.

1.

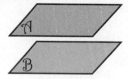

2.

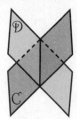

3.

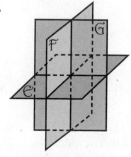

4.

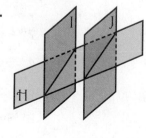

Compare Units

When converting area from one unit to another, you must remember that area is measured in square units.

$$1 \text{ square foot} = 1 \text{ foot} \times 1 \text{ foot}$$
$$= 12 \text{ inches} \times 12 \text{ inches}$$
$$= 144 \text{ square inches}$$

1 ft

1 ft

Customary Units for Area	
1 square foot (ft^2) = 144 square inches (in^2)	1 acre (a) = 4,840 square yards (yd^2)
1 square yard (yd^2) = 9 square feet (ft^2)	1 acre (a) = 43,560 square feet (ft^2)
1 square yard (yd^2) = 1,296 square inches (in^2)	1 square mile (mi^2) = 640 acres (a)

EXAMPLE 1

Which is the greater area, 3 yd^2 or 25 ft^2?

$3 \text{ yd}^2 = 3 \times 9 \text{ ft}^2 = 27 \text{ ft}^2$ *Think: 1 yd^2 = 9 ft^2*

$27 \text{ ft}^2 > 25 \text{ ft}^2$

$3 \text{ yd}^2 > 25 \text{ ft}^2$

Use the same principle to compare metric square units.

EXAMPLE 2

Which is the greater area, 5 km^2 or 5,000 m^2?

$5 \text{ km}^2 = 5 \times 1,000,000 \text{ m}^2 = 5,000,000 \text{ m}^2$ *Think: 1 km^2 = 1,000,000 m^2*

$5,000,000 \text{ m}^2 > 5,000 \text{ m}^2$

$5 \text{ km}^2 > 5,000 \text{ m}^2$

PRACTICE

Compare. Write <, >, or =.

1. 12,500 yd^2 ▨ 3 acres

2. 6 yd^2 ▨ 42 ft^2

3. 4 ft^2 ▨ 576 in^2

4. 5 yd^2 ▨ 6,500 in^2

5. 2.3 mi^2 ▨ 1,430 acres

6. 0.5 acre ▨ 21,700 ft^2

7. 30 cm^2 ▨ 3 m^2

8. 5 m^2 ▨ 75,000 cm^2

9. 6 km^2 ▨ 60 m^2

10. 100,000 cm^2 ▨ 1 km^2

Convert Between Measurement Systems

To convert between customary and metric units, you can use the following conversion factors.

Length	Mass	Capacity
1 in. = 2.54 cm	1 oz ≈ 28 g	1 fl oz ≈ 29.6 mL
1 mi. ≈ 1.6 km	1 lb ≈ 0.45 kg	1 qt ≈ 0.95 L

EXAMPLES

A How many kilometers are in 350 miles?

$350 \text{ mi} = \blacksquare \text{ km}$

$\dfrac{1 \text{ mi}}{1.6 \text{ km}} = \dfrac{350 \text{ mi}}{x \text{ km}}$ *1 mi ≈ 1.6 km. Write a proportion.*

$1 \cdot x = 1.6 \cdot 350$ *The cross products are equal.*

$x = 560$

$350 \text{ mi} \approx 560 \text{ km}$

B How many quarts does a 2-liter bottle of juice hold?

$2 \text{ L} = \blacksquare \text{ qt}$

$\dfrac{0.95 \text{ L}}{1 \text{ qt}} = \dfrac{2\text{L}}{x \text{ qt}}$ *1 qt ≈ 0.95 L. Write a proportion.*

$0.95 \cdot x = 1 \cdot 2$ *The cross products are equal.*

$0.95x = 2$

$\dfrac{0.95x}{0.95} = \dfrac{2}{0.95}$ *Divide both sides by 0.95 to undo the multiplication.*

$x = 2.11$

$2 \text{ L} \approx 2.11 \text{ qt}$

PRACTICE

Use the conversion factors in the table to answer each question.

1. How many grams are in 100 ounces?

2. How many kilograms are in 85 pounds?

3. How many fluid ounces are in 500 milliliters?

4. How many miles are in 30 kilometers?

5. How many centimeters are in 3 feet?

6. How many meters are in 5 miles?

7. How many quarts are in 285 liters?

8. How many kilometers are in 20 miles?

Measuring with Nonstandard Units

You can create your own units of measurement to approximate measures when you do not have standard measuring tools. You can measure distances like your stride, foot length, hand width, and finger width and use these units to estimate lengths.

Stride

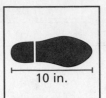
Foot length

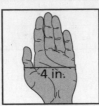
Hand width

Finger width

EXAMPLES

A The width of your desk is about 7 hand widths. Estimate the width of your desk in inches.

$$\frac{1 \text{ hand width}}{4 \text{ in.}} = \frac{7 \text{ hand widths}}{x \text{ in.}}$$ *Set up a proportion to find the distance in inches.*

$4 \times 7 = 1 \times x$ *Find cross-products.*

$28 = x$ *Multiply.*

The width of your desk is about 28 inches.

B The distance from your classroom to the library is about 24 strides. Estimate the distance from your classroom to the library in feet.

$$\frac{1 \text{ stride}}{33 \text{ in.}} = \frac{24 \text{ strides}}{x \text{ in.}}$$ *Set up a proportion to find the distance in inches.*

$24 \times 33 = 1 \times x$ *Find cross-products.*

$792 = x$ *Multiply.*

$792 \text{ in.} \times \frac{1 \text{ ft}}{12 \text{ in.}}$ *Use a conversion factor.*

66 ft

It is about 66 feet from your classroom to the library.

PRACTICE

Measure your stride, foot length, hand width, and finger width. Choose an appropriate unit for each object, and give an approximate measure for each object.

1. Width of a classroom

2. Diameter of a CD

3. Height of a classroom door

4. Height of a desk

5. Width of your textbook

6. Length of an unsharpened pencil

Significant Figures

Significant figures are the digits in a measurement that are known with certainty. When given a number, the significant figures are identified as follows:

- Nonzero digits
- Zeros at the end of a number and to the right of the decimal point
- Zeros between significant figures

Number	Significant Figures	Reasoning
230	two	The zero at the end of the number is not a significant figure because it is not to the right of the decimal point.
230.0	four	The zero at the end of the number is significant because it is to the right of the decimal point. The first zero is between significant figures.

When adding or subtracting, find the number with the least number of *digits* to the right of the decimal point. Round your answer so that it has the same number of digits to the right of the decimal.

When multiplying or dividing, find the number with the least number of *significant figures.* Round your answer so that it has that number of significant figures.

EXAMPLES

Write each answer with the appropriate number of significant figures.

A $25.3 - 7.12$

$$\begin{array}{rl}
25.3 & \leftarrow \textit{1 digit after the decimal} \\
-\ 7.12 & \leftarrow \textit{2 digits after the decimal} \\
\hline
18.18 & \\
18.2 & \leftarrow \textit{Round the difference to have one digit to the right of the decimal.}
\end{array}$$

B 1.1×0.2

$$\begin{array}{rl}
1.1 & \leftarrow \textit{2 significant figures} \\
\times\ 0.2 & \leftarrow \textit{1 significant figure} \\
\hline
0.22 & \\
0.2 & \leftarrow \textit{Round the product to 1 significant figure.}
\end{array}$$

PRACTICE

Determine the number of significant figures in each decimal.

1. 240   **2.** 0.0065   **3.** 210.00

Write each answer with the appropriate number of significant figures.

4. $2.3 + 2.46$ **5.** $12.3 - 2.54$ **6.** $110.5 + 10.34$

7. $22.30 - 2.04$ **8.** 2.5×0.4 **9.** $1.25 \div 0.05$

10. $4.2 \div 0.70$ **11.** 10×0.024 **12.** 4.2×0.040

Box-and-Whisker Plots

A **box-and-whisker plot** shows the distribution of data. You need five values to make a box-and-whisker plot.
- The **minimum** is the least value of the data.
- The **maximum** is the greatest value of the data.
- The **median** is the middle value of the data or the mean of the two middle values.
- The **lower quartile** is the median of the lower half of the data.
- The **upper quartile** is the median of the upper half of the data.

EXAMPLE

Use the data to make a box-and-whisker plot.

58, 60, 47, 56, 32, 78, 44, 72, 42, 35, 66

Order from least to greatest.	32, 35, 42, 44, 47, 56, 58, 60, 66, 72, 78
Find the minimum.	(32) 35, 42, 44, 47, 56, 58, 60, 66, 72, 78
Find the maximum.	32, 35, 42, 44, 47, 56, 58, 60, 66, 72, (78)
Find the median.	32, 35, 42, 44, 47, (56) 58, 60, 66, 72, 78
Find the lower quartile.	32, 35, (42) 44, 47, 56, 58, 60, 66, 72, 78
Find the upper quartile.	32, 35, 42, 44, 47, 56, 58, 60, (66) 72, 78

Step 1: Place a dot at the median, upper quartile, and lower quartile. Make a box connecting these points.

Step 2: Place a dot at the minimum and maximum.

Step 3: Connect the minimum and the maximum to the box with segments called whiskers.

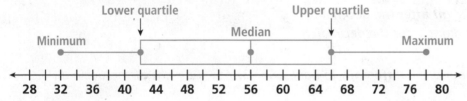

PRACTICE

Use the data to make a box-and-whisker plot.

1. 8, 6, 5, 4, 12, 9, 2

2. 56, 61, 45, 55, 63, 59, 46

3. 28, 12, 35, 22, 13, 33, 33, 17, 18, 22, 25

4. 78, 85, 68, 57, 72, 63, 79, 60, 66, 52, 78

Skills Bank

Sampling and Bias

A **population** is a group about which someone is gathering information.

A **sample** is part of a population. For example, if 6 students are chosen to represent a class of 24 students, the 6 students are a sample of the population of 24 students.

A sample is **random** if every member of the population has an equal chance of being chosen.

Bias is error that favors part of a population and/or does not accurately represent the population. Bias can occur from using a sample that is not random or from asking confusing or leading questions.

EXAMPLE

A Terence wants to know what students in his class think about the test they took. He asks all the students who sit in the back row. Explain whether the sample is random.

Since he selected only the students in the back row, other students did not have a chance to be selected. The sample is not random.

B Explain whether the following question is biased. "Do you think the corrupt mayor should be thrown out of office?"

The question is biased because it states that the mayor is corrupt, which leads people to believe that he should be thrown out of office.

C Janine wanted to know if students supported the current budget that moved funds from the athletic department to the arts department. She surveyed students on the baseball team. Explain whether the survey is biased.

The survey is biased because it samples students on the baseball team and they are not likely to want funds to be moved.

PRACTICE

Explain whether each sample is random.
1. To complete his survey, Paul placed the names of all students in his class in a hat. Then, without looking, he drew names out of the hat.
2. Dena got a list of the names and phone numbers of every senior at her school. The list was organized in alphabetical order. She surveyed the first 50 students on the list who responded to her call.

Explain whether each question is biased.
3. "Do you support the building of the new baseball stadium?"
4. "Do you support the new factory that will bring hundreds of new jobs to the community?"
5. Explain whether the survey is biased: To find out whether their customers will shop online, a store sent a survey to all shoppers on its email list.

Effects of Sample Size on Probability

Theoretical probability is a ratio of the number of ways an event can occur to the number of equally likely outcomes possible. Experimental probability is a ratio of the number of times an event does occur to the number of times an activity is performed.

As the number of trials increases, the experimental probability should get very close to the theoretical probability.

EXAMPLE

John, Sara, and Marcus flipped a coin a given number of times and recorded the results. Find the probability that the coin lands heads up in each experiment. Find the theoretical probability and compare the experimental probability to the theoretical probability.

John

Heads	14
Tails	6

Total   20

$P = \frac{14}{20} = 70\%$

Sara

Heads	22
Tails	28

Total   50

$P = \frac{22}{50} = 44\%$

Marcus

Heads	48
Tails	52

Total   100

$P = \frac{48}{100} = 48\%$

Theoretical Probability $= \frac{1}{2} = 50\%$

When more trials are performed, the experimental probability gets closer to 50%.

PRACTICE

Use the table for 1–2.

1. Color a sheet of white paper with a 10×10 grid as described in the table. (Each square of the grid should be large enough for a penny to fit within the square.)

2. Drop a penny onto the grid 20 times and record the color it lands on.

   a. Find the experimental probability of the penny landing on each color.
   b. Find the theoretical probability of the penny landing on each color.
   c. Compare the experimental probabilities from **a** with the theoretical probabilities from **b**.

Color	Number of Squares
Red	15
Blue	9
Green	16
Purple	5
Yellow	25

3. Combine your results with those of several classmates. Compare the experimental probabilities from the combined data to the theoretical probabilities. Explain how increasing the number of trials affected the experimental probabilities with respect to the theoretical probability.

Skills Bank

Mastering the Standards

for Mathematical Practice

The topics described in the Standards for Mathematical Content will vary from year to year. However, the *way* in which you learn, study, and think about mathematics will not. The Standards for Mathematical Practice describe skills that you will use in all of your math courses.

Mathematical Practices

1. *Make sense of problems and persevere in solving them.*
2. *Reason abstractly and quantitatively.*
3. *Construct viable arguments and critique the reasoning of others.*
4. *Model with mathematics.*
5. *Use appropriate tools strategically.*
6. *Attend to precision.*
7. *Look for and make use of structure.*
8. *Look for and express regularity in repeated reasoning.*

⑤ Use appropriate tools strategically.

Mathematically proficient students consider the available tools when solving a... problem... [and] are... able to use technological tools to explore and deepen their understanding...

In your book

Hands-on Labs and **Technology Labs** use concrete and technological tools to explore mathematical concepts.

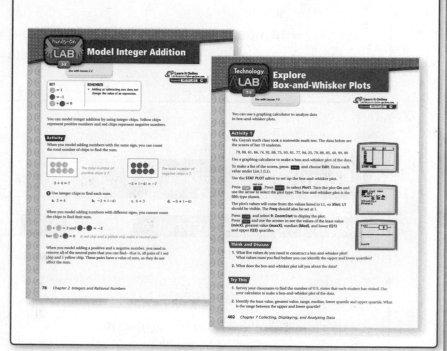

Getty Images/PhotoDisc

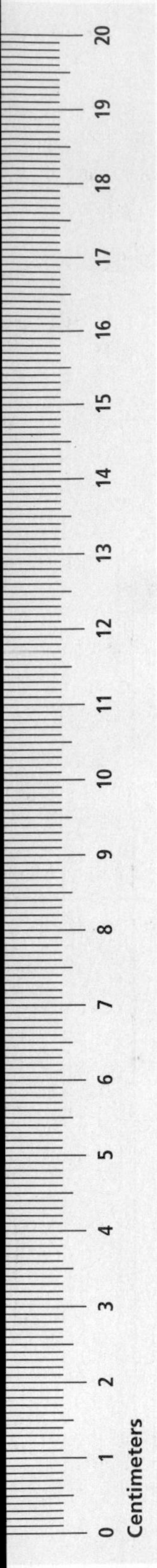

Table of Measures

METRIC	CUSTOMARY

METRIC

Length

1 kilometer (km) = 1,000 meters (m)
1 meter = 100 centimeters (cm)
1 centimeter = 10 millimeters (mm)

Capacity

1 liter (L) = 1,000 milliliters (mL)

Mass

1 kilogram (kg) = 1,000 grams (g)
1 gram = 1,000 milligrams (mg)

CUSTOMARY

Length

1 mile (mi) = 5,280 feet (ft)
1 yard (yd) = 3 feet
1 foot = 12 inches (in.)

Capacity

1 gallon (gal) = 4 quarts (qt)
1 quart = 2 pints (pt)
1 pint = 2 cups (c)
1 cup = 8 fluid ounces (fl oz)

Weight

1 ton (T) = 2,000 pounds (lb)
1 pound = 16 ounces (oz)

TIME

1 year (yr) = 365 days
1 year = 12 months (mo)
1 year = 52 weeks (wk)
1 week = 7 days

1 day = 24 hours (h)
1 hour = 60 minutes (min)
1 minute = 60 seconds (s)

Formulas

Perimeter and Circumference

Square	$P = 4s$
Rectangle	$P = 2\ell + 2w$ or $P = 2(\ell + w)$
Polygon	$P =$ sum of the lengths of the sides
Circle	$C = 2\pi r$ or $C = \pi d$

Area

Square	$A = s^2$
Rectangle	$A = \ell w$ or $A = bh$
Parallelogram	$A = bh$
Triangle	$A = \frac{1}{2}bh$ or $A = \frac{bh}{2}$
Trapezoid	$A = \frac{1}{2}(b_1 + b_2)h$ or $A = \frac{(b_1 + b_2)h}{2}$
Circle	$A = \pi r^2$

Centimeters

Formulas

Volume*

Prism	$V = Bh$
Rectangular Prism	$V = Bh$ or $V = \ell wh$
Cylinder	$V = Bh$ or $V = \pi r^2 h$
Pyramid	$V = \frac{1}{3}Bh$
Cone	$V = \frac{1}{3}Bh$ or $V = \frac{1}{3}\pi r^2 h$

Surface Area*

Prism	$S = 2B + L$ or $S = 2B + Ph$
Cylinder	$S = 2B + L$ or $S = 2\pi r^2 + 2\pi rh$
Regular Pyramid	$S = B + L$ or $S = B + \frac{1}{2}P\ell$
Cone	$S = B + L$ or $S = \pi r^2 + \pi r\ell$

*B represents the area of the base of a solid figure.

Temperature

Celsius (°C)	$C = \frac{5}{9}(F - 32)$
Fahrenheit (°F)	$F = \frac{9}{5}C + 32$

Other

Diameter	$d = 2r$
Simple Interest	$I = Prt$
Pythagorean Theorem	$a^2 + b^2 = c^2$

Symbols

$<$	is less than
$>$	is greater than
$\leq$	is less than or equal to
$\geq$	is greater than or equal to
$=$	is equal to
$\neq$	is not equal to
$\approx$	is approximately equal to
10^2	ten squared
10^3	ten cubed
2^6	two to the sixth power
2^{-5}	two to the negative fifth power
$2.\overline{6}$	repeating decimal 2.66666...
$|-4|$	the absolute value of negative 4
$\sqrt{\ }$	square root
\$5/h	the rate \$5 per hour
1:2	ratio of 1 to 2
%	percent

(x, y)	ordered pair
$P(\text{event})$	the probability of an event
$n!$	n factorial
$\cong$	is congruent to
$\sim$	is similar to
$\perp$	is perpendicular to
$\parallel$	is parallel to
$\overleftrightarrow{AB}$	line AB
$\overrightarrow{AB}$	ray AB
$\overline{AB}$	line segment AB
$\angle ABC$	angle ABC
$m\angle A$	measure of $\angle A$
$\triangle ABC$	triangle ABC
$^\circ$	degree
π	pi; $\pi \approx 3.14$ or $\pi \approx \frac{22}{7}$
A'	A prime

Selected Answers

1 Exercises

1. 7,000 **3.** 1,500 bottles of water
5. about 2 gallons **7.** 40,000
9. 20,000 **11.** 40 golf balls
13. 500 **15.** 0 **17.** 11,000
19. 40,000 **21.** 70,000 **23.** 400,000
25. 10 square miles
27. 40,000 square miles
33. 400; 36 rounds to 40, and 8 rounds to 10

2 Exercises

1. $58 **3.** about 12 gallons
5. 16 people **7.** 31 bags **9.** 24
11. $469\frac{2}{3}$ **13.** $674\frac{1}{3}$ **15.** $775\frac{13}{16}$
17. 71 hours **19.** every $84\frac{24}{34}$, or $84\frac{12}{17}$, minutes **21.** $88.50 **25.** A

3 Exercises

1. 8^3 **3.** 6^5 **5.** 5^5 **7.** 16 **9.** 625
11. 343 **13.** 2^6 **15.** 8^2 **17.** 6^5
19. 7^7 **21.** 4^2 **23.** 243 **25.** 81
27. 512 **29.** 256 **31.** 144

33. $16 \times 16 \times 16$ **35.** $31 \times 31 \times 31 \times 31 \times 31 \times 31$ **37.** $50 \times 50 \times 50$
39. $1 \times 1 \times 1 \times 1 \times 1 \times 1 \times 1 \times 1 \times 1$ **41.** $8 \times 8 \times 8 \times 8 \times 8$
43. 1,000,000 **45.** 6,651
47. 100,000 **49.** 512 **51.** 125
53. > **55.** < **57.** > **59.** 1,024 cells **61.** 8; 2^8, or 256 **65.** D

4 Exercises

1. 33 **3.** 50 **5.** 4 **7.** $138 **9.** 10
11. 32 **13.** 14 **15.** 25 **17.** 40
19. 24 **21.** 1,250 pages **23.** 18
25. 57 **27.** 1 **29.** 22 **31.** 64
33. 22 **35.** $(7 + 2) \times 6 - (4 - 3) = 53$
37. $5^2 - 10 + (5 + 4^2) = 36$
39. $9^2 - 2 \times (15 + 16) - 8 = 11$
41. $4^2 \times (3 - 2) \div 4 = 4$ **43.** 30 m^2
45. 300 m^3 **49.** J

5 Exercises

1. 40 **3.** 50 **5.** 320 **7.** 120 **9.** 156
11. 99 **13.** 108 **15.** 40 **17.** 50
19. 640 **21.** 108 **23.** 426 **25.** 138

27. 372 **29.** 328 **31.** 40 **33.** 60
35. 198 **37.** 111 **39.** 70 **41.** 70°F
43. 153 **45.** 198 **51.** 108 eggs
53. $208 **59.** 2,718 mi

Chapter Study Guide: Review

1. Distributive Property **2.** base, exponent **3.** order of operations
4. simplify **5.** 1,000 **6.** 6,000
7. 20,000 **8.** 800 **9.** $38\frac{11}{12}$
10. $291\frac{13}{29}$ **11.** $440\frac{11}{16}$ **12.** 1,281
13. 27 rows **14.** 5^3 **15.** 3^5
16. 7^4 **17.** 8^2 **18.** 4^4 **19.** 1^3
20. 256 **21.** 16 **22.** 216 **23.** 27
24. 1 **25.** 2,401 **26.** 125 **27.** 100
28. 81 **29.** 59 **30.** 11 **31.** 26
32. 17 **33.** 5 **34.** 45 **35.** $149
36. 30 **37.** 520 **38.** 80 **39.** 1,080
40. 40 **41.** 320 **42.** 168 **43.** 135
44. 204 **45.** 152

Selected Answers ... Chapter 2

1 Exercises

1. 56; 65 **3.** 24; 28; 32; 36
5. 23; 25 **7a.** 2 hr: $100 - 120$
miles; 3 hr: $150 - 180$ miles; 4 hr:
$200 - 240$ miles; 5 hr: $250 - 300$
miles **b.** between 350 and 420
miles **9.** 32° F; 50° F; 77° F **11.** 32
13. 13 **15.** 8 **17.** 56 **19.** 10
21. 110 **23.** 24 zlotys **29.** 38

2 Exercises

1. $4,028 - m$ **3.** $15x$ **5.** $\frac{p}{5}$
7. $(149)(2)$ **9.** the product of 345
and 196; 345 times 196 **11.** the
difference of d and 5; 5 less than d
13. $5x$ **15.** $325 \div 25$ **17.** $137 + 675$
19. $j - 14$ **21.** take away 19
from 243; 243 minus 19 **23.** 342
multiplied by 75; the product of
342 and 75 **25.** the product of
45 and 23; 45 times 23 **27.** the
difference of 228 and b; b less
than 228 **29.** $15 \div d$ **31.** $67m$
33. $678 - 319$ **37.** $d \div 4$ **41.** C

3 Exercises

1. $4n$ **3.** $5w$ **5.** $7n$ **7.** s^2 **9.** $n + 5$
11. $88n$ **13.** $n + 7$; $3n + 1$ **17.** G

4 Exercises

1. no **3.** yes **5.** yes **7.** 53 feet is
equal to 636 inches. **9.** no **11.** yes
13. no **15.** yes **17.** no **19.** yes
21. 300 m is equal to 30,000 cm.

Chapter 2

23. yes **25.** no **27.** no **29.** yes
31. no **33.** yes **35.** $17 \neq 350 \div 20$;
no, they do not have the same
amount of money. **37.** 6 **39.** 2
41. 3 **47.** H

5 Exercises

1. $x = 36$ **3.** $n = 19$ **5.** $p = 18$
7. 6 blocks **9.** $r = 7$ **11.** $b = 25$
13. $z = 9$ **15.** $g = 16$ **17.** 6 meters
19. $n = 7$ **21.** $y = 19$ **23.** $h = 78$
25. $b = 69$ **27.** $t = 26$ **29.** $m = 22$
31. $p + 20 = 36$ **33.** 880 m **37.** B

6 Exercises

1. $p = 17$ **3.** $a = 31$ **5.** $n = 33$
7. $y = 25$ **9.** $a = 38$ **11.** $a = 97$
13. $p = 33$ **15.** $s = 31$ **17.** $x = 36$
19. $a = 21$ **21.** $f = 14$ **23.** $r = 154$
25. $g = 143$ **27.** $m = 18$
29. 13 million **33.** D

7 Exercises

1. $x = 3$ **3.** $a = 9$ **5.** $c = 11$
7. 45 feet **9.** $a = 4$ **11.** $x = 4$
13. $t = 7$ **15.** $m = 11$ **17.** 6 feet
19. $y = 9$ **21.** $y = 8$ **23.** $y = 20$
25. $z = 40$ **27.** $y = 23$ **29.** $y = 18$
31. $y = 8$ **33.** $a = 14$ **35.** $x = 3$
37. $t = 6$ **39.** 15 to 177 segments
41. 4,000 light-sensitive cells **45.** C

8 Exercises

1. $y = 12$ **3.** $r = 63$ **5.** $j = 36$
7. $f = 60$ **9.** 90 min **11.** $c = 26$

13. $g = 98$ **15.** $x = 144$ **17.** $r = 81$
19. $c = 96$ **21.** $c = 165$ **23.** $c = 70$
25. $c = 60$ **27.** $\frac{w}{381} = 76$;
$w = 28,956$ m **33.** J

Chapter Study Guide: Review

1. algebraic expression
2. equation **3.** variable
4. 7, 6 **5.** 6, 10 **6.** 9, 18, 27, 36
7. 30, 33, 36, 39 **8.** 75, 80, 85, 90
9. $15 + b$ **10.** 6×5 **11.** $9t$
12. $g \div 9$ **13.** the product of 4
and z; 4 times z **14.** 15 plus x; the
sum of 15 and x **15.** 54 divided
by 6; the quotient of 54 and 6
16. m divided by 20; the quotient
of m and 20 **17.** 3 minus y; the
difference of 3 and y **18.** the sum
of 5,100 and 64; 64 added to 5,100
19. y minus 3; the difference
of y and 3 **20.** g minus 20; the
difference of g and 20 **21.** $3n + 1$
22. $n - 1$ **23.** yes **24.** no **25.** yes
26. yes **27.** $x = 6$ **28.** $n = 14$
29. $c = 29$ **30.** $y = 6$ **31.** $p = 27$
32. $w = 9$ **33.** 67 channels
34. $k = 45$ **35.** $d = 9$ **36.** $p = 63$
37. $n = 67$ **38.** $r = 14$ **39.** $w = 144$
40. 31 sports **41.** $v = 8$ **42.** $y = 9$
43. $c = 7$ **44.** $n = 2$ **45.** $s = 8$
46. $t = 10$ **47.** 50 pounds
48. $r = 42$ **49.** $t = 15$ **50.** $y = 18$
51. $n = 72$ **52.** $z = 52$
53. $b = 100$

Selected Answers ... Chapter 3

1 Exercises

1. 1 + 0.9 + 0.08; one and ninety-eight hundredths
3. 0.0765; seven hundred sixty-five ten-thousandths **5.** Osmium
7. 4.09, 4.1, 4.18 **9.** 7 + 0.08 + 0.009 + 0.0003; seven and eight hundred ninety-three ten-thousandths **11.** 7.15; 7 + 0.1 + 0.05 **13.** the Chupaderos meteorite **15.** 1.5, 1.56, 1.62
17. nine and seven thousandths
19. ten and twenty-two thousandths **21.** one hundred forty-two and six thousand five hundred forty-one ten-thousandths **23.** ninety-two thousand, seven hundred fifty-five hundred thousandths **25.** <
27. < **29.** < **31.** three hundredths **33.** one tenth
35. 4.034, 1.43, 1.424, 1.043, 0.34
37. 652.12, 65.213, 65.135, 61.53
39. Ross 154 **41.** Alpha Centauri, Proxima Centauri **45.** C

2 Exercises

1. about 12 miles **3.** 12 **5.** 5.4988
7. 120 **9.** from 44 to 46.5
11. about 450 miles **13.** 3.4
15. 5.157 **17.** 20 **19.** 6 **21.** from 14 to 17 **23.** 48 **25.** 17 **27.** $0.22, $0.10, $0.08, $0.04 **29.** (12 × 8) − (18 × 4) = 24, or about 24 cents
37. 6 inches in April, 10 inches in May, 2 inches in June

3 Exercises

1. 20.2 miles **3.** 12.65 miles
5. 5.6 **7.** 4.9 **9.** 3.55 **11.** 4.948
13. $567.38 **15.** 1.5 **17.** 18 **19.** 4.3
21. 2.3 **23.** 5.87 **25.** 9.035

27. 8.669 **29.** 0.143 **31.** 3.778
33. 3.8179 **35.** 1 **37.** 52.836
39. 29.376 **41.** 84.966 **43.** $72.42
45. 0.196 **49.** C

4 Exercises

1. $1.68 **3.** 0.24 **5.** 0.21 **7.** 16.52
9. 35.63 **11.** 2.59 km **13.** 0.027
15. 0.217 **17.** 0.00042 **19.** 0.012
21. 13.321 **23.** 26.04 **25.** 1.148
27. 2.5914 **29.** 0.009 **31.** 0.0612
33. 26.46 **35.** 1.6632 **37.** 0.2444
39. 4.1184 **41.** 14.06 **43.** 37.38
45. 62.1 **47.** 5.8 **49.** 4.65 pounds
51. 7.38 lb **55.** B

5 Exercises

1. 0.23 **3.** 0.35 **5.** 0.078 **7.** 0.104
9. $8.82 **11.** 0.22 **13.** 0.27
15. 0.171 **17.** 0.076 **19.** 0.107
21. 1.345 **23.** 0.236 **29.** when the divisor is greater than the portion of the dividend being divided into
31. C **33.** Subtract 5; 60.

6 Exercises

1. 5 **3.** 17 **5.** 6 **7.** 54.6 mi/h **9.** 6
11. 8 **13.** 217.5 **15.** 11 **17.** 5
19. 11.6 gallons of gas **21.** 6.3
23. 191.1 **25.** 184.74 **27.** 12.2
29. 12.2 **31.** 1,270 **33.** 1,125
35. 920 **37.** 2.15×10^7 **39.** about 232 bills; about $4,640 **45.** C

7 Exercises

1. 10 belts **3.** 2.25 meters
5. 8 bunches **7.** 3 packs **13.** C

8 Exercises

1. $a = 7.1$ **3.** $c = 12.8$ **5.** $d = 3.488$
7. 60.375 m² **9.** $b = 9.3$
11. $r = 20.8$ **13.** $a = 10.7$
15. $f = 6.56$ **17.** $z = 4$

19a. 1.6 meters **b.** $14.40
21. $q = 24.7$ **23.** $b = 4.2$
25. $a = 13.9$ **27.** $z = 13$
29a. 19.5 units, 21 units
b. 50.5 units **31.** 1.9×10^6 kg
33. 9 capsules **39.** H

Chapter Study Guide: Review

1. front-end estimation
2. clustering **3.** 5 + 0.6 + 0.08; five and sixty-eight hundredths
4. 1 + 0.007 + 0.0006; one and seventy-six ten-thousandths
5. 1 + 0.2 + 0.003; one and two hundred three thousandths
6. 20 + 3 + 0.005; twenty-three and five thousandths **7.** 70 + 1 + 0.03 + 0.008; seventy-one and thirty-eight thousandths
8. 90 + 9 + 0.9 + 0.09 + 0.009 + 0.0009; ninety-nine and nine thousand, nine hundred ninety-nine ten thousandths **9.** 1.12, 1.2, 1.3 **10.** 11.07, 11.17, 11.7
11. 0.033, 0.3, 0.303 **12.** 5.009, 5.5, 5.950 **13.** 101.025, 101.25, 101.52 **14.** 11.32 **15.** 2.3 **16.** 14
17. 80 **18.** 9 **19.** 2,000 **20.** 24.85
21. 5.3 **22.** 33.02 **23.** 4.9225
24. 2.58 **25.** 2.8718 **26.** 1.47
27. 6.423 **28.** $41.73 **29.** 9.44
30. 0.865 **31.** 0.0072 **32.** 24.416
33. 0.54 **34.** 10.5148 **35.** 2.05
36. 26.5 **37.** 5,678.4 lbs **38.** 1.03
39. 0.72 **40.** 3.85 **41.** 2.59
42. $3.64 **43.** 8.1 **44.** $6.1\overline{6}$
45. $3.87\overline{6}$ **46.** 52.275
47. 0.75 meter **48.** 14 containers
49. 9 cars **50.** 5.5 ft **51.** a = 13.38
52. $y = 2.62$ **53.** $n = 2.29$
54. $p = 60.2$ **55.** $5.00

1 Exercises

1. 1, 2, 3, 4, 6, 12 **3.** 1, 2, 4, 13, 26, 52 **5.** $2^4 \cdot 3$ **7.** $2 \cdot 3 \cdot 11$ **9.** 1, 2, 3, 4, 6, 8, 12, 24 **11.** 1, 2, 3, 6, 7, 14, 21, 42 **13.** 1, 67 **15.** 1, 5, 17, 85 **17.** 7^2 **19.** $2^2 \cdot 19$ **21.** 3^4 **23.** $2^2 \cdot 5 \cdot 7$ **33a.** 15 boys per team **b.** 5 teams of 9 players **35.** $3^2 \cdot 11$ **37.** $2^2 \cdot 7d$ **39.** $2^3 \cdot 3 \cdot 5 \cdot 7$ **41.** $2^2 \cdot 5 \cdot 37$ **43.** $2^2 \cdot 5^2$ **45.** 7^3 **47.** Birds **53.** 60

2 Exercises

1. 9 **3.** 7 **5.** 6 **7.** 4 arrangements **9.** 14 **11.** 2 **13.** 4 **15.** 12 **17.** 3 teams **19.** 12 **21.** 5 **23.** 2 **25.** 75 **27.** 4 **29.** 6 baskets **31.** 2 **33.** 9 **35.** 6 **37.** 6 rows **39.** 4 groups **43.** A

3 Exercises

1. 4(4 + 3) **3.** 5(3 + 4) **5.** 14(5 + 3) **7.** 2(3y + 4) **9.** 12(3n + 2) **11.** 8(4w + 1) **13.** Possible answer: 2(8 + 15); 2(15 + 8); 2 · 23; 46 **15.** Possible answer: 3(6x − 4x); 6(3x − 2x); 2 · 3x; 6x **17.** Possible answer: 8z + 8; 8 + 8z; 2(4z + 4); $2^3(z + 1)$ **19.** 16(3 + 2) **21.** 6(10 + 7) **23.** 2(16 + 17) **25.** 7(x + 4) **27.** 13(4v + 3) **29.** 16(3c + 4) **31.** Possible answer: 4(10 − 3); 2(20 − 6); 4 · 7; 2 · 14 **33.** Possible answer: x(9 − 7); (9 − 7)x; 2x; $3^2x − 7x$ **35.** Possible answer: 3 · 2p + 3 · 2; 6p + 6; 6 + 6p; 6(1 + p) **37.** equivalent **39.** equivalent **41.** not equivalent **43.** Possible answer: g + 15; 15 + g **45a.** Possible answer: 10 + 5h; 5h + 10; **b.** $40 **47.** Possible answer: 6x − 3

49. Possible answer: 8 · 4 **55.** Possible answer: 6 + 2f; 2f + 6; 2(f + 3)

4 Exercises

1. $\frac{3}{20}$ **3.** $\frac{43}{100}$ **5.** 0.4 **7.** 0.125 **9.** 0.21, $\frac{2}{3}$, 0.78 **11.** $\frac{1}{9}$, 0.3, 0.52 **13.** $5\frac{71}{100}$ **15.** $3\frac{23}{100}$ **17.** $2\frac{7}{10}$ **19.** $6\frac{3}{10}$ **21.** 1.6 **23.** 3.275 **25.** 0.375 **27.** 0.625 **29.** $\frac{1}{9}$, 0.29, $\frac{3}{8}$ **31.** $\frac{1}{10}$, 0.11, 0.13 **33.** 0.31, $\frac{3}{7}$, 0.76 **35.** $90 + 2 + \frac{3}{10}$ **37.** $100 + 7 + \frac{1}{10} + \frac{7}{100}$ **39.** $0.1\overline{6}$; repeats **41.** $0.41\overline{6}$; repeats **43.** 0.8; terminates **45.** $0.8\overline{3}$; repeats **47.** $0.91\overline{6}$; repeats **49.** > **51.** < **53.** < **55.** < **57.** $4\frac{1}{2}$, 4.48, 3.92 **59.** 125.25, 125.205, $125\frac{1}{5}$ **61.** Jill **63.** $\frac{1}{20}$ **67.** D

5 Exercises

1. $\frac{2}{3}$, $\frac{8}{12}$ **3.** $\frac{1}{2}$, $\frac{5}{10}$ **5.** 25 **7.** 21 **9.** $\frac{1}{5}$ **11.** $\frac{1}{4}$ **21.** 15 **23.** 70 **25.** 6 **27.** 140 **29.** $\frac{1}{4}$ **31.** $\frac{1}{5}$ **33.** $\frac{3}{4}$ **35.** $\frac{1}{2}$ **37.** $\frac{3}{6} = \frac{1}{2}$ **39.** $\frac{2}{3} = \frac{8}{12}$ **41.** $\frac{5}{20}$, $\frac{1}{4}$ **43.** $\frac{14}{35}$, $\frac{2}{5}$ **47.** Baskets and wreaths are $\frac{12}{72} = \frac{1}{6}$; jewelry is $\frac{32}{72} = \frac{4}{9}$; glass and pottery are $\frac{16}{72} = \frac{2}{9}$; paintings are $\frac{12}{72} = \frac{1}{6}$. **51.** B

6 Exercises

1. $2\frac{2}{5}$ **3.** $\frac{8}{3}$ **5.** $\frac{12}{5}$ **7.** $8\frac{3}{5}$ **9.** $\frac{20}{9}$ **11.** $\frac{13}{3}$ **13.** $\frac{25}{6}$ **15.** $\frac{19}{5}$ **17.** 4; whole number **19.** $8\frac{3}{5}$; mixed number **21.** $8\frac{7}{10}$; mixed number **23.** 15; whole number **25.** $\frac{53}{11}$ **27.** $\frac{93}{5}$ **29.** 3; 5 **31.** 13; 9 **33.** 2; 10 **35.** $28\frac{4}{9}$ yards **37.** = **39.** < **41.** $40\frac{1}{2}$; $50\frac{1}{2}$ **43.** $\frac{9}{5}$ **49.** J

7 Exercises

1. > **3.** = **5.** yes **7.** $\frac{1}{4}$, $\frac{1}{3}$, $\frac{2}{5}$ **9.** $\frac{1}{6}$, $\frac{1}{2}$, $\frac{2}{3}$ **11.** < **13.** > **15.** = **17.** > **19.** $\frac{3}{7}$, $\frac{1}{2}$, $\frac{3}{5}$ **21.** $\frac{1}{3}$, $\frac{3}{8}$, $\frac{4}{9}$ **23.** $\frac{2}{3}$, $\frac{7}{10}$, $\frac{3}{4}$ **25.** $\frac{1}{4}$, $\frac{3}{8}$, $\frac{2}{3}$ **27.** < **29.** > **31.** > **33.** > **35.** $\frac{3}{10}$, $\frac{2}{5}$, $\frac{1}{2}$ **37.** $\frac{1}{5}$, $\frac{7}{15}$, $\frac{2}{3}$ **39.** $\frac{2}{5}$, $\frac{4}{9}$, $\frac{11}{15}$ **41.** $\frac{5}{12}$, $\frac{5}{8}$, $\frac{3}{4}$ **43.** Laura; $\frac{3}{5} > \frac{4}{7}$ **45.** $1\frac{1}{8}$, $1\frac{2}{5}$, 3, $3\frac{2}{5}$, $3\frac{4}{5}$ **47.** $\frac{1}{2}$, $\frac{3}{4}$, $3\frac{1}{15}$, $3\frac{1}{10}$, $3\frac{1}{5}$ **49.** $3\frac{5}{7}$, $4\frac{2}{3}$, $4\frac{3}{4}$, 5, $5\frac{1}{3}$

Chapter Study Guide: Review

1. improper fraction; mixed number **2.** repeating decimal; terminating decimal **3.** coefficient **4.** 1, 2, 3, 4, 5, 6, 10, 12, 15, 20, 30, 60 **5.** 1, 2, 3, 4, 6, 8, 9, 12, 18, 24, 36, 72 **6.** 1, 29 **7.** 1, 2, 4, 7, 8, 14, 28, 56 **8.** 1, 5, 17, 85 **9.** 1, 71 **10.** 5 · 13 **11.** 2 · 47 **12.** 2 · 5 · 11 **13.** 3^4 **14.** $3^2 \cdot 11$ **15.** $2^2 \cdot 19$ **16.** 7 · 11 **17.** 5 · 11 **18.** 2 · 23 **19.** 12 **20.** 25 **21.** 9 **22.** 4 **23.** 4(5 + 16) **24.** 13(5 + 1) **25.** 7(5 + 4) **26.** 5(24 + 5) **27.** 5(3 + 10) **28.** 3(8 + 9) **29.** 6(5n + 3) **30.** 3(3b + 7) **31.** 10(3y + 2) **32.** 7(7m + 2) **33.** 3(8t + 15) **34.** 3(13 + 5x) **35.** $\frac{37}{100}$ **36.** $1\frac{4}{5}$ **37.** $\frac{2}{5}$ **38.** 0.875 **39.** 0.4 **40.** $0.\overline{7}$ **41.** Possible answer: $\frac{2}{3}$; $\frac{8}{12}$ **42.** Possible answer: $\frac{8}{10}$; $\frac{16}{20}$ **43.** Possible answer: $\frac{1}{4}$; $\frac{2}{8}$ **44.** $\frac{7}{8}$ **45.** $\frac{3}{10}$ **46.** $\frac{7}{10}$ **47.** $\frac{34}{9}$ **48.** $\frac{29}{12}$ **49.** $\frac{37}{7}$ **50.** $3\frac{5}{6}$ **51.** $3\frac{2}{5}$ **52.** $5\frac{1}{8}$ **53.** $3\frac{3}{4}$ **54.** > **55.** > **56.** = **57.** < **58.** $\frac{3}{8}$, $\frac{2}{3}$, $\frac{7}{8}$ **59.** $\frac{3}{12}$, $\frac{1}{3}$, $\frac{4}{6}$ **60.** $\frac{1}{3}$, $\frac{3}{8}$, $\frac{1}{2}$ **61.** $\frac{5}{6}$, $\frac{7}{8}$, $\frac{9}{10}$

Selected Answers

1 Exercises

1. 3 packs of pencils and 4 packs of erasers **3.** 36 **5.** 20 **7.** 48 **9.** 40 **11.** 63 **13.** 150 **15.** 8 **17.** 20 **19.** 18 **21.** 12 **23.** 24 **25.** 66 **27.** 60 **29.** 140 **31.** 12 **33c.** 12 **d.** Possible answer: 120, 144, 132 **35.** 12 and 16 **37a.** 120 **b.** 120 **c.** 4 **41.** B

2 Exercises

1. $\frac{5}{12}$ ton **3.** $\frac{3}{10}$ **5.** $\frac{13}{14}$ **7.** $\frac{1}{6}$ cup **9.** $\frac{7}{12}$ **11.** $\frac{9}{20}$ **13.** $1\frac{2}{15}$ **15.** $1\frac{1}{8}$ **17.** $\frac{7}{15}$ **19.** $\frac{7}{12}$ **21.** $\frac{1}{3}$ **23.** $\frac{28}{33}$ **25.** $\frac{7}{18}$ **27.** $\frac{1}{5}$ **29.** $\frac{2}{2}$ or 1 **31.** $1\frac{1}{8}$ **33.** $\frac{1}{2}$ **35.** $\frac{4}{7}$ **37.** $\frac{3}{4}$ **39.** $\frac{7}{8}$ **41.** $\frac{1}{6}$ gallon **43.** $\frac{9}{40}$ lb **49.** $\frac{11}{12}$ mi

3 Exercises

1. $\frac{3}{4}$ **3.** $1\frac{2}{3}$ **5.** $2\frac{3}{5}$ pounds **7.** $3\frac{4}{5}$ **9.** $7\frac{7}{8}$ **11.** $4\frac{13}{18}$ **13.** $1\frac{4}{5}$ **15.** $6\frac{2}{3}$ pounds **17.** $1\frac{4}{9}$ **19.** $8\frac{9}{11}$ **21.** $11\frac{2}{9}$ **23.** $12\frac{13}{18}$ **25.** $7\frac{1}{4}$ in. **27.** $7\frac{1}{3}$ **29.** $3\frac{8}{11}$ **31.** $11\frac{4}{7}$ **33.** $4\frac{11}{12}$ **35.** $1\frac{5}{6}$ **37.** $\frac{1}{12}$ **39.** $13\frac{5}{12}$ **41.** $1\frac{1}{12}$ yards² **43.** $1\frac{11}{12}$ yards² **47.** C

4 Exercises

1. $4\frac{1}{2}$ **3.** $5\frac{5}{8}$ **5.** $4\frac{1}{10}$ **7.** $57\frac{3}{4}$ in. **9.** $3\frac{5}{8}$ **11.** $4\frac{5}{6}$ **13.** $8\frac{7}{9}$ **15.** $6\frac{1}{4}$ feet **17.** $5\frac{1}{10}$ **19.** $7\frac{9}{10}$ **21.** $\frac{1}{3}$

23. 16 ounces **25.** $\frac{3}{8}$ in. **27.** $7\frac{7}{18}$ **29.** $5\frac{5}{12}$ **31.** $4\frac{1}{4}$ **37.** B

5 Exercises

1. $\frac{5}{6}$ **3.** $\frac{11}{14}$ **5.** $\frac{13}{15}$ **7.** $2\frac{1}{16}$ **9.** $21\frac{5}{7}$ **11.** $12\frac{7}{20}$ **13.** $\frac{15}{16}$ **15.** $\frac{7}{15}$ **17.** $1\frac{1}{18}$ **19.** $\frac{13}{14}$ **21.** $2\frac{2}{7}$ **23.** $15\frac{1}{2}$ **25.** $23\frac{1}{2}$ **27.** $3\frac{3}{5}$ **29.** $\frac{10}{27}$ **31.** $1\frac{1}{4}$ **33.** $\frac{1}{6}$ **35.** $13\frac{3}{4}$ **37.** $2\frac{2}{3}$ **39.** $17\frac{1}{2}$ **41.** $1\frac{17}{25}$ bags **45.** $1\frac{3}{7}$ **47.** 28 **49.** $1\frac{7}{8}$ **51.** $21\frac{3}{4}$ **53.** $3\frac{1}{2}$ cups of flour; 5 teaspoons of baking powder **55a.** $6\frac{1}{8}$ cups **b.** $1\frac{1}{6}$ cups **c.** $1\frac{3}{4}$ teaspoons **57.** 12 **59.** $1\frac{2}{3}$

6 Exercises

1. $\frac{7}{2}$ **3.** 9 **5.** $\frac{5}{13}$ **7.** $1\frac{5}{7}$ **9.** $2\frac{1}{6}$ **11.** $\frac{9}{50}$ **13.** $4\frac{4}{7}$ **15.** 10 **17.** $\frac{12}{11}$ **19.** $\frac{11}{8}$ **21.** $\frac{7}{6}$ **23.** $\frac{4}{21}$ **25.** $1\frac{5}{14}$ **27.** 12 **29.** $\frac{3}{10}$ **31.** $2\frac{22}{45}$ **33.** $\frac{2}{3}$ **35.** $\frac{1}{40}$ **37.** $1\frac{17}{25}$ **39.** $4\frac{2}{3}$ **41.** $\frac{3}{28}$ **43.** 16 bags **45.** yes **47.** yes **49.** $\frac{5}{2}, \frac{25}{4}$ **51.** $\frac{1}{5}, \frac{1}{5}$ **53.** The reciprocal of a fraction has the fraction's numerator as its denominator and has the fraction's denominator as its numerator. The product of a fraction and its reciprocal is 1. **55.** $\frac{11}{12}$ **57.** $1\frac{1}{14}$ **59.** $41\frac{19}{75}$ **61.** $24\frac{2}{9}$ in. **67.** H

7 Exercises

1. $z = 16$ **3.** $x = 7\frac{1}{2}$ **5.** 24 **7.** $x = 9$ **9.** $t = \frac{1}{10}$ **11.** $y = 20$ **13.** $j = 12\frac{6}{7}$ **15.** \$10 **17.** $y = 10$ **19.** $t = 16$ **21.** $b = 14$ **23.** $x = 9\frac{1}{3}$ **25.** $n = 12$ **27.** $y = \frac{2}{3}$ **29.** $\frac{3}{2}n = 9$; $n = 6$ **31.** 4 minutes **33.** 11 dresses **35.** 20 more pages **41.** B **43.** 35

Chapter Study Guide: Review

1. reciprocals **2.** least common denominator **3.** 30 **4.** 48 **5.** 27 **6.** 60 **7.** 225 **8.** 660 **9.** $\frac{33}{40}$ **10.** $\frac{3}{4}$ **11.** $\frac{1}{15}$ **12.** $\frac{5}{24}$ **13.** $3\frac{2}{3}$ **14.** $1\frac{1}{2}$ **15.** $5\frac{2}{3}$ **16.** $2\frac{5}{8}$ **17.** $6\frac{13}{14}$ **18.** $1\frac{1}{8}$ **19.** $4\frac{3}{4}$ feet **20.** $30\frac{3}{20}$ **21.** $14\frac{11}{12}$ **22.** $5\frac{5}{12}$ **23.** $3\frac{4}{9}$ **24.** $5\frac{7}{15}$ **25.** $3\frac{3}{10}$ **26.** 7 oz **27.** $1\frac{2}{3}$ miles **28.** $\frac{9}{10}$ **29.** $1\frac{1}{4}$ **30.** 2 **31.** $\frac{4}{21}$ **32.** $\frac{3}{20}$ **33.** $\frac{5}{9}$ **34.** 8 times **35.** $a = \frac{1}{8}$ **36.** $b = 2$ **37.** $m = 17\frac{1}{2}$ **38.** $g = \frac{2}{15}$ **39.** $r = 10\frac{4}{5}$ **40.** $s = 50$ **41.** $p = \frac{1}{9}$ **42.** $j = 1\frac{53}{64}$ **43.** 80 inches

1 Exercises

1. mean = 22 **3.** mean = 6.5
5. mean = 57, median = 54, no mode, range = 23 **7.** range = 19, mean = 508.2, median = 508.5, mode = 500 **9.** 11 **11.** 4 **13.** 70 **15.** 6, 7, 12, 15, 15 **19.** C **21.** 25

2 Exercises

1a. mean = 4.75, median = 5, no mode **b.** mean = 10, median = 7, no mode **3.** mean = 225, median = 187.5, mode = 240; median **5.** with: mean = 738.8, median = 810, no mode without: mean = 913.25, median = 906.5, no mode **7.** mean ≈ 118.29, median = 128, no mode **13.** 70

3 Exercises

1.

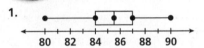

3. 8 **5.** 2
7.

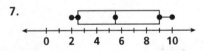

9. 8 **11.** 13.5 **13.** 4.3
15. 6 minutes **17.** 230 lb
19a. Tim: 1.5; Tony: 2.4;
b. Tim; a smaller mean absolute deviation means that the number of miles he runs each day is more consistent.
21. Possible answer: Increasing one number has less effect on the interquartile range than on the mean absolute deviation. The mean absolute variation is most affected by unusually large or small numbers.
23. B

4 Exercises

1.

Type of Instrument	
Trumpet	⊞
Drums	II
Tuba	I
Trombone	III
French horn	IIII

3.

Number of Years of Each Presidential Term				
Number (Intervals)	0–3	4–7	8–11	12-15
Frequency	7	22	12	1

5.

Pets	
Dog	⊞ I
Cat	⊞
Bird	IIII
Fish	III
Hamster	II

7.

Final Medal Standing at the Summer Olympic Games for the Top 25 Countries					
Number (intervals)	1–20	21–40	41–60	61–80	81–100
Frequency	14	8	3	0	2

9. histogram
11.

Populations of Australia's States and Territories	
Census	Frequency
0–999,999	3
1,000,000–1,999,999	2
2,000,000–2,999,999	0
3,000,000–3,999,999	1
4,000,000–4,999,999	1
5,000,000–5,999,999	0
6,000,000–6,999,999	1

13. no **17.** B

4 Extension

1. $0.00–$29.99 and $40.00–$59.99
3.

Amount ($)	Frequency	Cumulative Frequency
$0.00–$9.99	11	11
$10.00–$19.99	12	23
$20.00–$29.99	11	34
$30.00–$39.99	3	37
$40.00–$49.99	10	47
$50.00–$59.99	9	56

5 Exercises

1. normal **3.** In general, Jackson has better scores than Amy, but Amy is more consistent in her scores. **5.** normal **7.** Possible answer: About 50% of litters have between 3 and 5 kittens. **11.** D

Chapter Study Guide: Review

1. Variation **2.** frequency table
3. mode **4.** mean: 37; median: 38; mode: 39; range: 7
5. mean: 62.5; median: 50; mode: 50; range: 90 **6.** with outlier: mean ≈ 14.29; median = 11; mode = 12; without outlier: mean ≈ 10.33; median = 10.5; mode = 12 **7.** with outlier: mean = 31; median = 32; mode = 32; without outlier: mean = 35.75; median = 33; mode = 32
8. with outlier: mean ≈ 19.67; median = 14; mode = none; without outlier: mean =13.2; median = 13; mode = none
9. Data without Art score: mean = 87.5, median = 87.5, no mode
Data with Art score: mean = 86.4, median = 85, no mode
With the Art score added, the mean decreases by 1.1, the median decreases by 2.5, and there is still no mode.
10. Possible answer: 109, 121, 132, 136, 147 **11.** Possible answer: 136 − 121 = 15 **12.** Possible answer: 3.4
13. Number of Fish Identified at the Aquarium

```
            X
            X
        X  XX  X
        XXXX   X
        XXXXX  X  XXXX
    ┼┼┼┼┼┼┼┼┼┼┼┼┼┼┼┼┼┼┼
    4     8    12    16    20
```

14.

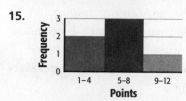

Points Scored			
Points (Intervals)	1–4	5–8	9–12
Frequency	2	3	1

15.

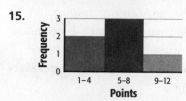

16. The distribution is symmetrical about the center. It shows a normal shape of distribution. **17.** The mean, median, and mode of the data set are all about 12.

Selected Answers

1 Exercises

1. 3:10 **3.** 41:16 **5.** the 8-ounce bag **7.** 19:3 **11.** the 15 lb bag **13.** 24 to 11, 24:11 **15.** 7 to 10, 7:10 **17.** 5 to 9, 5:9 **19.** $\frac{100}{101}$, 100:101, 100 to 101 **21.** 8:5 **23.** 5:8 **25.** 8:16 **27.** Wednesday **33.** The 24-ounce box is the better deal.

2 Exercises

1.

2	7
4	14
6	21
16	56

3.

96	48
48	24
24	12
12	6

5.

5	10	15	20
8	16	24	32

7.

24	12	6	3
16	8	4	2

9. 35 min

11.

8	15
16	30
24	45
32	60

13.

6	12	18	48	96
7	14	21	56	112

15.

11	22	33	44
25	50	75	100

17.

51	102	153	204
75	150	225	300

19. $\frac{8}{3}$ **21.** 24; 15 **27.** about 70,000,000 **31.** B

3 Exercises

1. (2, 3) **3.** (7, 6) **5.** (4, 5)

7–9.

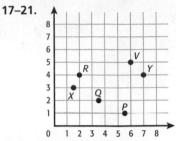

11. (3, 0) **13.** (1, 4) **15.** (11, 7)

17–21.

23. A **25.** C **27.** P **29.** (9, 8) **31.** (1, 5) **33.** (9, 0) **35.** $\left(5\frac{1}{2}, 0\right)$ **39.** D

3 Extension

1a. Possible answer:

Orbits of Satellite Over Time	
Time (hours)	**Number of Orbits**
1.5	1
3	2
4.5	3
6	4
7.5	5
9	6

b.

Orbits of Satellite Over Time

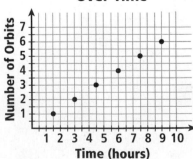

c. Possible answer: Jasmine switched the x- and y-coordinates. The satellite orbits Earth 1 time every 1.5 hours, not 1.5 times every 1 hour.

3. $\frac{\$8}{1\text{ h}}$

4 Exercises

3. 7 **5.** 35 **9.** 15 **11.** 55 **13.** 2 **15.** 3 **17.** 7 **19.** 3 **21.** $\frac{21}{6}$ **23.** 72 euros, 102 Canadian dollars, 752 yuan, 408 shekels, and 1,108 Mexican pesos. **27.** C

5 Exercises

1.

3.

5. $\frac{4}{5}$ **7.** $\frac{23}{25}$ **9.** 0.04 **11.** 0.64

13.

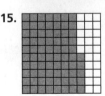

15.

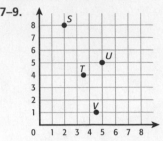

17. $\frac{3}{4}$ **19.** $\frac{18}{25}$ **21.** $\frac{16}{25}$ **23.** $\frac{17}{20}$ **25.** 0.44 **27.** 0.29 **29.** 0.6 **31.** 0.07 **33.** 0.02 **35.** 0.01 **37.** 0.7 **39.** 0.37 **41.** 0.08 **43.** 0.75 **45.** 1 **47.** 0.52 **49.** $\frac{3}{20}, \frac{13}{25}, \frac{71}{100}, 1$ **51.** 11% = 0.11 **53.** No **59.** H

6 Exercises

1. 39% **3.** 80% **5.** 44% **7.** 70%
9. 60% **11.** 60% **13.** 34% **15.** 62%
17. 30% **19.** 45% **21.** 12.5%
23. 74% **25.** 40% **27.** 4%, $\frac{1}{25}$
29. 45%, $\frac{9}{20}$ **31.** 1%, $\frac{1}{100}$
33. 60%, $\frac{3}{5}$ **35.** 14%, $\frac{7}{50}$
37. 80%, 0.8 **39.** 83.33%, 0.83
41. 34%, 0.34 **43.** 4%, 0.04
45. 26.67%, 0.27 **47.** < **49.** 5
51. > **53.** < **55.** about 48%;
about 52% **57.** 0.098, $\frac{7}{8}$, 90%
59. 0.21, $\frac{7}{25}$, 38% **61.** 17%, $\frac{5}{9}$,
0.605 **67.** D

7 Exercises

1. 24 **3.** 20 **5.** 8 **7.** 423 **9.** 171
students **11.** 11.2 **13.** 3,540
15. 0.04 **17.** 18 **19.** 13 **21.** 1.74
23. 39.6 **25.** 12.4 **27.** 6 **29.** 4.5
31. 11.75 **33.** 5,125 **35.** 80

37. 120 **39.** 0.6 **41.** 4.2
43. $4.80 **45.** 2.25 g **47.** 0.98
53. C

8 Exercises

1. 25% **3.** 60 **5.** 18% **7.** 50 **9.** 8%
11. $33\frac{1}{3}$% **13.** 300% **15.** 225
17. 100% **19.** 30 **21.** 22 **23.** 55.6%
25. 68.8 **27.** 77.5 **29.** 158.3
31. 5% **35.** 45 pieces **39.** She
needs to make more than $22,917
per month in sales. **41.** 75

Chapter Study Guide: Review

1. ordered pair **2.** percent
3. ratio
4. Possible answers: 2:4; 3:6; 6:12
5. 12 oz for $2.64
6. Possible answers:

3	6	9	12
10	20	30	40

7. Possible answers:

5	10	15	20
21	42	63	84

8. Possible answers:

15	30	45	60
7	14	21	28

9. $47.25 **10.** (4, 1) **11.** (3, 3)
12. $n = 9$ **13.** $n = 3$ **14.** $n = 14$
15. $n = 2$ **16.** 6 cups of bananas
17. $\frac{3}{4}$ **18.** $\frac{3}{50}$ **19.** $\frac{3}{10}$ **20.** 0.08
21. 0.65 **22.** 0.2 **23.** 89.6%
24. 70% **25.** 5.7%
26. 12% **27.** 70% **28.** 25%
29. 87.5% **30.** 80% **31.** 6.25%
32. 65% **33.** 68 **34.** 24
35. 4.41 **36.** 120 **37.** 27.3
38. 54 **39.** about 474 **40.** 125
41. 8% **42.** 12 **43.** 37.5% **44.** 8
45. ≈27.8% **46.** 7.96%
47. about $125

Selected Answers ... Chapter 8

1 Exercises

1. 108 **3.** 7 **5.** 3 **7.** 8 **9.** 3 **11.** 22
13. about 24 cups **15.** 48 **17.** 2
19. 2 **21.** 6,000 **23.** 3 **25.** 20
27. < **29.** = **31.** < **33.** = **35.** >
37. about 434 yards **39a.** 9 yd
b. 324 in. **41.** 3,520; 2 **43.** 8; 16
47. 4 pints **49.** Possible answer:
First, convert either the inches
to feet or the feet to inches so
that both lengths have the same
unit. Then compare. **51.** A

2 Exercises

1. 0.115 km **3.** 0.852 **5.** 3,500
7. 4,400 **9.** 0.05 **11.** 0.006
13. 0.110 **15.** 22,500 **17.** 2.460
19. 9.68 **21.** 0.782 **23.** 21.6 L;
21,600 mL **25.** $x = 0.23850$
27. 7,000 **29.** = **31.** < **33.** =
35. St. Louis Gateway Arch; 18 m
39. approximately 50 cups
41. 0.452 kg; 452,000 mg; 0.136 kg

3 Exercises

1. about 8.5 square units **3.** about
6 square units **5.** 100.1 in^2
7. 48 ft^2 **9.** 10 in^2 **11.** about
6 square units **13.** about 4 square
units **15.** 12.75 m^2 **17.** 260 ft^2
19. 0.75 cm^2 **25.** B

4 Exercises

1. 3 yd^2 **3.** 27 m^2 **5.** 26 ft^2
7. 88 cm^2 **9.** 3 ft^2 **11.** 72 in^2
13. 16 yd^2 **15.** 96 m^2
17. 5 square units **19.** 15 square
units **21.** 346.5 m^2 **31.** 175 cm^2

5 Exercises

1. 2,800 m^2 **3.** 57 square units
5. 640 yd^2 **11.** 40 square units

6 Exercises

1. 162 cm^3 **3.** 10 ft^3 **5.** 320 ft^3
7. $1 \times 1 \times 10$ and $2 \times 5 \times 1$
9. 79.36 in^3 **11.** 54 m^3 **13.** 71.72 ft^3
15. 480 in^3 **17.** 474.375 km^3
19. 20 ft **21.** 10 cm^3, 1 cm^3,
3.5 cm^3, 300 cm^3, 20 cm^3 **23.** pine
25. Alicia does not have gold.
29. 77.4

7 Exercises

1. 94 in^2 **3.** 56 cm^2 **5.** 2,640 cm^2
7. 326.56 ft^2 **9.** 376.8 m^2
11. $16\frac{1}{2}$ m^2 **13.** 133 cm^2
15. 11 km^2 **17.** 712.72 m^2
21. about 96 ft^2 **23.** about 190 cm^2
27. D

Chapter Study Guide: Review

1. perimeter; circumference
2. diameter **3.** customary system
4. in.; about five widths of your
thumbs **5.** mi; about 800 times
18 football fields **6.** lb; about 2
loaves of bread **7.** fl oz; about a
spoonful **8.** $\frac{1}{8}$ in. **9.** mm; about
32 times the thickness of a dime
10. mg; about 5 times the mass of
a very small insect **11.** kg; about
two textbooks **12.** L; about two
blender containers **13.** 2 cm
14. 15, 840 ft **15.** 6 yd **16.** 12 c
17. 3 gal **18.** 8 lb **19.** 4 T **20.** 4 lb
21. 144 in. **22.** 4 qt **23.** 99 ft
24. 250 yd **25.** 3,200 mL
26. 0.007 L **27.** 0.342 km
28. 0.042 kg **29.** 0.051 m
30. 71,000 m **31.** 681,296 g
32. 1 h **33.** 59,400 s
34. 105 days **35.** 12:10 P.M.
36. 105° **37.** Possible answer: 90°;
actual measure: 85° **38.** 33.9 in.
39. 6 ft **40.** 31.4 ft **41.** 9 m
42. 50.24 cm **43.** 11 ft

Selected Answers

1 Exercises

1. +5

3.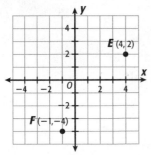
(number line: −4 −2 0 2 4)

5. (number line: −6 −4 −2 0 2 4 6)

9. 3 **11.** +50 **13.** +7 **21.** 10
23. 2 **25.** spending $83 **29.** +92
31. +25 **33.** 0 **35.** 105 **37.** 55

2 Exercises

1. > **3.** < **5.** −5, −4, 3, 7
7a. 3:30 A.M. **b.** 1°F **9.** > **11.** <
13. −8, 7, 15 **15.** −16, −9, −1, 13
17. −19, −3, 0, 8, 22 **19.** < **21.** >
23. < **25.** < **27.** −39, 14, 21
29. −26, −12, 0, 43
31. −73, −67, −10, 20, 82 **33.** C
35. San Augustin Cave, Dead
Sea, Mr. Rainier, Kilimanjaro,
Mt. Everest **39.** C

2 Extension

1. > **3.** < **5.** < **7.** > **9.** >
11. > **13.** $-7\frac{3}{4}$, $-2\frac{7}{10}$, 0, 0.21
15. $-4\frac{1}{10}$, −3, 2.25, $4\frac{3}{5}$ **17.** $-3\frac{1}{2}$,
−2.7, 0.09, $\frac{4}{5}$ **19.** −8.5, $-7\frac{1}{4}$, 1.25, $2\frac{2}{5}$
21. −8.25, −7, −2.5, $-4\frac{1}{5}$

3 Exercises

1. III **3.** I **5.** (1, 2)

7–9.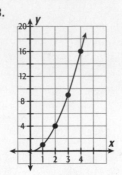

11. II **13.** I **15.** IV **17.** (−2, 4)
19. (4, 4) **21.** (−3, 0)

23.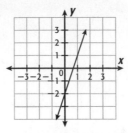

25.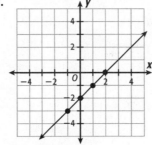

27.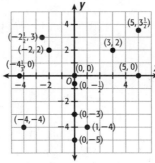

29. I **31.** III **33.** IV **35.** III
37–47.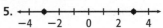

49. Gabon **55.** B

4 Exercises

1.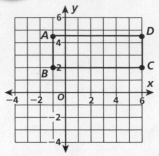

3. 18 units **5.** 22 ft **9.** 17 units
11. Square; 20 units **13.** 4, 8, 16;
when one side is doubled on the
square, the perimeter is doubled.
15. 18 units **19.** 22

5 Exercises

1. $A'(1, 7)$, $B'(3, 7)$, $C'(3, 5)$, $D'(1, 5)$
3. $A'(1, -4)$, $B'(3, -4)$, $C'(3, -2)$,
$D'(1, -2)$ **5.** $E'(0, 0)$, $F'(0, -3)$,
$G'(-3, 0)$ **7.** $H'(-1, -2)$, $J'(2, 2)$,
$K'(1, 0)$, $L'(-2, 0)$ **9.** $H'(-1, 2)$,
$J'(-4, 2)$, $K'(-3, 0)$, $L'(0, 0)$
11. $H'(-1, -2)$, $J'(-4, -2)$, $K'(-3, 0)$,
$L'(0, 0)$ **13.** translated up
3 units **15.** reflected across the
x-axis **19.** C

Chapter Study Guide: Review

1. output, input **2.** coordinate
plane, quadrants **3.** +10 **4.** −50
5. (number line: −4 −2 0 2 4)
6. (number line: −3 −2 −1 0 1 2 3)
7. (number line: −10 −8 −6 −4 −2 0)
8. (number line: −3 −2 −1 0 1 2 3)

9. 37 **10.** 14 **11.** 97 **12.** 13
13. < **14.** < **15.** <
16. –1, 2, 4 **17.** –3, 0, 4
18. –8, –6, 0 **19.** (–2, –3)
20. (1, 0) **21.** III **22.** II

23.

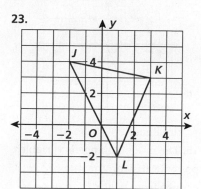

24.

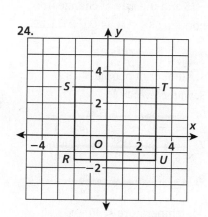

25.

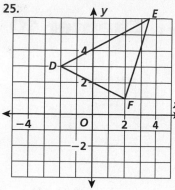

26.

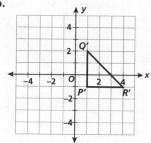

P' (1, –1), Q' (1, 2), R' (4, –1)

27.

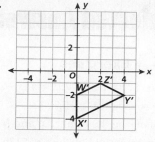

W' (0, –2), X' (0, –4), Y' (4, –2), Z' (2, –1)

28.

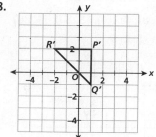

P' (1, 2), Q' (1, –1), R' (–2, 2)

Selected Answers ... Chapter 10

1 Exercises

1. 15 **3.** $j = b - 6$ **7.** $c = 12s - 2$
9. $p = 150m$ **11.** -54 **13.** $-3; 5$
15. Let c be the total cost and h be the number of hours. $c = \$125 + \$55h$ **17.** 9 hours **23.** G

2 Exercises

1. (1, 8); (2, 14); (3, 20); (4, 26)
3. no **5.** 2 **7.** 0
9.

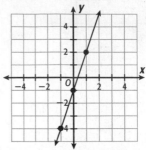

11. (1, −3); (2, −7); (3, −11); (4, −15) **13.** yes **15.** 1 **17.** 0
19. 2
21.

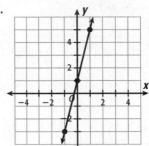

23.

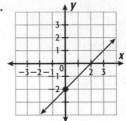

25.

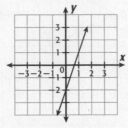

27. −3; −2; −1; 0 **29.** (1, 14)
31.

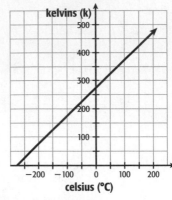

33. 219 kelvins **39.** H

2 Extension

1. independent: number of hours Erica works; dependent: Erica's paycheck
3. independent: daily amount of rainfall; dependent: growth of the grass
5. independent: number of hours Simon works; dependent: total charge; $f(h) = 10h$

3 Exercises

1. constant **3.** variable
7. constant **9.** variable
11.

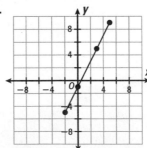

linear; 2

13.

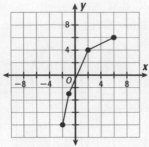

not linear
15. The rate of change is variable; possible answer: the rate of change from 9:00 A.M. to noon is -15 and the rate of change from noon to 5:00 P.M. is $\frac{44}{5}$. **21.** 1.25

4 Exercises

1. number of people ≤ 18
3. water level > 45
5.
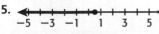
7.
9.
11. temperature < 40
13. number of tables ≤ 35
15.
17.
19.
21.
23.
25.
27.
29.
31.

35. $-200 \leq \text{depth} \leq 0$ **37.** $0 \geq$ *Manshu* depth measurement $\geq -32{,}190$ ft; $0 \geq$ *Challenger* depth measurement $\geq -35{,}640$ ft; $0 \geq$ *Horizon* depth measurement $\geq -34{,}884$ ft; $0 \geq$ *Vityaz* depth measurement $\geq -36{,}200$ ft **39.** B
41. 59 m/h **43.** $y = 5$

Chapter Study Guide: Review

1. inequality **2.** linear equation
3. function **4.** $y = 2x + 2$; 18
5. $\ell = 4w$, $\ell = $ length, $w = $ width
6. $(1, -3)$, $(2, -1)$, $(3, 1)$, $(4, 3)$
7. $(1, 8)$, $(2, 9)$, $(3, 10)$, $(4, 11)$
8. yes **9.** no **10.** variable
11. constant **12.** variable
13. constant **14.** variable
15. weight limit ≤ 9 tons
16. age > 200
17.
18.
19.
20.

Glossary/Glosario •••

A

ENGLISH	SPANISH	EXAMPLES
absolute value The distance of a number from zero on a number line; shown by | |.	**valor absoluto** Distancia a la que está un número de 0 en una recta numérica. El símbolo del valor absoluto es | |.	$\|-5\| = 5$
acute angle An angle that measures greater than 0° and less than 90°.	**ángulo agudo** Ángulo que mide más do 0° y menos de 90°.	
acute triangle A triangle with all angles measuring less than 90°.	**triángulo acutángulo** Triángulo en el que todos los ángulos miden menos de 90°.	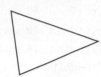
addend A number added to one or more other numbers to form a sum.	**sumando** Número que se suma a uno o más números para formar una suma.	In the expression $4 + 6 + 7$, the numbers 4, 6, and 7 are addends.
Addition Property of Opposites The property that states that the sum of a number and its opposite equals zero.	**Propiedad de la suma de los opuestos** Propiedad que establece que la suma de un número y su opuesto es cero.	$12 + (-12) = 0$
adjacent angles Angles in the same plane that have a common vertex and a common side.	**ángulos adyacentes** Ángulos en el mismo plano que comparten un vértice y un lado.	∠1 and ∠2 are adjacent angles.
algebraic expression An expression that contains at least one variable.	**expresión algebraica** Expresión que contiene al menos una variable.	$x + 8$ $4(m - b)$
algebraic inequality An inequality that contains at least one variable.	**desigualdad algebraica** Desigualdad que contiene al menos una variable.	$x + 3 > 10$ $5a > b + 3$
alternate exterior angles For two lines intersected by a transversal, a pair of angles that lie on opposite sides of the transversal and outside the other two lines.	**ángulos alternos externos** Dadas dos rectas cortadas por una transversal, par de ángulos no adyacentes ubicados en los lados opuestos de la transversal y fuera de las otras dos rectas.	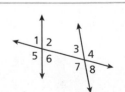 ∠4 and ∠5 are alternate exterior angles.

alternate interior angles For two lines intersected by a transversal, a pair of nonadjacent angles that lie on opposite sides of the transversal and between the other two lines.

ángulos alternos internos Dadas dos rectas cortadas por una transversal, par de ángulos no adyacentes ubicados en los lados opuestos de la transversal y entre las otras dos rectas.

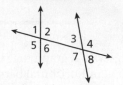

∠3 and ∠6 are alternate interior angles.

---

angle A figure formed by two rays with a common endpoint called the vertex.

ángulo Figura formada por dos rayos con un extremo común llamado vértice.

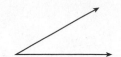

---

area The number of square units needed to cover a given surface.

área El número de unidades cuadradas que se necesitan para cubrir una superficie dada.

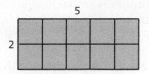

The area is 10 square units.

---

arithmetic sequence A sequence in which the terms change by the same amount each time.

secuencia aritmética Una sucesión en la que los términos cambian la misma cantidad cada vez.

The sequence 2, 5, 8, 11, 14. . . is an arthmetic sequence.

Associative Property of Addition The property that states that for three or more numbers, their sum is always the same, regardless of their grouping.

Propiedad asociativa de la suma Propiedad que establece que agrupar tres o más números en cualquier orden siempre da como resultado la misma suma.

$2 + 3 + 8 = (2 + 3) + 8 = 2 + (3 + 8)$

Associative Property of Multiplication The property that states that for three or more numbers, their product is always the same, regardless of their grouping.

Propiedad asociativa de la multiplicación Propiedad que establece que agrupar tres o más números en cualquier orden siempre da como resultado el mismo producto.

$2 \cdot 3 \cdot 8 = (2 \cdot 3) \cdot 8 = 2 \cdot (3 \cdot 8)$

---

asymmetrical Not identical on either side of a central line; not symmetrical.

asimétrico Que no es idéntico a ambos lados de una línea central; no simétrico.

---

average The sum of the items in a set of data divided by the number of items in the set; also called *mean*.

promedio La suma de los elementos de un conjunto de datos dividida entre el número de elementos del conjunto. También se le llama *media*.

Data set: 4, 6, 7, 8, 10

Average: $\frac{4 + 6 + 7 + 8 + 10}{5} = \frac{35}{5} = 7$

---

axes The two perpendicular lines of a coordinate plane that intersect at the origin.

ejes Las dos rectas numéricas perpendiculares del plano cartesiano que se intersecan en el origen.

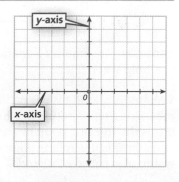

B

bar graph A graph that uses vertical or horizontal bars to display data.

gráfica de barras Gráfica en la que se usan barras verticales u horizontales para presentar datos.

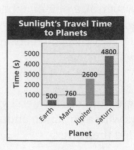

base (in numeration) When a number is raised to a power, the number that is used as a factor is the base.

base (en numeración) Cuando un número es elevado a una potencia, el número que se usa como factor es la base.

$3^5 = 3 \cdot 3 \cdot 3 \cdot 3 \cdot 3$; 3 is the base.

base (of a polygon or three-dimensional figure) A side of a polygon; a face of a three-dimensional figure by which the figure is measured or classified.

base (de un polígono o figura tridimensional) Lado de un polígono; la cara de una figura tridimensional, a partir de la cual se mide o se clasifica la figura.

Bases of a cylinder   Bases of a prism

Base of a cone   Base of a pyramid

bisect To divide into two congruent parts.

trazar una bisectriz Dividir en dos partes congruentes.

box-and-whisker plot A graph that shows how data are distributed by using the median, quartiles, least value, and greatest value; also called a box plot.

gráfica de mediana y rango Gráfica para demostrar la distribución de datos utilizando la mediana, los cuartiles y los valores menos y más grande; también llamado gráfica de caja.

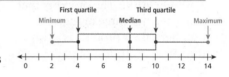

break (graph) A zigzag on a horizontal or vertical scale of a graph that indicates that some of the numbers on the scale have been omitted.

discontinuidad (gráfica) Zig-zag en la escala horizontal o vertical de una gráfica que indica la omisión de algunos de los números de la escala.

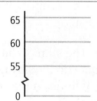

C

capacity The amount a container can hold when filled.

capacidad Cantidad que cabe en un recipiente cuando se llena.

Celsius A metric scale for measuring temperature in which 0°C is the freezing point of water and 100°C is the boiling point of water; also called *centigrade*.

Celsius Escala métrica para medir la temperatura, en la que 0° C es el punto de congelación del agua y 100° C es el punto de ebullición. También se llama *centígrado*.

ENGLISH	SPANISH	EXAMPLES
center (of a circle) The point inside a circle that is the same distance from all the points on the circle.	**centro (de un círculo)** Punto interior de un círculo que se encuentra a la misma distancia de todos los puntos de la circunferencia.	
center (of rotation) The point about which a figure is rotated.	**centro (de una rotación)** Punto alrededor del cual se hace girar una figura.	
chord A segment whose endpoints lie on a circle.	**cuerda** Segmento cuyos extremos se encuentran en un círculo.	
circle The set of all points in a plane that are the same distance from a given point called the center.	**círculo** Conjunto de todos los puntos en un plano que se encuentran a la misma distancia de un punto dado llamado centro.	
circle graph A graph that uses sections of a circle to compare parts to the whole and parts to other parts.	**gráfica circular** Gráfica que usa secciones de un círculo para comparar partes con el todo y con otras partes.	Residents of Mesa, AZ
circumference The distance around a circle.	**circunferencia** Distancia alrededor de un círculo.	
clockwise A circular movement in the direction shown.	**en el sentido de las manecillas del reloj** Movimiento circular en la dirección que se indica.	
clustering A method used to estimate a sum when all addends are close to the same value.	**agrupación** Método que se usa para estimar una suma cuando todos los sumandos se aproximan al mismo valor.	27, 29, 24, and 23 all cluster around 25.
coefficient The number that is multiplied by the variable in an algebraic expression.	**coeficiente** Número que se multiplica por la variable en una expresión algebraica.	5 is the coefficient in 5b.
combination An arrangement of items or events in which order does not matter.	**combinación** Agrupación de objetos o sucesos en la cual el orden no es importante.	For objects A, B, C, and D, there are 6 different combinations of 2 objects: AB, AC, AD, BC, BD, CD.
common denominator A denominator that is the same in two or more fractions.	**denominador común** Denominador que es común a dos o más fracciones.	The common denominator of $\frac{5}{8}$ and $\frac{2}{8}$ is 8.

Glossary/Glosario

ENGLISH	SPANISH	EXAMPLES
common factor A number that is a factor of two or more numbers.	**factor común** Número que es factor de dos o más números.	8 is a common factor of 16 and 40.
common multiple A number that is a multiple of each of two or more numbers.	**múltiplo común** Un número que es múltiplo de dos o más números.	15 is a common multiple of 3 and 5.
Commutative Property of Addition The property that states that two or more numbers can be added in any order without changing the sum.	**Propiedad conmutativa de la suma** Propiedad que establece que sumar dos o más números en cualquier orden no altera la suma.	$8 + 20 = 20 + 8$
Commutative Property of Multiplication The property that states that two or more numbers can be multiplied in any order without changing the product.	**Propiedad conmutativa de la multiplicación** Propiedad que establece que multiplicar dos o más números en cualquier orden no altera el producto.	$6 \cdot 12 = 12 \cdot 6$
compatible numbers Numbers that are close to the given numbers that make estimation or mental calculation easier.	**números compatibles** Números que están cerca de los números dados y hacen más fácil la estimación o el cálculo mental.	To estimate $7{,}957 + 5{,}009$, use the compatible numbers 8,000 and 5,000: $8{,}000 + 5{,}000 = 13{,}000$
compensation When a number in a problem is close to another number that is easier to calculate with, the easier number is used to find the answer. Then the answer is adjusted by adding to it or subtracting from it.	**compensación** Cuando un número de un problema está cerca de otro con el que es más fácil hacer cálculos, se usa el número más fácil para hallar la respuesta. Luego, se ajusta la respuesta sumando o restando.	
complement The set of all outcomes that are not the event.	**complemento** La serie de resultados que no están en el suceso.	When rolling a number cube, the complement of rolling a 3 is rolling a 1, 2, 4, 5, or 6.
complementary angles Two angles whose measures add to 90°.	**ángulos complementarios** Dos ángulos cuyas medidas suman 90°.	The complement of a 53° angle is a 37° angle.
composite number A number greater than 1 that has more than two whole-number factors.	**número compuesto** Número mayor que 1 que tiene más de dos factores que son números cabales.	4, 6, 8, and 9 are composite numbers.
compound inequality A combination of more than one inequality.	**desigualdad compuesta** Combinación de dos o más desigualdades.	$-2 \leq x < 10$

ENGLISH	SPANISH	EXAMPLES
cone A three-dimensional figure with one vertex and one circular base.	**cono** Figura tridimensional con un vértice y una base circular.	
congruent Having the same size and shape.	**congruentes** Que tienen la misma forma y el mismo tamaño.	
congruent angles Angles that have the same measure.	**ángulos congruentes** Ángulos que tienen la misma medida.	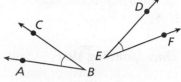 m ∠ABC = m ∠DEF
congruent figures Two figures whose corresponding sides and angles are congruent.	**figuras congruentes** Figuras que tienen el mismo tamaño y forma.	
congruent line segments Two line segments that have the same length.	**segmentos congruentes** Dos segmentos que tienen la misma longitud.	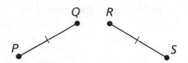
conjecture A statement that is believed to be true.	**conjetura** Enunciado que se supone verdadero.	
constant A value that does not change.	**constante** Valor que no cambia.	3, 0, π
coordinates The numbers of an ordered pair that locate a point on a coordinate graph.	**coordenadas** Los números de un par ordenado que ubican un punto en una gráfica de coordenadas.	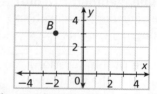 The coordinates of B are (−2, 3).
coordinate grid A grid formed by the intersection of horizontal and vertical lines that is used to locate points.	**cuadrícula de coordenadas** Cuadrícula formado por la intersección de líneas horizontales y líneas verticales que se usando por localizar puntos.	
coordinate plane A plane formed by the intersection of a horizontal number line called the *x*-axis and a vertical number line called the *y*-axis.	**plano cartesiano** Plano formado por la intersección de una recta numérica horizontal llamada eje *x* y otra vertical llamada eje *y*.	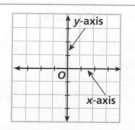
correspondence The relationship between two or more objects that are matched.	**correspondencia** La relación entre dos o más objetos que coinciden.	

ENGLISH	SPANISH	EXAMPLES
corresponding angles (for lines) Angles in the same position formed when a third line intersects two lines.	**ángulos correspondientes (en líneas)** Ángulos en la misma posición formaron cuando una tercera linea interseca dos lineas.	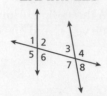 ∠1 and ∠3 are corresponding angles.
corresponding angles (in polygons) Angles in the same relative position in polygons with an equal number of sides.	**ángulos correspondientes (en polígonos)** Ángulos que se ubican en la misma posición relativa en polígonos que tienen el mismo número de lados.	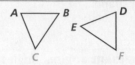 ∠A and ∠D are corresponding angles.
corresponding sides Sides in the same relative position in polygons with an equal number of sides.	**lados correspondientes** Lados que se ubican en la misma posición relativa en polígonos que tienen el mismo número de lados.	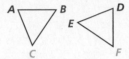 $\overline{AB}$ and $\overline{DE}$ are corresponding sides.
counterclockwise A circular movement in the direction shown.	**en sentido contrario a las manecillas del reloj** Movimiento circular en la dirección que se indica.	
cross product The product of numbers on the diagonal when comparing two ratios.	**producto cruzado** El producto de los números multiplicados en diagonal cuando se comparan dos razones.	For the proportion $\frac{2}{3} = \frac{4}{6}$, the cross products are $2 \cdot 6 = 12$ and $3 \cdot 4 = 12$.
cube (geometric figure) A rectangular prism with six congruent square faces.	**cubo (figura geométrica)** Prisma rectangular con seis caras cuadradas congruentes.	
cube (in numeration) A number raised to the third power.	**cubo (en numeración)** Número elevado a la tercera potencia.	$5^3 = 5 \cdot 5 \cdot 5 = 125$
cumulative frequency The frequency of all data values that are less than or equal to a given value.	**frecuencia acumulativa** Muestra el total acumulado de las frecuencias.	
customary system The measurement system often used in the United States.	**sistema usual de medidas** El sistema de medidas que se usa comúnmente en Estados Unidos.	inches, feet, miles, ounces, pounds, tons, cups, quarts, gallons
cylinder A three-dimensional figure with two parallel, congruent circular bases connected by a curved lateral surface.	**cilindro** Figura tridimensional con dos bases circulares paralelas y congruentes, unidas por una superficie lateral curva.	

degree The unit of measure for angles or temperature.

grado Unidad de medida para ángulos y temperaturas.

denominator The bottom number of a fraction that tells how many equal parts are in the whole.

denominador Número de abajo en una fracción que indica en cuántas partes iguales se divide el entero.

$\frac{3}{4}$ ← denominator

dependent events Events for which the outcome of one event affects the probability of the other.

sucesos dependientes Dos sucesos son dependientes si el resultado de uno afecta la probabilidad del otro.

A bag contains 3 red marbles and 2 blue marbles. Drawing a red marble and then drawing a blue marble without replacing the first marble is an example of dependent events.

dependent variable The output of a function; a variable whose value depends on the value of the input, or independent variable.

variable dependiente Salida de una función; variable cuyo valor depende del valor de la entrada, o variable independiente.

For $y = 2x + 1$, y is the dependent variable. input: x output: y

diagonal A line segment that connects two non-adjacent vertices of a polygon.

diagonal Segmento de recta que une dos vértices no adyacentes de un polígono.

diameter A line segment that passes through the center of a circle and has endpoints on the circle, or the length of that segment.

diámetro Segmento de recta que pasa por el centro de un círculo y tiene sus extremos en la circunferencia, o bien la longitud de ese segmento.

difference The result when one number is subtracted from another.

diferencia El resultado de restar un número de otro.

dimension The length, width, or height of a figure.

dimensión Longitud, ancho o altura de una figura.

discount The amount by which the original price is reduced.

descuento Cantidad que se resta del precio original de un artículo.

Distributive Property The property that states if you multiply a sum by a number, you will get the same result if you multiply each addend by that number and then add the products.

Propiedad distributiva Propiedad que establece que, si multiplicas una suma por un número, obtendrás el mismo resultado que si multiplicas cada sumando por ese número y luego sumas los productos.

$5(20 + 1) = 5 \cdot 20 + 5 \cdot 1$

dividend The number to be divided in a division problem.

dividendo Número que se divide en un problema de división.

In $8 \div 4 = 2$, 8 is the dividend.

divisible Can be divided by a number without leaving a remainder.

divisible Que se puede dividir entre un número sin dejar residuo.

18 is divisible by 3.

Glossary/Glosario

ENGLISH	SPANISH	EXAMPLES
divisor The number you are dividing by in a division problem.	**divisor** El número entre el que se divide en un problema de división.	In 8 ÷ 4 = 2, 4 is the divisor.
double-bar graph A bar graph that compares two related sets of data.	**gráfica de doble barra** Gráfica de barras que compara dos conjuntos de datos relacionados.	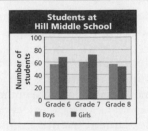
double-line graph A graph that shows how two related sets of data change over time.	**gráfica de doble línea** Gráfica lineal que muestra cómo cambian con el tiempo dos conjuntos de datos relacionados.	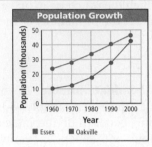

edge The line segment along which two faces of a polyhedron intersect.	**arista** Segmento de recta donde se intersecan dos caras de un poliedro.	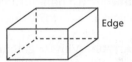
elements The words, numbers, or objects in a set.	**elementos** Palabras, números u objetos que forman un conjunto.	Elements of A: 1, 2, 3, 4
empty set A set that has no elements.	**conjunto vacío** Un conjunto que no tiene elementos.	
endpoint A point at the end of a line segment or ray.	**extremo** Un punto ubicado al final de un segmento de recta o rayo.	$\overset{A}{\bullet}\qquad\overset{B}{\bullet}$ $\overset{D}{\bullet}\longrightarrow$
equally likely Outcomes that have the same probability.	**igualmente probables** Resultados que tienen la misma probabilidad de ocurrir.	When you toss a coin, the outcomes "heads" and "tails" are equally likely.
equation A mathematical sentence that shows that two expressions are equivalent.	**ecuación** Enunciado matemático que indica que dos expresiones son equivalentes.	$x + 4 = 7$ $6 + 1 = 10 - 3$
equilateral triangle A triangle with three congruent sides.	**triángulo equilátero** Triángulo con tres lados congruentes.	
equivalent Having the same value.	**equivalentes** Que tienen el mismo valor.	
equivalent expression Equivalent expressions have the same value for all values of the variables.	**expresión equivalente** Las expresiones equivalentes tienen el mismo valor para todos los valores de las variables.	$4x + 5x$ and $9x$ are equivalent expressions.

ENGLISH	SPANISH	EXAMPLES
equivalent fractions Fractions that name the same amount or part.	**fracciones equivalentes** Fracciones que representan la misma cantidad o parte.	$\frac{1}{2}$ and $\frac{2}{4}$ are equivalent fractions.
equivalent ratios Ratios that name the same comparison.	**razones equivalentes** Razones que representan la misma comparación.	1/2 and 2/4 are equivalent ratios.
estimate (n) An answer that is close to the exact answer and is found by rounding or other methods.	**estimación (s)** Una solución aproximada a la respuesta exacta que se halla mediante el redondeo u otros métodos.	
estimate (v) To find an answer close to the exact answer by rounding or other methods.	**estimar (v)** Hallar una solución aproximada a la respuesta exacta mediante el redondeo u otros métodos.	
evaluate To find the value of a numerical or algebraic expression.	**evaluar** Hallar el valor de una expresión numérica o algebraica.	Evaluate $2x + 7$ for $x = 3$. $2x + 7$ $2(3) + 7$ $6 + 7$ 13
even number A whole number that is divisible by two.	**número par** Un número cabal que es divisible entre dos.	
event An outcome or set of outcomes of an experiment or situation.	**suceso** Un resultado o una serie de resultados de un experimento o una situación.	
expanded form A number written as the sum of the values of its digits.	**forma desarrollada** Número escrito como suma de los valores de sus dígitos.	236,536 written in expanded form is $200,000 + 30,000 + 6,000 + 500 + 30 + 6$.
experiment In probability, any activity based on chance.	**experimento** En probabilidad, cualquier actividad basada en la posibilidad.	Tossing a coin 10 times and noting the number of "heads."
experimental probability The ratio of the number of times an event occurs to the total number of trials, or times that the activity is performed.	**probabilidad experimental** Razón del número de veces que ocurre un suceso al número total de pruebas o al número de veces que se realiza el experimento.	Kendra attempted 27 free throws and made 16 of them. Her experimental probability of making a free throw is $\frac{number\ made}{number\ attempted} = \frac{16}{17} \approx 0.59$.
exponent The number that indicates how many times the base is used as a factor.	**exponente** Número que indica cuántas veces se usa la base como factor.	$2^3 = 2 \cdot 2 \cdot 2 = 8$; 3 is the exponent.
exponential form A number is in exponential form when it is written with a base and an exponent.	**forma exponencial** Cuando se escribe un número con una base y un exponente, está en forma exponencial.	4^2 is the exponential form for $4 \cdot 4$.
expression A mathematical phrase that contains operations, numbers, and/or variables.	**expresión** Enunciado matemático que contiene operaciones, números y/o variables.	$6x + 1$

F

face A flat surface of a polyhedron.

cara Lado plano de un poliedro.

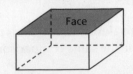

factor A number that is multiplied by another number to get a product.

factor Número que se multiplica por otro para hallar un producto.

7 is a factor of 21 since $7 \cdot 3 = 21$.

factor tree A diagram showing how a whole number breaks down into its prime factors.

árbol de factores Diagrama que muestra cómo se descompone un número cabal en sus factores primos.

```
    12
   /  \
  3 · 4
     /  \
    2 · 2

12 = 3 · 2 · 2
```

Fahrenheit A temperature scale in which 32°F is the freezing point of water and 212°F is the boiling point of water.

Fahrenheit Escala de temperatura en la que 32° F es el punto de congelación del agua y 212° F es el punto de ebullición.

fair When all outcomes of an experiment are equally likely, the experiment is said to be fair.

justo Se dice de un experimento donde todos los resultados posibles son igualmente probables.

When tossing a fair coin, heads and tails are equally likely. Each has a probability of $\frac{1}{2}$.

formula A rule showing relationships among quantities.

fórmula Regla que muestra relaciones entre cantidades.

$A = \ell w$ is the formula for the area of a rectangle.

fraction A number in the form $\frac{a}{b}$, where $b \neq 0$.

fracción Número escrito en la forma $\frac{a}{b}$, donde $b \neq 0$.

frequency The number of times a data value occurs.

frecuencia Cantidad de veces que aparece el valor en un conjunto de datos.

In the data set 5, 6, 7, 8, 9, the data value 6 has a frequency of 2.

frequency table A table that lists items together according to the number of times, or frequency, that the items occur.

tabla de frecuencia Una tabla en la que se organizan los datos de acuerdo con el número de veces que aparece cada valor (o la frecuencia).

Data set: 1, 1, 2, 2, 3, 4, 5, 5, 5, 6, 6
Frequency table:

Date	Frequency
1	2
2	2
3	1
4	1
5	3
6	2

front-end estimation An estimating technique in which the front digits of the addends are added.

estimación por partes Técnica en la que se suman sólo los números enteros de los sumandos. y luego se ajusta la suma para tener una estimacion mas exacta.

Estimate $25.05 + 14.671$ with the sum $25 + 14 = 39$. The actual value is 39 or greater.

Glossary/Glosario

ENGLISH	SPANISH	EXAMPLES

function An input-output relationship that has exactly one output for each input.

función Relación de entrada-salida en la que a cada valor de entrada corresponde un valor de salida.

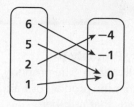

function table A table of ordered pairs that represent solutions of a function.

tabla de funciónes Tabla de pares ordenados que representan soluciones de una función.

x	3	4	5	6
y	7	9	11	13

 G

graph of an equation A graph of the set of ordered pairs that are solutions of the equation.

gráfica de una ecuación Gráfica del conjunto de pares ordenados que son soluciones de la ecuación.

greatest common factor (GCF) The largest common factor of two or more given numbers.

máximo común divisor (MCD) El mayor de los factores comunes compartidos por dos o más números dados.

The GCF of 27 and 45 is 9.

 H

height In a triangle or quadrilateral, the perpendicular distance from the base to the opposite vertex or side.
In a prism or cylinder, the perpendicular distance between the bases.

altura En un triángulo o cuadrilátero, la distancia perpendicular desde la base de la figura al vértice o lado opuesto.
En un prisma o cilindro, la distancia perpendicular entre las bases.

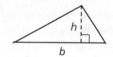

heptagon A seven-sided polygon.

heptágono Polígono de siete lados.

hexagon A six-sided polygon.

hexágono Polígono de seis lados.

histogram A bar graph that shows the frequency of data within equal intervals.

histograma Gráfica de barras que muestra la frecuencia de los datos en intervalos iguales.

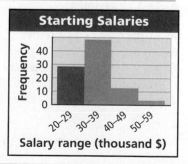

hypotenuse In a right triangle, the side opposite the right angle.

hipotenusa En un triángulo rectángulo, el lado opuesto al ángulo recto.

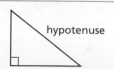

Glossary/Glosario **G13**

Identity Property (for Multiplication) The property that states that the product of 1 and any number is that number. | **Propiedad de identidad (de la multiplicación)** Propiedad que establece que el producto de 1 y cualquier número es ese número. | $5 \times 1 = 5$
$-8 \times 1 = -8$

Identity Property (for Addtion) The property that states the sum of zero and any number is that number. | **Propiedad de identidad (de la suma)** Propiedad que establece que la suma de cero y cualquier número es ese número. | $7 + 0 = 7$
$-9 + 0 = -9$

improper fraction A fraction in which the numerator is greater than or equal to the denominator. | **fracción impropia** Fracción cuyo numerador es mayor que o igual al denominador. | $\frac{5}{5}$
$\frac{7}{3}$

independent variable The input of a function; a variable whose value determines the value of the output, or dependent variable. | **variable independiente** Entrada de una función; variable cuyo valor determina el valor de la salida, o variable dependiente. | For $y = 2x + 1$, x is the dependent variable.
Input: x output: y

indirect measurement The technique of using similar figures and proportions to find a measure. | **medición indirecta** La técnica de usar figuras semejantes y proporciones para hallar una medida. |

inequality A mathematical sentence that shows the relationship between quantities that are not equal. | **desigualdad** Enunciado matemático que muestra una relación entre cantidades que no son iguales. | $5 < 8$
$5x + 2 \geq 12$

input The value substituted into an expression or function. | **valor de entrada** Valor que se usa para sustituir una variable en una expresión o función. | For the rule $y = 6x$, the input 4 produces an output of 24.

integer A member of the set of whole numbers and their opposites. | **entero** Un miembro del conjunto de los números cabales y sus opuestos. | $. . . -3, -2, -1, 0, 1, 2, 3, . . .$

interest The amount of money charged for borrowing or using money, or the amount of money earned by saving money. | **interés** Cantidad de dinero que se cobra por el préstamo o uso del dinero, o la cantidad que se gana al ahorrar dinero. |

interquartile range (IQR) The difference of the third (upper) and first (lower) quartiles in a data set, representing the middle half of the data. | **rango intercuartil (RIC)** Diferencia entre el tercer cuartil (superior) y el primer cuartil (inferior) de un conjunto de datos, que representa la mitad central de los datos. | Lower half Upper half
18, (23), 28, | 29, (36), 42
First quartile Third quartile
Interquartile range:
$36 - 23 = 13$

ENGLISH	SPANISH	EXAMPLES
intersecting lines Lines that cross at exactly one point.	**rectas secantes** Líneas que se cruzan en un solo punto.	
intersection (sets) The set of elements common to two or more sets.	**intersección (de conjuntos)** Conjunto de elementos comunes a dos o más conjuntos.	
interval The space between marked values on a number line or the scale of a graph.	**intervalo** El espacio entre los valores marcados en una recta numérica o en la escala de una gráfica.	
inverse operations Operations that undo each other: addition and subtraction, or multiplication and division.	**operaciones inversas** Operaciones que se cancelan mutuamente: suma y resta, o multiplicación y división.	
isosceles triangle A triangle with at least two congruent sides.	**triángulo isósceles** Triángulo que tiene al menos dos lados congruentes.	

L

ENGLISH	SPANISH	EXAMPLES
lateral surface In a cylinder, the curved surface connecting the circular bases; in a cone, the curved surface that is not a base.	**superficie lateral** En un cilindro, superficie curva que une las bases circulares; en un cono, la superficie curva que no es la base.	Lateral surface
least common denominator (LCD) The least common multiple of two or more denominators.	**mínimo común denominador (m.c.d.)** El mínimo común múltiplo de dos o más denominadores.	The LCD of $\frac{3}{4}$ and $\frac{5}{6}$ is 12.
least common multiple (LCM) The smallest number, other than zero, that is a multiple of two or more given numbers.	**mínimo común múltiplo (m.c.m.)** El menor de los múltiplos (distinto de cero) de dos o más números.	The LCM of 10 and 18 is 90.
like fractions Fractions that have the same denominator.	**fracciones semejantes** Fracciones que tienen el mismo denominador.	$\frac{5}{12}$ and $\frac{3}{12}$ are like fractions.
like terms Terms with the same variables raised to the same exponents.	**términos semejantes** Términos con las mismas variables elevadas a los mismos exponentes.	$3a^2b^2$ and $7a^2b^2$
line A straight path that has no thickness and extends forever.	**recta** Trayectoria recta que no tiene ningún grueso y que se extiende por siempre.	ℓ
line graph A graph that uses line segments to show how data changes.	**gráfica lineal** Gráfica que muestra cómo cambian los datos mediante segmentos de recta.	Marlon's Video Game Scores

ENGLISH	SPANISH	EXAMPLES
line plot A number line with marks or dots that show frequency.	**diagrama de puntos** Recta numérica con marcas o puntos que indican la frecuencia.	X X X X X X X X X 0 1 2 3 4 **Number of pets**
line of reflection A line that a figure is flipped across to create a mirror image of the original figure.	**línea de reflexión** Línea sobre la cual se invierte una figura para crear una imagen reflejada de la figura original.	Line of reflection
line of symmetry The imaginary "mirror" in line symmetry.	**eje de simetría** El <<espejo>> imaginario en la simetría axial.	
line segment A part of a line between two endpoints.	**segmento de recta** Parte de una línea con dos extremos.	A B
line symmetry A figure has line symmetry if one half is a mirror-image of the other half.	**simetría axial** Una figura tiene simetría axial si una de sus mitades es la imagen reflejada de la otra.	
linear equation An equation whose solutions form a straight line on a coordinate plane.	**ecuación lineal** Ecuación en la que las soluciones forman una línea recta en un plano cartesiano.	$y = 2x + 1$

M

mean The sum of the items in a set of data divided by the number of items in the set; also called *average*.	**media** La suma de todos los elementos de un conjunto de datos dividida entre el número de elementos del conjunto.	Data set: 4, 6, 7, 8, 10 Mean: $\frac{4 + 6 + 7 + 8 + 10}{5} = \frac{35}{5} = 7$
median The middle number or the mean (average) of the two middle numbers in an ordered set of data.	**mediana** El número intermedio o la media (el promedio) de los dos números intermedios en un conjunto ordenado de datos.	Data set: 4, 6, 7, 8, 10 Median: 7
metric system A decimal system of weights and measures that is used universally in science and commonly throughout the world.	**sistema métrico** Sistema decimal de pesos y medidas empleado universalmente en las ciencias y por lo general en todo el mundo.	centimeters, meters, kilometers, grams, kilograms, milliliters, liters
midpoint The point that divides a line segment into two congruent line segments.	**punto medio** El punto que divide un segmento de recta en dos segmentos de recta congruentes.	A B C B is the midpoint of $\overline{AC}$

ENGLISH	SPANISH	EXAMPLES
mixed number A number made up of a whole number that is not zero and a fraction.	**número mixto** Número compuesto por un número cabal distinto de cero y una fracción.	$5\frac{1}{8}$
mode The number or numbers that occur most frequently in a set of data; when all numbers occur with the same frequency, we say there is no mode.	**moda** Número o números más frecuentes en un conjunto de datos; si todos los números aparecen con la misma frecuencia, no hay moda.	Data set: 3, 5, 8, 8, 10 Mode: 8
multiple A multiple of a number is the product of the number and any nonzero whole number.	**múltiplo** El producto de un número y cualquier número cabal distinto de cero es un múltiplo de ese número.	
Multiplication Property of Zero The property that states that the product of any number and 0 is 0.	**Propiedad de multiplicación del cero** Propiedad que establece que el producto de cualquier número y 0 es 0.	$6 \times 0 = 0$ $-5 \times 0 = 0$
multiplicative inverse One of two numbers whose product is 1.	**inverso multiplicativo** Uno de dos números cuyo producto es igual a 1.	The multiplicative inverse of $\frac{3}{4}$ is $\frac{4}{3}$.

N

negative number A number less than zero.	**número negativo** Número menor que cero.	−2 is a negative number.
net An arrangement of two-dimensional figures that can be folded to form a polyhedron.	**plantilla** Arreglo de figuras bidimensionales que se doblan para formar un poliedro.	
numerator The top number of a fraction that tells how many parts of a whole are being considered.	**numerador** El número de arriba de una fracción; indica cuántas partes de un entero se consideran.	$\frac{3}{4}$ ← numerator
numerical expression An expression that contains only numbers and operations.	**expresión numérica** Expresión que incluye sólo números y operaciones.	$(2 \cdot 3) + 1$

O

obtuse angle An angle whose measure is greater than 90° but less than 180°.	**ángulo obtuso** Ángulo que mide más de 90° y menos de 180°.	
obtuse triangle A triangle containing one obtuse angle.	**triángulo obtusángulo** Triángulo que tiene un ángulo obtuso.	

Glossary/Glosario

ENGLISH	SPANISH	EXAMPLES
odd number A whole number that is not divisible by two.	**número impar** Un número cabal que no es divisible entre dos.	
opposites Two numbers that are an equal distance from zero on a number line.	**opuestos** Dos números que están a la misma distancia de cero en una recta numérica.	5 and −5 are opposites.
order of operations A rule for evaluating expressions: first perform the operations in parentheses, then compute powers and roots, then perform all multiplication and division from left to right, and then perform all addition and subtraction from left to right.	**orden de las operaciones** Regla para evaluar expresiones: primero se resuelven las operaciones entre paréntesis, luego se hallan las potencias y raíces, después todas las multiplicaciones y divisiones de izquierda a derecha y, por último, todas las sumas y restas de izquierda a derecha.	$3^2 - 12 \div 4$ $9 - 12 \div 4$ Evaluate the power. $9 - 3$ Divide. 6 Subtract.
ordered pair A pair of numbers that can be used to locate a point on a coordinate plane.	**par ordenado** Par de números que sirven para ubicar un punto en un plano cartesiano.	The coordinates of *B* are (−2, 3)
origin The point where the *x*-axis and *y*-axis intersect on the coordinate plane; (0, 0).	**origen** Punto de intersección entre el eje *x* y el eje *y* en un plano cartesiano: (0, 0).	
outcome A possible result of a probability experiment.	**resultado** Posible resultado de un experimento de probabilidad.	When rolling a number cube, the possible outcomes are 1, 2, 3, 4, 5, and 6.
outlier A value much greater or much less than the others in a data set.	**valor atípico** Un valor mucho mayor o menor que los demás valores de un conjunto de datos.	Most of data Mean Outlier
output The value that results from the substitution of a given input into an expression or function.	**valor de salida** Valor que resulta después de sustituir un valor de entrada determinado en una expresión o función.	For the rule $y = 6x$, the input 4 produces an output of 24.
overestimate An estimate that is greater than the exact answer.	**estimación alta** Estimación mayor que la respuesta exacta.	100 is an overestimate for the sum 23 + 24 + 21 + 22.

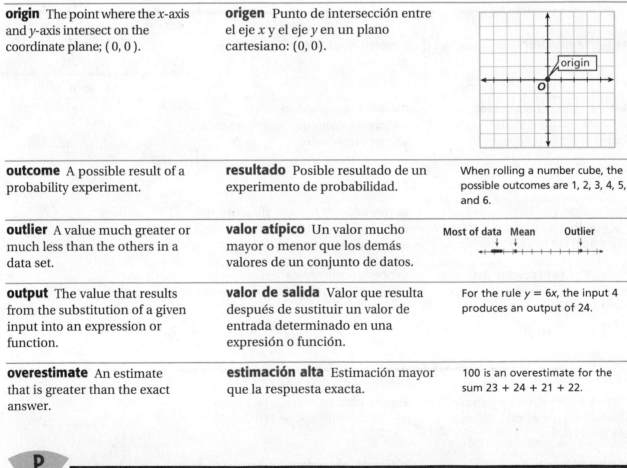

P

parallel lines Lines in a plane that do not intersect.	**rectas paralelas** Líneas que se encuentran en el mismo plano pero que nunca se intersecan.	*r* *s*

parallelogram A quadrilateral with two pairs of parallel sides.

paralelogramo Cuadrilátero con dos pares de lados paralelos.

---

pentagon A five-sided polygon.

pentágono Polígono de cinco lados.

---

percent A ratio comparing a number to 100.

porcentaje Razón que compara un número con el número 100.

$45\% = \frac{45}{100}$

---

perfect square A square of a whole number.

cuadrado perfecto El cuadrado de un número cabal.

$5^2 = 25$, so 25 is a perfect square.

---

perimeter The distance around a polygon.

perímetro Distancia alrededor de un polígono.

18 ft
6 ft
perimeter = 48 ft

---

permutation An arrangement of items or events in which order is important.

permutación Arreglo de objetos o sucesos en el que el orden es importante.

For objects *A*, *B*, and *C*, there are 6 different permutations: *ABC*, *ACB*, *BAC*, *BCA*, *CAB*, *CBA*.

---

perpendicular bisector A line that intersects a segment at its midpoint and is perpendicular to the segment.

mediatriz Línea que cruza un segmento en su punto medio y es perpendicular al segmento.

ℓ

A   *B*

ℓ is the perpendicular bisector of $\overline{AB}$.

---

perpendicular lines Lines that intersect to form right angles.

rectas perpendiculares Líneas que al intersecarse forman ángulos rectos.

n
m

---

pi (π) The ratio of the circumference of a circle to the length of its diameter; $\pi \approx 3.14$ or $\frac{22}{7}$.

pi (π) Razón de la circunferencia de un círculo a la longitud de su diámetro; $\pi \approx 3.14$ ó $\frac{22}{7}$.

---

plane A flat surface that has no thickness and extends forever.

plano Superficie plana que no tiene ningún grueso y que se extiende por siempre.

A   *C*
$\mathcal{R}$ *B*

plane *R* or plane *ABC*

---

point An exact location that has no size.

punto Ubicación exacta que no tiene ningún tamaño.

P
point *P*

---

polygon A closed plane figure formed by three or more line segments that intersect only at their endpoints.

polígono Figura plana cerrada, formada por tres o más segmentos de recta que se intersecan sólo en sus extremos.

---

polyhedron A three-dimensional figure in which all the surfaces or faces are polygons.

poliedro Figura tridimensional cuyas superficies o caras tienen forma de polígonos.

| --- | --- | --- |
population The whole group being surveyed.	**población** El grupo completo que es objeto de estudio.	In a survey about eating habits of middle school students, the population is all middle school students.
positive number A number greater than zero.	**número positivo** Número mayor que cero.	2 is a positive number. $$\xleftarrow{\;+\;+\;+\;+\;+\;+\;+\;+\;\rightarrow}$$ −4 −3 −2 −1 0 1 2 3 4
power A number produced by raising a base to an exponent.	**potencia** Número que resulta al elevar una base a un exponente.	$2^3 = 8$, so 2 to the 3rd power is 8.
prediction A guess about something that will happen in the future.	**predicción** Pronóstico sobre algo que puede ocurrir en el futuro.	
prime factorization A number written as the product of its prime factors.	**descomposición en factores primos** Un número escrito como el producto de sus factores primos.	$10 = 2 \cdot 5$ $24 = 2^3 \cdot 3$
prime number A whole number greater than 1 that has exactly two factors, itself and 1.	**número primo** Número cabal mayor que 1 que sólo es divisible entre 1 y él mismo.	5 is prime because its only factors are 5 and 1.
principal The initial amount of money borrowed or saved.	**capital** Cantidad inicial de dinero depositada o recibida en préstamo.	
prism A polyhedron that has two congruent, polygon-shaped bases and other faces that are all rectangles.	**prisma** Poliedro con dos bases congruentes con forma de polígono y caras con forma de rectángulos.	
probability A number from 0 to 1 (or 0% to 100%) that describes how likely an event is to occur.	**probabilidad** Un número entre 0 y 1 (ó 0% y 100%) que describe qué tan probable es un suceso.	A bag contains 3 red marbles and 4 blue marbles. The probability of randomly choosing a red marble is $\frac{3}{7}$.
product The result when two or more numbers are multiplied.	**producto** Resultado de multiplicar dos o más números.	The product of 4 and 8 is 32.
proper fraction A fraction in which the numerator is less than the denominator.	**fracción propia** Fracción en la que el numerador es menor que el denominador.	$\frac{3}{4}, \frac{1}{13}, \frac{7}{8}$
proportion An equation that states that two ratios are equivalent.	**proporción** Ecuación que establece que dos razones son equivalentes.	$\frac{2}{3} = \frac{4}{6}$
protractor A tool for measuring angles.	**transportador** Instrumento para medir ángulos.	
pyramid A polyhedron with a polygon base and triangular sides that all meet at a common vertex.	**pirámide** Poliedro cuya base es un polígono; tiene caras triangulares que se juntan en un vértice común.	

Glossary/Glosario

Q

quadrant The *x*- and *y*-axes divide the coordinate plane into four regions. Each region is called a quadrant.

cuadrante El eje *x* y el eje *y* dividen el plano cartesiano en cuatro regiones. Cada región recibe el nombre de cuadrante.

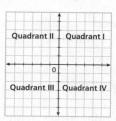

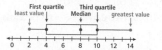

quartile Three values, one of which is the median, that divide a data set into fourths.

cuartil Cada uno de tres valores, uno de los cuales es la mediana, que dividen en cuartos un conjunto de datos.

quotient The result when one number is divided by another.

cociente Resultado de dividir un número entre otro.

In 8 ÷ 4 = 2, 2 is the quotient.

R

radius A line segment with one endpoint at the center of a circle and the other endpoint on the circle, or the length of that segment.

radio Segmento de recta con un extremo en el centro de un círculo y el otro en la circunferencia, o bien la longitud de ese segmento.

rate A ratio that compares two quantities measured in different units.

tasa Una razón que compara dos cantidades medidas en diferentes unidades.

The speed limit is 55 miles per hour or 55 mi/h.

rate of change A ratio that compares the difference between two output values to the difference between the corresponding input values.

tasa de cambio Razón que compara la diferencia entre dos salidas con la diferencia entre dos entrados.

The cost of mailing a letter increased from 22 cents in 1985 to 25 cents in 1988. The rate of change was
$$\frac{22 - 22}{1988 = 1985} = \frac{3}{3}$$
$$= 1 \text{ cent per year.}$$

rate of interest The percent charged or earned on an amount of money; see *simple interest*.

tasa de interés Porcentaje que se cobra por una cantidad de dinero prestada o que se gana por una cantidad de dinero ahorrada; ver *interés simple*.

ratio A comparison of two quantities by division.

razón Comparación de dos cantidades mediante una división.

12 to 25, 12:25, $\frac{12}{25}$

rational number A number that can be written in the form $\frac{a}{b}$, where *a* and *b* are integers and $b \neq 0$.

número racional Número que se puede expresar como $\frac{a}{b}$, donde *a* y *b* son números enteros y $b \neq 0$.

3, 1.75, $0.\overline{3}$, $-\frac{2}{3}$, 0

Glossary/Glosario

ENGLISH	SPANISH	EXAMPLES
ray A part of a line that starts at one endpoint and extends forever in one direction.	**rayo** Parte de una línea que comienza en un extremo y se extiende siempre en una dirección.	
reciprocal One of two numbers whose product is 1.	**recíproco** Uno de dos números cuyo producto es igual a 1.	The reciprocal of $\frac{2}{3}$ is $\frac{3}{2}$.
rectangle A parallelogram with four right angles.	**rectángulo** Paralelogramo con cuatro ángulos rectos.	
rectangular prism A polyhedron whose bases are rectangles and whose other faces are rectangles.	**prisma rectangular** Poliedro cuyas bases son rectángulos y cuyas caras tienen forma de rectángulos.	
reflection A transformation of a figure that flips the figure across a line.	**reflexión** Transformación que ocurre cuando se invierte una figura sobre una línea.	
regular polygon A polygon with congruent sides and angles.	**polígono regular** Polígono con lados y ángulos congruentes.	
repeating decimal A decimal in which one or more digits repeat infinitely.	**decimal periódico** Decimal en el que uno o más dígitos se repiten infinitamente.	$0.75757575\ldots = 0.\overline{75}$
rhombus A parallelogram with all sides congruent.	**rombo** Paralelogramo en el que todos los lados son congruentes.	
right angle An angle that measures 90°.	**ángulo recto** Ángulo que mide exactamente 90°.	
right triangle A triangle containing a right angle.	**triángulo rectángulo** Triángulo que tiene un ángulo recto.	
rotation A transformation in which a figure is turned around a point.	**rotación** Transformación que ocurre cuando una figura gira alrededor de un punto.	
rotational symmetry A figure that can be rotated about a point by an angle less than 360° so that the image coincides with the preimage has rotational symmetry.	**simetría de rotación** Una figura que puede rotarse alrededor de un punto en un ángulo menor de 360° de forma tal que la imagen coincide con la imagen original que tenga simetría de rotación.	

ENGLISH	SPANISH	EXAMPLES
rounding Replacing a number with an estimate of that number to a given place value.	**redondear** Sustituir un número por una estimación de ese número hasta cierto valor posicional.	2,354 rounded to the nearest thousand is 2,000; 2,354 rounded to the nearest 100 is 2,400.

S

ENGLISH	SPANISH	EXAMPLES
sales tax A percent of the cost of an item, which is charged by governments to raise money.	**impuesto sobre la venta** Porcentaje del costo de un artículo que los gobiernos cobran para recaudar fondos.	
sample A part of a group being surveyed.	**muestra** Parte de un grupo que es objeto de estudio.	In a survey about eating habits of middle school math students, a sample is a survey of 100 randomly-chosen students.
sample space All possible outcomes of an experiment.	**espacio muestral** Conjunto de todos los resultados posibles de un experimento.	When rolling a number cube, the sample space is 1, 2, 3, 4, 5, 6.
scale The ratio between two sets of measurements.	**escala** La razón entre dos conjuntos de medidas.	1 cm: 5 mi
scale drawing A drawing that uses a scale to make an object proportionally smaller than or larger than the real object.	**dibujo a escala** Dibujo en el que se usa una escala para que un objeto se vea proporcionalmente mayor o menor que el objeto real al que representa.	A blueprint is an example of a scale drawing.
scale model A proportional model of a three-dimensional object.	**modelo a escala** Modelo proporcional de un objeto tridimensional.	
scalene triangle A triangle with no congruent sides.	**triángulo escaleno** Triángulo que no tiene lados congruentes.	
scientific notation A method of writing very large or very small numbers by using powers of 10.	**notación científica** Método que se usa para escribir números muy grandes o muy pequeños mediante potencias de 10.	$12,560,000,000,000 = 1.256 \times 10^{13}$
segment A part of a line made of two endpoints and all points between them.	**segmento** Parte de una línea que consiste en dos extremos y todos los puntos entre éstos.	A————B
sequence An ordered list of numbers.	**secuencia** Lista ordenada de números.	2, 4, 6, 8, 10, . . .
set A group of items.	**conjunto** Un grupo de elementos.	

ENGLISH	SPANISH	EXAMPLES
side A line bounding a geometric figure; one of the faces forming the outside of an object.	**lado** Línea que delimita las figuras geométricas; una de las caras que forman la parte exterior de un objeto.	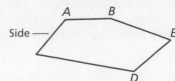
significant figures The figures used to express the precision of a measurement.	**dígitos significativos** Dígitos usados para expresar la precisión de una medida.	
similar Figures with the same shape but not necessarily the same size are similar.	**semejantes** Figuras que tienen la misma forma, pero no necesariamente el mismo tamaño.	
simple event An event consisting of only one outcome.	**suceso simple** Suceso que tiene sólo un resultado.	In the experiment of rolling a number cube, the event consisting of the outcome 3 is a simple event.
simple interest A fixed percent of the principal. It is found using the formula $I = Prt$, where P represents the principal, r the rate of interest, and t the time.	**interés simple** Un porcentaje fijo del capital. Se calcula con la fórmula $I = Cit$, donde C representa el capital, i, la tasa de interés y t, el tiempo.	
simplest form (of a fraction) A fraction is in simplest form when the numerator and denominator have no common factors other than 1.	**mínima expresión (de una fracción)** Una fracción está en su mínima expresión cuando el numerador y el denominador no tienen más factor común que 1.	Fraction: $\frac{8}{12}$ Simplest form: $\frac{2}{3}$
simplify To write a fraction or expression in simplest form.	**simplificar** Escribir una fracción o expresión numérica en su mínima expresión.	
simulation A model of an experiment, often one that would be too difficult or too time-consuming to actually perform.	**simulación** Representación de un experimento, por lo regular de uno cuya realización sería demasiado difícil o llevaría mucho tiempo.	
skew lines Lines that lie in different planes that are neither parallel nor intersecting.	**líneas oblicuas** Líneas que se encuentran en planos distintos, por eso no se intersecan ni son paralelas.	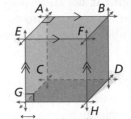 $\overleftrightarrow{AE}$ and $\overleftrightarrow{CD}$ are skew lines.
slope The constant rate of change of a line.	**pendiente** La tasa de cambio constante de una línea.	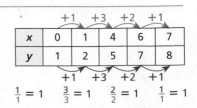

solid figure A three-dimensional figure.

cuerpo geométrico Figura tridimensional.

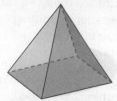

---

solution of an equation A value or values that make an equation true.

solución de una ecuación Valor o valores que hacen verdadera una ecuación.

Equation: $x + 2 = 6$
Solution: $x = 4$

---

solution of an inequality A value or values that make an inequality true.

solución de una desigualdad Valor o valores que hacen verdadera una desigualdad.

Inequality: $x + 3 \geq 10$
Solution: $x \geq 7$

---

solution set The set of values that make a statement true.

conjunto solución Conjunto de valores que hacen verdadero un enunciado.

Inequality: $x + 3 \geq 5$
Solution set: $x \geq 2$

$-4\ -3\ -2\ -1\quad 0\quad 1\quad 2\quad 3\quad 4\quad 5\quad 6$

---

solve To find an answer or a solution.

resolver Hallar una respuesta o solución.

---

square (geometry) A rectangle with four congruent sides.

cuadrado (en geometría) Rectángulo con cuatro lados congruentes.

---

square (numeration) A number raised to the second power.

cuadrado (en numeración) Número elevado a la segunda potencia.

In 5^2, the number 5 is squared.

---

square number A number that is the product of a whole number and itself.

cuadrado de un número El producto de un número cabal multiplicado por sí mismo.

25 is a square number since $5^2 = 25$.

---

square root A number that is multiplied by itself to form a product is called a square root of that product.

raíz cuadrada El número que se multiplica por sí mismo para formar un producto se denomina la raíz cuadrada de ese producto.

$16 = 4 \cdot 4$ and $16 = -4 \cdot -4$, so 4 and -4 are square roots of 16.

---

standard form (in numeration) A number written using digits.

forma estándar Una forma de escribir números por medio de dígitos.

Five thousand, two hundred ten in standard form is 5,210.

---

stem-and-leaf plot A graph used to organize and display data so that the frequencies can be compared.

diagrama de tallo y hojas Gráfica que muestra y ordena los datos, y que sirve para comparar las frecuencias.

Stem	Leaves
3	2 3 4 4 7 9
4	0 1 5 7 7 7 8
5	1 2 2 3

Key: 3|2 means 3.2

---

straight angle An angle that measures 180°.

ángulo llano Ángulo que mide exactamente 180°.

---

subset A set contained within another set.

subconjunto Conjunto que pertenece a otro conjunto.

ENGLISH	SPANISH	EXAMPLES
substitute To replace a variable with a number or another expression in an algebraic expression.	**sustituir** Reemplazar una variable por un número u otra expresión en una expresión algebraica.	
sum The result when two or more numbers are added.	**suma** Resultado de sumar dos o más números.	
supplementary angles Two angles whose measures have a sum of 180°.	**ángulos suplementarios** Dos ángulos cuyas medidas suman 180°.	30 150
surface area The sum of the areas of the faces, or surfaces, of a three-dimensional figure.	**área total** Suma de las áreas de las caras, o superficies, de una figura tridimensional.	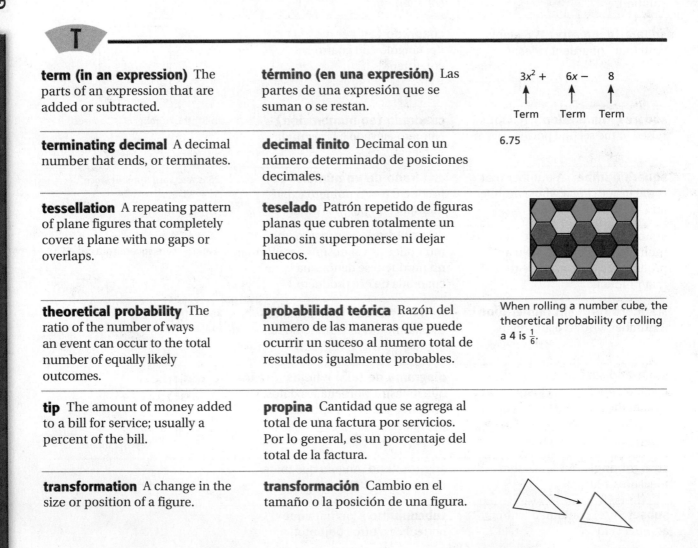 12 cm, 6 cm, 8 cm Surface area = 2(8)(12) + 2(8)(6) + 2(12)(6) = 432 cm²

T

ENGLISH	SPANISH	EXAMPLES
term (in an expression) The parts of an expression that are added or subtracted.	**término (en una expresión)** Las partes de una expresión que se suman o se restan.	$3x^2 +$ $6x -$ 8 Term Term Term
terminating decimal A decimal number that ends, or terminates.	**decimal finito** Decimal con un número determinado de posiciones decimales.	6.75
tessellation A repeating pattern of plane figures that completely cover a plane with no gaps or overlaps.	**teselado** Patrón repetido de figuras planas que cubren totalmente un plano sin superponerse ni dejar huecos.	
theoretical probability The ratio of the number of ways an event can occur to the total number of equally likely outcomes.	**probabilidad teórica** Razón del numero de las maneras que puede ocurrir un suceso al numero total de resultados igualmente probables.	When rolling a number cube, the theoretical probability of rolling a 4 is $\frac{1}{6}$.
tip The amount of money added to a bill for service; usually a percent of the bill.	**propina** Cantidad que se agrega al total de una factura por servicios. Por lo general, es un porcentaje del total de la factura.	
transformation A change in the size or position of a figure.	**transformación** Cambio en el tamaño o la posición de una figura.	

translation A movement (slide) of a figure along a straight line.

traslación Desplazamiento de una figura a lo largo de una línea recta.

trapezoid A quadrilateral with exactly one pair of parallel sides.

trapecio Cuadrilátero con un par de lados paralelos.

tree diagram A branching diagram that shows all possible combinations or outcomes of an event.

diagrama de árbol Diagrama ramificado que muestra todas las posibles combinaciones o resultados de un suceso.

trial Each repetition or observation of an experiment.

prueba Cada repetición u observación de un experimento.

In the experiment of rolling a number cube, each roll is one trial.

triangle A three-sided polygon.

triángulo Polígono de tres lados.

Triangle Sum Theorem The theorem that states that the measures of the angles in a triangle add to 180°.

Teorema de la suma del triángulo Teorema que establece que las medidas de los ángulos de un triángulo suman 180°.

triangular prism A polyhedron whose bases are triangles and whose other faces are rectangles.

prisma triangular Poliedro cuyas bases son triángulos y cuyas demás caras tienen forma de rectángulos.

U

underestimate An estimate that is less than the exact answer.

estimación baja Estimación menor que la respuesta exacta.

100 is an underestimate for the sum $26 + 29 + 31 + 27$.

union The set of all elements that belong to two or more sets.

unión El conjunto de todos los elementos que pertenecen a dos o más conjuntos.

unit conversion The process of changing one unit of measure to another.

conversión de unidades Proceso que consiste en cambiar una unidad de medida por otra.

unit rate A rate in which the second quantity in the comparison is one unit.

tasa unitaria Una tasa en la que la segunda cantidad de la comparación es una unidad.

10 cm per minute

unlike fractions Fractions with different denominators.

fracciones distintas Fracciones con distinto denominador.

$\frac{3}{4}$ and $\frac{1}{2}$ are unlike fractions.

Glossary/Glosario

variable A symbol used to represent a quantity that can change.

variable Símbolo que representa una cantidad que puede cambiar.

In the expression 2x + 3, x is the variable.

---

variation (variability) The spread of values in a set of data.

variación (variabilidad) Amplitud de los valores de un conjunto de datos.

The data set {1, 5, 7, 10, 25} has greater variation than the data set {8, 8, 9, 9, 9}.

Venn diagram A diagram that is used to show relationships between sets.

diagrama de Venn Diagrama que muestra las relaciones entre conjuntos.

---

vertical angles A pair of opposite congruent angles formed by intersecting lines.

ángulos opuestos por el vértice Par de ángulos opuestos congruentes formados por líneas secantes.

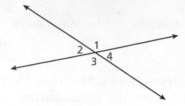

∠1 and ∠3 are vertical angles.
∠2 and ∠4 are vertical angles.

---

volume The number of cubic units needed to fill a given space.

volumen Número de unidades cúbicas que se necesitan para llenar un espacio.

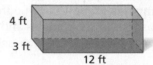

Volume = 3 · 4 · 12 = 144 ft³

---

x-axis The horizontal axis on a coordinate plane.

eje x El eje horizontal del plano cartesiano.

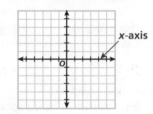

---

x-coordinate The first number in an ordered pair; it tells the distance to move right or left from the origin, (0, 0).

coordenada x El primer número en un par ordenado; indica la distancia que debes avanzar hacia la izquierda o hacia la derecha desde el origen, (0, 0).

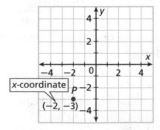

Glossary/Glosario

y-axis The vertical axis on a coordinate plane.

eje y El eje vertical del plano cartesiano.

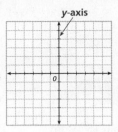

y-coordinate The second number in an ordered pair; it tells the distance to move up or down from the origin, (0, 0).

coordenada y El segundo número en un par ordenado; indica la distancia que debes avanzar hacia arriba o hacia abajo desde el origen, (0, 0).

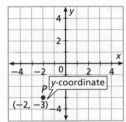

zero pair A number and its opposite, which add to 0.

par nulo Un número y su opuesto, que sumados dan 0.

18 and −18

Glossary/Glosario

Index ...

Index   (side tab)